THE AMERICAN DREAM

★ ★

CAN IT SURVIVE THE 21ST CENTURY?

JOSEPH L. DALEIDEN

Prometheus Books
59 John Glenn Drive
Amherst, New York 14228-2197

Published 1999 by Prometheus Books

Inquiries should be addressed to
Prometheus Books, 59 John Glenn Drive, Amherst, New York 14228–2197.
VOICE: 716–691–0133, ext. 207. FAX: 716–564–2711.
WWW.PROMETHEUSBOOKS.COM

03 02 01 00 99 5 4 3 2 1

Library of Congress Cataloging-in-Publication Data

Daleiden, Joseph L.
The American dream : can it survive the 21st century? / Joseph L. Daleiden.
p. cm.
Includes bibliographical references and index.
ISBN 1–57392–265–X (alk. paper)
1. Social prediction—United States. 2. United States—Population—Forecasting. 3. United States—Forecasting. 4. Twenty-first century—Forecasts. I. Title.
HN60.D33 1998
306'.0973—dc21 98–55176
CIP

Printed in the United States of America on acid-free paper

To my wife, Peg,
my daughters, Carolyn and Denise,
and my son, Rob,
who each in their own way
made invaluable contributions to this book.

Acknowledgments

It would be impossible to acknowledge all the people who directly or indirectly contributed to this book, since it reflects the thinking of literally hundreds of scholars, researchers, and policy analysts whom I have studied over the years. So I must limit myself to thanking those who reviewed earlier drafts of this work and whose criticisms and suggestions greatly enhanced the final product. I am especially grateful to have an iconoclastic friend such as Walter Buchmann, who is one of the most analytical thinkers it has been my pleasure to know, and has many times forced me to rethink my views.

Pete Smith provided insight into complexity of taxation. Bob Coen provided guidance on the thorny issue of social security. J. Robert Daleiden provided several excellent references on criminology. Denise Patten and Jeff Schramek helped edit an early draft. Finally, I benefitted from the many comments of Prometheus Books' editor-in-chief Steven L. Mitchell and the final copyediting of Joseph L. Mancuso.

Of course none of these fine people should be held accountable for the views expressed in this book. If anyone is to be hung, it must be the author.

CONTENTS

Introduction

What does the American dream mean to you? Over the years it has meant many things to many people: freedom from religious persecution; the opportunity to work one's own land; a chance for a fresh start; "a chicken in every pot and car in every garage"; the right to vote; equal opportunity; the chance to achieve fame, power, or fortune; on and on. The American dream is a term used in so many different contexts that today it is probably devoid of a common understanding.

For me, the term will always represent the dream expressed by Thomas Jefferson in the Declaration of Independence. He and the founding fathers shared the wild dream that they could establish a nation on the principle that all men had the "right to Life, Liberty and the Pursuit of Happiness." It has often been pointed out, and just as often ignored, that the Declaration did not say that all men have an unqualified right to happiness, as they did to life and liberty, but only "the pursuit" of happiness. (Any government or person who says that they can make us happy should be immediately suspected of promising what they cannot deliver.)

Equally as problematic, as it turned out, was the Declaration's promise that the three rights were to be granted to "all men." While the notion seemed straightforward enough, it took almost two hundred years before the term "all men" was generally accepted to include women, minorities, and children. Even today, being a society of fallible and imperfect human beings, we often fall well short in the application of these rights. During the last two hundred years European nations have also made great strides toward establishing these three rights, but 80 percent of the people on the earth today still live in societies that do not recognize them or are only just beginning to do so.

Protection of the American dream—as I define it—has not come easy. It took the self-sacrifice of millions of men and women who devoted, and often gave, their lives to ensuring that America was able to protect and extend such rights. It is with justifiable pride that we observe that our nation has survived a revolution, a devastating civil war, two world wars, and forty years of the Cold War with the American dream intact. Moreover, as we enter the twenty-first century there is only one major power in the world, and it is the United States. No nation can threaten our peace and harmony. As I write these words, the economy is strong, inflation almost nonexistent, the federal budget roughly in balance, and the percentage of people living in poverty is near an all-time low. In short, in most respects, the future of the American dream has never looked brighter.

It might seem odd, therefore, to write a book questioning whether our nation will continue to be dedicated to the preservation of the rights that define us. Yet as any student of history knows, the only constant in history is the rise and fall of civilizations. The demise of past societies many times appears due to their conquest by a superior military power. However, although the final *coup de grâce* could be identified in a historic battle, almost invariably the civilization had been in a state of decay for decades, maybe even centuries. This certainly was true for the Greeks and the Romans.

It seems one of the great ironies of life that success is often the breeding ground of failure, especially when that success is given rather than earned. The old adage is, "Shirtsleeves to shirtsleeves in three generations." Although it may take more than three generations, the rule may well hold true for societies as well as individuals.

Although for almost all of my thirty-year career I have worked as an economist, demographer, and long-term planner in the private sector, I had a short, but extremely illuminating position as consultant in the Office of Management and the Budget during the Carter administration. In almost all of my various assignments, I have been required to divert my attention from the cyclical ups and downs of the economy in an effort to uncover the underlying long-term socioeconomic trends. I have found that the most useful training in this regard has been demographics. The effects of demographic trends may take decades to be realized, but can often be forecasted with great accuracy by the trained observer.

For example, it took no psychic powers to predict in 1969 that the post-war baby boom would cause a host of socioeconomic problems for the United States during the decades of the 1970s and 1980s, including increased unemployment, lower real wages, higher crime, and increased taxes for infrastructure investment (e.g., schools, highways, sanitation, police and fire, etc.). Similarly, it was no feat of prescience when I forecasted in 1983 that the high birth rates in Mexico during the 1960s and 1970s would lead to waves of illegal immigration to the United States throughout the later part of the twentieth century and well into the twenty-first. These trends were so obvious that the only mystery was why our society did not recognize and deal with them far earlier. Perhaps former Canadian prime minister Pierre Trudeau was correct when he observed that it is the nature of politics to deal with urgencies rather than essentials.

I took a greater prophetic risk when I forecasted that the 1990s held the potential for being America's Golden Age. This prediction was based upon the observation that during the 1990s the dependency ratio (the number of people age 0 to 18 and over 65 relative to those age 19 to 64) would be the lowest in America's history. With so many in the labor force relative to children and old people needing to be supported, the economy could reasonably be expected to soar. In fact, based on the demographic trends alone, the economy should have begun a period of sustained growth by the mid-1980s. Why it took a decade longer to reach fruition than it should have will be explained later.

But although demographic trends are often easy to recognize, there are many other equally significant trends that are far more subtle and difficult to quantify, such as changes in societal values. For instance, who could have predicted the fallout from the 1960s sexual revolution? Moreover, as we move inexorably to a world economy, we are entering a realm where economic models based upon past correlations are of little value as guides to the future and may even be quite misleading.

To sort out the interaction of the numerous trends as we enter the twenty-first century is difficult enough. We must go a step further, however, and decide on the appropriate societal response early enough in an emerging trend to develop an effective remedy. We waited over a decade after the first of the baby boomers reached their high crime years (19 to 24 years of age) before expanding our judicial system sufficiently to cope with the problem. Had we moved expeditiously we might have avoided the soaring crime rates of the 1970s and 1980s.

My basic premise is that negative socioeconornic trends can be identified long before they reach crisis proportions. However, I am not nearly as confident that our nation can elicit the necessary social sacrifice and discipline to effect the required solutions. Neither political party today appears to possess the vision and leadership that our nation will need to effectively meet the challenges of the twenty-first century. One reason may be that the overwhelming majority of American people have removed themselves from the difficult task of self-government and seem willing to leave the task to professional politicians. Our voter turnouts are the lowest in our history and questionnaires on public issues indicate that although we may have entered the information age, in terms of the basic education necessary to be knowledgeable voters, we appear to be returning to the Dark Ages.

It is my hope that this book will serve as a wake-up call to all Americans to get involved in the process of government. We must learn to see through the double-speak of the latter-day snake-oil salesmen who have come to dominate both political parties. We must recognize that there are always difficult trade-offs to be made in life. We can't "have it all" if we are to leave something for our grandchildren. Before we "just do it" we must be prepared to live with all the consequences of our actions. We may only "go around once" but that fact does not free us from responsibility to our families and society. Above all we must resist having our values shaped by TV commercials and Hollywood!

We also must be realistic about what is achievable. We cannot "save" people, but we might enable them to save themselves. We cannot guarantee happiness for anyone, but we can offer more equal opportunity for our citizens to pursue happiness. We cannot solve the world's problems. At best we can try to preserve and improve on our own society and become an example for others. Whether they choose to follow or go their own way is their choice, not ours.

Finally, and perhaps most importantly, we must balance our desire to establish new rights with a willingness to accept the responsibilities that go with them. The moment we as a society become more concerned with the arguments over conflicting rights than we are over our relative responsibilities, we will have begun the long slide to social dissolution. As we will see in the course of this work, unless we continually strive to preserve the American dream as envisioned by our nation's founders, the dream could very easily become a nightmare. And we would have no one to blame but ourselves.

The Philosophical Basis for This Work

This volume is actually the third and concluding book of a body of work begun over twenty years ago. The first two books developed certain conclusions that are the starting point for the present volume. A summary of the conclusions of those two treatises, *The Final Superstition: A Critical Evaluation of the Judeo-Christian Legacy*[1] and *The Science of Morality: Balancing the Needs of the Individual, Community, and Future Generations*,[2] is provided in Appendix A. Basically, they argue the need for basing morality and socioeconomic policies on a rigorous logical empiricism. They demonstrate the danger of relying on religious doctrines based upon ancient superstitions and a woefully inadequate understanding of the factors determining human behavior. Moreover, many of the moral and social issues facing humankind today were not even considered years ago, nor were the options provided by new technology. Today, we are faced with a host of decisions that were of little or no concern to previous generations including: methods of population control, fertility drugs leading to multiple conceptions, *in vitro* conception, safe abortion, genetic engineering, artificial prolongation or termination of life, the ecological and environmental impact of human actions, the rights (if any) of other species, and so much more. Additionally, we have new insights into age-old problems such as the distribution of rights and responsibilities among sexes, races, socioeconomic groups, nations, and even generations.

Since rights and responsibilities are human creations, there are no transcendent principles we can rely upon to determine absolutely the priority or appropriateness of any socioeconomic policy. However, we can determine empirically that humans, like every other animal, seek survival of their species and the absence of pain—or, in a more positive sense, the feeling of happiness or well-being. Moreover, we argued that *society can optimize happiness for the greatest number of people in the long run by attempting to balance the needs of the individual, society, and future generations*. The happiness of future generations depends in large measure on the present generation preserving the environment. Although we cannot rely upon any absolute principle for ensuring the foregoing balance, a useful guideline to achieve this end is a modified form of John Rawls's principle of justice as expressed in his *A Theory of Justice. Modified Rawlsian justice is the principle that: "All social primary goods (liberty and opportunity, income and wealth, and the basis of self-respect) are to be distributed equally* unless *an unequal distribution of any or all these goods is to the greater {relative} advantage of the least favored."*[3] The modifier, relative, was added based upon empirical studies showing that once the basic necessities of life are met, the happiness of people depends less on how they exist in absolute terms than on how they perceive their economic welfare relative to others in their community.* Note also the key word "unless." In this volume it will be shown that an unequal distribution is indeed necessary to optimize happiness for humankind. The acceptable degree of inequality and the conditions under which inequality is permitted to arise are crucial topics that will be explored in depth. (For a fur-

---

*However it should be noted that if their socioeconomic welfare is less than others, they still can be happy if they feel that the opportunity exists for improving their relative status. Moreover, since it is perception rather than statistical reality that matters, *community* as used here refers to the group to which people closely relate. In the past it may have been their neighborhood or town. With the advent of TV, it may be the average TV lifestyle that sets the standard. This will, of course, lead to frustration for people who cannot match the fictitious TV life.

ther discussion of the basis for Modified Rawlsian justice I refer the reader to *The Science of Morality* and Appendix A of the present volume.)

Topics to Be Discussed

It is the purpose of the present volume to examine the existing socioeconomic trends and to suggest policies that improve the prospects for human happiness in the twenty-first century. It appears from the present trends in family cohesion, education, income distribution, violent crime, race relations, environmental degradation, and many other socioeconomic indicators that during the last twenty-five years in the United States, we have increased happiness for relatively few people.

At the time of this writing, the U.S. economy is performing well, with steady growth, relatively low unemployment and virtually no inflation. It is a relatively unique period in America's history due to the confluence of many temporarily favorable factors, as will be explained. However, the evidence would suggest that this economically comfortable time may be short-lived. It appears to be human nature, however, that whenever we are at or near the peak of a business cycle, as we presently are, people readily believe the Pollyannas who suggests that the business cycle has been vanquished, and the economy will just get better and better. Conversely, during a recession there is a tendency to believe the Cassandras who presage that conditions are bound to keep getting worse. The reality is that the economy will continue to undergo business cycles of varying lengths. However, this book is not concerned with short-term cyclical variations in economic activity. Rather, we seek to understand the underlying factors that will determine what direction our society is headed over the longer term, at least throughout the next century. Of course, it is impossible to predict the future, but we can extrapolate underlying trends and simulate the potential impact of various socioeconomic polices based upon an understanding of causal relationships.

Furthermore, when the pundits are saying that things will get better or worse, we should always ask, for whom? Too often economic and social indicators are depicted as averages and the problem with averages is that they can conceal extremes. If I am making $200,000 a year and you are making nothing, our average income is $100,000. I doubt if that average will be of any comfort to you. The goal of society should not be merely to increase socioeconomic conditions on average, if that means circumstances are getting better for some but worse for others. We want the rising tide of affluence to float all boats (or as close to all as we can reasonably come). In short, we seek nothing less than to increase the general happiness of our society.

There was every reason to believe that we should have been able to make significant progress toward the goal of increasing happiness for most members of our society during the past twenty-five years. Yet, despite the economic progress of the last few years, the United States not only may have lost a once-in-a-lifetime opportunity in this regard but, as many economists have pointed out, we are in danger of mortgaging the future happiness of succeeding generations. Furthermore, as will become clear in the course of this book, unless new policies are enacted immediately, our options will become ever more constrained and the necessary remedial steps to maintain even a sustainable society, let alone one that is improving its socioeconomic welfare, will become increasingly more draconian.

Although the platforms of both Republicans and Democrats have some policies that are of value and should be salvaged, both platforms are distorted by ideological considerations overriding a pragmatic approach to the nation's policies. As I will strive to make clear, if the entire platform of either party were achieved it would destroy our nation. But the present stalemate, which prevents either party from enacting its agenda, also threatens America's future. We must move forward with policies that reflect the needs of the future rather than perpetuating fallacious ideologies of the past.

The traditional view of the left maintains that since people are determined by their environment it is up to the government to change that environment. Liberals often believe that this can best be achieved by government programs of intervention involving education and training, regulation and income redistribution, i.e., especially in the form of entitlements. I know I will be accused of grossly oversimplifying the liberal view, but a close examination of their rhetoric and policies indicates that this is not too wide of the mark. A book such as *The Truly Disadvantaged*, by William Julius Wilson,[4] is representative of the liberal perspective.

The view of the political right involves two widely accepted premises. The first is that most of our present problems have been caused by government policies, especially the Johnson administration's War on Poverty and growth in government spending. Charles Murray's book *Losing Ground*,[5] which is a cogent statement of this view, has become the conservatives' Bible. The second premise of the right is, that because so much of behavior is a function of IQ and other hereditary tendencies, government polices can do little to improve the social situation. The answer is to rely on the market economy to reward individual merit. A primary role of government is to protect the lives and property of hardworking citizens by imprisoning the criminal element.

However, as will be demonstrated, although authors such as Wilson and Murray provide many insights, the reasons for the social trends of the past three decades are far more complex than they would lead us to believe. It is my contention that the present socioeconomic problems are a result of demographic trends (especially immigration); the social divisiveness and loss of respect for national leadership brought on by the Vietnam War and Watergate; the huge diversions of investment dollars to the defense industry in the 1970s and 1980s; the duplicitous method of financing the growth in defense and social welfare spending (especially Medicare and Medicaid) resulting in the largest deficits in our nation's history; the paradigm shift in moral thinking that has disjoined the crucial relationship between rights and responsibilities; the prohibition on consumption of certain drugs while promoting the consumption of others; the rise of fundamentalism; the growth of the information age; and the changes in international competition.

An examination of such complex and interactive causes is not what most people want to read. (Even many academicians hate such complex explanations because they are difficult, if not impossible, to quantify and mathematically model.) People want nice, simple explanations that focus the blame on someone else or imply a personally costless solution. Conservatives want to hear: "welfare mothers are the problem," or "it's foreign trade barriers," or "it's big government," or "we need more religion," or "taxes are too high," etc. Liberals like to hear: "it's greedy corporations," "it's society's fault," "it's due to prejudice," "we need to spend more money on education and childhood intervention," and the like.

Those who can't stand complexity and want simple answers will be frustrated by this book. But they probably wouldn't choose to read a book that is not guaranteed to reinforce their biases in the first place. Dyed-in-the-wool liberals and conservatives will find this book especially frustrating. It doesn't embrace an ideological position. Instead I have sought pragmatic rather than the ideal solutions, based upon empirical evidence rather than idle speculation or wishful thinking.[6] Most importantly, I have sought solutions that will balance the needs of individuals, community, and future generations. (The environment is, as will be explained, a surrogate for the needs of future generations.) If those solutions don't fit perceived ideological or religious views, then it is those views that must be changed, not the solutions.

This volume will demonstrate that there are socioeconomic policies that can significantly alter the present formidable long-term trends. Unfortunately, just as it took us over thirty years to get to our present predicament, it may take at least that long to correct the situation, *if we begin the required reforms immediately*. If we delay taking action for another decade or so we might find that the nation is in the same irreversible spiral of decline that has been the fate of former empires and great powers. Given the record of history and basic human nature, the odds of turning the situation around are not good.

I begin by presenting two possible State of the Union speeches delivered by the president to Congress in the year 2050. The first speech reflects the conditions that would exist if we merely extrapolate the present long-term trends. The prospects are not very encouraging, to say the least. The second speech shows what this country could be if, as a society, we display the courage to take the actions necessary to alter the path that we are on. *The key point to bear in mind is that to achieve the optimistic scenario described in the second speech we must take action today. The longer we wait the more difficult the solutions become to implement.*

The succeeding chapters discuss each of the required policy actions in detail. Chapter 2 outlines the objectives of all economic policies and how we can determine if the present policies are meeting these objectives. It shows that the implicit objective of present policy is to maximize the accumulation of goods and services for the present generation, irrespective of the long-term impact on future generations or even the happiness of this generation. The current use of Gross Domestic Product (GDP) to measure economic welfare is so flawed as to encourage socially detrimental policies and has little relationship to human happiness. Alternatively, broader measures of human welfare are examined that correlate more closely with gains in human happiness.

In chapters 3 and 4, we see that, contrary to the views of libertarian think tanks such as the Cato Institute, unless we can curtail population growth throughout the world and in the United States, the quality of life will seriously decline in the coming years for all but a privileged few. Here at home, it is especially important to reduce the number of births to those who are unable to provide an adequate home environment for healthy childhood development. Specific policies are explored, especially with regard to reducing the number of unwed mothers, teenage pregnancies, and children born to drug users.

Equally essential to reducing the growth of the U.S. population is a dramatic reduction or outright moratorium on immigration. Only about 7 percent of the legal immigrants are highly skilled, and even these could better serve humanity by using their skills to advance the interests of their home countries. The vast majority of legal immigrants and virtually all illegal immigrants tend to be low-skilled and poorly educated. Most politicians and academicians support the politically correct view that immigration is a noble tradition that serves both immigrants and indigenous and naturalized Americans. In moderation, this is true. However, it will be shown that the present level of immigration (the largest mass migration in the history of the world) depresses wage rates, robs job opportunities for black Americans, leads to huge increases in social costs for education and welfare, promotes interethnic conflicts and racial strife, accelerates environmental degradation and, ultimately, may lead to a separationist movement such as Canada has experienced with its French speaking population. Increasing border patrols and funding for the Immigration and Naturalization Service (INS), although of some value, is insufficient to cope with the crisis; additional legislation is proposed.

Chapter 5 examines the consumption trends in our economy and concludes that they are not sustainable. Not only will the preference of consumption over investment retard future growth, but it will continue to destroy the environment at an alarming rate. However, it is not all bad news; there has been significant environmental success in reducing acid rain and chlorofluorocarbons that are destroying the ozone layer. The greater difficulty we face is how to balance the responsibilities of the developed nations, which produce most of the world's pollution, with the desire for economic growth of the less developed countries (LDCs). If the LDCs followed the development path of the industrialized nations, the result will be the environmental devastation of our planet. How, then, can we convince the LDCs to protect their rain forests and environment when to do so may mean slower growth? The problem is not insurmountable, but requires that the more industrialized nations share the costs. If we begin the process today and spread the costs over the next half century, the drag on the economies of the developed nations will be barely noticeable. But if we wait until we are absolutely certain of global warming and its consequences before attempting to remedy the situation, it will probably be too late or, at the very least, it will force the next generation to absorb the costs of rectifying the situation in such a short time frame as to pose an excruciating burden on the economy.

Chapter 6 explores the causes and economic implications of the national debt. Several causes of the growth in national debt during the 1980s and early 1990s are examined, including continued growth in entitlements (especially health care), the 1982 tax cut, and the doubling of defense expenditures between 1980 and 1985. Special attention is given to the often overlooked or minimized relationship between past U.S. defense spending and the growth in debt.

Some economists, such as Robert Eisner, believe that the size of the present national debt is no cause for concern. The impact of the budget deficit and growth in the national debt are explained and the consequences of various proposals for closing the deficit are discussed. In the future, the primary impediment to a reduction in the nation's debt will be rising healthcare costs, so we examine the potential impact of proposed healthcare plans on the deficit. Although the need to further reduce the relative size of the national debt is indisputable, the means of reducing the debt are crucial to the outcome. We must ensure that the burden of debt reduction is not unfairly borne by the middle class.

The national debt is not the only form of debt that Americans have been incurring over the last three decades. There are actually eight sources of debt, all of which must be dealt with if the nation is to prosper in the long term. Of particular concern is the total debt, which includes business and consumer debt as well as the federal debt. Solutions to the debt problem will require sacrifices on the part of all Americans.

The best means of aiding the LDCs are also explored. It is essential that we stop the military arms build-up that undermines the economies of many LDCs and results in less rather than more security. The issue of LDC debt must also be dealt with if we are to reverse the continued decline of many countries.

Chapter 7 questions the notion that free trade is always the best policy. Both Japan and America experienced their most rapid growth during periods when their infant industries were protected by high tariffs. On the other hand, high protectionist tariffs appear to have retarded the growth of India and China. David Ricardo's theory of comparative advantage as the basis for proposing free trade is examined. The underlying assumptions of Ricardo's theory are found to no longer hold true. The implications for both the North American Free Trade Agreement (NAFTA) and the General Agreement on Tariffs and Trade (GATT) are examined and linked to our immigration policy. A modified free trade proposal is offered to reflect the realities of today's international marketplace, and to spread the benefits and costs of trade more equitably among countries and income groups within countries.

Chapter 8 examines the causes of poverty in the U.S. There are a host of interrelated causes involving demographic shifts, growth of international competition, the transformation from the industrial to the information age, dramatic cultural changes and misguided federal policies. Two of the most significant factors are found to be the explosive growth in mother-only families and the growth in low skilled immigrants. The latter group not only directly adds to the number of poor, but indirectly prevents others from moving out of poverty by depressing wage rates.

In chapter 9 we first review the theory of Charles Murray, and conservatives in general, that poverty in the United States was exacerbated by the War on Poverty. We find that although the 1960s War on Poverty, and the growth in the availability of welfare did indeed have unintended negative consequences, simply ending welfare will not be sufficient to end poverty. The impact of affirmative action policies is also reviewed and it is found that although initially beneficial to African-Americans who were to be the primary beneficiaries, affirmative action now actually works to the detriment of blacks and, hence, needs to be either significantly revised or, better still, scrapped altogether. The emphasis must shift from racial preferences to equal rights.

There are many steps that must be taken to reduce poverty, especially the growth in mother-only families and providing blacks access to jobs through policies that foster relocation of either jobs or people. To end the culture of poverty it will be necessary to tear down the high-rises and provide vouchers that can be used to obtain housing in the proximity of the jobs, particularly in the suburbs and rural areas where jobs are growing the fastest. At the same time we must slow the growth in unskilled and low skilled labor by significantly reducing immigration.

The causes of lower academic achievement are investigated in chapter 10. Again we find that demographic changes account for some of the decline. Just the fact that a greater proportion of graduating seniors are taking the SATs would result in a decline in average scores. However, affirmative action has also resulted in a "dumbing down" of course content. In grades K to 12 an excessive concern with the rights of children has resulted in a loss of classroom discipline that is essential to the learning environment. Unfunded mandates, such as mainstreaming children with an assortment of disabilities, has also resulted in dilution of teacher time. Finally, perhaps the biggest problem is the lack of parental support as demonstrated by interethnic studies.

Although a more equal distribution of financial support for schools would help marginally, the primary problem in most schools is not financial. However, vouchers are not the solution. An examination of the success of parochial schools demonstrates that the same environment could be created in public schools. In particular, control of the classroom must be returned to the teachers and control of the schools to the principals. Seriously disruptive students must be removed from the classroom and sent to specialized schools. Standardized testing must be implemented to assess academic achievement throughout the nation. Ineffective teachers must be removed from the classroom. Parents must take responsibility for their children's performance and ensure the completion of homework.

Although demographic factors and more rigorous law enforcement have reduced criminal activity significantly in recent years, crime rates are still far above the levels of the 1950s and unacceptably high relative to other developed nations. In chapter 11 we discover, not surprisingly, that many of the causes of poverty are also the causes for the increase in crime since the 1950s. The increase in crime is due to more than just demographic changes, however. The reaction against governmental authority as a result of the Vietnam War played no small part. We also find that the growth in crime between the turn of the century and 1933 was accompanied by a huge influx of immigrants and the establishment of Prohibition. During the last thirty years we also had a huge increase in immigration and a "prohibition," although this time aimed at drugs other than alcohol. It is time to rethink our drug policy. The War on Drugs has been a failure and has resulted in a huge increase in drug-related crimes. Although a certain percentage of the population will always seek to escape reality, European experiments with decriminalization of drugs demonstrate that we can significantly reduce drug-related crime.

Two of the most misunderstood problems facing America in the next century are the rising cost of health care and an underfunded social security system. Chapter 12 tackles both of these issues. The Health Care Reform of 1996 failed to deal adequately with either the need to provide affordable health care to the working poor, or the need to constrain total health care through some form of rationing. The long-term financial issues regarding Social Security are also misconstrued by many of the pundits. The true nature of the Social Security problem is examined and a reasonable solution is offered that provides the necessary financing that is equitable both among the different economic groups and between generations.

Americans believe that they are unduly burdened by taxes despite having one of the lowest aggregate tax rates of the industrialized nations. Chapter 13 dispels some myths regarding overtaxed Americans and suggests that we can raise the necessary revenues to reduce the national debt; replace our crumbling national infrastructure; and produce some ancillary benefits such as increasing conservation, reducing pollution, and ecological destruction, as well as curbing the use of the most dangerous drugs.

The final chapter explains that the present method of campaign financing results in Congress being held hostage to special-interest groups and will prevent passage of many of the meaningful reforms discussed in this book. The two-year terms in the House also hinder representatives from taking a longer-term perspective. At the same time the absence of term limitations results in Congressional inertia that resists change. Campaign finance reform, term limitations, and establishing four-year terms in the House become the sine qua non for implementing the reforms necessary to solve the perplexing problems now facing our nation. A final idea whose time may have come is the notion of the national referendum. As the population soars, the vote of each individual depreciates and power of the political professionals and special-interest groups is correspondingly augmented. If we want to retain a true democracy, we have to rethink how to involve our citizenry in the process of governing.

It might be argued that by taking on such a host of perplexing topics

I certainly must have bitten off more than I can chew. Any one of these topics would justify a lengthy book, and many have. However, I would counter that all the topics are related and that we cannot resolve any one of them without considering the impact of all of them together. In fact, trying to solve one problem without understanding the dynamic on all other parts of the system might only exacerbate the problems. For this reason, I have decided to tackle the problems as a socioeconomic gestalt. It is because of my background in long-term planning that I have been forced to read the many studies and analyses dealing with the nation's present problems and the means of coping with them. I am not so naive or conceited as to believe that I could single-handedly envision the answers to our nation's many problems. Rather, I have reviewed the solutions proposed by some of America's most brilliant minds over the past twenty years and have attempted to consolidate their analysis and insight into a meaningful new socioeconomic platform for the twenty-first century. I don't pretend that it is the definitive set of polices, but I do hope it will move the discussion forward from the moribund set of policies that presently threaten our nation's future.

NOTES

1. Joseph L. Daleiden, *The Final Superstition* (Amherst, N.Y.: Prometheus Books, 1994).

2. Joseph L. Daleiden, *The Science of Morality: Balancing the Needs of the Individual, Community, and Future Generations* (Amherst, N.Y.: Prometheus Books, 1998).

3. John Rawls, *A Theory of Justice* (Cambridge, Mass.: Harvard University Press, Belknap Press, 1971), p. 303.

4. William Julius Wilson, *The Truly Disadvantaged* (Chicago: University of Chicago Press, 1987).

5. Charles Murray, *Losing Ground: American Social Policy 1950–1980* (New York: Basic Books, 1984).

6. I choose the word *pragmaticism* in the philosophical tradition of C. S. Pierce, not the misconstrued *pragmatism* of William James for reasons that are explained in "Morality as Harmony." For the nonphilosophical reader this fine distinction can be ignored.

1

Two Scenarios for the Year 2050

State of the Union Address of the President to Congress, 2050, based upon an extrapolation of current trends:

Distinguished Speaker and Ladies and Gentlemen of Congress, in this my first State of the Union address, it pains me that before our nation completes its third century, I must portray the status of our great nation in such somber tones. Had my predecessors and the past members of the Congress demonstrated more courage and foresight in addressing the malignancies festering since well before the turn of the century, we may have avoided the dire situation in which we now find ourselves. At last, however, the American public has rejected the political parties responsible for the present crisis. The voters' decision to support the American Pragmatic Party signals the public's desire for a straightforward account of the present situation and a willingness to enact those policies necessary to save our endangered nation.

As my first action as president, it is my sad duty to call upon Congress to ratify the treaty with the secessionist southwestern states and recognize the Aztlan Republic as an independent nation. It is time to face the fact that despite more than ten years of a virtual police state to prevent their succession, it is has become impossible to ensure the safety of our citizens either in that area or elsewhere in our country. Although we condemn the terrorist acts employed by the rebels in their twenty-year war for independence, we must admit that the only way to stop this terrorist warfare is to concede to the will of the majority of the people in those states for self-determination. Already the efforts to prevent the breakup of the Union have cost over ten thousand lives. And despite our imprisonment of over 40,000 people and dozens of executions, the revolution is entering a much more dangerous stage. The rebels now threaten to contaminate major water supplies through the introduction of genetically manufactured microorganisms. Moreover, the miniaturization of nuclear weapons to fit into a brief case means that it is only a matter of time before we are faced with a major disaster unless this revolution is quickly resolved.

One of the more frustrating aspects of the present situation is that it was so clearly foreseeable from the experience of Canada and the Quebec secessionist movement. It is indeed a shame that we could not have learned from that experience and taken the steps necessary at the close of the twentieth century to avoid a repeat of that problem in our own country. Moreover, we knew the intent of the revolutionaries as long ago as 1994 when the Aztlan movement indicated its ultimate goal of forming an independent nation of the seven Southwestern states. Most unfortunately, no action was taken at the end of the last century to reduce the tidal wave of immigration that would so increase the Hispanic population in the Southwest as to make a move for independence inevitable. Now we have no alternative but to make the best of a deplorable situation. In addition to granting independence to the Southwest, we must make every effort to accommodate the millions of Americans in those states who wish to remain part of the United States and so want to migrate to the remaining forty-three states. Absorbing these people into our already overcrowded cities will present a host of additional problems, but at this time there is no alternative.

Our job might have been made easier if we had controlled our exponential population growth. It now appears inconceivable that in 1990 Congress increased the rate of immigration in the misguided belief that such action would add to the labor force and thus somehow prevent both the bankruptcy of the Social Security system in 2020 and improve business profits through a continued source of cheap labor. The result was, as you well know, that the population of the United States is now over 500 million and at present growth rates will reach one billion people early in the next century. To make matters much worse, the bulk of the population growth continues to be among the poor, uneducated, and less intelligent. Although it has long been taboo to discuss the genetic component of intelligence, the practice of subsidizing the birth rate among the poor and the addition of 150 million immigrants since 1990—most of whom were unskilled and uneducated—has had the unintended consequence of reducing the national average IQ by almost 10 points, and resulted in a rigid class-based society determined by intelligence.[1]

Furthermore, the growth in the number of unskilled workers competing for a dwindling number of low-skilled jobs has resulted in depressed pay scales that are barely sufficient to sustain life. If all this were not bad enough, the fantastic notion that every woman has a right to have children irrespective of her capability to support and care for them has resulted in the virtual disintegration of the American family. Less than 20 percent of African American children and less than 50 percent of white children now live in two-parent families. The incidence of abused and neglected children in the United States has reached a scale unprecedented in any society in the world. And, unfortunately, the magnitude of the problem is so large that there simply isn't enough money in the welfare system to to provide more than the basic necessities of life.

Finally, the battle for jobs has greatly aggravated the racial strife between whites, blacks, Asians, and Hispanics that has plagued our nation for the last sixty years. Many of our major cities have become virtual war zones as battles rage among rival ethnic gangs for control of the neighborhoods. As the number of people living in poverty increases unabated, drug trafficking continues to be one of our largest industries despite the expenditure of hundreds of billions of dollars over the last sixty years to fight this losing battle.

Perhaps the most distressing aspect of our current predicament is that it took so long to reach this crisis stage and yet no action was taken when the trends were clearly visible at the end of the twentieth century. It is a classic case of the boiling-frog syndrome. You have all heard the old anecdote that if you throw a frog into a pot of hot water the frog will immediately jump out. But if you put the frog in water at room temperature and then gradually turn up the heat, the frog will not sense the danger until it gradually succumbs to the heat and dies. As a nation we became accustomed to high crime rates, a shrinking middle class, greater poverty and homelessness, more child abuse, environmental degradation, and all the negative consequences of becoming an overpopulated nation like those we used to disparagingly refer to as third world countries. Finally, it became more than we could collectively stomach and so now you have elected the present administration with a mandate to take whatever action necessary to rescue the nation from its plight.

Therefore, after decades of inaction we are forced to adopt the following, admittedly draconian, policies:

First, we are sealing the borders to immigrants. Had we had a reasonable immigration policy over the past fifty years this drastic action would not have been necessary. But drastic times call for drastic measures. Therefore, in addition, no work visas will be granted and all aliens will be asked to reregister. A standardized tamperproof birth certificate, including encrypted thumb and retina prints will be created. This new proof of citizenship will be necessary for employment, social security, health care, and public education. Only foreign diplomats or noncitizens working on projects clearly in the long-term interests of this country will be permitted to stay in this country beyond the end of the year.

Second, childbearing will now require a license just as marriage does. The benefit of childbearing licenses will be two-fold: both to reduce the total number of births and to ensure that those couples who wish to have a child have received training in the basics of child care. Only couples will be eligible for childbearing permits and women must be between the ages of twenty-eight and thirty-five. One free permit will be issued per woman, unless it can be shown that a prior child has died. A second permit will cost $100,000 to defray the social costs inherent in providing education, energy, and pollution abatement associated with each additional person. Failure to follow this law will result in severe fines. A second conviction will result in sterilization.

Healthcare reform is the next item on our agenda. In the past, healthcare reform meant trying to give virtually unlimited care to all who requested it. However, with advances in technology it is now possible to extend the lives of almost anyone for many years if we are willing to incur the extraordinary costs. Despite this technological capability there are not enough government revenues to meet the virtually unlimited demand for life extending medical treatment. Also we do not have a sufficient number of doctors to provide the medical treatment, despite the decline in qualifications necessary to obtain a medical degree. Consequently, the only possible solution is to ration medical treatment. To that end I will be introducing the Medical Treatment Allocation Bill. This bill will set up administrative procedures for hospitals to follow in order to determine the medical treatment for which each patient is eligible depending upon the person's age and long-term prognosis. I know that such a procedure will cause grief for those who may be forced to forego life prolonging treatment. I also recognize that there is no alternative to lingering deaths for many terminally ill people since euthanasia remains illegal in many states. To those unfortunate victims, I extend my most heartfelt sympathy.

One of the few consolations in our current situation is in the area of nutrition. At least the United States is not faced with the food shortages now affecting so many regions of the world. It is unfortunate that because of our need to feed our own burgeoning population, even with the restrictions on beef production, the United States still has no surplus grain for export. Of course the loss of American grain exports has greatly exacerbated the shortage of food in many countries. This tragedy is all the more regrettable because it was so predictable. As early as 1997 almost one-third of the world's crop land—an area the size if China and India combined—had been abandoned due to overuse and was being replaced primarily by burning down the world's remaining rainforests. Any fool could have seen that such a practice was impossible to continue indefinitely. Yet nothing was done.

Even more serious than the loss of cropland and forests, has been the decline in fresh water, which threatens the very existence of many nations. As you know, most of the world's rivers run through more than one country, and the resulting wars over water rights have claimed an estimated eighty million lives in the last fifty years, with no end to the carnage in sight.

Even though the birth rates in every nation are now below the replacement rate of 2.1 children per couple, and worldwide population growth has stopped, we now recognize that our planet cannot even support the present nine billion people. But reducing population to the long term sustainable goal of five billion looks to be an extraordinarily difficult task. Not the least of our problems will be the need to support the aged population with a workforce only half the size of the dependent population of the world. It will require extraordinary growth in productivity at the very time that investment per capita is declining. The huge inequality between those countries that have failed to control their population in time (including most of Central and South America, Africa, and the much of the Middle East), and the rest of the world's nations, which succeeded in halting their population growth almost fifty years ago, has contributed to the enmity between the two groups of nations.

It is troubling indeed to find the United States powerless to play a leading role in the present worldwide strife. By foregoing our responsibilities during the first half of this century and continuing our policy of selling arms to every developing nation, we have severely undermined our ability to influence the course of world politics during the last half of the twenty-first century. From hindsight, it is apparent that our assumption that military superiority would be the determining factor in global conflicts was a tragic misunderstanding of the new realities. The plain fact is that nuclear superiority is no longer relevant in resolving international discord. And since our own economic plight is so precarious, we can ill afford to offer financial aid to any other nation, as we have so often in the past. Indeed, the question now is how to keep our own economy from further deterioration.

One of the most serious drains on our national resources has been the need to build dikes and relocate those people living along both seacoasts. The rise in sea level resulting from the atmospheric warming will require the relocation of over fifty million people and the building of new cites as much as 100 miles inland in some areas. I will soon be sending Congress proposed legislation to enforce energy conservation with a goal of reducing energy consumption and increasing the energy efficiency of machines and engines by 50 percent over the next twenty years. Had this legislation been enacted in the last century we could have reduced the global warming by as much as two-thirds and avoided the increased ocean levels that now threaten a significant proportion of the world's population located along coastal areas.

With the dramatic decline in the worldwide production of crude oil and natural gas, we must now also set a goal to meet half of our energy requirements through solar, geothermal, and wind sources. Nuclear energy will be required to fill a large portion of the other half of our energy needs. However, we still have not found a cost-effective answer to the disposition of nuclear wastes now that we have more than two hundred reactors retired in place throughout the country. The huge cost of ensuring the security of these retired reactors against a calamity caused by an act of nature or the work of terrorists might also have been avoided had the problem been given the attention it deserved in the twentieth century.

Another necessary priority of this administration, and one that will require a large portion of our national budget, is the expeditious clean-up of the 50,000 toxic waste dumps throughout the country. With one-third of the nation's groundwater already too polluted to drink, and with no hope of decontamination, we are facing severe water shortage in many areas of the country. We must, therefore, expend every effort to stop further contamination by cleaning up these poisonous waste dumps despite the enormous cost.

There is now a critical shortage of fresh water in 34 of the nation's 106 water-supply regions. Needless to say, we support the efforts of state and local governments in their enactment of laws providing severe penalties for any people who waste water in such senseless activities as washing cars or watering their lawns. However, at the present price of water approaching $12 a gallon in some parts of the country, only the very affluent can afford to be so wasteful.

As we are now all painfully aware, the high plains states stretching from the Dakotas to Oklahoma depended upon the underground water supply known as the Ogallala Aquifer. This water source has been steadily depleted for the last one hundred years and nothing was done to rectify the situation until it was too late. Then, in an act of desperation, it was decided to begin diverting water from the Great Lakes to the Plains states. The consequences of this ill conceived $100 billion project were all too predictable. We already knew what happened to the Aral sea in Central Asia when the same experiment was tried there. In a few decades, almost two-thirds of the Aral Sea had turned into a virtual desert. The same effect is now occurring in the Great lakes. Consequently, we must abandon the diversion of Great Lakes water and severely curtail grain production in the high plains states. With the loss of millions of acres of wheat production in the high plains states, we can ill afford to waste grain on inefficient sources of protein such as livestock. I am also asking Congress to continue indefinitely the moratorium on beef and pork consumption. Raising poultry will still be permitted, but to ensure a more equitable distribution, ration cards to purchase both poultry and fish will now be required.

Turning next to the issue of education, for as long as I can remember, every new administration has stated that it would make education a top priority. However, while giving lip service to that commitment, the federal government has spent less than 2 percent of the Federal Budget on education, forcing the burden onto the states and, more significantly, individual municipalities. Since the municipalities have widely differing tax bases it is not surprising that the quality of education varies dramatically from school to school. To make matters worse, the public education system first abrogated the teaching of values and morality, and then viewing with alarm the lack of moral behavior in our children, allowed the intrusion of religious beliefs in the classroom under the assumption that religions might have some special knowledge of appropriate moral behavior. This policy, coupled with a voucher system that allowed parents to send their children to any school of their choosing at state expense, has resulted in a system of cultural fragmentation and religious sectarianism that is not only divisive but has undermined the very basis of education. Instead of being taught how to think critically, we produced a nation of children conditioned to unquestioningly accept the pronouncements of their religious and civil leaders.

Given the general level of public apathy, economic and political ignorance, and rising religious fundamentalism, it was inevitable that a charismatic despot such as my predecessor would eventually come to power. Using the powerful psychological tools developed by the media to shape consumer views, and supported by the moral authority of religious leaders, he was not only able to win the presidency, but came perilously close to persuading the American public to repeal our cherished Bill of Rights on the false belief that his neo-Fascist policies would end the present economic chaos and bring about a new millennium. It was only his accidental death and the ensuing struggle for succession that allowed the truth of his plans to be revealed. That revelation, coupled with the ensuing economic collapse, appears to have been the necessary catalyst for the American people to awaken from their stupor and elect an administration that has resolved to begin the long road to reconstruction. The key to this reconstruction will be a complete revamping of the education system with the goal of increasing the quality of education in all schools, not just those of the rich, by stressing critical thinking, moral excellence, academic meritocracy, and job preparedness.

The United States now has over three million people in federal prisons, over 80 percent of whom were convicted on drug-related felonies. The expansion of the death penalty to sellers of drugs appears to have had minimum impact. Juries appear even more reluctant to find suspects guilty knowing that it means a sentence of death. Moreover, attempts to stop drug production by sending troops to Peru, Bolivia, and Columbia have resulted in revolutions in all three countries, each of which had to be put down by ruthless suppression and the installation of military dictatorships. What small measure of success we were able to achieve in reducing the smuggling of cocaine was more than offset by the growth in demand for the new manufactured drugs that are so concentrated as to be easily concealed for transportation throughout the nation. Over the last sixty years we have spent more than one trillion dollars on fighting the war on drugs yet we seem no closer to solving the problem. I have, therefore, requested the attorney general to convene a panel of psychologists, psychiatrists, criminologists, educators, and others who may have insight into the causes of drug abuse to seek new solutions to this perplexing national tragedy. The emphasis of the new approach will involve decriminalization of illicit drugs to remove the extraordinary profit incentives for drug sales, regulation and state sale of all drugs including alcohol and tobacco, rehabilitation of addicts, and the providing of job opportunities to youth that will dissuade them from getting started down the drug road in the first place.

There is much more that must be done to reconstruct our society than I have time to discuss this evening. Our infrastructure has been crumbling for almost a century, one-third of our citizens live in poverty, and our violent crime rate is the highest in the world. In short, in the space of the last seventy years our once great nation has come to reflect an average standard of living that is closer to the Less Developed Countries than that of the European Economic Community and the Pacific Rim Consortium. There is no excuse for this; all the advantages were in our favor, but a combination of short-term self-interest and ill-conceived utopianism have reduced our once mighty and united nation to a condition where it will take fifty to one hundred years of heroic effort to return the country to its former greatest. But let it not be said of us, as has been said of the previous generations: "They were endowed with the richest natural heritage of any people on earth, but through a combination of narrow minded self-interest and sheer stupidity, they managed to squander not only their own inheritance, but the fortune of generations to come."

We wish at long last to fulfill the vision of our nation's founders and justify the display of our most famous monument, Liberty Enlighteing the World.

Thank you.

State of the Union Address of the President to Congress, 2050, based upon policy reforms initiated in the year 2000:

Mr. Speaker, ladies and gentlemen of Congress, in preparing my text for this State of the Union message, I was initially perplexed by the realization that I had no dramatic new initiatives to propose. It seemed to me that I was going to have a hard time maintaining your interest throughout an address that, in essence, says that we are going to stay the course charted for us fifty years ago. To be sure, there are many complex issues that remain to be dealt with—which I shall address shortly—but the overall health of our nation today is testimony to the wisdom and foresight of our predecessors in all three branches of our government, as well as the self-sacrifice and perseverance of the American people. Allow me to review some of the policies that we will continue to pursue and the benefits which they are generating for our nation.

Just before the turn of the century, it became apparent that the short-term focus of our legislators was a function of a system that was held hostage by special-interest groups and a two-year congressional term that prevented any thought being given to the long-run good of the nation. Changing the House of Representative terms to four years, enacting term limits, subsidizing the candidacy of qualified office seekers with public money, eliminating Political Action Committees (PACs), and placing strict limitations on the total campaign expenditures, broke the back of the special-interest lobbies. By redirecting legislative attention on the long term, congressmen became cognizant of the crucial national trends that were apparent to anyone who took the time to study them since the 1960s. The results of this change in perspective was dramatic.

In the first place, the legislators recognized that unless we controlled the rapid growth in population, the United States would eventually overtake China as the world's most populous nation early in the twenty-second century. The result would have been an unmitigated disaster resulting in a declining standard of living for all but the elite, environmental devastation, class warfare, an imposition of rigid conformity to maintain order, and the subsequent loss of those individual freedoms we Americans have cherished since the nation's birth.

It is therefore with particular satisfaction that I can point out that our population continues to decline slightly each year since reaching a high of 350 million in 2040. We intend to sustain this downward trend which, at the present rate, would result in 200 million people by the middle of the next century. At that level, we will be able to make moderate but continuous improvements in our standard of living without further destruction of our environment. It is especially gratifying to note that we have been able to induce this population reduction without instituting any of the extreme measures that would have been required had we waited until the population soared completely out of hand before addressing the problem.

The stabilization of birth rates at two births per woman was achieved by eliminating the tax credit and welfare benefits beyond two children; instituting public education programs for responsible parenting aimed at teenagers; tying welfare benefits to the use of long-term contraception, such as the subdermal implant; free availability of all forms of birth control, such as RU–486 and other early abortion medications; and reintroduction of publicly funded abortions. Of particular success was the reinstitution into the nation's collective conscience of the time-honored tradition that it is shameful and morally reprehensible to have a child that a person cannot afford to sustain either emotionally or financially. This was reinforced by the laws prohibiting unwed mothers under the age of eighteen from keeping a child. Effectively, it forced them to either abort the fetus or give the child up for adoption. Changing public attitudes concerning abortion took some time in the face of opposition from religious fundamentalists, just as the acceptance of contraception did in the first half of the last century. Today it is universally recognized that abortion is not only a woman's right, but might be a moral obligation if the alternative of giving birth will result in serious hardship for the child.

The other population control policy—requiring that the quota on immigration be commensurate with our goal of zero population growth—has not only greatly increased job opportunities in our own country, but has placed pressure on other nations to reduce their own populations to sustainable levels as well. Certainly, the lack of immigrants has caused some temporary shortages in certain professions, and has even resulted in the loss of some businesses which sought to take advantage of cheaper labor elsewhere. Nevertheless, the reduced growth in the labor force has resulted in increased wage rates and lower unemployment, as the basic law of supply and demand always guarantees. Curbing the influx of cheap foreign labor coupled with the relocation of low-income housing outside of the central cities provided increased job opportunities to inner city poor while simultaneously resulting in the welcomed demise of the urban ghetto and its culture of poverty. Moreover, the increase in wage rates, spurred by the shortage of unskilled labor, coupled with limitations on welfare benefits, has resulted in a sustained and dramatic reduction in welfare recipients.

Many of you viewing this address remember the deplorable state of the world's environment at the turn of the twenty-first century. Deforestation, loss of topsoil, salinization, pollution of virtually every large body of water both above and below ground, destruction of the ozone layer, loss of plant and animal species at an alarming rate, environmental warming; the list goes on and on. It was no wonder that some scientists had the fanciful notion that the only hope for humankind was to build giant spaceships to carry humans to new planets in remote solar systems. Fortunately, reasonable people recognized the futility—not to mention prohibitive cost—of such a desperate gamble. As a nation, we decided to save ourselves from drowning in our own waste.

Perhaps the most daunting challenge of this century has been to save the environment from the ravages of our less ecologically conscious ancestors. Although some preliminary efforts were made in this regard during the last decade of the twentieth century, it soon became evident that, in the words of Preston Cloud, "We should not tackle vast problems with half vast concepts."[2] To salvage our fragile planet we had to develop an entirely new perspective of what responsibilities each generation has for its successors. We learned to adopt the perspective of Lester Brown who way back in 1981 espoused the view that we had not inherited the earth from our fathers, but rather are borrowing it from our sons and daughters.[3]

Reducing consumption to environmentally sustainable levels has proved a difficult goal, yet substantial progress has been made in recent years due no doubt in part by the shift in national focus away from Gross Domestic Product (GDP) as a measure of social growth. Our new Index of Social Welfare (ISW) is less biased toward consumption and measures the factors that more closely reflect improvement in aggregate human welfare, such as increases in literacy, employment, parenting hours, leisure time, environmental quality, etc., as well as decreases in infant mortality, divorce, juvenile suicides, crime, and mental illness. We now recognize that the goal of increasing GDP without reflecting the consumption of natural resources, the decline in the quality of air and water, the loss of species diversity, and the impact on the dozen other measures impacting the quality of life, was misleading at best. GDP also ignored the inherent value of maintaining full employment, opting instead to maximize total accumulation of products and services. Although the new ISW measure is not without its shortcomings and methodological difficulties, it appears to be moving the nation in the right direction.

More importantly, the ISW index results are now very close to the goal set by Congress in 2030. All major indices rose, including the number of high school and college students passing the National Proficiency tests, improvements in environmental quality, as well as the job and life satisfaction components. We have also witnessed declines in crime rates, infant mortality, unwanted pregnancies and involuntary unemployment. The composite ISW index now stands at 87, only three points below the national goal of 90, and for the first time surpassing the European and Pacific Basin Communities. When we compare this result to the 47 rating we registered when the Index was created, we can take justifiable pride in our nation's true progress in the past twenty years.

The new perspective derived from adopting the ISW produced a radically different economic paradigm. The simplistic cost/benefit analysis economists had used in the past to evaluate environmental and land-use issues guaranteed that the interests of future generations were discounted to the point of being all but ignored. Moreover, oftentimes businesses were able to derive private benefits from polluting while transferring the cost of pollution cleanup to society at large. This inequity required changes in cost accounting so that the person who benefits from pollution was the same person who incurred the cost, thus removing the incentive to pollute.

Forcing companies to pay the long-term cost of resource depletion and pollution resulted in either increased prices such that public consumption of the most damaging products was reduced or else inspired companies to seek improved technology to conserve resources and reduce pollution. Changes in cost accounting to include the long-term environmental costs of consumption means not merely that society now has the necessary economic incentive to recycle 60 percent of all the physical commodities that we consume, but that the nature of consumption itself is viewed very differently. Consumption of physical goods is now considered at best a necessary evil. The economic goal is to reduce rather than increase annual physical consumption rates. Preservation is the new ethos driving all economic decisions. Economists focus on the net- rather than gross-stock of physical capital, including natural resources. Durability is the primary quality of every product. Whereas it was once fashionable to buy a new car every two or three years, today's mark of status is the age of a person's car, just as in antique furniture. Turn of the century cars retrofitted with solar battery powered engines are now almost worth their weight in gold. Possession of many material goods is considered vulgar and crude.

Few people at the turn of the century recognized that the home computer would become a major factor in preserving the environment. But the information highway was the ultimate answer to the ever-increasing congestion and pollution from the nation's asphalt highways. Many people did not realize that one of the primary benefits of the shift to the information age was to switch consumer demand from the limited resource intensive goods to the inexhaustible and environmentally benign information services.

The technology of virtual reality now permits a person to have almost any vicarious experience without needing to expend large sums of money and utilize vast amounts of energy traveling around the globe. Of course, such experiences can prove psychologically addictive, but we learned long ago that addictive personalities will always find some means of escaping from reality whether by means of alcohol, drugs, or virtual reality. The best that a government can do is to protect society from any criminal consequences of addicts while offering the latter medical treatment and incentives to overcome their problem.

This administration will also continue the policies of the past several administrations that have reduced the national debt to an inconsequential level. Although conservatives tried to blame the deficits entirely on entitlement programs, and liberals tried to blame them wholly on defense spending, there were three causes that led to the huge national debt. First, was the huge ramp-up of defense spending based upon an erroneous belief that we were beset by a worldwide communist conspiracy which must be met by ever increasing spending on arms. In adopting such a far-fetched scenario, we effectively forced the Soviet Union to adopt a similar strategy thus launching an arms race that lasted until the Soviets went bankrupt. The second budget buster was the runaway healthcare costs precipitated by the utopian notion that every person was entitled to federally supported health care regardless of the cost. The third major cause of the deficits was the belief in the peculiar economic alchemy—the so-called supply-side economic theory—holding that by reducing taxes we could stimulate the economy to such an extent that total tax receipts would actually exceed the tax reduction. This age-old notion of getting something for nothing makes wonderful political rhetoric and ensured the election of presidents, but caused skeptics to question whether Lincoln might have missed the mark when he said you can't fool all the people all of the time. It appeared that you could fool most of the people most of the time, and that was enough.

Eventually, however, reason did prevail and by the turn of the century we were able to rein in the annual deficits and eventually reduce the national debt relative to GDP. The first step was to bring total defense expenditures down to 2.7 percent of GDP, about the level of our major trading partners. The surprising benefit was that in so doing we actually increased, rather than decreased, our national security. The United States became less tempted to directly intervene in the affairs of other countries not directly related to our national interest. The result was that America has now enjoyed the longest period of peace in our history and has won the respect and confidence of the world community. It is my intention to continue this successful policy and, in the absence of any foreseeable threat to our nation's security, reduce the portion of national output devoted to defense spending to 1 percent of GDP. This would still result in the spending of more on defense than the next four nations combined.

The second step toward solving our budget problem was to bring the growth of health care under control by limiting the lifetime payouts per capita and restricting certain medical procedures depending on the prognosis. This rationing of health care reflected the new public attitude that demanded increasing investment in preventive health care and reducing expenditures that only served to prolong the dying process.

Third, the nation finally got a Congress with enough backbone to demand that no new mandates be enacted without also requesting the taxes required pay for them. Congress also passed a value-added tax sufficient to pay for the federal programs that the public wished to continue. The VAT had the added benefit of reducing environmental destruction and increasing the savings rate.

Luckily, Congress and the president finally decided to make the tough decisions and take on health care and defense. The dramatic cutbacks in these two areas implemented at the turn of the century not only enabled us to balance the budget, but eventually freed up billions of tax dollars to invest in the most important resource of any country, its people. Education during the last century was sadly lacking in several respects. It was overly weighted in favor of funding for higher education to the detriment of primary and vocational education; it lacked training in societal values; the quality of education was unevenly distributed among social groups due to reliance on local funding; most standards of achievement were compromised due to misguided efforts to avoid discrimination; and discipline in the classroom was so compromised by the threat of lawsuits that teachers dreaded going to class. To make matters worse, the entire system of public education was endangered by efforts of religious groups that demanded we either introduce their doctrines into the curriculum or pull down the entire system of public education through the diversion of funding to private schools.

A comparison of American schools with those of Japan, Korea, and other Asian societies showed that there was nothing particularly mysterious in the failure of American education. Asian societies simply put in more days of schooling, more hours per day, more homework, more parental involvement, and certainly far more discipline. Somewhere in the 1960s the U.S. system got off track by thinking that school should be fun and that students should have a major say in how the schools should be run. So the first step of education reform was to give control of the schools back to the principals and teachers. Nationwide achievement standards were established. Funding for primary grades was increased and made more uniform across school districts. Unions were pressured to allow teachers to be constantly evaluated and those who failed proficiency tests in terms of academic knowledge or teaching skills were dismissed. Students who did not meet the achievement standards for college by age sixteen were slated for technical training. A smaller number of students went on to college and received advanced degrees. For those who did, greater emphasis was placed on a core curriculum and the physical sciences. Dollars saved on college education were pumped into more advanced vocational training and adult retraining programs. The result was a work force better matched to the needs of the work place; less wasted investment; and fewer frustrated, unemployed, and underemployed college graduates.

Additional investment was made in early childhood development programs to provide all children with a more equal starting point. By increasing investment in children, we sought to avoid the almost hopeless task of attempting to remedy a seriously disadvantaged adult. One of our most successful programs was making childhood development training mandatory for all those intending to have a child. This requirement, coupled with disincentives for people to have children that they would be unable to support, resulted in a dramatic decline of children born into poverty and deprived of a decent chance to succeed in life. Of course, to initiate many of these programs required a rethinking of what constitutes a "right" and a clarification of some very ambiguous language in the Constitution to reflect two hundred years of new knowledge and a very different world situation than the framers of the Constitution could have imagined.

Progress against crime during this half century has been truly remarkable. At the turn of the century, there were over one million inmates in federal and state penitentiaries; almost 80 percent of their crimes were in some way connected with drugs. Today we have been able to reduce the number of prison inmates by 75 percent despite a total U.S. population that is 20 percent larger. We can credit four social policies for this success: (a) the decriminalization of acts between consenting adults including prostitution and the sale and possession of drugs; (b) the inculcation of moral values in the education system, which reduced the propensity to antisocial behavior; (c) expanded knowledge of the causes of crime, both genetic and environmental, leading to an attack on the underlying casual factors such as hormonal imbalances, unemployment, gratuitous violence in the media, and the like; and (d) early childhood intervention which, at times, meant removing children from parents and placing them into institutions. When it became known that our society was serious about not tolerating negligent or abusive parents, and provided the means and incentives to avoid having unwanted children, the need for institutionalizing children dropped significantly.

It is especially gratifying to note that we were able to make such dramatic social gains in spite of (in fact, probably because of) our efforts to deal squarely with the Less Developed Countries (LDCs). Reduction of LDC debt through debt-for-nature swaps did much to save the world's dwindling rain forests. Technology transfers were used to help slow growth in pollution in the LDCs, while the developed nations took greater responsibility for reducing their own pollution. The reduction in trade barriers, without sacrificing environmental protections, proved more effective in improving the economies of the less-developed countries than all the previous international aid, even though it did reduce the demand for labor-intensive jobs in the developed nations. Surprising as it was to some, our efforts to persuade the World Bank to stop funding large projects in the LDCs proved more of a blessing for the LDCs than a curse. The megaprojects that the bank was so fond of encouraging almost inevitably proved to be economic failures, while also dislocating millions of people and proving disastrous for the environment. At our prodding, the World Bank changed its policy and supplied the funds for hundreds of thousands of small loans that provided indigenous people with the means to improve the productivity of their farms or start small businesses. The results have been gratifying.

Finally, the United States can be proud that we did our share in providing aid for birth control and family planning services throughout the world, thus significantly reducing birth rates in the LDCs. However, it will take another century to reduce the world's population to an environmentally sustainable level.

The policy of this administration will be to stay the course of those policies proven to be effective over the first half of this century. Although no new policy initiatives appear necessary at this time, we will continually monitor changes in the Index of Social Welfare, and when the empirical evidence warrants it, we will take appropriate action. As always, we will be driven by pragmatic rather than ideological considerations.

Thank you.

Which State of the Union will become a reality?

Both State of the Union addresses may appear far-fetched. But as the rest of this book will demonstrate, both scenarios are well within the realm of possibilities. At present, there is no doubt that we are on the course that will lead to the more pessimistic scenario. There are those who would argue that twenty years ago there were also prophets of doom who thought that by this time the world would have ended in nuclear holocaust. But note that it was specific actions on the part of both the United States and the former Soviet Union that avoided the catastrophe. Similarly, it was the introduction of a host of new environmental protection policies that halted the spread of some of the most dangerous pollutants such as dioxins, PCBs and CFCs. Likewise, it will take extraordinary changes in socioeconomic policies to come anywhere close to the optimistic second scenario. The difficulty is that many of the current trends are reinforcing (such as teenage pregnancy, mother-only families, poverty, and crime), so that to make a significant difference will take implementation of an integrated, comprehensive set of socioeconomic policies such as those discussed in the chapters that follow.

NOTES

1. I am well aware that it is politically incorrect to even consider the possible impact of genetics on IQ. However, Murray and Herrnstein have demonstrated quite convincingly that demographics can not only produce a decline in average IQ—a process they call *dysgenesis*—but that it is already occurring in the United States. Richard J. Herrnstein and Charles Murray, *The Bell Curve: Intelligence and Class Structure in American Life* (New York: The Free Press, 1994), chapter 15.

2. Preston Cloud, "Mineral Resources in Fact and Fancy," *Toward a Steady State Economy*, ed. Herman Daly (San Francisco: W. H. Freeman and Company, 1973), p. 51.

3. Lester R. Brown, *Building a Sustainable Society* (New York: W. W. Norton and Company, 1981), p. 359.

Chapter 2

Measuring the Welfare of Society and the Economic Fallacy

The traditional definition of economics is "a social science concerned with the problem of using or administering scarce resources (the means of production, i.e., land, labor and capital) so as to attain the greatest maximum fulfillment of our unlimited wants (the goal of production)."[1] Such a definition may seem clear enough but it is replete with ambiguities and omissions. First, there is an implicit assumption that we *should* attempt to fulfill unlimited wants through production. This assumption itself might pose an exercise in futility, since if wants are by definition unlimited, no amount of goods and services will fulfill them. There is another implicit assumption that fulfilling wants increases happiness, otherwise why would we care whether or not they are fulfilled? But as we will see, the relationship between fulfilling wants and increasing happiness is by no means as straightforward as it appears.

Second, the definition assumes that our collective *wants* (or consumer preferences in the parlance of economists) *are given*, not created, and there is no such thing as enough—more is always better. It ignores the capability of producers to create wants, which is a major function of advertising. Moreover, economic theory assumes that the consumer has "perfect information" regarding the costs of his preferences but ignores costs such as resource depletion or environmental damage.

Third, the definition of land traditionally includes natural resources such as minerals and forests but *excludes air and water*. Air and water were considered by economists as "unlimited" and hence "free goods." We know, of course, that pollution can destroy the quality of air and water, hence, the impact on air and water quality should be included in the cost of production. Alternatively, improvements in water and air quality should be included in measurements of output insofar as they fulfill basic needs.

Fourth, economics in the past has ignored the problem of waste from either the by-product of the production process or the disposal of goods after they are no longer functional, have become technologically obsolete, or we have just grown tired of them. Ecologists refer to the capacity to absorb wastes as the *sink function*. The capacity to absorb the growing mountains of waste, some of it quite toxic, without destroying our biophysical world will become one of the most important problems of the twenty-first century. Another way of characterizing the pollution and waste problems is to note that economics ignores the *problem of scale* with regard to economic activity. Again, traditional economics simplistically assumes that more is always better.

Fifth, by definition, economics (and neoclassic economic analysis*) ignores the *distribution* of the output of economic activity, yet this is a key point of disagreement in the economic theories of capitalism and socialism. Moreover, in considering the means of production we find that there is an inextricable link between production and distribution of goods and services. There is little doubt that meritocracy—rewarding people based upon their relative contribution—increases productivity and, hence, total output. At the same time, however, meritocracy leads to greater inequality in distribution and, if happiness is, in part, a function of each person's *relative* share of national output more so than their *absolute* share (once the basic necessities of life are achieved), then it is questionable as to whether the sole goal of economics should be to maximize production without giving some consideration to distribution.

Finally, and most significantly, economics is concerned primarily with optimizing consumption *today*. It is not concerned with the consequences for future generations. Economic models seek to attain Pareto optimality (named after the Italian economist Vilfredo Pareto) which is achieved when no further trading of consumer goods can make one individual better off without making another individual worse off. Note that this goal does not consider the fairness of the initial distribution of goods, nor does it consider the impacts of today's consumption on future generations.

This last point bears amplification because it may be the most serious failing of present economic theory. *Economic cost/benefit analysis assumes that*

*Neoclassic economic analysis, which is sometimes called marginal analysis, is the theory of how markets work to distribute goods and services. It is a result of a fusion of the theoretical work of the earliest economists such as Adam Smith, David Ricardo, and Thomas Malthus with the analysis of marginal changes in input, output, and prices of Alfred Marshall and Vilfredo Pareto. It is not concerned with the distribution of income.

the value of a good or service in the future is always worth less than it would be today. That is only true, however, from the perspective of people living today. It is a totally egocentric perspective—narrow self-interest run amuck. Taken to the extreme, there is no reason provided by economic theory why we should not consume all of the resources of world today and to hell with future generations. But as was demonstrated in *The Science of Morality*, when viewing the world from the perspective of Rawlsian justice, in which we attempt to develop ethical policies from a position of impartiality with regard to our present circumstances (from behind a "veil of ignorance"), we must give equal weight to the wants and needs of future generations. The economic perspective that goods and services tomorrow are less valuable than goods and services today I term *the economic fallacy*. We will return to this crucial failure of neoclassical economic theory time and again throughout this book.

In recent years, most economists have come to recognize the limitations of their science, yet often push them aside as externalities to be dealt with outside the framework of economic theory—a potentially fatal error when assessing economic policy. Other economists, especially in the new field of ecological economics, are seeking an interdisciplinary approach to wrestle with these crucial shortcomings. Still economics remains primarily focused on how markets for products and services work, and the goal of most research is how to most efficiently increase the total output of goods and services.[2] This focus on short-term maximization has led Harvard biologist Edward O. Wilson, considered to be one of America's greatest living scientists, to declare that "the greatest intellectual obstacle to environmental realism as opposed to practical difficulty is the myopia of most professional economists."[3]

The Use of Gross Domestic Product as the Measure of Social Welfare

As evidence of the obsession of economics with increased output, consider that the most important statistic the economic community tracks is the change in Gross Domestic Product (GDP). When adjusted for inflation, real- or constant-dollar GDP purports to reflect the value of all the goods and services produced in a given year. It is generally believed that such a measure can also serve as a rough gage of social welfare. The goal of economic policy has therefore become the long-term maximization of real GDP. But in so doing are we really maximizing social welfare? Social welfare is the aggregate of those factors that affect human happiness. However, there are many factors affecting human happiness that are not reflected in GDP measurements. These include: environmental quality, personal safety, health and longevity, and a host of intangibles such as peace of mind and self-fulfillment.

Social welfare is synonymous with the term "standard of living" in the broadest sense. Today, many economists and sociologists question whether GDP is even a satisfactory indicator of changes in economic output let alone the broader measure of standard of living. To the extent that it may be deficient, polices that are designed to maximize the growth of GDP may not improve social welfare; in fact, some such policies may be detrimental to social welfare and hence diminish human happiness.

It is my contention that GDP is so deficient as to be counterproductive when the increase in GDP per se becomes the primary goal of socioeconomic policies. To begin with, simply measuring aggregate GDP, even adjusted for inflation, does not tell us whether the people of a nation are growing richer or poorer. Many economists believe that *the real GDP per capita* is a more meaningful measure since it at least adjusts for the growth in the population. The growth in GDP for many less developed countries is being outstripped by the growth in their population, resulting in a decline in average GDP per capita. During the period from 1950 to 1973 growth in world GDP averaged about 4 percent, half of this due to population growth and half due to rising affluence. Between 1973 and 1980 world economic growth dropped to less than 3 percent with population growth the dominant factor.[4] Hence, there was little improvement in per capita real GDP worldwide. During the decade of the 1980s many LDCs made some progress. For example, Mexico increased its real per capita GDP by 2.9 percent per year. However, although Brazil's real GDP grew 2.1 percent per year, it was more than offset by growth in population so that, on a per capita basis, Brazil's GDP actually declined 0.1 percent per year throughout the decade.[5]

However, even real GDP per capita is not a useful measure of economic output, let alone social welfare. GDP per capita will increase with higher labor force participation rates even when real wage rates are falling. For example, in the United States GDP per capita rose in the 1970s when women entered the labor force as second household wage earners, often to supplement their husbands' declining real income. Hence, a better measure of economic output would be *real GDP per worker*. Likewise, we should look at how much income the worker actually has left to spend after paying taxes, i.e., *real disposable income per worker*.

To illustrate the dramatic difference in the various measurements, consider the following results for the U.S.:

1970–1997 Average Annual Growth Rate[6]

1. GDP	7.9 %
2. Constant Dollar GDP (inflation adjusted)	2.8
3. Constant Dollar GDP per Capita	1.8
4. Constant Dollar GDP per Worker	0.9
5. Constant Dollar Disposable Income per Worker	0.9

Note that real GDP and disposable income per worker increased between 1970 and 1997 by less than 1 percent per year. Furthermore, even this last measure, like any measure based upon GDP, is seriously flawed and overstates changes in social welfare for several reasons.

First, a certain portion of each year's production is going toward the replacement of the existing stock of investment. These expenditures only serve to maintain the existing level of physical capital; they do not increase the standard of living. This points out a major flaw in equating GDP with welfare. As economist Kenneth Boulding explains, at best GDP measures the *flow* of goods and services, but it is the *stock* of goods that contributes to human welfare.[7] ("Flow" refers to the annual output, while "stock" is the accumulated output of all past years.) Although Boulding's observation is insightful, it is not strictly correct. Much of the contribution to human welfare is in the form of services that are "consumed" at the time at which they are offered and thus are part of the flow rather than the stock of economic goods. Moreover, an increasing portion of GDP is comprised of services. Consider, for example, the growth in health care and education services over the past couple of decades. Nevertheless, with regard to *physical* goods it is the stock rather than the flow that is relevant. A better measure of economic welfare would be the change in the stock of goods adjusted for depreciation (net wealth) plus annual services on a per capita basis:

$$\frac{([\text{Net Wealth}_t - \text{Net Wealth}_{t-1}] + \text{Services}_t)}{\text{Population}_t}$$

where t is the current year and t – 1 is the prior year.

Second, GDP ignores the output of one of the most important sources of production in our society, the housewife (or househusband). Ironically, if parents hire someone to do the housework or to be a nanny to their children, it is counted in GDP, but if a woman does the work herself, it is not. The reason is that since she doesn't get a paycheck, it is very difficult to account for her contribution. However, her contribution to total output is no doubt considerable and has been estimated to equal 25 to 33 percent of total GDP.[8] When, beginning in the late 1960s, women entered the labor force in record numbers, the number of hours of housework, especially those associated with parenting, dropped dramatically. Even though it may have had a significant negative impact on the welfare of the nation's children (as will be shown), GDP increased as a result of the additional wages paid to the nation's women. Therefore, the shift of household functions such as child care, health care, food preparation, entertainment, and physical security from the housewife to the market economy resulted in a major increase in GDP. Nonetheless, it is at least questionable whether such a shift has increased net social welfare. It may have increased the welfare of many women who have jobs that they find rewarding and fulfilling. But for millions of men and women, a job is simply a necessary means of earning money to buy things that the homemaker used to provide "free" or that they have been conditioned to want. Furthermore, they are now taxed on the money they earn to pay for the previously "free" services. No wonder that, despite the increase in GDP, many Americans question whether their lives have improved. *After accounting for the addition to GDP of the unmeasured hours of labor of the housewife—which would increase GDP prior to 1970 more than afterwards—it is more than likely that real disposable income per worker was negative from 1970 to 1990.*

Economist Hazel Henderson points out that a third refinement that should be made to GDP is to adjust for depletion of natural resources analogous to a capital consumption allowance.[9] GDP treats the exhaustion of natural resources as if it were a good thing. Much of the apparent economic growth is an illusion based on the failure to account for a reduction in the nation's natural resources.[10] Economist Garrett Hardin suggests that we deduct from GDP an estimate of "Gross National Destruction (GND)."[11] This deduction should extend not only to loss of resources such as oil and gas, timber and farmland, but to air and water pollution as well. As mentioned previously, for too long economists have mistakenly considered air and water as free goods. But clean air and water are also limited resources and, therefore, have an economic cost that should be deducted from output.

On the other side of the ledger, Herman E. Daly and John B. Cobb Jr. criticize the convention of adding to GDP the defensive expenditures incurred to protect ourselves from the unwanted side effects of production.[12] Contrary to logic, if a firm spends money to clean up toxic wastes, it is considered a cost and reduces GDP, but if the government spends millions to clean-up toxic wastes, GDP increases because the expenditures are considered a purchase of goods and services.[13] For example, the clean-up of the Exxon Valdez oil spill increased GDP, but a system put in place by Exxon to insure that it wouldn't happen again reduces GDP! Even medical expenses resulting from the side effects of pollution, such as treatment for cancer, are counted as an addition to the nation's output rather than as a cost of producing that output.[14]

The same problem occurs when accounting for the costs of regulation without adding in any of the benefits of regulation. Regulations controlling toxic wastes reduce GDP, but there is no addition to GDP for the cleaner air and water that results from these controls. Pollution of underground water supplies is irreversible, but the cost of that pollution is not deducted from GDP until the effects of pollution necessitate expenditure for obtaining alternative water supplies. Hence, we need to measure the benefits of regulation against the costs, and the difference should be reflected in a measure of change in the welfare of the country. Such a measure should include the long-term value of clean air and water, not just the annual impact.

President Clinton took a step in the right direction when he directed the Bureau of Economic Development to devise a revised GDP measure that would reflect the cost of pollution and loss of natural resources.[15] In this connection, the National Biological Survey was instructed to inventory the biological and ecological resources of the nation. Clinton also directed federal agencies to look at all the benefits and costs of regulation, "those that are easily measured as well as those that are not."[16] Unfortunately, the Republican Congress, which appears to be biased against all forms of regulation, threatens to ignore the long-term benefits that are more difficult to quantify.

The seriously defective national accounting system distorts historic estimates of the nation's growth. In the 1950s and 1960s the absence of pollution control laws permitted producers to pollute with impunity and there was no deduction from GDP estimates. Then, beginning in the 1970s, tougher pollution control standards resulted in increased producer costs, such as for more fuel-efficient engines and catalytic converters to reduce hydrocarbon emissions, and additional waste treatment facilities to recycle water. The consequence was to reduce estimates of GDP growth even though there was a net benefit to social welfare. Theoretically, to avoid such distortion of GDP data, the cost of pollution should be deducted from past estimates of GDP, but as a practical matter this may be impossible. Similarly, additions to GDP should be made for economic benefits such as the reduced pollution due to improved automobile gasoline mileage.

Even an Improved Measure of GDP May Not Be a Valid Surrogate for Human Welfare

Supposing that we could construct a measure that adjusts for costs of resource depletion and pollution, changes in efficiency, changes in the stock of wealth, etc., and calculate the result on an inflation adjusted per capita basis; what would such a measure mean? Would it really be a measure of human welfare? Would it correlate with increases in human happiness? There is reason to doubt that it would. Surprisingly, studies have reported that self-reported happiness differs little from one society to another even when their material welfare, as measured by GDP, differs significantly. The studies reveal that above a very basic level of economic welfare, it is not the *absolute* level of affluence that contributes to personal satisfaction so much as the *relative* level of distribution within a society.[17] ***Although in any nation, wealthier people are generally happier than poorer people, increases in wealth in a given nation do not lead to increases in happiness, and wealthy nations are not, as a whole, happier than poorer ones.***[18]* A 1995 study showed that most Americans felt poorer then than they did thirty years before when real incomes were almost 30 percent lower than the 1995 levels.[19] Consequently, the percentage of Americans who reported they were "very happy" in 1995 was well below the 1965 level, and the number who reported that they were "not too happy" had risen over the thirty year period.[20] This lack of correlation between increased wealth and increased happiness is not unique to the United States. When Japan reached its peak of prosperity in the late 1980s, and the majority of Japanese believed that Japan had transformed itself from a poor nation to a rich one, fewer than 3 percent thought that Japan had become a happier nation.[21]

One reason that the level of economic affluence alone does not correlate with happiness is due to the *law of diminishing marginal utility*. At the very lowest levels of subsistence, each extra dollar can make a substantial difference in the lifestyle of a person. For example, a few extra dollars might mean the difference between being cold or warm at night, having enough to eat or suffering from malnutrition, etc. But as we move up the income spectrum an added dollar makes less and less difference. We all know the difficulty of increasing the enjoyment of the spoiled kid who already has more toys than he knows what to do with.

John Maynard Keynes believed that increased productivity would permit society to fulfill the basic "absolute needs" of human beings. These he defined as those needs which are felt regardless of the situation of other people (e.g., food, clothing, and shelter). There was a second class of needs, however: "those which are relative only in that their satisfaction lifts us above, makes us feel superior to our fellows."[22] Keynes rightly observed that such needs were insatiable. Economist John Kenneth Galbraith points

---

*As discussed in *The Science of Morality*, it might be argued that people will experience increased happiness as long as they have the *opportunity* to increase their economic status in absolute terms. But I know of no empirical evidence to support that hypothesis.

out that the production of goods actually creates the wants that goods are supposed to satisfy.[23] Even though advertising increases our wants, the satisfaction of those new wants does not necessarily increase a person's happiness (or does so only temporarily), but merely relieves the unhappiness created by the new want.

E. F. Schumacher, and advocates of smaller economies, argued that the major problem with modern economics is that it assumes that consumption (which is the flip side of production) is the end of economics. Schumacher advocated a Buddhist perspective in economics which would set as its aim to obtain the maximum of personal well being, i.e., happiness, through a minimum of consumption.[24] Most economists contend that increased happiness is too difficult to measure, so they set the goal of economics to maximize that which they can measure—the annual consumption of material goods.

Regardless of how much people have, they will always feel poor if they see that they have less than everyone else or they are conditioned to always want much more than they already have. Unfortunately, the whole purpose of advertising is to create new wants. Advertising does this most effectively by insinuating that a given product will allow people to satisfy their most fundamental needs. Virtually every product promises to increase personal security, sexual attractiveness, or the ability to dominate others by winning respect. Take the case of the typical beer commercial. The advertiser attempts to persuade us that beer = manliness = parties = girls = sex. Most automobile commercials have a similar message, the bottom line being that consumption determines happiness. Starting from this false premise, it is logical to mistakenly conclude that increased growth in GDP will naturally result in increased happiness.

Evaluating Economic Policies

This leads us to one of the central conundrums of economic policy. Most economic policies will create *relative* winners and losers, so how do we determine if a policy is desirable? In making this assessment we might turn to the concept of *modified* Rawlsian justice, which ***proposes that all are distributed goods equally except where an unequal distribution works to the relative advantage of the least favored.**** It is based upon the

*This should not be construed to be tantamount to proposing equal distribution. As a comparison of communist and capitalist societies in the post World War II era demonstrated only too well, a meritocracy that rewards extra effort and extraordinary performance will result in all people being better off than a system that effectively discounts performance.

assumption that this is the principle most people would accept if they would choose a guideline from behind a veil of ignorance with regard to their personal socioeconomic circumstances, i.e., they do not know whether they are rich or poor, black or white, young or old, smart or ignorant, etc., even whether they are part of this generation or some future one. Such an approach to distribution offers a basis for socioeconomic policy that most people would agree with if not biased by their present socioeconomic status. Adopting modified Rawlsian justice as the basis of social and economic policy will not necessarily lead to the maximizing of GDP, but could lead to greater happiness for all members of society, as opposed to increasing happiness for some at the expense of others.

An inherent difficulty with Rawls's theory is that people with a disposition for high risk may not choose to subscribe to Rawls's concept of justice. They may prefer a society in which people can risk everything—even life itself—for the chance to win big rewards. I find it doubtful that the majority of people would embrace such a strategy, but this is an empirical question that is worth further study. It does appear that the average disposition toward risk acceptance or aversion may differ from society to society, with European countries having a more skewed distribution of lower risk takers than the United States. To what extent this might be a function of genetic make-up or cultural conditioning is unknown.

In any case, in a democracy the political process determines the degree of trade-off between risk and reward inherent in the socioeconomic policies. This does not necessarily imply that the majority determines the desirable trade-off. A minority who possess a disproportionate share of political power may select policies that effectively fix one degree of trade-off for themselves and another degree of risk and reward for the rest of society. Therefore, when I assert that Rawlsian justice is a desirable criterion to be followed, I must confess that this doesn't follow as a derived hard and fast principle (as Rawls believed) but as a guideline that I seek to persuade others to accept by appealing to their sense of fairness. I believe that if we could inculcate this prospective into society, most people would be happier. At the same time, I admit that it flies in the face of the genetically induced desire for dominance—a winner-take-all predisposition. How can we accommodate those who are so disposed?

We might allow those who have a higher tolerance for risk to exercise that propensity by taking extraordinary chances with the understanding that society will not rescue them if they fail. Hence, if people want to bet their life savings on a high-risk business scheme they should be able to do so. But if they lose it all, they cannot expect any recompense from society. As demonstrated in *The Science of Morality*, it is essential that people be held accountable for their actions if we are to encourage prudent and prosocial behavior.

For socioeconomic policies to succeed in the long run, they must also promote the three harmonies referred to in *The Science of Morality*:

1. ***Individuals must, to some extent, have the opportunity to fulfill their basic biological needs to be in harmony with their genetic nature.*** This congruence requires more than simply meeting basic requirements of food, clothing, and shelter. It means providing the opportunity (not the guarantee) for people to fulfill other basic physiological and psychological needs such as personal security, sex, respect, a sense of belonging, etc. I emphasize the word, opportunity, because it is impossible for economic and social policies to guarantee success in attaining these goals. Furthermore, as will be shown, treating the attainment of these goals as inherent rights might be so counterproductive as to destroy the very incentives necessary for people to take the appropriate actions necessary to attain such objectives.

2. ***Fulfillment of the needs of individuals must be reconciled to the needs of others, i.e., to a reasonable extent, individual needs must be brought into harmony with societal needs.*** With any economic policy there will be winners and losers. It is impossible to meet 100 percent of everyone's needs and wants because they are bound to conflict with the needs and wants of others. Here, the goal is to mitigate against the extreme consequences of success and failure. The basis for this principle is similar to the logic underlying Rawlsian justice. Since our future circumstances are uncertain, prudent people will hedge their bets by foregoing the chances of extreme success to protect against the possibility of a horrible, subhuman existence. It is no different than the logic for taking out an insurance policy. The result of such logic would lead to some moderation of income distribution, but not to income equality if equality would result in such disincentives that all people in society would be severely disadvantaged due to the decline in general productivity. On the other hand, beyond some range of unequal income distribution, the diminishing returns of an added dollar of income may not add to the incentive for higher productivity but will only result in an increase in the general level of dissatisfaction.*

Economist Alan Blinder addresses this same issue when he questions whether it is better to have GDP growth of 4 percent and unemployment of 8 percent or GDP growth of 2 percent and unemployment of 4 percent. Blinder's answer is to opt for the higher growth rate and then take some of the proceeds that accrue to the winners of such a policy and redistribute

---

*Like Rawlsian justice, it cannot be maintained a priori that such harmony *should* be a basic principle, but we can assert that *if* we wish to optimize happiness in a society, this harmony *should* be pursued.

them to the losers.[25] I'm not at all certain that it is better to have higher growth than full employment. Moreover, although it is an article of faith with some economists that higher rates of growth will result in higher levels of employment, this is at least questionable. If population is held constant, growth in GDP per capita is primarily a function of increases in productivity. But growth in productivity, in turn, is primarily a function of substituting capital for labor (e.g., replacing assembly-line workers with machines, and to an increasing extent in the information age, the substitution of more efficient for less efficient capital—the constant updating of computers, software, and their application). In theory, the increase in productivity, and subsequently wealth, will result in the additional wealth being spent on additional goods and services, thus creating new jobs to replace the jobs that are lost. In reality, however, the process doesn't work out quite so neatly. The jobs that are lost oftentimes paid more than the jobs that are gained. The increased wealth that resulted from the increased productivity in the last decade has been concentrated into the hands of a smaller and smaller portion of the population. In addition, there is no guarantee that just because the jobs lost in the past were largely offset by the jobs gained, that it will be so in the future. One of the ways in which surplus labor was absorbed in the past was by reducing the average number of hours worked. Perhaps similar reductions in the average hours of work will be required in the future. (Some European countries are already down to a thirty-six-hour work week.)

An argument can be made that full employment should be a prime objective of economic policy because of the value of work in enhancing a person's self-respect and other social benefits such as reduced crime. It is very difficult to have self-respect without a job. For many people their self-identity is their job. They see themselves as "Carolyn, the teacher," "Denise, the lawyer," or "Rob, the police officer." Even the most menial of jobs can confer the satisfaction that the employed person is making a contribution to society, is self reliant, and is an asset to his/her family.

Furthermore, before we can seek to maximize economic growth, we must question the effect a given growth rate might have on the environment of future generations. This leads to a consideration of the third harmony that must be a goal of socioeconomic policy.

3. The aggregate needs of society must be fulfilled in a manner that is in harmony with the environment, i.e., aggregate consumption cannot exceed the carrying capacity of the environment. From behind a Rawlsian veil of ignorance, we don't even know whether we are a part of this generation or some future generation. It follows that Rawlsian justice would not seek to maximize output if it leads to destruction of the environment and jeopardized the happiness of future generations.

There was a time in the 1960s when the goal for economic growth in the United States was 4 percent a year. This exponential growth rate would result in expanding the production of goods and services by a factor of fifty in a century! Think about that a second. The U.S. annual output was $8 trillion in 1997. At a 4 percent growth rate, GDP would increase to $400 trillion annually over the course of one century. High rates of expansion are possible when starting from a very low base of production and a small population. But in a nation as mature as the United States, if the growth is driven primarily by consumption of physical goods rather than intellectual goods (such as art or education) or personal services, such an expansion would likely result in environmental destruction of unimaginable proportions. Reflections such as these lead us to consider ways of limiting or altering wants as an alternative to maximizing growth, a subject I will return to later.

In reflecting on Rawlsian justice and the three harmonies as the necessary precursors to human happiness, it is clear that maximizing GDP may not increase happiness, and in the long run may actually decrease human happiness. Obviously, there are many other measures that must be considered to determine whether progress is being made toward improving human welfare. These measures would include changes in infant mortality, teenage suicides, crime, longevity, employment, educational attainment, environmental quality, resource depletion, etc.

Alternative Measures of Social Welfare

There have been many attempts to combine a variety of factors for the purpose of attaining a truer reflection of changes in human welfare. Although some of the measures correlate with GDP over time, as we will see, there are notable discrepancies as well. Following are a few of the measures which attempt to correct for the deficiencies of GDP as a measure of human welfare and happiness.

Hicksian income, a concept developed by economist Sir John Hicks, is defined as "the maximum value which a man can consume during a week and still expect to be as well off at the end of the week as he was at the beginning."[26] Daly and Cobb applied this concept to national income as a measure of sustainable consumption. Hicksian income can be estimated by subtracting from GDP both the depreciation necessary to replace the stock of capital goods (which gives us Net National Product, NNP), and the depreciation which covers the consumption of natural resources, as well as the defensive expenditures necessary to protect against the unwanted side effects of production such as pollution.[27] Attempting to increase the growth rate of Hicksian income instead of GDP would increase the happiness of future generations by protecting them from rates of consumption that leave them with a depleted and polluted planet.

The United Nations *Human Development Report* ranked nations on an index that included life expectancy, adult literacy, and "purchasing power to buy commodities for satisfying human needs." The United States ranked sixth in this index, behind countries with lower GDP per capita such as Norway and Sweden.[28]

Japan has developed a *Modified GDP* that deducts the cost of pollution, crime control, addiction, etc., as social costs.[29] They plan to use this measure rather than GDP for assessing the impact of socioeconomic policy decisions.

The Overseas Development Council created a *Physical Quality of Life Index (PQLI)* that combines infant mortality, literacy rates, and life expectancy at age one.

The Fordham Institute for Innovation in Social Policy has developed an *Index of Social Health* comprised of sixteen indicators, including infant mortality rates, out-of-pocket healthcare costs for the elderly, teenage suicides, the high school drop-out rate, drug abuse, homicides, affordable housing, food stamps, child abuse, unemployment, average weekly earnings, the income gap between rich and poor, traffic deaths, and the number of children raised in poverty. The index, which stood at 73.8 in 1970, the first year of the series, reached a low in 1990 of 38.8. For 1992, the index improved slightly to 40.6; this was still 45 percent below the 1970 level, a pretty dismal performance over the past twenty-two years.[30]

Economists William Nordhaus and James Tobin developed an index that they called the *Measure of Economic Welfare (MEW)*. They began with GDP and then made three kinds of adjustments: "Reclassification of GDP expenditures as consumption, investment, and intermediate use; imputation for the services of consumer capital, for leisure, and for the product of household work; and correction for some of the disamenities of urbanization."[31] The separation of GDP into consumption, investment, and intermediate use is to isolate the consumption component that Nordhaus and Tobin believe is the only part of GDP that represents economic welfare. The reasons for the other adjustments are self-evident and we need not go into all the complexities of actually making these refinements. When comparing the results of their index to inflation adjusted GDP for the period 1929 to 1968, we find that the MEW grew only 1.1 percent per year compared to 1.7 percent average growth for real GDP. An even greater difference occurs when comparing the post World War II period of 1947 to 1965. Over this time, the MEW grew only 0.4 percent per year compared to the GDP average growth of 2.1 percent. Based on this comparison, the relatively steady growth in GDP did not yield the improvements in economic welfare that the GDP would appear to indicate. In fact, the growth in the MEW may still overstate improvements in human welfare since it does not deduct destruction of environment or negative aspects such as increased crime rates, family destruction, and overcrowding.

Xenophon Zolatas developed a measure of economic welfare that he termed the Index of *Economic Aspects of Welfare* (*EAW*). Like the MEW, the Zolatas index seeks to measure personal consumption, leisure, and household services. It also makes deductions for air and water pollution, resource depletion, commuting to work, and even half the cost of advertising. The last adjustment reflects the assumption of Zolatas that only half the cost of advertising represents a useful information service to consumers. Zolatas does not agree with Kenneth Boulding that it is the accumulation of goods that represents economic welfare and so the EAW ignores the stock of capital and focuses on the current flow of goods and services. In my opinion, this is a major weakness of the EAW index as a measure of social welfare or standard of living. However, the EAW does not purport to be a measure of the standard of living; it seeks only to measure the *annual* contribution to welfare. A more serious flaw of the EAW is its failure to reflect changes on a per capita basis. It is not an improvement in economic welfare if a society is consuming or producing more in the aggregate while average consumption is dropping. Despite these shortcomings, it is interesting to note that the EAW index grew only about 60 percent the rate of GDP from 1995 to 1997, i.e., about 2 percent per year.[32]

In an effort to correct the weaknesses of earlier indices of economic welfare, World Bank economist Hermann Cobb and theologian John Daly developed their own index which they call the *Index of Sustainable Economic Welfare* (*ISEW*). The ISEW starts with personal consumption and then makes numerous positive and negative adjustments as follows:

Personal Consumption (+/– Changes in distribution of income)

+ Household labor

+ Annualized stock of consumer durables

– Annualized expenditure for consumer durables

+ Public expenditures on health and education

– Defensive private expenditures on health and education

– Expenditures on advertising

– Costs of commuting

– Costs of urbanization (higher cost of land and housing)

- Costs of auto accidents
- Costs of water, air and noise pollution
- Loss of wetlands
- Loss of farmland
- Depletion of nonrenewable resources
- Long-term environmental damage due to use of fossil fuels (greenhouse effect, ozone loss and potential danger of wastes from atomic energy)

\+ Net capital growth

÷ Population

= per capita ISEW

Note that this measure considers the relative change in income distribution and consequently meets the guidelines of modified Rawlsian justice. Admittedly, some of these adjustments are controversial and the methods of estimating the adjustments at times may appear arbitrary. Nevertheless, the ISEW is a far better measure of changes in human welfare than GDP, and would be a better measure of the effectiveness of governmental policies. As such, it is instructive to contrast the results of the ISEW and GDP.

Comparing ISEW to GDP: 1950–1986 [34]

Year	*Per capita ISEW*	*Ann % Chg.*	*Per Capita GDP*	*Ann % Chg.*
1950	2488	N.A	3512	N.A.
1960	3052	2.06	4080	1.51
1970	3723	2.01	5294	2.64
1980	3672	-0.14	6477	2.04
1986	3403	-1.26	7226	1.84

During the period of the 1960s and 1970s both ISEW and GDP improved. One of the primary reasons for improvements in ISEW was the narrowing of the range in the distribution of income. However, disparity in income increased in 1970 and steadily worsened between 1976 and the last year estimated, 1986. Also during the 1970s, depletion of resources and failure to invest adequately to sustain the economy in the future resulted in a drop in the ISEW index by an average of 0.14 percent per year. In contrast, GDP was registering an average growth of about 2 percent a year. As the negative factors accelerated in the 1980s the ISEW fell an average of 1.26 percent per year even though GDP continued to increase 1.84 percent a year. Although Daly and Cobb's estimates don't go beyond 1986 there is little doubt that the disparate trends continued into the 1990s. The results correlate with what indexes of consumer confidence tell us and reflect how most people felt about their lives, i.e., that they did not improve during the 1980s and early 1990s, but actually got worse.

Although the mid-1990s probably would reflect an improvement in the ISEW, Daly and Cobb are pessimistic with regard to the long run. Their fear is that energy, which is now so cheap and abundant, will become more expensive. "The most fundamental problem in terms of sustainable economic welfare is the decline in the quality of energy resources as measured by the ratio of energy output to energy input. As a result of this entropic process, the discovery and extraction of oil will soon take more energy than is made available, thereby bringing to a close the era of cheap energy."[35] With the price of oil, in real dollar terms, sliding back to the level it was before the first oil shock of 1973, most people would be amazed at such a pessimistic outlook. Few people are aware that one of the reasons for the cheap oil today is Saudi Arabia's willingness to step up production and effectively dictate the lower price to the oil cartel as a reward to the U.S. for destroying the Saudis' most feared enemy, Iraq. How long the Saudis will be willing to continue flooding the world oil market to hold down the price is anyone's guess. Iraq also has substantial amounts of oil that the present embargo is keeping off the world market. Although the oil cartel is in disarray today as production hits an all-time high, the present rate of extraction cannot be maintained indefinitely. As we will see in chapter 5, world geological surveys indicate that within next twenty years the price of oil will increase significantly as the most easily accessible oil reserves are depleted.

I am not as pessimistic as Daly and Cobb regarding the long-term availability and cost of energy. There is a good chance that alternative sources of energy, including cleaner fission and possibly fusion, will one day provide an abundance of cheap energy. This will be discussed at greater length later in chapter 5. However, as we will see, there is little to be optimistic about when it comes to many of the other variables in the ISEW. The loss of wetlands and the diversity of species they support is a serious problem that will be accelerated if anti-environmental legislation, such as proposed by some in congress, is passed. Prime farmlands are also being continually encroached upon by urban sprawl. In many areas the nation's grasslands are being overgrazed. Ancient forests are fast disappearing. We have improved the water quality of many of our rivers and lakes, but contamination of underground water supplies by toxic wastes is being ignored because of the huge cost required for effective cleanup. There has been significant improvement in the sulfur dioxide pollution that leads to acid rain, and the most dangerous pollutants such as lead, as well as a reduction in chlorofluorocarbons (CFCs) that have been destroying the ozone layer, but the build up of CO_2 continues unabated. In short, although we have made gains in several areas, many measures of environmental quality are continuing to worsen.

Two major additional variables that need to be added to the ISEW index are changes in literacy rates and crime rates. Literacy rates have been declining in part due to the growth in immigration and in part due to the dissolution of the family and the decline of discipline necessary for success in school. Schools themselves have added to the problem, as will be shown in chapter 10, and have only recently begun a long overdue reform to reinstate the standards they all but abandoned in the 1970s. Crime rates have dropped significantly in the 1990s, but the outlook for the long-term remains uncertain.

In short, there may well have been some improvement in the ISEW in recent years, but it is too early to tell whether it is a temporary anomaly or an actual reversal in the long-term trend.

Summary

While the exact components of any index of human welfare are debatable, it is essential that such a measure be developed and used as the measure of the effectiveness of socioeconomic policies. If the goal of socioeconomic policies should be to measure changes in human happiness, we must move beyond maximization of GDP as our primary social goal. Although GDP can be measured on a per worker basis and adjusted for inflation, capital consumption, and environmental degradation, it still has little to do with social welfare once the basic amenities of food, clothing, and shelter are provided. To continue to rely on GDP as a meaningful measure of social welfare will not only fail to improve the happiness of the present generation but will have especially deleterious effects on future generations.

It is not just the measure of GDP that presents a problem for assessing social policies. It is a far more fundamental problem of economic theory. Economics assumes that the goal of society should be to fulfill unlimited wants. It also assumes that consumer wants are given rather than created, and that consumers have perfect information. Although all these assumption are questionable at best, and seriously undermine the usefulness of economics as the determinant of social policy, the most serious flaw of economics is its failure to adequately reflect the impact on future generations. The goal of neoclassic economic theory is to optimize production and consumption *today*. Finally, economic theory fails to account for the fairness in the initial distribution of goods and services. It ignores both the absolute and relative distribution of wealth. ***The failure to account for the impact of economic polices on human happiness, both for present and future generations, is a major shortcoming in using the growth of GDP as a surrogate for improvement in human welfare.***

There are a number of other measures that have been developed that are far superior to GDP in reflecting changes in social welfare. They include Hicksian income, the United Nation's Human Development Report, Japan's Modified GDP, the Physical Quality of Life Measurement developed by the Overseas Development Council, the Index of Social Health developed by the Fordham Institute for Innovation in Social Policy, Norhaus and Tobin's Measure of Economic Welfare, Zolatas's Index of Economic Aspects of Welfare, and Cobb and Daly's Index of Sustainable Economic Development. For the most part, these alternative measures indicate that the quality of life has not improved as indicated by the growth of GDP, and may have actually deteriorated over the last couple of decades. Therefore, our first policy recommendation must be to develop a more relevant measure of human welfare to replace GDP for assessing the consequences of socioeconomic polices.

NOTES

1. Cambell R. McConnell, *Elementary Economics: Principles, Problems, and Policies* (New York: McGraw Hill Book Company, 1960), p. 23.

2. For a full treatment of this issue, see John Gowdy and Sabrine O'Hare, *Economic Theory for Environmentalists* (Delray Beach, Fla.: St. Lucie Press, 1995).

3. Edward O. Wilson, *Consilience* (New York: Alfred A. Knopf, 1998), p. 290.

4. United Nations, *World Population and Prospects*, Dr. Herbert Block, "The Planetary Product" (Washington, D.C.: U.S. Department of State, Bureau of Public Affairs, October, 1979). Cited by Lester R. Brown, *Building a Sustainable Society* (New York: W. W. Norton and Company, 1981), p. 142.

5. U.S. Bureau of the Census, *Statistical Abstract of the United States, 1993* (Washington, D.C.: U.S. Government Printing Office, 1993), table 1388, p. 852.

6. President, *Economic Report of the President Transmitted to Congress, February, 1997* (Washington, D.C.: U.S. Government Printing Office, 1998). Calculated from tables B–1, p. 280; B–2, p. 282; B–31, p. 317; and B–35, p. 322.

7. Kenneth Boulding, National Academy of Sciences (NAS), "Energy Choices in a Democratic Society," in *Study of Nuclear and Alternative Energy Sources*, Supporting Paper no. 7 (Washington, D.C.: 1980). Cited by Brown, *Building a Sustainable Society*, p. 365.

8. The lower estimate is from Ann Crittenden Scott, "The Value of Housework: For Love or Money," *MS Magazine* (July 1972). Cited by John Kenneth Galbraith, *Economics and the Public Purpose* (Boston: Houghton Mifflin Company, 1973), p. 33. The higher estimate is from Robert Eisner, *The Misunderstood Economy: What Counts and How to Count It* (Boston: Harvard Business School Press, 1994) p. 22.

9. Hazel Henderson, *Creating Alternative Futures: The End of Economics* (New York: Perigee Books, 1978), p. 53.

10. Al Gore, *Earth in Balance* (Boston: Houghton Mifflin Company, 1992), p. 183.

11. Garrett Hardin, *Living Within Limits: Economy, Economics, and Population Taboos* (New York: Oxford University Press, 1993), p. 58.

12. Herman E. Daly and John B. Cobb Jr., *For the Common Good* (Boston: Beacon Press, 1989), p. 71.

13. Hardin, *Living Within Limits*, p. 73.

14. Ibid., p. 73.

15. President, *Economic Report of the President Transmitted to Congress* (Washington, D.C.: U.S. Government Printing Office, 1994), p. 184.

16. Ibid., p. 172.

17. Daly and Cobb, *For the Common Good*, p. 86.

18. R. A. Esterline, "Does Money Buy Happiness?" *Public Interest* 30 (1973): 3–10. Cited by James Q. Wilson and Richard J. Herrnstein, *Crime and Human Nature* (New York: Simon and Schuster, 1985), p. 330.

19. Andrew Brad Schmookler, "The Insatiable Society," *The Futurist* (July/August 1991).

20. Cynthia Crossen, "In Pursuit of Happiness, It Helps to Be a Well-Educated Woman," *Wall Street Journal*, March 26, 1996, p. B1.

21. John Gowdy and Sabrine O'Hare, *Economic Theory for Environmentalists* (Delray Beach, Fla: St. Lucie Press, 1995), p. 67.

22. John Maynard Keynes, *Essays in Persuasion*, "Economic Possibilities of Our Grandchildren" (New York: Norton, 1963), pp. 365–66. Cited by John Kenneth Galbraith, *The Affluent Society* (Boston: New American Library, 1958), p. 122.

23. Galbraith, *The Affluent Society*, p. 126.

24. E. F. Schumacher, *Small Is Beautiful: Economics as If People Mattered* (New York: Harper & Row, 1973), pp. 57–58.

25. Alan S. Blinder, *Hard Heads, Soft Hearts* (New York, Addison-Wesley Publishing Company, Inc., 1987), pp. 17–19.

26. Cited by Daly and Cobb, *For the Common Good*, p. 70.

27. Ibid., pp. 70–72.

28. United Nations Development Program Staff, *Human Development Report, 1992*, Inge Paul, Project Director (New York: Oxford University Press, 1992).

29. Henderson, *Creating Alternative Futures: The End of Economics*, p. 23.

30. *Chicago Tribune*, October 24, 1994, sec. 1, p. 16.

31. William Nordhaus and James Tobin, "Is Growth Obsolete?" In *Economic*

Growth, National Bureau of Economic Research, General Series no. 96E (New York: Columbia University Press, 1972), p. 5. Quoted by Daly and Cobb, *For the Common Good*, p. 77.

32. Xenophon Zolotas, *Economic Growth and Declining Social Welfare* (Athens: Bank of Greece, 1981), p. 107.

33. Cobb and Daly, *For the Common Good*, Appendix, pp. 401–55.

34. Ibid., Appendix, p. 419.

35. Ibid., Appendix, p. 455.

3

Population Issues and Policies

An understanding of the causes and consequences of demographic trends is fundamental to explaining economic results and formulating the appropriate socioeconomic policies. Nevertheless, many economists are so focused on the short-term business cycle, they all but ignore the demographic factors so crucial to understanding long-term economic trends (called secular trends in the arcane jargon of economists). For example, the increased U.S. unemployment rate of the 1970s was completely foreseeable by observing the timing of the baby boom between 1945 and 1958 and noting when this age cohort would begin crowding employment offices. The unemployment problem was exacerbated by the influx of women and minorities into the labor force after the Civil Rights Act of 1964. Yet, I attended dozens of economic symposiums and conferences in the 1970s where the discussion revolved around whether the higher unemployment rate was due to inappropriate fiscal or monetary policies; no mention was made of demographic factors. By failing to sufficiently consider the demographic factors, the unemployment situation of the 1970s and 1980s was tackled with a host of ineffective economic polices. This chapter will show why in the long term, population growth—both worldwide and in the United States—is the single most important factor affecting the welfare of society. To understand the impact of population growth on the U.S. economy, we must first examine the global trends and then turn our attention to the national trends and the policy implications.

WORLDWIDE POPULATION TRENDS

In 1970, the Club of Rome* predicted that, unless the world took immediate action, the planet faced a population explosion that would result in widespread famine, pollution, and exhaustion of natural resources. The growth in population has been less than the club predicted, in large part because of the efforts of China and several other nations to seriously curb their population growth. There has been famine, but it has been limited primarily to Africa, most notably Ethiopia, Somalia, and the Sudan. Even in these areas, famine has been due, in part, to the civil wars that have racked these countries for over two decades. Some natural resources have suffered a decline—especially forests and species diversity—but substitute materials and more efficient means of extraction have not resulted in higher prices for most raw materials such as oil or metals.

Since the dire consequences predicted by the Club of Rome, such as worldwide famine, have failed to materialize, some futurists and business economists such as Ben Wattenberg, the late Julian Simon and the late Herman Kahn, have been quick to point out that doomsday scenarios have been forecast since the time of Thomas Malthus but have never been realized. In fact, Simon and Wattenberg argue that growth in population has led to increased affluence worldwide. The explanation they offer is that more people result in more minds to solve the problems facing humankind. By this logic, China and India should be two of the most prosperous countries in the world. And, oh, those lucky people of Bangladesh—if only their population could continue increasing, what a wonderful future they will have! Conversely, countries such as Japan, Korea, and the nations of Western Europe, all of whom have dramatically slowed their growth in population, should have faired poorly since World War II. Clearly the theory of Simon and Wattenberg bears no relationship with the facts.

The fact is that anyone with a hand calculator can determine the ***impossibility of maintaining an increasing or even a constant rate of population growth.*** The theoretical reason is that a positive percentage change

---

*The Club of Rome is a group of scientists, economists, businessmen, international civil servants, as well as current and former heads of state from five continents. Their self-defined role is "to address new global imbalances caused by differing speeds of population and economic growth as well as the disruptive effects of global competition, resulting in unemployment in some countries and miserably low pay in others and leading to poverty and exclusion." Founded in 1968, the club's first report, "Limits to Growth," was published in 1970. It stressed the importance of the environment, and the essential links with the population and energy. The report sold twelve million copies in thirty-seven languages and was the wake-up call to the nations of the world that the rate of growth in world population (about 1.8 percent annually in 1970) was unsustainable.

results in an ever increasing growth in the *absolute* amount of change. In other words, if we increase a series starting at 100 by 3 percent annually, the series increases to 103, 106.1, 109.3, 112.3, and so on. Note that not only is the series increasing, but it is increasing by larger amounts each year. Now this small difference in incremental change might not seem much, but when we are dealing with large numbers over long periods of time it becomes explosive. Let me demonstrate with actual population data.

Suppose we extrapolate the 3.7 percent rate of growth the world was experiencing at the time the Club of Rome made its projections. Extrapolating that growth rate for the next two hundred years—just six generations—would result in the world's population exploding from 3.7 *billion* people in 1970 to 3.6 *trillion* people by the year 2270. That's 1,400 times more people.

Even maintaining the 1990s' significantly lower rate of growth of 1.48 percent*[1] *for 200 years would result in over 108 billion inhabitants on the planet, the equivalent of 100 new countries the size of China. The physical impossibility of maintaining such a rate of growth is seen by extrapolating the present growth rate out 800 years: it would result in 529 trillion people, enough to stand shoulder-to-shoulder over every foot of the earth's land mass![2] Even reducing population growth to only 1 percent per year would result in tripling the earth's population during the next century, approaching 38 billion people in two hundred years, and eventually reaching 4 trillion people—1000 Chinas—before 2700 C.E. Those who ignore the effect of compounding growth rates suffer from mathematical ignorance or historic myopia.

As Charles Darwin pointed out, "There is no exception to the rule that every organism naturally increases at so high a rate, that, if not destroyed, the earth would be covered by the progeny of a single pair."[3] Control of the overpopulation of other species is accomplished by high infant mortality rates. A sea turtle lays thousands of eggs over her life span, but most of her babies are gobbled up by predators almost immediately after birth; the result is that only about two live to reach reproductive age. Apes have only a few babies over their life span but are able to protect them much better than sea turtles can. Nevertheless, predators and illness kill off all but about two offspring before reproductive age. It all balances out nicely (or at least it did so until humankind reduced the survival rate of such species to less than two). An exception to the rule of reproductive balance are bacteria, such as E. coli, which keeps reproducing until it destroys the host and then, unless it finds a new host, the bacteria all die as well. It is not surprising then, that medical researcher Dr. Alan Gregg and others have compared the human organism behavior to that of cancer.[4] The problem stems from human success in reducing the infant mortality rate without also controlling the birth rate. This would ultimately result in a cancer-like growth. If left unchecked, our growth in population would destroy our host—our planet—and, of course, the human species as well. The issue is not whether the population must be slowed, but rather how fast and by what means.

A further difficulty with the present growth rate is that the reaction time to deal with the problem of runaway population has become shorter and shorter; and with time running out, so do our options for controlling population by less than draconian means. The table below shows that it took the entire history of civilization until the year 1830 to generate two billion inhabitants of our planet, but only 11 years to produce the fifth billion.

The Exponential History of Human Population Growth[5]

Population	*Time Span*	*Years*
1 Billion	0–1830	1,000,000
2 Billion	1830–1930	100
3 Billion	1930–1960	30
4 Billion	1960–1975	15
5 Billion	1975–1986	11
6 Billion	1986–1999	13 est.

Since about 1990 the population growth has slowed marginally. Instead of adding 80 million people each year, we are now adding about 75 million people.[6] But this is still more than the population of the Philippines. At the present rate, every decade the world will add population almost equivalent to that of India. *The total world population is doubling about every 50 years*. The situation would be much worse had China not undertaken its stringent population control policies. In large measure, it was China's lower growth rate and the decline in the birth rates of the industrialized nations that have prevented the dire predictions of the Club of Rome from being realized. In other words, because many nations have heeded the Club of Rome warnings the worst scenario has not been realized. Worldwide, we are still losing the war, however. To put things in perspective: in West Germany the total number of great-grandchildren the average couple can expect is 6, in Africa it is 258![7] At present rates of growth, Africa, Central and South America, and many Arab countries will be absolutely devastated. How tragic it is, then, to witness Pope John Paul II traveling to Africa and South America exhorting those poor people to refrain from contraception and abortion, or the late Mother Teresa obliviously bemoaning the fate of India's poor while refusing to allow her clinics to dispense contraceptives.

Assuming yields that the best farmers of the world are able to achieve on the world's most productive land (Iowa), in the best growing season, 10 billion people might be fed on a Western nation–style diet.[8] We would reach that population level in about fifty years if the current birth rate remained unchanged. Furthermore, there is no reason to believe that the rest of the world, much of which is farming very marginal land, can come anywhere close to the productivity of Iowa farms. Food per capita has been declining in Sub-Saharan Africa and Latin America for the past decade.[9] A far more somber assessment is offered by a Brown University study showing that if all the food in the world were distributed equitably, we could adequately feed six billion people on a vegetarian diet.[10] Joel E. Cohen offers only a slightly more optimistic view that perhaps 10 billion people may exist on a vegetarian diet, assuming no competition for grain from meat producing animals such as cows, pigs, or chickens.[11]

While it is true that the Green Revolution (the increase in agricultural productivity due to increased use of fertilizers and new hybrid crops) has provided a margin of temporary relief, it is also true that much of the increased food production has been bought at the cost of environmental destruction, such as the rapid destruction of the Amazon rain forest. Regrettably, the increased productivity brought about by the Green Revolution has also resulted in millions of farmers being displaced and forced to seek employment in the cities, giving rise to urban slums such as the notorious Brazilian *favelas*. Although the worst case scenario has been temporarily forestalled, the existing circumstances are none too encouraging. In 1993, one-third of the world's women were under fifteen years of age and so are just now entering their peak reproductive years.[12] Even with the declining trend in fertility rates world wide, the most optimistic forecasts show the world population reaching about eight billion by the year 2050 before beginning a long term decline.

It is pointless to argue as journalist Stephen Budiansky does, that the reason 700 million people throughout the world are presently suffering from malnutrition is not because the world cannot produce enough food, but because the poor have no money to buy food. Although free markets might help the situation in many nations, free markets alone will not solve the problem of population growth and malnutrition. It is not just food production that is required to alleviate poverty, but an entire economic infrastructure including housing, water and sanitation, transportation, communication, schools, industry, and the like. ***It is estimated that if the world population doubles, it would require a five- to ten-fold increase in economic activity to meet basic needs and minimum aspirations.***[13]

Developing an economy takes time. But time has run out for many of the less developed countries. Notwithstanding, the Pollyannas still turn a blind eye to the growth trends and argue that the only issue is one of economic distribution. They ignore the fact that population pressure has forced people to resettle in areas that will guarantee disaster on a monumental scale. For example, population pressure has forced people to settle in the Gangetic Delta in Pakistan, which is barely above sea level. Consequently, with absolute regularity tropical storms kill thousands of people. The same tragedy occurs in Bangladesh where an increase in population from 30 million to 118 million within just twenty years forced people to inhabit islands that inevitably are swamped during major cyclones. A 1970 cyclone left 300,000 dead; 10,000 died in 1985; and over 138,000 were killed in 1991. Such numbers are almost unimaginable; in this country it was considered a major tragedy when an earthquake or tornado kills a hundred people.

The Pollyannas ignore the 7 million homeless children who live and die in the streets of Brazil. Worldwide the number of street urchins may be 100 million.[14] The Pollyannas obstinately maintain that the 15 million infants who will die this year of malnutrition and curable childhood diseases are the result only of inequitable food distribution. Never mind that providing more food would only increase the population in those areas that are already growing out of control. As Alan Gregg morosely explains, "cancerous growths demand food; but they never have been cured by getting it."[15]

The population bomb has exploded, but most Americans fail to recognize the fallout. We are horrified by the continual warfare and deplorable living conditions in the third world. We lament the loss of Amazon rain forests and African wildlife. We decry the increased water and air pollution, the buildup of toxic waste, the destruction of the ozone layer, and worldwide soil erosion. We deplore the crime and poverty throughout the world. Still many people refuse to recognize that all the foregoing problems are directly related to population growth (and increased consumption per capita, as we will discuss in the next chapter).

Another of the ignored aspects of the burgeoning world population is the need to provide jobs for all these people. At present there are approximately one billion people who are unemployed or seriously underemployed throughout the world. If this were not bad enough, within the next ten years the world economies will have to generate almost 800 million additional jobs. If they fail to do so, the growth in the world's unemployed poor will be a major destabilizing force, what population expert Werner Fornos calls the "Aspiration Bomb." Yet the odds of generating so many jobs in nations where unemployment is already a major problem is very slight indeed.

Finally, it has become fashionable lately for some writers to lament the declining birth rates in the developed nations and predict dire consequences due to a population "implosion" (reduction).[16] Of course, a decline in population growth will present some new challenges, since a smaller population means fewer workers contributing to the support of a larger number of elderly from the previous generation. This is not news; it was recognized by demographers as long ago as 1970 when I studied demographics under the noted demographer Philip Hauser at the University of Chicago. At the time the general view was that the world's population would spike sometime in the twenty-first century and then precipitously decline. This is the normal trend in species that over populate, destroy their environment, and then suffer a population collapse. However, the hope was that by using our human intelligence we could anticipate and thus avoid such a traumatic prospect. By slowing the growth rate in population, we could avoid a spike and all its ramifications.

Trend line A below is a far easier trend to cope with than trend line B:

Figure 3.1

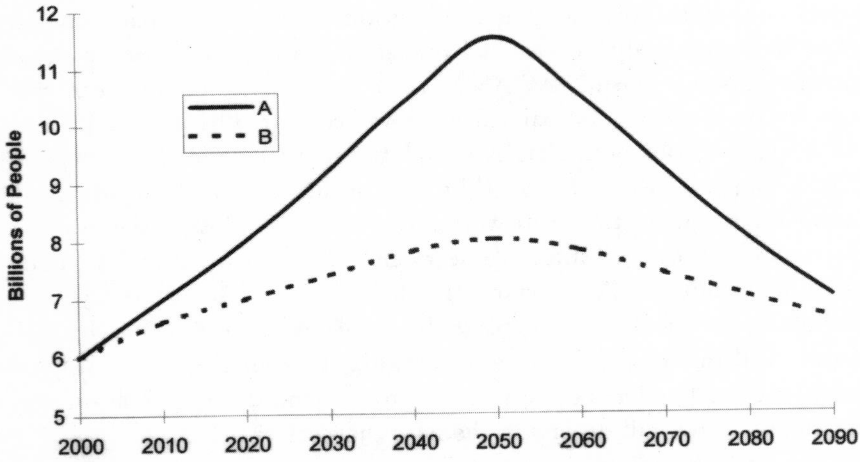

Line A is similar to what happened in Italy, where a huge baby boom in the 1945 to 1975 period was followed by a draconian drop in the birth rate. Italy was first overwhelmed with children to care for and not enough adults to provide the necessary supply of school teachers, police, social services, or infrastructure (schools, housing, roads, waste treatment facilities, etc.) to do the job adequately. This was followed by such a sudden drop in fertility rates that there may be insufficient labor to provide for the need of the aging baby boomers. There will be a shortage of doctors, nurses, healthcare workers and labor of various sorts to meet the needs of the retirees and aged. Periods of baby booms and bursts are always disconcerting to a society.

It should also be noted that our ability to support future generations of elderly is not dependent on increases in population. If that were true why do China and India have more problems than Europe? The ideal population trend would be a flat or slightly declining level in population. We can still improve the average standard of living with a declining population as long as the rate of growth in productivity exceeds the rate of decline in the population.

THE U.S. RESPONSE: THE LOST DECADE OF FAMILY PLANNING

If, in the year 2050, the president reports to Congress that world population has risen to the staggering number of eight billion, our children (and maybe some of those reading this book) will angrily ask, "why the hell didn't someone do something when the problem was containable?" The Christian Right did do something. It greatly exacerbated the problem by effectively persuading the Republican party to oppose funding for family planning services. As long ago as 1974, a study of population growth was ordered by President Richard Nixon. Called NSSM 200, it accurately predicted the growth in world population, the dire consequences for the economic development of the LDCs, and the worldwide environment destruction. Unfortunately for the world, out of fear of becoming immersed in the issue of population control and facing the ire of the Catholic Church and the Christian Right, Nixon decided to classify the study "Secret" rather than take appropriate action.[17] Stephen D. Mumford provides a well documented and disturbing account of how the Catholic Church has fought family planning throughout the world in an effort to safeguard its totalitarian claim of papal infallibility and supremacy in moral matters for all people, not just Catholics.[18]*

---

*As I noted in *The Final Superstition*, the Catholic Church has got itself in a box when, at the First Vatican Council of 1870, it tried to reverse its eroding authority by declaring the pope infallible on issues of faith and morals. This was a desperate, but temporarily successful effort to protect church authority from the spillover of the philosophically democratic notion that the authority of any institution must ultimately reside in those whom it governs. To compound its shameful claim of infallibility, the pronouncements of the popes during the last century clearly have condemned all forms of contraception and abortion. As a result, the pope cannot now renege on these issues without sacrificing the infallibility dogma. The horrendous consequence of papal intransigence is that the box the church got itself into has been turned into a coffin for millions of women whose lives would have been spared had they been permitted to avoid unwanted pregnancies through contraception. Tens of millions more have had their lives and those of their children condemned to a miserably marginal existence. It is a final and tragic irony that the major reason for the abortions the Church so unjustly condemns, is the insufficient availability of cheap contraception in the undeveloped nations due in large measure to papal intransigence.

In 1984, after being one of the prime supporters of family planning for many years—providing 40 percent of the world's family planning costs—the United States suddenly changed twenty years of policy by announcing at the United Nations' Conference on World Population in Mexico City that population growth was a neutral factor in economic development. Subsequently, the Reagan administration cut support for the United Nations Fund for Population Activities (UNFPA) and the International Planned Parenthood Federation (IPPF). Although the National Security Council and seventeen other U.S. government departments and agencies recommended expanded funding for these organizations, Reagan was swayed by the Catholic hierarchy who opposed all forms of contraception, and religious fundamentalists who objected that some of the aid was going to China where it might be used for forced abortions.[19] Even after two congressional investigations revealed that there were no such programs in China, and no government aid went for the one-half of one percent used by the IFPP to support voluntary abortions, President Bush continued to veto U.S. funds for international family planning programs.

Ironically, and tragically, the lack of U.S. funding for contraceptive and family planning programs had the result of greatly increasing the number of abortions in many countries. The World Health Organization estimates that there were approximately 45 million abortions in 1995, up 25 million from only five years earlier. Moreover, the lack of legal abortions has resulted in about 20 million of these abortions being performed in unsafe conditions. The consequence is the death of an estimated 70,000 women annually. Millions of others suffer from chronic morbidity afterwards. In Nigeria alone, 72 percent of all deaths of teenage girls are due to botched home remedy abortions. Reducing unplanned pregnancies could also save the lives of millions of women who bring unwanted pregnancies to term. According to the Population Reference Bureau, family planning could prevent 25 percent of all maternal deaths in developing nations.[20] Family planning improves the survival rates of adolescent girls by allowing them to postpone childbearing until maturity. The risk of dying in pregnancy and childbirth is twice as high for teenagers as for women in their twenties.[21] ***The failure of the United States and other developed countries to provide the relatively trivial funding required to provide adequate family planning services to every woman on the planet will be judged by history to be incredibly shortsighted and inhumane.*** The failure to make contraception universally available has already claimed the lives of tens of millions of women and resulted in an inestimable amount of unnecessary human suffering.

Almost a decade of population assistance was lost before Congress included $392 million in the 1994 budget for population development assistance, a paltry $40 million of which was earmarked for the UN population fund. Congress still would not allow more than $10 million to go to China.[22] In Clinton's 1995 budget, $635 billion was originally earmarked for family planning, but Congressmen Jesse Helms (R-NC) and the Christian Right opposed the funding. A bill was introduced by Senator Mitch McConnell (R-Kentucky) to again cut all U.S. aid for family planning programs. The 1997 funding bill slashed population spending to a mere $356 million.[23] The result: millions of additional unwanted children brought into a world where they will be forced to live a painful, marginal existence. As explained in *The Science of Morality*, the U.S. policy reducing funds for international family planning must be judged as highly immoral, not to mention extremely short-sighted even from a self-interested perspective.

THE 1994 CAIRO CONFERENCE: RECOGNITION OF RIGHTS BUT NOT RESPONSIBILITIES

The 1994 International Conference on Population and Development held in Cairo, although hailed as a major success by most nations, was actually only a small step forward in the world's effort to control population growth. The most significant success was the unanimous recognition that population growth was indeed a problem. Benazir Bhutto, Pakistan's prime minister at the time, set the tone of the meeting in her keynote address: "We are a planet out of control, a planet moving toward catastrophe."[24] Coming from the leader of a Muslim country, the recognition for slowing population growth was especially encouraging. Another heartening action was the Clinton administration's support of the joint statement that called upon "all countries to make assessible through the primary healthcare system, reproductive health to all, including family planning counseling services," thus reversing the disastrous position of the Reagan/Bush era with regard to family planning.

As usual, the Vatican tried to obstruct progress in population control. This tiny city-state should not even have been allowed into the conference since it is not actually a nation, but a protectorate. Comprised almost entirely of 1,500 old men, the Vatican has no business attempting to determine the reproductive rights and responsibilities of the world's women. Nevertheless, the Vatican was allowed into the conference, where it immediately allied itself with Iran, Libya, and other Islamic fundamentalist countries to oppose all forms of family planning involving contraception.[25] However, the efforts of the pope and ayatollahs to oppose family planning were overwhelmingly rejected by the world's nations. Only a handful of

Catholic and Moslem countries refused to endorse the final draft of the conference supporting family planning.[26]

Despite the Cairo Conference's success in gaining recognition for a woman's right to control her fertility, the Final Resolution of the conference suffered from two glaring deficiencies. First, it failed to recommend legalizing abortion. Instead it held that each country must determine its own policies with regard to abortion, noting only axiomatically that in those countries where abortion was legal, such abortions should be safe.[27] This lack of commitment to a woman's right to abortion was unfortunate not only because it perpetuates an unwillingness to recognize a woman's right to control her fertility, but also because abortion is the only recourse a woman has in areas where contraception is not available. Even if abortion is not the most desirable form of birth control, it is a far better alternative than having unwanted and neglected children.

The other major deficiency in the Final Resolution was the comment that "governments are encouraged to focus most of their efforts toward meeting the population and development objectives through education and voluntary measures rather than schemes involving incentives and disincentives."[28] Having more children than can adequately be raised by their parents or sustained by the environment violates the second and third harmonies required for improving human welfare. ***Given the strong biological urge to procreate, it may be necessary that societies provide offsetting incentives not to procreate. Such disincentives to procreation could include limiting tax deductions to two children, denying free education or other social services for a third child, or even forcing a couple to pay additional taxes to cover the social costs of having more than two children.***

Is Economic Development the Key to Reduced Population or Vice Versa?

The *demographic transition theory* provides a plausible alternative for those who oppose government involvement in population control. According to this theory, population growth undergoes two phases. In Phase I, the availability of medical services to fight disease results in lower mortality rates and rapid growth in population. In Phase II, economic development provides better education for woman and improved job opportunities for all people, thus providing sufficient income for people to care for themselves in old age. Since people do not need to raise as many children to provide for their parents in old age, the birth rate drops and population stabilizes. Consequently, the proponents of demographic transition theory believe that the population problem can be solved by simply fostering economic development. It has been estimated that the demographic transition to lower fertility rates occurs when annual income per capita reaches $2,000 (1990 dollars).[29] Unfortunately, a problem arises because few nations in Latin America, Africa, or the Middle East have broken through this theoretical income barrier. And they are not likely to do so precisely because of the rapid increase in their population—a classic catch-22.

Like so many half-baked theories, this one has an element of truth. When women become better educated and have greater job opportunities they tend to get married later and have fewer children. In Western economies, the increase in economic development did occur prior to the decline in the birth rate. This sequence occurred, however, in societies that had firmly established agricultural bases that were more than adequate to support the growth in population. These societies were also well into their industrial development before population began to exert significant pressure on their resources. The situation is quite different in the LDCs today. William N. Ryerson of Population Communication International explains that ***since World War II no country has gone from a developing status to a developed status without first reducing the birth rate.***[30]

Japan provides an alternative paradigm to the demographic transition as well as an example developing countries must emulate if they are to avoid disaster. From 1868 to 1940, the population of Japan grew from 32 to 73 million. Consequently, despite increased agricultural productivity and more land brought under cultivation, the average daily consumption of rice had dropped to bare subsistence levels. As early as the 1920s, Japanese politicians argued that there were only three avenues left to escape from the problem of surplus population: emigration, advance into the world markets, or expansion of territory.[31] Since immigration was precluded by the policies of other countries, and high tariff barriers effectively kept Japan out of world markets, Japan decided to pursue the third alternative of becoming a colonial power. The results were disastrous for the entire world. Unfortunately for Japan and the world, Japan never seriously considered a fourth alternative, population control, until after losing the war.

After the war, the Japanese dramatically reduced their fertility rate, attaining replacement level (2.1 children per woman) as early as 1950 and have maintained this level in the succeeding decades. The beneficial results of the new policy can be placed in dramatic perspective by contrasting economic development in Japan and Brazil since 1970.

Between 1970 and 1994 Brazil's economy (Gross National Product) grew by 194 percent in inflation adjusted terms, outpacing Japan's 165 percent growth. However, the growth of Brazil's population absorbed much of the benefit of this growth. On a per capita basis, Brazil grew only 77 percent compared to Japan's 132 percent, In other words, because Japan controlled its population growth, it grew almost twice as fast as Brazil on a per capita basis. Recall from the last chapter, that it is only real growth per capita that reflects an increase in living standards.

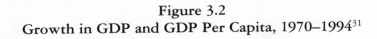

Figure 3.2
Growth in GDP and GDP Per Capita, 1970–1994[31]

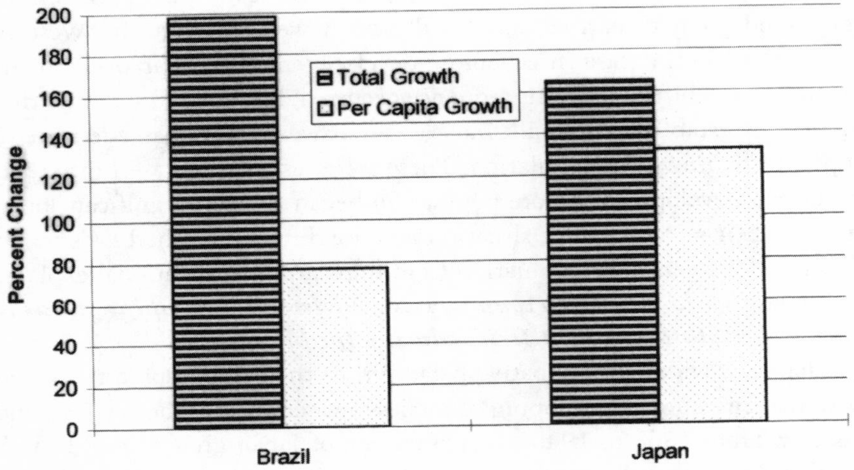

If we examine just the period from 1980 to 1994, the results are even more striking. During this period, Brazil grew 32 percent in real terms, but after adjusting for population, Brazil had virtually no growth on a per capita basis. Japan, on the other hand, grew not only 61 percent overall but, because it had very little population growth, per capita growth soared 50 percent. (As a point of reference, during the 1980–94 period real GDP of the U.S. grew 38 percent, about the same as Brazil, but our slower population growth yielded a per capita growth of 24 percent—not as good as Japan, but much better than Brazil.)[33]

Hence, the difference in the growth of prosperity between Japan and Brazil can be explained primarily in terms of their differential birth rates.* In the early 1990s, the population of most underdeveloped countries was growing about 3.4 percent per year. This means that their economies must grow that fast just to break even, with no real growth in income per capita.

---

*There has been some concern expressed in recent years concerning the potential impact of Japan's aging population. However, the high savings rate in Japan assures that they will not have trouble caring for their aged. Moreover, the problem is only temporary; eventually the number of aged will decline, reflecting the lower birth rate of forty-five years ago.

Japan, by comparison, was able to limit its population growth to less than 1 percent per annum since World War II. Thus, with a 4 percent average growth in GDP (adjusted for inflation), Japan was able to increase real income per capita by about 3 percent per year.

A study by the United Nations Population Fund (UNFPA) shows that the demographic transition theory has the causation exactly backwards. Slower population growth is a prerequisite to per capita income growth. In a study of 82 countries, it was discovered that the 41 countries with slower population growth increased per capita income by an average of 1.25 percent per year, while income per capita declined an average of 1.25 percent per year in the 41 countries with faster population growth.[34] Furthermore, R. T. Roosevelt, Director of Office of Population, U.S. AID, points out that South Korea, Thailand, Taiwan, and Indonesia have demonstrated that a policy of making contraception and quality abortion services available results in plummeting fertility rates followed by rapid economic growth.[35]

The experience of Thailand is instructive. Thailand concentrated its efforts to reduce population growth and pushed fertility rates down from 6.1 children per woman in the 1965–70 period to only 2.2 by 1987. Consequently, income per capita rose 4.4 percent over the same period.[36] Ryerson explains why lower birth rates result in increased per capita growth in the modern era: "[R]educed family size enables couples and nations to save a higher percentage of their income and invest it in education, government and industry—all of which lead to increased productivity."[37]

In light of all the evidence against the demographic transition theory, why is it still being touted? Basically, because it permits many liberals and conservatives from facing the fact that nations must provide incentives to reduce birth rates. Many neoliberals dislike any policy that seeks to influence a woman's choice with regard to her fertility and many conservatives of the religious right abhor the possibility that an incentive might result in more abortions. So both groups take solace in the myth of the demographic transition theory where everything works out just fine without government intervention.

Economist Lester Thurow concludes that the maximum sustainable population growth for LDCs is 2 percent per year.[38] Thurow points out that if Japan, Germany, and the United States continued to have population growth rates of 3 to 4 percent per annum, their standard of living would be no higher than 100 years ago.[39] As we shall see, many nations can no longer afford even a 2 percent per year growth rate. Although the benefits of a free market are many, there is no substitute for the availability of family planning and a well thought-out system of economic incentives to reduce population growth. Population control is a primary prerequisite to economic development. The greatest barrier to increasing living standards in Africa and Latin America and other Catholic countries such as the Philippines is the Vatican's continued archaic and, ultimately, inhumane policies against birth control and abortion. To the misfortune of Africa, it is the fastest growing region for the Catholic Church and its misogynistic policies. In the Philippines, the nation's spiritual leader, Cardinal Jamine Sin, forced the government to abandon its family planning campaign.[40]

But Aren't There Highly Populated Nations with High Living Standards?

The Netherlands is often used as an example by those who believe that population growth is a good thing, or at least neutral. Although it has a population density eighteen times that of the United States, the Netherlands enjoys a high standard of living. Paul Ehrlich explains that this argument, which he calls the Netherlands Fallacy, ignores the huge amount of physical resources acquired outside of the Netherlands's borders that are required to sustain its living standard.[41] "The Netherlands consumes the output equivalent of fourteen times the productive land contained within its borders."[42] Similarly, Japan sustains its standard of living by importing 70 percent of its corn, wheat and barley, 95 percent of soybeans, and 50 percent of wood from the rapidly vanishing rain forests of Borneo.[43] Biologist E. O. Wilson observes that so-called economic miracles "occur most often when countries consume not only their own material resources, including oil, timber, water and agricultural produce, but those of other countries as well."[44]

Most of the world's industrialized economies, including the United States, maintain their standard of living by using a very disproportionate amount of the earth's resources and generate much greater pollution per capita as well. This cannot continue forever. The poorer nations of the world are beginning to understand that if the rich nations are using a disproportionate amount of resources, they do so at the expense of the less developed nations. One result is that the disparity between rich and poor nations is growing larger rather than smaller. As the poor nations seek to catch up, they will find it increasingly more difficult to close the gap. Shrinking per capita resources and the need for more stringent standards to prevent further degradation of the environment will result in additional constraints on the LDCs, for example, limits on fish catches or the amount of pollutant emissions.

ARE WE NEARING A POPULATION MELTDOWN?

The evidence is growing that the population of the world is nearing, or perhaps has already exceeded, the long-term carrying capacity of our planet. University of California geologist Preston Cloud estimates that 6 or 7 billion people is the most the world can sustain at the standard of living of Western Europe.[45] The number would be considerably less at U.S. living standards. Ecologist David Piemental is not so sanguine. Piemental argues that for the entire world to live at the same standard as Western Europe would require the resources of another planet the size of Earth.[46] Based upon his analysis, the ideal population for our planet would be only about two billion people.

A study by William Rees, an urban planner at the University of British Columbia, estimated that it takes 10 to 15 acres of land to maintain the consumption of the average person living in a high income country. By 1990, however, the world's total ecologically productive land available was already down to 4.2 acres per capita.[47] In other words, if Rees is correct, there is no chance that the less developed countries will reach the consumption levels of the developed nations without a significant reduction in world population. Computer simulations by Jørgan Randers of MIT and Donella Meadows of Dartmouth University show that only if physical growth halts will the earth be able to support life.[48] The models also show that even with unlimited energy, growth in consumption must be stopped to control rising pollution. Finally, David C. Korten notes that if the world reaches a population of ten billion there will be no place for animal or plant life that are not immediately essential to human survival.[49] So we can kiss off the majority of animal species, especially the large mammals that compete with humans for food and habitat, such as those that exist in rainforests or the savannas of Africa. The nature films of the late twenty-first century will need to be shot in zoos.

In addition to the physical deprivation that a rapidly growing world must face, there are psychological problems as well. According to E. O. Wilson, studies of various species indicate that most kinds of aggressive behavior among members of the same species are exacerbated by overcrowding.[50] John B. Calhoun, a psychologist at the National Institute of Mental Health, studied the effect of overpopulation on the behavior of mice. He discovered that after a certain density is reached, juvenile behavior is extended into adulthood, parental care stops, aggressive behavior increases and, eventually, mating ceases and the colony becomes extinct.[51] Obviously, it is questionable whether we can extrapolate the behavior of mice to the human species. But there are enough similarities to the situation in our society today to give one pause. Calhoun believes that the human species is on a similar course. He predicts the world population will reach nine billion then drop precipitously over the next two hundred years to two billion people.

In my opinion, unless population growth is quickly brought under control the only way to avoid collapse will be through stringent population control and regimentation of all aspects of human behavior. Continued growth in population and the commensurate increase in the associated stresses on social stability will likely lead to more authoritarian governments. China is the logical paradigm here. The alternative, more voluntary, approach to reducing birth rates adopted by India has thus far proved far less successful.

The conclusion to be drawn from the above discussion is: ***freedom is inversely related to population.***[52] If societies wish to maintain whatever degree of freedom they presently enjoy, they will have to initiate both incentives and disincentives to persuade people to reduce their family size to no more than two children on average. In some overpopulated nations, they may need to reduce the number of children to less than the replacement rate until their population drops to a sustainable level.

Every Environmental Problem Is Worsened by Increased Population

The environmental impact (E) is a function of population (P), technology (T) and consumption (C):[53]

$$E = f(P,T,C)$$

Therefore, even if we make improvements in the types of technology employed, and reduce our per capita consumption, the environment can still deteriorate if population increases more than proportionally. We will explore the consequences of changes in consumption and technology in depth in chapter 5, but let's briefly explore some of the implications of the equation.

Assuming that fertility rates will continue to decline until they eventually reach replacement levels, the best estimates are that population (P) will reach 8 to 10 billion before leveling off or declining. Making a further assumption that consumption per capita (C) will increase no more than 2 percent per year (that's only two-thirds the growth rate of the past 25 years), total consumption will increase ten to thirteen times today's level over the next century. Thus, to hold pollution and environmental damage constant would require a ten- to thirteen-fold improvement in technology.

Unfortunately, most technologies do not advance like computer technology. They do not change by a factor of ten every few years. Quite the contrary, there has been very little improvement in environmental technology in the last fifty years. Our society still relies primarily on fossil fuel for its energy needs, and the increases in efficiency have been relatively slight. One of the primary reasons for the slow improvement in efficiency is the huge capital costs involved in reducing the pollution that results from use of fossil fuels.

Moreover, efforts to increase productivity by substituting fossil fuel–driven machines for human labor—one of the primary means of increasing productivity—will actually increase pollution and environmental destruction. Viewing the daunting task of increasing output by a factor of twenty—to maintain the level of consumption per capita in developed countries while increasing income and consumption in the LDCs above the poverty level—without increasing pollution, has led the U.S. Academy of Sciences and Britain's Royal Society of London to appeal to the world community to curb population growth and exert greater conservation efforts, "to avoid the possibility of irreversible damage to the earth's capacity to sustain life."[54] These scientists, who are most aware of the capabilities and limitations of technology, are not willing to make the leap of faith that technological improvements will offset the disastrous environmental trends resulting from increased population and consumption.

A cursory overview of present trends lends credence to their concerns.

Deforestation: The need to feed the burgeoning population of South America, Asia, and Africa is resulting in deforestation of an area the size of Austria every year. The primary reason for growth in deserts worldwide is due to the population exceeding carrying capacity of the land.[55] In Africa, the need for firewood is resulting in the persistent growth of the Sahara desert. In Indonesia and other parts of Asia, erosion has become a major problem as mountainsides are deforested to provide additional acreage for crops. In Central and South America, slash and burn techniques will destroy in six years forests that took sixty million years to develop. In Central America, 25 percent of all tropical rainforests have been destroyed since the 1960s to provide pasture land.[56] Tragically, the rainforest land serves as pasture land for only six to eight years before becoming completely nonarable. The ranchers then abandon the ruined land to burn more forests. Over a decade, the destruction of tropical forests is equivalent to the combined area of Malaysia, the Philippines, Ghana, the Congo, Ecuador, El Salvador, and Nicaragua.[57] ***At the current rate, by the middle of the twenty-first century all tropical forests will***

have been destroyed and the thin tropical soil eroded beyond productive use for farmland.

Species loss: The loss of tropical rain forests will result in an unprecedented increase in the rate of species extinction. There are an estimated 31 million plant and animal species in the world, although scientists have thus far catalogued only 1.4 million.[58] More than half of the estimated species live in the tropical forests. Considering that over 40 percent of the tropical rainforests have already been destroyed, the potential loss of species is a biological holocaust. E. O. Wilson estimates that we may be losing as many as 17,500 species each year and the trend is accelerating.[59] Aside from the esthetic loss, the potential medical benefits of these plants will never be realized. For example, rainforests are the source of 70 percent of all plants recognized by the National Cancer Society as having anticancer properties.[60] In 1997 scientists discovered that by slightly modifying the chemical formula for the poison produced by a rare species of tree frog, they could synthesize a nonaddictive alternative to morphine for relief of pain.

Pollution, Ozone Destruction, and Global Warming: Worldwide pollution and the spread of dangerous toxins have been discussed extensively in the environmental literature, and need not be repeated here. Suffice it to say that even formerly pristine areas such as the Galápagos Islands and Antarctica are being threatened by wind- and waterborne pollutants. There is no place to hide. There is one positive note, however. Due to the worldwide agreement to phase out chlorofluorocarbons (CFCs), the rate of increase in ozone depletion is declining. Scientists now believe that the ozone layer will begin to rebuild early in the twenty-first century. This is one catastrophe that may have been narrowly avoided through cooperation of the world's nations.

Global warming is the direct result of the energy it takes to support every additional person in the world. Specifically, the primary source of global warming is the buildup of gases in the atmosphere. The world is pumping six billion tons of carbon dioxide and other heat trapping gases into the atmosphere annually.[61] The loss of the world's rainforests contributes to the problem, as rainforests absorb carbon dioxide and produce oxygen. As we shall see in chapter 5, the evidence is indisputable that there is a trend in global warming. The debatable issues are what is causing it, how fast the warming trend is accelerating, and what the consequences will be. There is not yet scientific agreement that the warming is due primarily to the buildup of greenhouse gases as opposed to some cyclical trend due to other natural causes. However, the evidence pointing to CO_2 as the primary suspect continues to build. Moreover, by the time we can be certain as to the causes, it may be too late to reverse the trend. Therefore the case for global warming is not like a murder trial where we have to be certain beyond a reasonable doubt to find the suspect guilty. Rather we should seek to err on the side of prudence.

In 1996, the International Panel on Climate Change (IPCC), a group of 2,500 scientists reported on their collective studies on the potential for global warming. They estimated that the increase in average temperature would be 3.6 degrees Fahrenheit by the year 2100 if greenhouse gases were not reduced.[62] While this increase may not sound like much, it would be the greatest shift in temperature in the ten thousand years of human civilization. The effects of this warming are still subject to much debate, but there is increasing agreement that, at a minimum, the subsequent rise in sea levels throughout the world would threaten the habitat of hundreds of millions of people.

Although energy saving technological improvements may slow the warming trend, they are not enough. For example, even though China improved its energy efficiency 3.7 percent a year between 1979 and 1991, the increase in total output and population growth caused a 40 percent increase in total energy use just between 1980 and 1986.[63] In addition to energy saving technology, the world must switch from fossil fuels to less polluting sources of energy such as solar, wind, and geothermal.* Continued reduction in population growth is an essential prerequisite for reducing the growth in the demand for energy.

Water shortages: In recent decades, use of freshwater has been increasing 4 to 8 percent per year.[64] Freshwater pollution is due to three primary sources: excess nutrients from sewage and soil erosion, which cause algae blooms that eventually deplete the oxygen content of the water; pathogens from sewage that spread disease; and both heavy metals and synthetic compounds from industry, mining, and agriculture that accumulate in aquatic organisms, and eventually can be consumed by humans. Water shortages are becoming acute in many parts of the world, especially East and West Africa and North China.

In 1996, a World Bank report indicated that eighty nations, housing 40 percent of the world's population, already have water shortages that could cripple their efforts to expand industry and irrigate agriculture during the next few decades.[65] More ominously, a study by Robert Engleman and Pamela Leroy of Population International estimate that by the year 2025 up to fifty-two nations, containing 3.5 billion people, may be facing chronic water shortages.[66] Many countries do not have even that much time. The UN Habitat Conference warned that by the year 2000 or

---

*Utilization of the earth's interior heat. The main practical application is in finding natural concentrations of hot water for use in electric power generation and direct heat applications such as space heating and industrial drying processes.

shortly thereafter, a water crisis threatens because "many countries will have half as much water as they had in 1975."[67]

To make matters worse, roughly 95 percent of the world's urban areas are dumping untreated, or only partially treated, sewage into rivers and coastal waterways.[68] The world must brace itself for a "water shock" as wrenching as the oil shock of the 1970s. The World Bank has estimated it will cost $600 to $800 billion over ten years to meet even minimal water standards.[69] The water crisis will result in national conflicts over water rights, in some cases leading to warfare.

More People, More Minds, More Solutions?

Earlier, I mentioned it is alleged by some optimists that increasing population will actually improve the quality of life. Some economists have tried to support this view by pointing out that along with the increased population since the 1950s, the world's total output has increased five fold. But David Korten notes that over the same period, the number of people living in absolute poverty has kept pace with population growth: both have doubled.[70] While it may be true that average life expectancy has been lengthened because of the increase in modern medicine, it is questionable whether most people are any happier today than forty years ago. We may have simply increased the life span in which people can be unhappy. Or we may have purchased some or all of the increase in happiness from future generations by incurring large national debts and destroying the resources that would add to the security and happiness of our descendants. By this I do not necessarily imply raw resources—for which substitutes may be found—but natural resources such as open space, clean air and water, species diversification, etc.

The Pollyannas contend that a larger population will result in more potential geniuses to solve the myriad of problems facing humankind. The truth is that the chances of recognizing and developing the capabilities of a genius are inversely related to population growth. We will never know how many of the seven million children on the streets of Brazil may be potential geniuses. The most clever among them will learn how to cheat and steal to survive, but they will never make a positive contribution to society. On the other hand, as Japan has demonstrated by limiting their family size, a nation can devote the necessary resources to make certain that all of its children reach their maximum potential.

Is Population Stability Attainable?

In 1996 the world birth rate was 2.6 children per woman. Even if the birth rate continues to decline to an average 2.2 children per woman, the world population would still more than double to 12.5 billion in only fifty years and reach about 21 billion by the year 2150.[71] On the other hand, if the world could quickly reduce the average birth rate to 2.0, a population level of "only" 7.8 billion by the year 2050 would be achievable, after which there would be a slow decline in population to about the same level as today by 2150. A decade ago this seemed unlikely, but throughout the world countries are beginning to make significant progress at lowering their birth rates. For example, Kenya, which had the highest birth rate in the world, averaging eight children per family, has brought their average down to five. Their 2.8 percent growth rate is still far too high, but is a major step in the right direction. China halved its growth rate in the past ten years, to about 1 percent annually.[72] South Korea, Taiwan, and Cuba have made similar remarkable progress. The Caribbean dropped its population growth from 2 percent per annum to 1.5 percent. Even Central America made some progress, declining from 3.2 percent to 2.7 percent.

Conversely, reducing infant mortality in Africa worked to its disadvantage, as population growth increased from 2.7 percent to 3.0 percent annually. To put these numbers in perspective, consider that a growth rate of 1.5 percent rate would result in a doubling of population in forty-seven years. Kenya's 3 percent population growth leads to a doubling of population in just twenty-three years, while the 1 percent rate of Cuba would lead to a doubling in seventy years, and Italy's rate of less than 0.1 percent would not double its population for almost seven hundred years. (Ironically, the Vatican's pro-birth doctrines have been totally ignored by those in the pope's backyard.)

Current Worldwide Population Trends

Despite the progress made in slowing the world's population growth the question remains, will it drop fast enough to avoid disaster? Recent estimates are that world population will peak at 8 to 10 billion sometime in the twenty-first century. While this is better than the 12 to 15 billion forecast based upon the trend in 1980, it is not encouraging if the long-term carrying capacity of the earth is only about 2 billion people as some environmentalists believe. And, as China has painfully discovered, it is difficult to hold the fertility rate below 2.1 per woman (the zero population growth rate).

As explained, the key to reducing population growth is government sponsored family planning. At a minimum such programs must provide free, or at extremely low cost, a variety of forms of contraception including condoms, birth control pills, sterilization, and abortion on demand, coupled with an education program on how to correctly use each means. Using contraception to space pregnancies not only has the beneficial effect of reducing population growth, but also would result in a decline in maternal deaths by up to one half, thus reducing the number of orphans—a major problem in many countries today.[73]

Simply making contraception easily available is not enough. ***Every developing nation that has succeeded in reducing its birth rate has done so by aggressively promoting family planning.*** Costa Rica devoted 40 percent of its family planning expenditures to education, information services, and radio promotions. It succeeded in reducing its birth rate by 40 percent between the 1960s and 1980s.[74] In Thailand, manufacturers of condoms support sports teams. The traffic police distribute condoms free on New Year's Eve in a program call "cops and rubbers." By extremely aggressive advertising the number of people using birth control in Thailand has reached 65 to 70 percent and the birth rate has fallen from 3.2 percent in 1970 to a little over 1.0 percent by 1996.[75]

Even the Catholic LDCs are beginning to shed the yoke of Rome's opposition to contraception, but it is a race against time. Brazil has dropped the average family size from six children to three. Sixty-five percent of the people now use birth control. Most of the other South American countries are also making progress. In Central America, however, except for Mexico and Costa Rica, there has been little progress and the future of most of those countries is bleak. Mexico has reduced its average family size to 3.8 children with 45 percent of the population using birth control and 20 percent eventually choosing sterilization. The ambitious national goal is to reduce population growth to 1 percent per year by the turn of the century. Even 1 percent must be only the interim goal, with the ultimate objective of a negative growth rate since all indications are that Mexico has already exceeded its long-term carrying-capacity. As a consequence, the pressure for Mexicans to migrate to the United States will remain intense for many years.

Asia is a case of extremes, with some countries such as Korea, Japan, Taiwan, Thailand, and Indonesia making excellent progress while at the other end of the spectrum are countries such as India and Bangladesh. The latter nation is particularly unfortunate since 98 percent of the people know of at least one method of birth control, but the nation is so poor that only 40 percent have access to the means. Bangladesh is making some headway and has reduced its average family size from 7.7 children to 5.5.

However, unless much more progress is achieved, this hopelessly overpopulated nation will again double its population in only twenty-six years.[76] Bangladesh will never achieve demographic stability through economic growth. It requires an influx of family planning aid to make contraception free and strong government incentives to reduce fertility rates. If all else fails, they may have to adopt the Chinese approach.

Many of the Moslem countries, such as Iran, Jordan, Syria, Saudi Arabia, Oman, Yemen, and Kuwait are experiencing growth rates of up to 3 percent. Although, recently, progressive Moslem clerics have endeavored to show that contraception does not violate the Koran, the availability and knowledge of birth control is still extremely low. Pakistan was making progress but the rise of fundamentalism has turned back the clock. The population of Iraq continues to grow despite its apparent efforts to commit national suicide through its calamitous wars. Iran has finally awakened and, after a decade of promoting larger families, has now reversed itself by promoting family planning.

Finally, even Africa is beginning to reduce its birth rate, although in some countries more through war, famine, and disease (especially AIDs) than family planning. Whether Africa will bring its population growth under control through birth control or the consequences of disease and starvation is still an open question.

Availability of Birth Control Is Not Enough to Reduce Fertility Rates

In recent years, substantial progress has been made in providing contraception to the world's men and women. A major problem persists, however, in getting them to use it. According to John Bongaarts, president of the Population Council, there are only 87 to 100 million women in developing countries outside of China who indicate that they would like to delay their next pregnancy, but fail to use effective birth control even when it is available.[77] This is mainly a guess; other estimates indicate that about half of the world's married couples use some form of birth control, sterilization being the most popular.[78] Use of birth control is by no means evenly distributed around the globe. In Africa, only 25 percent of the women who do not want any more children are utilizing some form of contraception.[79]

UNICEF's "State of the World's Children" report for 1992 indicated that if women could decide on how many children to have, the rate of growth in the world's population would drop 30 percent.[80] This is somewhat misleading because to get the actual impact we must apply this percentage to the current growth rates. A 30 percent decline applied to a 1.7

percent growth would reduce the growth rate to 1.2 percent annually. Such an improvement would be insufficient to solve the population problem. We need to figure out how to reduce the other 70 percent of the growth. This is no easy task.

Charles Galton Darwin, the grandson of Charles Darwin, has postulated that *a purely voluntary control of population will, of necessity, fail as a means of population control.* The reason is due to the law of natural selection articulated by his illustrious grandfather. In this instance, adults who have a strong desire to produce children will produce more children than those who choose to use contraception. There is empirical evidence to support this theory which shows that "daughters of mothers who had more children than the norm for their generation also had more children than the average of their generation."[81] As explained in *The Science of Morality*, when one of the basic human desires is out of harmony with the needs of the environment, society must intervene by creating or exploiting other desires that will counter the biological need. The best way to achieve this is to increase the education of women and provide them with employment opportunities. Having alternative employment opportunities will enable them to satisfy the desire for security and material well-being that they would be unable to fulfill with a large family.

The opportunity to obtain good jobs may be enough for women of sufficient intelligence. It may not be enough for women whose only employment opportunities are low paying, undesirable jobs, unless they have no alternative source of support. Matters are made worse if the cost of having children is born by the community at large while the benefit (psychological or otherwise) is gained by the mothers. That is exactly how the present welfare system works in America. The situation would be exacerbated by free health care. ***To reduce the birth rate of poor women it is necessary to eliminate any subsidy for having children. There might even need to be positive or negative incentives to encourage women who cannot afford children to refrain from having them.*** Garrett Hardin goes so far as to suggest making aid to poor women contingent upon the adoption of fertility-reducing measures such as sterilization or an enforceable contract to have fewer children.[82] Hardin's suggestion might sound harsh, but we must always consider the far more disastrous consequences of overpopulation.

Equally as important as the education of women, is the availability of some form of social security. Where ample social security is available, one of the main incentives for having children—to care for the parents in old age—is removed. In such circumstances, the evidence suggests that people will reduce their family size to improve the material quality of their lives and that of their children.

ABORTION AS A MEANS OF CONTROLLING POPULATION

We already mentioned the Congressional action to cut off family planning funding to China because of their population policy and the allegations of forced abortions. Whether or not they are coerced, the religious right is opposed to permitting any abortions and is willing to destroy the entire family planning program solely because it permits abortions. The unintended result of past cuts in family aid is a greater number of unwanted pregnancies leading to an increase in the number of abortions worldwide. It is an ironic tragedy that in his unreasonable opposition to contraception, Pope John Paul II, more than any other person, is responsible for the excessive number of abortions worldwide. In countries where abortions are illegal, abortions are performed without adequate medical care, and often result in the woman's death and commensurate increase in the world's orphans.[83] No wonder scientist and writer Arthur C. Clarke has called the pope the most dangerous man in the world.

Under the dictator Ceausescu, Romania implemented a pronatalist policy similar to the pope's: the sale of contraception and abortion were banned. The result was a huge number of illegitimate and unwanted children. After the fall of Ceausescu, many of these children were adopted by Americans. Ireland effectively adopted a similar policy, and for the last century Ireland's major export was its surplus population. A tiny nation of only 3.5 million people, there are 80 million people of Irish descent throughout the world. In the future, nation's such as those in Africa and South America will not have Ireland's option of exporting their excess population. The numbers are so huge and growing so rapidly that only an insignificant fraction will have the opportunity to emigrate to other nations.

There is much irony in the religiously motivated decision regarding the U.S. policy of cutting funding for international family planning services. Conservative politicians have no qualms about sending billions of dollars in military aid to the LDCs that have often intensified wars and resulted in the deaths of thousands of men, women, and children. The same politicians that balk at destroying a group of fetal cells will often ignore the crushing poverty that must inevitably result if population growth is not brought under control. As Werner Fornos points out, if Ethiopia had launched a family planning program in 1970 which was half as effective as Thailand, the population in 1990 would have been reduced by 1.7 million, which equals the number of people forced to rely on emergency food aid from the rest of the world.[84] Moreover, the food aid was counterproductive since it only meant that those people survived to give birth to an even larger number which will starve during the next famine.

The Chinese Solution

In the early 1960s thirty million Chinese died of famine. Much of the problem was due to the failure of the collective farming system under Mao tse Tung. However, periodic famines existed long before Communism in China and the magnitude of the problem was growing with the size of the population. In the early 1970s, Chinese demographers realized that at the existing fertility rate the population would double to two billion people shortly after the turn of the century. They also knew that the inevitable check to this unsustainable growth was mass starvation. Drastic ills call for drastic remedies. The Chinese government decided that it had to dramatically slow population growth by the year 2000.

China's family planning efforts were impeded by the lack of the government's capability to care for people in old age, coupled with the custom that it was the son's responsibility to do so. Hence, when a couple had a daughter, they wanted to have additional children until a son was born. The government tried to institute elderly care programs, but lacked adequate means to do so, especially in rural areas. So China developed policies that would reward a couple for having only one child, penalize a couple for a second child, and severely penalize couples who were so socially irresponsible as to have a third pregnancy. More specifically:

- Salaries were increased for couples who had one child and promised to have no more.
- An adult grain ration was provided for one child, but less for additional children.
- A pension equal to 100 percent of their salary was provided to childless couples, 80 percent to one-child families, and less than 70 percent to two-child families.[85]
- Marriage licenses were only provided to men at age twenty-eight and women at age twenty-six.

Other, more coercive, measures were at times adopted by local authorities who were determined to meet population objectives. These involved making women report when they missed their period and, upon occasion, pressure to have an abortion. More distressing was the widespread practice of female infanticide by rural couples because pensions were not available to them, and because it was the only way the couple would be permitted to have another baby—hopefully a boy who would eventually care for them. It should be noted that female infanticide is strictly forbidden by the Chinese government. To stem this disturbing practice, the government has outlawed the use of ultrasound examinations to determine the sex of a fetus.

Although China's population control program has not been without pain, it has been extremely successful. Instead of 1.8 billion people by the year 2000, the population is now projected to reach only 1.2 billion.[86] The reduced growth in population may avoid the mass starvation of millions of people. Still, China's population is probably too large for long-term sustainability. It is estimated that the carrying capacity of China may be only 700 million.[87] There is no doubt that China's population control program is headed in the right direction and the United States has no right to criticize it. Instead, the United States should be attempting to curb its own population growth before American society reaches the point where we must implement the onerous policies of China.

U.S. International Population Control Policy Initiatives

The question is, can other LDCs achieve equally impressive results in slowing their population growth with less repressive measures? As stated, the key is to implement family planning programs before such drastic steps are necessary. It would be extremely useful if Catholic and Muslim prelates led the way by revising their dangerously outdated doctrines, but it is doubtful that such antiquated, authoritative religions will serve as anything other than an impediment to be overcome. However, effective, noncoercive population planning could be still be implemented in most of the underdeveloped world if the United States would reassert the leadership it once exerted.

The cost of providing the knowledge and means for family planning to all women worldwide is estimated to be only $17 billion per year, increasing to $21.5 billion by 2015.[88] ***This sum represents the total aid from all the developed nations. The U.S. share would only be about $1.8 billion.*** This is less than the cost of one Stealth bomber and would easily be recovered in savings from future emergency relief. (The funds could also be obtained by diverting some of the military aid provided to Israel, Egypt, and the LDCs.) Furthermore, reducing population growth will remove a major cause of national unrest which can lead to revolutions and international conflicts. It is to America's shame that we allowed the religious right to impede family planning aid for almost a decade, and now they threaten to do so again. ***It is in the self-interest of the United States to do all it can to support the LDCs through technical assistance and aid for family planning.***

The LDCs are equally to blame for their lack of family planning. They have devoted an exorbitant amount of money to military armaments. They could easily have financed family planning by redirecting a portion of their excessive military expenditures.

Space Colonization: The Solution to an Overcrowded Planet?

One final note: some wild-eyed optimists believe that after filling the earth to capacity we will just move to other planets, sort of like the Europeans who moved to the new world of the Americas. We already know, however, that there are no inhabitable planets in our own solar system. (Of course we could build some ecopod to house a few dozen or perhaps even a few hundred people on a barren and inhospitable moon or perhaps Mars, but only at a huge cost.) To find a livable planet, we need to travel to other solar systems, and there is the rub.

As Garrett Hardin explains, the nearest star to the earth is Alpha Centauri which is four light years away.* Traveling at the present rate of space speeds—about twenty-five *thousand* mph—it would take 114,000 years to get to Alpha Centauri. Even assuming we could boost the speed to twenty-two *million* mph—which may or may not be theoretically possible—it would take 125 years for the trip, i.e., four to five generations. And at the present birth rate, to keep the population of the earth from increasing further we would have to send off a quarter million people a day! Considering that it costs about $1 billion to build a submarine to house 140 sailors for a year, the cost of just one vehicle to house and support a quarter million people for 125 years is almost unimaginable. Even with economies of scale, one trillion dollars per spaceship would seem a bargain. And we would need to build one a day![89]

Finally, during those five generations of space travel, the voyagers would have to limit their population to replacement levels only (i.e., births – deaths = zero). But if we can get to zero population growth on the space vehicle, why not do it here on earth in the first place, saving all that absurd effort? It should be obvious to all but the most obtuse that the notion of

---

*There is no evidence that Alpha Centauri has any planets—in fact the odds are against it. The closest star with planets appears to be over eight light years away, and the likelihood that those planets are inhabitable is extremely small. Moreover, what if we discover there is already intelligent life on another planet? Does that give us the right to invade and conquer the indigenous people (assuming we could) so that we can export our surplus population? It never occurs to science fiction writers that from the perspective of any other planet with an indigenous population, we would be the space aliens. Perhaps only Native Americans can appreciate this irony.

populating distant solar systems to solve the earth's population problem is preposterous. Nevertheless, some people will clutch at any solution, no matter how absurd, to avoid taking the necessary actions dictated by circumstances.

SUMMARY

World famous entomologist Edward O. Wilson provides an excellent example of the dangers of maintaining a compound growth rate in population.[90] Imagine a pond in which you plant one lily pad. Suppose this lily pad doubles the second day and continually doubles every day for thirty days at which time the entire pond is covered in lily pads. On which day do the lily pads cover only half the pond? The answer is, of course, the twenty-ninth day! In other words, for those who don't understand compound rates of growth, the situation can look controllable just before disaster strikes. Even at the reduced rate of growth of recent years, the world population will double again in less than fifty years. In many LDCs, doubling of the population will occur in twenty to twenty-five years. Are we willing to risk the consequences?

The world's present rate of growth, or ultimately any positive rate of growth, will lead to increased strife among a growing population competing for shrinking land and water resources, greater income disparity, environmental destruction, and less freedom, as increasing population requires a proportional increase in rules and regulations to maintain order.

World population growth can be curtailed through wider availability of contraception and abortion. Just as importantly, the LDCs must improve the education of women, increase job opportunities for women, and provide minimum assistance to people in their old age.

Although the growth rate of the world's population has declined, an increase of seventy million people a year is still far too high to be sustainable. Africa, Central and South America, and many Moslem countries are in dire need of an immediate and dramatic reduction in their birth rates. The 1994 International Conference on Population and Development in Cairo, Egypt, took a small step forward in recognizing the seriousness and immediacy of the problem. Although the conference recognized the right of women to control their fertility, it failed to acknowledge the responsibility of women and men to reduce fertility rates. Further, it is unrealistic to think that population can be brought under control in many countries without introducing incentives to reduce fertility.

To support population control programs in the LDCs, the United States should immediately:

- Increase support to the UNFPA and the IPPF to at least $1 billion per year.
- Tie aid to LDCs to their efforts to implement effective family planning programs.
- Increase research and development for new contraceptives.[91]

With the adoption of the above recommendations, it would be possible to bring the world's population growth rate down from the present 1.4 percent per year to 0.5 percent in thirty to forty years. The optimal solution is a negative population growth rate for several decades after population peaks, until the world population falls back to the carrying capacity of the planet.

NOTES

1. United Nations estimate for the years 1990–1995, *Chicago Tribune*, November 17, 1996, sec. 1, p. 24.
2. Garrett Hardin, *Living Within Limits: Ecology, Economics, and Population Taboos* (New York: Oxford University Press, 1993), p. 121.
3. Ibid., p. 87.
4. Alan Gregg, "A Medical Aspect of the Population Problem," *Science* 121 (1955).
5. *The World Almanac and Book of Facts, 1998*, ed. Robert Famighetti (New York: World Almanac Books, 1998), p. 553. The 1998 estimate is from U.S. Bureau of Census, *Statistical Abstracts of Behavioral States, 1997* (Washington, D.C.: U.S. Government Printing Office, 1997), table 1334, p. 829.
6. U.S. Census Bureau estimates, *Chicago Tribune*, October, 10, 1996, sec. 1, p. 11.
7. *American Demographics* (December 1991): 4.
8. Stephen Budiansky, "10 Billion For Dinner Please," *U. S. News and World Report* (September 12, 1994) 58.
9. Robert S. McNamera, "The Population Explosion," *The Futurist* (November/December 1992): 10.
10. Brown University Hunger Program, "Hunger Report," cited in "Harvesting Hope," *ZPG Reporter* (October 1989): 1.
11. Joel E. Cohen, *How Many People Can the Earth Support?* (New York: W. W. Norton and Company, 1995).
12. "One-Third of Humanity Under 15 Years of Age," *ZPG Reporter* (August 1993): 3.
13. McNamera, "The Population Explosion," p. 10.
14. Werner Fornos, "Children of the Streets: A Global Tragedy," cited in World Population News Service, *Popline* (November/December 1991): 3.

15. Alan Greg, "A Medical Aspect of the Population Problem," *Science* 121 (1955): 681–82. Cited by Hardin, *Living Within Limits*, p. 174.

16. See for example, Barbara Crossette, "How to Fix a Crowded World: Add People," *New York Times*, November 2, 1997, pp. 1, 3. Nicholas Eberstadt has also picked up this theme.

17. Ed Dorer, "Suppression of NSSM 200," *The Humanist* (September/October 1992): 25.

18. Stephen D. Mumford, *The Life and Death of NSSM 200* (Research Triangle Park, N.C.: Center for Research on Population and Security, 1996). Michael Davies echoes the pope's own sentiment when he claims that, "His [the pope's] rule extends not merely to members of the Church, as most Catholics would imagine today, but to all men both as individuals and grouped together in a corporate body as a state." Michael Davies, "Religious Liberty and the Secular State," *Catholic Family News*, August 1996, p. 1. Cited by Mumford, p. 114. This is a perfectly logical conclusion if one first accepts the absurd assumption of papal infallibility.

19. Fornos, "Children of the Streets: A Global Tragedy," p. 67.

20. *Chicago Tribune*, February 6, 1997, sec. 1, p. 24.

21. Ibid.

22. World Population News Service, *Popline* (September/October 1993): 7.

23. *ZPG Reporter* (July/August, 1996): 8.

24. World Population News Service, *Popline* (September/October 1994): 1.

25. *Chicago Tribune*, August 18, 1994, sec. 1, p. 3.

26. *Chicago Tribune*, September 4, 1994, sec. 1, p. 15.

27. *Chicago Tribune* September 8, 1994, sec. 1, p. 7.

28. *The Final Document for the Conference on Population and Development*, Section 7.20. Cited by Donald Mann, "The Cairo Conference on Population and Development," *Negative Population Growth Position Paper* (August 1994): 1.

29. Paul Johnson, *Modern Times* (New York: HarperPerennial, 1983, 1991), p. 724.

30. William N. Ryerson, "What's Needed to Solve the Population Problem?" *The Social Contract* (Summer 1993): 277.

31. Hasimoto Kingkoro, *Addresses to Young Men*. Quoted in *Sources of Japanese Tradition*, ed. William T. deBary (New York: Columbia University Press, 1964), pp. 796–97. Cited by Paul Johnson, *Modern Times*, p. 189.

32. U.S. Bureau of the Census, *Statistical Abstracts of the United States 1980, 1995, 1996*, Gross National Product by Country, table 1334, p. 835; Population by Country 1995, table 1361, p. 845,

33. Ibid.

34. Paul Harrison, "Slower Population Growth Stimulates Economic Growth," World Population News Service, *Popline* (May/June 1992): 1.

35. R. T. Roosevelt, "Taking Contraception to the World's Poor," *Free Inquiry* (Spring 1994): 9.

36. Harrison, "Slower Population Growth Stimulates Economic Growth," p. 1.

37. Ryerson, "What's Needed to Solve the Population Problem?" p. 227.

38. Lester C. Thurow, "Why the Ultimate Size of the World's Population Growth Doesn't Matter," *Technology Review* (August 1986): 22.

39. Lester Thurow, *Head to Head* (New York: William Morrow and Company, 1992), p. 207.

40. Uli Schmetzer, "Philippine Church's Moral Code May Mask Political Purpose," *Chicago Tribune*, October 16, 1997, sec. 1, p. 10.

41. Paul R. Ehrlick and John P. Holdren, "Impact of Population Growth," in *Toward a Steady State Economy*, ed. Herman E. Daly (San Francisco: W. H. Freeman and Company, 1973), p. 82.

42. David C. Korten, *When Corporations Rule the World* (West Hartford, Conn., and San Francisco: Kumarian Press and Berrett-Koehler Publishers, Inc., 1995), p. 30.

43. Ibid., p. 33.

44. Edward O. Wilson, *Consilience* (New York: Alfred A. Knoff, 1998), p. 291.

45. Preston Cloud, "Mineral Resources in Fact and Fancy," in *Toward a Steady State Economy*, ed. Daly, p. 66.

46. *Chicago Tribune*, February 11, 1996, sec. 1, p. 4.

47. William E. Rees and Mathis Wackernagal, "Ecological Footprints and Appropriated Carrying Capacity: Measuring the Natural Capital Requirements of the Human Economy," in *Investing in Natural Capital: The Ecological Economics Approach to Sustainability*, ed. A. M. Jannson, M. Hammer et al. (Washington, D.C.: Island Press, 1994), p. 380. Cited by Korten, *When Corporations Rule the World*, p. 33.

48. Jørgan Randers and Donella Meadows, "The Carrying Capacity of Our Global Environment: A Look at the Ethical Alternatives," in *Toward a Steady State Economy*, ed. Daly, p. 283

49. Korten, *When Corporations Rule the World*, p. 35.

50. Edward O. Wilson, *On Human Nature* (Toronto: Bantam Books, 1978, 1982) p. 105.

51. Bruce Bower, "Population Overload: Mice Advice," *Science News* (May 31, 1986): 346–47.

52. Hardin, *Living Within Limits*, p. 294.

53. This is just a variation of Hardin's impact law which he gives as I = P x A x T, Hardin, *Living Within Limits*, p. 202.

54. *Wall Street Journal*, February 27, 1992, p. A1.

55. Hardin, *Living Within Limits*, p. 207.

56. World Population News Service, *Popline* (September 1987): 3.

57. Lester R. Brown, *State of the World, 1993* (New York: W. W. Norton and Company) p. 5. The latest satellite maps show that this might be a slightly high estimate, but what difference does it make whether we lose 17 million hectares a year, as Brown estimates, or only 14 million, the end result will still be the same.

58. *ZPG Reporter* (February 1991): 1.

59. Ibid., p. 1.

60. World Population News Service, *Popline* (September 1987): 3.

61. Mark Hertsgaard, "The Cost of Climate Change," *Greenpeace Quarterly* (Summer, 1996): 28.

62. Hertsgaard, "The Cost of Climate Change," p. 29.

63. *ZPG Reporter* (October/November 1993).

64. World Resources Institute, *World Resources 1992–93* (New York: Oxford University Press, 1992), p. 160.

65. Don Hinrichsen, "The World's Water Woes," *International Wildlife* (July/August 1996): 26.

66. Hinrichsen, "The World's Water Woes," p. 26.

67. *Chicago Tribune*, June 6, 1996, sec. 1, p . 8.

68. Hinrichsen, "The World's Water Woes," p. 27.

69. *Chicago Tribune*, June 6, 1996, sec. 1, p . 8.

70. Korten, *When Corporations Ruled the World*, p. 39.

71. E. O. Wilson, *Consilience*, p. 281.

72. U.S. Department of Commerce, Bureau of the Census, *Statistical Abstract of the United States, 1997*, table 1334, pp. 827–29.

73. Catherine Sweeney, "UNICEF Says Family Planning Saves Lives," World Population News Service, *Popline* (January/February 1991).

74. Brown, *Building a Sustainable Society*, p. 348.

75. U.S. Bureau of the Census, *Statistical Abstract of the United States 1996* (Washington, D.C.: U.S. Government Printing Office, 1996), table 1325, p. 827.

76. Fornos, "Children of the Streets: A Global Tragedy," p. 38

77. William N. Ryerson, "What's Needed to Solve the Population Problem?" p. 278.

78. Blyne Cuttler, "World's Choices for Birth Control," *American Demographics* (June 1991): 14. Cuttler estimates the following distribution of birth control methods:

Sterilization	35%
Intrauterine device	18
Pills	15
Condoms	10
Rhythm, withdrawal, abstinence	18

79. Bonnie Johnson, "Overpopulation and Reproductive Rights," *Free Inquiry* (Spring 1994): 13.

80. Ryerson, "What's Needed to Solve the Population Problem?" p. 278.

81. Jeffrey M. Wise and Spenser J. Condie, "Intergenerational Fertility Throughout Four Generations," *Social Biology* 22 (1975): 144–55. Cited by Hardin, *Living Within Limits*, p. 257.

82. Ibid., p. 164.

83. For a complete discussion of the ethics of abortion see Daleiden, *The Science of Morality*, chapter 15.

84. Fornos, "Children of the Streets: A Global Tragedy," p. 89.

85. Brown, *Building a Sustainable Society*, p. 160.

86. U.S. Bureau of the Census, *Statistical Abstract of the United States 1996*, Table 1325, p. 827.

87. *ZPG Reporter* (August 1990): 6.

88. Storer H. Rowley, "Tab to Curb Population: $17 Billion," *Chicago Tribune*, September 9, 1994, sec. 1, p. 3.

89. Hardin, *Living Within Limits*, pp. 10–11.

90. Wilson, *Consilience*, p. 286.

91. These are not unlike the recommendations of Werner Fornos, "Children of the Streets: A Global Tragedy," pp. 82–83.

4

U.S. Population Growth and Mass Immigration

As pointed out in the last chapter, demographic trends are of little interest to politicians or the general public. Politicians rarely look beyond the next election, which in the case of the House of Representatives is never more than two years away. The public is generally concerned with the crisis *du jour* and seeks to blame the nation's problems on corrupt and inept politicians. My experience in Washington indicates that most politicians are not corrupt or even inept (although, oftentimes, neither they nor their staffs know much about demography or economics). In our democracy most politicians merely reflect what the majority of their constituents want. Regrettably, their constituents are not only driven by self-interest, but are too often uninformed regarding the impact of demographic trends to seek an appropriate policy for America.

Consequently, although changes in the number and composition of the population is one of the most important factors regarding the ultimate success or failure of a society, it is the factor most often ignored. As the population of the United States continues its rapid growth and changes its demographic mix, many social problems have been exacerbated. But on a day-to-day basis the process has been so slow that it has avoided detection. (Remember the boiling-frog syndrome referred to in our imaginary State of the Union address in the year 2050.) Americans should know that:

- despite a slight increase since in wages since 1995, after adjusting for inflation average hourly wage rates in 1997 were still below the level of twenty-five years earlier;

- income distribution has become far more unequal;
- the environment continues to deteriorate in many parts of our nation;
- urban sprawl is destroying the best farmland in the world;
- open space is dwindling;
- public education is failing our children;
- we have made very little progress in reducing poverty; and
- crime continues at unacceptably high rates compared to the 1950s.*

Although increased population is not solely responsible for these problems, it strongly contributes to all of them. This is especially so when the growth in population is comprised of an increasing number of underskilled and poorly educated people. In the 1970s environmental organizations expressed a concern over population growth, and Americans generally scaled back the size of their families, until we were below the replacement level of 2.1 children per woman. However, most environmentalists, and Americans in general, completely ignored the growing impact of immigration.

U.S. Population Growth Is the Highest among Developed Nations

The United States now has the highest population growth rate in the industrialized world. We are adding about 2.3 million people every year. We are adding more people every decade than the total population of Australia and New Zealand (over 25 million people in the 1990s). To put this astounding growth into perspective: ***The U.S. population has doubled sixty-four times since the first census in 1790, which showed a population of 4 million people, until reaching our 1997 population of 269 million. If our population were to double only twice more, it would equal that of India. If current trends continue this will occur within the lifetimes of our grandchildren.***

Impossible you say? Back in 1978 when I worked as a consultant to U.S. Office of Management and the Budget, the Bureau of the Census projected that the U.S. population for the year 2050 would be less than 300 million. I had previously put together some projections of my own that reflected the increase in immigrants and their high birth rates and fore-

*Each of these trends will be documented in this or subsequent chapters.

Figure 4.1
U.S. Bureau of Census Projections

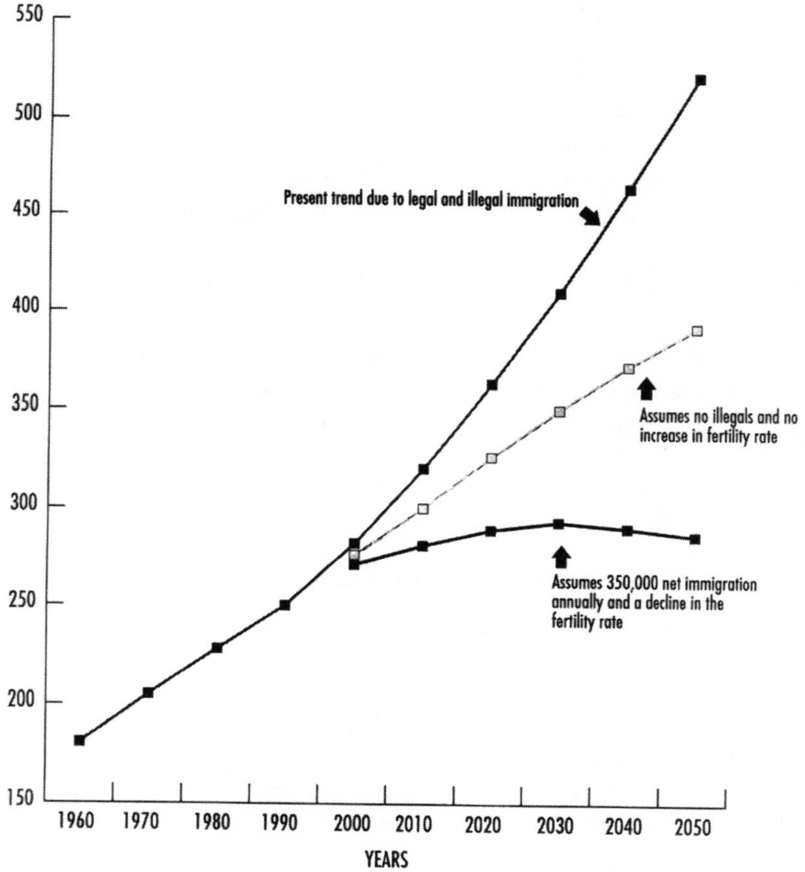

Source: U.S. Bureau of Census, Current Population Reports P-25-1104

casted a population of over 400 million by 2050. When I shared these projections with the Census Bureau, they were met with derision. I was told that I was an alarmist. As late as 1989, the Census Bureau's Middle Series projection for the year 2050 was only 299 million.[1]

By 1998, the Census Bureau's Middle Series projections jumped by 100 million people and now forecasts the population to reach almost 400 million people by 2050 as shown in figure 4.1. This projection still assumes net immigration below the average of the last decade and relatively constant fertility rates.[2] If the annual number of legal and illegal immigrants remains the same as today, and the number of births reflect the higher fertility rates of immigrants the United States (it takes two to three generations before immigrant birth rates drop to the average for American women), population could reach the Census Bureau's High Series projection of 519 million people by 2050—a 92 percent increase in the population in only fifty years.[3] Moreover, demographers Ahlburg and Vaupel sharply criticize the Census Bureau for its low fertility and immigration assumptions and conclude that under more realistic assumptions the United States will have a population of 811 million by 2080.[4] In short, only a major shift in U.S. immigration policies can prevent a population catastrophe in this country.

The extraordinary population growth in the United States is due in part to the uncontrolled population in the Less Developed Countries. figure 4.2 shows how Mexico's population problem has become America's population problem.

Figure 4.2
Comparison of Population Growth in the U.S. and Mexico, 1930 to 2000

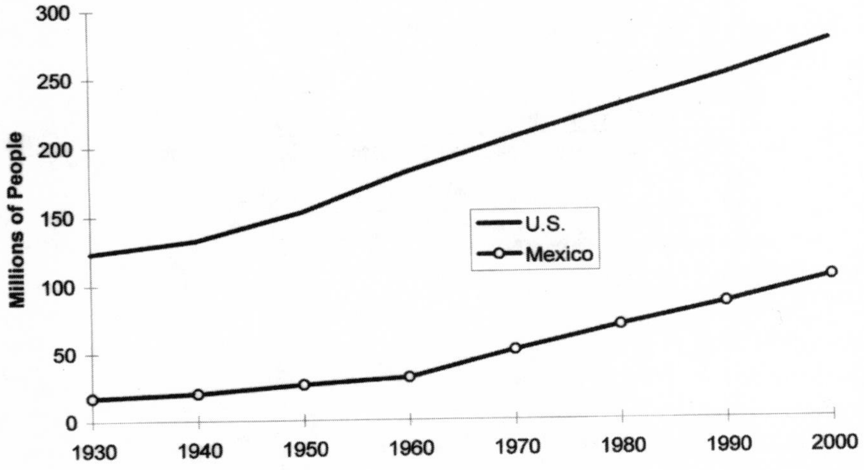

Nevertheless, it is *not* true that slowing population growth in the less developed countries will slow population growth in the United States. The reason is that there are about four billion people in the world who presently earn less than the average Mexican. ***Hence, even if the world could magically halt population growth tomorrow, there would be hundreds of millions of people still wanting to migrate to the United States and other industrialized countries (particularly Australia and Canada, the only other countries accepting large numbers of immigrants). This pressure on immigration will last as long as there is a substantial difference in the standard of living between the United States and the less developed countries.*** Moreover, it is foolish to think that the only way the problem will be resolved is to raise the standard of living in the LDCs. That will take a very long time, perhaps a century. It is more likely that during this time, while the standard of living of the LDCs rises, we will see the quality of life in the United States continue to decline (not GDP, but the more relevant measures discussed in the chapter 2).

As figure 4.3 demonstrates, even solving the problem of illegal immigration will be insufficient to stem the tide since illegals account for only about 25 percent of total immigration. We are presently being inundated with about 900,000 legal immigrants and refugees annually, and 300,000 to 500,000 illegals, for a total of 1.2 to 1.4 *million* immigrants per year. Unless the present immigration trends are significantly reduced, *America could add more people in the next sixty years than in the preceding four centuries since the founding of Jamestown in 1607.* Immigrants tend to have much larger families than the average American family, at least for the first two generations. When we factor in immigrant children and their children's children, it quickly accumulates to twelve to fifteen people for every immigrant allowed in. It is extremely important to realize that even if we were to stop all immigration tomorrow, the children and grandchildren of the immigrants of the last two decades will swell America's population by 75 to 100 million people during the next century.

Immigration was not a problem during the last century when there were open frontiers and we needed many strong backs to farm our lands, build our railroads, and work in our factories. Even today there are numerous examples of immigrants who are making a major contribution to our society. However, the majority of immigrants today, as in the past, are uneducated and unskilled. But now the American economy has entered the postindustrial, information age when there is a surplus of unskilled labor. We have sixteen million people either unemployed or involuntarily working at part-time or temporary jobs. We have thirty-six million Americans below the poverty level, most living in households where there is at least one working parent, but many of whom do not earn a living wage.

Figure 4.3
Legal and Illegal Immigrants, 1950–1997*

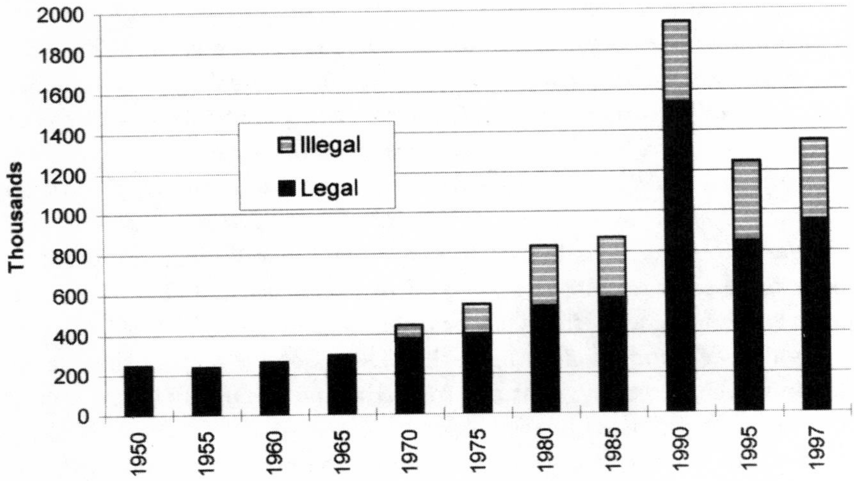

*The 1990 average reflects the amnesty given to illegal immigrants who entered the U.S. prior to 1983.

As shown in figure 4.4, the present immigration level is the highest in U.S. history and completely out of line with traditional immigration levels.[5] Except for the extraordinary periods between 1900 and 1915 and the ramp-up since the ill-conceived Immigration Act of 1965, during most of the twentieth century annual immigration ran in the two hundred and three hundred thousand range.

Congress Makes a Bad Situation Worse

Many liberals hate to say no to anyone who wants to immigrate to the United States; they believe that immigration helps the world's poor. And many conservatives like the idea of a continued supply of cheap labor. So what has Congress done to cope with this long simmering crisis? First, to cope with the problem of illegal immigration in 1986 Congress granted amnesty to illegal immigrants who entered the United States prior to 1983. Now there was a brilliant idea: solving the problem of illegal immigration by rewarding law breakers. Not surprising, the amnesty merely encouraged more people to enter illegally. After granting legal status to over three million illegals by 1990, several million new illegals flooded into the United States by 1996.[6] Having worsened the problem of illegals, the best Congress

Figure 4.4
Our Immigration Tradition

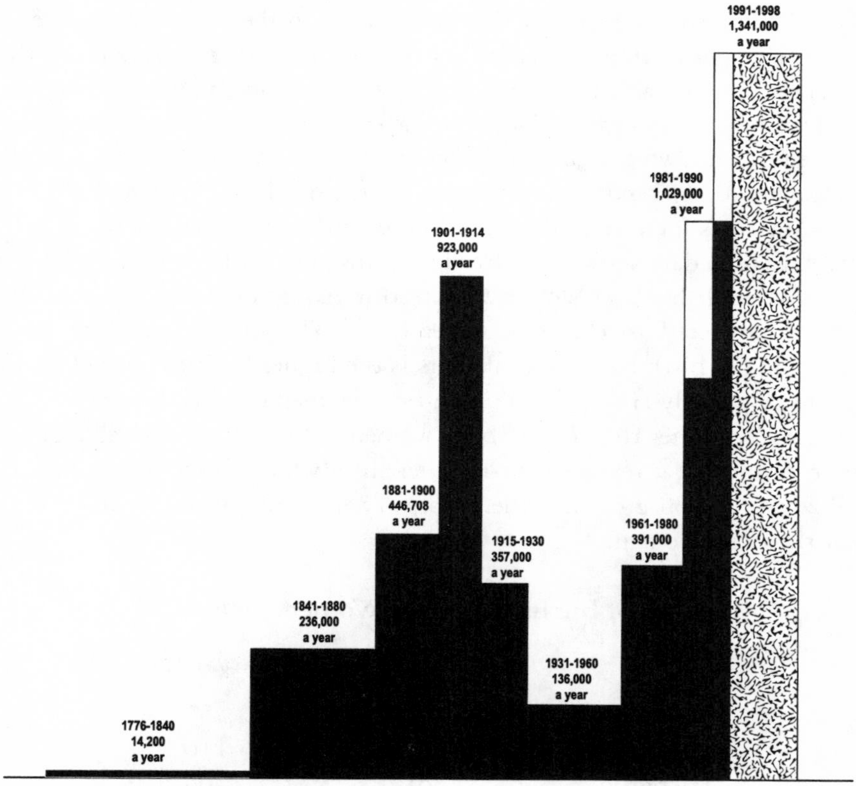

■ Actual (Source: Statistical Yearbook of the Immigration and Naturalization Service)
▨ Projected
□ Illegals based on Census Bureau estimate of illegals in country assuming they arrived after 1988-1991 amnesty

that special interest money could buy turned its attention to the problem of legal immigration. In 1990, legislation that started out to slow excessive legal immigration ended up being rewritten and actually increased the number of annual legal immigrants by 40 percent.[7] By 1997, U.S. legal immigration had soared to almost 1.0 million annually. Add to this upwards of half a million illegals, and that equates to approximately 1.5 million immigrants entering the nation every year, the largest number at any time in our nation's history!* Add the natural increase in population (births minus deaths) of 1.4 million to the flood of immigrants and it doesn't take a rocket scientist to see why U.S. population growth is soaring.

The United States is now the only country in the world that has yet to make a serious attempt to control its borders. The other two countries that accept any appreciable number of immigrants are Canada and Australia, and both of these nations have reduced immigration to protect jobs and the quality of life for their own citizens. Canada reduced its quota from 250,000 annually to about 200,000[8] and Australia cut its quota from 160,000 to 90,000.[9]

America's increase in immigration has also contributed to rising birth rates. Census data show that after bottoming out in 1976 at 1.7 children per woman, it has been slowly, but steadily rising, reaching 2.06 in 1996, and is projected to continue increasing.[10] The most significant factor affecting the birth rate in recent years is the higher fertility rates of immigrants, especially Hispanics. Foreign-born women have fertility rates 20 to 30 percent higher than native-born women.[11] In viewing the table below, bear in mind that replacement-level fertility (which would eventually stabilize population growth if there was no net immigration) is 2100 births per thousand women.

U.S. Births Per 1,000 Women, 1996[12]

	All Women	*Teenagers*†
White	1988	51
Black	2428	110
Hispanic	2977	104

†Ages 15 to 19.

Note also the relatively high fertility rate of Black and Hispanic teenagers. Exacerbating the problem is the cutback in all forms of family planning

*In fact the number may be even greater. A study by Lindsey Grant indicated that there were well over one million more airline passenger arrivals than departures each year in the United States. What happens to these surplus arrivals? There is no follow-up by immigration authorities. The suspicion is that many of these just blend in with other illegals.

services under Reagan and Bush, which, although reversed under Clinton, is still not getting the attention and funding that the problem warrants.

Despite the grave consequences of this runaway population growth, the general public and its elected representatives have yet to recognize the ramifications of adding anywhere from 120 to 250 million people in only fifty years—the equivalent of thirty to seventy-seven cities the size of Los Angeles, all with the problems associated with a mostly uneducated and underskilled populace.

The pressure on our borders will not end anytime soon. As mentioned in the last chapter, although Mexico is making strides to control its burgeoning population, they have a long way to go. Mexico's population is growing at more than double the U.S. rate and will have tripled in only forty years from 31 million in 1960 to 110 million by 2000, a rate far in excess of Mexico's ability to create jobs. In arguing for reductions in U.S. import restrictions, Mexico's president has said that either the United States exports jobs to Mexico or Mexico will continue to export people to the United States. Actually, unless we reform our immigration policies, both trends will accelerate. For instance, the removal of tariffs on exports to Mexico will result in an increase in American grain exports to its southern neighbor unless Mexican farms make substantial productivity gains. Unfortunately, achieving such gains in productivity would result in displacing tens of thousands of workers—more potential migrants moving north.

The situation is worse in Central America, whose population has grown 60 percent just in the decade between 1980 and 1990, from 22 million to more than 38 million. Unless there is a dramatic reduction in fertility rates, the population will almost double between 1990 and 2025.[13] The growth rate in Central America will guarantee be continued high unemployment and increased civil unrest. The result will be protracted pressure for migration to the United States, often as political refugees. The best national defense policy America could enact with respect to Central America is to convert our millions of dollars of military aid into family planning assistance and agricultural technology. Unless Mexico and Central America quickly reduce their respective birth rates, there will be continued political turmoil in the region and a flood of illegals into the U.S.

Furthermore, it is not only Mexico and Central America that will be generating increasing number of migrants. In 1994 there were 23 million political refugees worldwide[14] and over 100 million people seeking to migrate as a result of poverty, discrimination, violence, draught, and environmental destruction.[15] The number will grow dramatically in the next few decades. ***One estimate is that 1.25 billion of the 3 billion people living in LDCs will seek to improve their conditions by migrating to areas with more economic opportunity.***[16]

While we might sympathize with the plight of the world's poor, migration is not the answer. It will just result in swamping the industrialized nations to such an extent that they would all be impoverished. For example, other things being equal, if over the next twenty years the U.S. did take in 100 million new migrants, a 40 percent increase in population could reduce the potential United States per capita income by an equal amount. Now some might argue that I am ignoring the additional stimulus to economic growth caused by the immigration. But as we will see below, the cost of immigration will more than offset any benefits. Moreover, the relationship is not a linear one. In other words, an increase in immigrants will result in a greater than proportional increase in social costs. Finally, the incidence of the costs will not affect all segments of society equally. Those with the capital resources will benefit from cheap labor, while those who will face increased competition for jobs will lose out. The result will be increased income disparity between the haves and have-nots, and all the social unrest that will accompany such an outcome. In short, the United States will look more and more like a South American country in terms of the distribution of wealth.

The Economic and Social Consequences of Current Immigration Policies

It is more than mere hyperbole to characterize the present wave of immigration as an "invasion," as Wayne Lutton and John Tanton do, the "path to national suicide" as Lawrence Auster contends,[17] or as a "colonization of the United States" as Eugene McCarthy argues.[18] These are all apt descriptions of the current trend of mass immigration. Let's examine the probable consequences.

Reduced Job Opportunities and Depressed Wage Rates

To explain the overall impact of immigration on unemployment and wage rates, we need to review a little of the history leading up to the present employment situation. Those of us who were fortunate enough to enter the labor market in the early 1960s with a college degree had little trouble finding a well-paying job. Having selected a job, hard work was rewarded by relatively rapid advancement and a constant increase in salary even after adjusting for inflation. By the early 1970s all that had changed; unemployment rose sharply and average real weekly earnings steadily declined from 1973 through 1994. What happened?

Several adverse trends occurred simultaneously. Other countries became more competitive as the United States slowed growth in productivity by diverting investment and brain power to the defense industry. A decline in world trade barriers encouraged American businesses to invest in manufacturing abroad to take advantage of the lower wage rates in emerging nations, particularly Southeast Asia. U.S. businesses also went on an acquisition binge that enriched the deal makers while most often failing to achieve the promised economic benefits for the shareowners. Litigation became a more common road to enrichment than innovation. Several of these themes will be examined in the following chapters.

But in addition to all the foregoing problems there was a major shift in the demographics affecting job opportunities. The post World War II baby boom entered the labor force beginning in the mid-Sixties and carrying through the Seventies. As shown below, the twenty- to twenty-four-year-old age group would increase 55 percent between 1960 and 1970 and another 22 percent in the succeeding decade.

Percentage Change in Population for Selected Age Groups

Age Group	*1960–70*	*1970–80*	*1980–90*	*1990–2000*
15–19	43%	6.7%	–18.6%	17.6%
20–24	55	21.8	–14.2	– 5.9
25–34	10	39.5	13.6	–16.2

At the same time, civil rights created opportunities in the work force for minorities, but had an even more profound impact for white women. Their labor force participation rate jumped from 37.7 percent in 1960 to 51.5 percent by 1980.[19] Just the *increase* in white women in the labor force between 1960 and 1980 (14.7 million) was considerably more than the *total* number of blacks in the labor force by 1980 (9.3 million).[20] So we had the huge increase in baby boomers, women and minorities all trying to squeeze through the employment office doors at the same time. They couldn't all succeed in getting good paying jobs, because the supply of labor greatly exceeded the demand; unemployment jumped and wage rates began a twenty-year decline. After adjusting for inflation, and despite a slight increase in 1996 and 1997, average weekly earnings of workers in private nonagricultural jobs in 1997 were 21 percent below 1973.[21]*

*There was an increase in nonwage benefits during this period, but even accounting for benefits, average weekly compensation adjusted for inflation was essentially flat. In constant dollars, total compensation increased only 3.5 percent from 1979 (the earliest date this data is available) to 1997. If labor had received its share of total productivity growth over the 1979–1997 period, we would have expected compensation to increase about 25 percent.

Another factor exacerbating the rise in unemployment was the growing competitiveness of the rest of the world. The United States was virtually the only developed nation not devastated by World War II. As such, we completely dominated the world economy. By the mid-Sixties, Europe had been rebuilt and became a serious international competitor. By 1970, Japan and Taiwan had modernized and were coming on strong. During the 1980s the United States was flooded by imports from Korea and Taiwan, and then Thailand, Singapore, Malaysia, Indonesia, the Philippines, and China. Increased imports of manufactured goods began flowing in from Mexico, the Caribbean, and Latin and South American countries as well. All of these countries had far lower wage rates and so could more than compete in production of labor-intensive manufacturing products.

By 1980, U.S. competitiveness had also been weakened by a decade of high inflation that resulted in higher nominal wage rates (wages not adjusted for inflation). The higher nominal wages provided further incentive for companies to move their manufacturing operations to lower wage countries. Many of the jobs that remained in the United States continued to migrate from northern cities to the South, and from inner cities to the suburban and rural areas, effectively stranding inner city blacks.

In the mid-1980s, it appeared that the problem of excess labor supply, particularly in manufacturing, was going to improve. Inflation was brought under control and the number of new entrants to the labor force slowed as the "Baby Boomers" and the record number of women looking for work began to find jobs. However, the American worker now faced new threats: corporate mergers and acquisitions—a restructuring that resulted in a massive number of layoffs, and a sudden increase in immigration bringing in millions of foreign workers to compete with Americans for jobs at the same time that American job opportunities were moving elsewhere.

The cross-directional movement of job opportunities and people in the 1980s and 1990s is analogous to what happened within the United States in the late the 1950s and throughout the 1960s. Blacks seeking a better life were migrating North for jobs, while employers seeking cheaper labor were moving South.[22] The result was rapid population growth in the northern ghettos and a jump in the unemployment rates in Northern States. At least the migration of jobs stayed within the country, which allowed some of the benefits from increased Southern employment to be collected in the form of additional income taxes and redirected to aid Northern cities. In contrast, when jobs move out of the United States, there is no added revenue to be redistributed.*

---

*It is often argued that the U.S. benefits from the availability of cheaper foreign made products, but it is questionable whether it is enough to offset the extra costs that result from the huge influx of foreign workers. It certainly does not benefit the displaced American workers who will not have the purchasing power to buy the cheaper foreign goods.

The addition of approximately 30 million immigrants and their descendants between 1970 and 1995[23] amplified the downward pressure on wages due to the other demographic and economic trends mentioned above. A study by Donald L. Huddle of Rice University concluded:

> [E]mployers find it advantageous to hire illegal aliens in common and some semi-skilled jobs. First, illegal aliens often work harder, under more difficult conditions than will U.S. workers. Second, entry-level illegal workers are often paid less than the prevailing wage in an industry and always less than the union wage. Third, between one-fourth and one-half of employers, contractors, and subcontractors do not deduct any taxes from [the] workers' gross pay.[24]

One of the strongest proponents of immigration, business economist Julian Simon, was forced to admit that even if unemployment is not negatively impacted by immigrants, the large number of immigrants have lessened the need for employers to raise wages in order to attract sufficient workers.[25] George Borjas, an economist who specializes in immigration issues, estimates that ***immigration costs U.S. workers $133 billion a year due to depressed wages.***[26] Depressed wages, in turn, result in increased income inequality. Borjas estimates that recent immigration is responsible for one-third the growth in income inequality in the United States. This is the flip side of what happened after immigration was cut in the 1920s. Studies by economists Peter Lindhert and Jeffrey Williamson indicate that decreased immigration and lower fertility rates accounted for one-third of the decrease in income inequality during the period between 1929 and the Korean War.[27]

Some immigration proponents still refuse to accept the law of supply and demand, which tells us that, all other things being equal, an increase in the supply of labor will drive down wage rates. They cite studies conducted in the 1980s concluding that immigration does not have an impact on job opportunities or wage rates for native-born Americans.[28] However, these studies suffered from two serious shortcomings. First, they were often based upon data from the 1970 and 1980 censuses, which do not reflect the impact of the latest wave of immigration. Second, they generally employed a comparison of high-immigration cities with low-immigration cities. It has since been shown that the underlying assumption of such studies—that metropolitan labor markets in the United States are unconnected—is incorrect. Subsequent studies by demographers Randell Filer and William Frey have shown that natives who have been harmed by competition from immigrants and who are willing to work for less migrate to other cities.[29] Hence, a more comprehensive examination of the labor market impact is required to assess the impact of immigration.

More recent studies have shown that immigrants do indeed displace indigenous labor by both directly competing for jobs and by holding down the wage rate, thus making it more advantageous for people to remain on welfare. Examining the national impacts has caused Borjas to reverse his earlier opinion that immigrants do not have negative impacts on native wages and job opportunities.[30] By examining the impacts across occupation groups Steven Camarota and Mark Krikorian of the Center of Immigration Studies concluded that "a one percent increase in the immigrant composition of one's occupation reduces wages *at least* .7 percent."[31] (Several other such studies are cited in the endnote.)[32] According to economists Timothy Hatton and Jeffrey Williamson, all of the standard mainstream economic models now predict that migration will tend to lower wages in areas where large numbers of immigrants settle.[33]

There are several case studies that provide support for the predictions of economic models that real wages will decline if the supply of labor increases faster than the demand. A study by the United States General Accounting Office provided a dramatic example of how the process works. In 1977, approximately 2,500 black janitors in the Los Angeles area were unionized and earning a very respectable $12 an hour including benefits. However, a group of nonunion contractors began moving in to displace the blacks with Hispanic labor willing to work for $4.00 an hour. By 1985, the number of black janitors had declined to 600, of which only 100 were still protected by high wage contracts.[34]

Unskilled workers and African Americans are particularly hard hit by increased immigration. Labor economist Vernon Briggs Jr. of Cornell University has found that increased labor supply due to immigration prevents noncollege-educated males from finding jobs that pay enough to support a family and make marriage a viable option. Hence, immigration becomes one more factor contributing to the increase in illegitimacy.[35] Immigrants have displaced blacks in numerous unskilled jobs including farmworkers, garment workers, hotel maids, waiters, nursing assistants, orderlies, janitors, etc.[36] Oftentimes this is the result of a deliberate strategy on the part of employers who know they can replace blacks with other minority workers with impunity.[37] Studies by Joleen Kirschenman and Katherine Neckerman, among others, indicate that employers display a strong preference for immigrant workers over native workers in general and over black job seekers in particular.[38]

Based upon very conservative assumptions, the Center for Immigration Studies estimates about 2.1 million Americans were displaced by immigrants in 1992.[39] The cumulative impact would obviously be far higher. An estimated 55 percent of legal immigrants who enter the United States immediately enter the job market.[40] Since 1970, when the number of immigrants began increasing dramatically, many of the immigrant's children have entered the job market as well. Based upon labor force participation rates, the number of immigrants entering the labor force since 1970 would be well over 10 million. Some of these immigrants created new jobs, but a large number took existing jobs.

Immigration Hits Blacks the Hardest

Furthermore, the vast majority of jobs created by immigrants only go to other immigrants. For instance, according to Pyong Gap Min, a sociologist at New York Queens College, although the population in New York is 25 percent black, only 5 percent of the workers at Korean-owned stores are black. More than one-third of the employees are Mexican and Latin American immigrants.[41] In Los Angeles, which is 17 percent black, only 2 percent are hired by Korean-owned businesses. Some proponents of today's high levels of immigration claim that immigrants are only taking jobs that blacks won't do. This is simply not true. A 1995 study of fast food restaurants in Harlem revealed an average of fourteen job applicants for every minimum wage opening and most people had applied for four or five other jobs.[42]

One reason for the preference for Hispanics by immigrant store owners is that they are often able to pay Hispanics well below the minimum wage for six 12-hour days.[43] Another reason is that immigrant business owners are far more likely than white Americans to have a negative attitude toward blacks.[44] Immigrant-owned businesses are able to discriminate against blacks with impunity because state and federal civil rights agencies turn a blind eye to discrimination by minorities.[45] According to Philip Kasinitz, professor of sociology at New York's Hunter College, "No one has tried to enforce civil rights laws on immigrant enclave-business."[46] In fact, by giving job preferences to women and other minorities, affirmative action now works to the detriment of African Americans.

Immigrant businesspeople, especially Asians, have quickly learned to turn affirmative action to their advantage. Asian-American-owned businesses have more than doubled their share of contracts awarded under the Small Business Administration's so-called 8a program, getting 23.7 percent of the contracts in 1996, compared to only 10.5 percent in 1986. Black contractors, by comparison, have watched their share of the total contracts drop by more than a quarter.[47]

The displacement of blacks by immigrants is nothing new. In his book *The Case Against Immigration* Roy Beck documents the history of immigration and American blacks. Even before the Civil War, immigrants were used to displacing black workers in Northern States. After the Civil War, all the expected gains in employment and living standards that the newly emancipated slaves expected were soon wiped out by the importation of millions of immigrants. In 1870, 32 percent of black men in Cleveland had skilled jobs. Then, in the latter part of the nineteenth century, newly arriving immigrants formed unions that excluded blacks. By 1910 after several decades of increasing immigration, only 10 percent of the black men in Cleveland had skilled jobs.[48]

It is not just coincidental that the two periods that blacks made solid gains in both employment and wages were during the First World War when immigration was curtailed, and between 1940 and 1973 when immigration was also severely limited. During this latter period, tight immigration and low growth in the labor force enabled the black middle class to grow from 22 percent to 71 percent.[49] However, the increased growth in the labor force since 1970, due in part to the baby boom, but greatly exacerbated by immigration, reversed that trend. Especially since 1990 blacks have once again been losing job opportunities to immigrants. In Chicago, for example, black contractors and craftspeople have been quickly displaced by Hispanic, Polish, and Eastern European immigrants. An examination of employment trends in the Midwest over the period 1983 to 1995 shows that in virtually every major occupation group Hispanic employment was growing faster than black employment. In manufacturing and construction the trends were particularly noteworthy. During the 1990-91 recession blacks were more likely to be laid off, and during the economic recovery blacks were less likely to be hired than Hispanics.[50] Tragically, black leadership is so interested in gaining support from Hispanic and other immigrant voters, they have ignored the impact of immigration on their own people.*

Many years ago, both Frederick Douglass and Booker T. Washington advocated the hiring of unemployed blacks rather than importing additional white European workers. Washington argued that the South had two options: "We shall constitute one-third and more of the ignorance and crime of the South, or one-third its intelligence and progress, we shall con-

---

*Blacks have been negatively affected by immigration not only through lost job opportunities, but by diversion of educational resources to immigrants. A particularly perverse example occurred in California when black children in school districts that were primarily Hispanic were forced to attend bilingual education classes. Labor economist Vernon Briggs points out that other educational costs are more subtle but equally significant. "Namely, the societal goal of desegregated urban schools has been greatly retarded by the arrival of immigrant children because they have increased the racial isolation of inner city black children." Vernon M. Briggs Jr., "Income Disparity and Unionism: the Workplace Influences of Post 1965 Immigration Policy," in *The Inequality Paradox: Growth of Income Disparity*, James A. Auerbach and Richard S. Belous, eds. (Washington, D.C.: National Policy Association Report, #288, 1998), p. 118. Briggs cites several other analyses that arrived at the same conclusion.

tribute one-third to the business and industrial prosperity of the South, or we shall prove a veritable body of death, stagnating and depressing, retarding every effort to advance the body politic."[51] Douglass wrote, "The old employment by which we have heretofore gained our livelihood are gradually, and it may be inevitably, passing into other hands. Every hour sees the black man elbowed out of employment by some newly arrived immigrant whose hunger and whose color are thought to give him a better title to the place."[52]

Imagine what a different country the United States would be today had we heeded the prophetic words of these two visionaries! We didn't listen then and we are in danger of throwing away another historic opportunity. The same argument can be made today against accepting any more immigrants until we employ the current work force—including those presently on welfare—to its maximum capacity.

Of course, not only blacks are being unjustly discriminated against by the influx of minority immigrants, whites are as well. We have no valid reason for discriminating against whites in favor of migrants. Yet, a Hispanic or Asian migrant has an affirmative action advantage over a white person who is also trying to work his or her way out of poverty. Is it any wonder that many poor and middle-class whites are becoming increasingly more frustrated and hateful of immigrants and minorities? Or that they believe the government no longer represents their interests? ***The consequence of using affirmative action policy to provide an advantage for immigrants (80 percent of whom are defined as minorities) over American citizens will no doubt result in increased interethnic strife.***

Over the last twenty years, the demand for better-educated, higher-skilled workers has continued to increase. Has the education and skill level of immigrants kept pace? A master of statistical duplicity, immigration advocate Julian Simon argued that today's immigrants are on average better educated than those of years ago.* But using the averages disguises two very diverse trends among recent immigrants. On one hand, we have had an increase in the number of highly educated doctors, professors, and scientists migrating from India, the Philippines, Russia, and Southeast Asia. On the

---

*Simon's last analysis, *Immigration: The Demographic and Economic Facts*, suffers from the same kind of statistical chicanery and use of obsolete data as his earlier studies. For example, he uses 1980 Census data to bolster his claim that immigrants create more businesses than native born Americans. More recent data refutes this claim. Economics professor Herman E. Daly sums up the view of many of Simon's critics. "Julian Simon frequently exaggerates and makes mistakes, and he is frequently caught at it. . . . [But] by making mistakes faster than critics can correct them, he also maintains a permanent debating advantage, at least in some media. . . . [C]ritics have no choice but to keep on exposing his errors and exaggerations" (*Border Watch* [March 1973], p. 3).

other hand, the majority of immigrants today come from Mexico, Latin America, and the Caribbean, and have relatively low education and job skills. Aside from using averages that confuse the two distinct trends just mentioned, Simon failed to note that, not only has the average years of education for immigrants dropped relative to that of American workers (which has actually risen) but, more significantly, the educational level of immigrants has declined relative to that required by most jobs today. This is particularly true of illegals who were granted amnesty since 1986 and is reflected in the earnings of new immigrants. In 1970 recently arrived immigrants earned 17 percent less than the average American. Since then the gap has widened. The earnings of the most recent immigrants were 28 percent less than the U.S. average in 1980 and 32 percent less in 1990.[53]

A large portion of the immigrants compete for the lowest skilled jobs, and have effectively prevented the minimum wage from rising on an inflation adjusted basis. ***From 1974 to 1996 the minimum wage dropped 34 percent in constant dollars.**** As a result, entry-level pay for many jobs not only leaves a person well below the poverty line, but acts as a disincentive for a woman with children who tries to leave welfare to take a minimum wage job.[54] In addition to the expense of child care and transportation, she may lose her Medicaid insurance. As many women have learned to their chagrin, leaving welfare to take a job can result in greater poverty.

Recent Immigrants Are also Hurt by the Excessive Rate of Present Immigration

Ironically, the present high levels of immigration have worked to the detriment of immigrants themselves. Since the 1930s, when novelist John Steinbeck exposed the problem in his classic novel, *The Grapes of Wrath*, the migrant farm workers have been trying desperately to improve their lot. For a time in the early 1970s, it seemed as if they might succeed. By enduring many personal hardships and an extraordinary effort against seemingly insurmountable odds, Cesar Chavez's United Farm Workers Union made significant gains to improve working conditions and the hourly wage rate of farm workers, most of whom are immigrants. The agribusiness lobbied hard to reestablish the *bracero* program that would allow temporary foreign workers to pick crops at substantially reduced wages. Failing in that effort, the growers persuaded the government to raise quotas for legal immigration and

---

*In 1974 the minimum wage was $2.00 an hour. The 1997 minimum wage of $5.25 equals only $1.64 when adjusted for inflation. Therefore, minimum wage earners would still have lost 18 percent in purchasing power since 1974. In fact, at $5.25 an hour, on an inflation adjusted basis the minimum wage has risen only a nickel—or 7 percent—over almost half a century!

effectively turn a blind eye on the rising tide of illegals. The result was to effectively undermine the efforts of American farm workers who struck for higher wages. Real wages of citrus workers dropped by two-thirds from 1967 to 1988 according to labor economist Marshall Barry.[55]

In 1996, the United Farm Workers finally settled their eighteen-year effort to unionize Red Coach Lettuce. After adjusting for inflation, the UFW had to settle for a wage rate far less than they had asked for eighteen years earlier. According to a study by the California Institute for Rural Studies, based upon data collected by the U.S. Department of Agriculture and other government sources, the real wages of farmworkers in 1997 were about 25 percent lower than they were in 1976.[56] For many the decline in wages was far worse. In Salinas, California, the piece rate for picking broccoli remains 20 percent below the rate a decade ago, even before adjusting for inflation.[57] The reason for the decline in wages is no mystery: during the peak season, the United States has slightly more than 1 million farmworker jobs but 2.5 million farmworkers.[58] A U.S. Accounting Office study found that the tomato and tortilla industry constantly replaced immigrant workers with more recent immigrants or used the presence of new immigrants to hold down the wages of those who had worked in the previous year.[59] I find it frustrating that many of the same people who joined me in picketing stores carrying nonunion grapes and lettuce in the early 1970s are unable to see the linkage between the increased supply of labor and depressed wage rates. Today many of these same people are supporting the increased immigration that has undermined living standards of farmworkers and millions of other Americans.

Hispanic and black leaders are especially culpable in this regard. They appear far more interested in gaining more voters than improving the living standards of their exiting constituents. In the case of Hispanics, Bureau of Census data shows that household income for 1995 dropped 5.1 percent even though it was rising for every other American ethnic and racial group. Hispanics now constitute 24 percent of the nation's poor, up 8 percentage points from 1985.[60] The *New York Times* acknowledges that "the influx of million of Latin Americans—2 million between 1990 and 1994 alone, the Census reports—have pulled income down because immigrants tend to be poor."[61] ***The United States has adopted a policy of importing poverty, as if we did not have enough poor of our own. The most salient point is that, unlike the experience of immigrants during most of the post-World War Two period, the excessive supply of immigrants in recent years has resulted in average wages of immigrants decreasing rather than increasing.*** Yet not a single Hispanic congressman has shown the political fortitude or economic common sense to call for a reduction in immigration.

Pete Wilson, the former governor of California supported his state's agribusinesses in their successful effort to flood the state with cheap labor and California is now being haunted by his error. The inundation of immigrants during the past two decades placed a huge burden on the state's education and welfare systems and led to a host of other social ills.

It is not only unskilled and skilled blue-collar jobs that are threatened by immigration. An analysis by the Center for Immigration Studies in 1996 indicated that the influx of foreign-born scientists, engineers, and mathematicians into the United States has resulted in a glut on the market, depressing job opportunities and wage rates.[62] The Pew Health Professions Commission study warns of a surplus of 100,000 to 150,000 doctors, 200,000 to 300,000 nurses, and 40,000 pharmacists.[63] This 20 percent surplus is about equal to the share of immigrants who have entered the medical profession in recent years.* In 1997 the federal government began paying medical schools to train *fewer* doctors while still permitting foreign physicians to emigrate to the United States.

Although businesses are crying that they need immigrant labor for computer programmers, here, too, there is actually a surplus. There are about 40,000 new positions opening up in the software industry every year, while 51,000 computer science majors are graduating each year.[64] Yet the software industry has successfully lobbied for continual increases in temporary immigrant workers. The true motivation of the software industry is illustrated by American International Group, an insurance company that fired all 250 of its programmers and replaced them with programmers from India willing to work for about half the wage rate.[65] In short, employers and investors benefit from excessive immigration and cheap labor; most wage earners eventually suffer.

It is true that with less cheap labor it is more difficult for entrepreneurial types to start their own business. So be it. It is a far better social goal to pay Americans adequate wages than to allow a few to benefit at the expense of the many.

Many people believe we should stop illegal immigration but do not believe that legal immigration is a problem. Quite the contrary, even if we are able to reduce illegal immigration to zero, the excessive number of legal immigrants presents a serious problem. The U.S. Department of Labor estimates that we will create 18 million new jobs in the 1990s. Based upon present demographic trends 28 million young people will enter the labor market during the decade and perhaps as many as 10 million will leave the

---

*It is true that there is still a shortage of doctors in inner-city and rural areas, but building a surplus won't help much. As wage rates fall, fewer students will enter the profession. The answer is to provide incentives to work in these areas, such as permitting doctors to pay off their student loans by working in such areas, and a greater use of nurse practitioners.

labor market.[66] ***Hence, the growth in the number of jobs will approximate the number of new job seekers, excluding any immigration.*** With 7 million Americans still out of work in 1997, several million additional people who have given up looking for work, and perhaps 8 to 9 million workers involuntarily working at temporary or part time jobs, does it make any sense to permit the entry of another 9 million immigrants this decade? (Not to mention the estimated 5 to 6 million illegals).

Through shortsightedness we are squandering a major opportunity to reduce poverty in America. If we do away with welfare, economic theory suggests that unemployment will decline, irrespective of the growth in the population. An increase in supply relative to demand will force wages down. But faced with no alternative, people are willing to work at any wage that prevents starvation. (Of course, some may turn to crime as a preferable alternative to wages just above starvation level.) This leads us to the question, is a nation of employed poor that much better than a nation of unemployed poor? Isn't our real goal a nation of employed, decently paid workers?

Many people who do not understand economics believe that we can solve the problem by simply legislating a higher minimum wage. This is true, to some extent, during periods of tight labor markets. However, arbitrarily raising the minimum wage in periods of labor surplus will only result in higher unemployment. Moreover, if everyone's wages go up, but businesses are able to pass on the increase by raising prices, the wage earner is no better off.

Tight Labor Markets Are Key to Reducing Poverty and Increasing Income Equality

There is no getting around it, nothing helps improve the earnings of the American worker like tight labor markets. Let's take a concrete example. For several decades there was a shortage of nurses in this country. My wife was a nurse throughout this period and hardly a week went by when she did not get recruited by some hospital. To retain her services, her own employer was forced to provide generous wage increases. Collectively, hospitals bid up wages to the point where the nursing job became quite attractive to many women (and some men). As more entered the profession, the rapid increase in nurses' salaries declined. Today there is no major shortage of nurses, and wage rates are just about keeping pace with inflation. In a market economy, increased wages, or alternatively, increased productivity will solve a labor shortage whether it be for nurses or computer programmers. But employers would naturally take the easy way of importing a predictable supply of cheap labor.

As Roy Beck documents so cogently, the history of immigration is a continuous effort of employers to replace American workers with lower-wage immigrant labor. During periods of tight labor, some small employers might be forced out of business. But the more innovative businesses will spend additional money on recruiting and training employees from the inner city or elsewhere. This is exactly what occurred during World War II when businesses recruited labor from Appalachia and rural areas to work in their factories. Tight labor markets, such as existed during the period from 1940 to about 1968, could be a major factor in reducing poverty and enhancing equality of opportunity.

For as long as I can remember, economic discussions on what to do about joblessness and low wages have focused on how to create more jobs, i.e., to stimulate the demand for labor. The supply of labor was considered relatively constant. While this is true in the short run, over the longer term the supply of labor relative to demand can vary greatly. Tight labor markets are one of the most important prerequisites for increasing wage rates, reducing poverty, and increasing economic equality. This conclusion is supported by studies conducted by the Jerome Levy Economics Institute of Bard College and the Brookings Institute.[67] ***Hence, the most significant policy required to increase job opportunities and improve wage rates for Americans is to constrain immigration (including refugees and asylum seekers)—to about the average number of immigrants accepted annually prior to the surge in the 1970s, about 250,000 a year.***

As soon as wages begin to rise, as is normal in the latter stages of an economic recovery, the most likely reaction of employers will be to argue for increased immigration. Another equally predictable response is for the Federal Reserve Bank to construe wage increases as inflationary and respond by raising interest rates. The result would be to slow economic growth, thus raising unemployment and depressing wage rates. Such a policy distorts the distribution of wages and profits in a market economy in favor of the suppliers of capital. In a market economy, the negotiations for distribution of the benefits of production should be resolved by management and labor. If a shortage of labor improves labor's bargaining power and increases wages, so be it. It will only be inflationary to the point that a business can pass on the increased wages to its customers. However, in a competitive market, the smarter businesses will develop new techniques to improve productivity to offset wage increases. If the industry as a whole cannot offset wage increases, either profits will decline or the increased prices will reduce demand for that particular product. In any case, the market will self-correct if the Federal Reserve Board holds a neutral monetary policy. Any effort to curb price increases through higher interest rates only serves to interfere in the markets by punishing labor.

Higher Health and Education Costs

In southern California illegal immigrants cost the public $400 million in healthcare costs alone.[68] Prior to the passage of Proposition 187, any foreigner could come into the country, legally or illegally, and apply for the California program of Medicaid, receive treatment, and then return home leaving the U.S. taxpayers to foot the bill.[69] This is still occurring in many states. It is far too common for pregnant women to cross the border close to their due date or even while in labor. The baby is delivered free of charge at a county hospital and is automatically an American citizen eventually entitled to the benefits of any other citizen. Nearly two-thirds of the babies born in county-operated California hospitals during 1990–93 had parents who were illegal aliens.[70]

In 1982, the Supreme Court ruled in *Phyler* v. *Doe* that illegals were entitled to a free education.[71] Consequently, the cost of educating immigrants soared. Net U.S. education costs (after subtracting the revenue generated by immigrants) was estimated at $16 billion in 1993 and continues to grow rapidly.[72] California is a harbinger of what continued uncontrolled immigration will do to the country. In the last decade, its educational system has slid from the top in the United States to the bottom. In part this was due to the underfunding of the schools as a result of Proposition 13, which curbed property tax increases. But Proposition 13 was itself a reaction to the escalating educational expense caused in large part by being inundated with immigrants.[73]

A Rand Corporation study indicates that the growth in immigrant population is wreaking havoc in the America's school systems because immigrant children are overwhelming already financially strapped school districts.[74] Illinois will have to build a new school every month for the next twenty-five years to keep up with the rate of immigration.[75] Texas needs to build two schools a week; California must build a school a day![76] More than one-half of all the schools and public infrastructure constructed since 1970 has been built to accommodate immigrants.[77] This proportion will increase even more dramatically in the years to come.

By 1990 the cost of bilingual education alone has soared to $7.5 *billion*—over one thousand times the original estimates of $7.5 *million* when the program was introduced in 1968.[78] Bilingual education will exceed $10 billion by 1997 and is now the fastest growing component of those cities which have large numbers of immigrants. The Chicago School system offers bilingual education in nineteen languages: Arabic, Assyrian, Cantonese, Greek, Gujarati, Haitian-Creole, Hindi, Hmong, Khmer, Korean, Mandarin, Filipino, Polish, Russian, Serbian-Croatian-Bosnian, Spanish, Urdu, and Vietnamese.

The enormous increase in costs continues despite evidence that there are little or no benefits of bilingual education for primary school children. A study by the Office Of Planning, Budget, and Evaluation in 1975 sampled 286 bilingual education classrooms for at least four years. ***The study's conclusion was that most programs were planned to maintain minority language rather than transition to English, and students deficient in English did not gain proficiency.***[79] Studies in New York and California and, most recently, by the National Research Council, confirm that native-language instruction offers no special benefits to non-English speaking students. Christine Rossell of Boston University examined every study of bilingual education that meets minimum standards of validation and concluded that only 7 percent of them show bilingual education to be better than doing nothing at all for children who do not know English, while 64 percent show bilingual education to be worse than doing nothing. And none of the studies examined by Rossell shows bilingual education to be better than English as a second language or English immersion programs.[80] Furthermore, programs that emphasize cultural and ethnic differences in the classroom appear to be counterproductive, reinforcing stereotypes.[81] A far better and less costly solution is to offer additional training in English for elementary children—the so-called English as a Second Language (ESL). Secondary school children should be offered a six-month to one-year course in English before being admitted into mainstream classes. Of course, this would result in them falling a year behind their classmates, but that is part of the cost of immigrating to another country.

Projections are that by 2050 anywhere from 23 percent to 50 percent of the U.S. will be Spanish speaking.[82] Los Angeles is already the second largest Spanish-speaking city in the world with more Spanish speaking people than any city in Spain. In Dade County, Florida, the law establishing English as the official language has been repealed and every legal document must be printed in Spanish, Creole, and French at exorbitant public expense.[83] One cannot help wondering whether by the year 2050 the English language might be *excluded* from the classroom in Florida and certain Southwestern states, just as English was eventually excluded from Quebec schools.

Increased Crime and Racial Backlash

Most immigrants come to this country to find jobs. They are honest and energetic, and sacrifice much in order to find a better life for themselves and their children. But it cannot be denied that the current wave of immigration also has contributed to the increase in crime in America during the last two decades.* The U.S. Bureau of Prisons reports that 25 percent of the inmates of federal prisons in 1994 were noncitizens.[84] ***The incarceration rate among illegal aliens is three times the U.S. average.***[85] ***Since 1980 there has been a 600 percent increase in alien inmates, primarily due to drug-related charges.***[86] A 1987 Government Accounting Office report found that illegals accounted for 50 percent of the arrests by the Los Angeles Police Department.[87] Another GAO report in 1989 found that 40 percent of the crack cocaine market is controlled by aliens.[88] In 1980 Arizona prisons had 58 Mexican inmates; by 1997 the number had soared to 2,373.[89] In recent years, different ethnic immigrant groups have formed gangs specializing in various forms of crime: Colombians in cocaine; Mexicans in marijuana, smuggling immigrants, and auto theft; Nigerians in heroin trafficking as well as student-loan and credit card fraud; Chinese in heroin and smuggling immigrants; South Koreans in prostitution; Russians in drugs and insurance fraud; Jamaicans in cocaine.[90]

Despite the greater propensity for illegals to be involved in crime, some cities, such as Chicago, ordered their police departments not to cooperate with the Immigration and Naturalization Service efforts to deport criminal aliens. This policy was harshly criticized by the Chicago Crime Commission as contributing to the rising crime rate by making Chicago a "safe haven" for foreign born gangs. In 1996, Congress passed legislation to nullify such local policies. Still, most major cities now have such a large base of voting immigrants that they will not take any action that will offend immigrants, such as helping the INS apprehend illegals. As a result, these cities have set the course for their own demise. But as their schools and neighborhoods fall further behind the rest of the nation, they urge the federal and state governments to increase funding of city programs. Not unreasonably, many state legislators are reluctant to help the cities that are refusing to take the actions necessary to help themselves.

The other contribution immigration makes to crime is the open warfare that results when different ethnic groups fight over shrinking shares of the economic pie. One only has to witness the gang warfare in cities such as New York, Los Angeles, and Chicago where white, black, Hispanic, and Asian gangs are fighting turf wars. In Los Angeles alone there are an estimated 600 ethnic gangs with over 100,000 members.[91]

The huge number of legal and illegal immigrants even threaten the stability of ethnic neighborhoods once noted for their absence of crime. For example, Chinatowns in the nation's major cities are now suffering from the problems that plague inner city black neighborhoods, including unem-

---

*Ironically, an increase in crime can perversely increase GDP since policing costs are added to GDP as government purchases. This again demonstrates the deficiency of GDP as a measure of social welfare.

ployment, overcrowding, school dropouts, violent street crime, and gang warfare.[92] Dr. Haing Ngor survived the rein of terror in Cambodia under the Pol Pot regime to make the film *The Killing Fields* and win an academy award. In 1996 he was gunned down in front of his Chinatown home in Los Angeles, a city that is also rapidly becoming a killing field for immigrants as well as native born Americans.

A 1995 study by the Federation for American Immigration Reform (FAIR) compared five cities known for high immigration with five cities showing low immigration. The high immigration cities had twice as much unemployment, 40 percent more people living in poverty, twice as much welfare dependency, 60 percent higher rate of high school drop outs, twice as much violent crime, seven times as much crowded housing, three times the population density, more urban sprawl, and 30 percent longer commuting times.[93] In short, high immigration cities reflect a serious decline in the quality of life.

It is not only the big cities that have experienced the rise of gangs and crime. Small towns throughout the country—places that never had a problem—are now exposed to rising crime rates, particularly among immigrant youth. Storm Lake, Iowa; El Paso, Texas; Garden City, Kansas; Wausau, Wisconsin; and Worthington, Minnesota, all share common characteristics with Los Angeles, California: after a huge increase in immigration they had higher unemployment, depressed wages, greater need for public services, lower per capita taxes to pay for those services, and especially, higher drug usage, crime, and gang activity. In a public radio broadcast discussing the rise in crime in small towns, I was amazed that their analysis overlooked the obvious: every one of the cities they examined had been inundated by immigrants. The PBS commentators did not go to Spencer, Iowa, which is the sister city of Storm Lake. If they had, they would have learned that Spencer turned down the meatpacking industry that would have brought in the low-cost immigrant labor. As a consequence, Spencer avoided the problems of Storm Lake. Sure, Spencer hasn't grown like Storm Lake, but the residents don't have to worry about walking down their streets at night. They are a far happier town as a result.

Accelerating Environmental Destruction

It is difficult to say with any precision what the optimal population for the United States should be. Several studies suggest that we are already past the optimal level.[94] Although it is debatable what the optimal sustainable level is, there is no doubt that attaining a population of 400 to 500 million over the next fifty years will be environmentally devastating. Destruction of wetlands, forests, topsoil, underground aquifers, water and air quality will accelerate. On the other hand, if the population of the United States had remained at the 203 million level of 1970 and we had diverted the funds spent to meet the needs of immigrants on solving environmental problems instead, we would have met or been very close to meeting all of our environmental goals.

At present, America's 470 million acres of arable land works out to about 1.8 acres per person. Urban sprawl, erosion, and development will reduce America's available cropland to 290 million acres by 2050 according to David Piemental, a professor of ecology at Cornell University.[95] At the same time population will have doubled. These two trends will result in a decline of cropland to 0.5 acres per person. It is estimated that it takes about one acre of land per person to provide the highly nutritious American diet. The result of the decline in cropland will be to shift the United States from a net exporter of food to a net importer, and a commensurate drop in the standard of living for Americans.

Continued population growth due to immigration will also nullify the technological progress we are making to improve air quality. For example, tight restrictions on automobile exhaust have enabled Los Angeles to cut pollution per vehicle by 50 percent during the past thirty years. However, doubling the population of L.A. during that same period wiped out all the gains.[96] Total U.S. energy requirements have risen 27 percent since 1970, in lock step with population growth despite the tremendous increase in energy efficiency.[97]

Even the harm caused by natural disasters will increase as population grows. The hurricanes, floods, and earthquakes of the 1990s would not have been as devastating a couple decades ago for the plain reason that there were far fewer people living in those areas. If we settle people on flood plains and in hurricane- or earthquake-prone areas, such as the East and West coasts, it's not difficult to predict periodic tragedies of growing proportions.

Occasionally we hear the argument that since the environment is global it makes no difference whether people migrate from one country to another; the global impact is the same. Ridiculous! Let me demonstrate. It is indeed irrelevant to the environment in *other nations* of the world if 1 percent of the world's population were to move to the United States since it would reduce pollution in rest of the world by 1 percent, all things being equal. But 1 percent of the world's population in twenty years will equate to 100 million people immigrating to the United States, which would increase pollution by 37 percent (100m/270m minus the present population of the United States), again, all things being equal. Actually, the situation is far more grave, because we have to include the children of immigrants. Furthermore, all things are not equal. People who come to the

United States inevitably strive to reach its standard of living. Hence, their consumption and consequential environmental impact is far worse than if they had remained in their country of origin.

Moreover, as will be discussed in the next chapter, many measures indicate that the U.S. environment is under great duress even with the present population. For example, an Audubon Society study concluded that species loss in the United States is greater than in countries such as Brazil, Mexico, Indonesia, or Kenya.[98] So America must recognize the distressing dilemma that adding 100 million more immigrants will do little to improve the environment in other countries, while it could result in irreversible ecological damage here at home. As Roy Beck observes, if the federal government prohibited immigrants from settling any place where they would contribute to environmental deterioration, there would be very few places left for them.[99]

The Balkanization of America

The aforementioned economic costs do not include the less tangible, but possibly most worrisome cost of all. Garret Hardin observes that ethnic diversity and equality are mutually conflicting goals that have been achieved nowhere in the world. According to Lawrence Auster, the more likely outcome of cultural diversity is the "devolution of society into permanent divisions based upon ethnicity."[100] Arthur M. Schlesinger Jr. and Eugene McCarthy have also passionately warned that multiculturalism, which is so intellectually enticing as a goal, will in all likelihood degenerate into the balkanization of America into a bunch of warring ethnicities.[101] We have already been shocked at the racial backlash against immigrants that occurred in Germany and to a lesser extent in England and France. We have witnessed the horror of the ethnic wars that rocked the Balkan area and the previous Soviet Union. Eugene McCarthy points out that this is the inevitable conflict that results in the absence of a unifying culture. In the 1990s we have witnessed cultural clashes throughout the world:

- Tamils and Singhalese in Sri Lanka
- Serbs, Croats, Bosnians, andAlbanians in the former Yugoslavia
- Catholics and Protestants in Northern Ireland
- Greeks and Turks in Cyprus
- Basque separationists in Spain
- Corsicans and French

- Czechs and Slovaks in former Czechoslovakia
- Shiites and Sunnis in the Middle East
- Armenians and Adjerbaizianis in the former Soviet Union
- Moslems, Sikhs, and Hindus in India

It would be a serious miscalculation to believe that such conflict could not happen here. If continued immigration results in job displacement and greater poverty, a backlash is the inevitable result. Sociologist Stanley Lieberson noted that during the early years of this century when there was a high influx of Japanese and Chinese immigrants "the response of whites was of a violent and savage character in areas where they [the immigrants] were concentrated," but the hostility quickly ended when immigration policy was changed to stem the influx.[102] We have already witnessed an increase in hate crimes in recent years.[103] By 1997 hostility to immigrants was at the highest level in seventy years.[104] When the next economic recession occurs, the situation could become increasingly explosive.

The situation can only deteriorate if the high rates of migration continue. In small numbers, immigrants feel the need to assimilate and have been generally successful. Assimilation is a slow process at best. George Borjas's analysis of those immigrants and their descendants who came during the great wave of immigration during the first two decades of this century indicates that it takes about a century—four generations—for assimilation to occur.[105] Also, the process of assimilation did not begin until the numbers of immigrants were dramatically cut. There is little incentive for the Cubans of Florida or the Mexicans in many parts of the Southwest to assimilate. Why should they when in many areas they are the majority? The larger the number of immigrants from any ethnic group, the less they see the need for assimilation.

In another two decades, we may have such a large Spanish-speaking population in the Southwestern states that we will encounter the phenomenon that Canada experienced with the attempted secession of French-speaking Quebec. Already a militant Hispanic movement headquartered in Los Angeles called Casa Aztlan estimates that within twenty to thirty years they will have enough votes in California, Texas, New Mexico, and Arizona to win a secession vote to set up a new Hispanic nation or reunify with Mexico. On 90 percent of the public high school and university campuses in the Southwestern United States, there is a group called MEXA.* The

*Until 1997 they called themselves MEChA—Movimiento Estudiantil Chicano de Aztlan. In 1997 they changed the spelling of Chicano to Xicano and now call themselves MEXA.

preamble to the MEXA Constitution states that: Chicana/Chicano students of California must politicize our Raza [race] and continue the struggle for self-determination of the Chicana/Chicano people and the liberation of the nation of Aztlan."[106] Article II, Section 1 states that the "General Membership shall consist of any student who accepts, believes, and works for the goals and objectives of Me.Ch.A. *including the liberation of Aztlan, meaning self-determination of our people in this 'occupied state' and the physical liberation of our land*" (emphasis mine).

In a California conference entitled "The Immigration Crisis," Dr. Jose Angel Gutierrez from the University of Texas drew cheers from his audience when he shouted:

> Why do they come after us? Because we are fighting as a new Meztizo nation, not to be conquered. . . . We are going to build Aztlan—we are here again! . . . We are millions! Regardless of the outcome in the short term, we have to survive. There is an aging white America; they are not making babies. It is a matter of time. The most preferred minority (blacks) are not making babies, their numbers are declining. Their expectations exceed what they are entitled to. Asians are at our heels; don't get too comfortable. You've got to get ready to govern. You must believe that you are entitled to govern. They say you are Latinizing Los Angeles—I love it! Aztlan is our homeland! We are here again![107]

This rhetoric has the same tone as the white supremacy groups employ. Yet few people are willing to criticize such inflammatory racial rant. Apparently, such racial sentiments are politically acceptable if they are spoken by a minority group.

Is Dr. Gutierrez spouting just empty rhetoric? Although he is wrong about the number of blacks declining, Dr. Gutierrez is correct in recognizing that the fastest-growing group in America are Hispanics. If present trends continue, their numbers will rise from 22 million in 1990 to 81 million by 2050.[108] They will be primarily concentrated in just nine states: California, Texas, New Mexico, Arizona, Nevada, Florida, Illinois, New York, and New Jersey. If they continue to be on the bottom of the economic heap—and the socioeconomic profile of most of new immigrants suggest that they will be[109]—they will most likely blame the American "occupiers" of "Aztlan." The use of terrorism to achieve the goal of secession then becomes quite probable. We might recall that the last time a group of states tried to secede from the Union it was a bloody event indeed. Even if we can avoid a war of secession, the eventual outcome of present migration trends will be the "disuniting" of the United States to the detriment of all its citizens.

Michael Lind of the *New Republic* takes a somewhat different view, suggesting that Balkanization will not be the major problem if present trends continue. Rather, the problem will be "Brazilianization"—increased income inequality with a minority of white Americans forming an overclass, dominating an increasingly larger number of nonwhite poor.[110] Now that is a scenario ripe for social strife.

Even if the most dire prognostications are not realized, the huge influx of people from a culture with no tradition of common law, due process, or dissent within the law is bound to have serious consequences. As columnist Lawrence Harrison explains, Latin America does not even have a word for dissent. Disagreement is often seen as treason or heresy.[111] Until very recently, revolution has been the process employed for changing authoritarian governments, not the ballot box. Whether the move to democracy of recent years will be sustained remains to be seen.

The present migration patterns will even change the mix of religions in America, greatly increasing the power of the Catholic Church, which is a major reason Catholic prelates are so anxious to support sanctuary movements and virtually unrestricted immigration. Jesuit Father Richard Ryscavage, executive director of Migration and Refugee Services, boasted that immigration "is the growing edge of Catholicism in the U.S." and the influx of more than ten million migrants in the last decade "is the key to our future."[112]

Increased Net Cost to Taxpayers

Although an accurate financial assessment of immigration is difficult, Donald L. Huddle, professor emeritus at Rice University, has estimated that the net costs (tax revenues minus expenditures) to the taxpayers for immigrants arriving since 1970 reached $65 billion annually by 1996. If the present immigration trends continue, the projected cost over the period 1997 to 2006 will be $866 billion.[113] Other studies, such as that of the Urban Institute, dispute Huddle's estimates. The Urban Institute estimates that present immigration provides a net benefit of $27.4 billion per year.[114] However, the Urban Institute's more optimistic assessment is based upon several false assumptions: first, a much higher estimate of future wages received by immigrants, and hence taxes paid, than the current evidence supports; second, that there is no job displacement or impact on wage rates; third, the addition of millions of people will require no increase in infrastructure costs such as roads, sanitation, police, and fire protection, etc. Finally, the institute's study fails to accrue future social security payouts against present FICA taxes collected. Since most immigrants are of working age, this greatly overstates the benefits. Finally, the Urban Institute study overstates income taxes received from immigrants by inadequately reflecting the impact of the Earned Income Tax Credit. In 1986 over three million illegals were granted an amnesty that lead to eventual citizenship. A study of these immigrants showed that 69 percent had family income below the level set by the Earned Income Tax Credit and, as such, had to pay little or no income taxes.

According to many newspaper accounts, a 1997 study by the National Research Council (NRC) showed that immigration benefits Americans because the immigrants increase economic output by $1 to $10 billion annually.[115] This is a classic case of a half-truth. What most of the media choose to ignore is the study's estimate that immigrants cost Americans $14.8 to $20.2 billion annually due to the public services they use. Hence, what was widely reported as a gain for Americans was actually a net loss. But the real story doesn't end there.

Increases in output must be divided by the increases in population, because it is only when output *per capita* increases that Americans as a group benefit. The study shows that immigration produces a net cost of $10 to $14 billion annually, or about -0.13 percent to 0.18 percent. However, legal and illegal immigration now averages over one million people a year, resulting in population growth of 0.37 percent annually. Including the children of immigrants would substantially increase this rate. Since the number of immigrants result in population growing at the same time that net costs are increasing, the change in per capita output for America as a whole is declining even faster than the NRC estimates suggest.

The NRC's report also indicates that the depressed wages due to immigration result in lower costs of consumer goods. The fact is that immigration produces winners and losers. The winners are those who benefit from cheap labor, especially business owners and investors. The losers are those who constitute cheap labor (many of whom are immigrants themselves). This poses an ethical question that the NRC conveniently ducks: Is it right to make the poorest in our society even poorer, to benefit the richest in our society?[116]

Finally, the academy's report does not examine the effects of excessive immigration on the environment, future infrastructure requirements (such as more highways, schools, sanitation, and water treatment facilities), increases in crime and interethnic strife, social and cultural impacts, etc. By primarily focusing on short-term economic output and costs, ***the report fails to address the real question of today's unprecedented level of immigration: What impact will it have on the quality of life of future generations of Americans?***

Many studies on immigration seriously underestimate the long-term cost by assuming that immigrants do not use many welfare services. Such is not the case. A study by Lief Jensen indicates that foreign born residents were 56 percent more likely than native born Americans to be living in poverty, 25 percent more likely to receive public aid, and to have an average per capita income from public assistance of 13.6 percent more than natives.[117] Jensen's study was of immigrants arriving before 1988, and the shift in the mix of immigrants since then to the less educated and unskilled would increase the number of those likely to seek public aid. A 1995 General Accounting Office study concluded that immigrants were twice as likely to receive public assistance as the general population.[118] The welfare reform legislation passed in 1996 prohibited Social Security Supplemental Income (SSI) and food stamps for noncitizens who have not paid taxes for at least ten years, and in the future prohibits immigrants from receiving most other federal benefits during their first five years. However, overblown fears of disabled noncitizens starving in the streets resulted in Congress reinstating SSI for disabled noncitizens. Food stamps have been reinstated for immigrants in most states, and Clinton has proposed that the federal government again pick up the tab. Whether SSI will be reinstated for future noncitizens remains to be seen. But in any case, once the immigrants become citizens they will again be eligible. (During all the debate on the issue of welfare for immigrants there was virtually no mention of the responsibility of the children of immigrants or the immigrant sponsors to care for the disabled and elderly).* Moreover, even if we were to deduct all of the welfare-related expenditures in Huddle's study, the net cost would still equal about $40 billion annually, mostly due to education expense and displacement of U.S. workers.

To gain some perspective on the cost of immigration, let's try a very simple calculation. Assume an immigrant couple has only three children. (Obviously many immigrant families are much larger.) The average cost of sending a child to a Chicago public school is over $5,000 a year for elementary school and over $9,000 a year for high school. This is a significant understatement of the cost for an immigrant's child because we are not including the cost of bilingual education. Nevertheless, at these rates the cost of sending three children through grades K through 12 is $288,000! Now if we assume that both parents work and make $15,000 a year *each* (which is 50 percent higher than the minimum wage that many immigrants earn), their income tax would be about $1,600 annually. Most immigrants do not own their own homes, but they do pay property taxes indirectly since they are included in the landlord's charge for rent. There-

---

*Immigration regulations require that every immigrant (unless the person is a refugee) have a sponsor who has promised to take care of the new immigrant should the need arise. In the past this was a responsibility that sponsors took seriously. Today it is a meaningless gesture. To my knowledge there has not been a single case in recent years where a sponsor has been forced to live up to the legally binding promise of support.

fore, we can impute a comparable property tax of about $1,900 a year. We will also include an estimated $1,500 a year in sales taxes. (Both of these estimates probably overstate actual tax liability.) We need not add in FICA taxes, because they will get at least that amount back in future benefits. Adding all the taxes equals about $5,000 a year. ***Therefore, both parents would have to work almost fifty years just to pay enough taxes to cover their children's grade school and high school education.*** I've included nothing for the cost of additional infrastructure such as water; sanitation; waste disposal; streets and highways; police and fire protection; hospitals and jails; or any other federal, state, or local services. Nor have I included any costs due to displacement of other workers or any environmental costs. Of course it may be argued that many immigrants make much more than $15,000 a year or will in future years. But, on the other hand, many immigrants make less than this and actually are paying no taxes and getting an earned income tax credit! The conclusion is that since the majority of immigrants today are poorly educated and have few skills, they constitute a sizable net cost to our society.

Reducing America's Cognitive Average

Finally, if all of the foregoing liabilities of excessive immigration were not bad enough, Herrnstein and Murray report that the average IQ of Hispanic immigrants is only 91.[119] Although East Asians averaged IQs of 104, the far greater number of Hispanic immigrants mean that immigrants may act to drag down the national cognitive average. Since there is a tendency for IQs of immigrants to rise as they become acculturated, it is possible that these low IQs might rise with time. However, three factors reduce the odds of this hopeful outcome. First, the IQs of U.S. Hispanics who have been here many years also reflect this lower average.[120] Secondly, the large number of Hispanic immigrants appear to be preventing the normal acculturation process. Third, except for the Cubans who left immediately after Castro's rise to power, the overwhelming majority of Hispanics migrating to the United States are from the lower end of the socioeconomic scale in their country of origin, and therefore, are probably skewed toward the lower end of the IQ distribution as well.

Arguments in Defense of Immigration

There are ten common arguments made to support the present historically high level of immigration:

1. Although the total number of immigrants may be at an all-time high, the *rate* of immigration is actually declining.
2. We need immigrants to support an aging population.
3. Without immigration the United States faces a labor shortage.
4. Immigrants take jobs that Americans won't accept.
5. America is morally bound to provide political asylum for refugees and alleviate the overpopulation of other countries.
6. America is so big and rich that a few million more immigrants makes little difference.
7. Even though immigration reduces wage rates, lower wage rates are good for the American economy since it results in lower prices.
8. All borders should be scrapped, allowing citizens of each nation to "vote with their feet" thereby forcing oppressive or ineffectual governments to enact reforms to keep their population from fleeing.
9. The trend to a global economy is inevitable. Doing away with borders is just another step in this evolution.
10. It is against the American tradition to end immigration—we are a nation of immigrants.

Let's dismiss this last pseudoargument first. Garrett Hardin responds to such empty rhetoric boasting of our immigrant tradition by pointing out that *every* nation is originally a nation of immigrants.[121] Even the Native Americans came from Asia. The usual course of human events is that one group of migrants settle an area but eventually they are either driven out by a stronger group or repulse the invaders. Today, since there are no new lands to settle or be driven off to, the consequences of encroachment will be the bloody ethnic and racial rivalries that many other nations are experiencing.

Now let's turn to each of the other arguments in support of immigration.

The Rate of Immigration Is Actually Declining.

This is typical of Julian Simon's statistical deceptions. It is the level, not the rate of immigration, that is relevant. If we used the rate as the criteria for determining immigration, then the more populous America becomes the more immigrants we would permit, ad infinitum! Following Simon's logic, since adding one million immigrants to the population of India or China would represent an even smaller rate of increase than in the United States, those countries should be more willing to take in immigrants. Of course this is nonsense. The meaningful statistic is the absolute number of immigrants relative to the capability of the economy and the environment to absorb them.

Luckily, in the past Congress did not think in terms of constant rates of immigration. If it had sought to hold the rate of immigration constant since the turn of the century, the population of the United States would have reached 552 million by 1994—twice our actual population![122]

Immigrants Are Needed to Support the Aging Population

The aging population is not a new phenomenon and was predicted as long ago as 1960. Yet, like all long term trends, this inevitability was largely ignored until recently. Americans are living longer now due to amazing advances in medical technology. More significantly, the number of Americans over age sixty-five will soar as the post World War II baby boomers age. In 1990, there were 31 million people over sixty-five representing 12.4 percent of the population. By 2030 this number will double to 60 million.[123] The growth in the number of elderly will result in an enormous increase in expenditures for the aged, from 30 percent of the federal budget today to 60 percent by 2030. The question becomes, who will pay for this huge increase? One simplistic answer offered is to increase the size of the population under age sixty through immigration.

Some will admit that the current rate of immigration cannot continue indefinitely but believe that a temporary bubble of immigration would subsidize the aging baby boomers. Even if we accepted this reasoning, the time to increase immigration would be around 2010, not today. Accepting immigrants today over the age of thirty will just aggravate the problem because they will also be retiring around 2030.[124]

Furthermore, this argument assumes that immigrants will make a net contribution to Social Security. ***However, studies by the Rand Corporation indicate that the migrants result in a net cost to Social Security of about $1,000 per person annually.*** Only by screening immigrants to take in the most skilled and highly educated might they exert a net contribution. But such a discriminatory immigration policy will do little to help the poor of the world seeking entry to our nation, while at the same time it would drain the LDCs of the very talent necessary for their future development. Journalist Robert Verzala of the Third World Network Features agency argues that the U.S. is pirating third world doctors and other professionals. It costs $10,000 for the Philippines to train a doctor and the U.S. grabs the doctor without any compensation to the Philippines for its investment in his education.[125]

There are much better ways of coping with the problem of an aging population as will be discussed in chapter 12 on healthcare and Social Security.

Immigrants Are Needed to Cope with a Labor Shortage

The Immigration Reform and Control Act of 1986 attempted to control illegals by placing sanctions on employers who hire them. There was a loud outcry that the act would result in massive discrimination on hiring Hispanics, but such fears have proved groundless. Three years after the passage of the act, the Office of Special Council empowered to investigate charges of discrimination received less than 200 complaints of job discrimination.[126]

As mentioned, the 1986 immigration legislation was totally unsuccessful in slowing the flow of illegals; in fact the amnesty resulted in increased numbers of illegals crossing our borders. But employers wanted still more cheap labor, especially skilled labor. Demographic projections indicated a slower growth in the labor force during the 1990s, so businesses pressured Congress to raise the quota for legal immigrants in 1990 from 530,000 to 700,000 through February 1994, and 675,000 thereafter.[127] This included tripling the allotment for skilled and professional workers from 54,000 to 140,000 per year.* In addition, 65,000 temporary visas are granted each year for workers to do jobs for which, supposedly, there are no qualified Americans. In 1998, Congress increased the number of temporary visas to 115,000.

Were the increased immigration quotas justifiable? In a word, no! It is true that demographic projections indicated an easing in the growth of the labor supply, but this was following two decades of extraordinary growth in the labor force due to the influx of baby boomers, women, and minorities. We have already shown the deleterious impact the excessive growth in the supply of labor had on wage rates. The slowing in the growth of the labor force should have offered an opportunity for wage earners to make up some lost ground.

The use of immigrants and temporary workers to meet a short-term labor shortage is an effort on the part of employers to avoid one of the key features of a market economy. In a free market when there is an excess of labor relative to jobs, wages fall and profits rise. Employers and investors increase their share of the national income pie and think this is wonderful—capitalism at its best. Such has been the situation from about 1973 until 1994. But since then, the changing demographics of an aging labor force and higher economic growth has resulted in demand for labor exceeding the

*This number does not include refugees and asylees that would raise the annual total to almost one million annually.

supply in certain industries. Under such circumstances labor is able to command higher wage rates, threatening slower growth in profits. It is a way that the marketplace balances the power of labor and business over time. Businesspeople and investors are less than enthusiastic with this aspect of a market economy, and thus seek to avoid the consequences by crying for increased immigration. This is a flat-out attempt to change the economic balance so that it always favors the suppliers of capital.

As labor economist Vernon Briggs points out, union membership trends have historically moved in the opposite direction of immigration trends.[128] In the past, labor leaders such as Samuel Gompers were quick to recognize this ploy and fought to prevent the use of immigration as a way of undermining their bargaining position. Today, however, union leaders are supporting immigration. As one local labor leader told me, "We'll organize them and have more members." ***The union leaders either naively believe that just having more members increases their power, or perhaps they just like the idea of collecting more dues. In either case, labor unions are supporting the business strategy to undermine the bargaining power of labor and suppress wages.*** The unions even took out expensive full-page ads in major newspapers supporting increased immigration. Businesspeople were falling all over themselves in delight. They couldn't pay to get such extraordinary cooperation from the union leadership.

If I were a union member I would be outraged. But labor in general seems to be totally unaware of what's happening or too lethargic to do anything about it. If Karl Marx were alive today he would probably write that television (rather than religion) is the opiate of the masses.

The cumulative effect of immigrants and others who come to the United States on temporary work visas has greatly diminished opportunities not only for the unskilled, but for all Americans. For example, as many as 30,000 English-speaking software professionals, primarily from Australia, India, and the United Kingdom, are working in California on visas. They work for a fraction of the $50,000 to $100,000 salary a U.S. programmer makes, costing American programmers $2.4 billion per year.[129] Although hiring aliens to replace Americans is forbidden by law, the law is easily circumvented by hiring the aliens through another firm as temporary workers. One reason those on visas will work so cheaply is that they don't have to pay income taxes and can live like kings on their earnings when they return home.

If there were a true shortage of software professionals—or any other group—employers should readily agree to contribute $50,000 per temporary worker to a fund to educate Americans in software technology. Every time this suggestion has been made, employers have quickly sought to squelch it. Similarly, companies such as Microsoft have argued against paying to train new employees. Bill Gates wants society to pick up the cost of training while he reaps the benefits. When his programmers' skills become obsolete (in about ten years), Gates wants to dump his employees back on to society to support rather than pay the cost of retraining. Similarly, his company wants to hire only the top 2 percent of programmers. It is not his concern what happens to the other 98 percent. We are back to the problem of policies that yield private benefits while incurring public costs.

Even the jobs of college teachers who are not tenured are threatened. More than 50 percent of all United States college faculty under the age of thirty-six are foreign born.[130] Part of the reason for this excessive use of foreign born professors is due to a perverse result of affirmative action. As an example, at Stanford University departments were offered the funding of an additional faculty member for every two minority teachers hired. By 1993 it was discovered that half of the so-called minority teachers were foreign born, primarily from Asia.[131]

It is sometimes alleged that there would be a shortage of college teachers, especially in the sciences, if it were not for aliens who fill these slots. The reason for the temporary shortage in the 1970s and 1980s was due to the drain of engineers and scientists caused by the extraordinary defense buildup and the higher salaries paid by the Defense Department. But aside from these two areas, there has been a constant surplus of college graduates. In the period between 1984 and 1990, 20 percent of the graduates of U.S. universities took jobs in which they were underutilized. ***The forecast is that 30 percent of those graduating between 1994 and 2005 will have to settle for a job below their capabilities.***[132] The Institute for Higher Education and the Rand Corporation discovered that "universities in the U.S. are producing about 25 percent more doctorates in science and engineering than the U.S. economy can afford."[133]

In 1997, near the peak of the business cycle, labor markets finally began to tighten up as the employment rate fell below 5 percent. Still wage rates increased only slightly above inflation. If and when a shortage of labor does occur, it will result in raising wage rates to the level necessary to attract many of those on welfare by providing them with a living wage. In addition, bidding up the wage rates would be an incentive for more young people to go into technical jobs or job training right out of high school instead of going to college. This would reduce total postsecondary expenses for the nation and eliminate a large pool of disillusioned college grads who find that their college education was not economically justified.

It should also be noted that most immigrants are not coming to America to meet bona fide labor shortages. In 1993, 17 percent of immigration was supposedly based upon employer-identified needs. However, since this includes the migrants' families, the actual number of immigrants filling job needs was less than 9 percent.[134] In 1996, a U.S. Inspector General's audit found that letting in hundreds of thousands of temporary workers lowered wages and pushed out American workers. The audit concluded that the Foreign Labor Certification Program had become a "rubber stamp" for both skilled and unskilled aliens seeking to live and work in America. According to the report, "The program has become a stepping stone to obtain permanent resident status not only for the best and brightest but also for students, relatives, and friends."[135] The report recommended that the Labor Department eliminate the flawed foreign worker visa program.

Germany and Switzerland learned years ago that permitting the influx of foreign labor, even if only "guest workers," created more problems than it solved. They have long since given up trying to attract unskilled labor. Rather, they invest in less skilled manufacturing in other countries and perform the most skilled work at home. Japan follows the same practice.

Tight labor markets are the best thing that can happen to America. During World War II, the labor shortage drove the unemployment rate to 1 percent and enabled the middle class and the poor to dramatically improve their prospects. Everyone who wanted a job got one. There was no need for welfare for able-bodied people. Employers went to great lengths to integrate all Americans into the labor force. Women were taken into nontraditional jobs in record numbers. AT&T's need for telephone operators forced them to offer English classes to immigrants who had limited language proficiency. Tire companies in Akron, Ohio, recruited labor from the unemployed of Appalachia. The share of total wealth held by the top 0.5 percent of U.S. households fell from 32.4 percent in 1929 to 19.3 percent in 1949.[136] Some of this effect was due to the loss of wealth during the Depression, but most of the impact was due to the huge increase in earnings for working-class Americans during the tight labor markets of the war years. Middle-class Americans continued to improve their prospects until the early 1970s when the rapid increase in labor supply reduced their bargaining power and wealth again flowed disproportionately to the providers of investment and corporate managers. ***If we reduce immigration, the middle class will once again flourish.***

Immigrants Take Jobs that Americans Won't

The American agribusiness continues to argue that if it were not for immigrants there would be no one to pick fruits and vegetables or perform other menial work. The answer is, of course, ***that for the right wage rate, labor can always be found. Immigrants take jobs that Americans won't take at sub-***

standard rates of pay. At decent rates of pay and working conditions, Americans flock to apply for any work. Roy Beck describes how the Van Kuster Farms on Virginia's Eastern Shores, Bixby Orchards in Michigan, and A. Duda & Sons of Florida have solved their labor problems by offering decent pay and benefits such as health and life insurance, a daycare center, paid holidays, etc.[137]

It may be argued that if one company increases its cost of labor relative its competitors, it will be forced to raise prices and, hence, lose business. This is not necessarily true. A well run business frequently can figure out ways of improving productivity to offset the additional labor costs. (Just having a motivated labor force can often improve productivity.) In the agribusiness some growers have found that by diversifying to other vegetables that are picked at various times they can maintain a workforce almost year round. Some have found methods of mechanizing part of the job. Others have found that there are certain crops that are better to abandon to low-wage-rate third world countries. Major gains in productivity are most often achieved during periods of labor shortages. Necessity is truly the mother of invention.

Moreover, unionization can actually help the growers as well as the farm workers. When relatively standardized contracts are established, the growers do not have to worry that paying a living wage will drive them out of business because if all the growers raise their wage rates they can still maintain their profit margins. The cost of labor is such a small percent of the total cost of the product at the supermarket, that an increase in wages of the farm workers will have little, if any, impact on the demand for the product. In the case of lettuce, the harvest costs are only about 10 percent of the final price. Hence, a dollar increase in wages would raise the final price of lettuce to the consumer only 10 cents.

The notion that Americans will not do certain kinds of work is largely a myth. When it was announced that there would be 500 job openings at a new Chicago Sheraton Hotel, 9,000 applicants queued up all night to get a chance at landing one.[138] The announcement of a handful of openings for relatively unpleasant work in sewage treatment at the Metropolitan Water Reclamation District of Greater Chicago attracted 5,000 applicants hoping to land one of the jobs paying $12.88 an hour.[139] And we already saw that even jobs in Harlem paying only minimum wage had a huge surplus of applicants.

Certainly many welfare recipients would rather stay on welfare than take a job paying about the same as they are receiving in welfare benefits. Welfare reform is the way to solve that problem—and indeed the nation is finally stepping up to that issue. ***But forcing the able-bodied to work while at the same time bringing in millions of additional workers to***

drive down wage rates to below the poverty level is inequitable in the extreme. Under welfare reform, the states were required to have at least 25 percent of their welfare recipients working twenty hours a week within a year after the law was passed, and have 50 percent working thirty hours a week within five years. This plan will require finding two million jobs for unskilled, poorly educated people at a time when we are receiving over a million immigrants a year. Many of the states are considering creating public jobs to pick up the surplus labor. ***Creating jobs to absorb surplus labor while allowing millions of additional immigrants to enter the country is sheer economic folly.*** Yet, only a minority of Democrats and Republicans have noted the absurdity of such a policy.

Conservatives and liberals have spent the last two decades enacting immigration policies that betray working men and women. Is it any wonder that many Americans see the federal government as their enemy? The perverse impact of U.S. immigration policy is exemplified by the meat-packing industry. Beck carefully documents how new meat-packing plants, relying on immigrant labor from Southeast Asia and Mexico who were willing to work for half the pay rate, effectively undermined solid middle-class jobs of the established meatpackers.[140] In town after town, Americans were laid off as older meatpackers closed to be replaced with newer companies able to exploit immigrant labor. The net effect was not only to destroy the lives of those laid off, but to destroy the lifestyle of the entire town. While academicians hail the nebulous ideal of multiculturalism from their ivory towers, small towns throughout the country such as Storm Lake, Iowa; Rogers, Arkansas; or Wausau, Wisconsin, now have to deal with the problems of unemployment, gangs, drugs, and crime that were absent only a decade earlier.[141]

If, as a consequence of reduced immigration, employers cannot find adequate labor in rural areas or the suburbs, they will be forced to consider relocating to the city, providing transportation for employees to the suburbs, and lobbying to change zoning laws designed to prevent the construction of low-cost housing in the suburbs. All of these options are preferable to constantly increasing population and all the associated problems discussed in this chapter.

It is true that some immigrants are willing to take jobs requiring twelve-hour days, seven days a week at pay rates of only $2.50 an hour.[142]* Rather than take jobs that are virtually slave labor, people who qualify for welfare will find it more advantageous to stay on welfare. But do we really want to force Americans into the sweatshop conditions of the last century? Why not just reintroduce slavery? At least the slave owners had to incur

*Temporary and agriculture workers are not covered by minimum wage laws.

the costs of maintaining their own slaves. The modern exploiter of labor can fail to pay even the minimum necessary to sustain life and, in effect, ask society to make up the difference.

Slave owners worried about who would pick the cotton if they were forced to free the slaves. The answer then was the same as today: pay enough to attract labor or mechanize the task. Today's modern plantation owner lives in suburbia and worries, who will cut my lawn and be a nanny for my babies? The answer is, of course, pay enough to attract labor or do it yourself, but stop whining!

America Is Morally Bound to Provide a Sanctuary for Political Refugees and Alleviate the Overpopulation of Other Nations

Before the disastrous ethnic cleansing in Yugoslavia, there were an estimated 23 million refugees worldwide. But only 31,900 were identified by the international relief community as requiring resettlement in a third country because they were in immediate danger of death or persecution. Of the 112,573 refugees entering the United States in 1994, only 18,543 fell into this category.[143] Eighty percent of the refugees accepted by the United States never left their home country until they were notified of their acceptance as refugees. Obviously, they did not perceive themselves to be in *that* much danger.

Until recently all immigrants had to do when they set foot on American soil was to request political asylum. Once they are allowed into the country they would disappear: two-thirds never showed up for their hearings.[144] Of those who were accepted as refugees, it has become apparent that many were never in any real danger; they simply wanted to improve their economic opportunities. Fifty-one percent of the 2,190 refugees admitted through Chicago's O'Hare International airport during a twenty-eight month period between 1989 and 1991 were Russian. However, they were not fleeing from civil war or a danger of persecution. Rather, interviews revealed that "they were unable to get a good job because of their religious beliefs" or their children were "frequently insulted." A study by Michael Hedges of Russian refugees between 1989 and 1993 indicated that only 1 percent of the thousands of people accepted as refugees met the international criteria for true refugees.[145] Further evidence of the lack of real danger is the willingness of these bogus refugees to return home for vacation or to visit a sick relative.[146] Worse yet, the incredibly lax enforcement of refugee identification has allowed significant numbers of criminals from countries such as Russia to enter our nation and bring their crime syndicates with them.[147]

The basis for granting refugee status has been stretched so broadly that anyone who feels that they are persecuted for almost any reason can claim refugee status. Persecution of homosexuals, coercive abortions, and forced clitoridectomies are all repugnant practices. If we use those practices as the basis for granting asylum, however, we would have to take in anyone from China who opposes abortion, as well as most Moslem and African countries—about 80 percent of the world's 5.8 billion people.[148] Such a policy is *prima facie* impossible.

Other nations are severely restricting their intake of refugees. Britain has dramatically reduced the number of refugees granted asylum from 35 percent of those who applied before 1993 to only 4 percent of those who applied since then.[149] The United States should offer asylum only to people who are in immediate danger of their lives. Whenever possible we should seek to settle refugees in their home country with military protection, if necessary, under the auspices of the United Nations High Commission on Refugees. We are now spending as much to maintain refugees in the United States as our entire budget for foreign aid—about $13.5 billion annually.[150] ***It is far cheaper to protect refugees in their homeland—about six cents per day compared to $6.00 a day in the United States.***[151] ***Those who are admitted should be admitted on a temporary basis only and any children born while they are here (and children born of illegal aliens) should not automatically be granted citizenship.***

America Can Absorb Millions of Additional Immigrants with Ease

Some people look at America's rich farmlands and conclude that we indeed could support a population as large as India or China. That is partially true, but our environment could support such numbers only with a significant reduction of our own standard of living. The average American child has an environmental impact thirty times that of a child born in India.[152] Although it can be argued that Americans consume too much and waste too much, it is doubtful that we could reduce our environmental impact by a factor of thirty without a significant reduction in the standard of living.

As mentioned, the evidence suggests that the America may have already exceeded its long-term carrying capacity. Robert Costanza, co-founder (with Herman Daly) of the International Society for Ecological Economics, estimates that even if we were to totally rely on environmentally benign solar energy, we could still only permanently sustain a population of 85 million people at our present standard of living.[153] If we were to adopt the less environmentally destructive lifestyle of the Europeans,

170 million people could be sustained. Perhaps these estimates are too low. But the right number is probably much less than the 400 to 500 million population projected for the year 2050 based upon current immigration trends and fertility rates.

Lower Wage Rates Can Benefit the American Economy

Low wage rates are viewed by many businessmen and economists as good for the economy because it makes America more competitive internationally. Moreover, it has been argued that lower wages mean lower prices, thus benefiting the American consumer as well. Such arguments are intuitively appealing, but do not hold up under close scrutiny.

In the first place, exports account for only 10 percent of America's production of products and services. At present, 76 percent of all U.S. output is in the form of services, which are largely insulated from international competition.[154] Therefore, we need not be overly concerned with wage rates and international competition unless we become so ideologically committed to free trade that we myopically ignore the potential negative consequences. (This concern is addressed in chapter 7.) Second, the notion that low-wage rates result in low prices and, as such, are good for the economy is extremely simplistic. Most economic trends result in winners and losers. When wages are falling the winners are the suppliers of capital and the losers are the suppliers of labor. Since 1973 changes in wage rates have not kept pace with prices, consequently, the purchasing power of the average weekly wage earner has declined while that of managers and professionals has increased. Since the latter group are also the major suppliers of capital investment, they received a double benefit. The greater income inequality that has resulted during the past twenty-five years is evidence of this.

Finally, by considering wage increases and declines in employment as signs of inflation, the Federal Reserve Board (FRB) has effectively worked to prevent wage earners from improving their position. When profits increase, the FRB lets the economy roll but when wages increase the FRB puts the breaks on the economy and effectively punishes labor with higher unemployment. The issue of monetary policy is discussed in Appendix D, but, in short, the FRB should adopt a hands-off policy by expanding the money supply at a constant rate and let the free market sort out the respective shares of production that go to labor and capital. Neoclassical economic theory demonstrates that any short-term inflation would be self-correcting as higher prices are quickly offset by reduced demand. Past inflationary periods were not triggered by increased wage rates but by expansionary monetary policy.

Accordingly, neither the potential impact on prices or international competitiveness are valid justifications for increasing the labor supply through immigration.

The Dismantling of Borders Would Result in Less Repressive Regimes

A colleague of mine opposes immigration quotas because he feels that people should have the right to vote with their feet. By letting people freely migrate throughout the world, he believes it will put pressure on governments to be responsive to the needs of their citizens. There are two problems with this line of reasoning. First, even the most responsive government can do little to relieve the poverty of the LDCs in the short run. Thus, if people perceive that there is greater opportunity in a country like the United States, this is where they will want to come. However, the opportunity for the uneducated and unskilled is largely an illusion, unless they are willing to spend the rest of their lives cutting people's lawns. The number of decent-paying unskilled jobs will continue to shrink in the future. At the turn of this century 60 percent of the jobs were in agriculture; today about 1.5 percent of the jobs are in agriculture. The same is true for most of the other major uses of unskilled labor. From mining to manufacturing, mechanization has drastically reduced the need for unskilled labor. Gradually, even the service industries are destined for mechanization, primarily through computerization.

Second, by offering a safety valve for overpopulation or the exodus for those most dissatisfied with the present government, migration might reduce the urgency for the governments of the LDCs to solve population and other social problems. There is nothing that some governments would like better than to dump all their malcontents and trouble makers on someone else. (Remember the infamous Mariel boat lift when Castro cleared his jails and sent his criminals and mentally ill to the U.S.?)

Might John Rawls's justice support my friend's argument for open borders? Behind our veil of ignorance we could imagine that we might be a person in another country who would benefit by emigrating elsewhere. Shouldn't we, therefore, wish to establish the right for unconstrained immigration? On the other hand, we might just as well be a poor kid in the United States who is denied an opportunity for a job or whose wages are seriously depressed due to competition from immigrants.

From the perspective of Rawlsian justice our consideration of poor indigenous Americans offsets the needs of poor immigrants. The only way that immigration could be justified is if the talents the immigrants brought to the country not only benefited the immigrants but the indigenous workers as well. This might have been the case in the early days of our nation when the population was well below the carrying capacity of the country, although Native Americans might dispute this contention. It is certainly not the case today.

It is absurd to think that immigration is a way to alleviate poverty or overpopulation in the world. As Beck explains, over four billion people in the world live in countries where the average annual income is less than that of Mexico.[155] ***Every year, while the United States takes in a million immigrants, the aggregate population of the countries they came from increases by over 70 million people. So our excessive immigration does nothing to help relieve the plight of 99.9 percent of the world, while adding to the poverty of those in our own country.*** If we really cared about the world's poor we would spend more money on family planning assistance to the LDCs and the transfer of basic technologies, particularly in the areas of agriculture and water reclamation.

The Trend to a Global Economy Is Inevitable; Scrapping All Borders Is Just One Step in This Evolution

The trend is to a global economy, but it is a non sequitur to assume that this must be accompanied by eliminating borders. Every city in America is part of our national economy, yet cities have enacted zoning legislation to determine the density, and to some extent the living conditions, of the population they will house. In a sense, borders are a way for a nation to control its density and living conditions.

The *Wall Street Journal* has suggested the United States adopt a constitutional amendment to eliminate our borders. This is not surprising: an unlimited supply of cheap labor is the dream of many businesspeople. But let's see how it works out for labor. At present there are about 1.3 billion people in the world who earn less than $0.13 an hour; another 1.6 billion earn between $0.13 and $0.37 an hour.[156] At the other end of the spectrum, the average wage in the private economy for Americans was $12.26 an hour in 1997.[157] What would happen if we scrapped the borders? America would be flooded by immigrants until the average wage differential between the less-developed countries and the United States would reach an equilibrium level—an average of perhaps $2.00 an hour. In short, open borders would result in the population of America increasing several fold with a commensurate devastation of our environment and the impoverishment of the American laborer.

Someday when there is greater economic equality among nations, an open policy of migration might be feasible, but that day is a long way off. Today an open border policy is a prescription for disaster. The United States is the only nation in the world that doesn't appear to recognize that fact. We continue to take in more immigrants than the other 180 nations combined.[158] Our policy cannot be justified in terms of either economics or justice.

An Alternative to Immigration to Help the World's Poor

Few public policies are as emotionally charged as that of immigration. While working as a consultant to the Office of Management and the Budget, I also had responsibility for implementing an executive order requiring an urban and community impact analysis for any new law, agency policy, or major budget initiative. When I indicated that I believed immigration policies should be reviewed to determine their impact on America's cities I was branded by one young lawyer as a racist. For someone who was active during the civil rights movement of the 1960s and worked in support of Cesar Chavez's efforts to organize migrant farmworkers, this came as quite a shock. I explained that Canada had virtually shut down the immigration of U.S. citizens in the 1970s to protect job opportunities for Canadians, yet no one claimed that their policy was racially motivated or unfair. "That's different," was the retort, "they were only excluding whites." This person also had no complaint against Mexico's strict prohibition of immigration from Guatemala, I guess because Hispanics can't be construed as racists for discriminating against other Hispanics. Those with an ounce of common sense will realize that it is not racist to try to improve job opportunities for America's own poor. There are better ways to help the poor of other nations than by permitting unsustainable rates of immigration.

Japan demonstrates a more pragmatic practice with regard to immigration which is, at the same time, more just. Instead of encouraging immigration, which would not be feasible in a country as small as Japan, they export jobs by investing abroad. This not only benefits the Japanese culture and economy but has the advantage of improving the lives of other cultures while avoiding the necessity of indigenous populations leaving their families and societies to migrate to Japan.

Lowering trade barriers also allows poor nations to increase their exports to the United States while at the same time allows U.S. citizens to buy more goods at lower prices. The problem is that lowering trade barriers also threatens the jobs of employees in the U.S. industries that are affected by the lower cost of imports. This issue will be discussed at length in chapter 7.

As explained in the last chapter, the best and least costly action the United States can take to aid the world's poor would be to provide family planning assistance to help reduce their population growth. A $1 billion dollar investment toward international family planning would go far in providing the contraception necessary so women of the LDCs can control their birth rates. It is tragically irresponsible, therefore, when the Republican party caves in to the religious right and continues to oppose aid to international family planning.

Controlling Immigration: What Must Be Done

Every government commission since the time of the 1951 Truman Commission on Migratory Labor has concluded that too much immigration will work to the detriment of America's future. Nixon's Commission on Population Growth and America's Future concluded that there were no benefits from further growth in population.[159] The 1979 Congressional Select Commission on Immigration and Refugee Policy found that immigration was "out of control" and should be scaled back to 350,000 a year.[160] Most recently, Clinton's U.S. Commission on Immigration Reform chaired by the late Congresswoman Barbara Jordan, also recommended significant cuts in immigration.[161] Unfortunately, in each case the analysis and logic of the Commission was overruled by special interest groups who persuaded spineless presidents and congresspeople to avoid taking the actions necessary to ensure the future health and well-being of America. When faced with the future of America or their own political future, it is obvious which they felt was most important.

It is time to slow immigration so we can assimilate the millions of immigrants that have entered our country in the last three decades. Because of the pause following the Great Wave, by World War II the children of the immigrants who came at the turn of the century were successfully assimilated into the American society. This does not mean they gave up all of their traditions or that there were no ethnic neighborhoods. It did mean, however, that the majority saw themselves as Americans first and foremost. They felt obligated to learn the language (without bilingual education) and sought no special status or social benefits.

The American public is once again ahead of their political leaders on this issue. Polls continually show that 75 percent to 80 percent of Americans want to see immigration reduced. Surprisingly, and to the credit of Hispanic Americans, the Latin National Political Survey poll found that 79 percent of Mexican-born U.S. residents also recognized that there are too many immigrants.[162] There are several immigrants groups, however, such as the National Council of La Raza, that lobbied to increase the immigration rates in 1990 and will fight any new restrictions.

In 1996, the Simpson Bill, which proposed cutting immigration by only 10 percent, was defeated. Lobbyists opposing reduced immigration swarmed all over Capitol Hill. They represented religious organizations that receive tens of millions of dollars from the federal government to aid refugees and immigrants, businesses that seek cheap labor, and ethnic groups such as La Raza and the Mexican American Legal Defense Fund (MALDEF) who are liberally financed by philanthropic trusts such as the Ford Foundation. Legislators know that their reelection depends more upon the support of special interest groups than the majority of Americans who, although opposed to the current levels of immigration, do not place immigration high enough on their list of issues to determine their vote.

Charges of xenophobia or racism are a smokescreen to hide the lack of substantive arguments against controlling immigration. The proponents of today's immigration policies often like to truncate the immigration debate by charging that any one who seeks to reduce immigration or wants to change the rules is a racist or xenophobe. Name calling is often an effective ploy to stifle discussion in the absence of logic and facts.

Let's put the demands of the immigration lobbies in perspective. Suppose I decide I'm fed up with America and want to immigrate to France. Although they are under no obligation to do so, the French people generously agree to let me immigrate and offer me the opportunity of becoming a citizen. Rather than being grateful, a few weeks later I go to the appropriate ministries and present a list of my demands:

- I want the right to put my wife, parents, children (both underage and adults), brothers, and sisters all at the head of the list of future immigration applicants.
- I object to the French requirement that I be able to show that I have the means to support these relatives.
- I want my children educated in French schools at taxpayers expense *and* I insist that they have special English-speaking teachers and courses in English for an unlimited transition period while they learn to speak French.
- I want the French people to pick up any emergency medical costs.
- I demand that I and my American relatives be given priority in job hiring over French people.
- I want my relatives to be eligible for welfare if they can't find jobs, and my parents to be eligible for social security benefits. (These two last

requirements are denied and I grumble that it is typical of the mean-spirited French people.)

Its time for the majority of Americans to say "enough" to these absurd charges of xenophobia leveled at the most generous nation in the world and take control of our nation's future.

Steps to Reduce Immigration to Sustainable Levels

If we are to save the United States from duplicating the plight of other societies overwhelmed by mass immigration, the following steps must be implemented immediately. Some of these proposed actions were included in the bills presented to Congress, but were defeated by the pro-immigration lobbies. Several of these recommendations were also made by Lutton and Tanton in their book, *The Immigration Invasion*.

1. Determine the Long-term Population Goal for the United States that Is Commensurate with Environmental Sustainability

Eventual zero-population growth should be the goal. The only real issue is how fast we should achieve it. Even if we were to halt all immigration tomorrow, population will continue to grow for the next fifty years since there are more women of child-bearing age than old people. In addition, the 25 million immigrants admitted during the past fifty years will generate 70 to 100 million grandchildren.

2. Determine Immigration Quotas Based upon Long-term Population Goals

If the fertility rate were less than the 2.1 children per family replacement rate, ***immigration of about 250,000 to 300,000 per year would be sustainable and permit modest gains in the standard of living for all Americans over the long run without destroying our environment.*** Such a quota would be in line with the average immigration rate of 230,000 from 1776 to 1965 and leave America as the most generous nation in the world in terms of immigration.[163] Beck recommends a goal of 235,000, which would be sufficient to allow entry for adoptees, wives, and underage children of recent immigrants (200,000), refugees (30,000) and a small number of "brilliant workers" that U.S. businesses allegedly require (5,000).[164]

3. Eliminate the Employer Skill-based Set-asides for Immigration

Allowing employers to request immigrants with certain skills is the same as bringing in scab labor. It undermines the wages of American workers and robs developing countries of their best talent. Some businesses may not find the amount of skilled labor they need. They may have to relocate their operations abroad or even be forced out of business. There is no reason that we should seek to guarantee success for every person who would rather have their own business than work for someone else. Further, once we close the door to the smartest and best from other countries, they will seek opportunities commensurate with the needs of their homelands. This will certainly be better for developing nations than American foreign aid, which has been a dismal failure at improving the plight of the LDCs.

Beck provides a succinct summary of the results of current U.S. immigration policy: "By providing unending labor-force growth and population growth for thirty years, immigration has rewarded sweatshop owners, unscrupulous developers, and other environmental marauders, while disadvantaging business owners who have tried to be caring employers and good corporate citizens."[165]

4. End Chain Migration by Granting Preference Only to Underage, Unmarried Children, and Spouses of Legal Immigrants

This is another sensible recommendation of the Jordan Commission. Making family reunification a primary goal of immigration has resulted in a shift in the composition of immigrants since 1980 to about 85 percent Hispanic and Asian. The present nepotistic policy of granting preferential immigration to parents, brothers, and sisters, in addition to spouses and children, will continually skew the distribution of future immigrants in favor of Asians and Hispanics. It was wrong to give preferential treatment to Northern Europeans in the past. It is wrong to give preferential treatment to Asians and Hispanics today.

5. Establish an Employment Eligibility Verification System

About 40 percent of illegal immigrants do not sneak across our borders. Most illegals from Russia, Eastern Europe, Asia, and the Middle East enter our country legally, overstay their visas, and obtain false identification. The only solution is a job eligibility verification system. A national citizenship and legal immigrant verification system is no different than the system of social security cards or driver's licenses. You would not let someone buy a television on credit without an identification card (credit or debit card); why should someone be allowed to collect a paycheck or welfare check without some form of relatively secure identification? As of this writing, a few states are taking part in verification trials, however, business participation is on a voluntary basis. Those businesses that deliberately hire illegals obviously will not take part in such trials.

The Jordan Commission recommended that a national registry of Social Security numbers be created that an employer could consult to determine if a prospective worker had a valid number. Although any form of verification system is anathema to civil libertarians, they are responding with a knee-jerk reaction that both ignores the need and grossly exaggerates the potential problems of verification. Unless we have an enforceable verification system that includes all employers, we effectively have an open invitation for aliens to illegally enter our country. Virtually every country in the world has such a system except the United States. Are the liberties of the English, French, or Canadians impaired because they have systems to determine who are legal immigrants and citizens? Of course not.

6. End Affirmative Action for Immigrants

It makes absolutely no sense to grant preferential hiring status to an immigrant from Mexico or the Philippines over an immigrant from Poland or an indigenous American from Appalachia. There are more whites living in poverty than all other minorities. And, as we have seen, affirmative action has resulted in the hiring of immigrant minorities over African-Americans.

7. Eliminate All Benefits to Illegal Immigrants Except Emergency Medical Treatment

The Welfare Reform Act of 1996 was a step in the right direction but is slowly being eroded by a backpedaling Congress more interested in gaining the votes of immigrants than the welfare of present and future Americans.* A welfare system acts as a powerful incentive for immigrants who cannot find employment in the United States to remain here rather than

*The Welfare Reform Act of 1996 required welfare recipients to find a job within two years or lose their benefits. Generally they would be limited to five years of assistance during their lifetimes. The act placed further restrictions on immigrants, cutting off all welfare assistance, including food stamps. However, food stamps for out-of-work immigrants and welfare for disabled and elderly immigrants were reestablished in 1997.

returning to their country of origin. During the Great Wave of immigration between 1895 and 1915, about 40 percent of the immigrants returned home when they couldn't find a job. With the availability of welfare, immigrants arriving after 1965 rarely returned home. If we are going to provide welfare assistance to Americans, it only makes sense that we have a system to determine who is eligible, just as it is common sense to determine who should be eligible for a job.

8. Eliminate Automatic Citizenship for Children of Illegals

In 1994, the U.S. Census Bureau estimated that 503,000 births were to women who were not citizens.[166] National estimates of births to illegal immigrants is not known, but in California alone there were 78,386 births to illegals in 1995. The cost was estimated at $206 million, nearly 40 percent of the total child-birth costs covered by California's Medicaid system of healthcare for the poor.

France has repealed its law that automatically made every child born in France a citizen. The French realized that the higher birth rate of Moslems living in France threatens the French cultural traditions. Fundamentalist Moslems insist on female circumcision, polygamy, instantaneous divorce, and abolition of mixed sexes in the work place. Some Moslems were even calling for a separate Muslim state within France.[167] A similar situation is developing in the United States, where Hispanics are demanding bilingual education, bilingual publication of all public documents, special set asides for jobs, more subsidized housing, and—for the more radical Hispanics—a separate nation of Aztlan.

Some have argued that restricting automatic citizenship to children of American citizens is a violation of the Fourteenth Amendment to the Constitution. This is clearly not the case. The purpose of the 1866 amendment was to guarantee citizenship and the rights thereof to American blacks recently emancipated from slavery. It was never intended that the 14th Amendment would apply to foreigners as is clear from the Congressional Record of the time. In presenting the 14th Amendment, its author, Senator Jacob Howard (Michigan), specifically told Congress that it "will not, of course, include people born in the United States who are foreigners, aliens, who belong to the families of embassadors (sic) or foreign ministers. . . ."[168]

9. Increase INS Funding and Border Patrol Policing

The INS contends that Operation Gatekeeper, which installed a steel fence along the fifteen mile border near San Diego, cut the inflow of illegals in half. The evidence suggests, however, that it only pushed the immigrants further east. The fence needs to be extended along the 200 miles of border where 90 percent of the illegals cross. Call it a wall if you wish, but it cannot be compared to the Berlin Wall that kept people in, not out. A better analogy would be the Great Wall of China that was erected to protect China from the conquering hoards of Mongols.

The 1996 Immigration Reform Bill calls for increased INS funding and the addition of triple fencing to a small segment of the Mexican border. To effectively deter immigration we should divert at least one billion dollars from the $260 billion defense budget to defend against the most pressing threat to the future welfare of America.

10. Strengthen Border Patrols with the Use of the Armed Forces if Necessary

Why have armed forces in Europe or Japan when an invasion is occurring along the American border? If a million Mexicans amassed there tomorrow with the announced intention of invading, we would no doubt call out the army. But because they slip in over the course of several years, we fail to recognize the problem. Since the amnesty of the late 1980s, 2.3 to 2.4 million Mexicans have illegally taken up residence within our borders.[169] How ironic that an invasion that could never be achieved by force of arms, might be achieved by having thousands storm the borders every night for years.

Following America's Civil War, Congress felt that federal troops had become too deeply involved in law enforcement in the South and so passed the Posse Comitatus Act of 1878. The act forbids the use of federal troops to enforce the laws of the United States. The rationale for maintaining the law today is to avoid having military personnel, who are trained to operate under conditions in which constitutional freedoms do not apply, enforce laws within our borders, where such freedoms must be maintained. While recognizing this danger, unless other measures can be enacted to slow illegal immigration, we will have to repeal the Posse Comitatus Act to prevent a greater threat to our security of a continued invasion.

11. Deny Federal and State Funds to Municipalities that Refuse to Cooperate with the INS

Some cities, such as Chicago, Milwaukee, and San Francisco have declared themselves sanctuaries for illegal aliens. While Chicago is inviting tens of thousands of illegals to take residence, it is also begging the state and federal government for more aid for its schools and other public services. If

Chicago wants to be a sanctuary for illegals, it should not make the rest of the state's taxpayers pay for its ill-conceived policy.

12. Establish Refugee Centers within Warring Nations or Their Neighboring States Under the UN High Commissioner on Refugees

Providing food and housing for refugees in or near their home countries costs only a fraction of what it does to house them here and offers assurance that they will be repatriated when hostilities cease. One day's expense of settling a refugee in the United States would cover the needs of 500 refugees abroad.[170]

13. Sharply Delimit Who Qualifies as a Political Refugee

In 1975, at the height of the cold war, America received 2,432 political asylum cases. By 1996, expansion of the definition of what constitutes a political refugee encouraged 128,190 people to claim asylum. Only 13,532 cases were approved and 2,504 were denied.[171] The rest are pending, and most of these will never be resolved, but the claimants will just meld in with the other hundreds of thousand of illegals. Many of the LDCs have cruel and oppressive governments; unfortunately they account for 2 to 3 billion people. It is tragic, but the American government has to draw the line somewhere. Our inner cities are not much better off than an LDC. A nation's primary obligation is to its own citizens.

14. Return Refugees to Their Home Country after the End of Hostilities

About 17 percent of the total population of El Salvador were granted asylum during the many years of conflict there. Few have returned. The same situation occurred in Nicaragua. Refugees are never forced to return home. This laissez faire policy with regard to asylees encourages anyone who can't get into the United States through normal immigration channels to declare themselves a refugee.*

---

*The 1998 hurricane that devastated Honduras and Nicaragua might justify temporarily delaying the deportation of illegals from these two countries, but some immigration rights groups are trying to exploit these calamities as a way of seeking permanent amnesties for illegals from these nations.

15. Increase Aid for Family Planning to All Countries Seeking to Control Their Birth Rates

In 1996, Republican congresspeople introduced a bill to cut off all aid to international population programs and to eliminate the Agency for International Development which is responsible for administering U.S. support for population and family planning programs in the developing world. This is insanity. We should provide at least $2 billion for these programs. This is the price of just one of the B-2 bombers that the Pentagon says it neither wants nor needs, but that Congress insists on funding anyway.

Family planning is the most effective defense against the unrest that threatens every LDC. Ironically, and tragically, we give billions in military aid to LDCs, which only serves to increase their instability, and a pittance to assist them in coping with their overpopulation. Unless countries such as Mexico reduce their population growth, no amount of economic assistance will have any impact. Just to maintain their status quo, Mexico and Central America will have to create more jobs than America has created in the 1970s and the 1980s and achieve this in economies that altogether are only about 5 percent the size of the U.S. economy.[172]

Every country in the world is reassessing its refugee and immigration policies. Let's hope that the United States will have the wisdom to do likewise. Europe is taking down its borders, but only for the countries of the European Community, all of which have already brought their population growth under control. They are not opening their borders to immigrants from the LDCs. In contrast, almost all the immigrants coming to America's shores today are from the LDCs.

For those who worry about what this means for the ideal epitomized by the Statue of Liberty, they should remember that the original name for the statue was "Liberty Enlightening the World."[173] Today the message of enlightenment for other nations is that the United States recognizes the need to reduce our population growth to sustainable proportions, and it is time that every other country does so as well.

We must act quickly. Each day the immigration lobby is gaining strength. In places like Chicago immigrants represent the swing vote. As a result, Mayor Richard Daly will take no action that might jeopardize the immigrant vote regardless of the negative impact on the city. Instead he demands the state and federal government provide the city with more money that he can use to support immigrants. At some point the immigrant population will become the swing vote nationally and neither party will have the guts to take the action necessary to stop the immigration invasion. I only hope we haven't already passed the proverbial point of no return.

Reducing U.S. Fertility Rates

To stabilize the population at about 285 million by 2050 would require limiting net immigration to 350,000 a year and reduce the total fertility rate to 1.9 children per woman.[174] But the 1996 average fertility rate was 2.059 and has been rising for the past decade.[175] The increase was due to two factors. First, women are, on average, having children later in life, which resulted in an artificially low rate of birth in the late 1970s and early 1980s. Second, immigrants have higher fertility rates than native born Americans. This is especially true for Hispanics. (Hispanic-Americans average 2.9 births per woman. Hispanic immigrants have an even higher birth rate.)

It should be noted that the growth in population in the United States is not among the affluent or even the middle class. Population growth is driven by the higher-than-average birth rates of the poor, but it is not primarily due to unwanted and/or teenage pregnancies. Contrary to popular belief, the teenage pregnancy rate in the United States was in a steady decline for nearly twenty-five years until it increased slightly after 1985. The decline was due to the greater availability of contraceptives and abortion as well as an increase in the average age for marriage as more young women sought to go to college. Nevertheless, according to International Planned Parenthood, despite the twenty-five-year decline prior to 1985, the U.S. teenage pregnancy rate is still the highest of developed Western countries. Almost 75 percent of children born to teenagers will be raised solely by their mothers. The vast majority will also be raised in an environment of poverty and crime with little opportunity for achieving a happy life. Teenage pregnancy remains a problem of epidemic proportions, particularly among the poor, and must be addressed with strong sanctions.

The overall birth rate could be reduced even further—down to a level that would yield no further growth in population—by significantly cutting immigration and reducing unwanted births. As shown in the table below, in 1995 there were over three million unwanted births in the United States. These do not include unintended births, where a woman might have wanted a baby but just not at the time pregnancy occurred.

Unwanted Births, 1995[176]

	Number (000)	*Percent of Women 15–44 Years of Age*
All Women	3,387	5.6%
White†	1,660	3.6
Black†	940	11.4
Hispanic	578	8.6
Other	170	6.1

†Those living under poverty line.

The number of unwanted births remains unacceptably high in part due to the efforts of religious fundamentalists in pressuring the federal government to reduce the availability of free contraceptives and family planning services. For example, cuts in Title X Federal Funding resulted in a steady decline in family planning clinics since 1981.[177] Contrast the U.S. policy to that of Sweden, which supports a network of centers that provide contraceptives to school children. The result is a teenage pregnancy rate that is two-thirds less than the United States and far fewer abortions. ***In the United States, if only the women who wanted to get pregnant actually got pregnant and gave birth, it would mean over three million fewer births annually.***[178]* ***This would eliminate any increase in population due to natural growth (births minus deaths).*** Reducing federal financing of family planning services does not save tax dollars in the long run. A 1989 study showed that we spent $21.5 billion on families headed by teenage mothers.[179] There is no reason to believe that we are spending less today. The reason for limiting family planning availability is religious, not economic.

Of course the greater availability of contraceptives, by itself, will not solve the problem of unwanted pregnancies. A study based upon 9,480 abortions revealed that half the patients had used birth control during the month they conceived.[180] The same study showed that 82 percent of the

*The three million unwanted births have caused the proponents of mass immigration to argue that if we could eliminate all unwanted births, we could continue the policy of mass immigration without increasing total population. This simply isn't true. First, we don't have any good estimate of how many unwanted births would be eliminated by greater availability of family planning services. Certainly, despite the availability of contraception, the spontaneous nature of sex and religious taboos against contraception would still result in many pregnancies, and many women oppose abortion. Secondly, Hispanics are above the national average in unwanted pregnancies; but even subtracting unwanted pregnancies, their birth rate is 50 percent greater than whites. Therefore, not only will the number of immigrants swell the total population, but because over half of all immigrants are Hispanic, they will result in pushing up the overall birth rate for the nation.

women were unmarried, 75 percent were over the age of twenty, and 33 percent had an income under $11,000 as compared to 15 percent of the general female population who have an income below this level. In other words, unwanted pregnancies are not just a teenage problem. There are many women who take the proper precautions but still get pregnant, and many of these cannot afford to raise a child. It is futile to say that these women should simply refrain from sex. That will not happen. We can, however, prevent the population from surging due to millions of unwanted children born into impoverished conditions.

Despite the number of abortions performed each year in this country, the rising number of unwanted births is also due to the increasing difficulty in obtaining abortions, especially for poor women. Trends in state laws toward greater restrictions for abortions will have a significant impact on population growth, especially among the poor. According to the Alan Guttmacher Institute, there are presently about 1.6 million abortions performed in the United States each year. ***If it were not for the availability of abortions during the past thirty years, there would be over 40 million more people in this country today.*** Adoption would have accommodated only a small fraction of these children. A much larger proportion would have been born into poor families where their chances of living a happy, successful life would be minimal at best. All of the problems facing our society such as crime, unemployment, overcrowding, higher welfare costs, etc., would have been greatly exacerbated by millions of additional unwanted, and oftentimes neglected or abused, children. Conversely, all of these problems would have been ameliorated if fewer women were forced or persuaded to have children that they didn't want or were unable to care for.

Abortion is now legal for two-thirds of the world's population.[181] It is almost unimaginable that many United States states would seek to turn back the clock on women's rights at the behest of religious fundamentalists, papal authority, and political conservatives. To force women to bear children by granting rights to a preconscious organism is absurd and unjust. It is little more than theology and superstition dictating social policy.

In *The Science of Morality*, it was argued that there is no reason why rights should be symmetrical. It is reasonable and proper that women have the unrestricted right to avoid having babies they do not want, but women should not have the right to have a baby irrespective of their circumstances. The basis of this dichotomy is that since a fetus is not a person, it has no rights and can be aborted upon demand. On the other hand, intergenerational equity demands that future people should be guaranteed certain rights, such as, whenever possible, responsible and caring parents. These dichotomies may at first seem counterintuitive, but can be justified logically and empirically as being consistent with the goal of increasing human happiness.*

Aside from the problems of unwanted pregnancies, there is still a major problem of childbearing by teenagers and others who have neither the economic nor emotional wherewithal to provide for a child. Heretofore, most societies have taken the position that it is too dangerous to let the state interfere in such an important personal decision. For the state to direct whether or not a woman may have a baby is certainly a serious infringement on personal liberty. At the same time, most people would consider it wrong for a person to undertake a decision that has the ultimate result of bringing a child into the world with no thought or capability of providing the minimum support necessary to offer the child a chance of being happy. It is absurd that it is easier to have a baby than to get a driver's license. It is also paradoxical that society does a rigorous investigation of potential adoptive parents as to their capabilities, but tells a fourteen-year old girl that society has no interest whether or not she decides to have and raise a child.

Contrary to popular belief, there is no evidence to support the generalization that women have babies to obtain additional welfare payments. Far more important than the tangible incentives are the biological and psychological motivations. In addition to the biological instinct to procreate, for many young women having a baby is mistakenly thought to be a sign of maturity, and oftentimes about the only thing that an uneducated, unemployed women can take pride in. Other young girls share the mistaken notion that a baby will provide someone who they can love and who will love them in return.

Although young women do not get pregnant to obtain welfare money, the availability of welfare removes one disincentive to getting pregnant. Providing welfare is society's way of condoning their getting pregnant; denying welfare is society's way of showing disapproval, saying in effect, what you did is wrong and cannot be condoned.

Another consideration that cannot be ignored, although liberals often tend do so, is the cognitive capabilities of the groups with the highest birth rate. The evidence appears overwhelming that, on the average, people with

---

*Anti-abortion groups want to create a right to existence for fetuses. But fetuses are not people: they possess no sense of self-awareness. It is therefore impossible for a fetus to regret having its existence terminated. And if it is aborted, there can be no future person to regret not having existed; hence there is no person who could demand certain rights. On the other hand, in cases where the fetus is carried to term, there will be a future person who could regret being born in a situation where the possibility of happiness is extremely unlikely. We can imagine what it would be like being born to a women totally unequipped to provide for our basic needs. Therefore, in the interests of intergenerational equity we can decide to create rights for future people. For a complete discussion of this complex issue, see *The Science of Morality*, chapter 14.

lower intelligence are having more babies: there are 71 percent more babies among high school dropouts than among woman who have graduated from college.[182] ***If we could reduce the fertility rate of those without a high school degree to the rate of those with a high school degree, the overall fertility rate would drop to below the replacement rate (assuming no further immigration). Conversely, if we fail to reduce the birth rate among people of lower education and cognitive abilities, not only will population continue to increase, but it will gradually depress the average educational level and cognitive abilities of the population.***[183] The result, as demonstrated by the evidence in later chapters, will be to exacerbate every social problem now facing our nation.

Everyone agrees that something must be done to discourage women from having babies which they cannot care for properly, but we seem paralyzed as a society to do something about it. During the Eisenhower administration, a judge in Maryland promoted a plan to jail unwed mothers after their third child.[184] Many people might consider this a serious attack on a women's rights. But what about the right of a child to be brought into this world only when it has at least a minimum chance for happiness? All people, present and future, should at least have some minimum hope for success in the pursuit of happiness. This requires that they will receive a decent education both at home and at school. It also means that they will not be abused, and that there will be some minimal level of physical security. It means that they don't have to run the risk of birth defects by being born to women addicted to drugs or alcohol.

When the community must bear the burden of supporting potential children, the community should have a say in the conditions under which pregnancy should occur. As previously stated, women should have the right to refrain from having children. But the privilege of having a child must balance the interests of the mother with the interests of the future child and the interests of society, which shoulders so much of the costs of child bearing. It might seem that enforcement of such a principle jeopardizes the freedom of women. This need not be the case.

In the first place, efforts to reduce the number of births to women who are unable to adequately care for their babies does not necessarily imply an outright prohibition. A reasonable approach to discourage undesirable births utilizes positive incentives and social conditioning. For example, public service messages should be aired which effectively discourage girls under the age of eighteen from having children. ***Having a baby under age eighteen should be socially condemned as a form of child abuse.*** Having a baby at any age simply because "I want one," or "I feel a need to be a mother," without regard to the needs of the child should be exposed as a selfish act of self-gratification. ***"If you do not have the means to provide***

basic physical and psychological care for a child, don't have the child" should be the message conveyed to all women. Similarly, the myth that getting a girl pregnant is a sign of manhood must be shattered. "Real men don't father unwanted children," and "Only cowards run from responsibility," are new messages that must be conveyed to teenage boys. The schools should inculcate this message from the earliest grades. (The responsibilities of men with regard to fatherhood is further discussed in chapter 9.)

Next, society must provide free and readily available birth control and, since there is no fool-proof contraceptive, the RU-486 pill or its equivalent and abortion should be available through Medicaid. In 1993, Congress once again upheld the Hyde amendment that banned federal funding of abortions through Medicaid except in cases of rape or incest. The argument in support of the ban is that using federal funds in effect forces those morally opposed to abortion to provide funding for abortions. By this criterion Congress should eliminate the entire defense budget since some pacifist groups oppose such spending on moral grounds. In effect, we have Congressmen such as Henry Hyde and his colleagues on the religious right enforcing their theological views on poor women.

The year prior to the Hyde amendment there were about 275,000 federally funded abortions. So, from the time that abortion funding for the poor was cut off there have been millions of additional unwanted and frequently neglected and abused children born that society will end up subsidizing through welfare and, all too often, the costs of imprisonment as well. Ironically, those who oppose funding for abortions will frequently complain the loudest at the additional social costs that the unwanted children will cause.

Although it is impossible to precisely estimate the total number of unwanted children born to poor women because of the elimination of federally funded abortions, if the 275,000 federally funded abortions that occurred prior to the Hyde amendment dropped by only half there would be an additional 137,500 unwanted poor children born each year; that amounts to over one million per decade. The cost of subsidizing these children could be conservatively estimated at $50 billion over the decade.

Let's take the analysis a step further. The right-to-life supporters want to halt *all* abortions. If abortion had remained illegal, there would have been 40 million additional unwanted children since the *Roe* v. *Wade* decision of 1973. If we apply the ratio of prison inmates divided by the total population to the number of unwanted children, eventually it would result in at least 170,000 more prison inmates at a cost to the U.S. taxpayer of $5 billion a year. But of course we could expect a much greater proportion of unwanted children to wind up in prison. Assuming only 5 percent of unwanted children end up in prison for an average of eight years, would cost $480 billion to incarcerate them. Maybe this estimate is high, but it is only a small part of the social burden. We must add in the education and welfare costs of caring for millions of additional unwanted babies. ***Even if we were to assume that the vast majority of additional unwanted children would not wind up on welfare, a conservative estimate of all the social costs of the 40 million unwanted children who would have been born since 1973 would be over several trillion dollars.***

But the real tragedy is that a large number of unwanted children will be subject to abuse and neglect. When the right-to-lifers scream "adoption not abortion," the response should be, "Fine, we are looking to place about two million unwanted children each year, so either sign up or shut up."

The opposition to abortion clinics is similar to the hostility that Margaret Sanger encountered in 1916 when she established the first family planning clinic to provide contraceptives. The religious zealots are more successful in their fight against abortion because they are able to confuse the general population by equating human life with personhood. By attributing properties of personhood such as self-awareness to the fetus they attempt to create the illusion that there is some little person in the uterus who is just waiting to grow large enough to emerge.[185] However, neuroscience has determined that brain neurons do not even exist prior to four weeks in utero, and that brain synapses that make brain cell communication possible do not begin until the third month, and most are formed *after* birth.[186]

Dr. Dominick Purpura, Dean of Albert Einstein Medical School who has been studying human brain development since 1974, emphasizes that the minimum number of neuron and synaptic connections needed for the qualities of personhood does not even *begin* to occur until the middle of the last trimester.[187] Thus, the reaction of a fetus to an abortion is simply an involuntary muscular response. Despite the medical evidence that shows indisputably that a fetus does not possess even the rudimentary self-awareness to be deemed a person, the constant, unrelenting pressure of the religious right has resulted in a reduction of abortions, in large part because their terrorist attacks on abortion clinics have resulted in fewer doctors having the courage to provide abortions.* As a consequence, the number

---

*In October 1998, Dr. Barnett Slepian became the latest physician to fall victim to antichoice rhetoric. Dr. Slepian was gunned down by a sniper's bullet while standing in the kitchen at home with his wife and four children. Shortly thereafter, an antichoice web site drew a line through Dr. Slepian's name on its list of doctors and their "accomplices" who perform abortions. Although most antichoice organizations disavow murder as a way of achieving their objectives, as long as they describe abortion of fetuses as the murder of "babies," it is inevitable that some people will believe that it is morally justifiable to kill doctors who perform abortions. The anti-abortion assassins will argue that they are seeking to protect the lives of innocent "babies" just as an army can morally wage war on an aggressor. The failure in their logic, as explained in *The Science of Morality*, is that (1) fetuses are not people and hence have none of the rights of a person, including even the right to

of unwanted children has been increasing in recent years. (It also sends a message to other extremists: "terrorism can work!")

Evidence that the anti-choice advocates are reflecting a theological position rather than any concern over human suffering is apparent from their hysterical response to the French abortion drug RU-486. The drug has proved 96 percent effective when used up to three weeks after the women's first missed menstrual period. At this stage, the embryo is no more than a microscopic collection of cells, bearing a resemblance to a fertilized chicken egg. The benefits of RU-486 are inestimable. Not only would it be a major factor in reducing unwanted pregnancies and population growth but, according to Dr. Banoo Coyagi, the availability of RU-486 could substantially reduce the estimated 200,000 or more annual deaths in the Third World due to botched abortions.[188] Despite such advantages, Senator Jesse Helms and members of the religious right have succeeded in delaying the availability of RU-486 in the United States by almost a decade. Even worse, the anti-abortion lobby has persuaded the World Health Organization to withhold approval by threatening that the U.S. would retaliate by cutting contributions to its budget.

STABILIZING THE U.S. POPULATION

Estimates of the optimal population for the United States range from 100 million to 200 million.[189] Note that this is not the maximum population the United States could support. Reducing consumption per capita would allow for higher population. We could support over one billion people if we wanted to reduce our consumption to the level of the Chinese. However, as will be shown in the next chapter, America must reduce consumption levels in any case if we are to maintain our environment.

To reduce population to a long-term sustainable level, it is not enough that we promote the ethic that people should not have children they cannot afford. ***We must insist that people do not have more children than the environment can adequately support.*** Wealthy people sometime argue that since they pay more in taxes than they receive in social services, there are no constraints on the number of children they decide to have. This is patently false. Each additional person has an environmental cost that is rarely reflected in the traditional market costs. For example, each incremental person requires housing. The true cost of the dwelling is the long-term alternative use of that land. In the case of prime farmland, the true

life, and (2) if a society is to be preserved from anarchy, people cannot take the law into their own hands.

economic cost of the house and property is the lost capability of the land to produce food in perpetuity. Obviously, if society tried to levy such a price, conversion of farmland to housing developments would be prohibitively expensive.

There are many other ecological costs that are never imputed to the monetary costs of added children, nor is it feasible to do so. Therefore, the problem should be worked backwards, i.e., we should first determine the ecologically optimum population as best we can and then develop policies to reach that population. If, as appears likely, we are near or above the optimal population, we should seek to reduce population growth by promoting the two-child family as the desirable norm. Hence "two is enough" should be the goal not only of the less developed countries, but for all countries, including the United States. Having more than two children should be viewed as unethical. Those who wish to raise more than two children can always adopt. The ease of international adoption should be facilitated in this end.

A bill to stabilize the U.S. population was introduced by Richard L. Ottinger in 1981. This was before the myths of supply side economics and the possibility of unconstrained population deceived an economically and ecologically naive public. As the environmental and social costs of our current population policy becomes apparent, it is hoped that there will be renewed interest in slowing and even reversing the present ruinous population trend.

Demographer Anseley Coale suggests three preconditions for a sustained decline in fertility rates:

- the acceptance of rational choice as a valid element in fertility decisions;
- the perceptions of the advantages of reduced fertility; and
- knowledge and mastery of effective techniques of birth control.[190]

Coale's recommendations are useful but they do not go far enough. There are both direct and indirect ways to implement additional policies to reduce fertility.

1. Educating Women

One of the least coercive and best ways of lowering birth rates is to improve the education of women. As John Weeks explains, "virtually every study ever done on the topic has revealed that higher education is associated with lower fertility, no matter what the cultural setting, geographic region, or religious preference of the respondents. . . ."[191] Of course, this means true education, not just passing time at school. (The issue of improving education in general is taken up in chapter 10.)

In addition to improving general education, sex education needs to be totally revised. In most schools all that is taught is basic plumbing—the biological facts of life. Little or no time is spent in addressing the psychological and moral dimensions of sex. Sex education mostly involves how to make babies rather than how to avoid making them. Even discussing the need for condoms to prevent venereal disease and AIDs was prohibited in most public school districts until recently, and it is still opposed in many areas. It is a small wonder, then, that a 1991 poll conducted by the National Council of Negro Women and the Communications Consortium Center of 1,100 black, Latino, Asian, and Indian woman reported that 60 percent indicated that they never used any kind of birth control, and yet they believed they had no chance of contracting AIDs.[192]

2. Improving Job Opportunities for Women

Nobel prize winning econometrician Gary Becker offers evidence that as job opportunities for women increase, their propensity to have additional children decreases.[193] Moreover, investment per child in terms of education and training increases. Thus, increased job opportunities for inner city women would decrease both birth rates and welfare dependency for themselves and their children. During the last three decades, however, there has been a continued migration of jobs to the suburban rings of major cities. A primary reason for urban sprawl and the loss of job opportunities in the inner city has been federal and state subsidizing of inter- and intrastate highway systems. At the same time, no effort was made to build a public transportation system to take the inner city's work force out to the suburbs. The cost of owning and operating a car, plus the cost of day care for children, make working in the suburbs for minimum wage economically irrational.

Therefore, if we are to reduce welfare roles by enabling women to take low-paying jobs, then the temporary expedient must be a combination of federal subsidies for day care and the provision of more low-cost housing in the suburban ring. Yet, the cost of building an adequate public transportation system to provide access to and among the far flung suburbs is prohibitive. There is a better solution that would minimize additional government expenditures. Stopping the flow of cheap immigrant labor would drive up the wage rate to the point where it would be economically worthwhile for the inner city mother to either move to the suburbs or pay for her transportation expenses. Some businesses might find it more economical to move back to the city in search of available labor. A total ban on funding new highway construction and diversion of those funds to more cost effective mass transit systems into the central cities would also open new job opportunities for the inner city poor.

3. Denying Children the Right to Raise Children

Children under the age of eighteen who become pregnant must be told that they cannot keep their babies. They have only two choices: they must either have an abortion or find someone else willing to adopt their baby. This will, of course, offend those who believe that there is some God-given right for women to have babies. There is no such right nor should we create one. Our primary concern should be for the well-being of future children. Court-ordered subdermal contraceptive implants could also be used for seriously retarded individuals.

This appears to place all the responsibility for pregnancy on women. Where does the man's responsibility come in? The responsibility of men is discussed more fully in later chapters, but basically, men must be made to realize that if they get a woman pregnant, they have a moral and legal responsibility for sharing the burden of caring for any resulting children. Recent efforts by states to establish the paternity of children born out-of-wedlock, and then garnishing the wages of fathers who refuse financial support, is a step in the right direction. A man might argue that a woman tricked him into getting her pregnant by saying that she was taking contraception drugs when she wasn't. Too bad. The children should not be made to suffer for the lies of their parents. More importantly, if both men and women must bear responsibility for conception, then both men and women are more likely to take the appropriate means to avoid unwanted pregnancies. However, as a practical matter, women should understand that regardless of the law, it is relatively easy for a man to run from his responsibilities regarding a child and, hence, women may still be left with the burden of primary provider. The moral dictum we want to encourage is that children should not be born out of wedlock. It is the marriage contract that establishes the rights and responsibilities of men with regard to childraising.

4. Eliminating Tax Deductions for a Third Child

To maintain lower birth rates among all groups, there should be no tax deduction for dependents after the second child, except in the case of adoptions. Donald Mann suggests that the Earned Income Tax Credit be granted only to those parents who have no more than two children.[194]

Increased tax rates for more than two children might even be considered, again exempting adoptions.

5. Encouraging Women Not to Have Children

There are a wide range of incentives for not having children that might be considered. They include direct payments to women or couples for not having a pregnancy during a certain period of time, or payments to individuals who undergo voluntary sterilization. Ecologist Raymond B. Cowles suggested paying adolescent females not to have births.[195] According to the Urban Institute, the cost of raising a middle-class child is about $100,000, so a cash incentive could be a considerable amount and still save society money in the long run. A $5,000 payment to a teenage girl for a subdermal implant would not prevent her from having children later in life when she is more likely to be a suitable parent. Noncash incentives might include priority for subsidized housing for women with two or fewer children.[196]

Payment for voluntary sterilization would be the most effective and easiest policy to implement. Admittedly, however, it is not without its difficulties. If sterilization were offered to women who have no children, they might later regret their decision. If it were only offered to women with two children, there might be some women who would have two children just to qualify, but I think this is highly unlikely. To avoid the problems that India experienced with its sterilization program (many people apparently did not understand the procedure or its consequences), we would have to ensure that any such program involve informed consent. The primary obstacle to implementing such a policy would be opposition from most organized religions. Also, certain minority group organizations would raise the hue and cry that this is a form of racial genocide. Since any sterilization program would be voluntary, such a charge is groundless. In addition, since the present population growth rate of blacks is twice that of whites, and the growth of Hispanics four times the increase in whites, such an allegation is ludicrous.

6. If All Else Fails, Explore the Concept of Licenses to Bear Children

Before concluding the topic of population control, I would like to mention a recommendation made by Kenneth Boulding some years ago. Boulding suggested that licenses to have children be issued to individuals permitting 1.1 children (or 2.2 at marriage). People who do not or cannot have children can be rewarded financially by selling their rights to those who wish to have more than two children. (Herman Daly suggests changing the licenses from birth rights to survival rights to reflect the different infant mortality rates of the races.[197]) Making a decision to have a child based upon economics rather than only love for a child may sound cold and calculating. There is ample evidence, however, to show that the decision on how many children to have is based in large measure on economics anyway, or what is perhaps worse, simply filling a basic biological drive to procreate. How often do you hear a woman say "I want to have a baby," or a man say "I want a son"? This isn't just linguistic carelessness. These are very real biological and, to some extent, culturally determined needs. Although the feeling expressed is certainly understandable, it reflects the needs of women and men, not the needs of the future child. ***Having a child that cannot be cared for, or, as in the case of so many men today, fleeing from the responsibility to care for the child, is a despicable act and must be depicted as such in our social norms.*** Love is expressed by having children only when we can ensure that the child has the opportunity to become a happy and socially responsible individual.

I have not studied the issue of birth licenses sufficiently to have an opinion. However, the concept seems worthy of further consideration and should not be dismissed out of hand. It would be interesting to study the impact of such an experiment. But it is difficult to see how such a study could be designed since, unless it is nationwide in scope, people who want additional children could simply move to another locality to have them.

SUMMARY

The United States has the highest population growth rate of the industrialized nations. It is likely that we may have already exceeded the optimum population size in terms of long-term environmental sustainability. Today's excessive population growth is due to the lack of effective immigration policies and unsustainable birth rates, particularly among minorities. The influx of 1.0 to 1.3 million immigrants (legal and illegal) a year results in lost job opportunities for Americans, depressed wage rates, and higher social costs. Even reducing the number of legal immigrants to 550,000 a year as the Jordan Commission proposed will not solve the problem.

The present policy of relying on a constant source of cheap labor to hold down wages is nothing more than a pyramid scheme requiring an ever-growing population and all of its associated ills. The interaction between the supply and demand for any commodity will determine its price. This is probably the best known law of economics, yet it is amazing how often it is ignored in discussions of unemployment and wages. During the 1970s and 1980s, discussions about the cause and cure for the rising unemployment and falling real wage rates generally focused on the demand for labor (creating more jobs), while ignoring the demographic factors affecting the supply of labor, which, of course, is difficult to affect in the short run. However, to ignore the long-term supply of labor when formulating government policies is a serious mistake. To slow America's population growth to a sustainable level we must cap immigration at 250,000 people annually; strengthen the border patrol; create a secure method for identifying who is eligible to work; and eliminate most welfare benefits for illegal immigrants.

We must reject the siren song of multiculturalism and return to the proven concept of the melting pot, no matter how far short of that ideal we might fall. As Woodrow Wilson said, "You cannot become thorough Americans if you think of yourself in groups. America does not consist of groups. A man who thinks of himself as belonging to a particular national group in America has not yet become an American."[198] This is not to say that people cannot take pride in their ethnic heritage. It is just that they must first identify themselves as part of a larger community of Americans. In other words, it is time to drop the notion of hyphenated Americans. There are only Americans.

To reduce fertility rates, particularly among teenagers and unwed mothers, we need to provide even greater access to contraception and abortion. At the same time, teenagers should be offered both positive and negative incentives not to have children. Teenagers who have children should be denied welfare support; their only options should be adoption or abortion. Teenage boys should be impressed with the notion that getting a girl pregnant is a cowardly and despicable act. On the more positive side, fertility among the poor can be reduced by better education, more job opportunities, and both cash and noncash incentives.

It is not only the poor who must control their birth rates. Ecological constraints require that all people adopt the norm that two children is enough. Those who wish to raise more than two children should consider adoption. The tax deduction for more than two children should be eliminated (except for adopted children).

Finally, we should bear in mind that a growing population results in vote depreciation, i.e., the vote of each person counts for less. During the course of the twentieth century a tripling of the population has resulted in each of our votes being depreciated by about two-thirds. There was a time in this country when almost anyone could see the president. There was a time when people could at least meet with their senator. Now it is getting difficult to meet with even a representative. As we become more populous, the ideal of a nation of the people, by the people, and for the people recedes.

Today, neither Republicans nor Democrats are willing to take the bold steps necessary to solve the population problem. Once again there is an acute need for pragmatists to take control of their parties political agenda or else begin a new party that will reflect the needs of the twenty-first century.

NOTES

1. Gregory Spencer, *Projections of the Population of the United States, by Age, Sex, and Race: 1988–2080*, Series P-25, No. 1018 (Washington, D.C.: U.S. Department of Commerce, Bureau of the Census, January 1989), table F, p. 7.

2. U.S. Bureau of the Census, *Statistical Abstract of the United States, 1998* (Washington, D.C.: U.S. Government Printing Office, 1996), table 3, p. 9.

3. Ibid., Table 3, p. 9, High Series. The High Series assumes that fertility rates will increase from 2.05 in 1998 to 2.58. Since immigrants tend to have fertility rates over 3.0, the 2.58 is entirely possible. The High Series also assumes net immigration will rise to 1,370,000. Given estimates of outmigration of about 250,000, this means immigration would have to increase to 1,620,000 a year. Studies in Portugal, Greece, and Italy have shown that illegal immigration is in part a function of how many legal immigrants there are because legal immigrants frequently provide the means for illegals to enter a country and obtain jobs. Given present trends, the most realistic projection would be somewhere between the Middle and High Series.

4. Dennis A. Ahlburg and J. W. Vaupel, "Alternative Projections of the U.S. Population," *Demographics* 27 (December 1990): 648.

5. Data Supplied by Federation of Americans for Immigration Reform.

6. U.S. Immigration and Naturalization Service, "Estimation of the Unauthorized Immigrant Population Residing in the United States, October 1996," *Backgrounder* (January 1997): p. 1.

7. Wayne Lutton and John Tanton, *The Immigration Invasion* (Petoskey, Michigan: The Social Contract Press, 1994), p. 33.

8. *Wall Street Journal*, November 2, 1994, p. A6.

9. Lutton and Tanton, *The Immigration Invasion*, p. 125.

10. U.S. Bureau of the Census, *Statistical Abstract of the United States, 1997,* Table 94, p. 77.

11. Brad Edmondson, "The Boomlet's Still Booming," *American Demographics* (June 1991): p. 8.

12. U.S. Bureau of the Census, *Statistical Abstract of the United States, 1997,* table 94, p. 77.

13. Robert W. Fox, "Neighbor's Problem, Our Problems: Population Growth in Central America," *NPG Forum* (June 1990).

14. *Chicago Tribune*, June 11, 1995, sec. 1, p. 10.

15. "State of World Population Report," World Population News Service, *Popline* (July/August 1993).

16. John H. Tartan, M.D., "End of Migration Era," *NPG Newsletter* 18, no. 1 (Fall 1992): 8.

17. Lawrence Auster, *The Path to National Suicide* (Monterey, Va: The American Immigration Control Foundation, 1990).

18. Eugene McCarthy, *A Colony of the World* (New York: Hippocreene Books, 1992), pp. 63–73.

19. U.S. Bureau of the Census, *Statistical Abstract of the United States, 1991*, table 635, p. 386.

20. President, *Economic Report of the President Transmitted to Congress, February 1991* (Washington, D.C.: U.S. Government Pringting Office, 1991), table B–34, p. 325.

21. President, *Economic Report of the President Transmitted to Congress, February 1997*, table 47, p. 336.

22. During the period from 1940 to 1960, two million low-income, largely unskilled blacks moved from the South to the North in search of good paying manufacturing jobs. But between 1970 and 1977, 2.4 million skilled whites moved from the Northeast to the Southwest reflecting the growth in manufacturing jobs there, especially due to the growth in defense and aerospace industries.

23. Roy Beck, *The Case Against Immigration* (New York: W. W. Norton and Company, 1996), p. 15.

24. Donald L. Huddle, "Immigration and Jobs: the Process of Displacement," *NPG Forum* (May 1992): 4.

25. Julian Simon, *The Economic Consequences of Immigration* (Cambridge, Mass.: Basil Blackwell, Inc., 1991) pp. 230–32.

26. George Borjas, "Know the Flow," *National Review* (April 17, 1995): 49. See also, "Economic Benefits from Immigration," Working Paper No. 4955, National Bureau of Economic Reset (December 1994).

27. Peter H. Lindhert, *Fertility and Scarcity in America* (Princeton, N.J.: Princeton University Press, 1993), pp. 233–34. Jeffrey Williamson, "Kuznets Memorial Lecture," Harvard, 1991, cited by Beck, *The Case Against Immigration*, pp. 86–87.

28. See for example:

- Joseph G. Alonji and David Card, "The Effects of Immigration on the Labor Market Outcomes of Less Skilled Natives," *Immigration, Trade and Labor*, eds. John M. Abowd and Richard Freeman (Chicago: University of Chicago Press, 1991).
- Kristian F. Butcher and David Card, "Immigration and Wages: Evidence from the 1980s," *The American Economic Review*, 81, no. 2 (May 1981): 292–96.
- Thomas Muller and Thomas Espanshade, *The Fourth Wave: California's Newest Immigrants* (Washington, D.C.: Urban Institute Press, 1995).
- George J. Borjas, "The Impact of Immigrants on the Earnings of the Native-Born," *Immigration: Issues and Policies*, eds. W. M. Briggs and M. Trieda (Salt Lake City: Olympus Press, 1984).
- George J. Borjas, *Friends or Strangers: The Impact Immigrants on the U.S. Economy* (New York: Basic Books, Inc., 1990).

29. Rander K. Filer, "The Effects of Immigrants arrivals on Migratory Patterns of Native Workers," *Immigration and the Work Force*, eds. George Borjas and Richard Freeman (Chicago: University of Chicago Press, 1993). Also, William H. Frey and Liaw Kao-Lee, *The Immigration Impact on Population Redistribution within the United States*, Population Studies Center at the University of Michigan, Research Report Series (December 1996), no. 96–376.

30. George Borjas, Richard B. Freeman, and Lawrence F. Katz, "On the Labor Market effects of Immigration and Trade," *Immigration and the Work Force* (Chicago: University of Chicago Press, 1993).

31. Steven A. Camatora and Mark Krikorian, "The Impact of Immigration on the U.S. Labor Market" (Washington, D.C.: Center for Immigration Studies, 1997).

32. A few of the studies supporting the hypothesis that immigration displaces American jobs and reduces wage rates:

- Earnings of low skilled natives decline 12 percent for a 10 percent increase in immigrants in an SMSA. Joseph G. Altonji and David Card, "The Effects of Immigration on the Labor Market Outcomes of Less-skilled Natives." Cited by Donald L. Huddle, "Immigration, Jobs and Wages: The Misuses of Econometrics," *NPG Forum* (April 1992): 3.
- Cities with more immigrants have higher unemployment. David North in *U.S. Congressional Record*, Senate (S 19523-S 19525) December 20, 1979.
- Immigration results in 10 to 20 percent displacement of native workers, i.e., one million immigrants results in a loss of 100,000 to 200,000 American jobs. Harry E. Cross and James A. Sandos, *Across the Border: Rural Development in Mexico and Recent Migration to the United States* (LaJolla, Calif: Institute of Government Studies, University of California, 1982), p. 85.
- Influx of illegal workers result in lower wages and poorer working conditions in south Texas. Vernon Briggs Jr., "Mexican Migration and U.S. Labor Market" (Austin: Center for the study of Human Resources and the Bureau of Business Research, University of Texas, 1975), pp. 25–30.
- Illegal alien workers probably displace native workers. U.S. General Accounting Office, "Illegal Aliens: Limited Research Suggests that Illegal Aliens May Displace Native Workers" (Washington, D.C.: Government Accounting Office, April 1986), p. 35. Note that this conclusion ignores the potential impacts of the much larger number of legal aliens.
- Wage rate growth is slower in New York than cities with fewer number of immigrants. Adrianna Marshall, "Immigration in a Surplus Worker Labor Market: The Case of New York," New York University, Research Program in Inter-American Affairs, 1983.
- A study of five high-immigration cites (Houston, Los Angeles, New York, Miami, and San Antonio) compared to five low-immigration cities (Birmingham, Dayton, Memphis, Minneapolis, Pittsburgh) indicates that wage changes in high-immigration cities were 20 percent lower than the national average and wage changes in low-immigration cities were 18 percent higher than the U.S. average despite there being no difference in the cities' relative productivity (Walker, Ellis, and Barff, in *Economic Geography*).

- Lutton and Tanton conclude that "Vast pools of cheap immigrant labor have driven down wage rates in the New York metropolitan area. Jobs that once paid a salary that allowed an individual to support a family no longer do so" *The Immigration Invasion*, p. 27.
- Robert M. Solow of MIT received a Nobel prize for his economic model that explained why population growth impoverished a country. Solow showed that since 1965 the increase in immigration was pushing the United States into the fast-growing population trends of the Third World (Beck, *The Case Against Immigration*, p. 79).

33. Timothy J. Hatton and Jeffrey G. Williamson, "International Migration 1850–1939: An Economic Survey," in *Migration and the International Labor Market 1850–1939*, ed. Hatton and Williamson (New York: Routledge, 1994), p. 19. Cited by Beck, *The Case Against Immigration*, p. 25.

34. U.S. General Accounting Office, "Janitors in the Los Angeles Area," GAO/PEMD-88-13BR, March 1988, pp. 40–41. Reprinted in the *Social Contract* (Summer 1995): 258.

35. Vernon Briggs Jr., *Mass Immigration and the National Interest* (New York: M. E. Sharpe, 1992), pp. 214–215.

36. Beck, *The Case Against Immigration*, p. 181.

37. Ibid, p. 187.

38. Joleen Kirschenman and Katherine Neckerman, "We'd Love to Hire Them But: The Meaning of Race for Employers," in *The Urban Underclass*, eds. C. Jenks and P. Peterson (Washington: Brookings Institution, 1991); Katherine Neckerman and Joleen Kirchman, "Hiring Strategies, Racial Bias and Inner City Workers," *Social Problems* 38 (1990): 433–47. Cited by James H. Johnson Jr., and Walter C. Farwell Jr., "Growing Income Inequality in American Society: A Political Economy Perspective," in *The Inequality Paradox: Growth of Income Disparity*, eds. James A. Auerbach and Richard S. Belous (Washington, D.C.: National Policy Association Report, #288, 1998), p. 141.

39. Center for Immigration Studies, "The Cost of Immigration: Assessing a Conflicted Issue," no. 2–94 (September 1994): 16.

40. Lutton and Tanton, *The Immigration Invasion*, p. 126.

41. Jonathan Kaufman, "Immigrants' Businesses Often Refuse to Hire Blacks in Inner City," *Wall Street Journal*, June 6, 1995, p. A1.

42. Ibid., p. A9.

43. Ibid., p. A1.

44. Beck, *The Case Against Immigration*, p. 194.

45. Kaufman, "Immigrants' Businesses Often Refuse to Hire Blacks in Inner City," p. A9.

46. Ibid., p. A9.

47. Rochelle Sharpe, "Asian-American Gain Sharply in Big Program of Affirmative Action," *Wall Street Journal*, September 9, 1997, pp. A1, A8.

48. Beck, *The Case Against Immigration*, p. 171.

49. Ibid., p. 157.

50. Joseph L. Daleiden, Frank Latin, and Raj Pakkala, "Hispanics Gain

Employment at Expense of Blacks," Midwest Coalition to Reform Immigration, Working Paper 1.1, 1997.

51. Booker T. Washington, "Cast Down Your Bucket Where You Are," speech delivered to the Atlantic Cotton States and International Exposition (September 18, 1895). Reprinted in *The Social Contract* (Summer 1995): 242–44.

52. Frederick Douglass, *My Bondage and My Freedom* (New York: Dover, Black Rediscovery Series, 1969), pp. 454–55.

53. Frederick Rose, "Latest Immigrants Face Tough Job Problems," *Wall Street Journal*, November, 28, 1994, p. A-1.

54. Lutton and Tanton, *The Immigration Invasion*, p. 27.

55. Beck, *The Case Against Immigration*, p. 122.

56. Vincent J. Schodolski, "Farm Workers Earn Less Than in '76, Data Shows," *Chicago Tribune*, April 12, 1997, sec. 1, p. 12.

57. *New York Times*, March 31, 1997, p. 1.

58. Beck, *The Case Against Immigration*, p. 121.

59. U.S. General Accounting Office, "Illegal Aliens and Illegal Workers and Working Conditions of Legal Workers" (Washington, D.C.: Government Accounting Office, 1988), pp. 38–39. Cited by Beck, *The Case Against Immigration*, p. 63.

60. Carey Goldberg, "Hispanic Households Struggle as Poorest of Poor in U.S.," *New York Times*, January 30, 1997.

61. Ibid.

62. Center for Immigration Studies, "Foreign-Born Scientists, Engineers and Mathematicians in the United States," Washington, D.C., 1996.

63. Carol Jouzaitis, "Glut of Doctors, Nurses Predicted by Commission," *Chicago Tribune*, November 17, 1995, sec. 1, p. 20.

64. Norman Matloff, "A Critical Look at Immigration's Role in the U.S. Computer Industry," University of California at Davis (August 25, 1995): 6.

65. CBS News, "Slamming the Door," *48 Hours*, May 11, 1995.

66. Richard Lamb, "Immigration: The Shifting Paradigm," *The Social Contract* (Fall 1994): 55.

67. Richard B. Freeman, "Employment and Earnings of Disadvantaged Young Men in a Labor Shortage Economy," in *The Urban Underclass*, eds. Christopher Jenks and Paul E. Peterson (Washington, D.C.: The Brookings Institution, 1991), pp. 110, 119.

68. *Chicago Tribune*, July 13, 1993, sec. 1, p. 13

69. *Fair Immigration Report* (June 1993): 1.

70. Lutton and Tanton, *The Immigration Invasion*, p. 128.

71. Ibid., p. 11.

72. Donald L. Huddle, "The Net National Cost of Immigration in 1993," updated June 27, 1994. Methodology, notes, and exhibits, National Exhibit 3.

73. Harold Galleon, "Bursting at the Seams," *The Social Contract* (Summer 1993): 263.

74. Roy Beck, "More Confirmation of Immigrant Problems, But Symptoms, Not Source, Get Attention," *The Social Contract* (Summer, 1993): 279.

75. Leon F. Bouvier and Rosemary Jenks, *Shaping Illinois: The Effects of Immigration: 1970–2020* (Washington, D.C.: Center for Immigration Studies, 1996).

76. California Department of Education, "California Schools Busting at the Seams," September 3, 1991. Cited by Beck, *The Case Against Immigration*, p. 210.

77. Beck, *The Case Against Immigration*, p. 20.

78. Garrett Hardin, *Living Within Limits: Ecology, Economics, and Population Taboos* (New York: Oxford University Press, 1993), p. 285.

79. McCarthy, *A Colony of the World*, p. 109.

80 Linda Chavez, *Commentary* (September 1998): 12–130.

81. Linda Chavez, "The Failure of Bilingual Education," *Chicago Tribune*, July 30, 1997, sec. 1, p. 11.

82. The lower estimate came from the Census Bureau which has consistently underestimated the growth in the Spanish-speaking population. The higher estimate came form Carlos Fuentes, *The Futurist* (January/February 1993): 48–49.

83. Georgie Anne Geyer, "America Into Splinters," *The Social Contract* (Summer 1993): 247.

84. Lutton and Tanton, *The Immigration Invasion*, p. 61.

85. Ibid.

86. Ibid.

87. Ibid., p. 64.

88. McCarthy, *A Colony of the World*, p. 64.

89. Editorial, "Crossing the Border of Acceptability," *Chicago Tribune*, April 28, 1997, sec. 1, p. 12.

90. Special Report, "Global Mafia," *Newsweek* (December 13, 1993).

91. Lutton and Tanton, *The Immigration Invasion*, p. 77.

92. William Julius Wilson, *The Truly Disadvantaged: The Inner City, the Underclass, and Poverty* (Chicago: University of Chicago Press, 1987), pp. 36, 180.

93. The Federation for American Immigration Reform, *A Tale of Ten Cites* (Washington, D.C.: The Federation for American Immigration Reform, 1995), pp. xvii-xix.

94. For example, Donald Mann argues that the optimal population for the United States would be as low as 125 to 150 million. "Why We Need Smaller U.S. Population and How We Can Achieve It," *NPG Forum* (July 1992).

95. Jon Van, "Population Nearing Limit, Some Warn," *Chicago Tribune*, February 20, 1995, sec. 1, p. 3.

96. Meredith Berke, "An Environmental Income Statement for Immigration," *The Social Contract* (Summer 1993): 266.

97. Lindsey Grant, "Waiting for Al," *NPG Forum* (February 1995): 3.

98. Beck, *The Case Against Immigration*, p. 235.

99. Ibid., p. 235.

100. Lawrence Auster, *The Path to National Suicide: An Essay on Immigration and Multiculturalism* (Monterey, Va.: The American Immigration Control Foundation, 1990), pp. 60–61.

101. Arthur M. Schlesinger Jr., *The Disuniting of America: Reflections on a Multiculture Society* (Whittle Direct Books, 1991).

102. Stanley Lieberson, *A Piece of the Pie: Black and White Immigrants Since 1880* (Berkeley: University of California Press, 1980): pp. 368–69. Cited by Wilson, *The Truly Disadvantaged: The Inner City, The Underclass, and Poverty*, p. 33.

103. Southern Poverty Law Center, *Klanwatch* (April 1993): 1.

104. Southern Poverty Law Center, *Intelligence Report* 74 (August 1974): 1.

105. Beck, *The Case Against Immigration*, p. 49.

106. *Santa Barbara News Press*, October 22, 1995.

107. Dr. Jose Angel Gutierrez, speech given in conference entitled: "The Immigration Crisis, Proposition 187: A Post Election Policy Analysis on its Implications," sponsored by Ernesto Galarza Public Policy and Humanities Research Institute, University of California, January 13–14, 1995.

108. Leon Bouvier, Old Dominion University, unpublished estimates. Cited by Lawrence Auster, *The Path to National Suicide* (Monterey, Va.: The American Immigration Control Foundation, 1990), p. 24.

109. Latino immigrants average about 91 on IQ tests. Whether this reflects bias on the part of IQ tests has long been a subject of debate. Other immigrant groups have been able to improve their IQ scores over time. However, given the increasing correlation between IQ and economic attainment, it is a cause of concern. See Richard J. Herrnstein and Charles Murray, *The Bell Curve: Intelligence and Class Structure in American Life* (New York: Free Press, 1994), pp. 359–360.

110. Michael Lind, *The Next American Nation: The New Nationalism and the Fourth American Revolution* (New York: Free Press, 1995), p. 14. Cited by Beck, *The Case Against Immigration*, p. 223.

111. Lawrence Harrison, "We Don't Cause Latin American Troubles—Latin Culture Does," *Washington Post*, June 29, 1986. Cited by Auster, *Path to National Suicide*, p. 44.

112. *National Catholic Register* (November 8, 1992). Quoted by Lutton and Tanton, *The Immigration Invasion*, p. 144.

113. Donald L. Huddle, "The Net Costs of Immigration: The Facts, The Trends and The Critics," released by the Carrying Capacity Network (October 22, 1996).

114. Jeffrey S. Passel and Rebecca L. Clark, "How Much Do Immigrants Really Cost? A Reappraisal of Huddle's 'The Cost of Immigrants,' " The Urban Institute (February 1994): 1. See also, Jeffrey S. Passel, "Immigrants and Taxes: A Reappraisal of Huddle's 'The Cost of Immigrants,'" The Urban Institute (January, 1994): PRIP-UI-29.

115. National Research Council, *The New Americans: Economic, Demographic and Fiscal Effects of Immigration* (Washington, D.C.:National Academy Press, 1997).

116. An analysis by Steven Camarota of the Center for Immigration Studies examines just the incremental impact of immigration based upon the NCR analysis, i.e., he ignores the potential lost wage increases due to immigration. Based upon his analysis, he poses the ethical question: "Is it right to make the poorest 10 percent of the population 5 percent poorer so that the rest of society can be made two tenths of one percent richer?" See "Immigration's Effects on Jobs and Wages," *Immigration Review* (Summer 1997): 1–5.

117. Lief Jensen, *International Immigration Review* (Spring 1988). Cited by Lutton and Tanton, *The Immigration Invasion*, p. 9.

118. GAO/HEHS-95-58 (February 1995). It was not only Hispanics who were receiving welfare benefits prior to 1996. Twenty-nine percent of the Vietnamese immigrants were on welfare and 55 percent of Chinese senior citizens who came into the United States since 1980 were on welfare. Many were quite well off but have discovered that by transferring their assets to their children they could claim welfare benefits, such as Supplemental Security Income (SSI) and Medicare. In fact, the fastest-growing component of the budget until welfare reform was SSI. In 1994, nearly 738,000 noncitizen residents received SSI, up from only 127,000 in 1982; that's a 580 percent increase in only twelve years. By 1995, SSI and Medicaid to nonresidents was costing Americans $12 billion a year and was projected to rise to $67 billion by the year 2004. (Robert Rector, "A Retirement Home for Immigrants," *Intellectual Ammunition*, The Heartland Institute [May/June 1995]). It was hoped that the 1996 welfare reform would significantly cut that projection, but given the backpedaling of Congress, it is now questionable whether we can curb the growth of SSI significantly.

119. Herrnstein and Murray, *The Bell Curve: Intelligence and Class Structure in American Life*, pp. 359–364.

120. Ibid., p. 360. Although the mean IQ scores of native born Latinos are seven points higher than immigrant Latinos, they are still well below Asian and European immigrants, and almost one standard deviation below the overall national native born mean (i.e., their average score places them at the 84th percentile).

121. Garrett Hardin, "There Is No Global Population Problem," *The Humanist* (July/August 1989).

122. Leon Bouvier, *What If . . . ? Immigration Decisions: What Could Have Been, What Could Be* (Federation of American Immigration Reform, October 1994), p. 3.

123. Gregory Spenser, "Demographic Implications of an Aging United States Population Structure During the 1990 to 2030 Period," *Futures Research Quarterly* (Fall 1990): 26.

124. Beck, *The Case Against Immigration*, p. 153.

125. Robert Versola, "The West Is the Real Pirate," *World Press Review* (October 1992): 52.

126. Peter Skerry, "Hispanic Job Discrimination Exaggerated," *Wall Street Journal*, April 27, 1990.

127. Lutton and Tanton, *The Immigration Invasion*, p. 115.

128. Vernon Briggs Jr., "Income Disparity and Unionism: The Workplace Influences of Post 1965 Immigration Policy," *The Inequality Paradox: Growth of Income Disparity*, eds. James A. Auerbach and Richard S. Belous (Washington, D.C.: National Policy Association Report, #288, 1998), p. 112.

129. *San Francisco Chronicle*, July 6, 1992.

130. *Christian Science Monitor*, December 27, 1991. Cited by Lutton, *The Immigration Invasion*, p. 43.

131. Beck, *The Case Against Immigration*, p. 189.

132. "Bellboys with B.A.s," *Time*, November 22, 1993, p. 36.

133. Malcolm W. Brown, "Job Outlook Gloomy for Some Ph.D.s," *Dallas Morning News*, July 30, 1995. Cited by Beck, *The Case Against Immigration*, p. 147.

134. Federation for Immigration Reform, *Immigration Report*, May 1994, pp. 1, 4.

135. "Audit Says Visa Program Hurts U.S. Workers," *Chicago Tribune*, April 16, 1996, sec. 1, p. 10.

136. David C. Korton, *When Corporations Rule the World* (West Hartford, Conn., and San Francisco: Kumarian Press and Berrett-Koehler Publishers, Inc., 1995), pp. 62–63.

137. Beck, *The Case Against Immigration*, pp. 130–31.

138. *New York Times*, March 1, 1992. Cited by Federation for Immigration Reform, *Immigration Report* (April 1992).

139. *Chicago Tribune*, April 18, 1995, sec. 2, p. 1.

140. Beck, *The Case Against Immigration*, p. 111ff.

141. For a chilling description of how a peaceful town can suddenly be beset with problems usually associated with the inner city, see Beck, *The Case Against Immigration*, Chapter 6.

142. Kaufman, "Help Unwanted," p. A1.

143. Beck, *The Case Against Immigration*, p. 54.

144. Lutton and Tanton, *The Immigration Invasion*, p. 123.

145. Beck, *The Case Against Immigration*, p. 52.

146. Florian Moran, "Study of Immigrants Arriving in Chicago Between 1992 and 1995," Unpublished Monograph, 1996.

147. Beck, *The Case Against Immigration*, p. 52.

148. A federal judge ruled that Chinese immigrants should be allowed asylum because of Chinese abortion and sterilization policies. *Chicago Tribune*, August 8, 1994, sec. 1, p. 16. See also Lutton and Tanton, *The Immigration Invasion*, p. 130.

149. Ray Moseley, "Briton Retools Immigration Laws," *Chicago Tribune*, January 21, 1996.

150. Beck, *The Case Against Immigration*, p. 53.

151. Federation of American Immigration Reform, "What to Do about Refugees?" *Issue Brief* (March 1993).

152. Carole Douglis, "Images of Home," *Wilderness* (Fall 1993): 12.

153. Robert Costanza, "Balancing Humans in the Biosphere—Escaping the Overpopulation Trap," *NPG Forum* (July 1990).

154. Paul Klugman, *Peddling Prosperity: Economic Sense and Nonsense in the Age of Diminishing Expectations* (New York: W. W. Norton and Company, 1994), pp. 227–28.

155. Roy Beck, "Immigration by the Numbers," videotape (Petosky, Mich: The Social Contract Press, 1996).

156. E. O. Wilson, *Consilience* (New York: Alfred A. Knopf, 1998), p. 282.

157. President, *Economic Report of the President Transmitted to Congress, February 1998*, table B–47, p. 336.

158. Garrett Hardin, "There Is No Global Population Problem," *The Humanist* (July/August 1989). See also, Don Feddler, "Granddad and the New Tribe," *The Social Contract* (Summer 1993): 287.

159. Commission on Population Growth and the American Future, *Report of the Commission on Population Growth and the American Future* (Washington, D.C.: U.S. Government Printing Office, 1972).

160. *Select Commission on Immigration Policy and the National Interest* (Washington, D.C.: U.S. Government Printing Office, 1981).

161. U.S. Commission on Immigration Reform, *Legal Immigration: Setting Priorities* (June 1995).

162. Harold Galleon, "Bursting at the Seams," *The Social Contract* (Summer 1993): 265.

163. Beck, *The Case Against Immigration*, p. 16.

164. Ibid., pp. 243–49.

165. Ibid., p. 112.

166. Karen Brandon, "Citizenship a Hot Immigration Issue," *Chicago Tribune*, August 24, 1997, sec. 1, p.3.

167. Georgie Anne Geyer, "Europe Is Seeking New Commitments from Its Immigrants," *Chicago Tribune*, September 2, 1994, sec. 1, p. 21.

168. *The Congressional Globe*, "The Debates and Proceedings of the First Session of the Thirty-Ninth Congress," City of Washington, Congressional Globe Office, 1866. *The Congressional Globe* was the forerunner of the *Congressional Record.*

169. *Chicago Tribune*, August 31, 1997, sec. 1, p. 3.

170. Beck, *The Case Against Immigration*, p. 53. Beck quotes Roger Winter, director of the nonprofit U.S. Committee for Refugees.

171. U.S. Department of Justice, *1996 Statistical Yearbook of the Naturalization and Immigration Service* (Washington, D.C.: U.S. Government Printing Office, 1997), table 27, p. 87.

172. Lindsey Grant, "Free Trade and Cheap Labor: The President's Dilemma," p. 4.

173. Hardin, *Living Within Limits*, p. 276. The plaque encouraging the world to send us "your huddled masses yearning to be free," was added much later by a group of private citizens and never authorized or endorsed by the United States Congress. It was a noble-sounding sentiment, but in a world were the huddled masses number in the billions, it is pragmatically impossible.

174. U.S. Bureau of the Census, *Statistical Abstract of the United States, 1996*, table 3, p. 9, Lowest Series. Because of today's age distribution, the population would peak at about 291,000 in the year 2030 before declining slightly.

175. Ibid., tables 93 and 94, p. 77.

176. Calculated by author from *Statistical Abstract, 1998*, table 117, p. 89.

177. *ZPG Reporter* (August 1990): 3. See also *The Economist* (March 23, 1990): 30.

178. According to the U.S. National Center for Health Statistics, there were 17,077 unintended births in 1995, of which 19.6 percent were unwanted. *Statistical Abstract, 1998*, table 117, p. 89.

179. *ZPG Reporter* (December 1990): 7.

180. *ZPG Reporter* (December 1988): 2.

181. Lester R. Brown and Kathleen Newland, *Abortion Liberalization: A*

Worldwide Trend (Washington, D.C.: Worldwatch Institute, 1976). Cited by Brown, *Building A Sustainable Society*, p. 154.

182. J. A. Sweet and R. R. Rindfuss, "Those Ubiquitous Fertility Trends: United States, 1945–1979," *Social Biology* 30 (1983): 127–139. Cited by Herrnstein and Murray, *The Bell Curve: Intelligence and Class Structure in American Life*, p. 349.

183. Herrnstein and Murray, *The Bell Curve: Intelligence and Class Structure in American Life,* pp. 343–356.

184. Charles Murray, *Losing Ground* (New York: Basic Books, 1984), p. 19.

185. For a complete discussion of the distinction between human life and personhood and its relevance to the issue of abortion, see Joseph L. Daleiden, *The Science of Morality*, chapter 15.

186. James W. Prescott, "The Abortion of the Silent Scream," *The Humanist* (September/October 1986): 10.

187. Ibid.

188. "No Relief in Sight," *ZPG Reporter* (February 1991): 3.

189. For example, David Piemental, entomology professor at Cornell University, estimates 200 million for the United States and 2 billion for the world. (*Social Contract* [Summer 1993]: 286). The organization Negative Population Growth reports on a number of studies that would confirm their own recommended range of between 100 and 150 million people. (*Human Survival* 17, no. 1 [Spring 1991]: 1).

190. Anseley Coale, "The Demographic Transition," *Proceedings of the International Population Conference, Liege*, vol. 1, pp. 53–72. Quoted by John R. Weeks, "How to Influence Fertility: The Experience so Far," *NPG Forum* (September 1990).

191. Weeks, "How to Influence Fertility: The Experience so Far," p. 3.

192. *Chicago Tribune*, September 22, 1991.

193. Gary S. Becker, *A Treatise on Family* (Cambridge, Mass.: Harvard University Press, 1991), p. 15.

194. Donald Mann, "Why We Need Smaller U.S. Population and How to Achieve It," *NPG Forum* (July 1992).

195. Hardin, *Living Within Limits*, p. 272.

196. Weeks, "How to Influence Fertility: The Experience so Far," p.3. Weeks also mentions several other methods for undeveloped countries such as improved community infrastructure where community goals are met, or educational placement for first or second children but not higher-order births. For obvious reasons such incentives would not be appropriate or workable in this country.

197. Herman E. Daly, *Toward a Steady State Economy* (San Francisco: W. H. Freeman and Company, 1973), p. 158.

198. Bryce, *The American Commonwealth*, cited by Arthur M. Schlesinger in *The Disuniting of America: Reflections on a Multiculture Society*, p. 7.

5

Maintaining Sustainable Growth

In the last chapter we touched upon the environmental consequences of increasing the population (P) in the equation E = f(P,T,C). In this chapter we will examine the effects of increasing consumption (C) and changes in technology (T). In a sense, this chapter should not be necessary. There have been hundreds of books and thousands of studies to document the devastation that growth in population, increased consumption, and ill-advised technologies are inflicting on the world's ecosystems. Anyone who would like to review a fraction of this literature need only subscribe to World Future Society's publication *Future Survey*, a monthly review of recent books on a variety of subjects including ecology and environmentalism. Even a casual review of the literature is sobering, if not downright depressing. But we don't like to hear bad news, especially news for which we might be partially culpable. It means that we might have to change our behavior. We might even need to make some minimal sacrifice for the sake of future generations. A much more appealing message is offered by those who argue that the ecological problems are greatly exaggerated by "tree huggers" and "environmental kooks." According to those who believe that the free market can resolve all problems, if we do away with government regulations the market mechanisms will somehow take care of any ecological problems. Sure, the way it did the buffalo, cypress forests, and our nation's wetlands.

Ironically, just at a time when the environment has shown many signs of improving due to environmental legislation of the 1960s and 1970s, the nation was in danger of backsliding. In 1994, Republicans in Congress hoped to capitalize on what they perceived to be the new antienvironmental mood as exemplified by the growth of the "Wise Use" movement out West. Republicans sought to:

- rollback wetlands protection,
- stop reauthorization of the Endangered Species Act,
- kill the Superfund program to clean up toxic wastes,
- kill proposed revisions to the 1872 Mining Law, and
- kill any new pesticide legislation.

But it was soon made clear that the Republican leadership had misjudged the mood of the American people. Just because the environment slipped from the top of the agenda did not mean that Americans had lost interest in cleaning up their environment. Nevertheless, although Americans expressed dissatisfaction with the environmental record of Congress between 1994 and 1996, there is little doubt that the environmental movement has lost some of its steam. President Clinton has shown little leadership on environmental issues, which is most unfortunate. As we will see in this chapter, if present trends continue, the next generation may look back upon the present generation as the most ecologically destructive that the world has ever known.

The Role of Consumption in Increasing Human Happiness

Both John Stuart Mill and John Maynard Keynes predicted that the eventual satiation of human wants would result in an end to growth in consumption and, hence, the increased production of goods and services would gradually grind to a halt.[1] Much of Keynesian economic theory is devoted to stimulating demand for new goods and services on the assumption that recessions are induced by either overproduction or a decline in demand. The problem for Keynes was how to stimulate additional consumption. From their historical perspective, Mill and Keynes could not envision the impact of the increase in world advertising per capita by 220 percent in real dollars between 1950 and 1990.[2] Perhaps an even greater stimulus to consumption has been the impact of television. The stereotypical characters on TV reflect a level of affluence representative of only a tiny fraction of humankind, but are presented as if their standard of living were the norm.*

We now know that through the power of advertising there is no limit

* The family in the long-running TV sitcom *Married . . . with Children* was a perverse case in point. They were constantly whining about their terrible living conditions, yet, with their home in the suburbs and all their modern appliances, they possessed material abundance that the vast majority of Americans could only dream about as late as the 1950s.

to the material wants of humankind. Basic material needs—food, clothing, and shelter—were filled long ago for the majority of citizens in the industrial world. However, in *The Science of Morality*, we saw that survival of the species, as expressed through the mating urge, results both in a desire to dominate (primarily for males) and a need for security (more important to women). Both basic needs are grist for the advertiser's mill. One kind of domination takes the form of a race for acquisitions: "He who dies with the most toys wins," or at least has the best chance of attracting women. On the other hand, a million and one products from cosmetics to apparel exploit the desire of women to attract and keep their men. The tried and proven formula for advertising has always been "sex sells!"

Virtually every hope and fear of human nature is appealed to by the advertiser, with the ultimate message that happiness can be achieved through consumption. Economist Walter A. Weisskopf has pointed out the essential paradox in believing that material gain can produce lasting happiness:

> Economic growth and acquisition can lead only to . . . a temporary, homeostatic equilibrium. No lasting satisfaction or equilibrium can be reached on a psychological level. The "pleasure" of such need satisfaction presupposes a state of tension which is relieved by satisfaction. Without the emergence of tension no pleasure can be received from psychological need satisfaction. Without hunger the intake of food is not pleasurable.[3]

Hence, material satisfaction will result in only a fleeting moment of happiness. The consumption addicts have much in common with drug, alcohol, and sex addicts: they need a continual "fix" of acquisitions to keep their "high."

Does this mean that sustained happiness is impossible? It is if a person believes that happiness is dependent on gratification of material wants. However, millennia ago Buddhists and other ascetic sects learned that merely fulfilling material wants can never lead to happiness. Quite the contrary, they teach that lasting happiness can only be attained when we learn to curb our wants. This perspective has been confirmed empirically. Despite a doubling in per capita consumption by Americans between 1957 and 1990, regular surveys by the National Opinion Research Center of the University of Chicago report that people on average were no happier in 1990 than in the earlier surveys.[4] Other studies indicate that once the basic needs of food, clothing, and shelter are met, happiness is related to fulfilling psychological needs rather than increased consumption. These needs include satisfaction with family life, especially marriage; followed by satisfaction with work, leisure to develop talents; and friendships.[5]

Unfortunately, a Buddhist ethic defies the *raison d'être* of capitalism since it seeks to reduce wants rather than fulfill them (let alone create new wants). While a Buddhist economic policy might not be feasible, at least an enlightened socioeconomic policy could more accurately impute the full long-term costs to all goods and services. The higher costs would result in reduced consumption of products that damage the environment and, conversely, encourage the consumption of other more environmentally benign activities. To illustrate: when we build a highway through farmlands or wetlands we lose the use of that land in perpetuity and increase air pollution; such costs should be reflected in the cost/benefit analysis. To some extent this was the purpose of environmental impact statements. But whereas the environmental impact statement pointed out such costs, the costs were not actually charged to a developer or the taxpayer. It is only by making someone pay the costs up front, rather than deferring the costs to future generations, that we can prevent trading off the well-being of future generations for the gratification of the present generation.

For the most part, modern religions have all but thrown in the towel in their fight against materialism, although in recent years some have taken a renewed interest in the concept of human stewardship of nature. On the other hand, some of the fastest growing of today's religions, such as the Assemblies of God, have decided that rather than undertake the futile effort to fight the trend, they would harness it to their own advantage. Thus, their followers are encouraged to pray for material success, which in effect says, pray that you may be able to wallow in unconstrained self-indulgence.[6]

Not even the schools are safe from the insidious propaganda of the advertisers. Channel One is an advertiser-sponsored school television program. In between educational programs, advertisements for candy bars, fast food, and sneakers are pumped into the classroom for twelve minutes a day. The bait is a free satellite dish and video equipment if the school agrees that Channel one will be shown on at least 90 percent of the school days to 90 percent of the students. Twelve thousand schools signed up. It is not surprising that a survey found that since the programming is done in a classroom setting most students believed the products advertised must be good for them.[7]

Despite their protests to the contrary, neither liberals nor conservatives effectively take issue with the basic notion that materialism is the road to happiness. My experience has been that for all their preaching about saving the environment, liberal parents are just as likely as conservative parents to indulge their children's unlimited wants for TVs and stereos, ski trips, summer camps, computer games, roller blades, mountain bikes, the latest fad in clothing, and the like. The result has been an orgy of increasing consumption since World War II that has not been slowed by periodic recessions, declining growth in personal income, or skyrocketing national and personal debt. The rest of the world stands in wonder and oftentimes, dismay, at the appetite of Americans to digest a disproportionate amount of the world's resources while excreting ever growing mountains of waste. Consider for example:

- Although constituting only 5 percent of the world's population, the United States is responsible for 26 percent of the world's annual oil consumption.[8] If the entire world consumed oil at the U.S. rate of thirty barrels per person per year, the world's proven oil reserves would be exhausted in five years.[9]
- A child born in the United States will consume during his lifetime thirty times as much as one born in India, and contribute fifty times the pollution.[10]
- The U.S. produces and consumes about forty-seven times more goods and services per capita than China does.[11]

But why should we be concerned? Aren't these all measures of America's success? Isn't the rest of the world simply envious of our prosperity? Why should our consumption ever slow or stop? Economist Paul Samuelson once wrote that if we have the right fiscal and monetary policy, the United States can continue to grow at any rate we like. President George Bush must have believed Samuelson when Bush set a goal of doubling the size of the American economy in real terms in just ten years in his "Agenda for American Renewal." Cornucopians such as Ben Wattenberg and the late Julian Simon believe that there are no limits to economic growth. As evidence they note that all past forecasts of resource depletion have been wrong: for most resources such as chrome, nickel, copper, tin, and magnesium, the prices have actually declined. When adjusted for inflation raw material prices in 1990 were 30 percent below 1980 and 40 percent below 1970 prices.[12] The reason is due in part to productivity improvements in extraction, but primarily because of our ability to substitute cheaper, more abundant resources for more costly ones. For example, we use far less steel in cars today than two decades ago and more aluminum- and petroleum-based plastics. In fact, the total steel used in 1990 was less than that used in 1960.[13]

However, except for oil supplies (which will be examined in a moment), the issue is not raw material depletion per se. Popular economist George Gilder attempts to refute what he calls the materialist fallacy, "the illusion that resources and capital are essentially things which we can run out of, rather than products of the human will and imagination which in freedom are inexhaustible."[14] Of course, as long as substitutable materials are developed there can be no shortages. But what is the substitute for air, water, and land? And, just as importantly, the Cornucopians fail to give any value to the intangibles such as privacy, open space, or species diversity. (Where are the robins and song birds of my youth?)

I don't believe that we need to subscribe either to the position of those who say that economic growth must stop or those who believe that there are no constraints on consumption. Part of the problem is semantic. If by growth we mean consumption of material goods of certain kinds, such as automobiles, with no thought given to the recycling of the materials used to make those automobiles, then there is no doubt a limit. Even recycling might have limits since there may be a problem with the assumption of unlimited availability of energy, as well as the by-product of all production—heat. In contrast, if consumption takes the form of the arts, education, information or a variety of personal services, there is virtually no limit to growth since there is no practical limit to the imagination. Therefore, in the final analysis ***there is no reason why consumption per se cannot continue to grow, but the mix of what is consumed must change considerably. Specifically, in the future we will be consuming more services and less resource-intensive products.***

As demonstrated in chapter 2, although consumer expenditures contribute to economic growth as it is currently measured by GDP, growth in GDP is a poor surrogate for human welfare or happiness. Moreover, increased consumption expenditures on environmentally or morally damaging products (such as TV programs or computer games that promote violence) may actually result in a decline in a correctly construed measure of human welfare. On the other hand, ***our society can continue to grow forever in terms of better education, health, and cultural richness.***

The Need to Change the Mix of Consumption

So, the problem is not consumption per se, but the increasing consumption of resource- and energy-intensive products that destroy the environment and produce unacceptably high levels of waste and pollution as by-products. There are two key theoretical arguments that demonstrate that unconstrained physical consumption cannot be sustained:

- It is theoretically impossible to have unconstrained material consumption in a finite world. Resource limitations in terms of raw materials or energy will eventually limit growth.

- The effects of environmental destruction will eventually more than offset any benefits of increasing the amount of the present composition of consumption.

Do these arguments hold up under scrutiny? Let's see.

Is Unconstrained Growth in the Consumption of Physical Goods Possible?

First, let's examine the theoretical arguments against unconstrained growth in consumption. Economist by Hazel Henderson proposes the law of the limiting factor. She explains that a system is always constrained by the least available factor.[15] The supply of energy is frequently thought to be the limiting factor. However, the law of limiting factor would only be true in a closed system. The earth is not a closed system since it gets a continual supply of energy from the sun. As I will show, to the extent that we can directly harness the sun's energy, or reduce energy needs, we can avoid the limiting factor constraint.

Having unlimited energy does not, however, offer us unlimited consumption. The Second Law of Thermodynamics postulates that it is impossible to recycle energy, i.e., eventually all energy will be converted into heat. Therefore, the more energy we generate, regardless of its source, the more heat we will create. The result is an eventual raising of the earth's temperature and the host of potential problems that would result. As we will see, most scientists are concerned with the warming effects due to the buildup of carbon dioxide and other gases in the atmosphere. It is feared that the CO_2 buildup will result in global warming by preventing heat from radiating out into space. It is generally thought that the answer to this problem is merely to shift away from CO_2 emitting fossil fuels to sources of energy which do not generate the gas. But the Second Law of Thermodynamics forces us to be concerned with heat generation from any source. The only answer is to either conserve energy, and produce less heat, or utilize the energy coming from the sun, which would have been generated into heat in any case. We will return to the issue of energy, and its heat by-product as we examine the environmental consequences of growth in consumption. For now I'll just point out that even if we could recycle 100 percent of the products we consume, we would still be generating increasing amounts of heat.

Must Increased Consumption of Physical Products Lead to Environmental Disaster?

As mentioned previously, the reason for the present unsustainable trends in consumption is partly due to the failure of a market economy to adequately reflect the long-term environmental costs for certain forms of consumption. If all costs were included, prices would be driven up to the point where consumption would be reduced or technology altered to avoid environmental destruction. Although the world's scientists are virtually unanimously in their concern for the environment, there is still a barrage of misinformation coming from libertarian think tanks such as the Cato Institute, anti-environmental groups such as the Wise Use Movement, and commentators like Rush Limbaugh. Let's take a moment to review the evidence. We will examine the potential environmental consequences of continued growth in physical consumption as it impacts the following areas:

1. energy availability and consequences of growth in energy use
2. farmland and water
3. forests and species diversity
4. pollution and ozone depletion
5. global warming

1. Energy availability and the consequences of growth in energy use

Currently, the world appears to have a glut of energy, especially oil. Ironically, a major contributing factor to the favorable oil supplies of today was the formation of the Organization of Oil Exporting Countries (OPEC). In 1973, when the oil cartel finally decided to put the squeeze on the world's oil consumption, the United States was consuming 67 percent of the world's commercial energy. The shock of the sudden leap in oil prices from $2 a barrel to $12, and ultimately rising to $40 by 1979, caused a major rethinking of U.S. energy policies. For the first time, the Americans started to seriously conserve energy. (Interestingly, this conservation of oil was exactly what Juan Pableo Parez, the ecologist who created OPEC in 1960, hoped to accomplish.[16])

From 1950 until 1973, world oil production per capita climbed steadily from 1.5 barrels per person to 5.3 barrels. After 1973, when the OPEC nations slowed production and raised prices, the United States found that conservation could reduce demand for oil without seriously impairing economic growth. From 1973 until 1985, the economy grew 40 percent without increasing energy consumption. (As will be shown in subsequent chapters, the economy could have grown substantially faster and with even less energy consumption had it not diverted such a large portion of its research and development investment to defense). Beginning in 1983 there was a rapid decline in the price of oil relative to the price increases of all other goods and services. On an inflation-adjusted basis, this amounted to a 50 percent decline in cost of oil by 1986 (see figure 5.1). As a result, the federal government largely abandoned its efforts to improve energy efficiency. The result was that energy consumption began increasing again.[17]

Figure 5.1
Crude Oil Price Per Million BTUs in Constant (1987) Dollars, 1970–1997[18]

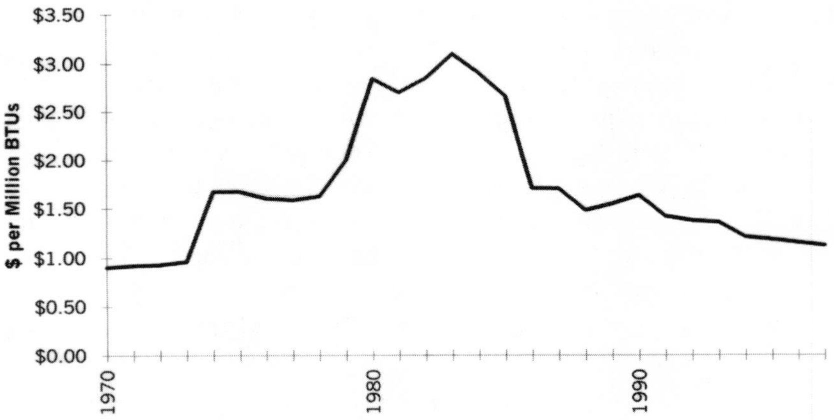

Although America reduced its oil consumption per dollar of real gross domestic product by 31 percent between 1973 and 1984, this trend turned around by the mid-Eighties and today we are still far less energy efficient than our major competitors, whether measured in terms of energy consumed per capita or energy consumed per dollar of GDP. (See figures 5.2 and 5.3.)

It is the energy intensive transportation sector that pushes up the nation's average. A comparison of the gas prices throughout the world (figure 5.4) shows the reason why U.S. drivers are not interested in conserving gas: it is simply too cheap in real dollar terms for U.S. drivers to be concerned with conservation. On an inflation adjusted basis, in 1997 gas was cheaper than it was in the 1950s.

If we were paying as much for gas as Italian drivers, Americans would be

Figure 5.2
Energy Consumed Per Capita in Tons of Coal Equivalent, 1994[19]

U.S.	11,391
Europe*	4,699
South America	1,184
Asia	1,009
World	1,993

*includes the Soviet Union, which in 1990 was running about 38 percent higher than the rest of Europe.

far more interested in conserving gasoline. James J. McKenzie of the World Resources Institute estimates that phasing in taxes on gasoline over a ten-year period to double the cost would reduce consumption by 25 to 45 percent.[20] Moreover, by adding a tax to make up part of the difference in price, we could subsidize mass transit projects and energy research, while at the same time reducing the number one source of pollution. A broader energy tax, such as the BTU tax that the Clinton administration proposed but failed to gain congressional support for, would reduce the amount of energy used for home heating and lighting, and reduce our dependency on foreign oil—the most important action we could take to improve our nation's defense. Instead of a BTU tax, or even a gas tax of $.50 to $1.00 per gallon (which

Figure 5.3
Energy Use: Oil Equivalent per Billion Dollars of GDP[21]

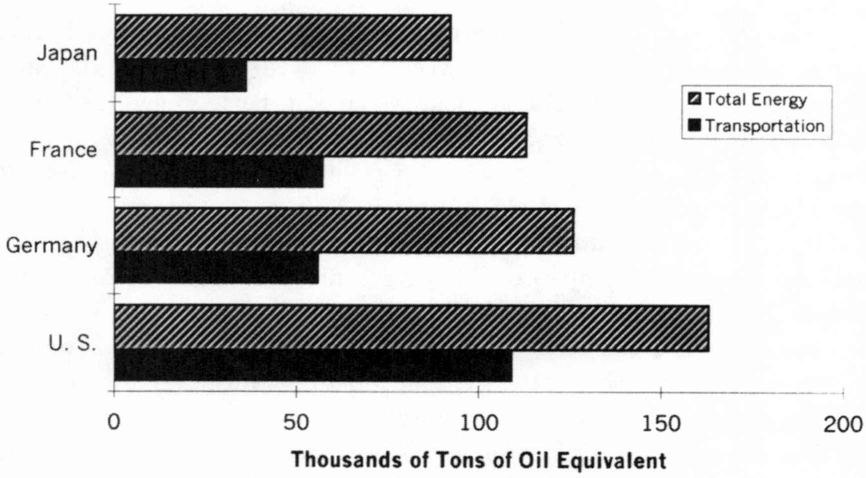

Figure 5.4
International Gas Price Comparison—1990[22]

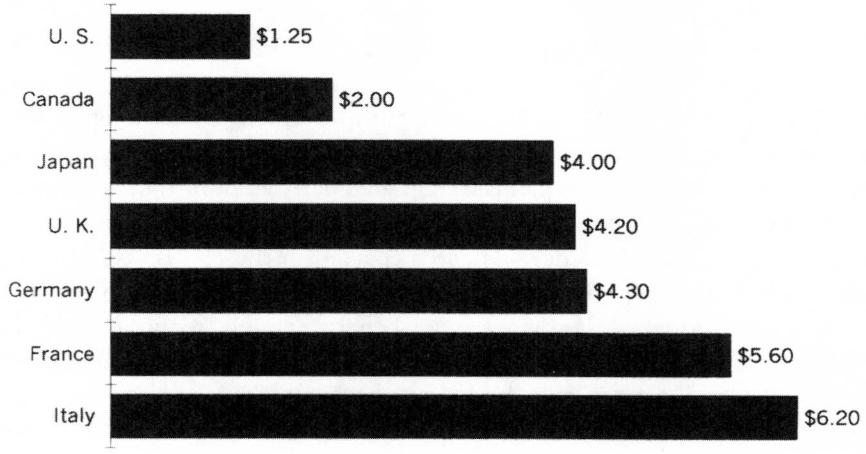

would also be used to reduce the national debt), Clinton had to accept an inconsequential tax increase in 1993 of 4.5 cents per gallon. In 1996, some myopic Republicans tried to rescind even this paltry increase.

Oil is the worst form of energy to rely upon given the volatility of the countries that supply most of it. Yet, after reducing our dependence on foreign oil slightly, we allowed oil imports to climb again until we had to go to war against Iraq to protect our oil interests in the Middle East (not that this was the only reason for stopping Iraqi aggression, but it was a major factor). Today, Americans still consume about 25 percent of the world's oil production.[23]

Oil is seriously underpriced in this country since it fails to account for all the hidden costs associated with it. Estimates of market costs not paid directly by U.S. drivers include $170 billion a year for road construction and repair, highway services, and parking. An additional $126 billion of externalities due to driving include air pollution, defense costs of protecting imported oil, traffic congestion, motor vehicle accidents, noise pollution, and land loss.[24] If these externalities were included, the price of oil and gasoline would be more than double what it is today.

If people had to pay the true price of oil they would be encouraged to conserve energy. And even a relatively small increase in efficiency results in dramatic oil conservation. After the oil shock of 1973, the government demanded that the automobile manufacturers increase fuel efficiency from the dismal performance of about 12 mpg for the average gas guzzler. After much wringing of hands and cries that the government goals were impossible to meet, the auto manufacturers finally got serious and without much trouble met the present standard of 27.5 mpg.* The Office of Technology Assessment estimates that a goal of 33 mpg could be reached by 2001 with existing technology, and with new technology it would be possible to reach 44 to 55 mpg by 2010.[25]

At the time of this writing oil companies believe that there are vast oil reserves in the coastal plains of Alaska and want to open up the Alaskan wilderness areas to drilling. Yet further improvement of automobile fuel efficiency from 28 to 40 miles per gallon would save 2.8 million barrels of oil a day—more than ten times the estimated daily amount that is believed to lie under Alaska's coastal plain.[26] The National Resource Council estimates that the fuel efficiency standards enacted in the 1970s saved American consumers $260 billion. Similar savings could be achieved by another such boast in mileage. If this were not benefit enough, reduction in U.S. demand would result in lower world oil prices, thereby benefiting those underdeveloped nations which do not have all the alternative energy options that we have.

Finally, by stretching out the existing stocks of oil, it provides more time to develop alternative, less polluting sources of energy. Failure to do so might result in the use of more coal as the major source of energy with the result that the CO_2 buildup would accelerate even faster.

1(a) Long term availability of oil

With oil so cheap today, it is easy to become lulled into believing that oil is a virtually inexhaustible resource. Nothing could be further from the truth. In 1948, M. King Hubbert, a petroleum geologist, introduced a new method of analysis that examined the incremental amount of energy it took to extract an additional barrel of oil. He noted that the amount of oil produced per unit of energy had been dropping for some time. (Again we can see the law of diminishing returns at work.) Based upon his analysis, he concluded that at some point the amount of energy to extract an additional barrel of oil would exceed the energy generated from that oil. New technology could improve extraction efficiencies to increase the total oil economically available, but it would just put off the inevitable. If Hubbert's calculations are correct, the growth in the rate of extraction, coupled with increases in the cost of extraction, would mean that 80 percent of all economically available reserves would be used up sometime prior to 2025.[27] The peak in production would occur sometime around the turn of the century. After peaking, the rising cost per barrel would result in a rapid

* Unfortunately, since the higher fuel standards do not apply to vans and recreational vehicles, which are the fastest-growing segments of the auto market, overall average fuel efficiency per vehicle has declined in recent years.

decline in oil production. More recent forecasts indicate that Hubbert's basic analysis is essentially correct, and half of the world's economically recoverable reserves will be used up sometime between now and 2017.[28] Unless alternative energy sources are developed before that time, the result will be a steady increase in energy costs with a commensurate decline in economic development, especially in those countries dependent upon oil as their primary energy source. We might hope that the result would be a renewed emphasis on energy conservation and reduction in pollution. The United States is more fortunate with regard to alternative energy supplies, particularly natural gas. Recent studies indicate that the amount of natural gas reserves is about twice earlier projections.[29] In terms of energy equivalents the supply of natural gas in the United States is two to three times that of oil. Even when added together, natural gas and oil reserves equal only about 15 percent of the energy equivalent of our coal reserves. Unfortunately, the pollution caused by burning coal, even with the most advanced pollution control technology available, makes coal an infeasible substitute source of energy.

Despite the benefits and need for conservation, the lower price of oil today has taken the urgency out of improving energy efficiency and since 1985 progress in this direction has ground to a halt. The reason for this inaction is simple: the lobbyists in Washington with some of the deepest pockets represent automobile and oil interests. Both political parties know that Americans are very short-term oriented, they will only react to a crisis. Any effort to encourage conservation by increasing the cost of oil by raising taxes on gasoline will be defeated in Congress.

1(b) Alternative sources of energy

There are abundant energy sources in this country that could be used to replace oil. All renewable sources of energy contribute about 10 percent of total U.S. energy and provided about one-third of the increase in total U.S. energy between 1979 and 1991.[30] We have approximately a seventy-year supply of natural gas at the current level of consumption that can be extracted economically with known technology, and another thirty-year supply that would require somewhat higher extraction costs.[31] Solar, wind, hydrogen, geothermal, and biomass all promise to be major sources of energy in the twenty-first century. Hydrogen made by directing sunlight through photoelectric cells could provide an unlimited source of energy. One study estimated that combining the various forms of commercially successful renewable energy could cost effectively meet most U.S. energy needs in the year 2030, by which time all of the exiting nuclear plants should have been retired.[32] Another analysis suggested that a circular area with a diameter of 240 miles, located in the Southwest, would be sufficient to manufacture hydrogen equivalent in energy to the entire fossil derived energy of oil, natural gas, and coal consumed in the United States during 1986.[33] Similarly, all the wind blowing across the Great Plains could theoretically meet all U.S. energy needs several times over.[34] Of course, such gigantic energy projects are not without their problems. Photoelectric generation can be substantially reduced by dust storms or even the high atmosphere dust from volcanic activity such as the 1991 eruption of Mt. Pinatubo in the Philippines. Windmill farms wreak havoc with birds such as the golden eagle. Hydroelectric dams can change the entire ecology of a region.

Ultimately, it is the judicious combination of alternative energy sources and conservation that can answer America's energy needs. Wind-generating power is growing at 13 percent a year and the new generation of wind turbines will generate electricity at a cost of 5 cents per kilowatt-hour, roughly equal to the cost of power generated by natural gas.[35] Solar energy costs also continue to fall and will soon be competitive with conventional power in certain areas of the country. Additionally, the United States has an almost limitless supply of coal, and new technologies such as fluidized-bed combustion and coal gasification can reduce much of the sulfur and nitrogen oxide emissions.

Nuclear energy's contribution to the world's electricity supply appears to have peaked at 17 percent, with just 34 nuclear power plants under construction in 1995 compared to 1,960 plants a decade ago. By the mid-1990s, Germany and India were installing more wind-generated capacity than additional nuclear capacity.[36] Here at home, there has been no new orders for nuclear reactors since 1978.

The failure to develop permanent repositories for nuclear waste and the danger of uncontrolled proliferation of nuclear fuels have not yet been satisfactorily resolved.* More than 40,000 tons of used nuclear reactor fuel have piled up at 71 civilian nuclear power plants in 34 states, with the amount growing each year.[37] It appears that the halting of nuclear plants was the correct economic decision despite the short term threat it created for energy supplies. As explained by the Worldwatch Institute, "nuclear energy is two to three times as expensive as the least-cost alternatives, including a new generation of small natural gas-fired generators that can be installed inside a factory or even an office building: the 'PCs' [personal computers] of the electricity industry."[38]

---

* Although sites for long-term storage of nuclear waste have been selected in Nevada and New Mexico, they are opposed by citizens in both states as well as some environmentalists and the issue has yet to be resolved by the courts. There are also unresolved issues regarding the safe transport of highly radioactive nuclear waste.

It is possible that nuclear energy will make a comeback in the future. The next generation Integra Fast Reactor (IFR) promised not only to be far safer than the old reactors, but could recycle its fuels and the plutonium from dismantled nuclear weapons, which would reduce radioactive waste by 90 percent. The remaining waste is only radioactive for 200 years rather than thousands of years.[39] However, given the current availability and low cost of imported oil, and the efforts to reduce the federal debt, in 1994 Congress cut further funding for IFR development. This is not necessarily bad. If energy costs adequately reflected the long-term price of resource consumption and pollution, energy conservation would be stimulated to the point where there would be no need for nuclear energy in any form.

Although all these sources might supply sufficient energy in the long run, they may not be sufficiently developed to close the gap between supply and demand in the short run. The Electric Power Research Institute calculates that if the U.S. demand for electricity grows at 1.4 percent per year, the country will need 250,000 megawatts of new capacity by the year 2010. This is the equivalent of 250 large coal or nuclear plants. Since the average power plant was twenty-six years old in 1995—about their expected life—we seem to have a problem. It will take a huge investment in energy generation to close the gap. ***Hence, despite the decline in oil prices in recent years, the cost of energy will likely rise substantially during the early part of the twenty-first century. To encourage conservation and ease the transition, the prudent solution is to begin raising energy prices now, thus encouraging conservation.***

The situation is much more serious in many third world countries where the lack of indigenous sources of energy, particularly fossil fuels, results in heavy reliance on imported oil. Nonetheless, a study by Robert Williams of Princeton University and a worldwide team of researchers concluded that with the proper investment in energy technology and conservation, the entire world population could live with the quality of energy services enjoyed by west Europeans. They could not, however, live in the energy wasteful style of Americans with larger homes and an automobile centered transportation system.[40] Moreover, solving the energy shortage of the third world often presupposes the introduction of nuclear energy. But do we really want to spread nuclear technology to every country? There is a significant danger in spreading nuclear technology to unstable countries involved in continual internal and external warfare.

At one time there was optimism that oil shale, which has eight times as much energy as the energy in coal, might save the day. But the environmental costs of exploiting oil shale have turned out to be prohibitive.[41] One potentially viable answer to the energy problem for many nations in the short run is the use of renewables such as wood and agriculturally based alcohol fuels. Renewables and solar energy are making gains throughout the world. By the year 2000, it is estimated that the energy contribution of all sources of renewables will surpass that of oil.[42]

At present, 58 percent of all federal subsidies for energy promote the use of fossil fuel. Another 30 percent is targeted for nuclear power. Only 3 percent is dedicated to improving end-use efficiency and 2 percent for emerging renewable sources of energy.[43] As a result, it is not surprising that today only about 8 percent of U.S. energy is supplied from renewable sources even though it is estimated that by doubling or tripling the research and development for renewable energy these sources could meet 40 percent of U.S. energy demands by the year 2030.[44] The pittance spent on energy research—less than $200 million per year—is inexcusable given the potential social benefits that can accrue from cheap and renewable energy sources. Regrettably, there are no major suppliers of energy who might benefit from research in alternative energy technologies, hence, there is no flock of lobbyists pressing Congress for funding of research in this area.

Back in 1978, while working as a consultant to the Office of Management and Budget, I was shocked to learn that almost half the budget of the Department of Energy went to provide fission material for nuclear bombs. Even more appalling was the pittance being invested in research to develop new sources of energy. I argued in favor of increasing the Energy Department's budget for research on alternative energy sources by a factor of ten. Even with such an increase, efforts to find alternative energy sources would have been under one billion dollars. My proposal was never seriously considered. During the Reagan years, energy department research was reduced further and redirected to such economically wasteful projects as the antiballistic missile defense system—the so-called Star Wars defense. The result was that the United States became steadily more dependent on foreign oil and eventually had to wage the Gulf War in part to protect its oil interests in the Mideast. Ironically, that month-long war cost more than was spent during fifteen years on alternative energy research. The Bush administration proposed an energy plan that completely ignored both conservation and improved energy efficiency. After the Republicans took control of Congress in 1994, they immediately proposed shutting down the Energy Department and virtually halted all research on renewable energy sources. ***The United States could make a major effort to exploit the advantage of alternative sources of energy, while at the same reducing pollution and strengthening its national defense, by diverting a portion of the defense budget to research in alternative energy.***

1 (c) Nuclear energy

For decades now the federal government has been subsidizing nuclear energy. The $15 billion in subsidies to the nuclear power industry[45] would have yielded a far greater benefit if these funds had been expended on conservation. As a source of energy, nuclear fission has proven to be inefficient and costly. It takes a large amount of coal and oil energy to extract uranium, which results in only a few percentage points of net energy increase.[46] Then we have to factor in the high cost of safety precautions due to the extraordinary dangers posed by nuclear energy. Finally, we must factor in the feasibility and cost of waste disposal, which has yet to be determined since the problem continues to be put off in the hopes that some miraculous solution will arise. Even excluding the cost of waste disposal, the real cost of nuclear energy rose an average of 14 percent a year during the decade of the 1970s compared to 8 percent per year for coal-fired plants.[47] The steep rise in the costs of nuclear plants effectively precluded any additional plants from being built in the last twenty years. In the meantime, the vast majority of nuclear plants are coming to the end of their useful lives. Worldwide, seventy-nine nuclear generating plants with an average life of only seventeen years have already been retired. The cost of decommissioning a nuclear plant were underestimated. In 1988, England estimated the cost of decommissioning at 2.6 billion British pounds. By 1992 the estimates had climbed astronomically to 22 to 23 billion pounds.[48] Had these estimates been available at the beginning of the nuclear age, far fewer nuclear plants would have been built. The retiring of plants coupled with the unprofitability of building new plants resulted in nuclear power generation actually declining since 1990.[49]

There are still many who defend nuclear energy. They point out that despite its real dangers—so dramatically demonstrated by the Chernobyl accident—the record of nuclear energy in this country provides evidence that it is safer than coal. They refer to the 100 to 300 deaths per year due to coal mining accidents, and the thousands of deaths that may result from sulfur dioxide pollution, not to mention the potentially dire consequences of adding huge amounts of CO_2 to the atmosphere. I will admit that strides in nuclear research offer the potential of making nuclear power an environmentally safe and efficient source of energy. The problem remains, however, of how this technology can be provided to the nations of the world without simultaneously giving them the power to make nuclear weapons. At present there is enough plutonium in the world to make 87,000 nuclear weapons.[50]

I often hear it wistfully expressed that if only nuclear fusion were at last economically feasible, all of our energy problems would be over.

Nuclear fusion offers the hope for an inexhaustible, nonpolluting source of energy. Even if nuclear fission or fusion do become an economically attractive source of energy, and we somehow guarantee that it will not be misused for making nuclear weapons, it still does not mean that we can ignore conservation. There is another issue that is often overlooked in dreams of unlimited supplies of energy: the danger of thermal pollution.

1(d) The thermal pollution problem

The basic laws of thermodynamics tell us that in transforming matter into energy there is always heat generated as a by-product. Transforming energy into work releases more heat. The result is that even at the modest increase of 3 percent per year, in three hundred years the world would add as much thermal pollution (i.e., heat) into the earth's atmosphere as we presently get from the sun.[51] It is hoped that in the absence of a buildup of the CO_2 which traps the heat, much of the heat would escape from the earth's atmosphere into space. Even if the increasing trend in greenhouse gases were stopped, however, the current CO_2 levels would linger for perhaps hundreds of years. Therefore, the addition of heat from any source will likely exacerbate the global warming trends discussed later. The consequences of adding thermal pollution must be studied further to understand all the possible implications. But until the answers are known, the prudent course of action is to follow a policy of energy conservation.

1(e) The use of mass transit to conserve energy

Since World War II, the United States has allowed the best mass transit system in the world to fall into shambles. Our mass transit is now antiquated and lagging far behind those developed in Germany, France, and Japan who have long recognized the valuable savings in energy and reduced pollution that result from an efficient transit system. The dismantling of the mass transit system began after the war when General Motors joined with Standard Oil, Firestone, and others who would benefit from auto sales, to form a jointly owned subsidiary to purchase and dismantle privately-owned urban rapid-rail transit systems.[52] According to congressional testimony, General Motors, "acting through subsidiary mass transit companies, acquired forty-six streetcar systems in forty-five cites and converted all to smog-producing bus operations."[53] In the succeeding years, the oil industry and automobile manufacturers joined forces with the Teamsters Union to lobby for the construction of the interstate highway system, as well as billions of additional dollars for the state and local highways that must be torn up every few years and rebuilt.

It is common knowledge that mass transit is far more fuel efficient than personal autos. Buses and trains can get from 150 to 200 passenger miles per gallon.[54] But the lion's share of federal and state transportation expenditures go to paving over more of America's landscape every year even though we cannot adequately maintain the highways currently in existence. In addition to repairs, highways have to be salted and cleared in the winter. Railroads and subways do not. Furthermore, the accelerating highway costs will be greatly exacerbated by the growth in population due to the current trend in immigration. A 50 to 100 percent increase in the population will result in a major increase in highway expenditures.

Two new kinds of transportation offer significant advantages over both highway and air travel. High Speed Rail (HSR) still relies on steel wheels on steel rails, but can improve speeds to 150 to 200 miles per hour. Even more impressive is the High Speed Magnetic Levitation (MAGLEV) systems that lifts the train off the "track," providing an incredibly smooth ride at speeds of 250 to 300 miles per hour.[55] Moreover, MAGLEV vehicles use only one-fourth to one-half as much energy per passenger mile as jets and automobiles.[56] Until recently, the cost of rebuilding the rail infrastructure would make such a futuristic transportation system prohibitive. But scientists at Sandia National Laboratories have developed a new system called SERAPHIM (Segmented Rail Phased Induction Motor) that could be built for one-fourth the cost of magnetically levitated trains. Preassembled ladderlike trellises could be attached to existing tracks, permitting new, lightweight magnetic trains to initially speed along at 125 miles per hour. Tracks could then be incrementally upgraded to allow speeds of 200 to 300 mph.[57]

Both technologies offer superior transportation alternatives to planes and autos for distances from 100 to 600 miles. They can avoid the time lost in airports and deliver their passengers to the heart of the business districts in major cities. The advantages become less with continued urban sprawl, however. As businesses become dispersed over larger areas, the desire to go from central city to central city decreases.

Myopic federal policies have encouraged urban sprawl for more than two decades now. More will be said about this later, but in a nutshell the policy of reducing taxation at the federal level places more pressure on the inner cities to make up the lost federal subsidies by raising taxes, primarily property taxes. Increases in local taxes causes more people to flee to the suburbs to avoid the higher tax rates. At the same time, using federal and state tax dollars to fund highways and new sewer and water systems subsidizes the flight to the suburbs. This policy has been going on with increasing momentum since the late 1960s. Most recently, there has been some return to the cities by those empty nesters discouraged by the traffic jams caused by the almost complete absence of public transportation in most suburban areas. Unfortunately, the harm has already been done as some of our nation's richest farm lands are buried forever under suburban shopping malls and parking lots. Twenty years of regressive federal policies will be all but impossible to reverse.

Despite the success of Japan's bullet train which has transported two billion passengers since 1964 without a single fatality, and France's HSR system which has transported 3.5 billion passengers between Paris and Lyons without an accident, the expiration of the High Speed Ground Transportation Act in 1975 resulted in the United States stopping research into such systems.* The Disney corporation is considering building a small MAGLEV system in Orlando, Florida, but the United States appears to be content to watch as Japan takes the lead in yet another area of technology.[58]

America is more interested in getting a man to Mars than getting a person to work on time. Instead of space stations we should be building a twenty-first century transportation system. ***Unfortunately, the balanced budget proposals will cut funding of mass transit, AMTRAK, and high speed rail development, which will force the states to spend even more money on highways.***[59] Another opportunity lost. The present transportation policy, coupled with population growth of 100 to 200 million people by the year 2050, is destined to result in an increasing number of gridlocks even though our government continues to increase expenditures for new highways and maintaining our existing highways. The lost productivity and significantly higher energy costs resulting from a grossly inadequate public transportation system will ultimately be just one more factor which, if not rectified, will reduce the quality of life for future generations. This is not presently apparent because, in the short run, less government spending on infrastructure and lower taxes may stimulate GDP growth (that grossly inadequate measure of social welfare).

1(f) Lack of leadership in developing alternative sources of energy and conservation

With the price of oil dropping in real dollar terms, America has relaxed its efforts at conservation, with virtually no leadership in Washington to champion the issue at the present time. In 1978, $221 million was allocated for conservation research. The Carter administration recognized the value of attaining energy independence and did get some legislation passed

---

* The 1998 derailment of a German high speed inter-city express that resulted in almost 100 deaths has had a chilling effect on development of high speed rail transport in the United States even though on a per-mile-traveled basis rail transport is far safer than commuting by auto.

to that end, such as tax credits for insulation and the use of solar energy. They also increased conservation expenditures to $569 million by 1980, still only .001 percent of the total budget. With the advent of the Reagan administration, conservation became a dirty word. By 1987, the budget for energy conservation had declined 50 percent to $281 million. By 1994, energy conservation increased to $738 million, which, after adjusting for inflation, would still be a 29 percent decline from the 1980 level.[60]

The lack of a comprehensive energy policy is a national disgrace. It has resulted in Americans consuming 2.5 times as much fossil fuel per unit of output as Japan and 1.7 times more than most European countries.[61] Japan had no need to rush into the Gulf War because even though it is not nearly as rich as the United States in energy resources, its extremely efficient conservation efforts and stockpiling of oil during peace time makes it much less vulnerable to temporary interruptions of oil supplies.

Although doing a far better job in conservation than America, other Western nations are still spending insufficient amounts of research money on energy conservation. The nineteen countries that are members of the International Energy Agency spend only 6 percent of their energy research funds on conservation. Only Sweden saw fit to devote 34 percent of its energy research on conservation.[62] With proper incentives for conservation, the nations of the world could save as much oil as OPEC now exports.[63]

1(g) Summary of policy initiatives to conserve fossil fuel energy and stimulate alternative energy sources

To summarize, the following policy initiatives must be immediately undertaken to ensure sufficient supplies of affordable, relatively clean energy.

- *Increase gasoline taxes by at least $1.00 per gallon to reflect the hidden social costs of oil and to encourage conservation.* The additional burden on the working poor could be offset by a tax credit.
- *Use Highway Trust Fund moneys to subsidize mass transit systems.*[64] (This and the following two recommendations were suggested by Al Gore in his book, *Earth in Balance*.)*
- *Institute policies that will encourage telecommunication companies to install the fiber necessary to build the nation's information superhighways.* This will encourage telecommuting and cut down on automobile usage.

*In the interest of space I will not elaborate on them here. The reader can read the rationale behind these recommendations in Gore's book.

- *Expand research into solar or battery driven cars.* Although such autos may not be practical for long trips or high speeds, they may prove extremely useful as a second car for shopping, commuting to work, taking the kids to school, etc.
- *Expend a minimum of $2 billion a year for research on renewable energy including solar, geothermal, hydro, wind, biomass, and photovoltaics.** Japan has made a heavy investment in alternative energy sources such as solar. By 1995, almost 30 percent of all Japanese buildings had solar collectors.[65] New technologies should be shared with third world nations to reduce their reliance on oil and, in places such as the sub-Sahara, scarce wood.
- *Reestablish tax credits for energy conservation measures such as insulation.*
- *Institute energy-saving commercial building codes such as requiring triple pane glass—or their equivalent—in northern climates.* It's a shame that this very logical and relatively inexpensive goal was not instituted twenty years ago before the commercial building boom of the 1980s. The result was another lost opportunity due to the short-term thinking and emphasis on maximizing profits so prevalent in America. However, as the glut of office capacity is worked down and new construction undertaken, there is a new opportunity in the commercial area. There is also still an opportunity to make small gains on residential construction.

Before leaving the subject of energy, I wish to dispute one commonly held myth: the belief that energy growth is necessary for job creation. This contention assumes that employment will always be increasing. But it is not true if the population stabilizes, which, as we saw in the last chapter, is essential for a sustainable society.[66] Moreover, as society advances further into the information age, the shift to the less energy intensive service sectors will require less energy per job.

2. Shortages of Farmland and Water

Randers and Meadows estimate that there are eight billion acres on our planet suitable for agriculture, only about half of which are already under production. Unfortunately, the other half would require immense investments of capital to settle, clear, irrigate, and fertilize before they could pro-

---

*Geothermal utilizes the heat from the earth's interior, biomass utilizes plant materials and animal waste, and photovoltaic involves producing a voltage when two different substances, such as semiconductors, are exposed to radiant energy such as light.

duce food.[67] As the most fertile farmlands are lost and more marginal lands brought into production, food production becomes increasingly more energy intensive due to the heavy reliance on the use of fertilizer and irrigation. Hence, there is a second-order impact since more energy means higher costs and more pollution, not to mention the loss of invaluable ecosystems. Consequently, the United Nations Food and Agriculture Organization (FAO) has concluded that in order to expand food output, the world must rely on more intensive use of currently cultivated land rather than new land development. ***To look at it from another perspective, dividing the 8 billion acres by the 5.3 billion world population allows for 1.5 acres per person. Randers and Meadows estimate that, based upon present average worldwide yields, about one acre per person is needed to provide a minimally adequate diet; 2.25 acres* per person would be needed to feed the world's population at U.S. standards.***[68] This means that at present yields, even assuming that we could bring all the land suitable for agriculture under production, the earth might adequately feed about eight billion people. If the nations of the world decide to convert all the rainforests to cropland (as they appear to be doing), farm marginal lands, and restrict our diets to that of the less developed countries, we could probably support a doubling of the earth's population. But why we should choose to do so is beyond my comprehension.

What about increasing productivity? The cornucopians are quick to point out the tremendous increase in yields per acre brought about by the "green revolution." Randers and Meadows estimate that another *doubling* of productivity would buy about thirty years of time if the population continues to grow at 2.1 percent per year.[69] This assumes that the amount of total arable land remains constant. Actually, the net arable land is declining as the most productive land is frequently being taken out of production and more marginal land is being added. Hence, even with the more recent reduction in the world's population growth rate to 1.4 percent per year and a quadrupling of productive capacity, the cross-over point between arable land available and the land required would occur not much more than sixty years from now.

This estimate may be optimistic. Much of the improved agricultural productivity in the past has been due to increased use of fertilizers and pesticides. Both of those contributors have reached the point of diminishing returns. As the table below shows, the incremental grain produced by additional fertilizer has been declining for four decades worldwide. It now seems to be leveling out.

---

* Note that this is more than twice the acreage per person required in the United States to provide adequate nutritional needs. The reason is that U.S. cropland has far deeper and richer soil than most places in the world.

Incremental Tons of Grain / Incremental Ton of Fertilizer[70]

	World Grain Production	*Increment*	*World Fertilizer Use*	*Increment*	*Incremental Grain/Response Ratio*
1934–38	651		10		
1948–52	710	59	14	4	14.8
1959–61	848	138	26	12	11.5
1969–71	1165	318	64	38	8.3
1978–80	1451	286	106	42	6.8
1988–90	1661	210	143	37	5.7
1994–96	1768	107	124	–19	–5.6

Fertilizer use in the United States peaked out in the late 1970s and world fertilizer use peaked in 1990.[71] A decline in the former Soviet Union's use of fertilizers is largely responsible for the worldwide drop in fertilizer use and the slow growth in grain production since 1990. However, China has already peaked out and even when the countries of the old Soviet Union increase their use of fertilizers it should only push off the eventual saturation point by a decade or so. We Americans may have already hit the optimal yields per acre, since yields have been relatively constant for the past decade.

Pesticides are following a similar trend. The United States now produces pesticides at a rate 1,300 times faster than we did when Rachel Carson wrote *Silent Spring* in 1962 warning of their danger. During the decade of the 1980s farmers increased their use of insecticides tenfold, yet the annual crop losses to insects doubled.[72] The reason is the extremely effective ability of crop pests to develop resistance to any pesticide. The losing battle is causing some farmers to revert to organic methods* of controlling pests. At any rate, fertilizer and pesticides will not be major contributors to increased productivity in the future for any nation except, perhaps, Africa. Genetic engineering of disease resistant and higher-yielding crops holds much promise. But remember, this promise has to be realized to make further productivity gains, and even with a quadrupling of productivity we still will come up short in food production by the middle of the twenty-first century.

Again, the foregoing may be an optimistic view. Brown estimates that cropland for cereal grains has been declining on a per capita basis and will continue to decline from .24 acres per person in 1950 to .13 acres in 2000, even assuming a 10 percent increase in total cropland between 1980 and the

---

*Organic farming produces food with the use of feed or fertilizer of plant or animal origin without employment of chemically formulated fertilizers, growth stimulants, antibiotics, or pesticides.

year 2000.[73] ***Already, although total grain production is still increasing, grain production per capita in 1996 was 8.6 percent below its 1984 peak.***[74] Again a major reason for this decline is the chaos in the old Soviet Union, but let's look at what is happening to the world's arable land. Between one-fifth and one-third of the world's cropland is losing topsoil at a rate that is undermining long-term productivity.[75] Twenty-five billion tons are disappearing every year. ***The loss of topsoil is occurring at a rate 18 times faster than nature can replace it.***[76] According to a United Nations survey of soil conditions around the world, 22 million acres can no longer support vegetation; 740 million acres require more restoration than developing nations can organize; and 2.3 *billion* acres—the size of the United States—require major reclamation efforts.[77] The causes of this catastrophe are livestock overgrazing, deforestation, and harmful agricultural practices such as overfertilization and ignoring fallow periods.*

The problem is not limited to the LDCs. ***In the United States, 34 percent of cropland is subject to serious erosion.***[78] The primary reason for this continued loss is that farmers know that the short-term cost of reducing soil erosion is three times the long-term economic benefits of doing so.[79] Consequently, farmers fail to rotate crops through pasture and hay, choosing instead to continuously grow corn and other row crops even though rotation would result in only 2.7 tons of topsoil loss per acre per year compared to the 19.7 tons lost for continuously growing corn.[80] Some fine tuning of conservation programs is warranted; in some areas the government is spending $3,000 an acre to improve land that is worth only $500 to $600 an acre.[81] More of the national budget needs to be devoted to soil and water conservation programs. Instead, the efforts to balance the budget have resulted in cuts in those areas. Such injudicious budget reductions may cost Americans lost future crop yields many times the short-term savings.

The loss of topsoil is exacerbated by urban sprawl as cities throughout the world are spreading into some of the most fertile and productive land. As Garret Hardin so dourly expresses it, "Asphalt is the land's last crop."[82] Worldwide, the growth in urban areas will consume land equal to the size of the cultivated areas of France in less than twenty years or 2 percent of the world's cropland.[83] Two percent may not seem like much, but it would provide food for 84 million people.[84]

In our own country, the situation is also critical. According to the Department of Agriculture, urban sprawl is consuming about two million acres of farmland a year.[85] As long ago as 1975, we had covered with blacktop or concrete an area the size of Ohio and Pennsylvania.[86] Given present trends, all the prime cropland in Florida will soon be put to other

*Leaving land unseeded during a growing season.

use. In Virginia, 24 percent of prime cropland will be lost.[87] Fifty percent of the best acreage in California will be destroyed by 2020 if present trends are continued. In Illinois, although the Chicago area population increased only 4 percent during the last twenty years, it spread out over a 40 percent larger land area—removing from production some of the richest farmland in the world. In the short span of time between 1985 and 1996, the United States lost or retired 26 million acres of farmland.[88]

Federal budget reduction efforts threaten the successful Conservation Reserve Program, which rewards farmers for improving the long-term productivity of their land by allowing a certain proportion to lay unplanted each year. In 1995, a total of 375,000 farmers in forty-seven states had 36.4 million acres in the program. As a result of the program, it is estimated that top soil erosion has been reduced by 700 million tons. The conservation program has also increased grassland protection and planted two million acres of trees.[89] Despite these significant benefits, the conservation program is continually being threatened with cuts, or eliminated altogether, by short-sighted politicians.

The destruction of wetlands is yet another cause of farmland loss through erosion. Erosion through poor wetland and soil conservation management has been occurring for decades. For instance, Iowa used to have sixteen inches of the best topsoil in the world, now its down to eight inches; most of the rest of it is somewhere in the Gulf of Mexico.[90]

2(a) Depletion of water tables pose threats to agriculture and world stability

In our country, there is a very real possibility of another dust bowl in the High Plains states. The dust bowl of the 1930s was caused by the increase in demand for grain during the First World War. To supply sufficient food for the troops, not only of our nation but France and Russia as well, the price of grain soared. Farmers responded to the inflated prices by intensively cultivating every acre of their land. When the periodic droughts hit the overworked and plowed-up land there was insufficient ground cover to hold the soil in place. Since the Thirties, many farmers supplement rainfall by irrigation from wells dug to tap into the underground water supply known as the Ogallala Aquifer. The world's largest underground lake—larger than any of the Great Lakes—provides water to portions of South Dakota, Nebraska, Kansas, Colorado, Oklahoma, New Mexico, and the Texas panhandle. This is the area that supports much of our nation's supply of wheat and beef. Tragically, this vital supply of fresh water is slowly being drained. ***Whereas wells fifty feet deep were sufficient to obtain water 40 years ago, today the wells must be 150 feet deep. The portion of the aquifer***

underlying 2.5 million acres in Kansas, Texas, and New Mexico is half depleted.[91] A USDA study of thirty-two counties in Texas estimates that any significant increase in fuel prices coupled with the continued water table depletion will more than offset the economics of irrigation.[92] At present rates of depletion, this invaluable natural resource, which took millions of years to create, will be dried up in 150 years or less.[93]

Some imaginative people have suggested that after depleting the Ogallala Aquifer, we can divert water from the Great Lakes to irrigate the plains states. In 1970, the Aral Sea was the world's fourth largest inland sea, comparable to Lake Superior. Because of a Soviet scheme to grow cotton in the desert, it now has shrunk by two-thirds, leaving ships that fished its depths stranded in what is now a growing desert.[94] By continuously trying to "fix" nature rather than adapt to it, we too can turn our Great Lakes into a desert.

It is not only America that is exhausting its underground water supplies. The aquifer under Mexico city is dropping eleven feet per year and the Beijing water table is dropping over six feet each year. Over 25 percent of Russian surface waters are seriously polluted.[95] Throughout the world, 1.2 billion people lack access to clean drinking water. Dirty water causes 80 percent of the disease in the developing world.[96] Over 2.2 billion people live without a sewage system, primarily because they do not have the water supply necessary for such a system. The situation can only get worse as the world's population increases. Despite the drop in water tables in many countries, irrigation throughout the world has resulted in adding more net farmland than what was lost through desertification. However, there is a danger of waterlogging and salination in areas with inadequate drainage. Estimates are that 10 percent of the world's irrigated land is waterlogged, reducing its productivity by 20 percent.[97] Equally serious, where as a result of irrigation the water table is too near the surface, evaporation through the thin topsoil results in the accumulation of alkali salt and minerals near the surface, reducing productivity or destroying the land completely. Such salination is reducing the productivity of soil in Israel, Egypt, Syria, Afghanistan, Turkey, Iraq, China, and Mexico.[98]

The lack of water is becoming yet another source of friction between nations. In 1967, when Jordan tried to dam the Yarmuk River reducing Israel's water supply, Israel destroyed the dam. A few years later, Israel diverted the flow of the Jordan to Lake Genezaret. The result was that 100,000 Israeli settlers have access to 26 billion gallons of water while one million Arabs have to make due with 36 billion gallons. According to water expert Joyce Starr, water may soon be more expensive than oil to the people of the Middle East.[99] Such international friction will not be limited to the Middle East. Of the 200 largest river systems in the world, 120 flow through two or more countries.[100]

In the United States, a similar situation is shaping up in the Southwest, which possesses only 6 percent of the nation's fresh water, but its growing population is using 36 percent of the nation's water supply. The result has been the "rerouting of rivers, wholesale destruction of wetlands, increased salinity in deltas and estuaries, degradation of ecosystems, and extermination of fisheries."[101] The situation cannot continue indefinitely. Las Vegas is presently the fastest growing city in the nation, yet it is scheduled to use the last of its water rights in twenty years.[102] They will then engage in a desperate battle to divert water from other areas and uses. While growing population is mainly the problem, much of the destruction is due to poor planning and plain wastefulness.[103] By 2025 as many as fifty-two nations with 3.5 billion people may experience chronic water shortages.[104]

Still another undesirable effect of present irrigation practices is the frequent diversion of water from wetlands, which are essential to wildlife. The United States has lost 50 percent of its wetlands in the lower forty-eight states since Colonial times.[105] Illinois has lost 85 percent of its wetlands, Missouri 87 percent, and Iowa 90 percent.[106] It is one reason that flooding along the Mississippi was so severe in 1993 and 1995. More importantly, the loss of wetlands constitutes a grave threat to wildlife. Wetlands provide the habitat for 40 percent of all U.S. endangered species and a majority of the nation's fisheries. For example, in Nevada the Stillwater wetlands once provided shelter for a quarter million migrating shorebirds each year. Diverting water for irrigation projects has reduced the Stillwater wetlands by three quarters. A few more severe droughts and the Stillwater will be completely dried up. If it does it will follow the plight of the Winnemucca Lake Wildlife Refuge, which dried up fifty years ago, never to return.[107]

Action must be taken to save America's dwindling wetlands. One-third of the Florida Everglades wetlands have been drained for agriculture. The diversion of the fresh water for agriculture and population growth has resulted in the devastation of one the richest biological communities in America as the waters became too salty for the aquatic life.[108] Now efforts are underway to spend $500 million to increase water flows by 20 percent[109]—an expensive solution to a problem that could have been adverted.

Rather than stemming the loss of freshwater and wetlands, in 1996 Congress came precariously close to making things worse. Although the 1972 Clean Water Act was well on the way to achieving its goals, the House decided to gut the act.[110] If the Senate had not killed the bill, it would have further reduced our wetlands, especially those that are wet only a part of the year or under one acre in size. While this sounds insignificant, a large proportion of water fowl and many other animals breed in these small, temporary wetlands. Under the proposed law these areas could be drained and developed. The "takings" provision of the new law (euphemistically entitled the Job Creation and Enhancement Act) would have forced the government to compensate property owners whenever a federal regulation threatens a 10 percent reduction in property values. It is theoretically right that we compensate individual land owners who incur the negative impact of regulations that benefit society as a whole. As a practical matter, however, it would have resulted in a deluge of legislation and significantly reduced the government's ability to regulate land use, such as the development of residential communities on wetlands. Again it was the Senate that killed this ill-conceived bill.

There is some good news regarding wetlands. The U.S. Fish and Wildlife Service estimates that the loss of wetlands between 1985 to 1995 was one million acres compared to three million acres lost between 1975 and 1985.[111] Even so, having already lost one-half of the wetlands in the United States, further losses should be prohibited.

Finally, in addition to depleting sources of water, we continue to pollute our lakes and rivers, primarily through urban and farmland runoff. Although there has been dramatic improvement in some lakes and rivers, according to EPA surveys conducted in 1992 and 1993, 40 percent of United States lakes, rivers, and estuaries are not clean enough for swimming or fishing (let alone drinking).[112]

2(b) Growth in per capita food production may have peaked

Despite the increased yields per acre, food production has barely kept pace with the world's growing population growth. It is not just a matter of local food shortages due to civil wars, droughts, or problems of food distribution, as the opponents of population control would have us believe. On a worldwide basis, per capita consumption of beef peaked out in 1977, mutton peaked way back in 1961.[113] Pork and poultry have increased, but the total meat consumption per capita has remained relatively constant since 1988. Since meat consumption per capita was relatively low in many parts of the world to begin with, it cannot be relied upon as the major source of protein in the future.

Fish consumption per capita increased slightly between 1970 and 1988, but the United Nations Food and Agricultural Organization (FAO) estimates that the 1989 fish catch was the maximum yield that can be sustained by ocean fisheries. Since 1988, fish consumption per person first dropped and then rose again to the 1988 level by 1994.[114] The total fish catch has remained relatively constant at 85 to 90 million tons, with all the growth in fish supplies coming from aquaculture. According to the FAO, only 31 percent of the world's fishing grounds are able to support the current levels of fishing.[115] Data from the FAO shows that the catch in all but two of the fifteen major fishing areas have fallen; in four areas the catch has shrunk by over 30 percent.[116] The size of the world's fishing fleet has doubled since 1970 and is now twice the size needed to bring in the maximum sustainable catch. Moreover, high technology fishing trawlers are able to catch whole schools of fish, thus eliminating the possibility of reproduction. In addition to the desirable eating fish, the huge nets gather up millions of other fish that are simply discarded. Such fish are an integral part of the ocean food chain and cannot be destroyed without threatening the entire chain. Twenty-seven million pounds of fish are discarded annually. Detailed analysis by the Center for Living Aquatic Resources indicates that such wholesale harvesting of the oceans fisheries is not sustainable.[117] Consequently, ***all fishing grounds in the Atlantic and Pacific Oceans and the Mediterranean and Black seas are in decline. Only the Indian Ocean's fish reserve is increasing, but probably not for long.***[118]

In addition to overfishing, fish supplies are threatened by oil spills as well as chemicals and pesticides washed into the sea by farming and industry. The results are predictable and potentially catastrophic. There is now a worldwide epidemic of algae, and formerly nontoxic algae are turning toxic. According to Theodore Smayda, Professor of Oceanography at the University of Rhode Island, this has become a major planetary trend.[119]

The declining supplies of fish per capita are particularly troubling because of the reliance on fish both as a food supply and a major economic component of many countries.[120] Skirmishes between countries are already occurring as they seek to protect their fish supplies from foreign vessels.

Increasingly, growth of the world fish supplies will come to depend on aquaculture (fish farms). The growth of fish stocks due to aquaculture in recent years has been impressive. The commercial production of salmon in 1997 was so extensive that it threatened the economic viability of the salmon fishing fleets.[121] Extensive aquaculture presents a host of new environmental problems, however. In addition to the demands for water resources, they have often resulted in destruction of wetland ecosystems. For example, clearing of mangrove swamps has destroyed the breeding grounds for countless terrestrial and aquatic fauna.[122]

The U.S. fish catch peaked at 400 million pounds in 1983 and has declined ever since to 282 million pounds by 1990.[123] In 1994, the Commerce Department was forced to prohibit fishing in 17 percent of the total fishing area off the coast of New England (the Georges Banks) due to depletion of cod, haddock, and yellow fin tuna.[124] Pollution is also a problem. The Chesapeake Bay oyster production has declined 90 percent since only 1987.[125] Fertilizer run off and a thousand other kinds of pollutants are constantly entering the watershed flowing into the Chesapeake.

Environmentalists have watched in dismay as one of the world's most productive fishing areas is turning into an open sewer.

Overfishing is a clear example of the phenomena called by ecologist Garrett Hardin the *tragedy of the commons*, the overuse of resources held as public trust. Hardin provides the following example.

Under English law in the Middle Ages, the pasture land around a village was public property. It was held in common to allow all people to graze their cows. This seemed an equitable arrangement, but it was doomed to disaster. It was only a matter of time when someone realized that if he were to increase the number of cows he grazed, the profit would all be his while the cost of feeding the extra cows would be borne by the entire community. As each person came to this conclusion, the number of additional cows added to the pasture land would eventually overwhelm and destroy the grazing land to the ruin of the entire village.

Actually, the disaster of overgrazing was averted because the English recognized the problem in time and passed laws regulating the type and number of beasts that could be grazed on common land; the process was known as "stinting."[126] Eventually, the English converted to a system of private property, whereby a man who allows his livestock to overgraze on his own land would soon realize that the cost exceeded the benefit.

Despite a philosophy that is respectful of nature, a similar fate befell Navajo sheep raisers. In the absence of private property, they overgrazed and destroyed a large portion of their range land. In the early 1920s, the father of conservation, Aldo Leopold, recognized the same situation was developing throughout the Southwestern areas of this country where there was common grazing. His concern for the destruction of the environment led him to write his now famous treatise, "The Land Ethic," in *Sand County Almanac*.[127] Although he recognized the destruction and argued that the land must be treated as if it has rights, Leopold did not link the problem to the potential conflict between self-interest and public interest. As Hardin explains, ***a disaster such as the tragedy of the commons will always occur when costs can be spread over the entire public while benefits accrue to the individual.***

2(c) Grasslands are also threatened by tragedy of the commons

The tragedy of the commons threatens the destruction of the America's grasslands, as well as its fisheries and forests. The Bureau of Land Management (BLM) manages 163 million acres of grasslands. More than 25 percent are judged to be in poor condition due to overgrazing, and another 50 percent are in only fair condition. Since the public at large (especially future generations) absorbs the cost of overgrazing while the individual rancher enjoys the benefits (at least in the short run), each rancher attempts to maximize his profits by allowing additional cattle to graze. The BLM attempts to control overgrazing, but has an up-hill battle against the powerful ranchers who graze their cattle on public lands and can bring political pressure to bear against BLM district managers who attempt to enforce the controls.

It is often suggested that the solution to the problem of overuse of the "commons" is to privatize all the public lands. One argument for privatization is that it would stop the supposed government subsidizing of grazing. It is pointed out that the government charges only $1.86 per month per animal unit whereas the owners of private grasslands charge $10 per month.[128] However, what such comparisons ignore is that the rancher using public lands must also buy a grazing permit for $1,000 per animal, which, if financed over thirty years comes to about $7.32 per month. Added to the monthly fee of $1.86 the total cost is $9.56, an amount comparable to the private land owners' fee. This is no mere coincidence; the private owners fee is set to be competitive with the government fee. It does not mean that the government fee is set at the right price, however. If the net effect is the destruction of federal grazing lands, the price is still too low. ***The "right" price is one which would maintain the grasslands in perpetuity. Any lower price is asking future generations to subsidize the existing generation.*** At a higher price the cost of beef would be driven up and the demand would fall until it reaches a level sustainable without further degradation of the grasslands.

What if private grazing lands could undercut the federal price and thereby gain a larger share of the grazing stock? This would not be a problem unless they allowed their own grasslands to deteriorate in the process. It is argued that this would not happen because the desire to derive future profits would prevent the owner of private lands from allowing their destruction. ***But the key to the success of an individual in a market economy is the time frame of the consequences.*** When negative impacts appear to be a long way in the future, people will lack the proper incentive to protect the interests of future generations. Therefore, to successfully protect the interests of future generations, the rules of the game must result in the consequences of a person's actions being felt in the short term—one hopes within a few years.

This is particularly essential for corporations that are driven by shareowners to maximize short-term profits rather than be concerned about the legacy they are leaving to the next generation. Go down to the bayou swamps around New Orleans and you will see huge areas of swamp grass that were once cypress forests. Although they were privately owned by lumber companies, it did not stop the companies from clear-cutting every last tree before moving on. Similarly, the Outer Banks of North Carolina were denuded to provide lumber for ship builders. Today, owners of ancient forests are content with clear-cutting century old redwoods and reinvesting in fast growing pines. In short, ***a market economy will not work to the advantage of the environment unless long-term costs are added to the costs of production.***

Returning to the issue of protecting grasslands, it should also be noted that beef is an extremely inefficient source of protein. It takes seven pounds of grain, or its equivalent, to add one pound of weight to a steer. On the other hand, only two pounds of grain are necessary to add one pound of weight to a chicken.[129] Therefore, it is good environmental policy to promote the consumption of chicken rather than beef. Increasing the grazing fees from $1.86 per month to $4.28, as Interior Secretary Bruce Babbitt proposed, would drive up the price of beef, and the subsequent fall in demand would reduce overgrazing and the degradation of public grasslands. Regrettably, an outcry from Western states legislators stymied the proposed increase.

The use of water from the Ogallala aquifer also will suffer from the tragedy of the commons unless each farmer and rancher is charged a water use fee significant enough to encourage conservation. If the water level drops, the charge must go up accordingly. Again, special interests groups will oppose such fees. It will be argued by some that, ultimately, market prices would reflect the higher cost of scarce water as the aquifer dries up. This is inviting catastrophe, since the depletion of the aquifer is reversible only in a geologic time frame. Recall the economic fallacy discussed in chapter 2: because a benefit in the future is worth less to today's generation than a benefit received today, the economic process of discounting future returns will always bias decisions against future generations. Market prices are least efficient where the time horizon is long or the effects uncertain. The market price for anchovies did not increase significantly until there was a complete collapse of the anchovy fish catch from 12 million tons to only two million tons in a one-year time frame. Then it was too late. Whether it was the American buffalo or ancient Redwood forests, a market economy sometimes requires government intervention to ensure that long-term costs are included.

3. Loss of Forests and Species Diversity

The figures on food production and available farmland would look much worse were it not for the efforts in many parts of the world—particularly Central and South America, but also Indonesia, India, and Africa—to add farmlands by destroying rainforests. To put it in perspective, E. O. Wilson explains that the world's surviving rainforests occupy an area about the size of the contiguous forty-eight U.S. states. During the 1980s these forests were being used up by an amount equivalent to the size of Florida each year.[130] The latest estimates are slightly less and indicate the world is now only losing an area the size of Ireland annually (27,000 square miles).[131] Brazil, Indonesia, and Zaire account for half of the world's rainforests. All three countries are systematically destroying their forests. Forests are also being stripped throughout Southeast Asia, Central America, Mexico, Central Africa, and the United States.

America must share responsibility for the systematic destruction of the world's forests. In 1991, a blue ribbon scientific panel of Congress found that the maximum sustainable harvest for National Forests in the Pacific Northwest would be 1.7 billion board feet of wood. The 1990 cut was 4.1 billion board feet, more than twice the sustainable level.[132] Conservative organizations such as the Heartland Institute argue that U.S. forests are not actually shrinking. They contend that there are more acres of forests in the United States than anytime since the 1950s. What they fail to acknowledge is that many of these so-called forests have been clear-cut and have no trees, but they are still called forests unless converted to other uses. In Maine alone, nearly 2,000 square miles—as much land as all of Delaware—were clear-cut between 1980 and 1992.[133] Moreover, millions of additional acres have been replanted with a single species of tree. The result is not a forest, but a tree farm incapable of supporting the diversity of animal and plant species housed by a forest.[134]

Most people are aware of the problem of deforestation but do not appreciate its magnitude or significance. They are unaware that forests reduce the greenhouse effect, prevent floods and erosion, maintain fisheries, and keep pests in check. They don't appreciate that the rich species diversity housed in the world's forests provide the ingredients for 40 percent of our prescription drugs, and may yet provide numerous new cures for many diseases and ailments of humankind. They do not realize that today only one-third of the world's ecosystems are still intact and that many species cannot survive a partially destroyed ecosystem even if small islands of trees are left standing. They fail to grasp that only 10 percent of our planet's land area contains more than one-half the species of animals and plants, and this is the area being clear cut or burned down today.[135]

Scientists have identified 1.5 million animal and plant species so far but they estimate that there may be as many as 30 million species in the tropical rainforests. ***At the present rate, our children will witness the complete and total destruction of the world's rainforests during the next sixty years.***[136] Loss of the rainforests means loss of animals and plants—up to 27,000 species are lost each year according to E. O. Wilson.[137] Wilson estimates that if the present trend continues, it could result in the loss of 50 percent of the world's species by the end of the next century.[138]

The crucial value of species diversity is not well understood. It is not just a matter of esthetics or to provide a livelihood for those involved in cataloging the myriad of species. There is a very practical value that diversity offers humankind. There is a great deal of hope and hype surrounding genetic engineering. But it must be understood that genetic engineering does not mean that scientists can create a new gene. They only recombine genes found in nature; that is why the supply of different genes is so crucial to their work. A couple of examples may help illustrate the vital importance of genetic diversity.

Most varieties of coffee beans grown in the Western Hemisphere are descended from a single Javan species sent to the island of Martinique in 1721. In 1970, the entire supply of coffee plants in Brazil, Central America, and Mexico was threatened by coffee rust disease. After frantically searching throughout the world for a strain of coffee plant resistant to the rust, researchers located a coffee in the forests of Ethiopia that was resistant to twenty-seven of the thirty-three varieties of coffee rust. If the rust problem had occurred twenty years later, the rust resistant species might have vanished with the destruction of the Ethiopian forests.[139] Similarly, the American barley crop was saved when only one of 6,500 varieties of barley was discovered to be resistant to the yellow dwarf virus. Coincidentally, this barley variety was also found in Ethiopia.[140] The crucial need to preserve genetic species to guard against future threats is why scientists are so concerned about protecting all the species they can. Of all the varieties of vegetables listed by the USDA in 1900, no more than 3 percent now remain. The agricultural monoculture practiced in most Western countries poses great risks in the face of new disease and pests.

Medicine is also crucially dependent on species diversity. More than 40 percent of all medicinals dispensed by pharmacies in the United States. contain substances originally extracted from animals, plants, ferns, and microorganisms. Yet fewer than 1 percent of all species have been examined for natural products that might serve as medicine.[141] Not long ago the anticoagulant drug hirudin, used in skin transplants and for treatment of rheumatism, thrombosis, and contusions, was derived from the saliva of a forest leech.[142] In 1997 it was discovered that by modifying the toxin produced by a rare variety of poisonous tree frog a new nonaddictive pain killer was created that is as effective as morphine. Not only the rainforests offer such a treasure of possibilities. The drug taxol, derived from the rare Pacific tree known as the yew, has been discovered to be an effective treatment for certain kinds of cancer. Unfortunately, over 90 percent of the slow growing yews have been destroyed by timber companies who regarded the trees as trash and burned them.

Efforts are now underway to investigate remedies used by aborigines in the Amazon and elsewhere. Scientists are discovering a fertile source of effective drugs that has been overlooked by arrogant developed nations that could not believe there might be anything we could learn from primitive peoples. However, despite the inestimable potential benefits derived from the diverse species sustained by the world's forests, the systematic destruction of forests continues unabated.

In 1991, the world consumption of wood was 3.4 billion cubic feet, 2.5 times the amount consumed in 1950. This increase reflects not only the growing population but also an increase of 33 percent more wood consumed per capita.[143] The two primary reasons for the loss of forests are the need for fuel and the need for farmland. Forty percent of the world uses wood for fuel.[144] As the number of wood users increases, the amount of forests shrinks proportionately. At the turn of this century 40 percent of Ethiopia was covered by forests. Today, less than 4 percent of its forests remain.[145] With the loss of forests, erosion is quickly wiping out the shallow topsoil that was laid bare. The result will be a wasteland. Not long ago Nigeria was a major exporter of tropical hardwoods. By 1985, it earned only $6 million on exports while spending $160 million on forest product imports. In 1947, Panama was 70 percent forested; by 1991, the portion of forest declined to 30 percent. By the year 2000, only 15 percent will remain forested.[146] In Central America, two-thirds of the forests have been cut down since the time of Columbus, over 60 percent of this decline occurred during the past sixty years.[147] The trends are depressingly similar worldwide. Erosion in the Philippines due to deforestation has resulted in flash floods that killed over 2,000 people in 1991.[148] In 1954, Russia had a scheme to turn vast tracks of virgin forests and grasslands in Siberia and Central Asia into farmland. The result of this ill-conceived experiment was to produce the biggest dust storms in history by 1960.[149] Even as remote an area as the Himalayas is being deforested as 70,000 trekkers a year cut trees for camps and fire wood, trashing what until quite recently was one of the most pristine spots in the world. Worldwide, in the late 1980s, only one acre of trees was being planted for every ten acres of forest cleared.[150] At this rate there will be a net loss of timberland equal to thirty Californias every decade.

Two other major uses of wood are home construction and paper, especially paper used in packaging. The United States is particularly guilty of overconsumption in both of these areas. ***The average size of a new house in the United States has grown 83 percent since 1949; the average home is 50 percent larger than the average European home and 100 percent larger than the average Japanese home.***[151] Contrary to expectations, office automation—especially the copy machine—has served to significantly increase the use of paper. The so-called paperless office has never been realized.

It is difficult for Americans to criticize the destructive practices of other nations when we have already destroyed almost 95 percent of the virgin woodland in the lower forty-eight states, and loggers are daily attacking the last ancient forests. But the consequences of deforestation are much worse in a rainforest than in the northern forests. The rainforest did not have the churning action of the glaciers to leave a thick, rich carpet of soil and nutrients. Only 5 percent of the nutrients of a rainforest are found in the forest floor; 95 percent are in the forest itself. Contrast this to American prairies where 95 percent of the nutrients are in the soil and only 5 percent in forest.[152] As a result, when the rainforests are destroyed to add agricultural land, the benefits are short lived. The thin soil provides low yields and is soon exhausted. The farmers then seek to move on, destroying still more rainforests. In trying to feed their growing populations by cutting down their forests, the equatorial countries are playing a game that they have no chance of winning.

In Brazil and elsewhere, even if the clear-cutting to gain more farmland is slowed, the danger is that it will result in a patchwork of thousands of fragments, none of which will be sufficiently large enough to adequately maintain many animal species. ***Ecologists are just beginning to understand that very large tracts are necessary to provide an adequate gene pool to support certain species. In the United States, the fourteen Western National Parks are too small to save all the animals that once inhabited them.***[153] Bryce Canyon has already lost one-third of its mammal species. Even though Yosemite National Park is over 2,000 square kilometers, it lost one-fourth of its mammals even before the disastrous fires of 1988. The only national park region in North America that shows no loss of wildlife is the Kootenay-Banff-Jasper-Yoho area which, at 21,000 square kilometers, is the size of New Jersey.[154]

Biologist Thomas Lovejoy has persuaded the Brazilian government to put aside parcels of land from 2.5 acres to 250 acres to study the impact of the size of a preserve on species diversity. Ultimately, Lovejoy hopes to obtain thirty preserves up to 25,000 acres in size, but he is running a race against time. In only sixty years, the Amazon rain forest and its incredible diversity may simply be a memory. The tragedy would be one of epic proportions. Trees can be replanted. South Korea undertook massive reforestation that reduced soil erosion within a decade.[155] China increased its forested area from 5 percent to 12.7 percent of the country between 1949 and 1978. Species extinction is forever, however. And it is the diversity of species, both animals and plant, that make a forest.

In the United States, just at the time the Endangered Species Act was having a major impact in protecting many species of animals, it was in danger of being significantly curtailed. Nearly 40 percent of the species protected by the act are now stable or recovering, including bald eagles, alligators, whooping cranes, and the cutthroat trout.[156] Still, many other species continue to decline rapidly. For instance, there has been a 50 percent decline in migrating songbirds during the last twenty years due to the fragmentation and destruction of forests throughout both North and South America.[157] If present trends continue, many of the world's most beautiful and unique animals will only be a memory or, at best, found in zoos. These include the tiger, hippopotamus, Black Rhino, Giant Panda, Red Panda, Asiatic Black Bear, Saiga Antelope, Red and Blue Lory Parrots, the Atlantic Blue Fin Tuna, etc.[158] The list is depressingly long.

Aside from all the practical reasons for saving the rainforests and preserving ancient forests elsewhere in the world, there is the unparalleled esthetic enjoyment that comes from walking through a real forest. A person need not go to remote regions of the world to view exotic animals to feel the exhilaration of nature. One of the great moments of my life was hiking through a redwood forest in Northern California. Walking among gigantic trees thousands of years old I experienced a sense of timelessness, peace, beauty, oneness with nature, and a general happiness that no paltry work of human artifice has ever provided me. The English nineteenth century philosopher John Stuart Mill best summed up the feelings of any person who has had the privilege of such an experience:

> Solitude, in the sense of being alone, is essential to any depth of meditation or character; and solitude in the presence of natural beauty and grandeur, is the cradle of thoughts and aspirations which are not only good for the individual, but which society could ill do without.[159]

3(a) Saving the Forests

As mentioned, some economists have suggested that in the long term conservation can only be achieved by privatization of public lands. The solution offered by libertarians and many free-market advocates is to sell all federal lands to private interests. This would be a tragic mistake. Although privatization can be an effective solution when long-term interests are not outweighed by short-term concerns, it will not be effective when the reverse situation holds. The past destruction of huge tracts of forests by timber companies who cut and ran without any effort to replant, or replanted only one species of trees, provides ample evidence of this fact.

To prevent the continued denuding of America's timberlands, Congress passed bills in 1897 and 1911 that forbade further sales of public timberlands. Subsequently, the U.S. Forest Service (USFS) was created to manage 168 million acres of timberland. To the disappointment of conservationists, the USFS has been less than effective in carrying out its charge. The primary reason is a failure to adequately charge for the sale of timber. ***Four out of five sales lose money.***[160] The reason is that when the forest service sells the right to cut down timber, it does not use the receipts to cover its cost. Rather, it charges its expenses to the taxpayer. Hence, if it costs the Forest Service $100 to manage the cutting of trees and it makes only $2 from the sale of timber, the Forest Service gets $102. It takes $100 from the taxpayer and only collects $2 from the timber company. It should, of course, collect the entire $102 from the timber company as a private owner would.

Simply privatizing national forests would do little to protect invaluable areas such as the redwood or hardwood forests. Given the hundreds of years necessary to grow redwoods, the most economical action of an entrepreneur would be to gradually sell off most of the forest, albeit at progressively higher prices. He probably could collect much more money from rich men who wish to line their family rooms in redwood than from poor people who could afford only a limited camping fee. The short-term *market solution* to the problem is to force the Forest Service to show a profit by at least covering their costs in timber sales. In contrast, the long-term *ecological solution* may be to restrict all sales in certain areas—in effect to greatly expand the national park system. At times the two solutions may be compatible. A Wilderness Society study found that tourism and recreation in the southern Appalachian Mountains contributed $379 million annually, as compared to $32 million from logging.[161]

Turning to the international problem, with only 10 percent of the tropical forests being logged on a sustainable basis today, what will it take to protect the remaining forests? We already discussed the debt-for-nature swaps suggested by Lovejoy. Alan Thein Durning, executive director of the Northwest Environment Watch, proposes returning the forests from control of national government to local communities to avoid the tragedy of the commons. Durning believes that the evidence clearly shows that the U.S. Forest Service has not been effective at protecting forests from exploitation by commercial interests. The same would hold true for other nations. Durning's solution is to return the forests to ownership of local people who, since they are dependent upon the health of the forests, will do a better job of protecting them. This might be true of indigenous tribal groups, but I don't think Durning's suggestion is sufficient to save the rainforests. I'll offer two reasons. First, it is not always true that a local indigenous group will seek to preserve forests. In most parts of the world, where population pressure is using up available agricultural land, such as in Zaire, the local residents continue cutting the forests to gain more farmland. Second, the tribal groups that are trying to defend their land against encroachment have often suffered the same fate as the Native Americans.

They have been beset by settlers and miners, and when they resist they have been slaughtered. It is true that Brazil and some other countries are trying to create a few reserves for native tribes, but how long can they hold back the demand for more land due to their surging growth in population?

Durning appears to recognize that merely returning forests to local control may not be enough and proposes additional protection from exploitation by private ownership through legally binding riders to land titles that forbid certain activities such as clear-cut logging and urban development. He also advocates community land trusts whereby a non-profit board manages the forest donated to it for the long-term benefit of the community.[162] This is similar to the approach of the Nature Conservancy, a U.S. organization that is now international in scope. It buys up land to be conserved and either manages the area itself or turns it over to a state with the proviso that it be preserved in its natural condition in perpetuity.

All of these ideas have merit, but ***the key to saving the world's forests, as well as our own, is educating people to the full long-term value of forests (not the discounted value used by economists) and reflecting that value in performing cost-benefit analysis for determining the best use of forest land and products.*** In estimating the costs we should include the cost of soil erosion as well as the loss of species diversity. The true costs of timber in tropical countries would be extremely high due to the dramatic ecological impact of timber cutting. It has been estimated that the full value of a mature tree in India is $50,000, while the true cost of a hamburger produced from pasture land cleared from rain forests is about $200.[163]

In estimating the value of forests we need to include the value of alternative uses, not only for the present generation, but for future generations as well. In the United States, the forest service now only receives the revenue for the sale of timber. If it also were credited with the user fees for hiking, fishing, hunting, etc., it would make more money than from timber sales. Furthermore, charging the full long-term costs of timber cutting would reduce the foreign demand for U.S. lumber. Other countries may decide to import more lumber from Siberia. So much the better for the Russians, if they have the wisdom to reflect the true costs. Maybe what the world needs is a timber cartel to enforce conservation such as the oil cartel was able to achieve for a short time. At the very least, we must end the subsidies that result in timber being sold for below present costs (let alone true future value).

In April of 1993, the U.S. Forest Service announced a plan to end unprofitable logging in sixty-two national forests and reduce annual harvests to 4.5 billion board feet by 1998 from the 7.3 million harvested in 1992.[164] This economically reasonable approach was met with extreme resistance by

Westerners who think that the forest are theirs alone, rather than the property not only of all present Americans, but future generations as well.

At the same time that we are saving the forests, society has a responsibility to help those who lose their employment as a result. The argument over the spotted owl is really an argument over jobs. What the loggers fail to appreciate is that when the last 5 percent of forests are cut down they will be without jobs anyway. But that is some years away and they are worried about putting food on their table today. With the proper assistance, they could be retrained and relocated to find employment elsewhere, assuming there were jobs available elsewhere. This takes us back to the need to ensure that population grows slower than employment demand by reducing the fertility and immigration rates.

While I can sympathize with the loggers, I have little sympathy for the timber companies or conservative pundits who try to bias the debate by pretending that it is a question of human needs versus those of an owl.* It is unfortunate that the media let them get away with obscuring the issue. For example, in the U.S. the spotted owl is a "keystone species" whose disappearance is indicative of the destruction of an entire ecosystem. Actually, ancient growth forests of the Northwestern United States are home to 667 species as well as 214 fish runs in three states.[165] The monoculture pine forests that would be planted in place of the ancient growth would be relatively sterile, lacking the variety of plant and wildlife that make up the older ecosystem.

Finally, to accomplish any of the above it is essential to shift the decision making from the relatively few people who benefit in the short run from deforestation to the many who will benefit by maintaining healthy forest ecosystems in perpetuity. Some people argue that it is the environmentalists who are already setting the U.S. policy agenda. That simply is not true. The wood products industry contributes $6 to Congressional candidates for every $1 contributed by the environmentalists and, as a result, the ancient forests continue to be cut down. To rectify the imbalance of power in environmental issues, as in so many others, will require serious campaign reform, a subject that will be addressed in the last chapter. Regrettably, in their almost fanatical effort to balance the budget without any cost to the present generation, Congress sought to obtain revenue by selling off public lands. Bills were introduced to create a commission to

---

*It might be argued that it is unreasonable to try to save every species. Certainly the world would not miss one of the many million insect species. The question is where to draw the line. Failure to protect species in Australia has resulted in the extinction of 28 percent of the nation's 102 indigenous animals. (*Chicago Tribune*, May 31, 1992, sec. 1, p. 10). I don't have an answer as to how to draw the line and would be interested in the thoughts of others on this perplexing issue.

identify national parks and forests to be closed or sold. The U.S. Forest Service and Bureaus of Land Management and Reclamation would be dismantled. Millions of acres of desert and range land would be turned over to the states, raising the probability that they will be turned over to development interests. This would be acceptable *if* the full cost were charged to the private interests wishing to purchase or use these lands. This means looking at the value of the land over several hundred years. However, failure of Congress to reform the Mining Law of 1887, under which mining conglomerates can claim land for as little as $2.50 an acre,* is indicative that this certainly will not be the case. It threatens to be the largest federal giveaway in history. Future generations will rightly accuse the present generation of stealing their heritage.

4. Pollution and Ozone Depletion

Chapter 3 discussed the impact of population growth on pollution. However, even assuming we are able to reduce world population to a sustainable level, if all nations continue to increase physical output per capita—which appears to be the primary goal of most nations of the world—pollution must continue to increase as well. In recent years, most people have become aware of the most obvious forms of pollution—dangerously contaminated air and water. The great danger is that when the most visible forms of pollution are controlled, the public will become complacent while the more insidious and dangerous forms of pollution go untreated. Years ago, when Cleveland's infamous Cuyahoga River caught fire, there was an immediate outcry and the level of flammable discharges and other contaminants was significantly reduced. Indeed, in many areas of the country, such as Lake Erie, the quality of surface waters has improved considerably. The use of regulations, such as the Clean Air Act of 1980, have also proved extraordinarily successful in improving air quality in many parts of the nation. The use of reformulated gasolines and cleaner burning power plants have resulted in a 29 percent decline in levels of six major pollutants over the last twenty-five years.[166] A decline in sulfur dioxide, the primary cause of acid rain that threatened lakes and forests in the Northeastern states, has been particularly gratifying. Still 80 million Americans live in areas that do not meet the standards of the Clean Air Act.

Despite our success in improving air quality, there are many areas

*This is not even restricted to American companies. In 1995 the provisions of the law forced the Interior Department to sell public land believed to hold more than $1 billion of minerals to a Danish mining concern. The total price: $275! To make matters even worse, the public is usually stuck with any cleanup costs after the mining firms are finished with their rape of the land. (*The Wall Street Journal*, September 7, 1995, p. B-6.)

where the environment continues to deteriorate at an alarming rate. For instance, the coral reefs off the coast of Florida are suffering from two lethal diseases—the white pox and the white plaque—which threaten to destroy the entire system of reefs. The diseases appear to be due to the sewage runoff from Florida Bay.[167]

Even more serious to the future of our nation is the silent, unseen pollution of underground water aquifers which supply 80 percent of the water in rural areas—because once underground water supplies are polluted no one knows if it is possible to clean them up. It is doubtful that they could "flush out" the contaminants as rivers and even lakes can. Just to build the facilities necessary to stop the continuing pollution and meet the requirements of the Clean Water and Safe Drinking Act would require almost $500 billion over the next twenty years.[168] Every day the problem—and eventual cost—is growing.

Already by 1976, 25 percent of the U.S. water supply was polluted beyond government standards.[169] Since then, 19,000 hazardous waste dumps have been steadily dripping their deadly toxins into the nation's water supply. Another 93,000 municipal and industrial dumps which are considered "non-hazardous"—meaning they theoretically contain no known sources of toxins—are also oozing into our underground water. Moreover, the non-hazardous label is largely a myth. For instance, millions of batteries containing highly toxic mercury, lead, and cadmium are discarded in these dumps. Who knows what potentially dangerous substances are slowly dissolving into our water supply? In addition, there are 2.3 million underground petroleum tanks of which 25 percent or more may be leaking.[170] Meanwhile, other nations such as France continue to dump radioactive waste in the sea without the vaguest notion as to the long term-consequences of their actions. Scientists are now discovering that plankton, algae, and sea animals concentrate radioactive substances by a factor of 1,000 to 1,000,000.[171] Thereafter, they pass through the food chain until they are eventually consumed by humans.

What to do with the accumulating wastes of the industrial age will be one of the biggest problems of the next generation. Every day each American produces more than twice his or her weight in waste.[172] In 1989, the Office of Technology Assessment estimated that 80 percent of existing landfills will be filled and closed within twenty years.[173] To reduce the amount of solid wastes many municipalities are looking to incineration as the answer. Unfortunately, incineration can increase air pollution with a witches brew of toxic chemicals, including dioxins and furons, arsenic, cadmium, chlorobenzenes, cholorophenols, chromium, cobalt, lead, mercury, PCBs, and sulfur dioxide.[174] The answer is, of course, to conserve and recycle, but up to now the cost of polluting was cheaper than the cost of recycling. This has to change. Polluters have to be taxed to cover the cost of their pollution. They will either try to pass the tax on to consumers through higher prices, in which case demand for their products and, ultimately, pollution will drop, or they will develop new manufacturing processes that reduce pollution.

David Korten suggests that a disposal tax that covers the cost of eventual disposal of a product and its packaging should be levied on every manufacturer.[175] The intent would be to encourage manufacturers to use recyclable packaging and, to the extent possible, recyclable products. While conceptually the idea makes sense, it might be quite difficult to implement given the millions of different products being produced.

The reduction of acid rain shows how with proper legislation, such as the Clean Air Act, progress can be made on saving the environment. Between 1973 and 1983, particulate matter in the air dropped by 50 percent, sulfur dioxide declined 27 percent, and airborne lead was reduced 77 percent.[176] However, as significant as these improvements were, the danger remains that cleaner smelling air might detract our attention from the potentially more serious problems of dangerous trace toxins such as those released by incineration, and the steady build up of CO_2 in the atmosphere.

The conservative reaction to the build-up of CFCs in the atmosphere is a textbook example of their response to pollution threats in general. First they denied that CFCs posed any problem despite all the evidence to the contrary. In her book *Environmental Overkill,* Dixie Lee Ray, the former governor of Washington State, claimed that because CFCs are heavier than air they cannot rise into the stratosphere to destroy the ozone layer.[177] Amazingly, such a statement ignores the fact that CFCs have been found in the stratosphere throughout the 1980s and 1990s. Scientist F. Sherwood Rowland correctly explains that winds in the atmosphere will evenly disperse all molecules in the air regardless of what they weigh.[178] In the book *Apocalypse Not* Ben Bolce and Harold Lyons argued that the amount of CFCs was inconsequential relative to other sources of pollution like volcanoes.[179] Again the scientific evidence refuted their position. The National Center for Atmospheric Research found little change in the amount of hydrogen chloride in the atmosphere after the huge eruption of Mount Pinatubo in 1991, although it was thought that the long-term trend could have been exacerbated by the particles of sulfuric acid from the eruption.[180] Finally, in 1994 NASA found the manmade gas hydrogen fluoride in the upper atmosphere, which scientists felt was conclusive evidence that the ozone hole was primarily caused by chlorofluorocarbons.[181]

The naysayers then maintained that the loss of ozone was not particularly harmful to humans if they would just add a little sunscreen.[182] It is true that even in the worst years ozone losses were expected to increase ultraviolet rays over the temperate zones by only about 8 percent. But it was not the damage done thus far that concerned the scientists, but the trend for the future. Moreover, it was not primarily the concern for increased skin cancer that caused scientific alarm, even though it was noted that in Queensland, Northeastern Australia, 75 percent of all people who have reached the age of sixty-five now have some form of skin cancer. Of greater concern was the possibility that additional ultraviolet rays might damage fish, shrimp, crab larvae, copepods, krill, zooplankton, and phytoplankton.[183] These latter two organisms are essential elements to the ocean's food chain. Some of the impacts of the diminished ozone may have been exaggerated, but Professor Ray Smith of the University of California at Santa Barbara found evidence of a 6 to 12 percent decline in the number of planktonic organisms while the ozone hole is open.[184]

One fact was indisputable: ***If the ozone layer is destroyed the amount of ultraviolet rays that would penetrate the earth's atmosphere would destroy most forms of life on the face of the earth.***[185] No prudent person would take such a risk. However, ultra-conservative demagogues such as Rush Limbaugh and Dixie Lee Ray seem willing. Despite the overwhelming evidence to the contrary, Limbaugh continued to quote discredited analysis, such as Ray's book, to say that there was no threat of ozone depletion.[186] This was alleged even after the 1992 analysis found that the ozone layer had declined another 2 percent to 3 percent setting a new record low. The ozone hole expanded over a wider area than ever before in the southern hemisphere; but in the northern hemisphere ozone concentrations were 9 to 20 percent below normal.[187]

Fortunately, the international community listened to the scientists and began restricting CFCs and other ozone destroying gases. The result was encouraging. By 1994, the evidence indicated that the buildup of chlorine and bromine in the atmosphere was slowing and should peak by the year 2000, after which a slow recovery of the ozone layer should begin.[188] Even so, scientist Michael Oppenheimer points out that the ozone layer will probably not return to normal levels for "several generations."[189] In short, we again have a case where strong governmental action has proved to be successful in averting a potential worldwide calamity, but ultra-conservatives are unimpressed. Since a catastrophe did not occur, some will no doubt claim that there was never any danger in the first place. Only after a calamity will the environmental activists ever be able to prove conclusively they were right. In the meantime, a substantial portion of the public would rather listen to the siren song of Limbaugh who says that most of the world's problems are either imaginary or caused by government policies.

Before leaving the subject of pollution, I would be remiss if I failed to note the devastating impact that the defense department has had on the environment. Not only is defense spending deleterious to the economy directly, but its impact on the environment adds another huge cost that is only now coming to light. Some environmentalists estimate that the world's armed forces are most likely the single largest polluters on earth.[190] The U.S. Department of Defense generates 400 to 500 thousand tons of toxins annually, more than the five largest chemical companies combined. Military nuclear reactors are responsible for an estimated 97 percent to 99 percent of all high-level nuclear wastes and 78 percent of all low-level wastes in the United States.[191] For years, under the shibboleth of "national security," the Defense Department was virtually exempt from the environmental standards demanded of industry. Cleaning up the military's garbage will result in yet another huge bill for the American taxpayer. ***Estimates of the nuclear decontamination costs at 4,500 contaminated sites are as high as $200 billion.***[192] ***Toxic waste clean-up may be another $20 to 40 billion.***[193] These costs are yet another liability we are leaving to future generations.

In addition to generating toxic and nuclear wastes, the military is a major consumer of energy. ***The U.S. military uses enough energy in twelve months to run the entire U.S. urban mass transit system for about fourteen years.***[194] Although politicians talk about "investing" in defense, from an economic perspective defense spending is not investment, but another form of consumption just like snowmobiles and powerboats. In fact, it is the most energy intensive form of consumption we can undertake.

5. Global Warming

The issue of possible global warming due to the buildup of CO_2 in the atmosphere is more difficult to resolve because the consequences are even more subtle, controversial and long term. Back in 1896 the Swedish chemist Svanti Arrhenius postulated that the buildup of carbon dioxide due to the burning of coal would result in the heating up of the planet. Arrhenius thought that this "greenhouse" effect would be beneficial to world agriculture much as a hothouse stimulates growth, and he was partially correct.

Today, however, most scientists are much less sanguine about the prospect of the earth's warming because even a relatively small change in temperature can have major consequences. For example, it is estimated that a drop in temperature of only 3 degrees centigrade (5.4 degrees Fahrenheit) started the last ice age.[195] In 1995, the Intergovernmental Panel on Climate Change (IPCC), composed of 2,500 scientists, estimated that present trends indicate a 2 to 6 degree Fahrenheit increase by the year 2100. The result could be a melting of one-third of the world glaciers and a potential increase in sea level of 6 inches to 3 feet.[196] The large range reflects the uncertainty regarding projections and the potential consequences of global warming. The possibility for disaster cannot be ignored, however.

More recent evidence suggests the prospect of a much worse scenario. A team from Victoria University in New Zealand concluded from fossil evidence that three million years ago the Antarctic ice melted completely, when average global temperatures rose only a few degrees. If that happened today, it could raise the world's oceans by 215 feet.[197] Of course, few, if any, scientists believe that the present warming will result in the Antarctic ice cap melting completely. However, even if such estimates are significantly overstated, consider that an increase of sea level by only twenty feet would threaten most of the coastal regions of the world. While some areas would be flooded with salt water, the additional heat will result in severe droughts in other areas. There are dozens of islands in the Pacific, Caribbean, and Mediterranean that sit only a meter or two above the water level "and will suffer an Atlantis-like fate if the warming trend causes sea levels to rise as scientists have predicted."[198]

Not all the effects of warming would be negative. A positive development has been the recent discovery that the warming has lengthened the growing season in northern climates by about a week. The longer period of growth permits plants to absorb more carbon dioxide, partially offsetting the increase in CO_2.[199] However, although the colder latitudes will warm up some, they are generally areas that have less topsoil than the areas that will incur the droughts. Hence, the overall food production of the world might be substantially reduced. Even a mere two foot increase in the world's oceans would result in making disasters common place. For example, a severe flood that occurred only once in a century would occur every twenty years. It is especially disconcerting if environmentalist and diplomat Sir Crispan Tickell is correct in his estimation that one-third of the world's population lives within thirty-seven miles of the coastal line.[200]

The consequences of shifts in temperature are more than just speculation. History is replete with examples of catastrophe caused by even minor changes in the average temperature. Albert Gore reports the calamitous consequences that can occur as a result of even minor changes in the weather trends. Some examples:

- In 1150 B.C.E., the Hekla 3 volcano erupted and the subsequent frigid temperatures and heavy rains for the next few years destroyed agriculture in Scotland and northern England, wiping out 90 percent of the population.[201]
- Around 209 B.C.E., a volcanic eruption in Iceland caused famine as far away as China.[202]

- The so-called Little Ice Age which lasted from 1550 C.E. until 1850 C.E. disrupted agriculture throughout Northern Europe. One of the hardest hit countries was Scotland. Failure of cod fishing and crops resulted in repeated famines and, by the year 1691, over 100,000 Scots migrated to Northern Ireland, displacing the indigenous Irish and leading to the 300-year confrontation between Catholics and Protestants.[203]

These changes took place when the average temperature varied by only 1 to 2 degrees centigrade.[204] With the earth as overcrowded as it is, a change in average temperature could result in cataclysms far greater than any in the past. Any efforts of one group of people to migrate to another nation would result in war. (Unless they decide to come to the United States.)

Given that the potential consequences of global warming could be extremely severe, why doesn't the federal government take the lead in seeking to remedy the situation? It would be facile to say that we elect leaders who lack the intelligence needed. Some would argue that the evidence of global warming is not compelling enough to warrant the economic dislocations that would occur as a result of a serious attempt to curb CO_2 buildup. Let's review it.

That the amount of CO_2 in the atmosphere has been steadily increasing is incontrovertible. Biochemist Charles David Keeling has been measuring the amount of carbon dioxide in the atmosphere over Antarctica for more than three decades. The now famous Keeling curve shows a steady increase in CO_2 since he began tracking it in 1958.[205] There was a noticeable slowdown in CO_2 buildup during the oil crises of the 1970s and early 1980s due to conservation efforts. But, the average increase in CO_2 was 4 percent a year prior to the oil crisis and the same trend has resumed since the mid-eighties when cheaper oil resulted in the United States and other nations relaxing their efforts on conservation.

Of course, there has always been CO_2 released by trees and plants during the night, but it was reabsorbed during the day and oxygen released through the process of photosynthesis. Now the additional burning of fossil fuels is destroying that balance. It is being thrown even more out of kilter by the destruction of the rainforests. Present projections are that the CO_2 in the atmosphere will again double within the next forty years.[206]

The second question is whether the increase in gases such as CO_2 will lead to a pervasive increase in the global temperature. Although it cannot yet be concluded that the warming trend of the last decade will continue, there is justifiable cause for concern. The evidence shows that summers in the last 50 years were warmer than any other fifty-year period throughout the last 12,000 years.[207] Ten of the top eleven warmest years on record have occurred between 1987 and 1998.* Not every year reflects an increase in temperature. There are bound to be variations from year to year, but the trend in temperatures for the last two decades is clearly upward.

Until recently the most significant evidence that contradicted the warming hypothesis comes from satellite measurements of the earth's lower atmosphere. The readings over the last nineteen years seemed to indicate a cooling of the lower atmosphere.[208] However, in 1998 it was discovered that the two-decade record of satellite data had been biased by the inevitable lowering of the satellites' orbits as they encountered atmospheric resistance. Correcting for this error, the satellite data now also indicates a warming trend, although not as much as the surface has.[209]

The inconsistencies of measurements have led scientists to begin collecting data from deep ocean probes. The deep probes are believed to be less affected by short-term fluctuations and give a truer picture of the underlying trend. Data from the ocean probes off of Antarctica, in the Indian Ocean, and in the South Pacific appear to confirm the warming trend predicted by computer models. Indian Ocean waters tested as deep as 3,000 feet have warmed by one degree Fahrenheit between 1962 and 1987. The result has been a rise in the Indian Ocean of 1.4 inches just due to thermal expansion.[210]†

There is also evidence that Antarctica has been warming for the past fifty years. In 1995, an iceberg the size of Rhode Island broke off from the Antarctic Peninsula.[211] Four major ice shelves along the Antarctic Peninsula have collapsed in the past fifty years.[212] A team of scientists analyzing a 400-year history of Arctic temperatures by analyzing tree rings, lake and ocean sediments, and ice cores concluded that there has been a naturally caused warming trend beginning about 1840. However, according to Ray-

---

*The years 1992 and 1993 saw a slight decline in the average temperature that many scientists ascribe to filtering out of the suns rays due to the dust sulfur particles from the eruption of Mount Pinatubo. But 1995 was the hottest year on record (*Chicago Tribune*, May 1, 1996, sec. 1, p. 12). The years 1997 and 1998 were also extremely hot, but that may be due in part to the Pacific currents known as the El Niño effect.

†In December 1998, the National Oceanic and Atmospheric Administration (NOAA) announced that evidence from cores drilled into Arctic ice packs and sediment layers on ocean and lake bottoms indicated that 1998 was the warmest year in the Northern Hemisphere in the past 1,200 years.

A second study appears to dash the hope that the warming trend will increase crop yields in northern latitudes. A 1998 National Science Foundation study shows that global warming may actually decrease crop yields by stimulating the growth of weeds and insects. Increasing crop yields in the far northern zones will be limited because of the poor soil quality, in many areas only a few inches deep. John J. Flika, "Study Shows '98 May Be Hottest in 1,200 Years," *Wall Street Journal*, December 8, 1998, p. B6.

mond Bradley of the University of Massachusetts, the warming trend appears to have accelerated in the twentieth century due to the increased burning of fossil fuels.[213] The Byrd Research Center at Ohio State University reported in 1992 that all mid- and low-latitude mountain glaciers are now melting and receding. Glaciers are disappearing all over the world. In the Alps, the ice masses have lost half their size since the middle of the nineteenth century. The upper layers of the world's oceans have warmed by 0.5 degree Celsius over the past fifty years.[214] And over the past century, the world sea level has risen by nearly eight inches.

Some scientists had hoped that the warming process might be self-correcting. For example, additional evaporation could produce more rain clouds which might result in a cooling effect. But it now appears that the additional vapor will only serve to prevent infrared heat from escaping into space.[215] On the other hand, the long-term warming trend might be masked by the decrease in ozone of recent years, which some scientists believe has resulted in more clouds to shield out the sun's heat. As the ozone rebuilds, it is feared that the warming trend will accelerate.[216]

The nonlinearity of the earth's climate makes it very difficult to be certain about any trend until more data is collected over a longer time. Hence, it cannot yet be determined with certainty that the warming trend of the last two decades is part of a longer term cycle due to causes we do not yet understand, or whether it is primarily the result of increases in CO_2. Scientists have, however, been able to test air bubbles in fossil ice and they indicate that over the last 160,000 years the concentration of CO_2 correlates with average global temperatures.[217] Correlation does not prove causation, but the preponderance of the evidence continues to support the warming theory. The models of climatic changes are becoming increasingly more accurate. They correctly predicted that the warming trend of the late 1980s would be checked or temporarily reversed by the eruption of Mount Pinatubo. And it was. According to a recent report of the IPCC, the research to date suggests that the warming of the last century, and especially of the last few years, "is *unlikely* to be entirely due to natural causes and that a pattern of climatic response to human activity is identifiable in the climatological record"(italics added).[218] The Max Plank Institute for Meteorology in Hamburg, Germany agrees. After studying temperature fluctuations of the last thousand years, Klaus Hasselmann and colleagues conclude that they were 95 percent certain that the warming of the past twenty years has been due to human, not natural, causes.[219]

Despite the growing body of evidence, the scientific community cannot be certain that the present trend in global warming is not a temporary phenomenon, or is due primarily to pollution, or will have the disastrous consequences that many scientists fear.[220] The quandary is that *if*

we wait until the evidence is conclusive it may be too late to reverse the trend. To illustrate, if the warming reaches Alaska, the resulting decay in the arctic tundra would release billions of additional tons of carbon into the atmosphere.[221] And, if the Antarctic ice sheet begins to melt, the darker water would absorb more heat from the sun, thus speeding up the warming process.[222]

So, what should be done? Some scientists propose solving technologically induced problems by the application of more technology. A former Soviet climate expert, Mikhail Budyko, suggests dumping sulfur dioxide gas into the stratosphere to act as a sunshade.[223] Unfortunately, he doesn't explain what to do about the sulfuric acid that would be mixed into rain water as a result. Other scientists have suggested dumping huge amounts of iron oxide in the oceans which would help dissolve more atmospheric CO_2 in the water. But they ignore Garrett Hardin's First Law Of Ecology: "We can never do merely one thing."[224] If in the long term we discover that loading the world's oceans with iron oxide has a disastrous impact on the ocean's ecology, how do we get the iron oxide back out? Or as noted biologist and ecologist Barry Commoner observed, "Everything is connected to everything else."[225] Ill-conceived draconian suggestions to stop pollution through more pollution are merely foolish efforts to avoid dealing with the problem of overconsumption.

In deciding on the proper course of action, we must consider the best and worst possible outcomes of pollution. Most importantly, we have to avoid any action that may produce irreversible harm to society. This can be achieved by developing a "payoff matrix" like the one developed by Robert Costanza.[226] Although Costanza developed his matrix to assess strategies for adopting new technology, we can use it for assessing the impact of pollution as well.

		Impact of increasing pollution	
		If Optimist Is Right	*If Pessimist Is Right*
Increase in Pollution	*High*	High	Disaster
	Low	Tolerable	Moderate

If we pursue a consumption policy that generates higher pollution but the impact on the world turns out to conform to the optimists' assumptions regarding the impact of pollution, there is a high payoff in terms of the increased standard of living. However, if the pessimists are right, then the higher pollution might lead to a world disaster. On the other hand, if we follow policies that reduce pollution and they reduce the overall wealth of society, even the worst case scenario would still be tolerable since we can provide the basic necessities of life (and much more) and generate very little pollution (assuming we control population growth). Given these possible outcomes, game theory would suggest that we pursue policies that assume the more pessimistic view of the potential impacts of pollution since the worst results are tolerable and we avoid a possible global disaster.

Of course, there are always those high-risk personalities who are willing to risk everything for the greatest possible gain. These are the people willing to jeopardize their life savings on an unknown penny stock or a spree at a casino. However, the vast majority of us will not take a fifty-fifty chance on our future happiness. We would not risk a life of poverty against even unlimited wealth on the mere flip of a coin. We would take the more prudent course of action and avoid such a potentially deadly game, accepting a moderate life style instead, especially when we know that great wealth is not a prerequisite for happiness. Risking the environmental destruction of our planet when we could at least have a tolerable existence even if our assumptions turn out wrong is no less a fool's game.

But while the optimum policy may call for sacrificing some GDP growth for lower pollution (about 1 percent per year less according to some estimates), self-interest leading to a tragedy of the commons becomes even more subtle and pervasive when the issue of pollution is considered. In this case, the "commons" is the environment. Since the cost of a cleaner environment is borne by everyone, while the benefits of pollution accrue to the individual polluter, self-interest will kick the common good to pieces. Economist Herman Daly refers to this process as the workings of the "invisible foot" in contrast to the presumed beneficial effects of classical economist Adam Smith's "invisible hand." Moreover, as Daly points out, the waste absorption capacity of the environment is not subject to partitioning or private ownership.[227]

In the long run, the only realistic answer is to reduce the production of pollutants by reducing consumption of environmentally damaging products and the consumption of fossil fuels. Raising gas mileage requirements of new cars, demanding reduced emissions, placing higher taxes on gas to encourage conservation, providing tax incentives for firms to reduce pollution, and providing tax incentives for insulation such as double and triple pane glass would result in a major reduction of the pollutants that may be causing global warming.[228] With such conservation measures, the Worldwatch Institute estimates that Americans could cut energy consumption by 50 percent, reduce carbon dioxide by 50 percent and save $200 billion a year in energy costs, all without much sacrifice.[229]

The key is to begin taking action today when we still have the luxury to slowly restrain emissions rather than waiting until we reach a crisis.

Economists believe that stretching the impact over a half century would result in a negligible impact on the economy. On the other hand, if we were to immediately freeze U.S. emissions to their 1990 levels it would be extremely costly according to Dale Jorgensen, an economist at Harvard University.[230]

As part of the Montreal Protocol on the Depletion of the Ozone Layer signed in 1987, the United States pledged to phase out CFCs. The results of that agreement, if the one hundred signatory nations honor it, will end the destruction of the ozone layer. The Montreal Protocol shows that pollution problems can be solved. But achieving international agreement to reduce CO_2 emissions will be far more difficult, since it will require reducing the consumption of all fossil fuel sources of energy. Nevertheless, in 1992, West Germany promised to cut CO_2 emissions by 25 percent within fifteen years. Similarly, Australia, Austria, Denmark and New Zealand have agreed to a 20 percent reduction in ten to fifteen years, and several other nations have agreed to hold emissions constant.[231] After initially expressing reluctance at making cuts, the United States made a political turnabout at the 1996 Geneva conference and called for strict control of greenhouse gases.[232]

At the 1997 conference on global warming in Kyoto, Japan, U.S. negotiators agreed to reduce emissions on carbon dioxide and other greenhouse gases to 7 percent below the 1990 level by a compliance date of between 2008 and 2012—a 30 to 35 percent decline from the projected level the U.S. would reach by that time based upon the present trends. The European Union agreed to an 8 percent reduction, and Japan and some other nations agreed to smaller cuts. However, the less developed countries were reluctant take action to reduce their levels of greenhouse gases. They pointed out that up to now most of the pollution had been caused by the more developed nations. Sixty percent of the world's population is meeting its basic needs in a sustainable manner. Conversely, 80 percent of the environmental damage has been caused by the 20 percent of the world's population from the industrialized nations.[233] The remaining 20 percent of the population are living in absolute deprivation. The LDCs feel that to force all nations to cut back on pollution equally would prevent them from closing the economic gap. Since industrialized countries have been the major cause of the accumulated pollution in the atmosphere, the LDCs felt that the industrialized nations should bear the brunt of reducing pollution. However, by granting the developing nations the freedom to pollute, it would encourage industries that cause the greatest pollution to relocate in the LDCs. To reduce worldwide pollution, it might be fair to place greater responsibility on the developed nations, but every country must incur some restrictions.

In the negotiations held in Buenos Aires, in November 1998, many of the Less Developed Nations (LDCs) began to realize that they, too, could benefit from pollution-cutting mechanisms created under the Kyoto Accord. Specifically, most LDCs agreed with the idea advanced by the United States that would give industrialized countries pollution credits for sharing clean technology with the LDCs and allow rich nations to buy pollution rights from their poorer but cleaner neighbors. Industrialized countries also promised to provide $2 billion over the next three years for emissions-tracking facilities in the Third World. However, the accords still lack a mandatory obligation on the part of the LDCs to cut emissions. The Pew Center floated the notion that emissions reduction in the LDCs should be determined by their available resources and present emission levels. The negotiators agreed to complete emission control mechanisms and accountability rules by the year 2000. ***The United States must demand that some level of responsibility be assumed by the LDCs if the accords are to work.***

In his monograph, *Sharing the Burden of Global Warming*, H. P. Young discusses the various theories for distributing the burden of controlling CO_2 emissions. He explains that there are three choices for controlling emissions: entitlements, taxes, and assessments. After ruling out taxes and assessments as not feasible to administer among countries, Young explores the various ideas for determining the extent of entitlements. He summarizes: "The *egalitarian* position is that emission rates per capita should be brought toward equity;* the *status quo* doctrine holds that current emission levels establish legitimate differences between per capita rates; the *contributions* doctrine maintains that excess emissions in the past constitutes a debt that must be paid off."[234] Believing that there is little political possibility that the developed nations would ever agree to this latter position, Young proposes a policy consistent with the first two positions:

> Countries with per capita emissions rates above the baseline would freeze their total emissions at levels established by some baseline date. Countries with per capita emissions below these levels would be able to expand up to but not beyond them. Emissions would be allotted to each country on an aggregate basis, and their internal allocation would be determined by each country's own policy. Countries would also be free to trade their allotments with others in order to enhance their efficiency.[235]

Of course, as noted above, if the underdeveloped nations are permitted to increase pollution while other countries must hold their emissions con-

---

*The implication is that the United States would have to cut annual per capita CO_2 emissions from 19.5 tons to only 4 tons by the year 2010. See David C. Korten, *When Corporations Rule the World* (West Hartford, Conn., and San Francisco: Kumarian Press and Barrett-Kochler Publishers, Inc., 1995), p. 34.

stant it will encourage emission-producing industries to migrate from developed to undeveloped nations. But this trend will continue anyway as manufacturing continues to migrate toward countries with the lowest labor costs. However, as pointed out in chapter 4, we must avoid the drastically disruptive impacts that would be caused by millions of immigrants migrating to the developed countries at the same time that jobs are moving to the LDCs.

Furthermore, Young recognizes that his policy recommendations might be insufficient where any net increases in total emissions is unacceptable as, for example, CFCs. In such cases he suggests that countries with per capita emission rates above the baseline must reduce their total emissions by amounts comparable to the increases of those less developed countries that are increasing their emissions.[236]

In the case of extremely dangerous emissions, however, Young's recommendation does not go far enough. For dangerous pollutants we must encourage all nations to reduce their emissions. To deal with the problem of seeking redress for past emissions on the part of industrialized nations, the industrialized countries would establish a joint fund that would invest in research and financial aid to help the LDCs implement lower emission standards. The Montreal Protocol established such a precedent.

Different policies might be established *within* each country to control pollution. The United States could set a tax rate equal to the marginal social damage from additional emissions. This is theoretically acceptable since it is compatible with a free market economy and would provide an economic incentive for individuals and firms to reduce their pollution. Where such a tax is difficult to administer, other techniques may be more appropriate, such as setting minimum miles-per-gallon efficiency requirements.

Title IV of the 1990 U.S. Clean Air Act amendments introduced a market based approach for controlling sulfur dioxide emissions. It begins by setting an overall goal for the level of emissions. Firms are awarded rights or allowances to pollute. An individual firm can choose to invest in technology to lower its emissions or purchase allowances from other firms, whichever is more economical. To encourage a net decline in total emissions, firms may be awarded only one pound of new pollution credits for every two pounds of pollution it eliminates. This market based approach has merit, but it remains to be seen if it can be monitored accurately enough to be effective.[237]

Internationally, reduced reliance on fossil fuels could be encouraged through fair trade negotiations by encouraging countries to stop subsidizing fossil fuel use. According to the Organization for Economic Development, governments worldwide pay $230 billion in annual fossil fuel "subsidies."[238] This estimate is quite low since there are innumerable indirect ways to subsidize fossil fuels, such as the cost of a strategic oil reserve, the military costs required to protect oil interests, subsidies for road and highways (often instead of more efficient public transportation), the inefficiencies inherent in state-controlled energy production (as in many LDCs), and environmental costs incurred by pollution.

By far, the most cost effective and least painful way to reduce pollution is to conserve energy. There are, however, three basic reasons that conservation is still such a low priority. The first is the fundamental human propensity to maximize today's happiness without regard to tomorrow. Second is the widespread ignorance on the part of most people regarding the real dangers of pollution. The ignorance is amplified by misinformation spread by industries who find it in their self-interest to stimulate consumption and ignore the consequences of pollution because the costs are borne by the general public. (Another example of the tragedy of the commons.) Third is the extraordinary leap of faith expressed by so many people that whatever problems we face will be solved by advances in technology.

Most importantly, as already shown, there is little evidence to support the argument that, after the basic necessities of life are met, continued material acquisition increases happiness proportionally. There are diminishing returns to consumption just as in every other aspect of life. Therefore, the impact on happiness due to increased consumption is not symmetrical, i.e., a large increase in per capita consumption does not afford the same degree of increase in human happiness as the potential destruction of the environment threatens a potential decrease in human happiness. Moreover, there are substitutes to pollution generating consumption that can result in greater increases in human happiness in the long run without posing any environmental danger. These include all of the arts, education, self-improvement courses, sports that are environmentally benign and consume little energy (such as baseball rather than off-road vehicles, or cross-country skiing rather than snowmobiling), etc.

Solutions to the Problem of Overconsumption

The problems are clear enough for anyone not too narrowly self-interested to see. However, the solutions are neither simple nor painless. Although there are many policies which could be enacted to rectify the problems, at present there is an insufficient constituency to persuade politicians that passing the needed legislation is politically feasible. Arrayed against ecologists and environmentalists are a host of powerful lobbies representing the oil, gas, and electric companies who generally oppose conservation efforts; loggers and ranchers who use federal lands at subsidized prices; trucking companies and the teamsters union who benefit from subsidized highways;

and some of the worst polluters such as chemical companies, paper mills, mineral mines, and certain manufacturers whose by-products are extremely toxic. However, these special-interest groups could be successfully opposed if the majority of citizens recognized the importance of saving the environment and made it a top priority. To do so, however, will require a major change in American values.

In the Old Testament, God grants man "dominion over the fishes of the sea and over the fowls of the air and the beasts and the whole earth, every creeping creature that moveth upon the earth" (Gen. 2:26). It is one of the central themes of Genesis that man is driven from Paradise to a hostile environment that must be dominated. In the New Testament, there is no mention of protecting the environment since it wasn't relevant in the thinly populated world of the time.[239] More recently, some of the more enlightened Christian and Jewish clerics are trying to reinterpret the Scriptures, substituting the concept of dominion with that of stewardship. This is encouraging, but hasn't yet translated into a new political paradigm. As scientist Bruce Murray pointed out in an address to theologians, none of the political philosophies dominant today embraces the values essential to a sustainable society. "Capitalism and Marxism have one thing in common: they both presume that man's fundamental needs are material."[240]

Americans are slow to grasp the need for a sustainable society. They still believe they live in what economist Kenneth Boulding terms a "cowboy environment" where we can take what we want from our environment and then move on, instead of a "spaceship environment" where of necessity everything must ultimately be recycled. Americans would do much better if they could reflect a little on the respect for the earth which is fundamental to Native American traditions. E. F. Schumacher urges a Buddhist attitude toward economics, one that would seek to cease the endless striving for material gain because the connection between materialism and happiness (beyond the basic necessities for survival) is merely an illusion.[241]

Americans are frustrated by the fact that they are working harder than ever but are not happier. One important reason for this, I maintain, is the American obsession with consumption. Americans work an average of 320 hours (or eight weeks) a year more than German workers, and economist Juliet B. Schor explains that, although U.S. productivity has doubled since 1948, Americans have not used the increased productivity to reduce their hours of work. Instead, the average American owns and consumes more than twice as much as in 1948. Astoundingly, Americans spend three to four times as many hours shopping as Europeans.[242] How did this sorry state come about?

The generation prior to World War II were actually excessive savers.

They had lived through the Great Depression, and when the war brought the United States out of its economic slump, they still could not buy much of anything due to rationing. By 1945 there was a fifteen-year tradition of not spending. This generation continued to be frugal and amassed considerable wealth. This accumulated wealth was lavished upon their children. At the same time, the first of the Baby Boomers to enter the labor force in the mid-1960s found jobs plentiful and their income and consumption continued to soar. Although the illusionary current dollar income continued to rise in the 1970s, growth in inflation-adjusted income per capita began to drop. But once Americans got into the habit of always having more, it was difficult to break. Increased consumption could be maintained because the vast majority of younger women entered the labor force and the two-income family became the norm. Then came the era of the credit card and easy, although extremely costly, credit. No longer was lack of money a constraint, as Americans continued to maintain their addiction to consumption by increasing their debt at an unprecedented rate. The ultimate consequence, as will be shown in chapter 6, was to acquire a mountain of personal, corporate, and government debt that will now take at least a generation to pay off. To make matters worse, we have become a generation of consumption addicts. Today, most Americans are willing to buy into any pseudoeconomic theory that promises to reduce debt without slowing consumption. This does not bode well for the nation's long-term welfare.

To be sure, it is not only Americans who have habits of consumption that threaten the environment. Many other nations—even the LDCs—pose an equally grave threat to the ecological health of our planet. When it comes to devastating pollution no one surpasses Russia and the nations of Eastern Europe. It will take a concerted effort on the part of all the nations of the world to prevent our planet from becoming an open sewer. It is up to the world's remaining superpower to take the lead. Just as the United States saved the world from totalitarianism during the Second World War, it must now take the initiative to save the world from ecological self-destruction.

Al Gore's Environmental Marshall Plan

In *Earth in Balance*, Al Gore suggested that the crisis in the world's environment requires the same degree of effort that America expended to save Europe from falling into chaos after the Second World War. While it cost the American people some money in the short run, the Marshall Plan paid rich dividends in European stability and U.S. trade in the long run. Gore's global "Environmental Marshall Plan" has three key elements:

1. Transferring of environmentally helpful technologies to the LDCs to achieve stable population and sustainable economic progress;
2. Linking the negotiations to save the rainforests in LDCs with reduction in greenhouse gases in developed nations;
3. Devoting 2 percent of GDP (approximately $100 billion) on environmental aid. This is equivalent to the proportion of GDP that was spent on the Marshall Plan after the war.[243]

With regard to the last point, although Gore acknowledges the problem of raising such money while the United States is $6 trillion in debt, he doesn't offer a solution. After the war, the United States was also in debt, but did not have the continued drain of social programs such as Medicare, Medicaid, and welfare. Equally important, we boldly scaled down the level of defense spending. In subsequent chapters, I will show how America can, indeed must, get the needed funding through reductions in defense spending, welfare, and health care, as well as increased tax revenue.

Gore's Environmental Marshall Plan has six strategic goals:

- Stabilization of the world's population.
- Development of environmentally appropriate technological policies in the fields of energy, technology, transportation, agriculture, building construction, and manufacturing. Note that "environmentally appropriate" might differ from nation to nation depending on availability of natural energy sources such as sunlight or wind, population density, amount of rainfall, unemployment, etc.
- A new system of economic accounting that assigns appropriate values to ecological consequences of individual, corporate, and national actions. This could be worked into the Index of Social Welfare proposed in chapter 2.
- A new generation of international agreements involving regulation, prohibitions, incentives, enforcement mechanisms, cooperative planning, etc.
- A cooperative plan to educate the world's citizens about the global environment and the factors that affect it.
- Establishment of social and political conditions in each country most conducive to emergence of a sustainable society. Although Gore doesn't say so, this might differ significantly in societies that are already overpopulated, such as China and India, compared to societies that have brought their populations under control, such as most of the European nations.[244]

Like all such comprehensive plans, the devil is in the details; still, I believe that conceptually it has merit. It implies, however, that the United States will first get its own environmental house in order, and that will take more effort than the American public has thus far been willing to make.

Summary and Recommendations to Establish a Sustainable Level of Consumption

In a market economy where prices accurately reflect costs there can be no long-term shortage of energy, since prices will rise to a point where conservation and production of alternative sources of energy will result in supply and demand reaching equilibrium. The more difficult issue is understanding the potential long-term environmental consequences of ever increasing energy usage.

Garrett Hardin observes that throughout human history exploitation of the earth has a familiar pattern: colonize—destroy—move on.[245] Like any generality this one can be debated. Certain cultures, especially relatively primitive cultures that had a stable population, were for the most part environmentally benign.* Perhaps a more apt description of the situation in America prior to the nineteenth century was that there was so much new land available that human population and consumption could grow without having to be particularly concerned about environmental damage. However, during the last 200 years, environmental damage has risen exponentially in the United States and throughout the world. In the United States, we destroyed almost 90 percent of our ancient forests, virtually all of the prairies, and over half of the wetlands. The nation's water supplies continue to deteriorate yet Congress came perilously close to eviscerating the Safe Water Drinking Act. Today, 116 million Americans drink water from systems that violate EPA standards and other rules governing safe drinking water. According to the National Academy of Scientists, today's water guidelines may be too lax to protect the health of small children.[246] Even America's future food supply is threatened as we continue to drain the world's largest underground lake—the Ogallala Aquifer—a crucial source of water for farmers in the High Plains states from the Dakotas to the Texas panhandle.

Although some progress has been made to reduce certain types of air pollution such as sulfur dioxide, the worldwide increase in carbon dioxide

---

*There were notable exceptions to this generality. In Hawaii, for instance, many species of birds were destroyed by native Hawaiians. And there is some evidence that the collapse of the Mayan civilization may have occurred in part because of population pressures that exceeded the carrying capacity of the land.

continues unabated. We are in danger of drowning in our own waste because, as Hardin observes, "there is no place to throw away to."[247] Erosion and overgrazing continue to threaten the long-term productivity of farmland, and hundreds of thousands of acres are lost each year to urban sprawl both in the United States and throughout the world. Destruction of the rainforests is accelerating, and at present rates will result in the complete eradication of the forests and the millions of plant and animal species—many yet undiscovered—that they house. More than two-thirds of the world's species of plants and animals are concentrated in just seventeen countries, most in Latin America and Asia.[248] Only two of the countries—the United States and Australia—are developed nations. In the LDCs, species habitats are being destroyed at an accelerating rate.

We have now reached a critical stage where only radical reforms may save us from an environmental cataclysm. When faced with the prospect of global warming there is an even more dangerous possibility that we pass some boundary of "dynamic equilibrium" which threatens the entire ecosystem.[249] For example, if warming reaches the point where the arctic tundra would melt, it could release huge quantities of methane that would accelerate further warming. In the case of rainforests, after a certain percentage are cleared, the initial effect would be flooding and erosion, but the long-term effect would be fewer rainstorms and eventual desertification with a commensurate loss of the remaining rainforests and the agriculture that replaced them.

By the time we are absolutely certain of global warming, it will be too late to reverse. Further, the costs of dealing with the resulting increase in sea levels, such as building dikes around the coastal areas of the world, or relocating 80 million of the world's population away from the existing coastlines, would be horrendous.[250] Therefore, we must develop policies on the basis of the existing evidence which indicates a strong probability that the warming trend of recent decades is not a natural cyclical phenomena but is caused by human pollution. The prudent course of action is to put in place a set of policies to immediately reduce pollution. Such policies will of necessity reduce consumption and waste. If properly formulated, they would have little negative impact on short-term human happiness while immensely improving the potential for happiness of future generations.

The basic factors affecting the environment are population, consumption, and technology. We can elect to allow the U.S. population to increase to the population of China if we are willing to reduce our consumption to the levels of China. I doubt if anyone would vote for that option. We have temporarily averted this problem by living off of the resources of the rest of the world. But this cannot continue as other nations strive to improve their own standard of living. We must also remember that higher consumption means less investment, which, in turn, reduces our ability to make the technological innovations necessary to protect the environment or improve our national productivity. Increased consumption is inversely related to improved technology.

To reduce consumption in developed nations to an environmentally sustainable level will require, first and foremost, that the price of all goods and services reflect their true long-term costs.[251] For those products that pollute, one method to reduce demand for them is to tax pollution. This Pigouvian tax—named after economist A. C. Pigou—would be equal to the marginal social costs of the pollution. Either the companies producing the products would figure out a way to reduce pollution, or they would be forced to raise prices to cover the tax, hence reducing demand for the product. In either case, pollution is reduced.

But what if collective demand for consumption of all products results in increased energy requirements that, in turn, would require a *permanent loss*, for example, a proposed dam that would flood Arches National Park? What is the lost value of species diversity? How do we put a price on the loss of a species of herb whose value is yet to be discovered? The present method of discounting the future in cost-benefit studies seriously underestimates the cost and benefits to future generations.

Economists Ciriacy-Wantrup and Bishop have proposed a *Safe Minimum Standard* approach to environmental policy.[252] They argue that ***whenever there is reasonable suspicion that an action may irreversibly harm the environment, we should err on the side of caution.*** This is not unlike the payoff matrix suggested by Costanza discussed earlier in this chapter.

To get a more accurate estimate of future costs we need to wed the discipline of economics with ecology. Kenneth Boulding and Nicolas Georgescu-Roegon have been instrumental in promoting the new science of ecological economics.[253] In 1988, the International Society of Ecological Economists was formed to further this effort.[254] Ecological economics recognizes that our planet has limits, that the Second Law of Thermodynamics cannot be ignored, and that every human action (especially in the area of socioeconomic policies) has many unintended consequences.

It is crucial in determining socioeconomic policies that we avoid the tragedy of the commons which will occur when environmental costs are borne by society at large while the benefits accrue to an individual. Whenever possible, costs should be charged to the specific consumer or generator of waste. For example, if we charged every person by the pound for the waste they generated, we would have few people using lawn catchers to collect their grass clippings. Differential charges for waste that cannot be recycled would lead to an effort of recycling that would match the environmentally beneficial results achieved in World War II when just about everything from paper to rags to scrap metal was recycled into war material. ***As demonstrated in*** The Science of Morality, ***the operating principle to achieve socially beneficial results is always to make the collective self-interests of individuals congruent with the environmental goals of society.*** In so doing, we balance the interests of today's generation against the needs of future generations.

David C. Korten proposes three principles that would lead to environmental sustainability:

1. ***The rate of use of renewable resources should not be allowed to exceed the rate at which the ecosystem is able to regenerate them.***
2. ***The rate of consumption of irretrievable, disposable, and non-reusable resources should not exceed the rate at which renewable substitutes are developed and placed into use.***
3. ***The rate of pollution emissions into the environment should not exceed the rate of the ecosystem's natural assimilation capability.***[255]

Implementing Korten's principles would result in establishing or increasing many charges that are either neglected or far below true costs. For example:

- setting emission charges for all types of pollution to levels proportionate to the potential long-term damage they inflict on the environment;
- imposing a virgin material fee at the point of manufacture or importation based on the quantity of nonrenewable virgin materials consumed in making the product;[256]
- increasing taxes to cover the full costs of gasoline usage, including oil depletion, pollution, defense of oil-producing nations, etc.;
- establishing utility rates that encourage conservation of resources for future generations (particularly water use charges to discourage water diversion projects and depletion of underground supplies);
- creating tax incentives for the development and implementation of alternative, less polluting sources of energy such as solar, wind, and geothermal;
- establishing tax incentives for better building insulation, such as triple-pane thermal glass.

Unfortunately, the framers of our socioeconomic policies are politicians who basically respond to the demands of their constituents. Oftentimes these demands conflict. For instance, everyone wants a cleaner environment, but few people want to pay for it either through reduced consumption or increased taxes for environmental cleanup. Moreover, the reduced consumption is felt immediately while the dangers of environmental degradation often appear to be in the distant future. As Gore so aptly stated, "The future whispers, while the present shouts."[257] Politicians most often respond to the shouts even when they suspect it will be harmful in the long run. As one congressman told me, "Look, if I don't do what my constituents want today, I wouldn't be here tomorrow to do any good whatsoever." There is some truth to this rationalization. It might indicate that we need to have longer terms in the House of Representatives, so that our political leaders are not so preoccupied with next year's election that they lose sight of what will benefit America most in the longer run.

There is no substitute for politicians of courage and foresight—increasingly rare character traits in this age of instant gratification. Harry Truman demonstrated such courage when he proposed the initially unpopular Marshall Plan to rescue postwar Europe. Gore has called for a Global Marshall Plan to save the world's environment. While some would argue that we cannot afford to undertake such an ambitious project, the evidence would suggest that we cannot afford *not* to undertake it. Destruction of our ecosystem poses a much greater danger to America than any foreign power. Moreover, we will get a far greater return on our investment by diverting some of the $270 billion annual defense spending to heal our damaged environment. This will, of course, be vigorously opposed by the narrow self-interest of business groups and others who push to fulfill their unlimited wants with no regard to future generations. They have formed numerous organizations with such environmentally friendly sounding names as The Wise Use Movement, National Wetlands Coalition, Keep America Beautiful, etc. The fight against the despoilers of the environment, will never be completely won but, like the protection of democracy itself, the environment can only be preserved by perpetual vigilance.

NOTES

1. Hazel Henderson, *Creating Alternative Futures: The End of Economics* (New York: Perigee Books, 1987), p. 340.

2. Alan Thein Durning, *Vital Signs, 1993*, Worldwatch Institute (New York: W. W. Norton and Company, 1993), p. 81.

3. Walter A. Weisskopf, "Economic Growth vs. Existential Balance," in

Herman E. Daly, *Toward a Steady State Economy* (San Francisco: W. H. Freeman and Company), p. 244.

4. Alan Thein Durning, "Are We Happy Yet?" *The Futurist* (January/February 1993): 21.

5. Ibid. Durning also cites Oxford University psychologist Michael Argyle's *The Psychology of Happiness* in which he concludes that the conditions of life that really make a difference are social relations, work, and leisure.

6. Robert Johnson, "Heavenly Gifts," *Wall Street Journal*, December 11, 1990, pp. A1, A6.

7. Donnella Meadows "Corporate Run Schools Are a Threat to Our Way of Life," *Valley News*, October 3, 1992, p. 22. Cited by David C. Korten, *When Corporations Rule the World* (West Hartford, Conn., and San Francisco: Kumarian Press and Berrett-Koehler Publishers, Inc., 1995), p. 156.

8. U.S. Bureau of the Census, *Statistical Abstract of the United States, 1997* (Washington, D.C.: U.S. Government Printing Office, 1997), table 934, p. 589. Latest data is for 1994.

9. Lester R. Brown, *Building a Sustainable Society* (New York: W. W. Norton and Company, 1981), p. 70.

10. Carole Douglis, "Images of Home," *Wilderness* (Fall, 1993): 12.

11. David and Marcia Piemental, *NPG Forum* (January 1990).

12. Lester Thurow, *Head to Head* (New York: William Morrow and Company, 1992), p. 41.

13. Ibid.

14. George Gilder, *Wealth and Poverty* (New York: Basic Books, 1981), p. 232.

15. Henderson, *Creating Alternative Futures: The End of Economics*, p. 184.

16. Lester R. Brown, *Building a Sustainable Society*, p. 64.

17. Dick Munson, "Philosophical Differences," *Northeast-Midwest Economic Review* (September 24, 1990): 7.

18. U.S. Bureau of the Census, *Statistical Abstract of the United States*, 1997, table, 933, p. 589.

19. Ibid., table, 934, p. 589.

20. Tim Walker, "Uncle Sam's Strategy," *Science News* (July 6, 1991): 10.

21. Jack L. Harvey, *Chicago Fed Letter*, Federal Reserve Bank of Chicago (November 1990): 3.

22. Merrill Lynch, *The Chartbook* (November 1990).

23. British Petroleum Co., Ltd., cited in Merrill Lynch, *The Chartbook* (August/September 1987): 5

24. James J. McKenzie, et al., *The Going Rate: What It Really Costs to Drive* (Washington, D.C.: The World Resource Institute, 1992). Cited in *Future Survey*, 14, no. 12 (December 1992): 7.

25. U.S. Congress, Office of Technology Assessment, "Improving Automobile Fuel Economy: New Standards, New Approaches" (Washington, D.C.: U.S. Government Printing Office, October 1991).

26. Dick Munson, "Philosophical Differences," pp. 3–8.

27. M. King Hubbert, "The World's Evolving Energy System," *American*

Journal of Physics, no. 49 (1981): 1006–29, and "Energy from Fossil Fuels," *Science*, no. 109 (1949): 103–109.

28. *Zero Population Reporter* (October/November 1993).

29. *Science News* (March 18, 1995): 171.

30. *U.S. Department of Energy, Annual Energy Review, 1991* (Washington, D.C.: U.S. Government Printing Office, 1991). Cited by Sir James Goldsmith, *The Trap* (New York: Carroll and Graf Publishers, 1994), p. 141.

31. Philip C. Cruver, "Lighting the 21st Century," *The Futurist* (January/February 1989): 32.

32. Solar Energy Research Institute, "The Potential for Renewable Energy," *Interlaboratory White Paper SERI/TP-260-3674* (Golden, Colo.: National Renewable Energy Laboratory, 1990). Cited by Goldsmith, *The Trap*, p. 142

33. Philip C. Cruver, "Hydrogen: Tomorrow's Limitless Power Source," *The Futurist* (November-December 1989): 25.

34. Durning, *Vital Signs, 1993*, p. 47.

35. "It's the Ecosystem Stupid," *National Wildlife* (February/March 1994): 43.

36. Nicholas Lenssen and Christopher Flavin, "Meltdown," *World Watch* (May 1986).

37. Associated Press, "Nuclear-power Wastes Piles Up with No Federal Storage Site in Sight," *Chicago Tribune*, January 31, 1998, sec. 1, p. 17.

38. Lenssen and Flavin, "Meltdown."

39. *Chicago Tribune*, March 10, 1991, sec. 7. p. 1.

40. Alan Durning, "Limiting Consumption," *The Futurist* (July/August 1991).

41. Garrett Hardin, *Living Within Limits: Ecology, Economics, and Population Taboos* (New York: Oxford University Press, 1993), p. 137.

42. Lester R. Brown, *Building a Sustainable Society*, p. 250.

43. Zero Population Growth, *Zero Population Growth Reporter* (October/November 1993).

44. Tim Walker, "Uncle Sam's strategy," *Science News* (July 6, 1991): 10.

45. *Common Cause* (January/February, 1989): 32.

46. Henderson, *Creating Alternative Futures: The End of Economics*, p. 86.

47. Charles Komanoff, *Power Plant Cost Escalation: Nuclear and Coal Capital Costs, Regulation and Economics* (New York: Komanoff Energy Associates, 1981). Cited by Brown, *Building a Sustainable Society: The End of Economics*, p. 74.

48. National Audit Office, "The Cost of Decommissioning Nuclear Facilities," London: HMSO (May 27, 1993). Cited by Goldsmith, *The Trap*, p. 146.

49. Nicholas Lenssen, "Nuclear Power at Virtual Standstill," *Vital Signs, 1994*, ed. Lester Brown et al. (New York: W. W. Norton and Company, 1994), p. 50.

50. Study by Rand Corporation and U.S. Department of Defense reported in the *Financial Times*, "Wonder Fuel to Burning Question," London, March 9, 1994. Cited by Goldsmith, *The Trap*, p. 162.

51. Albert A. Bartlett, "Fusion and the Future," Negative Population Growth newsletter—*Human Survival* (Fall 1990).

52. Lester R. Brown, *Building a Sustainable Society*, p. 323.

53. Stanley I. Fisher, *Moving Millions: An Inside Look at Mass Transit* (New York: Harper and Row, 1979). Cited by Brown, *Building a Sustainable Society*, p. 323.

54. Lester R. Brown, *Building a Sustainable Society*, p. 256.

55. Richard A. Uher, "Levitating Trains," *The Futurist* (September/October 1990): 28–32.

56. Richard D. Thornton, "Beyond Planes, Trains and Automobiles: Why the U.S. Needs a MAGLEV System," *Technology Review*, 94, no. 3 (April 1991). Cited in *Future Survey* (December 1991): 5.

57. *Science News* (July 29, 1995): 75.

58. Uher, "Levitating Trains," pp. 28–32.

59. *Wall Street Journal*, May 10, 1995, p. A8.

60. *Historical Tables, Budget of the United States*, Fiscal Year 1995, pp. 45 and 47. Estimate for 1995 from *Budget of the United States*, Fiscal Year 1996, table S–10, p. 204.

61. Merrill Lynch, *Weekly Economic and Financial Commentary* (August 13, 1990).

62. Lester R. Brown, *Building a Sustainable Society*, p. 309.

63. A. Lovins, J. Barnett, and L. Lovins, "Super Cars: the Coming Light Vehicle Revolution," paper presented at the European Council for an Energy Efficient Economy, Rungstedgard, Denmark (June 4, 1993). Cited by Goldsmith, *The Trap*, p. 139.

64. Al Gore, *Earth in the Balance* (Boston: Houghton Mifflin Company, 1992), pp. 326, 333, 345.

65. Lester R. Brown, *Building a Sustainable Society*, p. 233.

66. Daly, *Toward a Steady Economy*, p. 261.

67. Jørgen Randers and Donella Meadows, "The Carrying Capacity of Our Global Environment: A Look at Ethical Alternatives," *Toward a Steady State Economy*, ed. by Herman E. Daly, p. 285. I converted their estimates for hectares to acres which are more familiar to American readers: one hectare equals about 2.5 acres.

68. Randers and Meadows, "The Carrying Capacity of Our Global Environment: A Look at Ethical Alternatives," p. 284.

69. Ibid., p. 285.

70. Food and Agriculture Organization, U.S. Department of Agriculture. Brown, *Building a Sustainable Society*, p. 119. The 1988–90 and 1994–96 estimates are from Brown, et al., *Vital Signs, 1997*, pp. 27, 39.

71. Brown, et. al., "Fertilizer use keeps dropping," *Vital Signs, 1994*, Worldwatch Institute (New York: W. W. Norton and Company, 1994), pp. 42–43.

72. R. Hindmarsh, "The Flawed 'Sustainable' Promise of Genetic Engineering," *The Ecologist* (September 1991): 198–99. Cited By Goldsmith, *The Trap*, p. 105.

73. Brown, *Building a Sustainable Society*, p. 33.

74. Lester R. Brown et. al., "World Grain Harvest Sets Record," *Vital Signs, 1997,* Worldwide Institute (New York: W. W. Norton and Company, 1997), pp. 26–27.

75. A lower estimate is found in UN Conference on Desertification, "Economic and Financial Aspects of the Plan of Action to Combat Desertification," Nairobi, Kenya, August 29–September 9, 1977. Upper estimate based on Brown's analysis of later data for U.S., USSR, Africa, and other regions. Lester R. Brown, *Building a Sustainable Society*, p.5.

76. David and Marcia Piemental, *NPG Forum* (January, 1990): 3.

77. M. Stroch and J. Raloff, "The Dirt on Erosion," *Science News* (April 4, 1992): 215.

78. National Agricultural Lands Study, co-chaired by the USDA and the Council on Environmental Quality, "Soil Degradation: Effects on Agricultural Productivity," Interim Report No. 4 (Washington, D.C.: November 1980). Cited by Lester R. Brown, p. 5.

79. Paul Rosenberg, Russell Knutson, and Lacy Harmon, "Predicting the Effects of Soil Depletion from Erosion Control," *Journal of Soil and Water Conservation* (May/June 1980). Cited by Lester R. Brown, *Building a Sustainable Society*, p. 21.

80. Lester R. Brown, *Building a Sustainable Society*, p.19.

81. *Wall Street Journal*, May 10, 1995, p. A8.

82. Hardin, *Living within Limits*, p. 110.

83. Ibrahim Nahal, "Some aspects of Desertification and Their Socioeconomic Effects on the ECWA Region," presented to the UN Conference on Desertification by the Economic Commission for Western Asia, Nairobi, Kenya, August 29–September 9, 1977. Cited by Lester R. Brown, *Building a Sustainable Society*, p. 29.

84. Lester R. Brown, *Building a Sustainable Society*, p. 28.

85. *National Wildlife* (February/March 1994): 42.

86. Roy Beck, "Washington Notepad," quoting David Piemental of Cornell University, *Social Contract* (Summer 1993): 286.

87. M. Rupert Cutler, "The Peril of Vanishing Farmlands," *New York Times*, July 1, 1980. Cited by Lester R. Brown, *Building a Sustainable Society*, p. 27.

88. U.S. Bureau of the Census, *Statistical Abstract of the United States*, 1997, table 1110, p. 678.

89. "Voice of the People," *Chicago Tribune*, February 19, 1995, sec. 4, p. 2.

90. Gore, *Earth in the Balance*, p. 3.

91. E. O. Wilson, *Consilience* (New York: Alfred A. Knopf, 1998), p. 284.

92. Kenneth B. Young and Jerry M. Coomer, "Effects of Natural Gas Price Increases on Texas High Plains Irrigation," 1976–2025, Agricultural Report No. 448 (Washington, D.C.: USDA, Economics Statistics, and Cooperative Service, February, 1980). Cited by Lester R. Brown, p. 26.

93. Based 1980 U.S. Geological Survey estimates of 3.25 billion acre feet of water, and current depletion rates of 500 to 600 million acre feet every 25 years. See Robert W. Fox and Ira H. Mehlman, *Crowding Out the Future* (Washington, D.C.: Federation for American Immigration Reform, 1992), p. 48.

94. Gore, *Earth in the Balance*, p. 20.

95. Murray Fishback and Alfred Friendly Jr., *Ecocide in the USSR: Health and*

Nature Under Siege (New York: Basic Books, 1992). Cited in the *Amicus Journal* (Fall 1992): 448.

96. John Vidal, "No, Apocalypse Now," *The Guardian* (June 1, 1996). Reprinted in *The World Press Review* (August 1996): 8–9.

97. United Nations Conference on Desertification, "Economic and Financial Aspects of the Plan of Action to Combat Desertification," Nairobi, Kenya, August 29–September 9, 1977. Cited by Lester R. Brown, *Building a Sustainable Society*, p. 25.

98. Gore, *Earth in the Balance*, p. 112.

99. "New Politics of Thirst," *Der Spiegel*, reprinted in *World Press Review* (November 1992): 18–21.

100. Ibid.

101. Carole Douglis, "Images of Home," *Wilderness* (Fall 1993): 19.

102. *Chicago Tribune*, July 24, 1994. sec. 1, pp. 1, 12.

103. Sandra Postel, *Last Oasis*, as cited by Douglis, "Images of Home," p. 19.

104. Don Hinrichsen, "The World's Water Woes," *International Wildlife* (July/August 1996): 24.

105. *Chicago Tribune*, September 18, 1997, sec. 1, p. 13.

106. *National Wildlife* (February/March 1994): 42.

107. Jonathan Weiner, *The Next One Hundred Years* (New York: Bantam Books, 1990), p. 181.

108. *Chicago Tribune*, August 9, 1994, sec. 1, p. 10.

109. "It's the Ecosystem Stupid," *National Wildlife* (February/March 1994): 43.

110. *Wall Street Journal*, May 17, 1995, p. A4.

111. *Chicago Tribune*, September 18, 1997, sec. 1, p. 13.

112. *Chicago Tribune*, December 15, 1995, sec. 1, p. 10.

113. Food and Agriculture Organization, cited by Lester R. Brown, *Building a Sustainable Society*, p. 52.

114. Ann E Platt, "World Fish Harvest Hits New High," *Vital Signs 1996*, ed. Brown et al., p. 31.

115. Ray Mosely, "Seas Riches a Dwindling Infinity," *Chicago Tribune*, September 2, 1996, sec. 1, p. 1.

116. Peter Wilson, "Net Loss: Fish, Jobs and Marine Environment," *Worldwatch Paper*, no. 120 (July 1994): 6. Total fish harvest hit a new high in 1994 at 109 million tons.

117. "Fishing: Out of Control?" *Science News* (June 8 1996): 367.

118. Ibid., p. 13.

119. *Wall Street Journal*, November 22, 1991, p. B1.

120. "Fishing: Out of Control?" *Science News* (June 8, 1996): 367.

121. Bill Richards, "Fishermen in Alaska Awash in Salmon, Strive to Stay Afloat," *Wall Street Journal,* September 4, 1996, p. A1.

122. Crispino A. Saclauso, "Brackishwater Aquaculture: Threat to the Environment?" *NAGA, The ICLARM Quarterly* [International Center for Living Aquatic Resource Management] (July 1989), cited by Anjali Acharya, "Aquaculture Production Rises," *Vital Signs, 1996*, p. 32.

123. "Year of the Unfortunate," *National Wildlife* (February/March 1992).

124. *Wall Street Journal*, December 6, 1994, p. A1.

125. "It's the Ecosystem Stupid," *National Wildlife* (February/March 1994): 41.

126. Susan Jane Buck Cox, "No Tragedy of the Commons," *Environmental Ethics* (Spring 1985): 49–61.

127. See also Aldo Leopold, "Some Fundamentals of Conservation in the Southwest," *Environmental Ethics* 1, no. 2 (Summer 1979): 131–141.

128. *National Wildlife* (February/March): 42.

129. Lester R. Brown, *Building a Sustainable Society*, p. 253.

130. E. O. Wilson, *The Diversity of Life* (Cambridge, Mass.: Harvard University Press, Belknap Press, 1992). See also Wilson, *Consilience*, p. 293.

131. Wilson, *Consilience*, p. 293.

132. "The Year of the Unfortunate," *National Wildlife* (February/March 1992).

133. Bill McKibben, "An Explosion of Green," *Atlantic Monthly* (April, 1995: 72).

134. Jon Margolis, "Pondering the Link Between Our Forests and Our Humanity," *Chicago Tribune*, September 5, 1994, sec. 1, p. 11.

135. Weiner, *The Next One Hundred Years*, p. 169.

136. Gore, *Earth in the Balance*, p. 119.

137. Wilson, *The Diversity of Life*, p. 3.

138. E. O. Wilson, *The Diversity of Life*, cited by Gowdy and O'Hare, *Economic Theory for Environmentalists*, p. 166.

139. Alan Thein Durning, "Saving the Forests, What Will It Take?" *Worldwatch Paper*, no. 117 (December 1993): 24.

140. Gore, *Earth in the Balance*, p. 139.

141. Wilson, *Consilience*, p. 295.

142. Durning, "Saving the Forests, What Will It Take?" p. 16.

143. Ibid., pp. 32–34.

144. Lester R. Brown, *Building a Sustainable Society*, p. 37

145. Werner Fornos, *Gaining People, Losing Ground* (Washington, D.C.: The Population Institute, 1987), p. 14.

146. Nathaniel Sheppard Jr., "Panama Forests Fall to Indifference," *Chicago Tribune*, March 10, 1991, sec. 1, p. 1.

147. *Popline* (September/October 1992): 4.

148. *Wall Street Journal*, November 7, 1991, p. A1.

149. Paul Johnson, *Modern Times* (New York: HarperPerennial, 1983, 1991), p. 676.

150. Fronos, *Gaining People, Losing Ground*, p. 18.

151. Durning, "Saving the Forests," p. 35.

152. Gore, *Earth in the Balance*, p. 117.

153. Weiner, *The Next One Hundred Years*, p 174.

154. Ibid.

155. Lester R. Brown, *Building a Sustainable Society*, p. 181.

156. Lisa Drew, "25 Messages from Wildlife," *National Wildlife* (April/May): 11.

157. Ibid.

158. World Wildlife Fund, "Wildlife for Sale," *Focus* (November/December): 4–5.

159. John Stuart Mill, *Principles of Political Economy* (1848), quoted by Hardin, *Living Within Limits*, p. 118.

160. *The Economist* (October 22, 1988): 24.

161. Bill McKibben, "An Explosion of Green," *Atlantic Monthly* (April 1995): 9.

162. Durning, "Saving the Forests," p. 14.

163. Thomas Gladwin, Leonard N. Stern School of Business, New York University, New York, private communication, September 5, 1993; Center for Science and the Environment, The Price of Forests (New Delhi, 1993). Cited by Durning, "Saving the Forests," p. 20.

164. *National Wildlife* (February/March 1994): 44.

165. Durning, "Saving the Forests," p. 45.

166. John J. Fialka, "EPA's Bower Says Air Quality Has Been Improved," *Wall Street Journal*, December 18, 1996, A11.

167. *Chicago Tribune*, December 18, 1996, sec. 1, p. 11.

168. *National Wildlife* (February/March 1994): 41.

169. *New York Times*, May 13, 1973. Cited by Henderson, *Creating a Alternative Futures: The End of Economics*, p. 256.

170. *The Economist* (October 4, 1986): 36–37.

171. E. F. Schumacher, *Small Is Beautiful: Economics as If People Mattered* (New York: Harper & Row, 1973), p. 137.

172. Gore, *Earth in the Balance*, p. 147.

173. *Science News* (October 6, 1990): 218.

174. Gore, *Earth in the Balance*, p. 156.

175. David C. Korten, *When Corporations Rule the World* (West Hartford, Conn., and San Francisco: Kumarian Press and Berrett-Koehler Publishers, 1995), p. 288.

176. Alan S. Blinder, *Hard Heads, Soft Hearts* (New York, Addison-Wesley Publishing Company, Inc., 1987), p. 136.

177. Barbara Ruben, "Back Talk," *Environmental Action* (Winter 1994): 14. Cited by Dixie Lee Ray with Lou Guzzo, *Environmental Overkill: Whatever Happened to Common Sense?* (Washington, D.C.: Regnery Gateway, Lanham, 1993).

178. Ibid., p. 14.

179. Ben W. Bolch and Harold Lyons, *Apocalypse Not, Science, Economics and Environmentalism* (Washington, D.C.: Cato Institute, 1993).

180. Ibid., p. 14.

181. "Volcanic Source of Chorine Is No Longer an Issue," *Chicago Tribune*, December 20, 1994, sec. 1, p. 3.

182. Boyce Rensberger, "A Reader's Guide to the Ozone Controversy," *Skeptical Inquirer* (Fall 1994): 489.

183. Weiner, *The Next One Hundred Years*, p. 158.

184. Boyce Rensberger, "A Reader's Guide to the Ozone Controversy," p. 495.

185. Rensberger, "A Reader's Guide to the Ozone Controversy," p. 491.

186. *Environmental Action* (Winter 1994): 14.

187. *National Wildlife* (February/March 1994): 40.

188. *Science News* (September 17, 1994): 187.

189. *National Wildlife* (February/March 1994): 40.

190. Michael Renner, "Assessing the Military's War on the Environment," in Lester R. Brown, *State of the World, 1991* (New York: W. W. Norton and Company, 1991), p. 132.

191. Renner, "Assessing the Military's War on the Environment," p. 143, and Center of Defense Information, "Nuclear Threat at Home: The Cold War Lethal Leftovers," *Defense Monitor* XXIII, no. 2 (1994).

192. Center for Defense Information, "Nuclear Threat at Home: The Cold War Lethal Leftovers," *Defense Monitor* XXIII, no. 2 (1994).

193. Renner, "Assessing the Military's War on the Environment," p. 150.

194. Ibid., p. 137.

195. Weiner, *The Next One Hundred Years*, p. 102.

196. *Chicago Tribune*, October 25, 1995, sec. 1, p. 8.

197. *National Wildlife* (February/March 1994): 40.

198. *Science News* (March 31, 1991): 201.

199. R. Monastersky, "Warming Reaps Earlier Spring Growth," *Science News* (July 13, 1996): 21.

200. Gore, *Earth in the Balance*, p. 74.

201. Ibid., p. 59

202. Ibid.

203. Ibid., p. 69.

204. Ibid., p. 73. Unfortunately, after he became vice president, Al Gore appears to have forgotten his own lesson regarding the socioeconomic consequences of mass migration. Never once did he speak out against the excessive number of immigrants coming to the United States during the 1990s, and he did not support the Jordan Commission recommendations to reduce immigration to more sustainable numbers. Obviously, being a good team player under Clinton meant more than saving the country from overpopulation.

205. Weiner, *The Next One Hundred Years*, p. 29.

206. Gore, *Earth in the Balance*, p. 93.

207. Ibid., p. 105.

208. R. Monastersky, "Planet Posts Temperature Record for 1997," *Science News* (January 17, 1998): 38.

209. William K. Stevens, "Revised Satellite Data May Back the Theory of Global Warming," *Chicago Tribune*, August 14, 1998, sec. 1, p. 20.

210. "Deep Sea Tests Off of Antarctica Add Weight To Global Warming Reports," *Chicago Tribune*, April 13, 1997, sec. 1, p. 18.

211. *Chicago Tribune*, March 2, 1995, sec. 1, p. 3.

212. "Antarctic Warmth Kills Ice Shelves," *Science News* (February 17,

1996): 108. By 1949, satellite photos indicated that the ice shelves were breaking up faster than anyone predicted. *Chicago Tribune*, April 8, 1999, sec. 1, p. 9.

213. Associated Press, "Arctic Thaw Not New, But Greenhouse Gases reportedly Accelerating Process," *Chicago Tribune*, November 14, 1997, sec. 1, p. 20.

214. "The Calamitous Cost of a Hotter Word," *Der Spiegel*, reprinted in *World Press Review* (July 1995): 9.

215. Gore, *Earth in the Balance*, p. 90.

216. "Cloudy Effects of Ozone Loss," *Science News* (December 24, 31, 1994): 427.

217. Wilson, *Consilience*, p. 285.

218. *Chicago Tribune*, September 10, 1995, sec. 1, p. 10.

219. "The Calamitous Cost of a Hotter Word," *Der Spiegel*, p. 10.

220. Some scientists, such as British Antarctic Survey member David Vaughan, believe that it would take 200 years, at current warming rates, before the problem would become serious. *Chicago Tribune*, July 10, 1997, sec. A, p. 21.

221. Weiner, *The Next One Hundred Years*, p. 75.

222. Ibid., p. 116.

223. Ibid., p. 230.

224. Ibid., p. 199.

225. Barry Commoner, *The Closing Circle* (New York, Knopf, 1971), p. 33.

226. Robert Costanza, "Balancing Humans in the Biosphere: Escaping the Overpopulation Trap," *NPG Forum* (July, 1990): 3.

227. Daly, *Toward a Steady State Economy*, p. 17.

228. Weiner, *The Next One Hundred Years*, pp. 218–19.

229. Ibid., p. 218.

230. G. Pascal Zachary, "Greenhouse Emissions, Pose Tricky Problem," *Wall Street Journal*, March 10, 1997, p. A1.

231. Ibid., p. 202.

232. R. Monastersky, "Stage Set for Curbing Greenhouse Gases," *Science News* (July 27, 1996): 27.

233. Alan Durning, "Asking How Much Is Enough?" in *The State of the World, 1991*, ed. Lester R. Brown (New York: W. W. Norton and Company, 1991), pp. 153–69. Korten, *When Corporations Rule the World*, p. 279.

234. H. P. Young, *Sharing the Burden of Global Warming (Draft)*, School of Public Affairs, University of Maryland, pp. 19–20.

235. Ibid., p. 20.

236. Ibid.

237. Donald A. Hansen and William A Test, Chicago Fed Letter, May, 1992, No. 57. See also Jeffrey Taylor, "New Rules Harness Power of Free Markets to Curb Air Pollution," *Wall Street Journal* (April 14, 1992).

238. Deroy Murdock, "There is More to Global Warming than Meets the Eye," *Headway Magazine* (December/January 1998): 19.

239. Lynn White, "The Historical Roots of Our Ecological Crisis," *Science* (March 10, 1967).

240. Bruce Murray, "Prophet of Tomorrow's Redirected Technology," *Chris-*

tian Science Monitor, November 3, 1976. Cited by Brown, *Building a Sustainable Society*, p. 350.

241. E. F. Schumacher, "Buddhist Economics," in Daly, *Toward a Steady State Economy*, pp. 231–38.

242. Juliet B. Schor, *The Overworked American: The Unexpected Decline in Leisure* (New York: Basic Books, 1992). Cited by *Future Survey* (April 1992): 8.

243. Gore, *Earth in the Balance*, pp. 300–304.

244. Ibid., pp. 305–307.

245. Hardin, *Living Within Limits*, p. 17.

246. Vicki Monks, "Safe Drinking Water: Will Congress Weaken the Law That Protects Your Health?" *National Wildlife* (April/May 1995): 29.

247. Hardin, *Living Within Limits*, p. 201.

248. Laurie Goering, "Much of World's Life Held by Few," *Chicago Tribune*, December 9, 1997, sec. 1, p. 17.

249. Gore, *Earth in the Balance*, p. 47.

250. A major United Nations scientific study indicated that global warming in the next century, through heat expansion and melting glaciers, will likely cause oceans to rise one or two feet by the year 2000. "Island Nations Losing Ground to Oceans," *Chicago Tribune*, June 25, 1997, sec. 1, p.9.

251. Although most economists would agree with this recommendation in theory, they effectively circumvent it by using a discount rate that grossly understates the long-term costs when compared to present benefits. Even a discount rate of 5 percent would result in a $100 cost fifty years in the future being reflected in present dollars as only $8.75 cents; in 100 years it would be reflected as 76 cents. In other words, if we were seeking to measure the benefits of an action that yields a net benefit today of $100 but results in pollution over the next 100 years of, say $5 a year, the total pollution costs discounted at 10 percent per year would be only $50, indicating that we should go ahead with the project. But if we used a discount rate of 5 percent, costs would equal the benefits and at any lower discount rate the costs would exceed the benefits: for example, a 3 percent discount rate over only 50 years would still yield a net loss to the project of -$30. Of course the benefits may be more than for one year and subsequent year benefits must be discounted as well.

252. V. V. Ciriacy-Wantrup and R. Bishop, "Common Property as a Concept in Natural Resource Policy," *Natural Resources Journal* (October 1975): 713–27. Cited by Gowdy and O'Hare, *Economic Theory for Environmentalists*, p. 116.

253. See Kenneth Boulding, "The Economics of the Coming Spaceship Earth," *Toward a Steady State Economy*, ed. Herman Daly (San Francisco: W. H. Freeman, 1973), and Nicholas Georgescu-Roegen, *The Entropy Law and the Economic Process* (Cambridge, Mass.: Harvard University Press, 1971).

254. Hardin, *Living Within Limits*, p. 56.

255. Korten, *When Corporations Rule the World*, p. 272.

256. Gore, *Earth in the Balance*, p. 349.

257. Ibid., p. 170.

6

THE MANY FACETED DEFICIT

In 1976, I gave a lecture at DePaul University in which I forecasted that around 1985 America would enter a virtual Golden Age of economic growth and social harmony. My optimism was predicated on demographic trends indicating that during the late 1980s the post World War II baby boom generation would be entering its peak earning years and the dependency ratio (the ratio of people aged 0 to 18 and over 65, to those between 18 and 65) would be the lowest at any time in our history. The significance of this demographic profile is that when the relative number of potential labor force participants (those between 18 and 65) rises relative to those either too young or too old to be in the labor force, society has more "surplus" wealth to use to meet its other demands. With a record number of job holders in both a relative and absolute sense, tax receipts would rise relative to disbursements, providing more revenue to address social ills and rebuild the nation's aging infrastructure (e.g., school buildings, mass transit, water and sewage, waste disposal, bridges and highways, etc.). Unfortunately, history has shown that my anticipation of an economic Golden Age was a bit premature, and unless Americans reduce the unforeseen rise in immigration, it may turn out to be short-lived.

In the twenty-year period from 1950 to 1970 hourly earnings adjusted for inflation rose from $5.34 an hour to $8.03, an increase of 50 percent.[1] During the next twenty-seven years, from 1970 to 1997, real hourly wages dropped to $7.54, a decrease of 6 percent.[2] Real per capita disposable income fared much better, boosted by more hours worked (including sometimes a second job), two-income families, higher wages for upper managers (especially at the higher levels), and investment returns for those who had adequate savings to invest. From 1950 to 1970 per capita disposable income adjusted for inflation rose 59 percent; from 1970 to 1997 it rose 62 percent.[3] Average family income also rose, primarily due to the increase in two-worker families which have now become the norm.

Figure 6.1
Comparison of Hourly Wages and Disposable Income per Capita 1950–70 and 1970–97

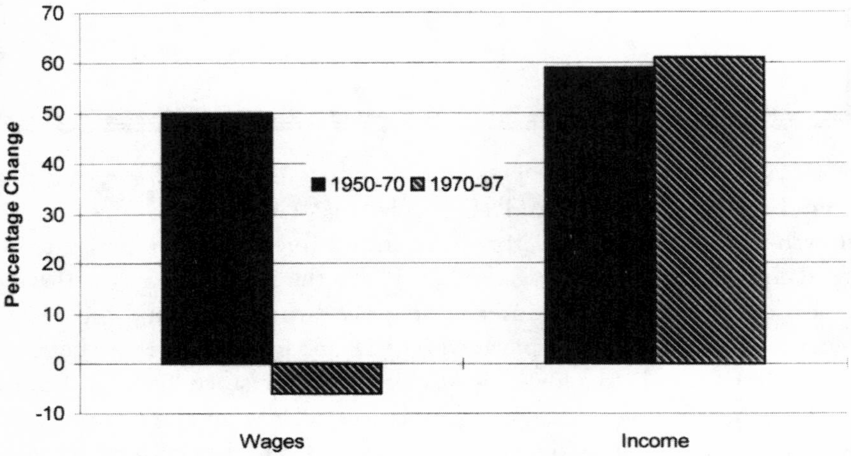

The striking difference between hourly wages and disposable income is one of the reasons why conservatives and liberals interpret the results of the last two decades so differently. Conservatives cite the disposable income or family income estimates while liberals note the trend in hourly wages. The correct interpretation of the numbers is that the average American family has been able to improve its economic welfare, but there has been a price to pay in terms of more hours worked and reduced parenting hours as women entered the work force in record numbers. It also tells us that those who have been able to save and invest have made out extremely well while those at the lower end of the economic spectrum, especially single wage-earner households, have lost ground. We will return to these issues in chapters 8 and 9.

For our present purposes we need to understand that ***the growth during the 1980s was achieved primarily through the economic stimulation of massive federal deficits which, even after a budget surplus is attained, will continue to exert a fearful cost to our society and result in significant redistribution of wealth from the middle and lower classes (who are taxed to pay the interest on the debt) to the upper classes (who***

as owners of government securities receive the interest on the debt). Moreover, the balance of trade, which was positive throughout the 1960s and only slightly negative in the 1970s, suddenly registered an enormous deficit of over $100 billion annually by 1984.[4] Productivity growth slowed during the 1980s to 1.2 percent a year, about half the post World War II average.[5] America's biggest growth industry, aside from defense and health care, became the publication of the thousands of books and articles lamenting the loss of our competitive edge. Japan became the new leader of the world economy in terms of growth rate, if not in absolute size. And a new Democratic administration was swept into office on the slogan "It's the economy, stupid."

Beginning with the U.S. recovery from the 1990–91 recession, the economic circumstances of America and Japan appeared to have been reversed. After the collapse of Japan's stock market in 1990, its economy has been mired in near recession conditions for the past decade. The United States, on the other hand, entered into its longest post World War II economic recovery. By 1999, U.S. unemployment had declined to 4.4 percent, inflation was almost nonexistent, and the stock market, reached a record high.

Despite the plethora of encouraging economic news, there are several disconcerting notes. Not all Americans have shared in the growing prosperity. As noted earlier, except for the most recent period from 1997 to 1998, income quality has steadily increased over the past twenty-five years. Moreover, part of the decrease in the unemployment rate was attributable to welfare reform, which, although it did force welfare recipients into the workplace, it also forced many people to take such low-paying jobs that it has done little to reduce poverty. Additionally, the economic repercussions of the 1998 financial meltdown of many Asian nations has yet to be fully felt in the United States, while our balance of trade continues to deteriorate. Fears that the Year 2000 problem would wreak havoc with the economy began to increase as we entered 1999. Such fears, regardless of whether they prove to be well founded, could easily spawn a recession. A recession could reverse the tenuous income gains made by the poor and the middle class in recent years. Finally, as we shall see, the nation has not yet come to grips with financing the explosive growth of Social Security and Medicaid, both of which face huge deficits early in the twenty-first century. In short, the United States is far from attaining the economic Valhalla some pundits try to portray.

In this chapter we will focus on the issue of the national debt which, although it occupied center stage in the late 1980s and early 1990s, is all but ignored as we approach the turn of the century. We will examine the causes and the consequences of the federal debt, which is now about six trillion dollars, and most importantly, what should be done about it. Since at first glance the annual federal budget appears to be roughly in balance, both the president and Congress seem to have lost a sense of urgency in reducing the national debt. Should this be a cause for concern?

There is a wide range of opinions with regard to how we should manage the debt issue. On the one hand, we have many congresspeople who believe the answer is a Constitutional amendment to balance the budget. Some propose to balance the budget by increasing taxes, but most want to achieve a balanced budget primarily by reducing expenditures. Presidential candidate Bob Dole promised in 1996 to cut taxes 15 percent and still balance the budget. He based this contention on the same economic theory employed by Ronald Reagan, which George Bush had termed "voodoo economics." But by the time he ran for president, Dole apparently became a believer in what is commonly called "supply side" economic theory. However, supply side economics is by no means accepted by most economists. Herbert Stein, a former chairman of the Council of Economic Advisors, labeled the proposal of reducing taxes while advocating a balanced budget hypocritical.[6]

At the other extreme on the debt issue, some liberal economists, such as the late Robert Eisner, argue that we really shouldn't worry much about the size of the national debt. Like a bit of inclement weather, it may not be as comfortable as we like, but at worst it is a minor inconvenience that has no serious consequences.

I will attempt to show the fallacy in both extreme positions. Although some national debt per se may not be cause for concern, the present magnitude can indeed be a serious impediment to the future development of our nation. However, I contend that the debt can be managed without the proposed Constitutional amendment to balance the budget, which is likely to do more economic harm than good.

To understand the implications of the annual budget deficits and the cumulative national debt, we must first understand how it arose, the short- and long-term consequences on national productivity, and the implications of the various policy options to reduce the debt. Although many discussions of the issue gloss over the distinction between deficits and debt, let me be quite clear: A *deficit occurs* when *annual* government expenditures exceed *annual* revenues (for all practical matters tax receipts). The *national debt* is the total *cumulative* indebtedness of the nation. The debt is financed by having the treasury department sell bonds and notes to individuals and institutions both here and abroad. (Whether the bonds are sold to Americans or foreigners is an important distinction as we will see.)

Hence, the first fact to note is that a deficit in any one year is relatively unimportant; it could always be made up by a surplus (revenues exceeding expenses) in subsequent years. Every business and individual runs a cash-flow deficit when they make a major investment in a new factory or buy a house. Second, the significance of a given level of debt is measured *relative* to the income and assets of a person or business. A bank would willingly lend a person the money to buy a $300,000 home if he was making $100,000 a year, assuming no other major indebtedness, but would be foolish to make such a loan to a person who is earning only $20,000 a year or is already deeply in debt.

Moreover, economist Howard M. Wachtel reminds us that the national debt is not the only debt that must concern us. Wachtel refers to the "seven deadly debts"[7]:

1. Federal (national) debt
2. Corporate debt
3. Consumer debt
4. Bank debt
5. Foreign-held debt from U.S. trade deficits
6. Infrastructure "debt"
7. Third World debt

To this list I would add (8) pension fund debt. Many municipal and corporate pension funds are significantly underfunded. Although the stock market rally since 1990 has gone a long way to close the gap, particularly for corporate pension funds, a significant drop in the value of their portfolios could again threaten the pensions of millions of workers.

As I shall show, all these debts are related, but it is the total of the first four measures of indebtedness that is particularly relevant. Also, bear in mind that one of the conclusions of *The Science of Morality* was that justice demands that we attempt to make decisions from the perspective that we do not know whether we are a member of today's generation or a future generation. ***Therefore, in the interest of intergenerational equity we can only justify borrowing from future generations if in so doing we expect to generate a return on that loan to offset the costs to the next generation.***

Having once incurred the debt, regardless of the justification at the time, we are then faced with the most equitable way of reducing the debt, assuming it needs to be reduced. We must also consider whether a very gradual or immediate reduction in the debt is preferable in terms of the consequences for the economy. As we will see, the answer depends in part on where we are in the business cycle, since to remove the stimulus of a deficit during a recession could prolong and deepen the recession, whereas balancing the economy during the latter stages of a recovery could have the beneficial consequences of slowing an overheated economy and reducing inflationary pressures.

Is There Ever a Good Reason to Deliberately Increase the National Debt?

To start this discussion we need to review a little elementary economic theory. One of the basic laws of classical economic theory is Say's Law (named after French economist Jean-Baptiste Say). Say posited that the production of goods and services (supply) must equal the aggregate purchases of those goods and services (demand). In short, supply creates its own demand. At first blush this seems reasonable enough: the money that is paid to the factors of production—investors and labor—can be used to purchase that which is produced. Therefore, if more is produced (supply increases), there are more wages and profits to buy the increased production (demand increases).

Classical British economist John Maynard Keynes demonstrated a serious shortcoming of Say's Law, however. Keynes showed that if people saved money, not all the production may be purchased. As inventories build, production will be cut back. If production is cut back, less investment is made and wages may be cut or the labor force may be laid off. The subsequent drop in demand means that even more inventories are accumulated, necessitating further cuts in production and wages. If producers react quickly enough they might cut prices sufficiently to increase demand and work down inventories to the point where they have to increase production. However, there is a lot of guesswork here, as producers try to anticipate how buyers are going to react. There is a tendency for businesspeople to project the future by mere extrapolation, i.e., tomorrow is going to be like today. Therefore, they will tend to overproduce when times are good and underproduce when times are bad, thus exacerbating cyclical activity.

Keynes worried about periods when supply would exceed demand, leading to the downward spiral of economic activity that periodically led to severe recessions. Keynes reasoned that the government could mitigate recessions by stepping in to increase demand by spending more money than it collected in taxes, hence running a deficit. The government could increase aggregate demand by either cutting taxes without cutting government expenditures or by increasing expenditures without raising taxes. In either case it would run a budget deficit, but the economic spiral would be reversed. The increased demand would trigger an increase in production and economic recovery would begin. Then, when the economy was performing well, the government could gradually pay off the deficits by reducing spending or increasing taxes.

Until the 1930s, it was generally believed that the government should always run a balanced budget and, except for periods of war, that was generally the case. In fact, the effort to run a balanced budget during the early part of the Great Depression actually made the economic situation far worse by reducing aggregate demand. Although the Roosevelt administration was partially swayed by the new Keynesian theories regarding the stimulative economic impact of deficit spending, Roosevelt was still afraid to run a deficit of the magnitude called for by the circumstances. Deficit spending during the Depression averaged only about $3 billion a year,[8] not enough stimulus to break the back of the economic slump. Then, with the outbreak of the Second World War, the United States was forced to undertake massive deficit spending. Beginning in 1942, the annual deficit jumped to $21 billion and ran at about $50 billion for each of the next three years (over $400 billion annually in constant 1987 dollars). As soon as the war was over, the federal government again aimed for a budget surplus and achieved that goal by 1947. The total debt added throughout the fifteen years of depression and World War II was $200 billion (about 1.8 trillion in 1987 dollars). By 1950 the total national debt was $257 billion.

During the 1950s and early 1960s the federal government had a few surplus years, and in other years ran relatively small deficits. The result was that although the national debt increased a bit, it was growing far slower than the overall economy. Moreover, Roosevelt's creation of unemployment insurance added a built-in stabilizer to the economy by helping to maintain aggregate demand during a business slowdown. A second stabilizer was the income tax system itself, which resulted in less taxes collected during a recession and more taxes collected during an expansion. If the government kept its expenditures relatively constant throughout a business cycle, it would run a deficit during slowdowns and a surplus during economic expansions. Many economists thought they now had a system that would permit fine tuning of the economy and prevent the major cyclical swings of the past. (There was still sharp disagreement on the role of monetary policy, however.)

During the Vietnam War the deficits began rising again, up to $25 billion a year, kicking the total debt up to $484 billion by the war's end in 1975 ($929 billion in 1987 dollars). To make matters worse, the Johnson administration tried to finance both the war and his new Great Society programs by increasing the money supply. The result was that the money supply was growing faster than production, and prices began to rise. From there, the debt continued to climb slowly throughout the succeeding Carter administration. But none of this experience prepared us for the decade of the 1980s.

The 1980s and the Short-lived Theory of Supply Side Economics

In 1980 Ronald Reagan was elected President. He had three primary goals: to increase defense spending, to cut just about everything else, and to reduce taxes. But the Democrats controlled Congress and they had different goals; first and foremost was to protect entitlement programs, especially health care. Many Democrats also did not want to adopt the politically unpopular position of standing in the way of tax reductions. How then would it be possible to reconcile these contradictory goals of increasing military spending, maintaining social programs, and cutting taxes? The honest answer was that it was impossible. But too often the art of politics is to convince a gullible public to accept the impossible as possible.

David Stockman, Reagan's Director of the Office of Management and Budget, promised the Senate Budget Committee in April 1981 that, rather than incurring a $60 billion deficit by cutting taxes and increasing defense spending, the budget would be balanced by 1984 through budget reductions "to be announced later." Of course, this raised the eyebrows of not a few skeptics. In addition to unspecified budget cuts, the Reagan administration based its budget on the new school of economic thought known as supply side economics. Referring to Say's law that supply creates its own demand, the supply siders said Keynes had it all wrong. We shouldn't be focusing on stimulating demand. Rather, we should seek to increase supply, and this could be achieved by cutting taxes.

Of course, Keynes also indicated that the economy could be stimulated by cutting taxes, if it resulted in a deficit. But the supply siders said that it was not necessary to run a deficit, supply would increase by cutting both taxes *and* government spending. This contention was based upon an observation made by economist Arthur Laffer, known as the *Laffer Curve*. Basically, Laffer observed that the amount of the tax revenue collected by the government would be zero at either a tax rate of 0 percent or 100 percent. In the case of 100 percent, Laffer argued that if in any year the government taxed all income, people would have no money to purchase goods or services, hence there would be no production, no jobs, and therefore no taxes to collect in the subsequent year. But, of course, this would only be true if government burned all the money it collected. In the real world, government uses tax revenues to buy goods and services or to redistribute income. In either case, the economy keeps moving forward.

Laffer probably realized this, but made a second, more plausible assumption. At some rate of taxation, people would find it not worth their time and effort to work as much or invest as much. Therefore, if we are at or past that disincentive rate of taxation, we could encourage more work and investment by lowering the tax rate. The additional work and investment would stimulate the economy so that the additional taxes collected by having more people working would be greater than the taxes lost through the lower rates. This may very be true at tax rates of 90 percent (most people would not wish to work for only an additional 10 percent in income), but the crucial assumption the supply siders made in 1980 was that the U.S. tax rates were already so high that they depressed work and investment.

Was there any empirical support for this argument? Absolutely not. Nevertheless, the hypothetical Laffer Curve was a rationale that some conservatives could seize upon to justify cutting taxes. And after the tax cut of 1981 revenues did rise slightly, hence, the supply side proponents claimed they were right. Although revenues went up, they did not increase nearly as much as in the recovery from other recessions, nor sufficiently to prevent the deficit from accelerating. From 1981 until 1984 corporate and personal tax revenues grew an average of only 1.4 percent a year although the total economy grew by 5.8 percent.* If tax revenues had kept pace with GDP, the economy would have generated $70 billion more in taxes, more than one-third of the $185 billion budget deficit for 1984.

"Don't blame us for the increased deficits," the supply siders argued. "The reason for the increased deficits was due to increased federal spending. Had the federal government decreased spending as well as decreasing taxes, the economy would have been stimulated and the deficits would have decreased." "Au contraire," replied the Keynesians, "the economic stimulus that resulted in economic growth throughout the 1980s was in large part due to the deficit spending of the federal government just as Keynesian theory predicts." So who's right? Let's examine the evidence.

First, there is no evidence that tax rates were at the level where they affect people's willingness to work or invest. When we add state taxes to federal taxes, the combined tax rates differs significantly throughout the United States, yet no study has been able to show a difference in individuals' propensity to work or invest because of the difference in state taxes. Nor has there been any evidence to show that a difference in the propensity to work over time correlates with changes in tax rates. (In fact, when disposable income has declined for whatever reason, the number of hours

*I did not include Social Security taxes because they were not directly affected by the change in tax rates. Although Social Security taxes did increase at a much faster rate due to the growth in employment that resulted from the faster economic stimulus of deficit spending, the supply side theory held that income taxes should have grown as fast. This analysis shows that cutting income taxes does not stimulate the economy to sufficiently offset the lost revenue due to the lower income tax rates.

worked has increased to make up the shortfall.) Recent research by Austan Goolsbee of the University of Chicago and others indicates that higher tax rates for the wealthy do increase total tax revenue. Despite their efforts to dodge taxes, at least 60 percent of the tax increase gets collected.[9]

International comparisons do indicate that in countries with higher tax rates unemployed people spend a longer time between jobs, but this appears to be a function of the unemployment benefits they receive rather than the relative tax rates. Certainly, if people are paid unemployment benefits equal to 80 percent of what they made by working, there is little incentive to get a job. But motivation is quite different if the alternatives were to incur an 80 percent tax rate or have no income or public benefits whatsoever. The key here is not the tax rate per se, but the difference in the net rewards of working versus not working.

Second, there is a large body of empirical evidence that supports the Keynesian hypothesis that whenever the government engages in deficit spending, the economy will be stimulated in the short term, hence total tax revenues will increase, albeit not enough to offset the deficit. This is exactly what happened during the Second World War and many times since. Whether the federal government increases spending or the private sector does, as long as aggregate demand increases, the economy will expand.

The major shortcoming of supply side theory is that it tends to look only at the impact of changing tax rates on disposable income and ignores the impact of the change in federal spending. If the federal government cuts taxes and federal spending by an equal amount, the incremental increase in aggregate demand could be zero, even though disposable income increases.* ***The key point is not whether the federal government or the taxpayer spends an additional dollar, but on what it was spent.*** If a dollar is spent on consumption it has a far different impact than if it is invested. To illustrate, consider which would have the greater impact on future economic growth: $4,000 invested in educating a future scientist or engineer, or $4,000 spent on a snowmobile? Both have some immediate economic stimulus, but with very different long-term impacts. Increased consumption of products and services does not increase long-term productivity nearly as directly, or in the same magnitude, as increases in investment. (Increases in consumption do ultimately lead to some increased investment and productivity, since the snowmobile manufacturer dedicates some of his profits to making more snowmobiles.)

---

*In fact, if the government spends a dollar it provides slightly more economic stimulus than by cutting taxes by a dollar. The reason is that initially all of the government's dollar goes to increased demand, while the individual will save some small amount, and, therefore, the demand for goods and services is stimulated by a slightly lesser amount.

It is essential that we not forget that all real per capita increase in wealth is the result of increased productivity. Everything else is merely shifting dollars (or the goods and those services that those dollar purchase) from one group of people to another group. The real question is not whether our tax rates have reduced the incentive to work, but whether shifting dollars from public to private spending (or vice versa) will increase national productivity.

It is my contention that in the 1980s we had the *worst* of both worlds. Increases in public spending were primarily devoted to defense and health care, both of which have a relatively low (and in the case of defense a potentially negative) impact on productivity. And the low savings rate of the 1980s indicates that most of the increased income from the tax cuts went to consumption, rather than investment. A major reason that the economy did as well as it did was due to the economic stimulus caused by the deficit spending which, in effect, increased the standard of living by borrowing against future generations.* However, not everyone benefited equally from the reallocation of tax dollars that always accompanies deficit spending. Certainly, those that made use of subsidized health care or were employed in the defense industry benefited, as did those in the upper-income brackets who were not only the primary beneficiaries of the tax break, but also received interest on the treasury bonds issued to finance the deficit. The middle-income group and their children are the ones who have and will continue to bear the bulk of the debt burden.

Most economists warned that supply side economics was a cruel hoax: lower taxes would not increase GDP enough to generate sufficient tax revenue to cover the tax cut. They believed that the resulting budget deficits would keep interest rates too high for long-term economic growth, and the high interest rates would drive up the value of the dollar vis-à-vis other currencies, reducing demand for U.S. exports and exacerbating the trade deficit. That is exactly what happened. Of course, the trade impacts did not affect the economy much at first because the fiscal stimulus of deficit spending spurred American consumption, thus jolting the economy out of the 1980 recession, precisely as Keynesian economics predicted. The supply siders argued that the tax cut would increase savings and investment. But it was consumption, not savings, that increased. Consumption increased from $1.9 trillion in 1981 to $2.4 trillion in

---

*There was, of course, another key factor. The Federal Reserve Board raised the Federal Funds rate (the rate the FRB charges member banks to borrow money) from 7.9 percent in 1978 to 16.4 percent by 1981, which threw the economy into a recession but broke the back of inflation. Increases in consumer prices declined from 13.3 percent in 1979 to 3.8 percent by 1982. After interest rates gradually fell, companies were again encouraged to undertake investments to improve productivity and increase output.

1984, while savings dropped from $159 billion to $131 billion over that same period.

The net result of the failed experiment with supply side economics, and the inability to offset the increase in defense and health care with cuts elsewhere in the budget, was that between 1980 and 1990 the aggregate federal debt jumped from $908 billion to $3.2 trillion, an increase of 238 percent.

Some hopeful observers believe the experience of the tax hikes in 1990 and 1993* will have driven the final spike through the heart of supply-side theory. The supply-siders issued dire warnings that the two tax hikes would depress the economy, reduce tax receipts, and increase the budget deficits. However, the tax hikes succeeded in reducing the deficit, reducing interest rates, and stimulating the economy (through added government spending). The 1990 tax increase slashed the deficit by at least $482 billion over five years, and the 1993 hike cut the deficits another $433 billion over five years.[10] Even Stephen Moore, a CATO Institute supply-sider, conceded that the deficit would be higher if taxes hadn't been raised. However, he speculates that the economy might have grown even faster. But that could not have happened, because Fed Chairman Alan Greenspan and the Federal Reserve Board were prepared to check any faster growth to prevent inflation. As it was, the Fed raised interest rates in 1997 to cool down an overheating economy.

THE GROWTH OF FEDERAL EXPENDITURES DURING THE 1980S

There were several factors which caused the explosion of federal debt in the 1980s. The five major factors include (1) the tax cuts already discussed, (2) the doubling of the defense budget in the early 1980s, (3) the spiraling costs of Medicare and Medicaid, (4) the bailout of the savings and loan institutions, and (5) the increase in interest payments on the debt. ***These five factors account for about 87 percent of the increase in federal expenditures between 1980 and 1990. As*** table 6.1 ***shows, by 1990 income security (including federal pensions), national defense, Medicare and***

---

*The 1993 tax hike was particularly interesting. It raised tax rates only on the top 1percent of income earners. It might appear that the top marginal rate was raised to 39.6 percent, but this understates the actual impact. After including the Medicare tax of 2.9 percent for the self-employed upper-income folks, and the phasing out of upper income deductions for dependents, business expenses, medical expenses, interest on home mortgage and state income taxes, the effective marginal tax rate becomes 50.5 percent for wealthy people in California and 55 percent for those in New York (Mike Evans, "Deficits and Democracy," *Industry Week*, May 19, 1997, p. 78).

Medicaid, and interest on the budget accounted for more than two-thirds of the entire federal budget. Since 1990, the decrease in defense expenditures has been more than offset by the increase in income security and health care.

Table 6.1[11]
Distribution of Budget by Function (Billions of $)

	1980	1985	1990	1995	2000
National defense*	$160	$288	$337	$315	$319
Income security	86	128	147	225	266
Commerce	9	4	67	-17	12
Education	32	29	39	54	63
Health	55	99	156	275	367
Other	80	93	82	117	126
Interest†	55	134	200	265	292
Total	477	770	1028	1227	1445
On-budget					

*Includes International Security Assistance, which equals about $6 billion annually and Veterans Benefits, which will rise from $21 billion in 1980 to $44 billion by the year 2000. Although I believe it is proper to include Veteran's Benefits in defense, if I were to exclude them it would not materially affect our analysis or conclusions.

†Includes net interest plus the Social Security trust fund interest received.

Note that I have not included Social Security outlays in this analysis. If we include the outlays we must also include the FICA taxes received. This is how the federal budget is usually shown and as a result the budget is shown to be roughly in balance by 1999. However, the Social Security trust funds are required to pay out future benefits—indeed we are not accumulating enough of a surplus to cover the projected benefits. Hence, ***the correct accounting procedure should be to accrue future payouts and include that in the budget. On this basis the budget shows not a surplus, but a continued deficit of over $100 billion.*** Therefore, we get a clearer understanding of the relative impact of the budget components that contributed to the deficits by excluding both Social Security revenues and expenditures. We will explore the problem of social security and its solution in depth in chapter 12.

We now need to explore the major categories of the federal budget expense growth shown in table 6.1 in more depth.

Defense Growth

While working as an economic consultant to the Federal Government's Office of Management and the Budget (OMB) I was asked to sit in on its review of the federal agencies' 1980 budgets. Each agency was subject to a severe grilling by the OMB staff assigned to challenge every line item on the agency's budget as OMB tried to reduce total federal spending. But when we came to the Defense Department's budget I was surprised to find out that the budget reviewers were actually housed at the Defense Department and seemed to be more responsible to the assistant secretary of defense than to the director of OMB.

In the absence of any serious challenge to the defense budget, an OMB staffer and I questioned the potential social and economic impacts of spending a planned $160 billion on defense for fiscal year 1980. I argued that such large expenditures were reducing private research and development, investment in plant and equipment, and investment in urban infrastructure. At the same time, the best and brightest of our scientists and engineers were being pulled out of universities and the private sector to work on lucrative defense contracts. My concerns were always met with the answer, "This is a matter of national security and therefore takes precedence over any other issue."

As dismayed as I was at how little oversight was exerted to insure the necessity of spending $160 billion, my experience did not prepare me for the incredible hemorrhage of federal tax dollars that was to flow to defense during the Reagan years. (A brief history of post-war defense spending and its economic consequences is provided in Appendix B.)

In 1980, Ronald Reagan won the presidency using the tried-and-true scare tactics of the Red Menace. Within six years his administration had pumped the Defense Department budget up from $134 billion to $273 billion annually, an increase of more than 100 percent. The increase in defense spending over the decade of the 1980s was the single largest category of expense increase, exceeding even the combined increase in income security and health care. (Since 1990, defense-related expenditures have declined, but by the year 2000 they will still account for 22 percent of the entire budget—19 percent if we exclude veterans' benefits.)

Citing the annual increase does not adequately reflect the cumulative impact of the rise of defense spending in the 1980s. During the decade, Americans spent $3.6 trillion on defense (in 1995 constant dollars). The Reagan budget forecasts planned on continuing to increase annual defense expenditures to $400 billion annually by 1992 with no end in sight.[12] The Bush administration trimmed defense spending in real dollar terms and Clinton continued the cuts. But by the mid-1990s further cuts were generally opposed by both parties.

The Clinton administration's defense strategy is that we must be prepared to fight two full-scale wars simultaneously without any aid from our NATO allies. This strategy ignores the fact that with the collapse of the Soviet Union there is no nation or group of nations strong enough to fight a war of such a magnitude. Outside of Western Europe, Iraq was thought to have the largest army in the world and it took only a few weeks to annihilate it. In 1997, the $270 billion U.S. defense budget (excluding veterans benefits) exceeded that of the next six largest armies combined. The Russian military budget had dropped substantially to $69.5 billion by 1995 and was expected to be cut further, while China spent $63.5 billion on defense.[13] The next several countries in the ranking are our allies including France, England, Germany, and Japan. In short, there is no military justification for the present level of U.S. military overkill.

Even though Clinton's 1996 budget sought to increase defense expenditures by $25 billion over the next five years to mollify congressional hawks, it was not enough. The House sought to spend $80 billion to fund forty B–2 Stealth bombers that the Pentagon and Air Force have told Congress repeatedly that they don't need or want. As Ron Dellums (D-Calif.) said during the debate, "I hear the sizzle of pork."[14]

Some specific initiatives that would yield substantial tax savings include the following:

1. *Substantially cut U.S. troops in Europe, Japan, and Korea.* With the Soviets withdrawing all troops from Eastern Europe, it makes no sense for America to have more than a skeleton force there. At the end of 1997 approximately 100,000 U.S. troops were stationed in Europe along with an even greater number of civilian employees and military dependents.[15] The Center for Defense Information estimates that the 60 percent of our total defense budget that goes to our efforts to support NATO (about $160 billion in 1998) is greater than all the other NATO military budgets combined. Given the many problems we face at home, such an expenditure is patently absurd. These expenditures are enough to house every homeless American, provide adequate drug rehabilitation, and rebuild crumbling roads and bridges.

An additional 100,000 troops are stationed in Japan (64,000) and Korea (37,000). These are also unnecessary. The South Korean army is far more sophisticated and powerful than their North Korean adversary, and Japan faces no danger from Russia, as Japan's own defense program tacitly reflects. The Japanese air force is rapidly becoming one of the best in the world.

2. *Develop a nonintervention pact with Moscow whereby both countries agree not to support either revolutionary forces or incumbent governments with any form of military assistance.* Admittedly, this is a difficult agreement both to nego-

tiate and enforce. But the time is right. Both countries have much more to gain than to lose by such an agreement.

3. *Continue the present moratorium of all nuclear tests, both above and below ground.* Russia has sought this goal for some time. It is in our best interest to agree since we are far ahead of Russia and all other countries in nuclear weapons technologically, and such an agreement maintains that advantage at no cost. This would be one of the easier treaties to monitor. It would also protect us from the potential escape of radiation from underground tests as has occurred in the past.

4. *Continue mutual nuclear disarmament.* India tried to derail the present effort to develop a worldwide ban on nuclear testing, arguing that the ban must be coupled with a goal of total nuclear disarmament. However, *total* nuclear disarmament will not happen, nor should it. Neither the United States or Russia is going to risk its strategic superiority over the rest of the world by total nuclear disarmament. However, both countries can significantly reduce their nuclear stockpiles without any risk to national security.

In the mid-1980s there were about 50,000 nuclear weapons worldwide. The United States had about 26,000 weapons (including 4,000 inactive weapons) and the nations of the former Soviet Union about 20,000. With the fall of the Soviet Union there has been a reduction of nuclear weapons on both sides, but not nearly the reduction we might have expected.[17] Both the United States and Russia have 8,000 to 9,000 nuclear warheads. The START 3 treaty, which neither country appears to be seriously considering at this time, would reduce warheads to about 3,500. Senator Jesse Helms continues to push for the Anti-Ballistic Missile system in violation of the ABM treaty. There is no way Russia will cut more nuclear weapons if the Americans insists on pursuing Star Wars.*

Aside from ourselves and Russia, France, and the United Kingdom have the most nuclear missiles. China has from 225 to 300; India, Israel, South Africa, Pakistan and possibly North Korea, have added limited nuclear capability. India and Pakistan also are developing medium-range missiles to deliver their nuclear bombs. Several other countries, including Iran and Iraq, and possibly Brazil, were actively seeking to develop the bomb. West Germany has been guilty of supplying the technical know-how and facilities necessary to develop nuclear capabilities to anyone willing to pay. The United States should make it clear that unless Germany makes a determined effort to police its export of nuclear capabilities it will have the gravest consequence for future German-American relations. Further prolif-

*Not content with maintaining the nuclear threat, Helms has also used his position to prevent the Senate from voting to ratify the Chemical Weapons Convention signed by 120 countries. He prefers that the U.S. sit on its stockpile of 30,000 tons of chemical weapons.

eration could be halted by a United Nations threat of embargo against any nation that tests a nuclear weapon. Of course, an embargo cannot be effective unless most of the world goes along with it. Past embargoes proved ineffective against dictatorships such as Iran or Cuba. In the case of democracies, however, businesses and citizens affected by the embargo will quickly bring pressure on the government to alter its policies.

5. *Accelerate base closings around the world and in the United States.* America has 360 large military installations throughout the world plus hundreds of smaller installations. Only a fraction of these are needed for adequate security. Most of these bases were established to meet a Soviet threat prior to the advent of the intercontinental ballistic missile. They need to be assessed in light of the new world order.

One of the biggest obstacles to base closings in this country is the threatened loss of jobs that causes each congressional representative to fight for bases in his or her home state. However a study of seventy-five base closings between 1961 and 1975 showed that although 68,800 Defense Department civilian employees lost jobs, 78,800 new civilian jobs were located on the former defense facilities, including education, air transport, and light industry.[18] Although reduced defense spending will hurt some regional economies, at least temporarily, it will benefit others. One of the primary reasons for the economic success of the South and West during the last 30 years was the huge influx of defense dollars. Conversely, many of these tax dollars to support defense came from the Northeast and Midwest areas. The net outflow of tax dollars from these areas amounted to $19.3 billion in 1989.[19] Slowing this constant outflow of tax dollars from the Northeast-Midwest region has already had a significant benefit for their economies (except for Massachusetts which was a prime beneficiary of Navy contracts), and reduced the need for other forms of federal assistance in these areas.

6. *Assuming the status quo in the world situation, continue to reduce defense spending to $200 billion.* The Center for Defense Information (CDI) estimated that the we could have reduced military personnel worldwide from 2,050,000 in 1995 to 1,200,000 by the year 2000, cut spending by $500 billion over this period, and still have fulfilled all essential military requirements.[20] Total defense expenditures could drop to as low as $175 billion by the year 2002 if our government stopped trying to be the world's policeman.[21] Taking a slightly less aggressive approach to cutting defense, holding the defense budget at $200 billion in constant dollars would still leave us spending far more on defense than any combination of possible enemies. A budget of $200 billion would be $66 billion less than the 1997 defense budget. The House has approved a 1997 defense spending authorization of $265.6 billion. Adjusted for inflation, this amount is still

higher than defense expenditures in the 1970s after the end of Vietnam War, even though there is now no Soviet Union or other external threat to justify that level of expenditure. Ironically, it is even $11.3 billion more than the Pentagon requested! Once again we can hear the sizzle of pork.

Expensive systems such as the Stealth bomber, Stealth fighter, and the Seawolf submarine must also be reviewed in terms of their need relative to other more pressing priorities such as education, crime, and replacement of the nation's physical infrastructure. The cost of new weapons is staggering. It will cost $80 billion for only forty B–1 bombers—two hundred times the cost of a World War II bomber. Fighters cost one hundred times more today than in the Second World War.[22] Seawolf submarines cost $2.4 billion each.

Do we need all this added high-tech capability? A 1996 General Accounting Office Study concluded that during and after the Persian Gulf War (1991) the Pentagon dramatically oversold its most expensive high-tech aircraft and missiles. Claims made by the Pentagon and its main military contractors for the Stealth fighter, the Tomahawk land-attack missile, and laser-guided smart bombs "were overstated, misleading, inconsistent with the best available data, or unverifiable." The GAO concluded that the costly systems didn't necessarily perform better than old-fashioned, cheaper "dumb" bombs.[23]

Furthermore, the primary contest of the twenty-first century will be an economic war, not a military one. The country that spends the most on civilian research and development, not defense R and D, will be the victor. As England discovered to its dismay, a nation whose productivity falls 1 percent per year below its competitor nations will eventually drop from an industrial leader to a mediocre economy.[24]

By reducing America's military strength at this time, the world may actually be more, rather than less safe. Having an overly dominant military power encourages hegemony and military adventurism. As for our role as the world's policeman, to the extent that it can be accomplished at all—which is doubtful—that is more properly a function for the United Nations. It is obvious that Europe and South Korea do not think they are faced with any external threats and are unwilling to pay the United States for the protection we provide. (Japan is the exception, since they do pay approximately the cost of our protection.)

Furthermore, it is one thing to want to be able to defend yourself from potential enemies. It is quite another to want the capability of waging multiple wars around the world. We can adequately accomplish the first at a fraction of the cost now being expended. With regard to the second goal, a robust economy can quickly meet any such threat if it appears that one is developing. But such a fear is far-fetched at best. A much more realistic danger is that within fifty years we will be a nation faced with a major shortage of uncontaminated water. Again, it is a matter of getting our priorities straight.

Income Security

There is so much misleading information with regard to income security that to understand this category we need to examine it in some detail. In the first place, it comes as shock to most people to discover that the federal government provides as much or more in subsidies to the rich than it does to the poor. Neil Howe and Philip Longman calculated that in 1991 households with over $100,000 in income received an average of $5,690 worth of federal cash and income benefits, whereas households with under $10,000 in income received an average of $5,560.[25] The benefits to the wealthy do not show up as a line item in the budget, however, because these are taxes not collected as contrasted, for example, to the earned income tax credit for the poor, which is an actual payout of net tax refunds to those earning below a certain level. Yet, the effect of not collecting taxes or of paying a tax credit are exactly the same in terms of the impact on the federal budget's bottom line.

If we just examined the actual federal outlays between 1980 and 1991, average benefits in constant dollars to low-income households declined 7 percent while during the same period the real value of benefits to households with income over $200,000 doubled.[26] The reason is primarily due to the benefits received by the elderly regardless of their income. In other words, the increase was due primarily to increases in Social Security payments, Medicare, and federal pensions.

When most people think of welfare they think of Aid to Families with Dependent Children (AFDC) and assume that such welfare is a major portion of federal spending. The truth is that AFDC accounted for barely over 1 percent of all federal spending in 1995.[27] Food stamps and housing assistance would add another 4 percent.[28] The biggest chunk of assistance to the poor is Medicaid, which was $96 billion, or over 6 percent, of the 1995 budget.[29] All social welfare spending would amount to about 15 percent of the budget. Except for Medicaid, the absolute amount expended upon the poor has been declining for more than a decade in inflation adjusted terms, and even more so on a per capita basis. *Business Week* estimated that, adjusted for inflation, Federal appropriations for nonentitlements such as AFDC and food stamps were 40 percent lower in 1994 than 1981.[30] Other areas with steep declines in real dollars include:

- 62 percent reduction for housing,
- 59 percent reduction for employment and training,

- 29 percent reduction for block grants to states and municipalities,
- 54 percent reduction for energy assistance,
- 26 percent reduction for legal services.[31]

For almost two decades now there has been an increasing clamor for welfare reform. The general belief is that growth in welfare has been a major contributor to the budget deficit. The correct answer depends on how we define welfare. As seen above, the items that most people think of when they hear the term welfare have been declining. The two areas accounting for virtually all of the increase in welfare—in the broadest sense of the term—are Medicare and income security (unemployment payments, not Social Security). Between 1990 and 1995 income security jumped by $75 billion, accounting for 32 percent of the increase in total spending for the period. Two of the primary drivers of this growth were the increase in the Earned Income Tax Credit (EITC), which rose by $12 billion, and Supplemental Security Income (SSI), which grew by about $15 billion. The growth of the EITC reflects the fact that many of the jobs created after the 1990–91 recession were so low paying that they could not raise a person out of poverty. The low wages were due to the excessive growth in the labor force relative to the demand for labor, as we discussed earlier.

The increase in SSI reflects the growing number of elderly immigrants who have been coming to retire in America. According to the General Accounting Office, over one-third of the recipients of SSI in 1995 were immigrants. Many of these people were not poor or could be supported by their children, but by deeding their assets to their children, they could claim SSI benefits. Moreover, based upon the trend, SSI was projected to increase from $12 billion in 1995 to $67 billion by 2004. The 1996 Welfare Reform Bill sought to deny SSI to immigrants as well as food stamps and other benefits. However, most of the cuts were later reversed. The other reductions resulting from Welfare Reform—although not insignificant—had only a minor impact on the overall budget.

Immigration has had another major impact on the growth of welfare costs since the majority of immigrants are poor. Economist Robert Samuelson estimates that a quarter to a half of the increase in poverty since the early 1970s was due to immigration. He points out that between 1973 and 1994 the number of people with incomes below the poverty line rose by 15 million, of which 6 million (40 percent) were Hispanic.[32] Obviously, all immigrants are not Hispanic and all Hispanics are not immigrants. However, Hispanics account for over half of all immigrants, and as a group have the least marketable skills among immigrants. Moreover, immigrants compete with indigenous Americans, thereby depressing wage rates, which results in a greater number of American citizens falling under the poverty level, and this also increases welfare costs. If we want to significantly reduce welfare without simultaneously increasing the number of people living in poverty, we must reduce immigration. From every prospective, the U.S. immigration policy of the last two decades makes no sense.

Savings and Loan Bailout

In the 1980s, the public was outraged at the crass greed displayed by S & L officials who attempted to parlay the savings of the public into their own personal wealth by undertaking extraordinarily high-risk investments until their whole financial house of cards came tumbling down. Over four hundred S & L officials were eventually charged with some form of wrong-doing. But we are mistaken to conclude that the S & L fiasco was due to an unusually large number of greedy financiers. An objective analysis of the S & L debacle reveals that it was seriously flawed federal policy that prompted the self-interest, which is inherent in human nature, to go seriously awry. Basically, the federal government removed regulatory constraints, while keeping in place federal guarantees on bank loans. The problem S & Ls were those that had no stringent state regulations to fill the gap left by dropping federal regulation. Texas is a prime example. In effect, a bank manager was provided an incentive to lend money for high-risk projects that might yield a high return. After all, he knew that the savers really had little risk of losing their money since, even if the bank failed, the federal government would guarantee their savings. I say this not to exonerate the behavior of all S & L presidents but, in general, it was misguided federal policies that produced the S & L fiasco.

In 1980 the number of troubled S & Ls could have been bailed out for $15 billion. But the Reagan administration ignored the situation, choosing to believe that any problem in banking could be cured with less, rather than more, regulation. They might have been right *if* the administration removed federal deposit insurance at the same time it removed the regulations on the loan policies of S & Ls. Without federal deposit insurance, a bank would have had to purchase private insurance and the private insurer would have provided the oversight to make certain the S & L wasn't making unwise loans. Ironically, the administration so much in support of a market economy effectively instituted a policy that completely subverted the checks and balances of a free market. The result added approximately $146 billion to the federal debt between 1986 and 1991. And the total cost was expected to reach about $250 billion. (It accounted for $58 billion of the 1990 Commerce expenditures in the functional budget shown in table 6.1). Eventually, the federal deposit insurance costs are expected to return to the normal $2 billion annual level. Still, the cost of the bailout will be reflected in the interest on the federal debt for years to come.

Health Care

In the first half of the 1990s, soaring Medicare and Medicaid costs replaced defense as the primary budget driver. From 1980 until 1990 federally financed health care tripled from $55 billion to $156 billion; between 1990 and 1995 it rose by another $119 billion to $275 billion. In 1997 the Congressional Budget Office estimated that Medicare and Medicaid would grow by 8.4 percent and 7.7 percent respectively through the year 2002.[33] Healthcare costs are indeed the number one issue of the 1990s and beyond, amounting to almost half of the total projected increase in the budget between 1995 and the year 2000.[34]

Federal expenditures on health care were projected to reach almost $381 billion by year 2000, more than 21 percent of the total budget outlays. (After congressional negotiations, this amount was reduced slightly.) The cost of Medicare is 150 times the estimates made when the program was created.[35] If we add the amount of private expenditure on health care, the projections of healthcare costs are indeed staggering. As figure 6.2 shows, total federal, state, and private healthcare spending exceeded $1 trillion in 1996, and based upon the current rate of growth would exceed $1.2 trillion by the year 2000.[36]

Figure 6.2[37]
Health Care Expenditures 1950 to 2000 (Billions of $)

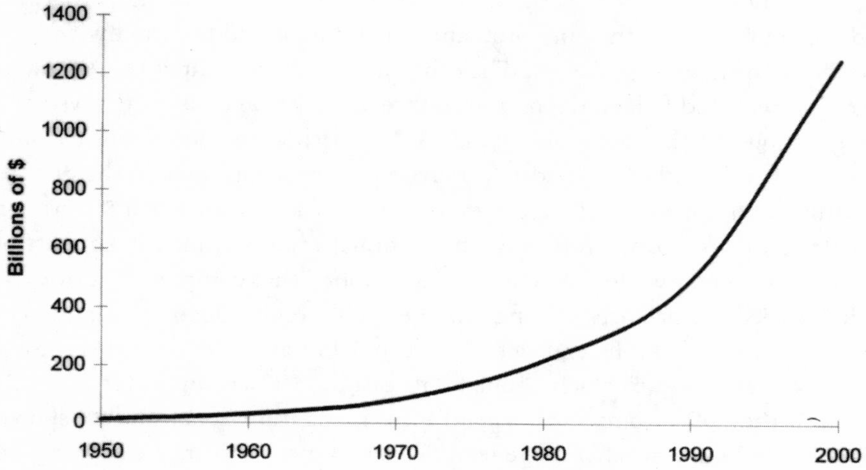

Although the growth of Health Maintenance Organizations (HMOs) significantly reduced the growth of healthcare costs in 1996, pressuring doctors and patients to join HMOs will not be sufficient to significantly curb the long-term trend in rising healthcare costs. The primary reason is that the continued introduction of new technology to extend life will result in added demand for healthcare expenditures. Moreover, there is little doubt that continued legislative efforts will be made to extend healthcare coverage for many more people.* In 1997 there were still over forty million Americans who had no healthcare coverage during the year. There are also a number of proposals to improve access to healthcare for people fifty-five to sixty-four years old. All such legislation, whatever its other merits, will raise healthcare expenditures. We will take an in-depth look at the issue of health care in chapter 12.

Interest Charges

Finally, the failure to fund the higher federal spending through higher taxes resulted in borrowing to such an exorbitant extent that the interest costs are now one of the major causes of further growth in the national debt. ***From 1980 to 1990 net interest increased from $52 billion to $184 billion annually, a growth rate of over 13 percent per year. From 1990 to 1997 interest costs rose to $244 billion annually—a much improved annual rate of only 4 percent.*** Still, when we net out the interest received due to trust fund surpluses (primarily Social Security), increased interest expense on the rest of the budget accounted for about 29 percent of the total increase in federal expenditures between 1990 and 1997. On this adjusted basis the interest on the national debt in 1997 was $285 billion accounting for 22 percent of the total outlays, compared to only 13 percent in 1980.†

Even though the annual deficits are shrinking, as long as we run deficits, the national debt will continue to grow. If interest rates rise again, the debt will grow even faster due to the payments of interest on the debt—every 1 percent increase in interest rates would increase the debt by $40 billion.

---

*For example, the Health Care Insurance Portability and Accountability Act (HIPAA) passed in 1996 helped workers maintain continuous coverage by limiting exclusions of preexisting conditions and by expanding guaranteed issue and renewability requirements, which prohibit insurers from denying coverage or renewal on the basis of health status or claims experience.

†Since the trust funds are collecting interest, the net interest for 1997 was only $244 billion, or 15.2 percent of the total outlays.

Deficits are Understated Due to Social Security Surplus

To make matters worse, the deficit estimates do not adequately portray the situation, because they reflect the *"unified" or total budget.* The unified budget concept was established in 1969 to account for all of the federal government trust funds, including those for Social Security. Tax revenues are accumulated in trust funds to provide for a future liabilities. In the case of Social Security, a huge surplus is necessary today to provide adequate old age pensions to the generation of baby boom workers when they retire.

In budget terminology, trust funds are called an *off-budget* item. The annual deficit is calculated both including and excluding the present surplus in the trust funds. However, the most commonly used estimate of the federal deficit in Congressional discussions and the popular press is the unified budget deficit which *includes* the surplus in the Social Security trust fund. In 1997, the Social Security and disability trust funds ran a surplus of about $75 billion.[38] ***If we netted out all the "off-budget" receipts and expenditures and consider only the "on-budget" items, the deficit for 1997 would have been $103 billion rather than the $22 billion commonly quoted. Instead of running a projected $8 billion surplus in the year 2000, the on-budget deficit is projected to run a $105 billion deficit.***[39] Adding these trust fund surpluses to the budget without also accruing the cost of future payouts presents the danger that the government will, in effect, steal from future generations by using the present budget surpluses to fund other projects. As we will see, the most accurate portrayal of the federal budget is to keep Social Security payments and benefits in a separate budget, and report not only annual receipts and payouts, but equally important, report the net of projected future receipts against future payouts.

But are the Deficits a Problem?

As scary as these numbers seem on the surface, some economists believe that we should not be overly concerned with their magnitude. In part it depends upon how one views the data. Figure 6.3 shows the annual deficits in five-year increments since 1935. The picture between 1980 and 1990 was indeed alarming. However, the annual deficit peaked in 1992 at $292 billion and has been steadily declining ever since. The decline reflects the strong economic growth since the 1990–91 recession, major cuts in spending, and the tax increases passed by Bush and Clinton.

Moreover, the raw data may give a misleading picture regarding the rel-

Figure 6.3[40]
Total and On-budget Deficits, 1935–2000

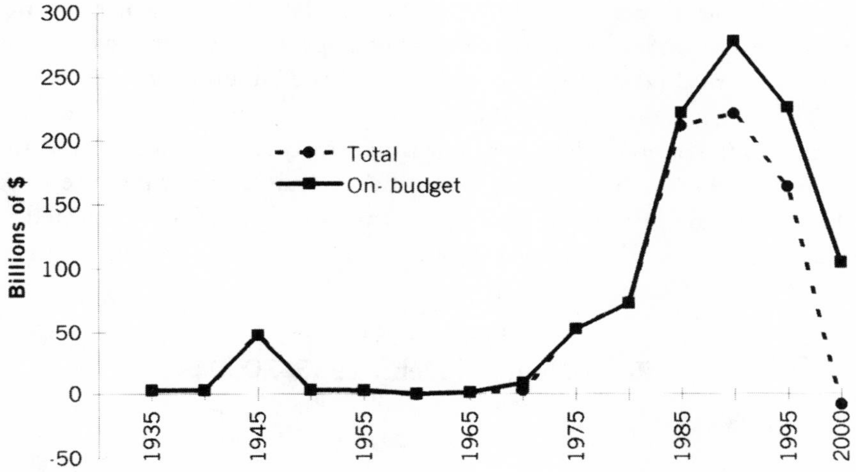

ative magnitude of the deficits in the last two decades compared to previous deficits. Economists will point out that there has been significant inflation over this period and, hence, a more accurate view of the annual deficits would adjust for inflation, i.e., be shown in constant dollars. Furthermore, since the economy is much larger today than in the past we are able to borrow more each year. To adjust for inflation and growth of the economy we need to view the deficit as a percent of total GDP as shown in Figure 6.4.

Figure 6.4[41]
Deficit as Percent of GDP, 1935–2000

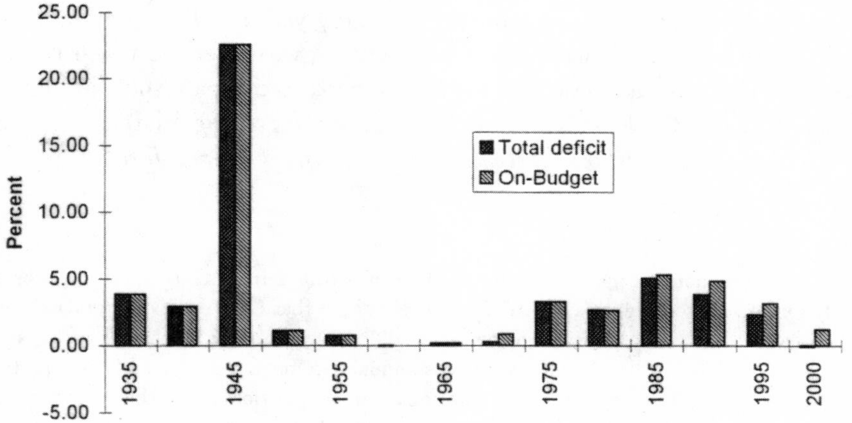

Here we see that as a percentage of total output, the 5.2 percent registered when the deficits were over $200 billion annually was much smaller than the relative 1945 deficit, which amounted to 23 percent of GDP (the all-time high was 30 percent of GDP reached in 1943). Even when viewing the higher on-budget deficit, it does not appear particularly worrisome from a historical perspective. So what was all the hubbub about?

The problem is that even though the *annual* increase (i.e., the annual deficits) to the national debt was increasing slowly relative to the GDP, the *cumulative* debt (i.e., the total federal debt) grew at a blistering pace since 1980, as shown in figure 6.5, reaching $5 trillion in 1996 and projected to be about $6 trillion by the year 2000.

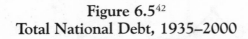

Figure 6.5[42]
Total National Debt, 1935–2000

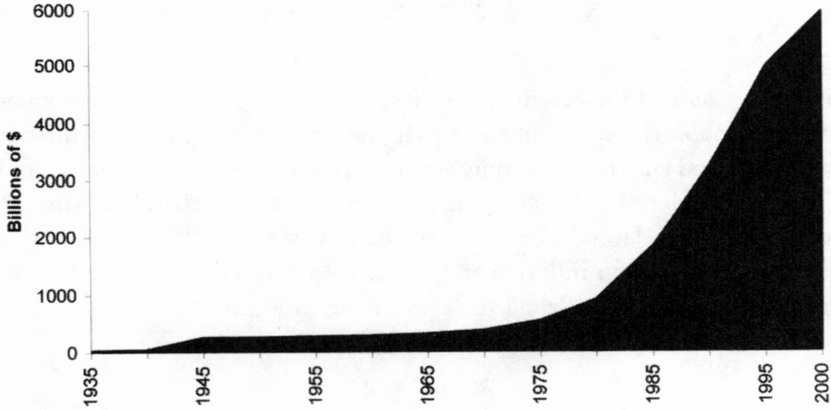

It is like the man who keeps borrowing every year until one day he finds he is up to his neck in debt. But if he is getting wealthier every year maybe he can afford the added debt. So again we need to compare the cumulative federal debt to GDP.* The question is, *is the debt growing* relative *to the size of the economy? If it is, then it would become increasingly more difficult to support the debt burden.*

*Some economists may complain that by comparing debt to GDP, I am inappropriately mixing a "stock" with a "flow." They might argue that I should divide total debt by the nation's total wealth rather than one year's GDP. However, what I am doing is the same as a bank does when it review's a borrower's annual income as a measure of his liquidity and debt-carrying capacity. We never want to be in the position where the country must sell its assets to fund its debt, for in doing so we are selling the next generation's legacy.

Figure 6.6[43]
Debt as Percentage of GDP, 1935–2000

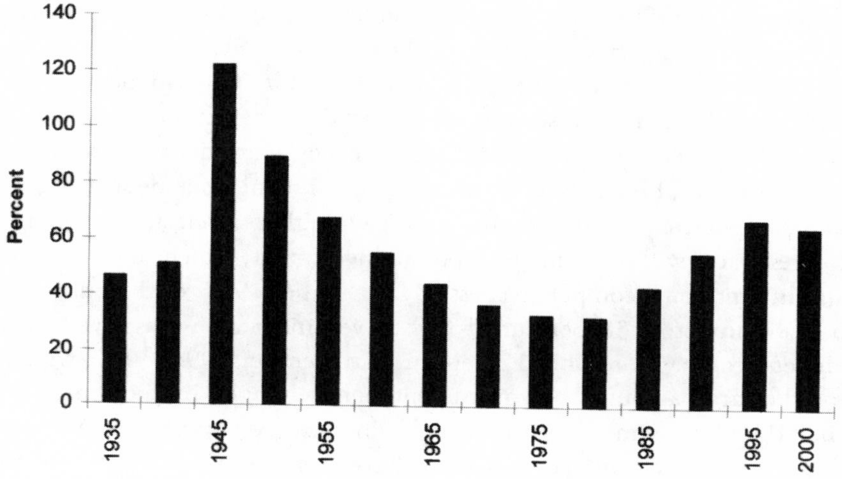

As figure 6.6 shows, as a percent of GDP, the national debt peaked in 1995 at 65 percent of GDP, about the level of 1955, and much lower than the 122 percent level just after the Second World War (or the roughly 100 percent that Japan was running in 1998). In the absence of a major tax cut, the ratio should continue to decline. However, much of the projected decline is due to the accumulation of the huge Social Security surplus, which will eventually evaporate when the baby boomers retire. By 1998 it looked like the rapid growth in the economy would generate enough tax dollars to close the total deficit by 1999. But if there is a recession, this picture could change rapidly; and remember, we still have not closed the "on-budget" deficit which is the more meaningful estimate.

Even when the annual deficits were at their highest some economists, such as the late Robert Eisner of Northern University, were not concerned about the magnitude of either the deficits or the growth in the federal debt. Let's examine their arguments.

1. *In addition to being much lower than during World War II, as a percent of GDP our national debt is not higher than many of our international competitors, such as Japan.* Economist Lester Thurow points out that this is true but irrelevant, since the other major industrial nations have a much higher savings rate then we do. Therefore, they can run deficits and not have to worry that the funding of the debt would deprive funds needed to sustain the private sector for investment. The Japanese save so much that they could afford to not only cover their own debt, but a significant portion of the U.S. debt as well.[44] Ultimately, then, the problem is not so much the mag-

nitude of the debt per se, but the lower rate of investment of Americans in their own economy. As the baby boomers hit their prime earnings years, domestic savings and investment should increase. This indeed began during the mid-90s even though the annual savings *rate* has not increased as economists expected. Indeed, it is at a postwar low.

2. *We can borrow from abroad to finance the debt.* This is true only if the U.S. risk-adjusted interest rates are higher than the rest of the world. But since the government is competing with corporations when seeking to borrow money, higher interest rates on government-issue debt means that U.S. corporations will also have to pay higher interest rates. Higher interest rates will discourage corporate investment, which reduces growth and international competitiveness. By the end of 1997, of the public debt held by investors 38 percent of U.S. government debt was owed to foreigners, compared to only 17 percent at the end of 1994.[45] If it were not for the large amounts of government bonds bought by foreigners, plus their direct investment in American businesses, the growth rate in jobs and GDP during recent years would have been much slower. In fact, throughout the nineteenth century, America was a net debtor nation and it was foreign investment that did much to finance the building of the railroads and to develop the frontier of the U.S. economy.

Each year the United States must pay approximately $85 billion in interest on the $1.3 trillion of debt owned by foreigners. The interest may be more than offset by the additional output generated by the investment but, all things being equal, we would rather such investment returns go to Americans investing in their own country.[46] Borrowing from abroad also puts the U.S. economy at risk if the need for capital abroad causes foreigners to redeem their U.S. bonds. The result would be a net outflow of investment from the United States, thus reducing our growth rate.

Eisner points out that because all U.S. debt to foreigners is denominated in U.S. dollars, there is no danger of having to default because we can simply increase the supply of money to pay off the debt.[47] But such a strategy of devaluing our currency would be inflationary and discourage further investment from abroad.

3. *The U.S. economy can grow faster than the debt, thus shrinking the debt in relative terms until we generate so much incremental revenue that we can eventually pay it off.* Thurow argues that this is impossible because to grow faster than the growth in debt would require a productivity growth of 4.6 percent a year.[48] The average growth for U.S. productivity is only about 1 percent per year over the past twenty-five years.[49] (In the last couple of years, however, productivity has increased over 2 percent annually.)

4. *A large portion of government spending—e.g., spending on infrastructure, research, and education—is investment, not consumption. This investment should*

not be included in current spending (and, hence, added to the deficit) any more than capital equipment purchases for a private firm are counted as expense. To the extent that government expenditures are investment, more investment is better than less investment.

Unlike many countries, the United States does not differentiate between annual consumption expenditures and capital investment expenditures in the National Income and Product Accounts.[50] All expenditures are treated as annual cash outlays, but whereas consumption is used up in the year, investment lasts many years. According to Eisner, in 1992, $520 billion, 25 percent of government expenditures, could be deemed capital expenditure.[51] This would include, for example, investment in sanitation facilities, airports, highways and bridges, or any public works. When businesses invest in plant and equipment they depreciate the expenditure over its useful life and only charge the annual depreciation against current year revenue. There is no reason why government should not follow the same accounting system for budget purposes. Failure to do so biases spending decisions against capital investment and is one of the reasons why as a nation we have failed to maintain investment in infrastructure such as mass transportation, highways and bridges, sanitation facilities, school buildings, etc.

Eisner would go further and, again following the example of business, count government research and development expenditures as investment. He would also treat educational expense as investment in human resources in the same manner, to be amortized over the working life of the person.[52]

According to Eisner, the $255 billion deficit estimated for 1993 should have been reduced by $80 billion for R & D, education, and training. Moreover, Eisner argued that on balance the deficits have been good for the economy over the past three decades, primarily because they resulted in less unemployment.[53] He estimated that if the economy were stimulated to the point where unemployment dropped to 5 percent, the deficits would be cut by $100 billion annually.[54]

As Eisner puts it: "What really counts is not the size of the deficit or the amount of private saving as currently measured. What is critical is what households and business and government are spending for. It makes a big difference if individuals turn out to be big borrowers and spenders to gamble in Las Vegas or to buy durable goods or new houses or finance their children's education."[55]

There are several problems with Eisner's arguments. He is correct in saying that it matters more what the money is being spent on than whether it is spent by individuals or their public representatives. Eisner is right in pointing out that some federal expenditures should be considered as capital investment, just as business accounting treats plant and equipment and R &

D spending. We have concluded as much in our discussion of measurement of GDP in chapter 2. It all depends on what they buy. Clean air and water, more efficient and safe public transportation, safer streets and schools, and the like, all can make major contributions to human happiness. But his assumption that 25 percent of the federal expenditures are investment rather than consumption is at least debatable. Although no doubt some of federal expenditures are true investments in infrastructure and human capital, and therefore will contribute to future production, the two fastest growing components of the budget today are health care and interest on the debt. But it is questionable whether the increase in health care has led to a generally healthier, more productive work force. A large proportion of the increase is due to inefficiencies in the present system, rising prices, and increased expenditures on the elderly. Also, defense expenditures, which were a primary source of the growth in the deficit in the 1980s, are not investments since they do not increase the productive capacity of the economy (even though there may be some indirect spin-off technology improvements).

Furthermore, although Eisner predicted that reducing the deficit in 1994 would result in slowing the economy,[56] the opposite occurred and the economy grew so fast that the Federal Reserve Board had to raise interest rates to keep it from overheating.

Businesses recognize that the standard income statement by itself can give a very false perspective on the health of the business. Cash flow (which conceptually is simply the cash intake and outflow each year) is an equally important perspective regarding the viability of a business (some would argue even more so). And even though a government is not like a business, because federal debt is primarily held by its citizens and the government can control the value of that debt by regulation of the money supply,* no government can simply ignore the size of its debt. Regardless of what the federal government spends money on, it is a cash outlay and must be financed. At the very least, the financing of the deficit causes a redistribution of wealth from those who pay the interest on the debt (in the form of taxes) and those who receive the interest (those who purchase government bonds).

Nor can we ignore the fact that if the federal government is already deeply in debt its options are limited with regard to fiscal policy to stimulate the economy or to meet special additional requirements such as a war, a banking collapse, or aid to bolster the economies of other countries (such as the 1995 bailout of Mexico that avoided their financial collapse). Even monetary policy is constrained by a large burden of debt because any increase in interest rates to slow an overheated economy will increase the

*Of course, the government can also raise taxes to repay the debt.

interest on the debt and, hence, the size of the deficit.

In summary, although the size of the national debt is not as dangerous to the future of our nation as many people believe, over the long run the national debt must grow slower than the nation's output of good or services if the nation is to prosper. Note that this does not imply that the level of federal spending is too high, only that if we wish to maintain any given level of spending we must ultimately finance it through additional tax revenue or other offsetting expense reductions.

Another, more recent concern is the amount of debt held by foreign institutions. Although foreign purchase of our debt stimulates the American economy, we must remember that the interest on that debt is flowing out of the U.S. economy instead of being recycled within it. In addition, when foreign demand for American debt is satiated, the United States will have to raise interest rates to attract more capital. Based upon historic trends, if not for the recent crisis in Asian markets, the United States may have been very close to that level.

Finally, in any discussion of national debt we cannot consider the federal debt in isolation. It must be viewed in the context of state and local government debt, including pension funds, as well as business and consumer debt.

State Deficits

Aside from the deceitful way in which the income tax cuts of the early 1980s were presented to the American people with regard to expected federal budget impacts, they had a covert impact on state and local government budgets as well. As will be discussed more fully later, over the years states and urban areas had become increasingly more dependent on federal grants and transfer payments to provide basic services. As whites fled to the suburbs, the declining tax base of urban areas forced the federal government to step in to make up the loss. Had it not done so, the decline of America's central cities would have been even worse than it was. Faced with a decline in their tax base, the cities would have had to rely upon sales taxes and property taxes, both regressive in terms of their impact, since the poor- and middle-income earners devote a larger proportion of their income to consumption and, therefore, pay a higher proportion of their income for these two taxes than do the rich.* Increasing other taxes, such as payroll taxes or personal property taxes, would drive out businesses. Therefore, the only hope of the cities, aside from cutting services, was increased support from the federal government.

The budgets of the states and of local governments are quite misleading. They always appear to run surpluses, but that is only because of the receipt of federal grants-in-aid. If it were not for federal infusion of dollars, state and local governments would show a continual deficit since 1970. The federal transfer payments rose from $6.5 billion in 1960 to $223.8 billion in 1997.[57] Excluding the federal grants, the aggregate deficit of state and local governments would have grown from $3 billion in 1970 to $113 billion by 1996.

Figure 6.7[58]
Comparison of Federal Grants to State and Local Government Budget Surpluses 1960–1997

As shown in figure 6.7, by 1980 the cities were receiving $80.5 billion

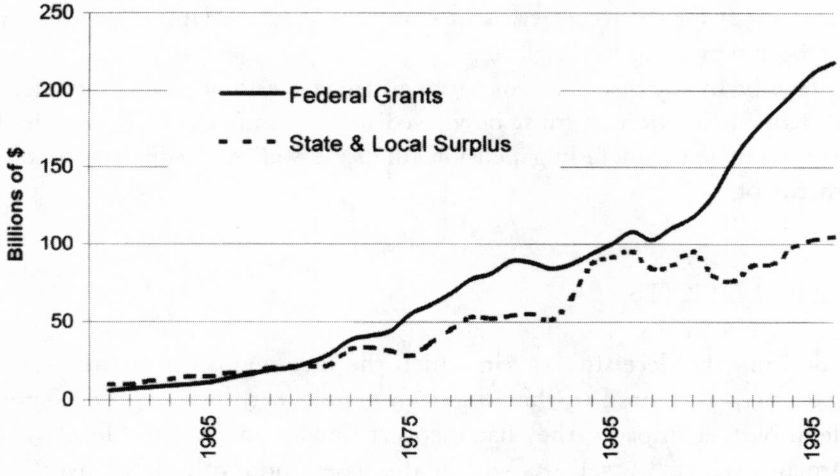

grants-in-aid, amounting to about 24 percent of their total receipts.[59] In the decade that followed, attempts to offset the spiraling defense and healthcare expenditures resulted in a decline in the growth of aid to states and localities. Adjusted for inflation, the federal government subsidies to states and localities were cut by 16 percent. Particularly hard hit were major urban areas that incurred cuts in almost every category, including education and training, mass transit, welfare assistance and criminal justice. The Reagan administration knew that its voter support lay in sub-

*It is sometimes thought that since lower wage earners are more apt to rent than the wealthier people, they are less likely to pay property taxes. However, economists generally agree that property taxes of real estate owners are passed on to renters in the form of higher rents.

urban and rural areas that generally gave little thought for the fate of the central cities. Moreover, the central cities often had little support from state legislatures whose members would have had to raise state income taxes to fill the vacuum left by cuts in federal aid.

By 1988 federal grants fell to 17.6 percent of total state and local funding. States and cities that began raising taxes to make up the shortfall soon ran headlong into a taxpayer rebellion. The strain on the cities forced the Bush administration to again increase grants-in-aid, and this was accelerated under the Clinton administration. By 1996, federal aid reached $218 billion, or 20.7 percent of the state and local government receipts. Without the federal aid, the states would have run a $113 billion deficit in 1996, and even with the federal help many states such as California are still in serious financial trouble.[60]

Pension Fund Deficits

Although few people were aware of the problem, by 1994 state and local pension plans across the country were more than $125 billion short of the money they will need to meet their pension promises.[61] Adding in the shortfall in pension funds for federal civilian and military employees, the total shortfall was a staggering $1.24 trillion.[62] No wonder Dennis Spice, who heads the Illinois State pension plan, predicted that "public-pension underfunding will be the healthcare crisis of the next century."[63] A major cause of the projected pension fund shortfall was the liberal contracts with public employees predicated on the assumption that the public would be agreeable to picking up the tab through increased taxes. Taxpayers proved to be not so docile as public employees and the elected officials negotiating the contracts assumed. Tax freezes and tax cuts meant there would be insufficient funds to cover future pensions.

Since 1994 many states and municipalities were able to close their pension fund shortfalls. This was due in large part to the extraordinary rally in the stock market. The growing economy also increased tax receipts to states and municipalities. Still, if the stock market were to stumble badly, the shortfalls would reappear. Moreover, pension funds must also cover medical plans for retired employees. With the present rate of growth in medical costs, many pension plans are still far from healthy.

Just as in the case of solving the projected Social Security shortfall, the issue is one of intergenerational equity. The pensioners argue that to cut benefits is to effectively say that they were lied to when they were promised a certain level of benefits. On the other hand, the present generation of young people ask why they should pay for the economic sins of their fathers. In the private sector corporations were able to divert some of the improved cash flow to fund pension plans by reducing the real wages paid to employees over the past two decades. In essence, then, present employees have increased funding of their pensions whether they knew it or not. However, as real wages rise and profits shrink, corporations may again try to skimp on adequately funding pension plans.

In the long run, pension benefits for public employees should not continue to be indexed to inflation, unless the Consumer Price Index is modified to reflect the different market basket of goods and services that retired people actually require. (Most private sector companies have already made this change.) For example, elderly homeowners do not need to buy new, larger houses and so they shouldn't incur the weight of the increase in housing prices. But renters are not so lucky. It would be more equitable to offer the two groups a different inflation adjustment for their pension, but it would be impossible to administer, it would invite all sorts of chicanery (such as declaring a small apartment in Florida as the principle residence), and be so politically unpopular as to make passage impossible. The question of how to treat homeowners and renters more equitably is discussed in chapter 13 on tax reform.

Corporate Debt

We discussed the fact that increased corporate and consumer debt contributes to the negative economic impact of the federal debt. What are the causes and consequences of the long term growth in corporate and consumer debt?

If the increase in corporate debt was to raise investment to bring new products and services to the market, we would have little reason for concern. However, one of the major causes for the increased U.S. corporate debt was the takeover mania of the 1980s, or what I have dubbed the *MBA syndrome*. Rather than seek the laborious and difficult task of developing new products and services, and the markets that will buy them, it was thought that an easy road to increased corporate (and more often personal) wealth was simply to buy a company and float junk bonds* to cover the purchase. The profits would supposedly come from synergies between the two companies or by getting rid of the fat in the target company. Unfortunately, more than two-thirds of these takeovers lost money for the purchasing company shareowners.

*Junk bonds are those bonds that offer higher interest rates because they run a higher risk of default. Generally, junk bonds are those rated "ccc" or lower by bond-rating services, although some analysts would advise investors to beware of "B" rated bonds.

I've often listened to investment mangers wax eloquent about the benefits that the acquisition craze was going to generate for America. Yet after the orgy of acquisitions in the 1980s, U.S. productivity growth was no higher than in the 1970s—still struggling along at about 1 percent per year.[64] Productivity did not improve much in the 1990s even with the major corporate restructuring that cut out hundreds of thousands of management jobs. Such cutbacks of bloated bureaucracies have a one time impact in improving efficiency and could have been accomplished by efficient management. Perhaps the need to pay off the debt resulting from the acquisitions resulted in reduction of corporate bureaucracies, but the increase in international competition would eventually have produced the same result.

In the long run, the key to sustained earnings growth is increased research and development to increase productivity and develop new products and services. Unfortunately, all too often companies laden with debt after an acquisition have had to cut R & D, capital investment, or marketing to meet their interest payments. Between 1983 and 1990 corporations increased their debt-to-net-worth ratio* from 66 percent (just slightly above the post World War II average) to an extraordinary peak of 90 percent before finally turning down.[65] As a percentage of cash flow, interest payments rose from 23 percent in 1981 to 30 percent by 1989.[66] This left less for investment, especially R & D. As economist Paul Krugman explains, the primary effect of the mania of corporate leveraging (going into debt to expand the company) and buyouts was the redistribution of wealth from workers to stockholders.[67]

I do not contend that acquisitions are never a good idea. There are many thoughtful acquisitions that have made good economic sense. On the other hand, the vast majority of acquisitions appear to have done little more than enrich lawyers, financiers, the management of the acquired company who were given golden parachutes,† and the management of the acquiring company who feel entitled to larger salaries because they are managing a larger operation. I am not even including all the inside traders whose obscene personal enrichment became a role model for a whole generation of business school majors.

Some might feel that the growth of the economy in the 1990s was evidence of the benefits of the previous decade's mergers. Indeed there is some evidence that to repay the huge debt, corporations began a downsizing of

---

*This ratio uses net worth based upon historic costs. If I had used the ratio of debt to net worth based upon market value, it would, of course, be much lower, but the trend would be similar, increasing from 29.5 percent in 1980 to 53.4 percent in 1994.

†Special one-time payments to managers who lose their jobs due to an acquisition. For top management these payments can be many millions of dollars.

white-collar jobs that was long overdue. However, aside from the information industry that continued an incredible growth in productivity, most industries improved profitability by holding down wages, either by moving jobs offshore to lower-wage job markets, or by suppressing wage demands by threatening to move. Many companies are also able to gain special tax concessions from city and state governments as incentives to stay at their present location or to relocate to other cities and states. Overall U.S. productivity continued to inch up at only about 1 percent a year through most of the 1990s.[68]

During the 1991 recession, corporations slowed their acquisitions and began getting their financial houses in order. By 1997 the ratio of debt to net worth had declined to a more financially secure level of 73 percent.[69] Much of the 1990s saw profits rapidly improving. But toward the end of the decade, the improved cash-flow positions of many corporations once again wetted their appetites for the take-over game. It looks like the cycle will begin all over again.

Consumer Debt

In tandem with governments and business, all of whom decide to plunge into debt, consumers also join the leap into the seductive waters of easy credit. Why save for the future when you can have it all today? What can we expect from a nation, whose citizens are mesmerized by thousands of hours of TV advertising and consumption-enhancing programming? Before leaving college these TV-conditioned consumers have credit cards thrust upon them and they are off to the consumption races. Unfortunately, at the same time real wages failed to keep pace with their expectations. Even two-wage families did not produce enough income to enable them to keep up with the television "Joneses" who reassure them that they can have it all.

The result was an explosion of personal debt from $1.5 trillion in 1981 to $5.5 trillion by 1997, a more than threefold increase.[70] The total of mortgages and consumer credit rose from 67 percent in 1981 to 86 percent of disposable personal income in 1991, and continued to inch up to 92 percent by the end of 1997.[71] A substantial and growing portion of this debt, about 80 percent, was due to home mortgages. Normally, increased home ownership reflects an increase in one's standard of living. Unlike most other forms of consumption, home ownership is often considered a form of investment since housing usually appreciates over time. However, although houses may increase in value, they do not produce anything else. Therefore, increased investment in homes does not increase the productivity of the nation and so from an economic perspective is a form of consumption rather than investment. Furthermore, to the extent that home prices might be overinflated and subsequently suffer a decline, as occurred in the late 1980s, the decline in value can seriously impact the financial position of families and, consequently, future consumption, investment, and economic growth.

Of greater concern than growth in mortgages was the jump in consumer credit from $350 billion in 1980 to $797 billion by 1990.[72] During the 1990–92 recession the increase in debt slowed but resumed its climb after the recession, reaching $1.2 trillion by the end of 1997.[73] Not surprisingly, this formidable increase in personal debt was accompanied by an equally distressing increase in personal bankruptcies. Bankruptcies hit 580,459 by 1989, more than doubling in a decade.[74] The 1990–91 recession increased bankruptcies another 55 percent to 889,840 before declining after the recession. However, in a break with past trends, as the economic recovery gathered steam bankruptcies again soared, reaching 989,172 by 1996.[75] It will be interesting, and probably distressing, to see the impact of the next recession on consumer solvency.

A related concern is that as the economy improves there is a tendency for people today to increase their relative indebtedness rather than pay off outstanding debts as their parents were inclined to do. In 1989, just prior to the last recession, installment debt rose to 17.3 percent of personal income. During the recession people worked down their debt (or filed bankruptcy); by the end of the recession installment debt had dropped to 15.6 percent of personal income. Once out of the recession people began taking on more debt until by the end of 1997 it had increased to 17.5 percent. Although even then installment debt accounted for only 8 percent of the nation's total debt,[76] it is of concern because when the consumers get too far in debt they eventually have to reduce their consumption to pay their creditors and this can trigger an economic recession in our consumer-driven economy.

Total Debt

In total, business and consumer debt added another $10 trillion to the federal government's debt of $5.4 trillion in 1997, bringing the total U.S. debt by the end of 1997 to the fantastic sum of $15 trillion.[77] (See figure 6.8.) This does not include projected future pension and Social Security shortfalls. If we included such accrued liabilities, the total debt would be over $16 trillion or twice the level of the total output of the economy in 1997 (GDP = $8.1 trillion).*

---

*The federal debt shown here is only the public held portion of the federal debt as reported in the Flow of Funds report of the Federal Reserve System. It excludes the por-

Figure 6.8[78]
Total Nonfinancial Debt, 1945–1996

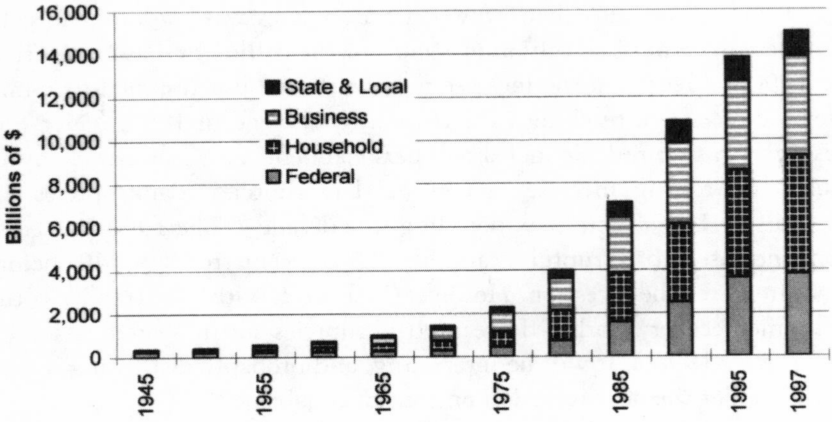

As figure 6.8 shows, each segment of the economy has contributed to the growing debt burden. During World War II the federal government accounted for 72 percent of total debt while the shortage of consumer goods depressed household borrowing to 8 percent of the total debt. Immediately after the war, consumer and business expanded their borrowing, while the federal government began paying back the debt used to finance the war. By 1960, federal government debt had dropped to 33 percent of the total debt, while consumers and business each accounted for 29 percent. The federal government's share of debt bottomed out at less than 20 percent in the late 1970s, and then began to climb again, peaking in 1995 at 26 percent. Business and consumer debt also grew, reaching 37 percent and 31 percent, respectively. The share of debt due to state and local borrowing was always relatively small, increasing from about 4 percent in 1945 to a peak of 11 percent in 1970 before declining to 7.5 percent by 1997. The key point to note here is that while most people were worrying about increases in the federal debt, they should have been at least equally concerned about the growth of consumer debt. In fact, by 1998 concern for consumer debt should have eclipsed our concern for the federal debt. By the end of 1998, savings as a percentage of disposable income fell to zero for the first time since the Great Depression.

---

tion of the debt that is held by the government in trust funds. This is a questionable practice since those trust funds are actually a liability against future tax revenue. If we were to include trust fund liabilities it would increase total debt by about $1.6 trillion in 1997 (*Economic Report of the President Transmitted to Congress, 1998*, table B–81, p. 376).

Figure 6.9
Distribution of Nonfinancial Debt by Sector, 1945–1997

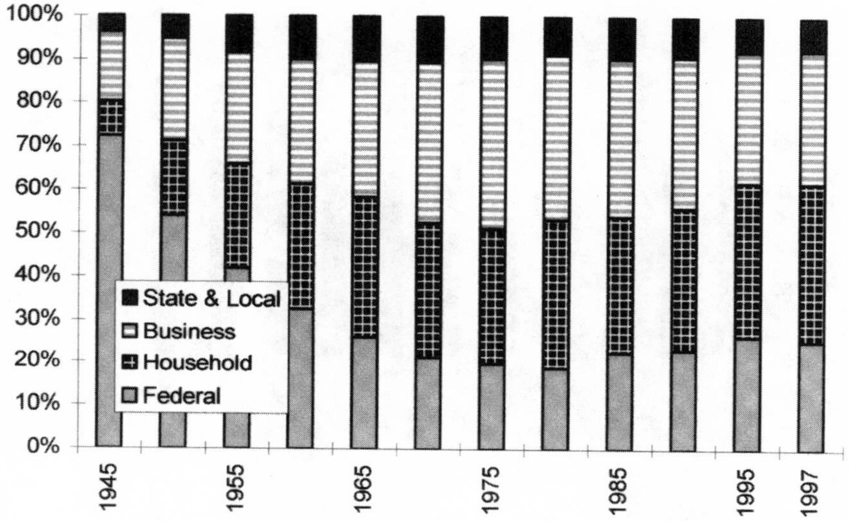

Figure 6.9 illustrates how the mix of debt by sector has changed since World War II.

To place the total debt burden in proper historical perspective, we must again view it as a ratio to total GDP. The total cumulative debt relative to GDP, as shown in figure 6.10, is one way of viewing our nation's economic health.

The data here is limited, because we don't have estimates prior to 1945, but the evidence indicates that we might have a problem. After the Second World War, total nonfinancial debt stood at 1.7 times the annual GDP and then dropped to about 1.37 times GDP after the Korean War and held there until rising slightly in the mid-1970s. Between 1980 and 1990, debt soared from 1.42 to 1.9 times GDP, the highest level in U.S. history. Since 1990 the ratio has continued to increase, although at a slower rate as the annual deficits began to decline. By the end of 1997 the ratio stood at 2.06 and even if the federal budget starts generating true surpluses, total debt will decline only slightly. Such a high level of debt is not necessarily a fatal economic disease like cancer; it is more like a bad case of the flu that could develop into pneumonia if we are not careful.

A cyclical recession does not cause me concern, since it will be self-correcting. *The real problem is the lack of savings in preparation for retirement.* The baby boomers entering retirement will be problem enough; the fact that many are not adequately prepared will worsen the problem. Then, too, their

Chart 6.10[79]
Ratio of Nonfinancial Debt to GDP, 1945–1996

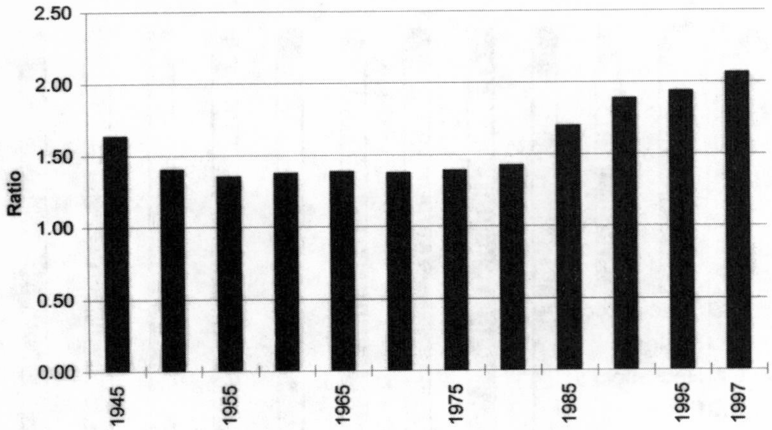

children not only do not have the savings to help their parents, but because of the new job environment where people jump from job to job, they will not receive significant corporate pensions. This means they have to save more money in their private IRAs and Roth accounts* to make up the deficiency. Self-reliance is the watchword for the twenty-first century, but I am afraid that the urge to have it all today will result in a large percentage of the population finding out that old age will not permit retirement, or certainly not with the lifestyle to which they have become accustomed.

Although the relative size of the total debt does not portend an economic apocalypse as some doomsayers claim, neither can it be ignored. The present level of debt limits the options for businesses, consumers, and of government. In the case of business and consumers, a high level of debt keeps interest rates high and thus limits their capacity to undertake certain projects. It also transfers wealth from spenders to lenders. It is sometimes argued that whereas businesses and individuals are constrained by debt, because if they can't make their payments they can be forced into bankruptcy, the money creation powers of the federal government always permits it the last recourse of creating more money. But the mere creation of money without a corresponding increase in real output per unit of input (productivity) will result in inflation. In the process of making our dollars worth less, the gov-

*Individual Investment Accounts (IRAs) allow an annual contribution of $2,000 which is a tax deductible. The earnings and capital gains on an IRA account are tax deferred. In a Roth account, the annual contribution is not tax deductible, but all growth in earnings and capital gains are tax free.

ernment would be effectively assessing a hidden tax. For example, an expansion of the money supply by 10 percent at a time when the growth in national productivity was 2 percent would, all other things remaining equal, be the equivalent of a 8 percent tax. In fact, a primary reason for creating the semi-autonomous Federal Reserve System is to remove this insidious form of taxation from the hands of the politicians. Too often throughout history, governments have sought to reduce their debt by devaluating their money to repay the debt in cheaper dollars. The result can be an inflationary spiral that eventually leads to a total economic collapse.

During the last two decades the Federal Reserve Bank has wisely ruled out the option of "monetizing the debt," e.g., increasing the money supply much faster than output, and rekindling an inflationary spiral. Therefore, the only legitimate options for the federal government are to finance the debt through higher taxes or reduce the growth in government expenditures. Whether raising taxes or cutting expenditures, economic pain is inflicted on the public; the only question is how that pain is distributed among the various constituencies. Congress has chosen to cut expenditures. Many of the budget cuts will result in fewer dollars going to state and local governments. This forces the latter officials to make the difficult choice of cutting services or raising taxes. Most municipalities do a little of both. Since most state and local taxes (such as property, sales, and flat-rate state income taxes), are regressive, it means that the real pain of balancing the budget will fall on the middle class and the poor.

Investment and Infrastructure Debt

It is an amazing fact—and an indictment of our educational system—that not one person in a hundred in this country has the vaguest idea of how wealth is created. I've heard people express the opinion that the government or the Federal Reserve System can create jobs or wealth. Actually, the government can only redistribute wealth or, at best, affect the economic climate in which wealth is created; and the FRS only controls the growth of the money supply, which is not the same as wealth. People know their own wealth is somehow related to their paycheck, but do not understand the underlying factors that determine the paycheck.

Increases in the total wealth of a nation is a function of its productivity. Productivity (P) is the change in the ratio of output (all the goods and service a nation produces) to input [all the capital investment (C), labor hours (L) and other resources (A), including land, air and water, used in the process of production]. For the mathematically minded:

$$\Delta P = \Delta (O / [C+L+A])$$

To understand how changes in productivity equate to changes in per capita wealth, take the example of a primitive society where everyone spends all their time hunting for food. There is no time to spend on making any other goods except those essential to the hunt. There is no wealth as such—nothing that can be accumulated and handed down from generation to generation.

Now take the first step to an agrarian society. Spending less time to produce the equivalent amount of food is an increase in productivity. In between planting and harvesting people have some spare time to do other things, like making pottery, tools, clothes, and so forth. Such items can be accumulated and handed down from generation to generation. Thus there is wealth creation. Note that money is incidental to the creation of wealth. The function of money is to facilitate the exchange of such items by providing a common medium for expressing the relative value of various items of production.

Growth in productivity is largely a function of how much a society invests in its people and technology. If we examine the developed economies of the world, we will see that there is a high correlation between rates of savings and investments and rates of productivity growth, with Japan leading the world for the period 1970–1990, and Southeast Asian countries leading since then. The United States is at the low end of the range, although we have improved after the 1990–1991 recession, mainly due to corporate downsizing.[80] All three sectors of our economy are to blame for the underinvestment. Consumers did not save enough to invest, businesses were more interested in buying out other businesses than investing in new products and processes, and government was diverting tax dollars to forms of consumption such as defense and health care, rather than infrastructure investment. Many states and local governments also had to short-changed infrastructure investment to meet increasing health and welfare benefits as well as operating expenditures (primarily salaries and wages) for education, police, health, and welfare.

The substitution of machines and computers (capital) for labor is the primary driver of long-term productivity growth. However, the evidence suggests that public infrastructure expenditures—especially transportation and schools—also play an important role. During the 1970s and 1980s, America had less public investment and less productivity growth than Japan, Germany, France, the United Kingdom, Italy, and Canada.[81] Federal Reserve Board economist David Alan Aschauer showed that for the period 1953 to 1984, the slowing growth of infrastructure investment was accompanied by a declining profit rate:[82]

	Capital Outlays as % of GDP	*Profit Rate*
1953–59	1.9	10.9
1960–64	2.2	11.6
1965–69	2.3	13.3
1970–74	1.4	9.8
1975–79	0.7	9.1
1980–84	0.4	7.9
1985–89	0.4e	8.2e

e = estimate

Aschauer's thesis is that the increase in public capital stock makes private capital stock more productive. For example, public expenditures on transportation are necessary to enable producers to bring their goods to market. A poor transportation system raises the cost of delivery. *According to Aschauer, because of the present infrastructure deficiency, an extra dollar of public capital would have a greater impact on total output and private sector profitability than a dollar of private investment.* This may also be true of government investment in human capital. Certainly investment in education, training, and job placement that would result in people obtaining gainful employment could yield an exceptional return compared to the negative impact of supporting people on welfare.

Joseph A. Pechman, senior fellow at the Brookings Institute, explains that the controlling principle for determining government outlays is that they "not exceed, or fall short of, the level at which the benefits to the nation's citizens of an additional dollar of expenditures would be the same for public and private use."[83] While this principle is indisputable, making that evaluation is far from easy due to the subjective nature of determining "benefit." It is complicated because on one hand there are billions of dollars spent on advertising to persuade us that consuming beer will greatly increase our enjoyment of life, but there are relatively few dollars being expended to persuade the public that more money for education, cleaner water, or the arts will increase our happiness and welfare. Hence, there is a bias in what society views as a benefit.

Short-changing investment in better roads and mass transit, cleaner air and water, and the like, has been a serious problem for the past thirty years. The National Council for Public Works graded U.S. infrastructure as follows:

Highways	C+
Mass Transit	C–
Aviation	B–

Water Resources	B
Water Supply	B–
Waste Water	C
Solid Waste	C–
Hazardous Waste	D

These poor grades were awarded in 1994 and, given the need to balance the federal budget, a tight rein on federal expenditures has prevented any significant improvement.

Ironically, the one area that continues to get the lion's share of public infrastructure expenditures is the area that may be least conducive to increased welfare and interstate highways. ***The interstate highway system was, in effect, subsidized transportation for the trucking industry and urban sprawl. It has resulted in decimating the nation's highly efficient railroad system as well as other forms of mass transit, greatly facilitating the flight of business and workers from the central cities to the suburbs, necessitating increased infrastructure investment in water and sanitation for suburban use, and resulting in the loss of millions of acres of valuable farmland and wetlands.*** Additionally, it has encouraged the production of millions more cars requiring still more highways to prevent gridlock. The net result is that America, which had the world's most energy efficient transportation system before World War II, now devotes a significant portion of federal and state budgets to maintaining one of the world's least energy efficient transportation systems.

Despite the huge increase in highway investment, the share of federal civilian fixed investment to GDP is only about half what it was in the 1960s.[84] ***In fact, after subtracting depreciation, infrastructure investment is virtually zero, meaning we are wearing out our physical plant faster than it is being replaced.***[85] As long ago as 1986, it was estimated that after two decades of declining infrastructure expenditures, the cost of repairing the nation's bridges, highways, public transportation, schools, water and sanitation facilities, and the like, would be more than $1 *trillion.*[86] The cost today may be twice that much. Twenty percent of the nation's bridges are structurally deficient and 20 percent of our highways are in poor to medium condition.[87] In addition, the physical plant of our inner-city schools and hospitals is a national disgrace. The longer we delay, the more expensive it will be to make the needed rehabilitation.

Yet with a $6 trillion national debt how can we prevent further decay of infrastructure? To make matters worse, much of the most dilapidated infrastructure is in major cities. But the proportion of the population living in the nation's central cities has steadily declined. According to the Census Bureau, in 1950 only one quarter (26 percent) of the nation's population lived in the suburbs, by 1990 almost half of the population (48 percent) have moved to the suburban ring. By the year 2000, it will be over 50 percent. The result has been a shift in political power to the suburbs. As the tax base declines, the cities are on the horns of a dilemma: if they increase taxes it will drive property owners to the suburbs, but if city services and infrastructure decline, this will also drive people to the suburbs. They clearly need help from the federal government. However, as the political power shifts to the suburbs, they tend to vote Republican, encouraging budget cuts and the use of block grants to the states. Since the suburban and rural interests tend to control state legislatures, it will result in further reduction in funding for the cities.

Representative Ray LaHood (R-IL) has proposed that the federal government make use of its money-creating authority to supply state and local tax-supported bodies with interest-free loans for capital projects and to pay off existing debt.[88] To avoid the inflation associated with an overly expansive money supply, the Federal Reserve would still be responsible for setting the target for the overall growth in the money supply. The overall money growth would then be allocated between growth in public-supplied moneys controlled by the Treasury Department and private funds controlled through the traditional Fed regulations. By avoiding the fees and commissions of bond underwriters, the proponents estimate that it will save billions of dollars in taxes. The proposal has been endorsed by the U.S. conference of Mayors. Representative LaHood introduced legislation in 1996 that would create $360 billion over a five-year period, but the legislation died in committee.

The proposal is worth considering; however, it presents several problems. First, by subsidizing infrastructure such as highways, sewers, and sanitation, it may encourage continuation of urban sprawl. Second, it increases the necessity for federal supervision to determine the credit worthiness of municipal bodies to borrow. At present, this is the job of the various bond underwriters. The relative interest rates charged different municipalities tells the investor the degree of risk associated with a particular municipality. Furthermore, without the incentive of the potentially higher cost of obtaining capital, where is the incentive for a city to be financially responsible? If the federal government is made responsible for determining whether or not to grant a loan, there will always be an element of politics involved. Third, if the demand for public funding exceeds the supply of new money how does the federal government prioritize which projects get funded? Finally, there is danger of the cities arbitraging the federal loans, i.e., they obtain the money from the federal government and then temporarily place it in higher yielding investments until the money is spent. There would be a temptation to drag out a project to milk the investments. The alternative is for the federal government to pay the money as the bills come due, but this might become an administrative nightmare. Despite these potential problems, the idea has sufficient merit to warrant in-depth study and a trial, perhaps in a smaller state.

Equitable Policies to Reduce the National Debt

As mentioned, the present size of the national debt doesn't bother some economists. So what if the government has to borrow a great amount of money each year to finance its programs? Since most of the debt is financed by Americans, our children will receive the interest on all those treasury bills and notes.[89] That may be true for upper class children who will probably inherit some T-bills from their parents. But it isn't true of the children of the poor who will only pay the taxes to cover the interest on the debt. Even the middle class is in danger of getting shut out. Many of the T-bills are bought by pension plans, and we might expect the middle class to benefit from the interest paid into those plans. But as we pointed out earlier, if retirement plans are underfunded, it is questionable whether the middle class will get as many dollars out of their pension plans from the interest on the debt as they pay in taxes to cover the interest. Also, an increasingly larger number of people are not covered by any pension plan; and due to high turnover rates and lack of pension portability,* many people will never accumulate enough service with any one company to receive even a minimally adequate pension.

In short, a large federal debt and its associated interest costs can have a significant unplanned redistribution of income. This is one more reason why we might wish to reduce the national debt. The politically contentious issue is how to understand what underlies the federal government spending and to look for further budget cuts to reduce the national debt; we therefore must examine the budget in more depth. Table 6.2 provides details of the major

---

*Historically, employees became eligible for a pension only after attaining a certain number of years of service with a company, usually 25 or 30, and also reaching a certain age, such as fifty-five or sixty. Employees who voluntarily or involuntarily left a company and were not pension eligible were given termination pay. Termination payments were a small fraction of the amount of pension employees might have received had they been given an amount proportional to the employees' salary and/or years of service without any minimum eligibility requirement. Pension portability would provide a worker who left a firm with an amount equal to that which the firm had accrued toward the employee's eventual pension. The employee would roll over the amount into a personal pension plan that would continue to grow through reinvested interest and dividends. By this means, even employees who are forced to take many different jobs over their working lives would be able to accumulate a pension.

budget components based upon President Clinton's 1999 budget. Subsequent negotiation's with Congress will no doubt change these amounts slightly primarily in the area of health care. (After excluding the Social Security surplus needed to finance future pensions, there will still be a $105 billion deficit. (The problem of future Social Security shortfalls will be discussed in chapter 12.)

Table 6.2
1980–2000 Budget Outlays by Function[90]
(Billions of $)

Function	1980	1995	1980–95 Change	2000	1995–2000 Change
1. Defense* & Veterans	$160	$315	155	$319	4
2. International affairs*	8	11	3	9	–2
3. Science, space & technology	6	17	11	18	1
4. Energy	10	5	–5	0.2	–5
5. Natural Resources & Environment	14	22	8	24	2
6. Agriculture	9	10	1	11	1
7. Commerce & housing	9	–16	–25	12	28
8. Transportation	21	39	18	43	4
9. Community Develop.	11	11	0	10	–1
10. Education, training & employment	32	54	22	63	9
11. Health & Medicare	55	275	220	367	92
12. Income security†	87	225	138	266	41
13. Admin. of Justice	5	16	11	26	10
14. General Government	13	14	1	17	3
15. Net Interest	55	265	210	292	27
16. Offsetting receipts	–19	–38	–19	–32	6
Total On-Budget Outlays‡	477	1227	750	1445	218

*Defense includes $6 billion for International Security Assistance
†Excludes all social security which is off-budget—$409 billion in the year 2000.
‡Totals may not add due to rounding

The first point to note is that only health care, income security, and the interest on the debt show any significant increase, and most areas of the budget reflect substantial decreases if adjusted for inflation. (The commerce and housing increase is an artifact of the unusual negative amount in 1995 due to savings and loans repaying some of their bailout loans.) The four largest components of the budget—defense, health care, income security, and interest—amount to 86 percent of the total budget. So any significant cuts must come from these areas.

Although defense was projected in the 1995 budget to decline $27 billion by 1999, by the time of the 1999 budget the cuts had been restored and defense spending increased slightly by the year 2000. Adjusted for inflation, defense spending is still projected to decline but, as pointed out earlier, defense spending could be slashed further without endangering our national security.* On the other hand, a large reduction in defense spending might have adverse economic consequences in the short run due to the displacement of jobs in both the armed forces and the defense industry. Some of this impact could be modified by transferring a portion of the expenditures to needed infrastructure projects. Of course, reallocating dollars will slow the reduction of the fiscal deficit, but they will reduce the infrastructure deficit.

If it is so obvious that defense should be cut, why isn't it? The answer is that defense is the biggest pork barrel in the budget. No matter how much Newt Gingrich cried about federal waste, he fought tooth and nail to keep the F–22 Stealth Fighter in the budget because it was to be built in his state. About $1.3 billion will be spent on amphibious assault ships that the Navy doesn't even want, because the ships will be built in the home state of Trent Lott, the Senate Republican leader. The Democrats have their hands in the pork barrel as well: Dick Gephardt, House minority leader, wants the C–17A transport plane and FA–18 fighter to be constructed in his district, and so forth.

The increase in income security primarily reflects the growth in federal retirement pensions (for both civilian and military personnel), increases in trade adjustment assistance, unemployment compensation, and temporary assistance for needy families. This last item refers to the welfare–to–work program which is expected to cost $17 billion by the year 2000. In addition, we will be paying $25 billion for the Earned Income Tax Credit (EITC) in the year 2000 to the working poor. ***Most of this combined outlay of $42 billion could be saved if we cut immigration of low-skilled people. The reduced labor supply would force wage rates up to the point where workers would receive a livable wage.*** Conversely, if present immigration trends continue, we should expect even higher federal outlays for the EITC.

Regarding the increase in federal pensions, although an adjustment to pension policy might be made affecting future employees, and cuts in the number of federal employees would affect future growth in this component, it would not reduce the budget until some time in the future (after the present retired employees receiving pensions die).

One of the most significant savings in future budgets was to have been

---

*The war in the Balkans will undoubtedly result in increased defense spending.

the reduction in benefits to immigrants. However, because of concerted pressure from immigrant rights organizations, Congress decided to reestablish SSI and food stamps to immigrants. The specter was raised that without continued assistance, elderly and disabled immigrants would be thrown into the street to starve. In the hysteria that surrounded this discussion the crucial fact that every immigrant has a sponsor that promises to take care of them was completely ignored. ***As a result, we can expect that many immigrants will continue to encourage their parents to come to America to retire at the taxpayer's expense.***

The largest projected increase in federal expenditures is in health care. Since health care is the fastest growing part of the budget, Congress has finally decided that even this area must be slashed. They plan to reduce the projected growth rate from 10 percent to 5 percent, which would require reducing the prior projected annual expenditures for Medicare and Medicaid in the year 2002 by $62 billion and $53 billion, respectively.[91] Virtually all of the savings are to come from forcing recipients of the two programs to join HMOs or contribute to tax-free Medical Savings Accounts (MSAs) to pay future medical bills. It is ludicrous to think that this action, by itself, will yield anywhere near the projected budget reductions. In failing to face the harsh realities head on, Congress wants to take credit for an assumed budget reduction without taking the difficult action necessary to hold down the rise in health care costs as the baby boomers age.

The third largest line item in the budget is interest on the debt, which can't be reduced except by decreasing total debt, not just balancing the budget, and could increase substantially if interest rates rise. It should also be noted that the interest shown in table 6.2 is $57 billion higher than the net interest shown in the federal budget accounts because I excluded the interest the government is receiving from the off-budget Social Security trust fund surplus. Other on-budget trust funds, such as the federal employee trust funds, are also in surplus. In fact, ***the interest on the public debt, excluding all interest from trust funds, is projected to be $369 billion in the year 2000, making it equal to the total of health and Medicare expenditures.***

Foreign aid is another area that is often thought to offer a major opportunity for budget reductions. Polls have shown that Americans think that U.S. foreign aid amounts to 15 to 20 percent of our federal budget.[92] This is just another example of how uninformed most Americans are about how their tax dollars are spent. ***Total foreign aid, including the $6 billion of international security assistance that should be included under defense, is projected to be only $15 billion in the year 2000, less than 1 percent of the total budget!*** Adjusted for inflation, it has been dropping every year since 1980 and is projected to continue to decline.

Of the $9 billion that can appropriately be called foreign aid, over one-third goes to the Middle East, primarily Israel and Egypt. Here there is room for reduction. Israel has less population than the metropolitan Chicago area yet in 1993 received $4.2 billion in direct aid (including $1.3 billion off-budget assistance) and $2 billion in guaranteed loans (which, if history is any guide, will never be repaid).[93] Yet any effort to cut this clearly disproportionate aid will be successfully opposed by what is arguably the most influential Washington lobby, the American Israel Public Affairs Committee (AIPAC). As former Illinois congressman Paul Findley learned, any congressman who opposes AIPAC will soon be out of a job.[94] Instead of cutting aid to Israel, House Republicans want to continue cutting the paltry aid that goes to support the world's family planning programs, from the $600 million in 1993 to $356 million in the 1997 budget.[95] Yet family planning aid is probably the most efficient use of tax dollars in the entire budget in terms of reducing poverty and the international unrest that accompanies overpopulation.

Relative to the other industrialized nations, U.S. foreign aid is indeed miserly, ranking sixteenth in aid as a percent of GDP and dropping.[96] The excuse that we cannot afford to help sounds just a bit hollow. America is twice as rich on a per capita basis as we were when John F. Kennedy was President, and three times richer than we were at the end of World War II when it provided the Marshall Plan, yet it says it can only provide token support for aid to Russia ($1.0 billion), Eastern Europe ($0.4 billion) or the LDCs ($3.0 billion).[97] Just diverting 10 percent of the defense budget would increase foreign aid six-fold and, if judiciously spent (such as providing aid to countries who agree to reduce arms spending and expand family planning services), could do more for the peace of the world than ten times as much spent on armaments.

There are, Of course, other areas of the budget where savings might be generated through greater efficacy or by eliminating programs that offer the prospect of little benefit, such as the latest aerospace boondoggle, the space station. Originally estimated to cost $8 billion by Ronald Reagan, who first proposed the space station, the price tag had soared between $40 to $96 billion by 1988 when the first of the forty-four space shuttle trips was launched to construct the station. That's one heck of a range, and indicates that no one really knows what it will cost. My guess is that it will exceed $100 billion. This staggering amount of money could provide free family planning services to every woman in the undeveloped nations of the world for ten years. Why blow it on a space station? Supposedly the space station is needed as a staging area for a manned flight to Mars. However, as discovered with the moon landing, although it makes good theater for the masses, we can learn about all we wish to know with unmanned probes at a tiny fraction of the cost.

In the meantime, there is an unexplored area deep in the Pacific ocean about the size of the United States that, based upon the few probes made into this area, appears to be teaming with strange and wondrous life forms. Not only could exploration of this underwater world be conducted for a small part of the cost of space research, but the potential benefits for humankind of underwater research is considered by most scientists to be far greater. Unfortunately, there is no lobby supporting deep ocean research to match the powerful aerospace industry lobby, and oceanic research does not offer sufficient entertainment value to a generation raised on *Star Trek*.

It is ironic that Congress insists on cost-benefit analyses for environmental regulations designed to save our planet, but no such analysis is demanded for exploration of space even though all of the evidence suggests that there is no value to be found in the inhospitable environments of the other planets in our solar system.

Taxes

Even though selected budget cuts accompanied by tax increases would reduce the national debt, the American public doesn't want to hear of it. It is usually the death knell of any politician if he or she even hints at raising taxes. So it is little wonder that to get re-elected many politicians perpetuate the myth that we can reduce the debt while cutting taxes. One reason that the annual deficits have been reduced in the last decade is that presidents Bush and Clinton did demonstrate some political courage by raising taxes.

There are ways of raising tax revenue that are more palatable and equitable than increasing income taxes. An eminently reasonable method of raising additional tax revenue would be to tax imported oil to the level where the price per barrel is the same as 1980, i.e., $36 a barrel. Since imported oil now costs about $16 a barrel this would result in a tax of $20 a barrel. With annual imports of oil running about 1.7 billion barrels this would provide about $34 billion in annual revenue. Even at $36 a barrel, the price will be less than one-half the 1980 price in real dollar terms. The economic effects will be minimal because conservation will be stepped up to offset the higher cost, just as happened in the early 1980s before the real dollar cost of oil dropped to the point where conservation efforts were relaxed. An even higher tax might be justified on the basis that the higher price will reduce the demand for imported oil, and the reduced reliance on imported oil can be offset by the reduced military expenditure to protect this unreliable source of energy.

A fairly stiff tax on the imported oil is a winner from every perspectives:

- it will reduce consumption of oil, and hence CO_2 buildup, thus improving the environment;
- it reduces dependence on foreign oil, and thus increases U.S. security;
- it improves the balance of trade;
- it decreases the federal debt.

As an alternative way of achieving a similar end, economist Lester Thurow proposes that gasoline taxes be raised by $1 a gallon, to about the same rate as every other industrial democracy. The present price of gas, if adjusted for the change in the overall consumer prices, is about the same as in 1970 before the oil embargoes, as shown in figure 6.11. In fact, ***adjusted for inflation, people today are paying about 25 cents per gallon, the same price as in the 1950s.*** Gas is such a bargain that people no longer worry about fuel efficiency. The trend has once again turned to gas guzzlers: this time in the form of recreational vehicles and vans which are exempt from federal gas mileage standards.

Thurow estimates that a one-dollar increase in gasoline tax would raise about $116 billion.[98] Regrettably, all that Clinton could get past Congress was a pathetic 4.3 cents a gallon tax increase. Most people could not even guess the price of gas within four cents of the actual price at any given point in time.

Some other taxes suggested by the organization Common Cause include:[99]

- tax beer and wine at the same rate as distilled spirits	$21 billion
- tax cigarettes $.32 a pack	$15
- raise income tax on the highest income families by 5%	$30
Total Revenue	$66 billion

Although these are worthy suggestions, they will be vigorously opposed by the tobacco and alcohol lobbies. Senator Jesse Helms (N.C.) will support taking away children's lunch programs but not the subsidies for the tobacco industry in his state. No matter how he tries to deceive the voters, the cold truth is that he would rather see children addicted to nicotine than well fed.

State and local governments will also oppose increasing federal taxes on items such as gas, alcohol or tobacco, which they view as a source of local tax revenue. However, these added taxes of $66 billion, coupled with a $60 billion from a 50 cent increase in gasoline taxes, would have resulted in a balanced budget in 1996. Further slowing in defense and healthcare costs,

Figure 6.11[100]
Price Per Gallon Adjusted for CPI

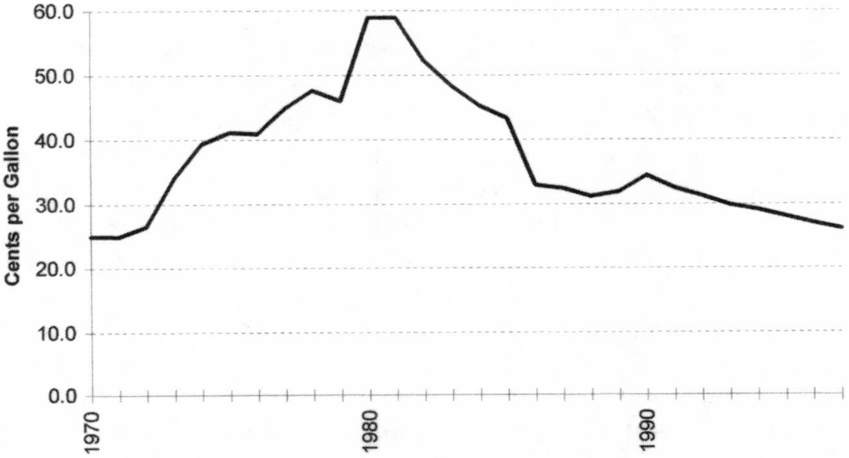

together with continued growth in the economy, would result in dramatically reducing the national debt over the next decade. However, what would not be accomplished is the closing of the deficits in infrastructure investment (including human capital) and progress in saving the environment. The only way to effectively raise sufficient revenue to meet these ends will be discussed in chapter 13.

Summary

During the 1980 to 1992 period the gross federal debt rose $3 trillion. This is greater than the total of all the debt incurred since the birth of our nation. The $4.2 trillion spent on defense during this period contributed in no small measure to this deficit. The other two major factors were the growth in healthcare expense, and the 1981 tax cuts.

The 1980s witnessed not only an explosion in federal debt, but business and consumer debt as well. The result was that we entered the 1990s with the highest total debt relative to GDP of any time in our nation's history. When seeking to place the blame, there is enough to go around for everyone. Conservatives kept increasing defense expenditures and trying to reduce taxes instead of increasing them to cover the shortfall. Liberals prevented cuts in welfare and supported the growth of health care without the taxes to pay for it. The elderly succeeded in getting an overly generous inflation adjustment built into Social Security, while opposing all efforts to limit benefits. Most Americans of all political stripes continued to increase their personal debt with little thought for the future.

By 1998 the annual deficits had improved significantly and were predicted to continue to improve. However, if the temporary Social Security surpluses were subtracted, the remainder of the budget was still running an annual deficit of about $100 million in 1998. Moreover, the U.S. taxpayer is left with a national debt of about $6 trillion that results in a redistribution of income from taxpayers to those in this country and abroad who receive the interest payments on the debt. Thus, it is desirable to reduce the national debt further, but to do so will require substantial restraint on spending on the part of federal, state and local government, as well as individuals and businesses.

Not only has the United States been running deficits in each sector of society, but the shift of federal expenditures to cover defense, health care, and interest on the debt has resulted in an infrastructure deficit as well. We have not maintained our highways, public transportation, airports, sewage and water treatment, schools, etc. We have been particularly lax in cleaning up the mountains of toxic wastes that run the risk of polluting our underground water supplies. Finally, we have made inadequate investment in human capital in terms of training and education.

Although budget forecasts show decreases in the national debt relative to GDP, they do not include the potential impacts of providing health care to the tens of millions of working Americans now at risk. Moreover, the annual deficits are being grossly underestimated by the inclusion of the temporary surpluses from social security. Ultimately, the federal government will have to raise additional revenue unless it abdicates more programs to the states, in which case the revenue shortfalls become a state and local government problem. Increases in taxes on alcohol and tobacco will help, but a significant increase in the tax on oil or gasoline is essential.

Notes

1. President, *Economic Report of the President Transmitted to Congress, 1991* (Washington, D.C.: U.S. Government Printing Office, 1991), table B–44, p. 336.

2. President, *Economic Report of the President Transmitted to Congress, 1998,* table B–47, p. 336.

3. President, *Economic Report of the President Transmitted to Congress, 1991*, table B–27, p. 317, and *Economic Report, 1998*, table B–31, p. 317.

4. President, *Economic Report of the President Transmitted to Congress, February 1998,* table B–103, p. 398.

5. President, *Economic Report of the President Transmitted to Congress, February*

1996, table B–46, p. 338.

6. Russ Feigned, "A Dissenting View," *Chicago Tribune*, December 20, 1994, sec. 1, p. 27.

7. Howard M. Wachtel, *The Money Mandarins: The Making of a Supernatural Economic Order* (Armonkey, N.Y.: M. E. Sharpe Inc., 1990). Cited in *Future Survey* (April 1991): 8.

8. President, *Economic Report of the President Transmitted to Congress, February, 1991,* table B–76, p. 375.

9. R. C. Longworth, "Rethinking the Reagan Creed," *Chicago Tribune*, September 5, 1998, sec. 2, p. 1.

10. Roger Lowenstein, "How Budget Balancers Join the Jobless," *Wall Street Journal*, August 7, 1997, p. C1.

11. U.S. Office of Management and Budget, *Budget of the United States Government, Fiscal Year 1998, Historical Tables* (Washington, D.C.: U.S. Government Printing Office, 1998), table 3.2, pp. 50–64. Year 2000 projections are from *Budget of the United States, Fiscal Year 1999,* table 33–2. Outlays by Function, Category and Program, pp. 292ff.

12. *Chicago Tribune*, February 21, 1988.

13. U.S. Arms Control and Disarmament Agency, World Military Expenditures and Arms Transfers, annual, *Statistical Abstract of the United States, 1997* (Washington, D.C.: U.S. Government Printing Office, 1997), table 1389, p. 1995.

14. Michael Lillian, "Defense Hawks Keep B–2 Funds Flowing," *Chicago Tribune*, September 8, 1995, sec 1, p. 3.

15. Department of Defense, *Defense Almanac* (November 1997): 18.

16. The Defense Department either doesn't know or won't reveal the amount the United States spends on its involvement with NATO. This estimate is from Chris Hellman of the Center for Defense Information.

17. Center for Defense Information, *Defense Monitor* XXIV, no. 8 (September/October 1995).

18. Roger Bolton, "Impact of Defense Spending on Urban Areas," unpublished manuscript.

19. *Northeast-Midwest Economic Review* (February 4, 1991): 3.

20. The Center for Defense Information, *Defense Monitor* XXIV, no. 7 (August 1995): 6.

21. Ibid.

22. Paul Kennedy, *Rise and Fall of the Great Powers: Economic Change and Military Conflict from 1500 to 2000* (New York: Random House, 1987), p. 442.

23. "Pentagon Overstated Precision of Smart Weapons, GAO Says," *Chicago Tribune*, July 9, 1996, sec. 1, p. 6.

24. Kennedy, *Rise and Fall of the Great Powers,* p. 446.

25. Neil Howe and Philip Longman, "The Next New Deal," *Atlantic Monthly* (April 1992): 88–89.

26. Ibid.

27. U.S. Office of Management and Budget, *Budget of the United States Gov-*

ernment, Analytical Perspectives, Fiscal Year 1995, "Federal Programs by Agency and Account," Family Support Payments to States, p. 353.

28. U.S. Office of Management and Budget, *Budget of the United States Government, Fiscal Year 1995*, table 3.2, p. 52

29. U.S. Office of Management and Budget, *Budget of the United States Government, Analytical Perspectives, Fiscal Year 1995*, "Federal Programs by Agency and Account," Grants to States for Medicaid, p. 351.

30. *Business Week*, August 1, 1994, p. 20.

31. U.S. Office of Management and Budget, *Budget of the United States Government, Analytical Perspectives, Fiscal Year 1995*, "Federal Programs by Agency and Account," Grants to States for Medicaid, p. 351.

32. Robert J. Samuelson, "Immigration and Poverty," *Newsweek* (July 15, 1996): 43.

33. Jackie Calmes, "Budget Office Sees Slower Growth in Health Programs," *Wall Street Journal*, January 17, 1997, P. A4.

34. U.S. Office of Management and Budget, *Budget of the United States Government, Fiscal Year 1996*, table S–18, p. 217.

35. Garrett Hardin, *Living Within Limits: Ecology, Economics, and Population Taboos* (New York: Oxford University Press, 1993), p. 243.

36. "Health Care Costs Reach $1 Trillion," *Chicago Tribune*, January 13, 1998, sec. 1, p. 5.

37. The 1989 forecast of the National Leadership Commission on Health Care was that costs would reach $1.5 trillion by the year 2000. But there has been a slowing in growth the last couple of years, so I revised the year 2000 estimate downward. Cited in *The Futurist* (July/August 1990): 13.

38. U.S. Office of Management and Budget, *Budget of the United States Government, Fiscal Year 1998, Historical Tables*, table 13.1, p. 252 (includes old age and survivors insurance fund and the disability insurance trust fund).

39. U.S. Office of Management and Budget, *Budget of the United States Government, Fiscal Year 1999*, table S–15, p. 367.

40. U.S. Office of Management and Budget, *Budget of the United States Government, Fiscal Year 1999*, table S–15, p. 367. Earlier years from *Budget of the United States Government, Fiscal Year 1998, Historical Tables*, table 1.1, p. 20.

41. U.S. Office of Management and Budget, *Budget of the United States Government, Fiscal Year 1998, Historical Tables*, table 1.2, pp. 21–22.

42. President, *Economic Report of the President Transmitted to Congress, 1996*, table B–74, p. 367 and *Budget of the United States, Fiscal Year* 1999, table S–15, p. 367.

43. President, *Economic Report of the President Transmitted to Congress, 1998*, table B–78, p. 373. *Budget of the United States, Fiscal Year 1999*, table S–15, p. 367.

44. Lester Thurow, *Head to Head* (New York: William Morrow and Company, 1992), p. 265. See also Herman E. Daly and John B. Cobb Jr., *For the Common Good* (Boston: Beacon Press, 1989), p. 223.

45. President, *Economic Report of the President Transmitted to Congress, 1997*, table B–89, p. 384.

46. Eisner points out that $40 billion in interest would equal 1 percent of GDP (in 1994), but the investment that generated the $40 billion in interest would reduce unemployment by 0.3 percent, thus more than offsetting the interest cost. *The Misunderstood Economy: What Counts and How to Count It*, p. 79.

47. Ibid., p. 75.

48. Thurow, *Head to Head*, pp. 100–102.

49. President, *Economic Report of the President Transmitted to Congress, February, 1997*, table, B–47, p. 354. Productivity increased to 1.9 percent in 1996 and 1.7 percent in 1997 (*Wall Street Journal*, February 11, 1998, p. A2), but whether the United States can maintain even this modest improvement remains to be seen.

50. Eisner, *The Misunderstood Economy*, p. 30. In addition to overstating annual federal "expenses," not including business or household investments in the national income and product accounts overstates consumption and understates savings.

51. Ibid., p. 52.

52. Ibid., p. 54.

53. Ibid., p. 106.

54. Ibid., p. 94.

55. Ibid., p. 57.

56. Ibid., p. 107.

57. President, *Economic Report of the President Transmitted to Congress, 1998*, table B–85, p. 380.

58. Ibid.

59. Ibid.

60. Ibid.

61. Leslie Scism, "Coming Up Short," *Wall Street Journal*, April 6, 1994, p. A1.

62. Ibid.

63. Ibid.

64. Merrill Lynch, "Special Analysis," January 11, 1990. p. 7.

65. Board of Governors of the Federal Reserve System, "Balance Sheets of the U.S. Economy, 1945 to 1994," C. 9 Flow of Funds, June 8, 1995, pp. 36–37 and *Flow of Funds Accounts of the United States*, Report Z1, "Balance Sheet of Nonfarm Nonfinancial Corporate Business," table B.102, p. 103.

66. Merrill Lynch, *Weekly Economic and Financial Commentary*, October 30, 1990, p. 5.

67. Paul Krugman, *The Age of Diminished Expectations* (Washington, D.C.: Washington Post Briefing Company, 1990), p. 91.

68. President, *Economic Report of the President Transmitted to Congress, 1998*, table B–49, p. 338.

69. Board of Governors of the Federal Reserve System, Flow of Funds Accounts of the United States, "Balance Sheet of Nonfarm Nonfinancial Corporate Business," table B.102, p. 103.

70. President, *Economic Report of the President Transmitted to Congress, 1998*, table B–76, p. 371 and table B–77, p. 372.

71. Calculated from Board of Governors of the Federal Reserve System, *Flow of Funds Accounts of the United States*, Report Z1, December 11, 1997, table D.3, p. 8 and *Economic Report of the President to Congress, 1998*, table B–31, p. 317.

72. President, *Economic Report of the President Transmitted to Congress, 1996*, table B–73, p. 366.

73. President, *Economic Report of the President Transmitted to Congress, 1998*, table B–77, p. 372.

74. U.S. Bureau of the Census, *Statistical Abstract of the United States, 1985*, table 881, p. 520, 1997, table, 856, p. 549.

75. U.S. Bureau of the Census, *Statistical Abstract of the United States, 1997*, table 856, p. 549.

76. Bernard Wysocki, "Large Consumer Debt Isn't a Huge Concern," *Wall Street Journal*, July 28, 1997 p. A1.

77. Board of Governors of the Federal Reserve System, *Flow of Funds Accounts of the United States*, Report Z1, December 11, 1997, table D.3, p.8.

78. Ibid., table L.1, p. 50, and Report Z1, table D.3, p. 8.

79. Ibid.

80. President, *Economic Report of the President Transmitted to Congress, 1994*, p. 37.

81. David Alan Aschauer, "Prescription for Productivity: Build Infrastructure," *Chicago Fed Letter* (September 1988).

82. David Alan Aschauer, "Is Public Capital Stock to Low?" *Chicago Fed Letter* (October 1987).

83. Pechman, *Federal Tax Policy*, p. 20

84. President, *Economic Report of President Transmitted to Congress, 1994*, pp. 29–30.

85. Eisner, *The Misunderstood Economy*, p. 93.

86. Philip Longman, "Age Wars," *The Futurist* (1986): 8–11.

87. President, *Economic Report of the President Transmitted to Congress, 1994*, p. 41.

88. For more information on this proposal contact Sovereignty, 1154 West Logan St., Freeport, Illinois, 61032.

89. Eisner, *The Misunderstood Economy*, p. 100.

90. U.S. Office of Management and Budget, *Budget of the United States, Fiscal Year 1998*, *Historical Tables*, table 3.1, pp. 47–64, and *Budget of the United States Government, Fiscal Year 1999*, table 33–2, p. 292ff.

91. *Wall Street Journal*, May 10, 1995, p. A8.

92. R. C. Longworth, "Washington, the Rest of Us Worlds Apart," *Chicago Tribune*, November 17, 1998, sec. 1, p. 15.

93. *Washington Report on Middle East Affairs* (June 1994): 46.

94. Paul Findley, *They Dared to Speak Out: People and Institutions Confront Israel's Lobby* (Westport, Ct.: Lawrence Hill Books, 1985, 1989).

95. World Population News Service, *Popline* (July/August 1996): 1.

96. Philip L. Geyelin, "The Adams Document and the Dream of Disen-

gagement," *Estrangement, America and the World*, ed. Sanford J. Unger (Oxford University Press, 1985), p. 203.

97. U.S. Office of Management and Budget, *Budget of the United States, Fiscal Year 1995*, p. 218.

98. Daniel Bell and Lester Thurow, *The Deficits: How Big? How Long? How Dangerous?* (New York: New York University Press, 1985), p. 119. Since in making his estimates, Thurow assumed 1985 consumption levels, the additional taxes would be significantly higher today.

99. *Common Cause Magazine* (January/February 1989): 32.

100. U.S. Bureau of the Census, *Statistical Abstract of the United States*, 1997, table 765, p. 501 deflated by the CPI and rebased to 1970 = 100.

7

Rethinking Trade Policies

There may be no topic in economics that is more misunderstood by the general public than that of international trade. The conventional wisdom today is that trade is good and more trade is even better. The unasked question is, good for whom? In this chapter we will see that the benefits of trade depend upon the conditions under which trade occurs and that by no means do all people benefit under "free trade." But first we need to understand the term, "balance of trade," and what assumptions are implicit, but usually ignored, when ascertaining who wins and who loses when nations trade goods and services.

There are four components that make up the balance of trade: merchandise, services, investment income, and unilateral transfers (which include the transfers of goods and services under the U.S. military grant program). Figure 7.1 shows the changing composition of these elements over the last two decades.[1] Although improving somewhat in the earlier part of the 1990s, the net trade deficit was $155 billion in 1997 in part due to the collapse of the Asian currencies, making imports from Asia cheaper to Western economies and exports more expensive to Asian nations.[2]

The lion's share of the trade deficit is in merchandise. The merchandise balance shifted to a deficit beginning in 1970, but a serious problem did not begin until 1980. The merchandise deficit bottomed out at $160 billion in 1987 and was improving until the recession in Europe slowed European demand for American exports between 1991 and 1993. The dramatic decline in the value of the dollar in early 1995 relative to the yen was expected to decrease American imports from Japan and improve our overall balance of payments in the future. However, even as the relative value of

Figure 7.1[3]
Balance of Payments Components, 1970–96

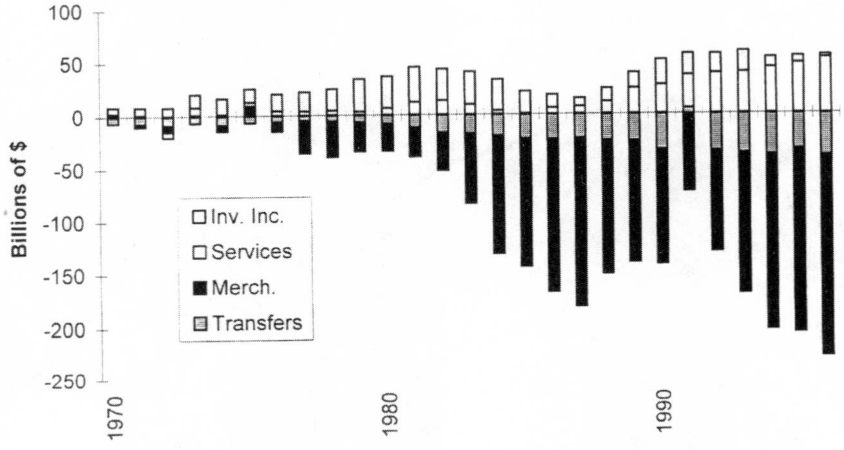

U.S. imports from Japan were declining, imports from China increased to the point where the U.S. deficit vis-à-vis China will soon exceed that of Japan.[4] By the end of 1996 the total merchandise deficit was almost $200 billion.[5] The decline in Asian currencies will no doubt worsen the merchandise deficit in the next few years.*

The overall balance of payments deficit would be even greater if it were not for the growing surplus the United States ran in the services component during the last two decades. From only a few billion dollars in the 1970s, we increased the surplus in this area to over $50 billion by 1996. The completion of the Uruguay round of the General Agreement on Tariffs and Trade (GATT) was expected to strengthen our position still further since for the first time services were included in the trade agreement. This will increase demand for U.S. technological know-how in the areas of accounting, construction, consulting, and telecommunications.[6] However, it is an open question whether in the long run such transfer of knowledge comes back to bite us in the form of merchandise deficits as we enable countries to better compete with us in areas of production.

Annual net investment income (income derived from U.S. investments abroad) has been dropping steadily from its high of $31.5 billion in 1980 to only $2.8 billion in 1996.[7] Figure 7.2 shows the reason. There has been a significant shift in U.S. assets owned abroad vis-à-vis the rest of the world's assets owned in America during the last two decades.[8] Whereas

*A 50 percent decline in the value of Asian currencies means that the price of U.S. exports to Asia increases by that amount and the price of Asian exports to the U.S. decreases by that amount.

Figure 7.2[9]
Net International Investments in the U.S., 1984–96

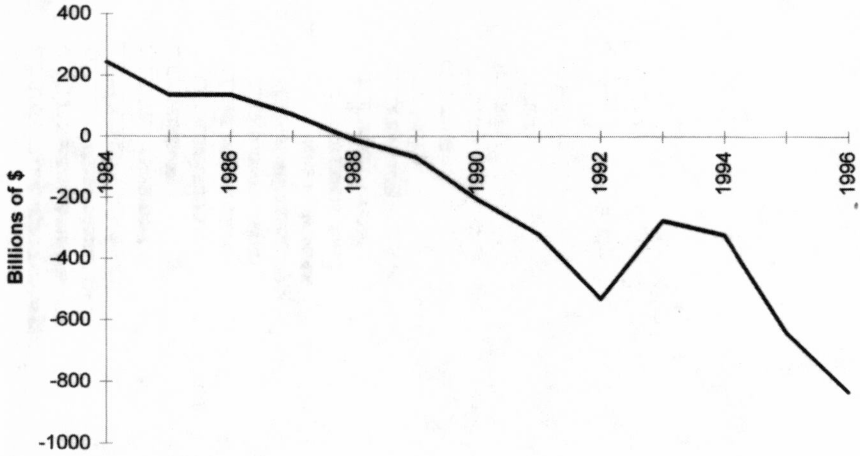

U.S. investment abroad used to exceed the rest of the world's investment in here by a wide margin, the situation was reversed by 1988. By the year 2000 net investment income will probably turn negative.

Contrary to popular belief, Japan does not own more U.S. assets than any other country, that honor goes to the United Kingdom. However, Japan has passed Great Britain as the number one investor in the United States on an annual basis, and Japan's investment is almost four times as great as the amount of U.S. annual investment in Japan, but that is primarily due to the purchase of Treasury bills, not capital investment in businesses. (We invest the most in the UK.) Whether this is good or bad for our economy cannot be answered unequivocally. On the one hand, overseas investment here creates jobs that are essential for economic growth, but on the other hand the profit from the products of foreign investments which are sold in the United States flows out of our country. On balance, foreign investment is better than no investment, but not as beneficial to Americans as American investment in our own country.

Moreover, to gain the proper perspective we must compare the amount of direct foreign investment coming in with the amount of U.S. investment in foreign nations, and the investment should be adjusted to reflect the market value of those investments or the replacement costs. As figure 7.3 shows, U.S. private investments in foreign countries is about the same as foreign investment here. The reason that total investment in figure 7.2 shows a growing imbalance is due to the amount of U.S. treasury securities held by foreign governments. Here we see the relationship between the national debt

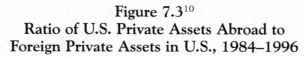

Figure 7.3[10]
Ratio of U.S. Private Assets Abroad to Foreign Private Assets in U.S., 1984–1996

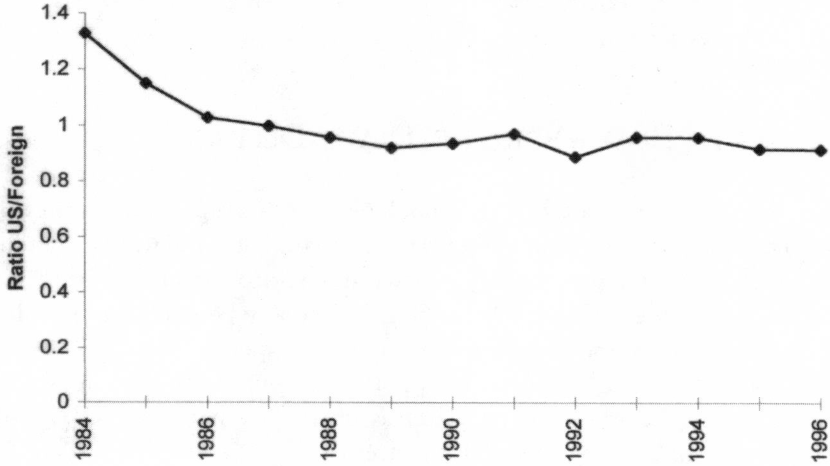

and trade balances. The purchase of U.S. treasury bonds by foreigners has helped finance our government deficits, kept interest rates lower than they would have been, and provided investment capital to support U.S. growth. However, it results in interest payments going overseas and, in the long run, it reduces U.S. growth and economic welfare. It also makes our economy less stable, because if Japan gets in enough financial trouble and it needs to sell U.S. bonds to raise capital, it can impair America's ability to finance our debt. The result would be to drive up interest rates, reduce corporate investment in plant and equipment, and slow our own economic growth.

The myth in the 1980s was that the Japanese were buying up America. The Japanese were able to increase their investment in the United States because they saved their money while Americans were spending their income as fast as they got it. However, Japan's U.S. investments reached a high in 1988 which turned out to be the peak of the last business cycle. The value of Japan's U.S. investments fell significantly in the 1990–91 U.S. recession and Japan has been far more circumspect in their American investments since then. Japan accounts for less than 2 percent of U.S. stocks.[11]

In summary, foreign private investment in the United States is about equal to our private investment in foreign countries and is no cause for concern. On the other hand, foreign purchases of U.S. treasury bonds to finance our debt, although necessary, is not in the long-term best interest of America. The primary problem is the debt, not foreign ownership.

The last area of the balance of payments deficit, unilateral transfers, includes the transfer of goods and services under the military grant program. This has grown from $8.3 billion in 1980 to $40 billion by 1996, a 380 percent increase, and amounted to 26 percent of the 1997 deficit.[12] Cutting unilateral transfers is warranted now that the Cold War has been over for almost a decade.

WHO IS TO BLAME FOR THE TRADE DEFICITS?

When the economy falters everyone looks for a scapegoat: inefficient workers, greedy management, restrictive government regulations, onerous taxes, etc. Over the past twenty years our favorite target has been the Japanese and, more recently, China. Somehow many people have been led to believe that Japanese success has been at our expense. Politicians point to the lopsided trade balances to support this contention. But let's step back a moment. Trying to assign blame assumes that that trade deficits are necessarily bad. Are they a cause for concern?

First, let's put the issue of trade in perspective. In 1997 total imports of goods and services amounted to $1,048 billion or 13.0 percent of GDP compared to only about 3.0 percent in 1960. But when we net out our $938 billion of exports, the trade in goods and services balance in 1993 was only -1.4 percent of GDP compared to about 1.0 percent in 1960.[13] Hence, trade is becoming a more significant portion of America's economic activity, but the overall imbalance—although swinging from positive to negative over the last thirty-five years—is insignificant relative to the U.S. economic output.

Second, those who claim that our trade deficits are caused by unfair trade practices of trading partners such as China and Japan don't understand how U.S. saving and investment ultimately determine the demand for imports and exports. If imports increase relative to exports for whatever reason (including trade practices that we might deem unfair), the result is a decline in the value of the nation's currency relative to its trading partners. A decline in the value of currency increases the price of imports. The increase in price lowers demand for imports reestablishing the trade balance. Hence, under floating exchange rates a nation's openness to trade has no long-term impact on trade balances. Then what does?

Ultimately, trade balances reflect the difference between national savings and investment. If the total savings of the private and public sectors of a country is less than its investments, it has to borrow from abroad. Such borrowing drives down the value of its currency relative to other nations. The relative increase in the prices of imports thus eventually would produce a trade surplus. So much for theory; now let's examine the key factors affecting U.S. trade balances over the past thirty years.

In the 1970s rampant domestic inflation raised the price of our products relative to the rest of the world, thereby reducing worldwide demand for our products; the lower level of exports relative to imports resulted in a trade deficit. However, as predicted by trade theory, the exchange rate soon reflected the higher inflation by lowering the value of the dollar relative to other currencies. The price of exports began to drop relative to imports and America's trade deficits began to improve in the early 1980s.

Next, the soaring U.S. federal deficits required us to increase our borrowing from foreigners by offering higher interest rates on Treasury bonds. By 1987 annual foreign investment in the United States exceeded our investment abroad by $156 billion. To increase their investment in America, foreigners had to buy dollars. The increased demand for dollars drove up their value relative to other currencies. The change in the exchange rate reduced the price of imports entering out shores and increased the price of U.S. exports resulting once again in soaring trade deficits.

In the 1990s the decreasing budget deficits meant that our government could reduce its borrowing from abroad even though the size of the national debt meant we were still making hefty interest payments to foreign holders of our debt. Following the 1990–91 recession, American consumers went on a spending binge, reducing their savings rate from the already low level of 6.2 percent in 1992 to zero by the end of 1998. At the same time, the crisis in Japan (coupled with that country's high savings rate), followed by financial havoc throughout Asia, resulted in foreign investment dollars seeking a safer haven in the United States. Hence, net capital flows to America increased significantly. These increased capital flows and the reduced saving rate of U.S. consumers once again resulted in a growing trade deficit. Note that nowhere in this explanation do we mention the trade practices of other nations. They simply are not relevant to the issue of trade deficits. (This is not to say that trade practices cannot have a major impact on certain industries or on specific groups of consumers.)

Throughout the rest of this discussion of trade policies, four points should be kept in mind:

> ***1. Together, the net of trade balance and investment flows will always equal the difference between savings and investment in the United States. When there is a shortfall of investment resulting in increased capital flows into a country the net capital flows are exactly equal to the country's excess of exports over imports.***
>
> ***2. In general, it is not the policies of our trading partners that determine whether we have a trade deficit or surplus, but our own rate of consumption, investment, and saving. However, to the extent that public policies raise the cost of production, such as environmental laws***

or the requirement for businesses to provide health insurance to their employees, it can place those companies at a disadvantage to their foreign competitors. Society must make a decision as to how much health care it wants relative to how many foreign made VCRs and TVs. This is no different than any other decision consumers must make with or without trade.

3. Taken just by itself, the balance of trade tells us nothing about the relative health of the U.S. economy or the welfare of the American people.

4. Productivity improvements are the basis for economic growth, not trade policies.

This last point bears a little more elaboration. We have already discussed the crucial role of productivity improvement in generating economic growth. As pointed out, growth in U.S. output per hour dropped from an average of 2.7 percent per year during the 1953–1973 period, to only 1.2 percent per year in the 1973–1997 period.[14]* Such a result would have come as quite a shock to the optimistic social theorist Herman Kahn who, predicted that productivity growth would reach 4 percent per year by the end of the century. Instead, for the last two decades productivity growth has averaged about 1 percent per year, the slowest in a century.[15] What went wrong?

Productivity growth slowed for two reasons: (a) overconsumption (especially defense-related consumption in the 1980s), and (b) the failure to invest in not only plant and equipment, but also equally important infrastructure replacement and human capital. Although government regulations are often offered as an explanation for the slow growth in productivity, there is no substantive evidence to support this contention. As economist Paul Klugman notes, if regulation produces slower productivity growth, why do European economies boast substantially higher productivity growth than we do even though their economies are much more regulated than ours?[16] Neither can we blame the oil shocks, as some economists have tried, since the price of oil has declined to below the 1973 level in real dollar terms.[17] This leaves us with overconsumption and its flip side, undersavings and investment, as the culprits.

The data below shows that we have failed to come even close to Japan in the rate of savings or capital investment over the period 1985 to 1996. Differences in the 1960s and 1970s would be even more pronounced.

---

*A more comprehensive measure of productivity which includes both factors of production, labor and capital, indicates that productivity growth between 1973 and 1992 was even lower, only 0.4 percent per year. (*Economic Report of the President, 1994*, p. 44.) It has probably improved since 1992, perhaps to about 1 percent annually.

U.S. and Japan, Selected Comparisons, 1985–1996[18]

	Real GDP Growth	Investment Rate*		Savings Rate per capita†	
	1985–96 Avg.	*1985*	*1996*	*1985*	*1996*
U.S.	4.7%	18.8%	17.0%	7.2%	4.9%
Japan	6.0%	27.5%	29.6%	15.6%	13.2%

The savings rate estimates are not strictly comparable. For example, much of Japan's savings are in the form of personal pensions since the Japanese receive very little in the way of social security or corporate pensions. However, even adding U.S. pension plans and social security, the rate of saving in America is still much less than Japan.

It is no wonder, then, that at least until the early 1990s, Japan was the fastest growing of the world's developed economies. During that period Japan invested 60 percent to 70 percent more of its GDP than the we did.

But if investment is the key to productivity, which is the source of increased national wealth, why have the economies of Japan and other Asian nations faltered so badly in the late 1990s? The answer is not, as some Wall Street pundits have claimed, that America's emphasis on short-term planning is better than Asia's long-term focus. The reasons were more complex. First, many Asian nations speculated heavily in land. Investment in land, unlike investment in new technology, does not increase productivity. In fact, land speculation can be a virtual pyramid scheme where the only reason for the increase in value is that the returns to the first investors spark an escalation of investment—a bubble that must eventually pop. At one time it was estimated that the land occupied by the Imperial Palace was valued at more than all of Canada, and the total real estate value of Tokyo was greater than all of America. Such estimates may be exaggerated,

---

*Perhaps a better measure of America's investment in future productivity would be private investment net of depreciation. There are problems in getting accurate measurements of depreciation and the estimates tend to be very volatile on a year-to-year basis. However, we might note that net private investment averaged 7.4 percent of GDP in the 1960s and 1970s but dropped to 5.5 percent in the 1980s and averaged only 2.9 percent for the 1990–1993 period. Not a good harbinger of future productivity growth. (Calculated from *Economic Report of the President, 1994*, tables B–1, p. 268, and B–17, p. 288. The Annual *Economic of the President* no longer reports net investment, possibly because the data required for its calculation is questionable.)

†Purchasing power parity basis. The goods and services produced in different countries should be valued consistently if the differences observed are meant to reflect real differences in the volumes of goods and services produced. The use of purchasing power parities (ppp) is intended to achieve this objective. PPPs show how many units of currency are needed in one country to buy the same amount of goods and services in another country.

but the truth is that real estate prices in 1998 were 75 percent less than their peaks.[19] To make matters far worse, the inflated real estate prices were used as collateral for loans that were made in overly inflated stock deals. When the bubble burst, as all bubbles do, the combined losses of stock and real estate were estimated at about $5 trillion.[20] Tragically, many other Asian nations failed to learn from Japan's disaster and followed the same ruinous policies.

Second, as William Perry, former U.S. defense secretary and now a professor at Stanford University, pointed out, Japanese industry made huge bets in the 1980s and 1990s on semiconductor memory chips which have become a commodity, developing artificial intelligence which has never succeeded to the extent the Japanese hoped, and high definition television which has yet to take off.[21] The failure of these three major areas of Japanese investment underscores the dangers of an industrial policy, where the government gets involved in promoting certain technology rather than have technology driven by the marketplace.

Third, Asian nations almost all have extremely lax banking regulations. Nobody really knows what is going on. If much of the banks' assets are in overinflated land values, this shaky foundation can bring down the whole economy. In many respects Japan and the Asian nations suffered a fate similar to America's own savings and loan debacle in the early 1980s. Recall that our government had to initially ante up almost $500 billion to bail out our S & Ls after we stopped regulating them while still guaranteeing investor assets. The situation in Asia was far worse because of the incestuous relationship between government, banks, and big business. Moreover, since a large proportion of Japan's economy hinges on exports, both to the other Asian nations that are also in trouble, and to the United States which now has an average wage rate below that of Japan, Japan's troubles are not going to vanish overnight.

In fact, Japan's trouble may get worse before they get better. It took the Great Depression to teach America about the dangers of excessive investment on margin and the dangers of inadequate bank regulation. It is entirely possible that Japan will have to undergo a depression before it gets its financial house in order. If it does slide into a depression, its high rate of savings—so essential to Japan's long-term growth—will actually work against it in the short run. The Japanese may need to undertake major federal public expenditures, just as America did to jolt them out the Depression. (Remember that even the public works programs in the 1930s were insufficient to end American's depression. It took the massive deficit spending of World War II to really get the American economy pumped up again.)

Although Japan (and most of Asia for that matter) might have some extremely rough years in the near term, it would be foolish to assume that

Japan and other Asian countries will not take the necessary steps to correct their present problems. It may take a decade or more to fix their banking system and recover their momentum, but eventually a wiser and competitively tougher Japan and Asia will emerge.

America has its own Achilles' heal that, in the longer run, puts us at a greater disadvantage: our anemic savings rate. Americans will do almost anything to keep up their voracious consumption habits. The two-worker family has become the norm, yet savings rates are lower than ever. For many women jobs were a chance to fulfill career aspirations and maximize their potential. For many other women, jobs were the only means by which household income could continue to grow and permit them to pay for the new "necessities of life" such as VCRs, stereos, giant screen TVs, late model import cars, etc.

The federal government has been singularly unsuccessful in getting Americans to save more even during the best of times. Over the past forty years the personal savings rate reached a high of 9.5 percent in 1973 and 1974, fluctuated throughout the 1970s and then began the long decline to zero by the end of 1998.[22] Surprisingly, there appears to be no relationship between savings and the changing demographics over this time. We might have expected the aging of the baby boom to result in increased savings. But apparently when the baby boomers are not spending on themselves, they are spending on their kids.

Economist Lester Thurow points out that, historically, a relatively meager personal savings rate was partially offset by U.S. firms saving more of their cash than foreign firms.[23] As explained earlier, this is no longer the case since the 1980s as American firms thought that increasing their debt (called leveraging up) was an easy way to reduce taxes and improve earnings. Total private savings was 17.6 percent of GDP in 1980. The rate has dropped steadily since then to 14.7 percent by 1996.[24] Thurow believes that if we are to improve U.S. productivity, the goal for private national savings (consumers and businesses) should be 25 percent of GDP.[25]

When Americans worry about the rate of foreign investment here at home, they focus on the wrong issue. It is not that foreign countries invest too much, but that we invest too little. At one time about two-thirds of the money borrowed from foreign investors was due to the low U.S. savings rate, and the other one-third was borrowed to finance the federal deficit. If it were not for foreign investment, the cost of financing the U.S. debt would be much higher and the growth of our economy much slower. Two interesting trends have taken shape in the last few years. First, although U.S. direct investment abroad is still 25 percent higher than foreign direct investment in the United States, our borrowing from abroad is 88 percent higher than foreign borrowing from the United States (even excluding the borrowings from abroad to finance our national debt). In other words, our growth in recent years has been dependent to a significant degree on investment from foreigners.

Second, American manufacturers have been out-sourcing parts and components to foreign factories, especially in Asia and South America. As a consequence, when the currencies of these countries took a tumble, although our imports rose and worsened the trade deficit, since the price of those imports fell, profits increased for American producers of finished products, such as autos and computers. This is one reason the U.S. stock market has outpaced U.S. economic growth.

THE UNITED STATES LAGS BEHIND JAPAN AND GERMANY IN CIVILIAN RESEARCH & DEVELOPMENT

To be of maximum value it is not enough just to increase capital investment; those investments must embody more advanced technology then that of our world competitors. This requires a continued increase in research and development expenditures. The United States has seriously neglected research and development for the past two decades, especially in the production processes. Some economists try to obscure this fact by pointing out that the average real increase in corporate R & D during the decade of the 1970s was 3.9 percent annually, while it increased to an average of 4.8 percent during the 1980s.[26] The problem with this analysis is that the 1980's average is skewed by the early part of the decade which grew at 8.2 percent from a very low base due to the 1980 recession. During the last half of the 1980s the National Science Foundation estimates that R & D grew just over 1 percent per year.[27]

Some of the more upbeat analysis also fails to note that a significant portion of the R & D spending during the 1970s and 1980s was in the defense industry. In fact, the federal government provided for about 66 percent of the funds for basic research and about two-thirds of this amount (about 44 percent of all R & D) was directed to the Department of Defense. During this period our major international competitors were focusing on civilian rather than military R & D. In 1995 the Germans and Japanese were still spending a greater portion of their GDP on civilian R & D than we were, although the gap has closed slightly in recent years:

Percentage of GDP Spent on Civilian R & D, 1995[28]

Germany	2.5
Japan	2.8
U.S.	2.0

The 1995 federal budget sought to partially redress the imbalance by shifting federal R & D to civilian projects. By 1995, civilian R & D was expected to have increased from 33 percent to 45 percent of all federally funded R & D.[29] However, total R & D expenditures were constrained by the need to reduce the deficit.

Evidence of the impact of slower growth in U.S. research and development is shown in the growing share of U.S. patents granted to foreign nationals:[30]

15% in 1960
25% in 1970
38% in 1980
47% in 1990
43% in 1994

To stimulate U.S. R & D, in 1994 Clinton restored the investment tax credit for R & D and increased federal civilian R & D by one billion dollars—a paltry sum, but given the budget deficit, about all he could do. He also asked the defense department to shift 10 to 20 percent of its weapons research to commercial technology transfer activities with industry.[31] So far it is difficult to assess the results of these initiatives.

Wage Rates

There was a time when U.S. productivity was so far above that of our international competitors that we could afford to pay far higher wages and still deliver higher quality products at lower costs than our competitors. However, with productivity increasing so slowly for the past two decades, foreign competitors have caught up and sometimes exceeded our output per hour. Even if they only come close to our level of productivity, if their labor rates are lower, they can underprice us. For many industries that is the case today.

The comparative wage rates in America improved markedly during the latter half of the 1980s, in part because of lower increases in hourly pay in manufacturing, and in part because of the falling value of the dollar. In the late 1990s, the sharp plunge in the currencies of Japan and the Asian nations increased relative U.S. wage rates.

As table 7.1 shows, although our hourly labor rates in 1997 were still considerably below German manufacturers and slightly below the Japanese, we pay several times the hourly wages of countries such as Mexico or the newly industrialized Asian nations such as Hong Kong, South Korea, Singapore, or Taiwan. To put it in more recognizable terms, in 1997 the average American factory worker earned $19.01 an hour, while the average Chinese worker earned $0.33 in that same hour.[33]

Table 7.1
Index of Hourly Compensation Costs (Including Benefits) in Manufacturing[32]

	1985	*1994*	*1997*
United States	100	100	100
France	58	100	93
Germany*	74	160	153
Canada	84	92	NA
Britain	48	80	NA
Japan	49	125	105
Mexico	12	15	NA
Asia†	12	34	NA

*Formerly West Germany only
†Newly industrialized countries

While credit is given to management for improving competitiveness of U.S. businesses vis-à-vis our trading partners, it was the American laborer who paid the price with cuts in inflation-adjusted average weekly earnings and periodic layoffs. During this period executive compensation rose exorbitantly. For example, in 1996 alone average pay for CEOs rose 39 percent, while average pay for salaried employees rose less than 3 percent. The difference in wage costs between management and labor is higher in the United States than any other industrialized nation. ***Japanese CEOs earn only sixteen times more than the average worker compared to the U.S., where CEOs make as much as 160 times more than the average employee.***[34] Even worse, American CEOs get paid huge amounts in good years and not much less in bad years. By contrast, in Japan top managers are expected to take substantial voluntary pay cuts rather than eliminate jobs when a company gets into trouble. When GM president Robert Stempel, who received $2.18 million in direct and deferred compensation, announced that GM was going to wipe out 74,000 jobs, Peter Drucker observed that "in Japan, someone like Mr. Stempel would have announced his resignation by now."[35] In short, U.S. executive compensation adds to the costs of our products, while they are not subject to the greater risk and responsibility which is supposed to justify the higher pay.

Moreover, it was U.S. executives who decided on the acquisition mania of the 1980s and increased their corporate debt to unprecedented levels. During the decade, 28 percent of U.S. corporate assets changed hands—a total of $1.3 trillion.[36] The consequence of this acquisition binge was to make the takeover artists rich while increasing corporate debt to such unprecedented levels that corporations had to curtail investment in R & D and capital modernization programs. From 1970 until 1991, inflation-adjusted R & D expenditures in private industry grew about 5.3 percent per year. But from 1991 to 1995 private R & D was essentially flat.[37] Profits were increased by cutting back expenditures across the board, including investment.

THE JAPANESE BOGEYMAN

It is generally felt by American businesspeople that Japan's past success was due largely to restraint of trade practices. Like its predecessors, the Clinton administration pressed the point by threatening retaliation. Let's examine the evidence.

It is alleged that the Japanese are guilty of dumping: charging lower prices for goods sold abroad than in Japan.[38] One 1991 survey found that two-thirds of the products exported to the United States were, on average, 37 percent cheaper than the prices of those products in Japan.[39] The intent of such a policy is both to reduce internal consumption and to increase market share abroad. Americans have reason to resent a duel pricing policy that, if eliminated, might increase exports to Japan by 20 percent.[40] However, from the Japanese perspective it is just good business to take losses to increase the volume of business to the point where economies of scale result in lower unit costs, increased sales, and increased long-term profits. We think such a practice unethical; the Japanese view it as sacrificing today's profits to for greater benefits tomorrow. It is easy to see why Americans favor making such a practice illegal. It is more difficult to see why it is unethical. True, it does restrain trade, but then so did America's system of high protective tariffs which was so successful during the last century in protecting our own infant industries against European competition.

Americans may argue that such activity is illegal because pricing below costs was once employed by big businesses to drive smaller competitors out of the market. Once the monopolies controlled the market they could then raise prices to whatever they deemed appropriate. It was the outrageously high prices rather than the absence of competition per se which provided the rallying point in America to adopt laws making such anticompetitive practices illegal. However, even after dominating the market, the Japanese have not abused their position by raising prices. Tere are two reasons: (a) the decline in the unit costs that comes with increasing volume of sales permits handsome profits even without raising prices, and (b) many countries have much lower wage rates than Japan so if Japan fails to improve its productivity and hold down its prices, these countries will underprice Japan.*

*Japan's strategy of basing prices on future costs works particularly well if we assume that relative labor costs rather than comparative advantage (to be explained later in this

The only basis for declaring such a system as unethical is if Japan agrees not to practice this policy and then does so surreptitiously. At times this has been the case. For example, Japan agreed to antidumping regulations to avoid the U.S. retaliatory tariffs on Japanese imports. Once they make such an agreement, they are bound to honor it. However, it is questionable whether Japan's occasional dumping practices have been significant in affecting our balance of trade with them. Krugman notes that although it may seem that the we are awash with Japanese exports, ***Japan exports only 14 percent of what it produces, less than any other major industrial country except the United States.***[41] Conversely, Japan does import many goods, especially raw materials. Unfortunately for us, Japan does not import many of the finished goods we export.

American manufacturers might argue that if it isn't Japan's export policies that are to blame for the trade deficit, its protectionist import policies are. Unlike Germany, which imports 17.9 percent of its GDP, Japan only imports 5.7 percent.[42] And the percentage has shrunk as the Japanese economy has grown. But before condemning Japan for rampant protectionism, it should be noted that Japan has the fewest number of quotas and the lowest tariffs of any industrialized nation. It didn't refrain from buying U.S. cars during the past two decades because of restrictions. It didn't buy them for the same reasons that Americans stopped buying them: for too many years American auto manufacturers produced an inferior product. The perception of poor American quality became so ingrained that many Americans didn't believe the claims that U.S. cars were of equal quality to the Japanese even after American auto manufacturers improved their models. (Indeed Consumer Union's survey indicates that American-made cars in general still have worse repair records than Japanese cars.)[43] To make matters worse, American manufacturers did not want to mass produce cars with steering wheels on the right even though Japan, like England, has left side driving. American manufacturers wanted guaranteed high volume sales before they would take the chance of redesigning their cars.

It is also charged that the Japanese distribution system is an inadvertent barrier to bringing U.S. goods to the Japanese market. Japan doesn't have large discount chains like Walmart or Sears. The Japanese consumers are loyal to the family-owned store. The relationship between the proprietor and his customers is more important than price. Japan has thousands of small retailers that make it extremely difficult and costly to market goods in Japan. It is less efficient, but provides more jobs and is in accord with their culture. This hardly constitutes a case for protectionism. Yet

---

chapter) is the prime determinant of export and imports. However, if the standard of living in a nation is to increase—at least in terms of quantity of goods consumed—there will be pressure by the workforce to increase wages. This already has happened in Japan.

pressure from America is threatening the traditional Japanese distribution system. It is only a matter of time before Walmart or other discount distributors make inroads into Japan's retail trade.

What can or should we do about Japan's practice of charging less for exports than home consumption? Our present policy is to not only enforce the antidumping policies, but to demand that Japan import more from us. We can try and make any trade agreement that the Japanese will buy. But let's not pretend that somehow we occupy the moral high ground. We don't have to buy anything from Japan and vice versa.

U.S. businesspeople also complain that although it isn't Japan's fault; Japanese labor is of higher quality than U.S. workers. However, the evidence suggests that when Japan builds an auto company in the United States, it is run about as efficiently as in Japan. Japan invests more in human capital than we do (although not as much in education—an important distinction, as we shall see). The Japanese also gain more loyalty from their workers in part because of the large difference in wages paid by the more successful firms. The loyalty also reflects the practices of Japanese companies to reduce management salaries and resort to other cost-cutting measures before layoffs. One survey found that 75.7 percent of Japanese firms cut costs other than wages to cope with business deterioration compared to 55.4 percent of U.S. companies.[44] If personnel cuts are inevitable, the Japanese make a greater effort to shift employees to other companies. The result of such policies is that in 1998 after almost a decade of near recession conditions, the Japanese unemployment rate was still only a little over 4.0 percent. Company loyalty is also ensured by the lack of a national social security pension system, thus making Japanese employees more dependent on their employers. These practices are changing, however, because international competition is forcing Japan to lay off employees to remain competitive during its current recession. The pain of restructuring is just beginning in Japan. The Japanese are learning that once their average wages approximated those in the United States, they have to adopt our labor practices to remain competitive.

The real issue regarding trade with Japan—or any nation—is whether trade without tariffs or other trade barriers, i.e., free trade, is always in our best interests.

Reevaluating the Theory of Comparative Advantage

It is almost an article of faith among economists that international trade benefits all nations, hence the United States should remove all tariffs, quotas, and other barriers to free trade. Regrettably, as we shall see, it is not quite that simple. The tide of international trade does not necessarily lift all boats.

Support for international trade rests largely upon the classic *theory of comparative advantage* initially developed by English economist David Ricardo in 1817. Ricardo attempted to prove that trade is always mutually advantageous to trading nations, even if one nation is more efficient in producing every product than another nation.[45] To understand this nonintuitive proposition, Ricardo offered an example of England and Portugal. Assume that the two countries produce only two products, cloth and wine, and that the labor required for producing the products is as follows:

Hours of Labor

	England	*Portugal*
One bolt of Cloth	100	90
One case of Wine	120	80

Note that Portugal is more efficient (has an *absolute advantage*) in producing both cloth and wine. Yet it would still be to Portugal's advantage to produce only wine and import cloth form England because it has a *comparative advantage* in wine, i.e., it can produce more wine by devoting all its resources to that activity while importing cloth from England. Suppose, for example, instead of requiring a total of 170 labor hours to produce one bolt of cloth and one case of wine (90 hours + 80 hours), Portugal could expend 160 hours to produce two cases of wine and then trade one of them to England for a bolt of cloth. Portugal would have saved 10 hours of work, which could be used to produce other goods. England would agree to such a trade because, instead of spending 220 hours to produce one bolt of cloth (100 hours) and one case of wine (100 + 120 hours), England could make two bolts of cloth for 200 hours, trade one bolt to Portugal for a case of wine, and have an extra 20 hours to produce other goods.

The exact terms of trade would fall somewhere between the internal cost ratios of the two countries: for England 120/100, i.e., one case wine = 1.2 bolts of cloth; for Portugal 80/100, i.e., one case of wine = .8 bolts of cloth. Anywhere between the range of one case wine = .8 to 1.20 bolts of cloth and both countries benefit. Of course, England will try and drive toward trading .8 bolts of cloth for a case of wine while Portugal will try and get closer to 1.2 bolts per case of wine.[46] All things being equal (the infamous *ceteris paribus* assumption of economists), the two countries would arrive at an agreement somewhere in the middle, about 1.04 bolts of cloth per case of wine.

So much for economic theory. But there is a catch: ***Ricardo's theory is based upon certain key assumptions that many economists tend to ignore: (a) capital must not be allowed to cross borders from a high wage country to a low wage country, (b) trade between participating countries should be roughly in balance, (c) each country must have full employment with roughly comparable wage rates, and (d) no mass migration is permitted.***[47] We can easily see some of the problems that arise when these conditions are not met. In the first place, investment capital will always flow to the nation that maximizes the return to investors. This might be a good thing since it would help the development of an underdeveloped country. Unfortunately, it did not always work that way, since deals were often cut with corrupt third world governments to hold down wages and the undeveloped nations had to absorb many of the external costs such as infrastructure investment or destruction of their environment. Moreover, frequently the higher level skills such as engineers and supervisors were exclusively maintained by the developed nation so that the workers from less developed countries would not form rival corporations. That changed when the United States and European countries began training indigenous people and even encouraged them to attend our universities.

There was another impediment to industries moving to LDCs: the danger of nationalization of industry, which was commonplace with the rise of socialism. Once this threat was passed, capital began flowing in ever larger amounts to politically stable countries with low wage rates. The advantage of low wage rates can be augmented when the costs of pollution or resource depletion are not charged to the corporation but borne by society at large.

The third and fourth assumptions of Ricardo's theory were that labor in each country approaches full employment with roughly equivalent wage rates, and labor is relatively immobile. If these assumptions do not hold, then neither does Ricardo's theory. ***If wage rates are not roughly comparable among countries, then capital will move from high-wage countries to low-wage countries.*** The result will be that a trade advantage in labor intensive products accrues to the country with the lowest labor costs.[48] To take our earlier example, if England is paying wages of $10 an hour while Portugal is paying $1 an hour, investment will flow to Portugal to make both cloth and wine. The return on the investment will accrue to England's investors and their increased wealth will have some secondary benefit to England's workforce, but it is doubtful that the out-of-work English wine and cloth makers will find jobs with equivalent pay to the jobs they lost.

The flow of capital from high-wage to lower-wage countries worked to America's advantage in the last century as capital flowed into America from England to finance the building of our railroads by Irish and Chinese immigrants working for virtual slave wages. In the post World War II era, it has worked to the advantage of lower-wage, recently industrialized countries. However, what has saved the United States from feeling the full economic consequences of this trend has been the countervailing impact of our movement to the postindustrial information age where the education of the labor force becomes a prime consideration. The lack of an indigenous, highly educated labor force in the LDCs has kept many industries from migrating to some of the undeveloped countries. As the educational level of the newly industrialized countries continues to increase, however, this too will change as well. For example, more information technology work is flowing to Ireland, England, India, and other English-speaking countries (which in the future will be most of the world).

The possibility of mass migration between nations was never contemplated by Ricardo when formulating his famous theory. However, he does point out that the ease of mobility of capital and labor is the reason that the theory of comparative advantage does not work among regions within a country. Such was the case in the United States during the 1960s. The difference in wage rates and the ease of mobility resulted in investment and jobs moving to the South to take advantage of cheaper, nonunion labor, while blacks continued to move north seeking jobs. Furthermore, the better welfare system of the North resulted in labor staying there rather than following the jobs south again.

To some extent this same trend is developing in world markets. Up until 1970 there was a substantial outflow of investment from America to other nations, particularly those with cheaper labor. It did not go to Japan in any appreciable amount because the high savings rate there generated sufficient capital internally with such low interest rates, so that Japan did not try to attract outside investment. (Indeed it might be argued that foreign investment in Japan was deliberately discouraged.)

With the reduction in trade barriers resulting from the North American Free Trade Agreement (NAFTA), we might expect a situation similar to that of the North/South movement in the United States where Mexican migrants continue to move north at the same time that the low-skilled jobs which they seek move south. We have already witnessed the explosive growth in the Maquiladora program along the Mexican border that allows factories to bring unfinished parts and components into Mexico tariff free for final processing and assembly prior to re-export to the United States, where only the value added by the processing is subject to tariff. Between 1980 and 1992 the number of plants on the Mexican side of the border has grown from 620 factories employing 119,550 workers to 2,200 pants employing over 500,000 workers. This is not surprising, since the average wage rate for Mexicans is $1.64 an hour compared to $16.17 for Americans.[49] We can't expect the wage rate for Mexicans to increase very quickly.

Since 1992 the Mexican government has denied its workers the right to form independent labor unions, and the growth of the Mexican labor force is still much faster than their economy can create jobs. Hence, the pressure will be on Americans to lower wage rates. With the removal of tariffs we can expect many more labor intensive industries to relocate to Mexico, or at the very least to use this threat to depress wage rates at home. The American Maquiladora Fund has targeted U.S. companies resisting the move abroad. The fund plans to buy such companies and relocate their manufacturing operations to Mexico.

Noting that certain of Ricardo's assumptions may not hold in the modern world, some economists believe that any comprehensive trade theory should recognize what is known as the *factor price equalization theorem*, which holds that under plausible assumptions the elimination of trade barriers will result in the returns to all the factors of production tending to equalize.[50] This means that when trade occurs between a high-wage and low-wage country, the real wages of the high-wage country will eventually decline.* The key assumptions are that investment and technology will freely flow between nations.

Some economists are skeptical that technology is that easily transferred to low-wage, low-skilled countries. They also point out that the wage rates of unskilled workers have fallen in both traded goods industries and in industries unaffected by trade. However, this is to be expected since a surplus of labor in any sector of the economy tends to drag down wage rates in any other sector that can utilize those workers.[51] With regard to the transfer of technology, one need only observe how fast Japan, and then Taiwan, Hong Kong, Singapore, and South Korea, have been moving up the technology curve. With transnational corporations controlling one-third of the global output,[52] it is virtually impossible to prevent the rapid transfer of technology. Daly and Cobb point out that, ***"Those who advocate free trade and free capital mobility are simultaneously advocating equalization of wages."***[53]

The worldwide General Agreement on Tariffs and Trade (GATT) will accelerate the migration of investment in labor-intensive industries to low-

---

*Swedish economists Eli Hecksher and Bertil Ohlin developed a theory of trade between countries where there was significant differences in the relative levels of different factors of abundance such as labor, capital equipment, and neutral resources. In the 1940s, MIT economist Paul Samuelson extended their analysis to show that if countries share the same production technology, not only will the prices of the products they produce be driven to the same level, but so will the prices of the factors of production: the wages earned by workers and the rate of return earned by investors. Gary Burtless, Robert Z. Lawrence, Robert E. Litan, and Robert J. Shapiro, *Globaphobia* (Washington, D.C.: Brookings Institution, the Progressive Policy Institute and Twentieth Century Fund, 1998), p. 61.

wage nations. The long-term impact of such U.S. capital outflow on American wage rates could be even more traumatic than it has been over the past twenty years, as workers are forced to accept real-dollar wage reductions to prevent firms from picking up and leaving for cheaper labor elsewhere. Not only the direct wages, but worker benefits will be cut as well. Although a strong propnent of free trade, economist Gary Burtless admits that international trade has been one factor in the growing inequality of income in the United States. Between 1969 and 1993 the gap between those earning at the ninetieth and tenth percentiles climbed 67 percent in most trade-affected industries and only 17 percent in the least trade-affected industries.[54] Sir James Goldsmith, a leading opponent of GATT, points out that so far America has faced low-wage competition primarily from Taiwan, Hong Kong, South Korea, and Singapore, all of which have a combined population of only seventy-five million people.[55] What happens if we increase the productivity of the four billion people who live in the world's LDCs? Daly and Cobb paint an even bleaker picture. Lower wages mean less income taxes, so government services would also have to be scaled back here at home. At the same time, governments will become increasingly less able or willing to tax capital out of fear that the subsequent lower returns will result in increased capital outflows. Hence, they may be forced to place an increasingly higher proportion of the tax burden on the backs of the labor force.[56]

Again, consider the situation between the regions of America. Declining incomes in the northern cites resulted in reduction in services such as education, health care, unemployment, and welfare. Some of these cuts were mitigated by the federal government moving in to take up the slack through grants-in-aid to state and local governments and transfer payments to individuals. The federal government could do this because the loss in income tax revenue in the North was at least partially made up by the growth in taxable income in the South. However, the growth in Mexican tax dollars will not help unemployed American workers. The only alternative is to increase taxes on those reaping the benefits of the higher returns on their investments abroad, but in 1997 Congress again cut taxes on capital gains. Thus we can expect the trend in increased income inequality to continue.

There are other problems with the theory of comparative advantage. First, even years ago all things were rarely equal as Ricardo's theory assumed. Earlier, for example, I referred to the problem of trade with Central American countries. Since the Central American nations produced primarily just a few cash crops such as sugar, bananas, and coffee for export, they soon became dependent upon imports for all the other necessities of life such as clothing and food (especially grains). Thus they were in a very weak bargaining position. It was far easier for U.S. citizens to give up coffee or bananas than for Central Americans to give up grain and clothing. To make matters worse, since no single country supplied the lion's share of any product, the United States could leverage one country against another. America followed the same policy on oil until the oil-exporting nations got wise and formed a cartel that, for a few years anyway, could act like a monopoly and demand higher prices for its oil.

Basically, two strategies have been proposed for developing nations. The *import substitution strategy* proposed by Argentine economist Paul Prebisch suggests concentrating on locally produced substitutes for goods that a country currently imports. The alternative is an *export strategy* that has generally been favored by the World Bank and International Monetary Fund. They have sought to build domestic industries primarily dedicated to serve foreign export markets. Neither strategy is correct for all countries under all circumstances. Each country needs to tailor the strategy to its own resources and level of development.

Self-sufficiency—at least for an extended period of time—is essential to be able to bargain from a position of strength. Ironically, it is not only the small, less-developed countries of Central America that must bear this lesson in mind. Japan built a solid agricultural and industrial base before it began to work on export industries. Even then it employed high tariffs to slow imports until it built up a solid trade advantage, and only then began opening its internal markets to foreign competition. It was hardly Ricardo's model, but it worked spectacularly well. Again, the key to success is basic self-sufficiency. Through the use of conservation and the buildup of strategic oil reserves, Japan, although having no oil of its own, weathered the two major oil crises far better than the United States. We had become so dependent on foreign oil that we felt compelled to declare a "right" to third world oil and threatened to take it by force if the Arab nations either cut off the supply or raised the price too high.

Goldsmith proposes an intriguing alternative to the free trade model endorsed by most economists. He suggests that we divide the world into trading areas comprised of nations that are relatively similar in terms of development and wage structure.[57] For example, the United States, Europe, and Japan could comprise a region, as would South American or Southeast Asian countries. Products would be freely traded within a region, while the different regions would enter into bilateral trade agreements. Businesses wanting to sell their products within a region would have to produce locally, importing capital and technology, and creating local employment and development.[58]

THE IMPACT OF TARIFFS ON THE U.S. ECONOMY

During the nineteenth century, a time when America was growing from a tiny country of thirteen sparsely populated colonies to a world economic power, the United States followed a largely protectionist policy for its infant industries. Tariffs provided over half the federal government revenue right up to World War II.[59] Generally, foreign products were kept from our shores by the high tariffs, while raw materials and specialty goods were let in. The policy was, in effect, not all that different from the one employed by Japan a century later. As a result of U.S. tariff policies, between 1860 and 1914 exports grew sevenfold while imports only grew fivefold.[60] Still, by 1913 only 8 percent of GDP was derived from foreign trade.[61]

Although the system of high tariffs worked to our advantage for well over a century, we carried it too far in 1928. The enactment of the Smoot-Hawley tariff to protect U.S. farmers from agricultural imports led to reprisals by other nations, which further restrained the market for U.S. exports. By 1935, U.S. exports to Europe had dropped to $21 billion from a peak of $58 billion in 1928.[62]* In the 1950s economists convinced politicians that the collapse of the export market was a contributing factor to the Great Depression. The result was a new federal policy to reduce tariffs, not only on farm goods, but across the board. The subsequent success of the American economy in the post World War II era (which was due in large part because we were the only major economy in the world not ravaged by the war) emboldened economists to take the theory of competitive advantage to its logical extreme and argue for dismantling all tariffs. Through successive rounds of tariff reductions as a result of the GATT negotiations, U.S. tariffs dropped from an average of 40 percent in 1945 to less than 6 percent in 1998.[63] But it is at least questionable whether dismantling our tariffs to such an extent provided a net benefit to America.

Some economists, such as Ravi Batra, think it is not just coincidental that, during the period from 1869 to 1900 when U.S. tariffs averaged 45 percent, GDP quadrupled, average per capita income doubled, and real wages rose 50 percent.[64] Contrast this result to the period after the tariff reductions: from 1973 to 1993 average real weekly earnings fell 19 per-

---

*How much of this decline was due to European reprisals as opposed to the general spreading of the depression internationally is still subject to debate. Alfred Eckes Jr., former chairman of the U.S. International Trade Commission and professor of contemporary history, argues that foreign reaction to Smoot-Hawley was largely limited to diplomatic protests: "Contrary to conventional wisdom, Smoot-Hawley produced little retaliation or discrimination against American exports." *Opening America's Market: U.S. Foreign Trade Policy Since 1775* (Chapel Hill, N.C.: University of North Carolina Press, 1996).

cent.[65] During the same period real wages rose in Germany and Japan in part because they were less open to manufactured imports.[66] Our changing balance of trade with China provides additional evidence of the impact of lower trade barriers coupled with substantially higher wage rates. In 1980 the United States granted most-favored nation status to China, lowering tariffs from 40 percent to 6 percent.[67] As a consequence, by 1997 our trade deficit with China rivaled that of Japan.

It would be simplistic to suggest that America's stagnant wage rates were solely due to the decline in tariffs. Unfortunately for econometricians trying to measure cause and effect, several negative events began around 1973 that make it virtually impossible to quantify their respective influences. In 1973 oil prices quadrupled, the United States was attempting to fight the inflation that resulted from increasing the money supply to finance the Vietnam war, and the demographics resulted in a flood of baby boomers entering the work force. Additionally, in the 1980s productivity was depressed by the diversion of investment to defense, and immigration began to spin out of control.

By themselves, trade barriers do not guarantee economic success. India and Pakistan had protective tariffs of 313 percent and 271 percent respectively, after their independence,[68] yet neither economy flourished like the Japanese. The other conditions of low birth rate, a national commitment to increased productivity through mechanization, and a stable political order were all lacking.

But Don't Lower Prices on Imports Benefit Americans?

There is another argument against tariffs advanced by most economists. It holds that the lower wage rates paid in countries such as Mexico result in cheaper products for U.S. consumers. Since Americans can now pay less for those products, their standard of living increases despite lower wages. On the other hand, protectionist laws such as tariffs or import quotas drive up the prices of imports. Quotas on Japanese cars drove up their price by $2,500 in 1984, which added $5 billion to the bills of U.S. customers.[69] Economist Alan Blinder argues that protectionism, particularly quotas, are an inefficient way to save U.S. jobs, even of poorly paid workers. Quotas result in U.S. consumers paying much more than the annual salary of the jobs that are protected. For example:

	1984 Cost per Job Saved[70]
Textiles	$ 42,000
Automobiles	$105,000
Televisions	$420,000
Steel	$750,000

It would seem that all Americans would be better off by dropping protectionist policies that save jobs and provide a cash payment to the employees laid off due to foreign competition so that they can look for other jobs.

The Organization for Economic Cooperation and Development (OECD) and the World Bank estimated that the application of GATT tariff reductions would increase world income[71] by $213 billion a year. This amounts to only 0.7 percent of world income but, more importantly, not all or even most of the world's population share in this benefit. The problem is that the beneficiaries of cheaper prices are not necessarily those who lose jobs or face drastic wage cuts because of free trade. Even if average income rises, certain groups will be adversely effected.

Daly and Cobb fear that in the case of NAFTA, wage earners will share the lower living standard with Mexican workers, while the suppliers of investment dollars benefit from cheaper prices and cheaper labor both here and abroad.[72] Blinder's response is that the majority of citizens who benefit from the free trade *could* help workers who are hurt by such policies as lengthening the eligibility for unemployment insurance, job retraining, and providing subsidies for relocation.[73] For example, the American Jobs Protection Act would prevent employers from closing a plant or relocating to another country without giving prior notice to employees, providing them time to seek other employment.[74]

The notion of providing assistance to workers negatively affected by increased free trade is far from new. The Trade Adjustment Assistance Act (TAA) was established in 1962 and revised in 1988 to offer weekly cash benefits to eligible workers enrolled in a training program or completing training. Together with unemployment insurance, these weekly cash benefits may last up to eighteen months. It has been suggested by Gary Burtless and other economists that TAA be converted into a time-limited earnings insurance that would provide trade-displaced workers with a supplemental payment to cover a portion (perhaps 50 percent) of the difference between the wage of their old job and their new job for up to two years. To ensure that displaced workers get another job as soon as possible, the cash supplement would only kick in after they take a new job. The primary problem with all such solutions is that they involve increasing the federal bureaucracy, and it is extremely difficult to determine whether or not trade was the reason for layoffs in many businesses that may derive some portion of their revenue from the other products directly affected by increased trade.[75]

Economist Paul Krugman falls somewhere between Blinder/Burtless and Daly/Cobb on the issue of protectionism. He agrees that the danger of one nation enacting tariffs to protect its industries is that other nations might retaliate with higher tariffs of their own. However, because of the relatively small amount of America's total GDP that is derived from exports, Krugman argues that a "tariff war which would cut trade in half would do no more economic harm than a mild economic recession."[76] Moreover, there are times when Krugman sees a justification for protectionist policies: "if the pattern of international trade and specialization largely reflects historical circumstances rather than the underlying national strengths, then government policies can, *in principle*, shape the pattern to benefit their domestic economies."[77]

Even if society were willing to provide monetary compensation for the jobs lost, it still may not offset the social benefits of a fully employed, relatively well paid work force. I share the concern of Goldsmith who believed that modern trade policy has resulted in "the poor of the rich countries subsidizing the rich in poor countries."[78] Goldsmith draws the common sense conclusion that "it surely must be a mistake to adopt economic policies which make you rich if you eliminate your national workforce and transfer production abroad, and which bankrupts you if you continue to employ your own people."[79] ***What we would like to do, if at all possible, is to introduce economic policies, such as free trade, at a slow enough pace so that employment can adjust through the market mechanism with a minimum of government interference through new federal programs.***

ENTER THE MULTINATIONAL CORPORATIONS

Much of economic theory, such as Ricardo's comparative advantage, was developed before creation of the mammoth multinational firms of today. These huge corporations owe allegiance to no national government and seek to monopolize industries on a global scale. Their strategy is straightforward: "to produce products where costs are the lowest, sell where markets are the most lucrative, and shift the profits to where tax rates are the least burdensome."[80] They are often larger and more powerful than the nations in which they operate. The aggregated sales of the world's ten largest corporations exceed the aggregate GDP of the world's smallest hundred countries.[81] Of the world's hundred largest economies half are multinational companies.[82] They can leverage their position to gain major tax concessions and subsidized infrastructure. Then, if they see a better deal—such as cheaper labor elsewhere—they can skip town.

Take the case of Proctor Silex. In the 1970s it pressured Moore County, South Carolina, to provide tax breaks, ease environmental regulations, and float a $5.5 million bond issue to provide sewer and water hook-ups for its new factory. But in 1990 Procter Silex moved to Mexico to take advantage of cheaper labor, leaving behind 800 unemployed Moore County workers, drums of toxic wastes, and a large public debt.[83] Before we condemn Procter Silex we must consider its alternatives. If it was faced with international competition with lower-cost labor, Procter would soon find its profits and market share eroding. Eventually, it would be forced out of business. Hence, it is not necessarily the evil intentions of Procter Silex that must be blamed, but the workings of the international market.

Even the best intentioned companies must cope with the unrelenting workings of international trade. The clothes manufacturer Levi Strauss received awards for its nonexploitive work practices in developing countries. The company once rejected a $40 million-per-year production contract with China to protest that country's human rights violations. Yet during the 1980s shrinking profit margins forced Levi Strauss to close 58 U.S. plants and lay off 10,400 workers. It tried to keep 34 U.S. plants open even though, if profitability was the only criterion, all these plants should have been relocated.[84] By 1999, it was forced to lose the rest of its U.S. operations.

A further complicating element is that multinational companies muddy the issue of bilateral trade agreements. According to a *Wall Street Journal* analysis, foreign companies control about three-fourths of China's exports. Half is produced directly in foreign-owned Chinese factories, and another one-fourth is produced in other countries but sold through China. Hence, it is difficult to say exactly how much one country sells to another and who ultimately benefits. For example, even though China's exports have dramatically increased, much of that increase has not been at the expense of the U.S. domestic factories, but the movement of manufacturing jobs from Japan, Taiwan, and South Korea.[85]

The problem with unrestricted international trade is that it will tend to average out wage rates throughout the world just as the difference in wage rates between North and South in the United States narrowed significantly after World War II. Weighting by their respective populations, averaging America's and Western Europe's wage rates (about $20 an hour) and the wages earned by workers in China and in LDCs (less than $1 an hour) would result in average world wages falling to about $4 an hour. This leaves the United States between Scylla and Charybdis: either keep moving up the technology curve, which results in a shrinking number of good paying jobs (mainly for the cognitive elite who develop and learn the higher-skilled technologies) or reduce wage rates to meet world competition. There has been a long debate as to whether wage rates have fallen in real dollar terms over the past twenty-five years due to (a) increased technology, (b) world competition, or (c) immigration. The answer is of course (d) all of the above, because all the trends are intrinsically related and reinforce one another.

Daly and Cobb's solution to the problem of unrestricted international trade is to require quotas that limit imports to rough equality with exports.[86] Even Blinder admits that protectionism may be justified in the case of infant industries that need to move up the learning curve to gain the economies of scale to compete. But in this case tariffs are more desirable than quotas because a tariff at least provides money to the U.S. treasury.[87]

My own view is that in the long run, the U.S. wage rates are bound to be depressed by lower wage rates throughout the world. The low wage rates of Asia, Mexico, and South America in particular will drag down U.S. wages. As these countries become more politically and financially stable, investment capital for labor-intensive businesses will flow south. However, although the loss of unskilled and semi-skilled jobs may be inevitable, the speed of implementation can be slowed to mitigate the pain. Indeed, until recently, the United States continued a mildly protectionist policy: duty free imports dropped from 54 percent in 1950 to 30 percent in 1981, but from 1975 through the mid-1980s the percentage of U.S. imports subject to some sort of protection rose from 8 percent to 21 percent.[88] Then came the Urguay round of the GAIT negotiations and NAFTA. By 1997, U.S. tariffs overall were at a relatively low level of about 3 percent.[89] There is no reason to seek further tariff reductions at this time.

The Uruguay Round of GATT

The General Agreement on Tariffs and Trade (GATT) was established in 1950 with the purpose of dropping tariffs from an average of 50 percent to 5 percent over the next forty years. Through tough bargaining sessions over that period, substantial progress has been made in attaining that goal. The last round of negotiations, known as the Uruguay Round, was completed in 1994. The United States was generally pleased with the outcome; our officials believe that the lower worldwide tariffs will generate from $100 to $200 billion of added annual revenue for the United States by 2005.[90] We were particularly gratified with the reduced agricultural subsidies in foreign nations, greater protection for intellectual property rights, the phaseout of textile quotas, outlawing protection of heavy industry and new rules for trade of services.

However, there was some concern about establishing a new international body, the World Trade Organization (WTO), to resolve trade disputes—the fear being that it might be biased toward the less developed nations. The greater concern should be that the WTO will be biased in favor of the multinational corporations and effectively reduce environmental protection and social policy to the lowest common denominator—what David Korten calls "a race to the bottom." Under the GATT provisions any member country can challenge any law of another country that it believes deprives it of benefits it expected to receive from the new trade rules. The challenge will be reviewed by a three judge panel of trade experts—generally lawyers who have made careers representing corporate clients on trade issues.[91] You can bet none of the judges will be ecologists or sociologists. The burden of proof rests with the defendant country to demonstrate that its law is not a restriction of trade as defined by GATT. There is no appeal process—the panel's recommendations are automatically adopted by the WTO sixty days after release unless there is a unanimous vote by the over 100 member countries to repeal them—not likely.

Let me offer three examples of the potentially disturbing consequences of such a biased arrangement. International tobacco companies forced Korea to lift its ban on tobacco imports. The subsequent competition and its focus on stimulating demand through advertising resulted in the percentage of male teenage smokers in Korea increasing from 1.6 percent to 8.7 percent.[92] The result will be hundreds of thousands of additional deaths due to cancer. As a second example, consider that global health and safety standards will be set by a group known the Codex Alimentarius Commission. The Codex standards permit DDT residues on food products up to fifty times that permitted by U.S. law.[93] If the United States tries to enforce its more restrictive laws, it will be considered a restraint of trade.

The third example—and by far the most troublesome—occured in April 1996 when the WTO ruled against the U.S. Clean Air Act, ordering Washington to change its rules on how clean gasoline must be in order to be sold in the United States. The WTO argued that the Environmental Protection Agency's regulations discriminate against foreign oil companies that don't want the added expense of cleaning up their gas before exporting it to the United States. If we give in to this ruling we will not only endanger our own citizens but effectively give up sovereignty with regard to our environmental standards.

I don't want to overstate my concerns with the WTO. Some people worry that international tribunals such as the WTO are a threat to U.S. sovereignty. In the final analysis, however, the WTO cannot compel any nation to abide by its decisions. The worst that can happen to a country that does not choose to abide by the rulings of the WTO is that the complaining countries choose to withdraw some concession that they made previously. It might also be worth noting that to date the United States has been the most active complainant.[94]

In the minds of many economists, the most significant problem with the WTO is that China has still not agreed to comply with its decisions. To be effective in adjucating trade disputes, China must be brought under the WTO. Some of the practices of China that would almost certainly be outlawed by the WTO include the state-owned companies maintained by state subsidies and loans, China's willingness to use its large market to compel the transfer of technology, and its failure to enforce intellectual property and labor rights.

Despite some reservations about the WTO, economists were almost universally pleased with the outcome of the GATT negotiations. Nevertheless, the worldwide benefits are not as unambiguous as economists would have us believe. Of particular concern is the danger that the more efficient American agricultural business will drive farmers throughout the world out of business. Sir James Goldsmith has pointed out that the present world rural population is about three billion people. Goldsmith believes that as a result of the GATT tariff reductions as many as two billion people will be driven off their farms into urban areas or mass migration.[95] A similar situation exists in Mexico, where the loss of tariff protections as a result of implementation of the NAFTA will probably result in a major displacement of the peasant population. The consequence will be the migration of hundreds of thousands, perhaps millions, of peasants to the already overcrowded slums of Mexican cities, and ultimately, north to America. But this doesn't concern economists who are focused on the impact on GDP growth under the assumption—which we showed in chapter 2 was fallacious—that GDP is an adequate surrogate for human welfare.

Economists will argue that this is the same kind of alarmist rhetoric that was expounded by labor organizations who feared that the mechanization of jobs would create vast numbers of unemployed. To the contrary, it can be shown that the economic stimulus created by mechanization has resulted in economic growth and the creation of whole new industries resulting in more, rather than fewer, jobs. However, the agrarian revolution, coupled with relatively high fertility rates, has resulted in overcrowding of the world's cities. Even in those areas with the most favorable results, such as Japan and Southeast Asia, it is debatable whether, on balance, the quality of life in terms of happiness has actually improved significantly. With the increase in material goods has come increased stress to compete, increased pollution, and the loss of cultural traditions that have given meaning to the lives of many people.

I do not wish to be a latter-day Luddite throwing my wooden shoes into the wheels of free trade. If implemented in a gradual and circumspect manner, free trade can have major benefits, especially for the third world countries who will be able to take advantage of their lower wage rates to compete with America. ***The lowering of our trade barriers has already been a much greater help to third world nations than the precious little we provide in foreign aid or loans from the World Bank.*** Between 1975 and 1995 the number of desperately poor people in East and Southeast Asia has declined from 717 million to 348 million. According to the World Bank, South Korea, Taiwan, Hong Kong, and Singapore have eliminated absolute poverty.[96]* Despite this impressive result, free trade is not a panacea for the LDCs and has many undesirable side effects that must be dealt with. Of crucial importance is the need to ameliorate the dislocation of peasants from rural to urban areas, and far greater efforts are needed to reduce fertility rates so that the benefits of economic growth are not swamped by a burgeoning population.

It is especially important not to hasten the decline of trade barriers any faster than we already have. ***Extending NAFTA to include all of Central and South America is not warranted at this time.*** Even if we adopted Blinder's recommendations to assist those who lose their jobs to foreign competition, there would be lags, as there always are, in implementing such policies. We need to adopt free trade policies *gradually* to give our social institutions time to cope.

The remaining tariffs of other countries have little negative economic impact on the United States. As I explained earlier, the trade imbalance created in the 1980s was not due primarily to the trade policies of Japan. Rather, it was due to the host of other missteps in U.S. policies, especially the inflation triggered by federal spending on defense and social programs coupled with expanding the money supply to finance that spending when the economy was already overheating. After a decade of deteriorating trade balances, in the mid-1980s the Federal Reserve Bank sought to improve the balance of payments by increasing the money supply to bring down the value of the dollar. (The Fed can adopt such a policy without rekindling inflation when there is slack in the economy.) The fall in the dollar resulted in the expected increase in export demand from 12 percent of U.S. production in 1986 to 20 percent by 1990.[97] Net exports accounted for 90 percent of U.S. growth during the 1990 recession. We reached a balanced trade position with almost every country except Japan. Unfortunately, Japan's overpriced investment markets were readjusting at the same time, driving down the price of the yen.[98] The decline in the yen prevented improvements in trade balances with Japan during the early 1990s. Since

---

*Based upon a poverty line estimate of $1 a day at 1985 prices.

1993 the value of the yen has risen, and although trade balances have not improved much in absolute terms, the trade balances have shown significant improvements relative to total GDP. As a percentage of total GDP the overall negative U.S. trade balance has declined from 3.6 percent in 1987 to about 2.0 percent by 1997.[99]

Improving the Competitive Position of the United States

We will conclude this chapter with several policy recommendations that could improve American competitiveness vis-à-vis our major trading partners over the long term without disadvantaging emerging economies.

1. Stimulate Savings

Between 1960 and 1980 the U.S. personal savings averaged about 8 percent of disposable personal income, but declined to 5 percent by 1989 and, despite the growth of personal income in the 1990s, had dropped to zero by the end of 1998, the lowest rate since the Great Depression.[100] Some forms of savings that are not included in income, such as capital gains, pensions, and social security, have been increasing, so the picture may not be quite as bleak as it first appears. Nevertheless, capital gains can disappear quickly in a sudden stock market drop and the pensions are needed for retirement. If we aggregate all forms of savings, Germany saves on average 67 percent more than we do, and Japan saves a 100 percent more.[101] The problem therefore is how to get Americans to save and invest more.

Japan appears to have a problem of too much savings. Insufficient consumption can result in recession. But in the long run excessive rates of consumer spending cannot be maintained; foreign investment cannot always be depended upon to make up the shortfall, and sooner or later the lack of investment dollars drives up interest rates, causing firms to decide not to undertake certain projects. The slowing growth of investment results in less productivity, increased unemployment, and, finally, reduced consumption. Of course the danger is that a downward spiral gains momentum and results in a full-scale depression.

As shown in chapter 4, mass immigration can also maintain an economic boom, which is the case in the United States today. Ultimately, however, relying on population growth to maintain economic growth is a pyramid scheme that will exert its toll on future generations and must eventually collapse.

The first step to stimulate savings and investment has already been taken by changing the tax code to encourage savings by avoiding taxes through vehicles such as IRAs and Roth accounts. Of course this will be of little help to the tens of millions of Americans who are struggling to make ends meet and have virtually no discretionary income.

In many cases, however, we find that people are spending money on the new "necessities" of life created by the advertising industry, such as VCRs, CD players, exercise equipment, $120 basketball shoes, and exorbitantly expensive designer clothes, etc. As a society we spend billions on encouraging consumption—why not some expenditure on increasing savings? At the very least, we must teach consumers how to compute the long-term economic costs of their consumption. I'll bet there isn't one out of a hundred graduate students who realizes that investing $15,000 at 8 percent instead of spending it on a new car would net them over $326,000 by the time they retire at age sixty-five.

Another, more controversial, policy recommendation would be to disallow *consumer advertising as an expense when calculating taxable income deduction*, effectively raising the cost and, hence, reducing the amount of advertising. It might be argued that elimination of the tax deduction for advertising would only mean that the cost will be pushed off on the consumer in the form of higher prices. But since we are arguing for lower consumption, raising prices is not necessarily bad. Moreover, since advertising dollars are expended disproportionately on those goods which have very elastic demand (i.e., the quantity demanded is inversely correlated with prices and the substitution of other goods), the price increases would fall disproportionately on luxury goods, which is exactly what we want. As a side benefit, elimination of the deduction for advertising expense would provide additional tax revenues. To avoid providing a benefit to foreign manufacturers advertising their goods in the United States, an alternative would be to place a tax surcharge on all advertising rather than eliminating the expense as an income tax deduction.

Obviously such a proposal will raise a howl from businesspeople. They would seek to escape such a tax by claiming that their advertising is public information and argue that the government is taxing their right to free speech. Of course free speech does not mean that it should come at no cost. There is a right to own private property as well, yet it is taxable. If businesspeople would put aside their short-term self-interest they might recognize that in the long run even they would benefit from less consumption in favor of more savings and investment.

2. Reduce the Cost of Capital

Most economists feel that the Japanese benefit from a lower cost of capital. Different rates of taxation explain variation in the cost of capital between the United States and Japan. Although Japan taxes corporate profits at a higher rate than we do, Japan's tax rate on dividends is much lower than the combined federal-state tax rate on dividends here. Because of a tax credit equal to 10 percent on dividends received, the effective marginal personal income tax rate on dividends is only half of one percent. According to a study by The Institute for Political Economy, the low dividend tax rate, coupled with the fact that most personal interest income in Japan is excluded from taxable income and that capital gains from the sale of securities are exempt from tax, means that "capital source income in Japan is virtually untaxed at the personal level."[102] The study concludes that adopting the Japanese system would lower the cost of capital in America by 16 percent, which would result in an increase of 5 percentage points in the profit margins for U.S. corporations.[103]

Like every other economic issue there is a dissenting voice to the notion of Japan's lower cost of capital. Carl Kester and Timothy Luehnman question if Japan had such an advantage in raising low-cost capital, why did it quickly increase the capital it raised in foreign markets from 560 billion yen to 1.4 trillion yen after the relaxation of its Foreign Exchange Control Law in 1981? By 1985, foreign bond issues rose from 20 percent to 50 percent of all new issues. From such evidence Kester and Luehnman remain "skeptical that a prolonged difference in the cost of capital favoring Japan existed at any time during the past twenty years."[104]

Despite the reservations of Kester and Luehnman, the preponderance of evidence would suggest that Japan can attract more capital at a lower cost than we can. The real interest rate (the nominal rate minus the rate of inflation) in Japan has been negative for most of the postwar era.[105] The higher savings rate and resulting lower cost of capital is one of the primary reasons for Japan's long-term success.

3. Eliminate Incentives for Debt Financing

The 1980s merger mania was exacerbated by the interest deduction for debt financing. Leveraged takeovers often were prompted by little more than the desire to siphon off the cash of a profitable company and replace equity with debt. This offered no net productive value to the nation. Although reducing the cost of capital may stimulate investment, it should be accomplished in such a way as not to reward shifts between debt and equity holders. All the cost of capital, whether interest paid on debt or dividends paid on earnings, should be deductible as business expense, or else neither should be deductible.

4. Reduce the National Debt and Increase Infrastructure Investment Through a Value-Added Tax

The single most important step we could take to improve the long-term performance of our economy is to enact some form of consumption or value-added tax as discussed in chapter 13. It would generate the revenue needed to reduce the national debt, while discouraging consumption rather than investment. The immediate impact would be to slow economic growth, but if implemented during a period of rapid economic growth, it would prevent the economy from overheating and result in steadier growth over the long term.

5. Ease Antitrust Laws to Permit Joint Research and Development Efforts

Many economists in the early 1990s advocated some variant of a limited industrial policy. Lester Thurow points out that if we matched Germany, we would have spent $140 billion to help industries in 1991.[106] Krugman believes that we should adopt an industrial policy that would pump $10 billion of federal money into a consortia of firms dedicated to greatly expanding research and development efforts.[107] Until recently it was thought by some analysts that Japan's industrial policies—what David Haberstan calls "state guided communal capitalism"[108]—was a major reason for its past success. I disagree. Japan's industrial policy was a minor factor, if indeed it helped at all. Instead of the federal government getting involved in business planning, the same end could be achieved by easing antitrust laws to allow consortia to integrate their planning and development to meet foreign competition. ***The whole purpose of antitrust legislation is to foster competition and avoid monopolies. Hence, where there is significant competition from abroad, there is little reason to worry about collusion of American firms to meet that competition.*** Clinton's move to relax antitrust laws to allow U.S. business groups to do joint research is a step in the right direction. Thurow advocates permitting financial institutions to acquire a dominant or majority position in industrial firms and conglomerate or vertical supplier-groups, such as those that exist in Japan, but not single industry groups (for example, J. P. Morgan's efforts to control the entire U.S. steel industry).[109]

Another area for federal involvement is in basic research having long-term and speculative payback. This is an area that firms are reluctant to undertake, as, for example, in the area of superconductors or nuclear fusion. The difficulty here is how to disseminate the benefits of such research broadly without foreign firms also gaining the knowledge virtually free of charge.

Finally, the Clinton administration has proposed the creation of one hundred manufacturing technology centers that would provide advice to small and medium manufacturers from people with extensive industrial experience.[110] It is appropriate that the federal government adopt policies to facilitate the dissemination of information while not getting directly involved in business planning.

6. Protect and Assist Workers Injured by Foreign Competition

Protectionist measures should not seek to protect the highest-paid workers, such as steel and auto, since by paying higher prices for imports it means that the average-paid workers are subsidizing the highest-paid workers.[111] Rather, we need to protect semiskilled jobs and gradually lift the protection as the supply of unskilled labor declines. Of course, this assumes that we are adopting policies to reduce the growth in unskilled and semiskilled jobs, such as strict immigration enforcement and incentives for the poor and uneducated to reduce their birth rates.

It is also essential that where workers are being adversely affected by the removal of tariffs, we don't try to protect the industry, but rather, try to ease the transition of laid off workers to new jobs. This means increasing trade adjustment pay; providing up to two years of retraining; maintaining medical insurance; and, when appropriate, a relocation allowance.[112]

7. Build Far More Progessivity into the Tax Structure

A progressive tax structure, that taxes higher income earners at commensurately higher rates, will force those who benefit from the increased worldwide competition to provide the necessary help to the losers. Again, the subject of taxation will be covered in depth in chapter 13.

8. Rethink Our Commitment to the WTO

The United States should not under any circumstances allow an international organization to endanger Americans by dictating a relaxation of our environmental policies. On the other hand, we should increase pressure on China to join the WTO.

Trade Policies and LDC Development

One argument for dropping U.S. tariffs is that it will increase U.S. demand for products from the Less Developed Countries, thus stimulating their economies. This is true, but the flip side is that, if the LDCs must also lower their trade barriers on exports from the United States, some LDC home industries will be unable to compete with the highly mechanized U.S. products despite the lower cost of labor in the LDCs. This is certainly true for many agriculturals products. There are two other ways to help the LDCs that would benefit all nations of the world: reducing LDC debt and halting arms sales to LDCs. These two actions are interrelated, since arms sales to the LDCs is a major factor contributing to their debt burden.

After three decades of U.S. aid to the LDCs, many are in worse shape than ever. In 1980 the total debt of the LDCs was about $400 billion and climbing rapidly.[113] By 1989 their debt had more than doubled to $850 billion—about 44 percent of their GDP.[114] The continued increase in LDC debt resulted in a net flow of capital from south to north since 1983, despite the billions of dollars in foreign aid from Northern Hemisphere nations. By 1994, growth in exports had improved for many nations, particularly those in Asia and South America. The growth in LDC debt had slowed, reaching about $1.0 trillion by 1994, while their GDPs were rapidly increasing, thus resulting in a welcomed decline in their critical debt service ratio (debt payments as a percent of exports).[115] Then in 1997 the picture changed again, as many Asian nations slid precariously close to bankruptcy. The International Monetary Fund was called upon to bail them out, but it demanded major economic reform in return, especially banking reform to curb the hemorrhage of bad loans. It is too early to know if the IMF funding and national reforms will be enough to put the troubled nations back on the road to recovery.

There are several ways in which LDC debt—and the debilitating interest charges—could be permanently reduced.

The first step in reducing LDC debt is to reduce the global military buildup. The problems facing developing nations have all been made infinitely worse by their escalated military spending, which rose from 6 percent of Third World GDP in 1965 to 20 percent by the mid-1980s.[116] ***Between 1985 and 1989 the value of all the aid given to the less developed countries by the developed nations was $166 billion, but the value of the weapons sold to the LDCs was $195 billion.***[117] ***In other words, the LDCs would be ahead by $29 billion if they had received no aid and bought no additional weaponry.*** According to James Grant, the present rate of military spending, if devoted to economic development, would be enough to end absolute poverty on this planet within ten years.[118] Such a forecast is probably simplistic since we have discovered that just throwing money at the problem of poverty will not necessarily solve it. Nevertheless, instead of using money wisely to at least alleviate poverty, military dollars are devoted to destroying human life. Since the end of World War II, there has been an estimated twenty million deaths due to military actions; 90 percent of the casualties of these wars were civilian.[119] Increasingly, the wars are internal conflicts—only 3 of 82 conflicts between 1982 and 1992 were wars between states. It is arguable that the increase in expenditures is as much a cause as a result of the numerous wars going on throughout the world. At the very least, the newer weapons make the wars much more destructive.

The former Soviet Union and the United States had a hand in more than a few of the wars prior to the fall of the U.S.S.R., not necessarily in starting them, but certainly exacerbating the carnage by military support of the two sides of the conflict. In the early 1960s, President Kennedy created the Agency for International Development (AID) whose purpose was ostensibly to assist economic development of poorer nations. However, from the beginning ideological criteria were used to determine who received our aid. Basically, to get AID dollars a country had to spurn any socialistic leanings. It did not matter much whether the country embraced democracy, just so it supported free markets. What at its inception was meant to be an economic development program very quickly became a military development program as well. By 1966, 38 percent of the aid went to military programs such as training police and security forces.[120]

In the late 1970s, the Carter administration sought to establish some basic humanitarian criteria, albeit naively in some cases, and reduced aid to some of the most oppressive dictatorships such as Guatemala and Uruguay. But the Reagan and Bush administrations soon scuttled any efforts to tie aid to humanitarian practices. They greatly increased the flow of arms to countries such as El Salvador, Guatemala, and the insurgents in Angola and Nicaragua. American ignorance of world events was a great benefit to their misguided efforts in those years. Just as long as an election was held, no matter how rigged, it was assumed that the country was a democracy. More often than not, after an election, the military remained firmly in control. It is a difficult heritage to escape. Colonel Byon Disrel Lima of Guatemala expresses the sentiment of many military men in Central and South American nations: "There is a civilian wave in Latin America now, but that doesn't mean military men will lose their ultimate power. Latins take commands from men in uniform."[121] U.S. policies could have much to do with whether or not the colonel's prediction is accurate.

Since 1987 when Cold War rivalry pushed arms sales to an all-time high of $78.6 billion, sales of military hardware have dropped dramatically to $30.2 billion. Most of this reduction came from a decline in Russian sales. They have virtually exited the business of exporting death. For the United States, on the other hand, it has been business as usual. During the decade of the 1980s we provided over $128 billion in weaponry and military assistance to more than 125 of the world's 169 countries, irrespective of these countries' records on human rights.[122] In 1995, we sold $13.3 billion, or 44 percent, of the total $30.2 billion of international arms.[123] French sales ran a close second. In contrast, Russian arm sales had declined to about $1 billion.[124] Rather than trying to maintain the lead in military sales, it is in the best interest of the world and the United States to slow the weaponry spiral throughout the third world. Not only is it inherently destabilizing, but we can be virtually certain that some of those guns will eventually be aimed at U.S. forces, just as U.S. arms were in Iran and Iraq.

We appear far more interested in short-term profits than world peace. In 1997 the Clinton administration decided to change the long-standing policy and permit the sale of high-tech weapons to Latin American countries. Clinton's only justification for this irresponsible action was that if we don't offer such weaponry for sale, other nation's will. This is akin to a "hit" man's rationale that if he didn't accept a murder contract, someone else would.

Many people might dismiss the notion of a moratorium of military sales to the third world as unrealistic, but a historic event occurred in Oslo, Norway, in April 1998, when African and Western nations, including the United States, endorsed measures to control the spread of light weapons to Africa. The Oslo resolution would result in a moratorium on automatic rifles, machine guns, hand grenades, mortars, and shoulder-fired missiles in West Africa. Of particular note was that the agreement was not a work of major outside powers but came from eighteen African nations.[125]

Some specific recommendations to reduce the international military buildup include:

1. Seek a worldwide ban on military aid to all nations. This would include the elimination of all grants or loans for arms sales to third world nations. These nations must come to realize that there is no such thing as a reasonable or just military solution to political differences either between countries or within a country.

2. Work to establish a worldwide moratorium on weapon sales and transfers. This will not be easy but is essential to prevent other nations from filling the void if we reduce our sales. The major exporters of weapons after the United States, are France, United Kingdom, Germany, China, and Israel.

3. Until such a moratorium can be established, all nations should be required to report all sales to the UN Staff Committee. This can help focus political pressure against sales.

The second step in helping the LDCs to become self-sufficient is to

recognize that most of their debt will never be repaid, and so the lender nations might as well write off at least half of it. The combined debt of the sub-Sahara LDCs is equal to their GDP, and growing at a faster rate. In this situation they have no chance of lifting themselves out of poverty. Worldwide, the total value of all LDC indebtedness is only about 1 percent of the net wealth of the creditor nations. The interest on the debt also equals about 1 percent of the creditor nations' GDP. So the write-off is no great loss. Of course, the incidence of the write-off doesn't impact equally on all sectors of the economy; rather it falls on the commercial banks where it would have a substantial effect. Nevertheless, for several years now the commercial banks have recognized that they will not get repaid and have been writing off a substantial portion of the loans. Paul Krugman suggests that the debt of the most troubled nations could be halved at a cost to the American taxpayer of about $10 billion.[126] He reasons as follows.

Worldwide, loans to the most heavily indebted nations amount to about $400 billion. Say we decide to write off about $200 billion. It is generally recognized that the loans are worth, at best, 35 to 40 cents on the dollar. This means that the debt on the books of the creditor banks has already been reduced to $80 billion. U.S. banks account for about 40 percent of the lending, the equivalent of $32 billion. Moreover, by canceling half the debt, the probability of the debtor nations paying off the other half of the debt increases substantially. Therefore, at a cost to the United States of probably only $10 to $20 billion dollars, we have substantially eased the debt burden on the LDCs and may give their economies a chance to begin growing again. Note, too, that such a bailout is only a fraction of our $250 billion S & L bailout. Growth in LDCs will provide growth to U.S. export markets as well, thus effectively repaying the U.S. economy for the write-off.

Another intriguing idea is the concept of "debt for nature swaps" suggested by biologist Thomas Lovejoy. Lovejoy proposes that conservation organizations buy debt obligations from commercial banks at heavily discounted rates of 15 percent to 30 percent of the face value. The LDCs' central banks then issue new bonds in local currency at something less that the value of the original debt, which are used by indigenous environmental groups to undertake conservation projects.[127] One example of this approach was the Dutch government's purchase of $33 million worth of Costa Rica's debt in exchange for $10 million of local investments in reforestation, watershed management, and soil conservation.[128]

There are those who believe that the problem of third world debt was primarily caused by the process of granting the loans to uncreditworthy customers in the first place. If we had not meddled with the free market mechanisms, these loans would not have been made and the LDCs wouldn't be in their present mess. There is no doubt some truth to this allegation. However, to think that relying totally upon free markets to solve the LDCs' development problems is a little naive. A free market does not guarantee sustainable economic development and can often result in worse rather than better conditions for vast numbers of people. The fatal error of those who believe that free markets are the be-all and end-all to the problems of the LDCs is the mistaken assumption that the various factors of production, or in the case of international trade, the various trading partners, have the wherewithal to bargain equitably. In purely competitive markets this may be true, but pure competition is a theoretical abstract that does not exist in the real world.

In the real world, small or economically weak LDCs have been persuaded to focus on production of one or two cash crops—such as coffee, rubber, sugar cane, or cotton, or certain minerals such as oil or copper—to maximize their exports and ability to obtain international currency. The problem with this strategy is that it makes the country totally hooked on exports. If for any reason the price of exports declines, the country can be in a desperate situation, since it has also become totally dependent on imports for the necessities of life, such as food or fuel. If the exports are not essential to the more advanced countries who are purchasing them, and the imports are essential to the LDC, the former countries have the latter over a barrel. This is the situation with the Caribbean and Central American nations vis-à-vis the United States.

The small nations have little impact on either the price America is willing to pay for imported produce, or the cost that the LDCs must pay for U.S. exports. There are, of course, other markets as a source of exports and imports, but with the United States constituting such a relatively large portion of the world market, the bargaining power of the Caribbean and Central American countries is severely constrained. The unequal bargaining power is one reason that the oil-producing nations formed a cartel to try and balance the negotiating power of producers and consumers. For a while the cartel appeared to even be gaining the upper hand, but it was very short-lived, because the cartel could not prevent its most cash-strapped members from increasing production, thus driving down prices.

Free markets have generally improved the welfare of the LDCs. Except for sub-Saharan Africa, the LDCs have made substantial advances in the last twenty years:

- life expectancy rose from forty to sixty years
- child mortality rates halved
- literacy rates have doubled
- family planning increased from 9 percent of the LDC population in the 1960s to 45 percent today (in fact this has been a primary cause for the other benefits listed)

- the share of the LDCs' world industrial output rose from 5 percent to 20 percent
- average wage rates of nonindustrial countries rose from only 10 percent of manufacturing wages received by workers in the United States in 1960 to about 30 percent of U.S. wages by 1992. (Of course, some of the increase in the LDC wages was achieved at the cost of declining real wages in the United States.)[129]

However, although a free market has proven to be the most efficient in determining what is produced and how much it should cost, it is not the answer to all of society's needs. In philosophical parlance, it is a *necessary but not sufficient* condition of societal advancement. In any state of social development, it is sheer folly to pretend that effective government is unnecessary. Left purely to its own devices, the market economy can cause great tragedy. Left unchecked, sophisticated advertisements can ruthlessly exploit the ignorance of consumers in the LDCs. For example, in Kenya women gained the impression from the billboards advertising cola that it had healthful properties. Many substituted cola for their own milk, which resulted in infants dying of malnutrition.[130] For years the Nestlé corporation successfully persuaded many African women that Nestlé infant formula was better for babies than mother's milk. But when the women mixed the formula in polluted water their babies got dysentery. Still, it took many years and pressure from all over the world before Nestlé changed its marketing program.

Furthermore, in many LDCs the short-term perspective of the marketplace has resulted in ruthless and devastating ecological destruction. For example, harvesting of hardwoods in Malaysia and Indonesia is denuding huge tracts of mountain forests that will cause permanent soil erosion. And we have already discussed the consequence of the slash-and-burn techniques to gain land for farming and grazing throughout the remaining rainforests in Latin America. Often, there is not a problem of too much government in the LDCs, but governments that are either uneducated or beholden to numerous special interest groups (not totally unlike our own government).[131]

The third step to LDC self-sufficiency, is to ensure that their population growth does not exceed the carrying capacity of their country. In many countries of Latin America, the Middle East, and Africa this condition does not hold. It is doubtful that the market economy by itself will enable the countries of sub-Saharan Africa to significantly reduce their poverty in the foreseeable future. In 1988 the total GDP of the forty-five countries in this part of the world (excluding South Africa) was only equal to the GDP of Belgium, about $138 billion. There has been little improvement since then. Over a quarter of the African families live with chronic hunger.[132] Such miserable conditions are by no means limited to Africa. The World Bank estimates that over 1.1 billion people earn less than $370 per capita annually.[133] Clearly, the problems of the most troubled of the LDCs have already led to tragic consequences. Ecologist Garret Hardin maintains that the population in many areas of the world is in excess of their environment's carrying capacity. Only through a sharp decline in population is there any chance for Africa and other desperately poor LDCs to rise from the depths of poverty.

SUMMARY

Although Americans complain about many of trade polices in countries such as Japan, most of the Japan's competitive advantage during the 1960–1990 period cannot be blamed on unfair trade practices. Rather, Japan's success was primarily due to greater savings and investment in the private sector and a willingness to defer gratification, whether it be by lower consumption or greater effort in education and work. A lower wage rate also helped at one time. That is no longer the case in Japan, although it still provides an advantage to other Asian countries.

The necessity for the federal government to borrow from abroad to finance the national debt contributes to our trade deficit as well. The inability of highly leveraged U.S. firms to invest in the research and development and capital improvements necessary to retain their competitive edge has exacerbated the trade problem. While protectionist policies have been a factor in the U.S. trade deficits with certain countries such as Japan, the major contributor to our trade problems is our national debt, overconsumption and the flip side—undersaving. On balance, investment by foreign firms has aided our economy in the short run; however, in the long-term it would be better if those investments were made by U.S. firms.

Federal policies to increase the competitiveness of U.S. firms will have only limited success at best. Much of the responsibility for success or failure lies in the policies of our corporations, firms, and citizens. Japanese firms pay out only 30 percent of their after tax profits as dividends while U.S. firms pay out 82 percent.[134] In Japan, profits are further lowered by immediately expensing investments rather than depreciating investments over many years. U.S. firms are under pressure to pay higher returns to their investors, and investors want their profits now, not ten years from now. Unless the U.S. populace can begin taking a longer-term view, they are bound to lose out to those countries who do, despite our success in the last half of the 1990s.

Although there is much discussion in the press concerning America's balance of trade deficits, a $200 billion deficit in an economy that produces $8 trillion annually amounts to only 2.5 percent. Moreover, in the long run floating exchange rates ensure that the trade deficits are to a large extent self-correcting. ***The real issue regarding international trade is not the trade deficit, but how lowering trade barriers affects certain groups of workers and what can be done to minimize the economic pain to those displaced as jobs move abroad.*** In the long run, lower trade barriers will benefit Americans as well as other counties, but in the short run, reducing trade protection too quickly will result in dislocation of workers in many industries and, unless remedies are established to retrain workers, it will result in greater income inequality and social unrest. Some short-term assistance may be provided to displaced workers, but the emphasis must be on incentives that encourage laid-off workers to quickly find new jobs. We should avoid costly and ineffective government programs and, to the greatest extent possible, rely on the market to find new work. ***The very worst policy we can implement in reducing trade barriers is to increase immigration at the same time. The result will be more competition for jobs being displaced, and less likelihood that businesses will be willing to retrain workers from industries negatively affected by trade.***

The LDC debt should be largely written off in exchange for arms reductions, debt for nature swaps, or increased efforts to control population. Aid to LDCs should primarily be in the form of family planning and short-term loans to carry nations through financial turnarounds, such as the 1995 U.S. loan that saved the Mexican economy (and has been repaid early).

In addition to cutting our own military expenditures, we must work to reduce the world's outlay on arms. ***In 1995, world military expenditures were $800 billion.***[135] Dropping expenditures by only 3 percent a year and reinvesting that amount in development programs could yield a cumulative world peace dividend of $1.5 trillion over a seven-year period.[136] According to Dr. Oscar Arias, the former president of Costa Rica, who won the 1997 Nobel Peace Prize, "if we just redirected $40 billion a year over the next ten years to fighting poverty, all the world's population would enjoy basic services such as education, health care, and nutrition."[137] Conversely, at the present level of spending, the world has little chance of alleviating the plight of the peoples of the LDCs.

NOTES

1. President, *Economic Report of the President Transmitted to Congress, 1998* (Washington, D.C.: U.S. Government Printing Office, 1998), table B–103, p. 398.

2. U.S. Bureau of the Census, *Statistical Abstract of the United States, 1998* (Washington, D.C.: U.S. Government Printing Office, 1998), table 1302, pp. 786–87.

3. President, *Economic Report of the President Transmitted to Congress, 1998*, table B–103, p. 398.

4. U.S. Bureau of the Census, *Statistical Abstract of the United States, 1998*, table 1323, pp. 801–802. Projections based upon extrapolations by author.

5. Ibid., table 1302, pp. 786–87.

6. President, *Economic Report of the President Transmitted to Congress, 1994*, p. 47.

7. President, *Economic Report of the President Transmitted to Congress, 1998*, table B–103, p. 398.

8. Ibid., table B–107, p. 403.

9. Ibid.

10. Derived from data in *Economic Report of the President, 1998*, table b–107, p. 403, and *Flow of Funds Accounts of the United States*, table B–100, p. 104 and table B–102, p. 105. Business includes only nonfarm, nonfinancial business.

11. *Wall Street Journal*, April 9, 1992, p. A–4.

12. U.S. Bureau of the Census, *Statistical Abstract of the United States*, *1998*, table 1302, pp. 786–87.

13. Calculated from the *Statistical Abstract*, *1998*, table 1317, p 798, and table 715, p. 451. Much of what has been lost in export goods has been offset by an increase in services.

14. Calculated from the *Economic Report of the President, 1994*, table B–47, p. 322, *Economic Report of the President, 1998*, table B–49, p. 338, and U.S. Bureau of the Census, *Statistical Abstract of the United States*, *1998*, table 689, p 433. During 1996 and 1997 productivity edged up to 2.0 percent annually.

15. Paul Krugman, *The Age of Diminished Expectations* (Washington, D.C.: The Washington Post Company, 1990), p. 5.

16. Ibid., p. 19.

17. Ibid., p. 17.

18. U.S. Bureau of the Census, *Statistical Abstract of the United States, 1997*, table 1355, p. 836, and table 1357, p. 837. Investment rate is the ratio of gross fixed investment to GDP; Savings rate is the ratio of savings to disposable income.

19. Michael A. Lev, "Weakened Japan Inc. Faces Tumble," *Chicago Tribune*, January 18, 1998, sec. 1, pp. 1, 8.

20. Ibid.

21. Bernard Wysocki Jr., "As Innovation Revives, Some See Complacency," *Wall Street Journal*, March 23, 1998, p. Al.

22. President, *Economic Report of the President Transmitted to Congress, 1997*, table B–26, p. 316, and Bernard Wysocki Jr., "Low U.S. Savings: How Big a Problem?" *Wall Street Journal*, December 21, 1998, p. A2.

23. Lester Thurow, *Head to Head* (New York: William Morrow and Company, 1992), p. 94.

24. Calculated from the *Economic Report of the President, 1998*, table B–1, p. 280, and B–32, p. 318. If we included government savings, the rate would be just

slightly higher—16.6 percent—because the state and local budget surplus and consumption of fixed capital at all levels of government more than offsets the federal deficits. However, adding back depreciation, because it is not a cash outlay, in one sense seriously overestimates savings, because we have to replace these assets sooner or later.

25. Thurow, *Head to Head*, p. 94.

26. Claude E. Barfield, "US R & D Spending: Getting Behind the Numbers," *New York Times*, March 4, 1990, reprinted, *American Economic Institute*, no. 15, 1990.

27. Ibid.

28. The National Science Foundation, *Science and Engineering Indicators, 1996*. Cited by The *Wall Street Journal*, September, 19, 1996, p. Al.

29. U.S. Office of Management and Budget, *Budget of the United States, 1995* (Washington, D.C.: U.S. Government Printing Office, 1995), p. 116.

30. U.S. Bureau of the Census, *Statistical Abstract of the United States, 1998*, table 852, p. 547. Data prior to 1980 from Combs-Morehead Associates, Inc., *Competitive Intelligence* (July/August 1990): p. 1. Taken from U.S. Patent Office Data.

31. President, *Economic Report of President Transmitted to Congress, 1994*, p. 196.

32. U.S. Bureau of Census, *Statistical Abstract of the United States, 1996*, table 1356, p. 846. Estimates for 1997 from Morgan Stanley as reported in *Wall Street Journal*, January 26, 1998, p. Al.

33. Morgan Stanley estimates as reported by Michael M. Phillips, "U.S. Firms May Lose Labor Cost Advantage," *Wall Street Journal*, January 26, 1998, p. Al.

34. Jill Abramson and Christopher J. Chipello, "Compensation Gap," *Wall Street Journal*, December 30, 1991, p. 1. Citing compensation expert, Graef Crystal, "In Search of Excess." Also see Thurow's *Head to Head*, p. 138. Thurow estimates that American CEOs make as much as 119 times as much as the average worker.

35. Jill Abramson and Christopher J. Chipello, "Compensation Gap," p. 1.

36. Walter Adams and James Brock, *Dangerous Pursuits: Mergers and Acquisitions in the Age of Wall Street* (New York: Pantheon Books, 1989). Cited in *Future Survey* (November 1990): 9.

37. Calculated from data in *Statistical Abstract of the United States, 1991,* table 992, p. 589, and *Statistical Abstract, 1996*, table 958, p. 602.

38. For an excellent examination of the reasonableness of antidumping laws see Gary Burtless, Robert Z. Lawrence, Robert E. Litan, and Robert J. Shapiro, *Globaphobia* (Washington, D.C.: Brookings Institution, the Progressive Policy Institute and Twentieth Century Fund, 1998). The authors point out that antidumping laws forbid the following practices:

(1) Foreign producers are forbidden to charge higher rates at home than in foreign markets. But if anyone should complain it should be the producer's home market.

(2) Foreign producers are forbidden to sell at less than average costs plus an allowance for profit. But economic theory suggests that under competitive conditions firms should sell at marginal costs, not average costs.
(3) American firms are not required to meet standards imposed on foreign firms selling in the United States.
(4) Since firms set prices in foreign markets in foreign currency, fluctuations in the exchange rate can result in foreign producers suddenly finding themselves guilty of dumping.

After reviewing the dubious rationale behind the antidumping laws, the authors ask the rhetorical question, "Is antidumping law redressing an unfairness or creating one?" p. 102.

39. President, *Economic Report of President Transmitted to Congress, 1994,* p. 219. Also see Lester Thurow, who estimates that the price of tradable products are 86 percent higher in Japan than for those same goods in the United States. Thurow, *Head to Head*, p. 117.

40. President, *Economic Report of the President Transmitted to Congress, 1994*, p. 219.

41. Krugman, *The Age of Diminished Expectations*, p. 75.

42. R. C. Longworth, "Japan Takes a Solitary Path," *Chicago Tribune*, October 7, 1996, sec 1., pp. 1, 6. Data for 1993 from OECD.

43. Consumer Reports, *1995 Buying Guide*, pp. 325–366.

44. Japan Productivity Center, "Survey: U.S. Puts Profit First, Japan Favors Employment," *Productivity in Japan* (Winter 1989): 5.

45. David Ricardo, *On the Principles of Political Economy and Taxation* (London: John Murray Albemarle Street, 1817), chapter VII, pp. 128–36.

46. See for example, Herman E. Daly and John B. Cobb Jr., *For the Common Good* (Boston: Beacon Press, 1989), pp. 212–13.

47. David C. Korten, *When Corporations Rule the World* (West Hartford Conn. and San Francisco: Kumarian Press and Berrett-Koehler Publishers, Inc. 1995), p. 79.

48. Ricardo, *On the Principles of Political Economy and Taxation*, p. 134.

49. Korten, *When Corporations Rule the World*, p. 129.

50. Gary Burtless, "Technological Change and International Trade: How Well Do They Explain the Rise in Income Inequality?" in *The Inequality Paradox,* eds. James A. Auerbach and Richard S. Belous (Washington, D.C.: National Policy Association, 1998), p. 60.

51. ". . . the *job losses* of thousands of similar workers in traded goods industries may tend to push down the wages of *all* (sic) workers—even those in the service sector—in a particular skill category" Burgess et al., *Globaphobia*, p. 10.

52. Goldsmith, *The Trap*, p. 37.

53. Daly and Cobb Jr., *For the Common Good*, p. 226.

54. Burtless, "Technological Change and International Trade," p. 76.

55. Goldsmith, *The Trap*, p. 42.

56. Robert Reich, "The Inequality Paradox," in *The Inequality Paradox,* eds. Auerbach and Belous, p. 4.

57. Goldsmith, *The Trap*, p. 40.

58. Goldsmith, *The Trap*, p. 41.

59. John G. Swartout, "The Free Trade Charade," *The Social Contract* (Fall 1993): 31.

60. Paul Kennedy, *The Rise and Fall of the Great Powers*, p. 245.

61. Ibid., p. 244.

62. Ibid., pp. 282–83.

63. Burtless et al., *Globaphobia*, p. 4.

64. Dr. Ravi Batra, *The Myth of Free Trade: A Plan for Economic Survival* (New York: Charles Scribner Sons, 1993). Book review by John Swartout, "Challenging the Free Trade Gospel," *The Social Contract* (Fall 1973): 72.

65. President, *Economic Report of the President Transmitted to Congress, 1994*, table B–45, p. 320.

66. Thurow, *Head to Head*, p. 53.

67. Swartout, "The Free Trade Charade," p. 31.

68. Little et al., *Industry and Trade in Some Developing Countries* (London: Oxford University Press, 1970). Cited by Paul Johnson, *Modern Times*, rev. ed. (New York: Harper Perennial, 1991), p. 157.

69. Alan S. Blinder, *Hard Heads, Soft Hearts* (New York: Addison-Wesley Publishing Company, Inc., 1987), p. 117.

70. Rebecca M. Blank and Alan S. Binder, "Macroeconomics, Income Distribution and Poverty," in ed. S. Danziger, *Antipovery Policies: What Works and What Does Not* (Cambridge, Mass.: Harvard University Press, 1896), p. 187

71. I. Goldin and D. van der Mensbrugghe, "Trade Liberalization: What's at Stake" (Washington, D.C.: World Bank and OECD, 1993). Cited by Goldsmith, *The Trap*, p. 33.

72. Daly and Cobb Jr., *For the Common Good*, p. 220.

73. Blinder, *Hard Heads, Soft Hearts*, p. 124.

74. *Chicago Fed Letter* (September 1992): 2.

75. Burtless et al., *Globaphobia*, pp. 143–50.

76. Krugman, *The Age of Diminished Expectations*, p. 7.

77. Ibid., p. 67.

78. Goldsmith, *The Trap*, p. 37.

79. Ibid., p. 28.

80. Korten, *When Corporations Rule the World*, p. 126.

81. Paul Hawken, *The Ecology of Commerce* (New York: HarperCollins, 1993), p. 92.

82. R. C. Longworth "Corporate Giants Dwarf Many Nations," *Chicago Tribune*, October 7, 1996, sec. 1. p. 1.

83. Andrew Cohen, "The Downside of Development," *The Nation* (November 4, 1991): 544–46. Cited by Korten, *When Corporations Rule the World*, pp. 128–29.

84. Korten, *When Corporations Rule the World*, p. 233.

85. Joseph Kahn, "Foreigners Build China's Trade Surplus," The *Wall Street Journal*, April 7, 1997, p. Al.

86. Daly and Cobb Jr., *For the Common Good*, p. 230.

87. Blinder, *Hard Heads, Soft Hearts*, pp. 126–27.

88. Ibid., p. 110.

89. Joseph Kahn, "Foreigners Build China's Trade Surplus," p. Al.

90. President, *Economic Report of the President Transmitted to Congress, 1994*, p. 233.

91. Korten, *When Corporations Rule the World*, p. 174.

92. Paul Hawken, *The Ecology of Crisis: A Declaration of Sustainability* (New York: Harper Business, 1993), pp. 99–100. Cited by Korten, *When Corporations Rule the World*, p. 174.

93. Mark Ritchie, "GATT, Agriculture, and the Environment: The U.S. Double Zero Plan," *The Ecologist* (November/December 1990): 216. Cited by Korten, *When Corporations Rule the World*, p. 179.

94. Burtless et al., *Globaphobia*, pp. 100–101.

95. Sir Thomas Goldsmith, "Europe Should Keep its Farmers," *The Social Contract* (Summer 1993): 244.

96. World Bank estimates as reported in the *Wall Street Journal*, August 27, 1997, p. Al.

97. Merrill Lynch, *Chart Book* (November 1990): 8.

98. Merrill Lynch, *Weekly Economic and Financial Commentary* (December 4, 1989).

99. President, *Economic Report of the President Transmitted to Congress, 1998*, table B–103, p. 398, and table B–1, p. 280.

100. *Economic Report of the President, 1998*, table B–32, p. 319. Year end 1998 from National Bureau of Economic Research.

101. Thurow, *Head to Head*, p. 160.

102. David Brazell, Aldona Robbins et al., "The Cost of Corporate Capital in the United States and Japan," Institute for Political Economy, The Krieble Foundation, 1985, p. 23.

103. Brazell and Robbins, et al., "The Cost of Corporate Capital in the United States and Japan," p. 4.

104. W. Carl Kester and Timothy A. Luehnman, "The Myth of Japan's Low-Cost Capital," *Harvard Business Review* (May/June 1992).

105. Japan Statistical Bureau, "Principle Interest Rates on Postal Savings," in *Japan Statistical Yearbook, 1986* (Tokyo: The Bureau, 1986), p. 418. Cited by Thurow, *Head to Head*, p. 126.

106. Thurow, *Head to Head*, p. 38.

107. Krugman, *The Age of Diminished Expectations*, p. 76.

108. David Haberstam, *The Next Century* (New York: William Morrow, 1991)

109. Thurow, *Head to Head*, p. 286.

110. President, *Economic Report of the President Transmitted to Congress, 1994*, p. 197.

111. Blinder, *Hard Heads, Soft Hearts*, p. 115.

112. Sheldon Friedman, "Terms of Adjustment," *N–MW Economic Review* August 1992): 8–9.

113. U.S. Bureau of the Census, *Statistical Abstract of the United States, 1991*, table 1486, p. 862, and *1997*, table 1388, p. 860.

114. Sandra Postel and Christopher Flavin, "Reshaping the Global Economy," in Lester R. Brown et al., *State of the World, 1991* (New York: W. W. Norton and Company, 1991), p. 171.

115. U.S. Bureau of the Census, *Statistical Abstract of the United States, 1997*, table 1388, p. 860.

116. Michael Renner, *Assessing the Military's War on the Environment*, in Lester R. Brown et al. *State of the World, 1991* (Washington, D.C.: Worldwatch Institute, 1991), p. 133.

117. "World at War, 1992," *Defense Monitor* XXI, no. 6 (1992).

118. James P. Grant, *The State of the World's Children 1990* (New York: Oxford University Press, 1990). Cited in *Future Survey* (December 1990): 3.

119. United Nations Development Program Staff, *Human Development Report 1994* (New York: Oxford University Press, 1994), p. 47. Cited by David C. Korten, *When Corporations Rule the World*, p. 20.

120. Wolfe, *America's Impasse*, p. 189.

121. *Wall Street Journal*, October 30, 1985, p. 1.

122. Center for Defense Information, *Defense Monitor* XX, no. 4 (1991).

123. "World Arms Sales Rose 15% Last Year," *Chicago Tribune*, October 9, 1996, sec. 1, p. 9.

124. Center for Defense Information, "International Arms Sales: Race to Disaster," *Defense Monitor* XXII, no. 9 (1993).

125. New York Times News Service, "Africans, West Endorse Small Weapons Moratorium," *Chicago Tribune*, April, 5, 1998, sec. 1, p. 8.

126. Klugman, *The Age of Diminished Expectations*, pp. 87–88.

127. United Nations Food and Agriculture Organization, "Fertilizer Yearbook," Rome, Various Years. Cited by Postel and Flavin, "Reshaping the Global Economy," p. 176.

128. Postel and Flavin, "Reshaping the Global Economy," p. 176.

129.Burtless, et al., *Globaphobia*, p. 68.

130. Hazel Henderson, *Creating Alternative Futures: The End of Economics* (New York: Perigee Book, 1978), p. 104.

131. See Robin Broad and Walden Bello, "Development: The Market is Not Enough," *Foreign Policy*, no. 81 (Winter 1990–91): 144–62.

132. David Ewing Duncan, "Africa: The Long Decline," *The Atlantic Monthly* (July 1990): 20–21. Cited in *Future Survey* (April 1991): 13.

133. World Bank Staff, *World Development Report, 1990* (New York: Oxford University Press, 1990). Cited in *Future Survey* (December 1990): 4.

134. Thurow, *Head to Head*, pp. 126–27.

135. Merrill Goozner, "Nobel Laureates Press to Curb World Arms Trade," *Chicago Tribune*, May 29, 1997, sec. 1, p. 4.

136. United Nations Development Program Staff, *Human Development Report, 1992* (New York: Oxford University Press, 1992). Cited in Future Survey, October, 1992, p. 5.

137. Goozner, "Nobel Laureates Press to Curb World Arms Trade," p. 4.

8

Poverty and Welfare: Causes

Income can be viewed in either absolute or relative terms. In other words, we can look at how much money people earn (and whether they are making more or less than years ago after adjusting for inflation), or we can look at the distribution of income (whether the spread between the rich and poor is increasing or decreasing). Actually both measures are relevant. It is of little consolation that all people are relatively equal if they were all getting poorer, as in the case of many socialist countries before the collapse of communism. Conversely, when everyone is gaining substantially in wealth, as in the case of Saudi Arabia, they are content with a huge disparity between the nation's ruling elite and its citizens. But, as I argued in *The Science of Morality*, when the standard of living is relatively stagnant or increasing only slowly, distribution of income is more important to happiness than the absolute level. If a person is driving a new Chevy, while all his friends are driving new BMWs, he will probably feel deprived. But take that same person and surround him with friends driving ten-year old cars and he'll probably feel fortunate to have any new car. So what has been the recent history in America?

At first glance it would appear that the U.S. worker has done fairly well over the last couple of decades. After adjusting for inflation and taxes, average per capita disposable income rose 44 percent between 1973 and 1997.[1] By 1995, the U.S. GDP per capita was $26,448, placing us second in the world economy, 21 percent more than Japan and 29 percent more than Germany on a purchasing power parity basis.[2] But, as we saw in chapter 2, on a per worker basis real disposable income rose only 17 percent—that's less than 1 percent per year. The average per capita income is inflated by the growth in the percentage of women in the work force over that time.* In 1996, the proportion of mothers working full time, year round had climbed to 39 percent of households with kids, from only 17 percent in 1963.†

During the twenty-two years from 1950 to 1973, the average weekly earnings adjusted for inflation *increased 48 percent*. Then beginning in 1973, average inflation-adjusted weekly earnings began a long decline—by 1997 they had *dropped 21 percent* from the level of 1973.[4] Despite the increasing number of women entering the labor market after 1973 to bolster household earnings, family income grew less than 1 percent a year compared to a 3 to 4 percent annual average during the 1950s and 1960s.‡ Partially offsetting the contribution to family income by women entering the labor force was the increase of mother-only families.

The decline in the real wage rate neglects to account for the increase in employee benefits, however. During the highly inflationary period of the 1970s unions decided they would be better off bargaining for better benefits that would not be subject to taxes rather than seeking large wage increases. Hence, by 1994, although the average wage rate was only $13.12 an hour, employees received another $5.26 in benefits.[5] Most of the increase in fringes occurred between 1973 and 1980. After inflation was licked, unions had a new worry—layoffs due to restructuring or businesses

---

*Some economists, such as Robert Samuelson, make much of the fact that *household* income adjusted for the decreasing size of the average household shows a significant increase over the 1970–1996 period. However, much of the increase may be due to the rise of two–income families. On the other hand, average household income is negatively affected by the increase in mother-only families, and is also affected by growth in the number of aged people living alone. For all these reasons, use of household income is a difficult, if not impossible, statistic to interpret.

†Many economists believe that the estimated decline in real wages is overstated. They argue that the estimates of the Consumer Price Index, which is used to adjust wages for inflation, were much to high. However, to be responsible for the difference in real wages over the two periods, the overestimation of the CPI would have to be much greater in the second period compared to the earlier period. Moreover, as Freeman explains, every other country in the Organization for Economic Cooperation and Development (OECD) deflates their wages by a similarly constructed price index, yet they show a significant increase in real wages since 1973. (Richard B. Freeman, "Is the New Income Inequality the Achilles' Heel of the American Economy?" in *The Inequality Paradox: Growth of Income Disparity*, eds. James A. Auerbach and Richard S. Belous (Washington. D.C.: National Policy Association, 1998), p. 221.

‡In 1997 and 1998 the tighter labor markets have resulted in inflation-adjusted wages rising 2.6 percent annually, and the wages of the lowest-paid workers rose at a faster rate than wages of higher-paid workers. Coming at the end of a seven year economic recovery this is not surprising. It would be remarkable if the trend persisted over the next decade. (David Wessel, "Inflation-Adjusted Wages are on the Rise for Typical U.S. Worker, Shifting Trend," *Wall Street Journal*, July 17, 1998, p. A2).

relocating abroad in pursuit of cheaper labor. So many unions were willing to settle for small increases in wages and fringe benefits in return for increased job security. With the surplus labor situation of the late 1980s and early 1990s, management found that it did not have to give either. After a year and a half strike at earth mover manufacturer Caterpillar, workers found that they had to go back to work with nothing to show for their effort. Caterpillar beat the union by threatening to replace all the striking workers with new, lower-paid, workers or else picking up and moving the company's operations out of the country.

After adding in benefits, total compensation between 1979 and 1997 remained almost constant, increasing only 3.5 percent on an inflation-adjusted basis.[6] (That's not an annual rate but the total increase over eighteen years!) The situation is even worse because the averages disguise the growing inequality in fringe benefits; fewer low-paid men and women are now receiving pensions or employer-paid health insurance.

Percent of Work Force Receiving Benefits[7]

	1979	*1993*
Pensions		
High School Dropouts	39%	21%
High School Graduates	57%	45%
Health Insurance		
High School Dropouts	58%	35%
High School Graduates	78%	62%

Changes in average wages conceal the very different trends that occurred among wage groups. Although average real wage rates fell, the decline was particularly severe for the lowest-income people, especially those receiving the minimum wage. Not only did their wage rates decline in real dollars, but their average annual hours of work also declined. In short, the poorest 25 percent of Americans in 1995 were worse off than the bottom 25 percent in 1973. On the other hand, well-educated women saw significant increases in employment, hours of work, and hourly rates of pay since 1973.[8] The result was that women in the top 20 percent of the wage distribution had their earnings increase 25 percent between 1979 and 1993.

Average income also obscures the increasing disparity in the income consequences for the rich and the poor over the past two decades. See figure 8.1. Note that in the 1966 to 1979 period the lowest quintile of American families were able to increase their income by 22 percent, while in the 1980 to 1997 period they saw their income decline by one percent. At the other

Figure 8.1[9]
Changes in Average Real Family Income by Quintile

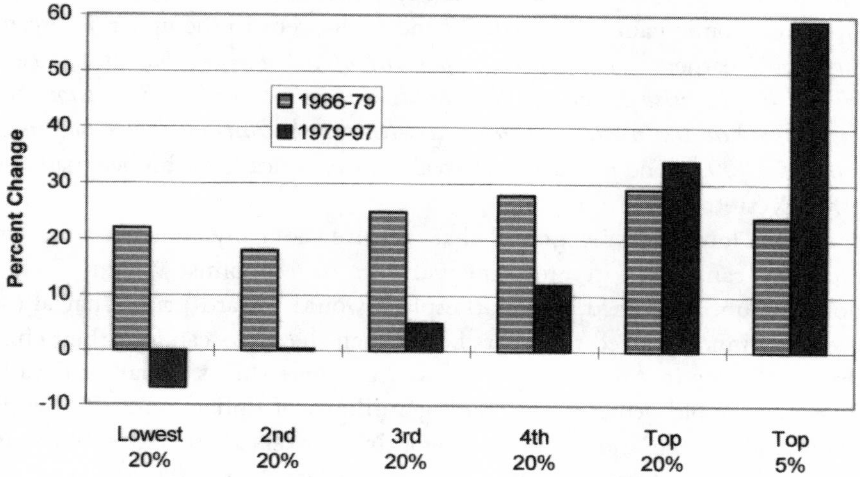

end of the spectrum, the average income of the top quintile saw their income increased by 29 percent between 1966 and 1979, and then continued to grow by 34 percent between 1979 and 1997. One often overlooked reason for the increase is that upper-income men tend to marry the highly educated women who received substantially increased employment, hours of work, and wage rates as mentioned above. It is not surprising, therefore, that highly educated, two-wage families should have significantly increased their income relative to poorly educated, mother-only families.*

By 1997, the medium income of the American family was $45,347, less than 2 percent higher than the 1989 peak of $44,647. The top 5 percent of all households received 21 percent of all income, while the bottom 40 percent of the households received only 14 percent of all income.[10] Income inequality reached its peak in 1993. Since then income in each quintile has increased, with the largest gains in the lowest quintile.[11] This is usually the case late in an economic cycle. Near the peak of the economic cycle the increased demand for labor will enable lower-income people to increase their real wages. Nevertheless, given the underlying trends, we can expect a continued increase in inequality in the twenty-first century as long as the United States maintains its policy of importing labor to depress wage rates.

The economic disparity is even greater in terms of total wealth than in

*These data include only income, not capital gains appreciation. During the 1980 to 1997 period the decline in interest rates depressed income growth of the top 20 percent of families. However, were we to include stock market appreciation, the wealth of the top 20 percent grew much more than 26 percent.

terms of annual income. According to economics professor Edward Wolff, the share of the total wealth held by the richest 1 percent of the families doubled between 1979 and 1992. Richard Freeman calculates that 99 percent of all the economic gain between 1979 and 1994 went to the upper 5 percent of income earners.[12] ***In 1996, 42 percent of all marketable assets were owned by the elite 1 percent that holds a minimum of $2.3 million per family, while the medium family wealth for the nation as a whole was only $52,000.***[13] The inequality of wealth in America is far higher than any other Western nation.*

It has long been recognized that, despite the many benefits, a market economy can result in great inequalities. As economist Arthur Okum noted, if unconstrained, the marketplace would "award prizes that allow the big winners to feed their pets better than the losers can feed their children."[14] Today in America we see instances where this is actually the case. Twenty-year old athletes are making millions of dollars annually, while many young men and women are working for less than $10,000 a year. Even college graduates are often working for less than $20,000 a year.

The increasing disparity, not only between rich and poor but between rich and middle class, is reflected in the Louis Harris polls that are used to calculate an Alienation Index. Feelings of economic inequality explain much of the increase in the index from 29 in 1969 to 65 in 1993,[15] and again demonstrate that it is changes in *perceived* relative income rather than actual or absolute income that mostly determine a person's sense of personal well-being or happiness.[16]

As mentioned in chapter 6, when arguing whether Americans are better or worse off than years ago, liberals tend to ignore the increase in average income while conservatives try to downplay the growing spread in income and wealth. One conservative writer observes that the income distribution in Minnesota is about the same as Sweden. But this is a disingenuous selection of data. Minnesota is one of the most egalitarian states in the union. Taking a different view, Paul Krugman notes that the income distribution in metropolitan areas is more unequal than at any time since the 1930s and it is rapidly increasing.[17]

Whether we are viewing income or wealth, is an increase in inequality necessarily a bad thing? This is an extremely difficult question since there is no "right" degree of inequality. This issue of income inequality was dealt with at length in *The Science of Morality*, and we will not repeat it here.[18] We concluded in that discussion that human happiness will be optimized if income inequality is enough to provide incentives for people to maxi-

---

*It is important to note that even if the income or wealth of all groups grew by the same percentage, the absolute difference in wealth would continue to grow.

mize their efforts to improve the nation's productivity and, hence, increase national welfare, but inequality must not be so great as to cause divisive class conflict or relegate one segment of society to a life of misery. Admittedly, quantifying this criterion will not be easy. Until a more definitive criterion can be developed, perhaps the Harris poll's Alienation Index could be used as a surrogate.

There is little doubt that a meritocracy that distributes benefits based upon relative contribution is necessary to provide the incentives to increase effort and output. However, at some point it is doubtful that increases in income (or relative inequality of income) results in greater personal effort. In Japan, where the distribution of income is not nearly so skewed as in the United States, there is no evidence to suggest that people do not work as hard—quite the contrary. Throughout Europe the distribution of income and wealth is also more equitable, and yet their productivity would appear to rival ours. And here at home the greater dispersion of income that has occurred during the past twenty years has been accompanied by less rather than greater productivity.

The number of Americans living below the poverty level increased from 23 million in 1973 to 35.6 million in 1997.[19] Meanwhile the 400 richest Americans increased their net worth to $220 billion, a 41 percent increase in just the two years from 1986 to 1988.[20] According to *Business Week*, in 1980 corporate CEOs made 42 times what factory workers received. By 1994, the CEOs made 53 times the average factory worker's pay, compared to German CEOs who made only 21 times the average worker's income, and Japan's CEOs who received 20 times higher compensation.[21] For the largest U.S. companies, the difference was even more staggering, with the CEOs making 225 times the average worker's salary.[22] To put this in perspective, the CEOs made in one day what the average (not the lowest-paid) American worker made in a year. Michael Eisner, the Chairman of Disney, received $770 million in 1996 compensation.[23] That is the equivalent of the median income of 17,907 families! What makes it particularly disconcerting is that in many cases CEOs received huge compensation packages even when they led their corporations into serious economic trouble.

If it were not enough that average weekly earnings for American workers were falling, the Reagan and Bush administrations decided to cut income tax rates for the rich and stick it to the poor. Between 1980 and 1990 the average tax bite fell 15 percent for the top 1 percent of income earners, and 5 percent for the top 20 percent. At the same time the government increased taxes by 16 percent for the 20 percent of American wage earners at the bottom of the income ladder.[24] (It was even more if we include the changes in the FICA [Social Security] tax rates.) This is an interesting approach to resolving poverty! It gives new meaning to the cliché of kicking a man (and women and children) when they are down. The Clinton administration reversed this situation somewhat by increasing the tax rate for the wealthiest from a maximum of 33 percent to 39.5 percent and decreased the taxes on the lowest-income earners by raising the income levels whereby a person would qualify for the Earned Income Tax Credit.*

There has been much talk concerning the growth in jobs during the 1990s. Although a Labor Department study indicated that two-thirds of the jobs created since the 1990–91 recession were better-than-average-paying jobs, it did not address whether the jobs created by the economy were better than those lost due to downsizing following the recession.[25] More than 12 million white-collar workers lost their job between 1991 and 1996.[26] One study found that those laid off generally found new jobs but at an average wage of 30 percent less than before.[27] Another study found that median weekly wages for rehired workers were 8 percent lower than for the job they held two years earlier, and career workers stood to ultimately lose 25 percent.[28]

The drop in the unemployment rate from 7.5 percent in 1992 to 4.3 percent by December, 1998, while encouraging, is also somewhat misleading since the official unemployment rate does not count those who have given up the search for jobs. David Dembo and Ward Morehouse of the Council of International Affairs estimate that the jobless rate, based upon a common sense definition of the unemployed as those who want a job and are not able to find work, was 16 million people in 1991, or 13 percent, about twice the official unemployment rate.[29] Additionally, even after recovery from the 1990-91 recession, several million people were underemployed, i.e., they had temporary or part-time employment (at little more than minimum wage and often with few or no benefits), but were seeking full-time employment. In the early 1980s, fewer than 600,000 Americans were working in temporary jobs; by 1998 the ranks of temps had swelled to 7.2 million.[30] How many of these are involuntary is not known.

Finally, it should be noted that had we not had such a huge increase in immigration, the increase in jobs would have had a far greater impact on reducing our poverty figures. Economist Robert Samuelson estimates that "perhaps a quarter to a half of the increase in poverty since the early 1970s reflects immigration."[31] He notes that of the 15 million increase in people

---

*The Earned Income Tax Credit (EITC) is calculated so that when income (adjusted for the normal tax deductions) falls below the minimum level where a person must pay a tax, the government would pay a proportional subsidy. A more complete discussion of the EITC is provided in chapter 13.

under the poverty level between 1973 and 1994, six million were Hispanic. Of course, not all immigrants are Hispanic and not all Hispanics are immigrants. But Hispanics account for the lion's share of immigrants, both legal and illegal, and are much more likely to be unemployed than Asian immigrants or those from Eastern Europe.

Racial Differences in Income

Charles Murray points out that black workers improved their income relative to whites throughout the period from 1955 to 1980. In 1955 the median income of blacks was 61 percent that of whites. By 1980 black median income reached 75 percent of the income for whites.[32] Most of this gain occurred after 1965, despite Murray's claim that the social legislation of that year failed to improve economic conditions for minorities. Moreover, Murray's analysis stops in 1980. Since 1980, year-round, full-time black female working black males have been able to improve their median income from 70 percent that of whites to more than 78 percent by 1996. Black females, while they started out more equal to whites in their income levels, have lost some ground. The median income for a year-round, full-time worker dropped from 93 percent of her white counterpart in 1980 to 87 percent by 1996.[33] These statistics seriously understate the actual difference in black/white earnings since the average black man or woman is far more likely not to have worked (or to have found only part-time employment) than the average white man or woman. Hence, the annual income difference is much larger than the difference in weekly wages.

This fact is reflected in the average family income of whites and blacks. In inflation-adjusted dollars, blacks improved their median family income 48 percent from the decade between 1960 and 1970. During the 1960s black family income improved not only in absolute terms, but in relative terms as well, rising from 55 percent of the white average income to 63 percent.[34] However, by 1996 not only did blacks fail to make any further improvement in real average family income but, relative to whites, they slipped slightly to 59 percent.[35]* Moreover, as the case with whites, the growth in inflation-adjusted income slowed considerably as well.

It is often thought that the primary reason for the differential in family income is the declining number of two-earner families among blacks. Only

---

*Actually, this understates the decrease in black family income relative to whites, because Hispanics are generally counted as whites. Since they are the fastest growing segment in our society over the last twenty years, and their income is about the same as blacks, they tend to pull down the white average. Throughout this chapter and the next this fact should be kept in mind when viewing differences between white and black average income.

one out of three black children were living with both parents in 1996.[36] But studies by sociologists Christopher Jenks and William Julius Wilson show that this is indicative of a deeper problem—the inability of black women to find black men who earn a decent income. So many black men are unemployed and underemployed that the pool of black men capable of supporting a family is depressingly small. It is especially disconcerting to note that despite the progress of blacks in moving into professional, technical, and managerial positions—in percentage terms they increased faster than whites since 1983[37]—the ratio of black unemployed to white unemployed in 1996 was higher than in 1948:[38]

	Black Unemployment Rate	White Unemployment Rate	Ratio Black/White
1948	5.9	3.5	1.7
1997	10.0	4.2	2.4

The situation for black youth is far worse. At the end of 1996, 34 percent of blacks between the ages of sixteen and nineteen were looking for full- or part-time work and were unable to find it, compared to only 14 percent of whites in the same age range. For the twenty to twenty-four-year-old group, the unemployment rate was still a very unsatisfactory 19 percent—more than double the 8 percent of their white counterparts.[39] The crucial question is, why do blacks still incur such high rates of unemployment thirty years after the Civil Rights Act of 1964? The answer must wait until the next chapter.

Poverty in America

According to the Swiss-based World Economic Forum, the United States regained its title as the world's most competitive economy in 1994.[40] This is not surprising since the employment cost index, which is a measure of the cost of labor (including benefits), remained virtually constant between 1980 and 1993 after adjusting for inflation and has risen only slightly since then.[41] But becoming the world's most competitive economy was not without pain. One of the major reasons for the improvement in U.S. competitiveness was that, while top management was increasing its average pay dramatically, nonmanagement employees were receiving little benefit from the increased productivity. To make matters worse, so many manufacturing jobs were lost and eventually replaced with low-paying service sector jobs that the average real weekly earnings continued to plunge. In

Figure 8.2[44]
People Under the Poverty Level—Number & Percentage

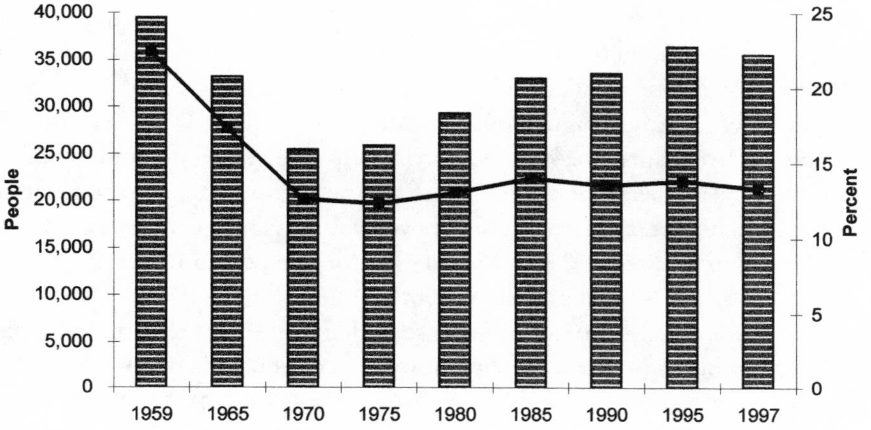

1973 inflation-adjusted weekly earnings topped out at $315; by 1997 they had dropped to $261, a 17 percent decline.[42] Those at the bottom of the socioeconomic spectrum were most negatively affected during the 1980s. The number of Americans below the poverty line increased from 24.5 million in 1973 to 35.6 million in 1997, an increase of over 50 percent.[43] Figure 8.2 shows the trend in poverty over the past three decades. Both the number and the percentage of people living in poverty dropped during the early 1960s, even before the war on poverty. The number of people in poverty continued to decline through the early 1970s, then in absolute numbers, it began rising again while remaining about constant in percentage terms. Moreover, if not for immigration, the number under the poverty level would have dropped more substantially. Note, however, that even in 1997 the 36 million people living in poverty was still below the 39 million living in poverty in 1959, and the percentage of people living in poverty was well below the 1959 level. Nonetheless, by the end 1997, about one out of seven Americans (13.3 percent), were still living below the poverty level.

Conservatives often argue that the earned income used to define poverty does not include benefits from the government such as food stamps, welfare payments, housing subsidies, etc. Nor does it include illegal income. However, if we were to include these amounts, we would be confounding poverty with the means of coping with poverty. If the poor had sufficient income, society would not need to provide these welfare benefits. Nevertheless, if we *included* all forms of government benefits such as the Employment Income Tax Credit (EITC), welfare, health care, food stamps, school lunches, etc., it would reduce the number living in poverty from 36.5 million in 1996 to 27.1 million or 10.2 percent of the population.[45] On the other hand, if we were to *exclude* all forms of government transfer payments, including social security, we would have 57.5 million or 21.6 percent of the population below the poverty line.

Moreover, many people would consider the poverty line is calculated too low. When a survey asked people what income they felt should constitute the poverty level for a family of four the respondents set the level at 24 percent higher than the actual poverty line. The poverty level for a family of four was set at $16,036 in 1996; for one person under age sixty-five it was $8,163—that's $680 a month.[46]

Understanding who is poor is essential if we are to develop suitable polices for reducing poverty. A popular misconception is that poor people are primarily black, urban, and jobless. However, the truth is that there are more poor whites than blacks, although not in percentage terms; poverty rates are higher in rural areas (21.1 percent) than urban areas (14.7 percent), although the absolute number living in poverty was greater in urban areas.[47] Over half of the adult poor have jobs, although often only temporary or part time. Let's fill out the picture of the nation's poor more completely.

In 1997, with the economy surging, there were still 6.7 million unemployed job seekers, about 5 million who had given up looking for work, and 4.0 million who were involuntarily working part time. That equates to a total to 15.7 million or 11.5 percent of the labor force. Another 10 million were working at the minimum wage. After adjusting for inflation, a minimum wage of $5.15 represents a 21 percent reduction since 1974 (and a 30 percent decline from the 1968 high). ***As a consequence, during the 1960s and 1970s a full-time wage earner receiving the minimum wage earned enough to keep a family of three above the poverty line, but by 1990 it took two full-time workers making the minimum wage to keep their family above the poverty line.***[48] The young were particularly hard hit. According to a U.S. Census Bureau report, among full-time workers in the age group eighteen to twenty-four, 47 percent earned less than a poverty level wage, compared to 23 percent in 1979.[49] It would take a minimum wage of $6 an hour to reach the poverty level for a family of three.

Although, as mentioned, there are more poor whites than poor blacks, the proportion of those under the poverty level is almost three times higher for blacks and Hispanics. Also, the poverty of blacks is less likely to be temporary, reflecting longer-term unemployment for blacks.

Number and Percentage Below Poverty Level, 1996[50]

	Number (000)	*Percentage*
Whites	24,650	11.2
Blacks	9,694	28.4
Hispanics	8,697	29.4

There was a time when poverty of the aged was a major concern of the nation. In 1970, approximately 25 percent of the aged were under the poverty level, compared to 12.5 percent for the national average. But despite all the criticism it has received, the introduction of Social Security was a tremendous benefit to the aged. By 1995 the percentage of aged who were below the poverty level was cut in half to 10.5 percent, falling below the national average of 13.8 percent.[51] Actually, the situation of the elderly is even better than that, since many older people have little annual income but sufficient total wealth to live on. For example, many seniors own their homes mortgage free and have substantial savings.

America's children have fared far worse than the elderly. The number of children living in poverty rose since 1970 to a high in 1993, when 22.7 percent of the children were living in poverty, before beginning to decline in both relative and absolute terms:

Children Under 18 Living in Poverty, 1970–1996[52]

	Number (millions)	Percentage of Children Under 18
1970	10.2	14.9
1993	15.0	22.7
1996	14.5	20.5

Again, contrary to common belief, there are actually more white children living in poverty than black children, although the percentage of blacks under the poverty level is far higher.

People Under 18 in Poverty, 1996[53]

	Number(millions)	Percentage in Poverty
Whites	9.0	17.8
Blacks	4.5	39.9
Hispanics	4.2	40.3

As might be expected, the greater the number of children in a family, the greater the probability they will be living in poverty:

Families Below Poverty Level[54]

Size of Family	*Number Below Poverty (in Thousands)*	*Percentage*
Two people	2688	9.5
Three people	2020	12.6
Four people	1723	11.9
Five people	1095	17.3
Six people	451	22.0
Seven or more	415	34.6

The conclusion to be drawn here is clear: reducing family size would reduce the number of families living under poverty. However, even if we were to eliminate all families over four people we would have reduced the total families in poverty by only 18 percent. The causes of poverty are far more complicated than just having a large family.

THE CAUSES OF POVERTY AND INCOME INEQUALITY IN AMERICA

Most economists are by nature reductionists, seeking to explain complex human phenomena with a relatively few quantifiable variables. It is extremely difficult to isolate the relative impact of a dozen trends because of their interaction with each other.[55] But it is exactly because the problems of today were caused by the confluence of many negative factors that they are proving to be so resistant to simple solutions. The numerous causes responsible for changes in income inequality over the past thirty years can be categorized as follows:

1. Demographic Factors
    - (a) the impact of the baby boom
    - (b) internal migration within the United States
    - (c) increased immigration into the United States

2. International Factors
    - (a) increased competition from low-wage countries
    - (b) changes in the trade laws

3. Technological Factors
    - (a) the shift from the industrial age to the information age
    - (b) genetic factors, i.e., differences in cognitive capabilities

4. Cultural Factors
- **(a) the rise of mother-only families**
- **(b) the rise in the use of drugs**
- **(c) the establishment of the so-called culture of poverty**

5. Fiscal Policies
- **(a) the growth and decline of welfare**
- **(b) changes in the tax structure**

6. Racial Impacts—past and present

There are other causes that have been suggested by some authors, such as changes in the rate of unionization, the minimum wage, and the growth of nonwage income, but as we shall see these are the consequences of the factors listed above and not independent factors.

Of course, we would like to know the relative weight of each of these factors. However, in examining the numerous studies correlating income inequality to the causes listed above, I found that, in total, the causative factors would explain for more than 100 percent of the variance in income inequality. Hence, in the discussion that follows, the numerical values suggested in the various studies must be considered only indicative of their relative significance rather than precise estimates of their actual weight.

1. Demographic Factors

(a) Impact of the Baby Boom

The post World War II baby boom lasted until 1958 and had several unanticipated consequences. Although demographers cautioned that the baby boom would have major societal impact, the country was slow to react as the boomers overwhelmed the schools in the 1950s and early 1960s, as well as the law enforcement and judicial systems, as will be examined in later chapters. Our present concern is the impact that the baby boom had on poverty and income inequality beginning in the early 1970s as the labor force swelled with record numbers of new job seekers.

Between 1960 and 1970 although the total U.S. population rose 13 percent, the number of twenty to twenty-four-year-olds rose by 54 percent.[56] At the same time, the new affirmative action laws encouraged young women (who had also swelled in numbers due to the baby boom) to enter the labor force at record rates. Between 1960 and 1970, the labor force participation rate for women rose from 37.7 percent to 43.3 percent, and continued to climb throughout the next two decades, reaching 57.5

percent by 1990 before beginning to level off. By 1997 it stood at an all-time high of 59.6 percent.[57] In 1960, only 32 percent of the families had working wives, but by 1990, 68 percent of the wives worked. In the 1950s and 1960s civilian employment grew about one million jobs a year. But due to the changing demographics during the 1970s, the annual growth in the labor force doubled to more than two million a year.[58] As table 8.1 shows, on the whole the economy performed quite well in this regard, eventually creating 13 million new jobs between 1960 and 1970 (a 19.6 percent increase), another 21 million jobs between 1970 and 1980 (26 percent), and 19 million jobs between 1980 and 1990 (19.6 percent).[59]

Table 8.1[60]
Growth in Labor Force, Employment, and Over 16 Not in Labor Force*

	Growth In Labor Force	*Growth in Employment*	*Growth in Over 16 Not in Labor Force*
1960–70	13,143	12,900	6,698
1970–80	24,169	20,625	6,491
1980–90	18,900	19,490	2,518
1990–97	10,457	10,765	3,513

* All totals are in thousands.

Despite the rapid growth in jobs between 1970 and 1980, the job market could not expand fast enough to accommodate the large number of new entrants. When the baby boomers entered the labor market between 1970 and 1980, labor force growth exceeded job growth by 3.5 million people (24.2 – 20.6). This does not include the 6.5 million increase in people over age sixteen who were no longer in the labor force, many because they gave up hope of finding a job. Hence, the surplus of labor force, minus the employed, plus the increase in those no longer in the labor force, grew by 14 million between 1970 and 1980. Between 1980 and 1990 this surplus was significantly reduced. Employment growth slightly exceeded the growth in the labor force by 0.8 million. However, to obtain and keep jobs, workers had to take cuts in real hourly wages.

Blacks were particularly hard hit by the labor surplus: tight labor markets have traditionally helped blacks more than whites, while slack labor markets hurt blacks more than whites.[61] In periods of excess labor supply, employers are able to hire workers with greater experience, education, and skills than the jobs actually demand. For example, in the 1980s many recent college graduates were working as secretaries, and many Ph.D.s were taking entry-level management jobs. By the 1990s the glut of Ph.D.s became so excessive that many colleges began replacing retiring well-paid full-time professors with low-paid part-time professors. In many colleges adjunct professors make only $2,000 to $3,000 per course.

Many blacks obtained jobs in the 1960s and advanced quickly, as did whites, because they beat the flood of baby boomers into the labor markets. However, when the blacks of the baby boom era reached the labor market, they found that not only did they have to compete for jobs with white males, but with the influx of white females as well. In a perverse and unanticipated way, affirmative action laws ultimately worked to the disadvantage of blacks. Implementation of the laws required quotas to be set for hiring and promotions of minorities and women proportional to their number within the population. Since there were six times more white females than black males in the labor force, the quotas for hiring white women were also six times greater. Because white women had many of the same environmental and educational advantages as white males, black males soon found that they were once again at a disadvantage—this time through the very laws that were supposed to help them. Then with most immigrants qualifying for affirmative action (over about 80 percent being Hispanic, Asian, African, or Indian), American blacks were once again relegated to the back of the employment bus.

At the same time black job opportunities were declining, the density of teenage population in the inner city high-rise was experiencing a volatile rate of growth. Between 1969 and 1982 the number of central city poor climbed by almost 60 percent, from 8 million to 12.7 million.[62] A great number lived in public housing, particularly the infamous high-rises. In societies where there is relatively high employment, small family size and a strong sense of prosocial behavior, such as Japan or the Netherlands, such density of population poses few problems. But the U.S. inner cities are quite different. Here we have a high concentration of poorly educated, unemployed youth lacking a centuries' old traditional sense of moral discipline or work ethic. Instead, there is a strong belief that the deck has been stacked against their chance for success, as indeed it was for the last 400 years in this country. Given that history, it is all too easy to avoid accepting personal responsibility for one's actions. Such concentrations of moral anarchy and deep resentment have proved to be a fertile breeding ground for social pathology.

Past discrimination in housing has exacerbated the problem. William Julius Wilson notes that only 32 percent of poor whites live in poor urban neighborhoods, while 68 percent of poor blacks do.[63] The high-rise destroys the sense of community so critical for developing a feeling of social responsibility. Every effort to ameliorate the conditions in the inner city high-rises has failed. At best, crime can be constrained somewhat with strict policing, but that is hardly conducive to developing prosocial behavior.

(b) Internal Migration in the United States

During and after World War II, blacks moved to northern industrial cites in record numbers to take advantage of the relatively high-paying jobs. Wilson believes that the movement of blacks into higher-paying manufacturing jobs in the north from the 1940s through the 1960s had more to do with improving opportunities and income for blacks than equal employment legislation.[64] There was a downside to the migration as well. The northern inner city ghettos grew beyond the capabilities of the cites to provide basic services such as adequate schools and police protection. Faced with increasing taxes to meet these needs motivated many whites to flee to the suburbs. Then, as the postwar boom in manufacturing slowed and many industries began to relocate in the South to take advantage of the lower pay scales, the lack of welfare benefits and job discrimination in southern states discouraged black workers from following the jobs back South. As firms continued to exit the inner cities of the north, black unemployment soared.

Also beginning in the early 1960s the new continuous-line processes that required sprawling single-level factories made the old multistory factory buildings in the major industrial cities obsolete. The new interstate highway system and the availability of cheap land and low taxes prompted the construction of new factories in the suburbs. Between 1947 and 1972 the thirty-three most populous central cities lost 880,000 manufacturing jobs, while manufacturing jobs in the suburbs grew by 2.5 million. Not only manufacturing jobs were lost to the suburbs. The same cites lost 867,000 retail and wholesale jobs while the suburbs added millions of such jobs.[65] ***After an in-depth review of the data, John D. Kasarda concluded that nearly all growth in entry level and other low-skilled jobs accrued in suburbs and nonmetropolitan areas far removed from growing concentrations of poorly educated urban minorities.***[66]

To make matters worse, the lack of available housing—in part due to discrimination, in part due to the high cost—left inner city blacks stranded. Virtually all public transportation was directed into the central city. To have a job in the suburbs required a car. According to a Chicago study by the Mayor's Office of Employment and Training, only 18 percent of welfare recipients in Chicago had access to a car; less than one-third even had a valid driver's license.[67] Federal Highway Administration data show that 26 percent of households below poverty level don't have cars.[68] Public transportation is relatively efficient when commuting within central cities, or from the suburbs to the city, but urban sprawl often makes commuting to suburbs from the inner city using public transportation impossible or extremely difficult.

Barbara Brown, a graduate student at Baltimore's Morgan State University, tested the trials of reverse commuting. Using public transportation in the Baltimore area to suburban jobs took over two and a half hours one way. It required leaving at 5:30 in the morning and involved buses, trains, walking, and waiting to arrive at a job by 7:52. The round-trip commute cost $10.35 to get to a job paying $6.50 an hour.[69] With the influx of cheap immigrant labor to depress the wages and the high cost of getting to work, it was no longer an economically logical choice to travel to low-paying jobs in the suburbs.

The movement of jobs to the suburbs while blacks were left in the city is known as the *spatial mismatch hypothesis.* The validity of this hypothesis has been questioned in a study by David T. Ellwood, who showed that few blacks from Chicago's West Side take jobs in the nearby Western suburbs.[70] However, Ellwood fails to take several other factors into account, such as the labor surplus that developed during the baby boom era, which allowed employers to hire qualified white employees from suburban communities. Most importantly, Ellwood fails to take into account the cost of transportation. For instance, after deducting the cost of transportation from a Minneapolis neighborhood to suburban Bloomington, an $8 an hour telemarketing job drops to only about $4.60 an hour. This is clearly not sufficient to encourage someone to give up a welfare check.[71]

In addition, inner city residents do not have access to the suburban job network. A study by John Kain found that suburban manufacturers do not advertise their vacancies in venues where inner city blacks would learn about them.[72] Moreover, the informal network is the primary way people learn about job openings. As an example of how efficiently it works, I once asked the Chicago Botanical Gardens' Personnel Director why they had no black gardeners, only Hispanics, despite being located in an area fairly close to large concentrations of black labor. She told me that whenever there was a job opening a Hispanic employee was quick to notify a relative—even one living across the country—and a Hispanic applicant was there to apply in a day or two.

(c) Increased Immigration to the United States

We already touched on the impact of excessive immigration in chapter 4. The impact of the baby boom on the labor supply was exacerbated by the addition of 27 million immigrants between 1973 and 1996. One reason that median income has not risen in the last twenty-three years, which is almost always overlooked in discussions on the subject, is that adding millions of poor and unskilled immigrants will inevitably lower average income. This is in addition to the impact on wage rates of increasing supply relative to demand. Poverty among the foreign born in 1990 was 50 percent higher than that of native born Americans.[73] Furthermore, since lower-income immigrants, especially Hispanics, have larger families, it will result in more children falling under the poverty level. In fact, 41 percent of children under the poverty level have foreign born parents. Therefore, this does not reflect a failure of U.S. economic policies, but an overly rapid influx of immigrants.

The more invidious impact of this huge increase in immigration was a devastating blow to the aspirations of millions of Americans, especially blacks. My own analysis suggests that blacks lost jobs to immigrants as older manufacturers closed down or moved to collar counties or rural areas. Between 1983 and 1994, Midwest blacks lost 22,000 manufacturing jobs while Hispanics gained 140,000 jobs.[74] An examination of the yearly changes in employment reveals that most of the loss of black jobs occurred during the 1990–91 recession. After the recession, most of the job growth went to Hispanics. The reason is that many of the firms that closed during the recession were located in or near the central cities, while many of the fastest growing firms during the recovery were in collar counties or rural areas. These employers recruit Hispanic labor from California and Texas, rather than blacks from the inner city. Moreover, there is a reluctance of blacks to leave their inner city neighborhoods to move to primarily white areas.

In the construction industry in the Midwest, blacks gained 14,000 jobs between 1983 and 1994, while Hispanics gained 27,000 jobs. Whites gained 347,000 jobs. A substantial portion of these were immigrants from eastern Europe, especially Poland, Romania, and Russia. Interviews with small contractors indicate a preference for immigrants because they are willing to work for less and under more difficult conditions, such as winter. Here again, immigration is destroying the opportunities affirmative action was suppose to provide African Americans.

The continued excessive number of immigrants will virtually ensure a growing black underclass in American society, which welfare reform will not change. Of course it is not only blacks that will suffer, but the poor of every race. For example, with welfare reform the Chicago area will have seven people looking for every entry-level job.[75] Similar imbalances between job seekers and available jobs exist throughout the country.[76] Continued immigration will only add to these numbers, greatly increasing America's underclass.

Morton Bahr, President of the Communication Workers of America, observes that high wages are correlated with the percent of unionized workers.[77] What Bahr and union leaders in general fail to realize is, historically, unions lost power and membership whenever immigration was high. Although they would like to, unions cannot escape the iron law of supply and demand. When the supply of labor surges relative to demand, real wage rates will fall. First the wave of the baby boom hit the labor force, then the immigrants flooded in. The percentage of private sector employment has dropped steadily over this time to 10 percent in 1996.[78] Labor economist Vernon Briggs points out that the dramatic increase in workers' real earnings that occurred in the 1920s until the Great Depression was in large part due to the immigration quotas of 1921 and 1924.[79] In contrast, a 1995 study by the Bureau of Labor Statistics found that "immigration accounted for approximately 20 to 25 percent of the increase in the wage gap between low- and high-skilled workers during the 1980s in the fifty largest metropolitan areas of the United States."[80]

Union leaders today are either extraordinarily uninformed regarding the impact of immigration, or they are so politically motivated that they are concerned in gaining support from immigrant workers and don't care that today's excessive immigration is reducing real wages and job opportunity for their existing union members.

2. International Factors

(a) Increased Competition from Low-wage Countries

While America was focused on winning the Cold War with the Soviet Union, many Eastern Asian nations were improving their systems of education to provide a fertile ground for the transfer of technological information from the West. All at once it was not only inexpensive, unskilled, labor-intensive goods that were invading U.S. markets, but high-tech hardware as well. And it wasn't just Japan, but Taiwan, Korea, Singapore, and Hong Kong who were providing it. Meanwhile other nations also began to improve their status in world trade: Thailand, Indonesia, Malaysia, Brazil, and Mexico are just a few of the LDCs who will be major competitors of the United States during the next fifty years. The increasing international mobility of capital and technology, coupled with low wage rates, make all of these countries formidable competitors, especially for manufacturing jobs.

Manufacturing jobs were also lost through the lack of U.S. investment in many industries. The inflationary spiral which roared through the 1970s, coupled with the diversion of research and investment from consumer products to defense spending, seriously impaired America's ability to compete in world markets. The result was loss of jobs during this time, particularly the better-paying, semi-skilled manufacturing jobs. The reduction of tariffs, although increasing the wealth and purchasing power of many Americans, accelerated the loss of high-paying manufacturing jobs that had provided economic opportunities for the less educated. On the other hand, as explained in the last chapter, tariff reductions increase high-skilled job opportunities by stimulating the sale of information industry products.

(b) Changes in the Trade Law

We already discussed in the last chapter the problems that reductions in tariffs present to a high wage country such as the United States. Here I will only mention that Gary Burtless of the Brookings Institution estimates that "the globalization of the U.S. economy is unlikely to explain more than one-fifth the huge rise in wage or income inequality since 1969."[81] Burtless believes that changing technology has played a far more significant role.

Before leaving the discussion of the impact on international trade, however, I wish to comment on the impact of such trade on corporate downsizing. While there is little doubt that many corporations seriously threatened by international competitors were forced to lower costs by downsizing, it would be a mistake to assume that international competition was the only or perhaps even most significant reason for much of America's corporate downsizing. The other major factor was the impact of acquisitions beginning in the early 1980s.

The acquisition frenzy of the 1980s had an invidious effect on job opportunities for both women and minorities. In general, the acquisitions did little more than saddle most of the purchasing companies with a mountain of debt. Mergers, acquisitions, and leveraged buyouts completed in just one year (1988) cost $266 billion yet resulted in no new products and in most cases little, if any, increases in productivity.[82] Over two-thirds of acquisitions were unprofitable. The need to return to profitability was a prime motivation for the corporate restructuring that took place in the 1990s. This allowed older white males to take advantage of special voluntary retirement programs and walk away with a nice pension. But their jobs were either eliminated or downgraded so that their replacements—often white women, much less frequently black males or females—received far less pay for equivalent and oftentimes greater responsibilities. The cuts were particularly severe in middle management. During the period July 1990 to February 1993, about 480,000 middle manager jobs were lost, most after the 1990 recession ended. This was the first time a greater proportion of white-collar employees were cut than blue-collar labor. Although accounting for only 19 percent of payrolls, middle managers represented 29 percent of the jobs eliminated.[83]

Although the ax fell hardest on white-collar employees, nonmanagement employees did not escape untouched. During the 1980s, the National Labor Relations Board ruled that the new owners of companies could scuttle existing union contracts.[84] That, coupled with the desire to plunder pension funds, was often sufficient reason for an acquisition.*

Indeed, there were times when employment cutbacks were necessary to improve a corporation's competitive position in world markets. Not infrequently, however, the work force reductions were made in the very area necessary to ensure the long-term success of the corporation, such as product development. To become more competitive, firms found that they could lower wages by outsourcing functions that were not central to their business. The outsourcing exacerbated the loss of good paying jobs due to restructuring.

3. Technological Factors

(a) The Shift from the Industrial Age to the Information Age

Burtless believes that technological change has had a greater impact on income inequality than globalization of the world's markets.[85] Economist Alan B. Krueger estimates that two-thirds of the increase in earning inequality among male workers since 1979 is the result of widening earnings differences among workers who have the same amount of education and previous work experience.[86] The computer, which initially slashed the ranks of clerks who collected and processed data, in the last couple of decades has enabled companies to dramatically thin the ranks of middle managers as well.

Although productivity improvements during the last two decades have been low by historical standards, this is in large part due to the growth of service industries that are not so readily mechanized as agriculture and manufacturing. However, productivity growth in manufacturing continues to reduce the jobs needed in that sector. Today the United States produces as much as it did a decade ago with a third fewer workers.[87] Between 1969 and 1993, the civilian labor force increased by 47 million.[88] Over the same period, the number of manufacturing jobs declined by 12 percent, a loss of

---

*During the 1980s nearly two thousand corporations collectively removed a total of $21 billion of "excess" funding from company pension accounts. Much of this money was used to repay the debt accrued in making buyouts. Many of these pension fund raids were to obtain money to pay off the debt required to make the leveraged buyout. The deal makers risked nothing, made a fortune in the process, and left the corporate employees and shareowners holding the bag. Donald L. Bartlett and James B. Steele, *America: What Went Wrong?* (Kansas City: Andrews and McMeel, 1992), p. 163.

over two million jobs.[89] By 1995 blue-collar jobs were only 17 percent of the labor force, compared to 35 percent in 1965.[90]

It is almost an article of faith among economists that productivity growth is an unqualified good. It is true that per capita growth in GDP is a function of increased productivity. Yet it does not follow that increased productivity benefits all people. It all depends on how the benefits of productivity increases are distributed. It is generally assumed that increased productivity in one sector of the economy will so increase wealth that it will create jobs in other sectors. But many of the new jobs may pay much less. Hence, the distribution of increased wealth for the nation as a whole may accrue to the investors in the new processes, not the displaced workers. During the industrial revolution, when huge gains in productivity were made in Britain by mechanizing the production of textiles, much of the subsequent increase in unemployment was shifted to India by placing prohibitive taxes on India's domestically produced textiles.[91] Displaced workers in Britain also migrated to America and elsewhere, just as in our own country victims of the industrial revolution migrated West. But the age when migration to new frontiers solves unemployment is long over.

In recent years, the loss of high-paying manufacturing jobs was partially offset by increased jobs in services and retail trade. In 1993, service sector jobs accounted for 60 percent of the job growth, although still accounting for only 30 percent of all jobs.[92] While professional and skilled service jobs are high paying, most services and retailing jobs pay far less than positions in manufacturing. According to the Bureau of Labor Statistics, the average earnings of Americans who lost jobs in 1993 and 1994 and found new ones fell 14 percent. The decline for factory workers was 19 percent.[93]

Furthermore, the growth in high-paying technical information jobs such as computer programmers and systems analysts required higher education in scientific and technical disciplines. Since blacks are significantly underrepresented in these disciplines, they garnered a lower number of well-paying job opportunities.[94] Moreover, because of the labor surplus, firms could become more choosy in who they hired: in general they wanted college educated people with good work records, which left many blacks out in the cold.

(b) Genetic Factors, i.e., the Difference in Cognitive Capabilities

Information technology requires more education and greater intelligence than was necessary to work on an assembly line. A strong mind rather than strong back will be the key to success in the future. In their controversial book *The Bell Curve: Intelligence and Class Structure in American Life,* Herrnstein and Murray advance the hypothesis that job requirements in the information age will cause America to bifurcate into an affluent and powerful cognitive elite and a relatively poor underclass of cognitively disadvantaged; that low IQ is related to unemployment and poverty appears to be indisputable. Even holding socioeconomic background constant, young white males who had an IQ two standard deviations below the average (i.e., in the bottom two percent of the population)* were twice as likely to be out of the labor market.[95] Not surprisingly, those with such low IQs were more than twice as likely to be living in poverty.

The most controversial aspect of Herrnstein and Murray's analysis is their observation that blacks in the United States average about 15 points lower than whites on IQ tests (1.21 standard deviations, or roughly in the lowest 14 percent of the population).[96] The critics of Herrnstein and Murray allege that this result is due to the bias built into IQ tests. For example, the verbal portion of the test contains words that are not familiar to poor people, and blacks in particular. But the low-scoring groups tend to do worse on the nonverbal portions of the test that do not require middle-class vocabulary. For example, a typical nonverbal problem requires determining the next digit in a sequence of numbers such a 2, 4, 7, 11, 16. For some reason, lower IQ people have problems determining the next digit, particularly in reverse order sequences. Unlike vocabulary, such a result could not be attributed to cultural bias in the tests.

The particular point that has outraged their critics is the suggestion by Herrnstein and Murray that cognitive capabilities are accounted for in large measure by heredity. They state that studies would indicate that inheritance accounts for between 40 percent and 80 percent of IQ results, and although they lean toward the higher number based on the study of twins,[97] they admit that both genes and environment contribute to the racial differences. They further admit that the evidence does not yet justify an estimate of the relative impact of the two variables.[98] Despite this caveat, their willingness to lend credence to the impact of heredity has earned them the enmity of many liberal columnists and book reviewers. Columnist Joan Beck called their book "sociological pornography"[99] and Ellen Goodman flatly denies that genes can have any impact on IQ, although she offers no evidence to the contrary.[100] Other reviewers have argued that some of the studies the authors referenced in support of their argument might be tainted by the prejudice of the researchers.

A 1997 analysis by Bernie Devlin, Michael Daniels, and Kathryn

---

*One standard deviation (SD) refers to the percentage of observations that fall 33.5 percent above or below the arithmetic mean average in a normal distribution. Two standard deviations equal 48 percent above or below the average. Hence, being one SD below the average would place a person in the lower 16.5 percent of the population, and two SDs below the average would place a person in the lowest 2 percent of the population.

Roeder of Pittsburgh's Carnegie Mellon University that combined more than 200 earlier studies concluded that genes accounted for 48 percent of the factors that determine IQ.[101] The study also found that conditions during prenatal development also affect intelligence. Some newspapers jumped on this latter finding as a refutation of Herrnstein and Murray's book. This hardly seems the case. True, the Devlin analysis lends less credibility to the notion that genes are the primary determining factor in IQ. But it does not refute the *Bell Curve*'s central thesis that with the economic trend to jobs with greater cognitive content, those with low IQs will tend to fall further behind economically. Just as importantly, it does not refute the hypothesis that poverty is linked to IQ. Since the poor often not only have low IQs but fail to provide the proper prenatal and early childhood care for their children, their children will also have low IQs in addition to other traits, such as impulsiveness, which greatly reduce the children's chances to break out of the cycle of poverty.

As Herrnstein and Murray readily admit, it is important to bear in mind that the difference in IQ *within* groups of whites and blacks is greater than the difference *between* the two groups. Economist Thomas Sowell offers the reasonable hypothesis that ***"heredity accounts for more variation within the general population and environment accounts for more variation between the general population and particular subgroups."***[102] Most importantly, we cannot draw the inference that any specific white person will have a higher IQ than any specific black person. ***Obviously, therefore, any decision on whom to employ based upon skin color is plainly wrong from a statistical as well as moral and legal perspective.*** Moreover, many jobs require more skills than just cognitive ability. IQ tells us nothing about a person's creativity, imagination, leadership qualities, interpersonal skills, self-motivation, diligence, or the like.[103] ***Nevertheless, it cannot be denied that if we were perfectly fair in hiring people for certain jobs based upon cognitive ability we might expect a difference in the distribution of whites and blacks in those jobs. Moreover, if high cognitive jobs paid more money on average, we could not conclude that the average difference in income between races is solely a function of unjustified racial discrimination as Derrick Bell would contend.***

Herrnstein and Murray state that the relationship between IQ and jobs may be due to three reasons: (a) IQ often reflects educational attainment, but it is education itself that determines job success; (b) IQ is related to job status because we live in a world of artificial credentials; or (c) IQ does reflect cognitive ability and cognitive ability has market value.[104] They clearly support the third premise, citing studies of adopted siblings placed in different homes. The results indicate that the biologically related siblings resembled each other in job status even though they grew up in different homes, while the job status of unrelated siblings growing up in the same home was not correlated.[105] However, this study was conducted in Copenhagen where the cultural differences were far less distinct than in the United States. IQ studies of adopted children in the United States reflect an average gain of 6 points.[106] Black children adopted by white families have an average IQ score of 106.[107] In contrast, one French study examined the change in IQ scores of children from very deprived families (the lowest 2 percent in IQ) to very advantaged families (the top 2 percent). It produced a shift of almost twenty points.[108] Still Herrnstein and Murray report that, "as a group, adoptive children do not score as high as the biological children of their adoptive parents."[109]

From these and many other studies we can deduce that environment can affect IQ scores directly to some extent, especially the environment of a child at a very early age. There is a growing body of evidence that prenatal and early childhood nutrition have an especially significant effect.[110] It also has been established that low-birth-weight babies can have lower IQs.[111] Smoking, alcohol, and drugs can all contribute to low birth weight, as can undetected infections in the mother. Since low-IQ women are more likely to engage in such dangerous habits, as well as suffer from infections while pregnant, there is an environmental linkage that will also affect a child's IQ, which will falsely appear to be due to heredity.

A hotly debated question today is to what extent, if any, could social policies such as early childhood intervention improve IQ? Even a small rise in average IQ would have a profound effect on the lives of the poor. According to Herrnstein and Murray a mere increase of three points in the average IQ would result in: poverty rates falling 25 percent; males in jail declining 25 percent; high school dropouts dropping 28 percent; a 20 percent reduction in children living in poverty; and an 18 percent decline in welfare recipients.[112] Moreover, even if only 40 percent of IQ is determined by environmental factors, there is ample room for improvement of average IQ of this magnitude through changes in the environment.

Herrnstein and Murray examine some popularized intervention programs such as Operation Head Start, the Perry Preschool Program, and the Carolina Abecedarian and Milwaukee day care projects. In general, while there is sometimes a significant increase in IQ and socialization benefits, the results appear often to be only temporary.[113] At other times, the sample size and study methodology have proved questionable, placing definitive conclusions in doubt. However, the evidence suggests that it is possible to boost IQs with extremely early childhood intervention—within the first three years. If so, Head Start programs begin too late.

Research at the Carnegie Corporation in New York indicates that the children's environment from the day of their birth—and possibly even before—affects the number of brain cells, the connections among them, and the way the connections are established.[114] Stressful environments can cause the death of brain cells involved in learning and memory. Children rescued from deprived or stressful environments can display cognitive benefits in only eighteen months. When extremely high-risk children entered educational programs, by six months of age, their incidence of mental retardation was cut by 80 percent. According to Craig Ramey, a developmental psychologist at the University of Alabama at Birmingham, by age three these children had an IQ 15 to 20 points higher than children of similar backgrounds without such programs. By ages twelve to fifteen the effect was greater still.[115] More recent research at Columbia and Northwestern universities indicated that poverty accounted for 52 percent of the IQ gap between black and white children. The children's home environment, and how much learning stimulation it provided, explained most of the rest.[116]

The problem is that it takes a massive dose of childhood intervention that must continue throughout their educational career, to achieve the desired results and such intervention is extremely costly. Society will be unable or unwilling to make the investment necessary when the numbers of those with low IQ people are in the tens of millions. Therefore, only a tiny fraction of at-risk children will be reached with the intensive intervention programs needed to significantly affect the intellectual development of children living in poverty. The vast majority of child care facilities in the United States are rated poor to mediocre by the Families and Work Institute; only 9 percent of child care arrangements are rated as good quality.[117] Hence, although federal and state programs to aid the poor through childhood intervention may be of benefit, as would more equitable investment in education of the poor (to be discussed in chapter 10), results of such efforts are not encouraging with respect to their capabilities to eliminate, or even substantially reduce poverty. Those living in poverty in the inner cities have an average IQ of about 80.[118] The notion of wholesale intervention in the lives of tens of millions of families simply isn't feasible. Moreover, the IQ studies show that even after controlling for differences in IQ, black poverty rates are twice as high as those for whites.[119] Simply improving IQ, assuming that is possible, is not enough to close the gap. There are clearly a host of other problems that must be solved if we are to reduce poverty in America.

This does not mean that we should give up trying to change the environmental factors that contribute to poverty, especially those incentives that perpetuate actions that contribute to poverty. However, it does suggest that we should also take care not to subsidize higher birth rates among the poor. Rather, ***we must adopt policies that will discourage people from having children if the parents are unable or unwilling to make the nec-***

essary investments of time and effort to aid the child to develop the cognitive skills to succeed in life. Some people will argue that such an approach is discriminatory toward blacks. But as pointed out earlier, there are more poor whites than blacks, and there soon will be more Hispanics as well. This policy is aimed at people such as the white woman I recently saw on a talk show whose seventh child suffered from fetal alcohol syndrome and will require $2 million of care over the child's life. This woman, her children, and society in general would have all been better off if she had been persuaded to have no more than two children, or possibly none at all.

4. Cultural Factors

(a) The Demise of Personal Responsibility and the Rise of Mother-only Families

Christopher Jenks suggests an interesting hypothesis regarding the increase in dysfunctional behavior that leads to poverty and crime. According to Jenks, the American middle class has contributed to antisocial behavior by becoming more tolerant of such behavior.[120] This misconstrued tolerance is especially exhibited by well-educated liberals who chant the "don't blame the victims" mantra. They understand that behavior is a function of genetics and the environment. But if a person is determined by genetics and environment how can they legitimately be held responsible for their behavior? I dealt with this subject in depth in *The Science of Morality*.[121] The conclusion reached was that even if we live in a deterministic world (and the evidence would suggest we do) where people cannot be said to have free will or be morally responsible for their actions in the philosophical sense, ***society must, nevertheless, hold them responsible for their actions to provide the necessary psychological motivation to behave in a socially responsible manner. It is a quintessential rule of developing prosocial behavior, in both children and adults, that we do not (except under extraordinary circumstances) decouple an action from its consequences.*** However, during the late 1960s and early 1970s an overconcern with the sociological factors that contribute to poverty and crime oftentimes was expressed in terms that excused irresponsible and antisocial behavior. A case in point was the social acceptability of unwed motherhood.

Despite overwhelming evidence that being an unwed mother more often than not put a child at risk, a large number of women thought they had a "right" to have a baby, and most of the rest of society decided to condone such irresponsibility. For example, when a young girl got pregnant, instead of social censure and ostracization (such as taking her out of high school), in the 1970s she was supported in her decision to have a baby. This was carried to the point in the 1990s of throwing baby showers for unwed mothers, which is, in effect, tacit approval of the unwed mother's irresponsible behavior. The result was a virtual epidemic of unwed mothers.

Births to Unwed Mothers[122]

	1960		1995	
	Births	*Percent*	*Births*	*Percent*
White	82,500	2.3	785,000	25.3
Blacks	138,744	23.0	421,000	69.9

The situation is actually worse than these numbers represent because even if a child is fortunate enough to be born to a two-parent family, the chances are that the union will not last. ***In 1997 a black child had about a one in seven chance of growing up in an intact family—that's a mere 15 percent. Eighty-five percent of black women with children under age six have never been married. About 75 percent of Hispanic women and 56 percent of white women are in the same situation.***[123] The only good news is that the percentage of children born to unwed mothers seems to have leveled off and the actual number of children born to unwed mothers has been declining slightly since 1990.

Although illegitimacy was not a major problem for white women in 1960, it has quickly become a problem, as 35 percent of white mothers are now having children out of wedlock, about the same proportion as unwed black mothers thirty years ago. Moreover, the rate of increase in unwed white mothers has been about three times that of blacks, so that today there are many more unwed white mothers than unwed black mothers. In short, like poverty, it is not just a problem for blacks.

But so what? The media has tacitly given their sanction to unwed mothers and castigated Dan Quayle for daring to criticize the TV character Murphy Brown for deliberately becoming an unwed mother (perhaps the most intelligent thing he said during his tenure as vice president). Maybe the concept of the traditional two-parent family is irreversibly doomed and fathers in America will become an anachronism. This is the view expressed to me by a young black professional woman. In her opinion, aside from breeding purposes, men were quite superfluous to child-raising. As evidence she cited the lack of child-raising involvement by fathers in some tribes in Africa. It was apparent that she was attempting to justify a situation that she felt to be inevitable by ignoring all the relevant evidence to the contrary. Is her opinion outlandish or reflecting a growing sentiment? If her thinking becomes the mainstream thought of the future, American society is indeed doomed. How do I know? Just check the evidence: for starters, the misfortune of living in a mother-only family greatly increases the likelihood of the child living in poverty.

Children Under Six Living in Poverty, 1996[124]

	Number (million)	*Percent of Families Type*
All Races		
Two parents	2.0	11.5
Mother-only	3.0	*58.8*
Whites		
Two parents	1.6	10.9
Mothers-only	1.5	*54.4*
Blacks		
Two parents	0.1	13.6
Mother-only	1.4	*64.1*
Hispanic		
Two parents	0.9	32.2
Mother-only	0.7	*72.4*

Over half of all children under age six who live in mother-only families live below the poverty level. Such evidence is overwhelming: single parenting is the number one reason for children living in poverty irrespective of race.* Michael Novak points out that if household types in 1989 had been the same as they were in 1969, median income would have risen $3,200 and the poverty level would have dropped to 10 percent.[125] The Murphy Browns of this world are an anomaly and present a foolishly optimistic view of what lies ahead for the children of single mothers. The truth is that single parenting is most often a prescription for disaster, especially in the case of unwed mothers:

- Unwed mothers comprise almost four-fifths of the welfare rolls.[126]
- Only about 16 percent of unwed mothers get any support from the father.

---

*Between 1990 and 1995 there is some indication that there has been an increase in two-parent families. But it is too early to tell whether this means the trend of the last twenty years has turned around (*Chicago Tribune*, March 10, 1996, sec. 1, p. 20).

- 30 percent of children of unwed mothers and 22 percent of the children of formerly married mothers will repeat a grade in school.[127]
- Children of single-parent families are more likely to require treatment for emotional and behavior disorders.[128]
- The lack of a male parent also appears to correlate highly with the increase in juvenile delinquency and the four-fold increase in the incidence of violent crime among teenagers.[129]
- The increase in unwed mothers correlates all too well with the more than four-fold increase in the rate of child abuse from 10 per 1,000 in 1976 to 45 per 1,000 in 1993.[130]

In addition to the problems mother-only families present for their children, they also place a burden on society: the cost to the U.S. taxpayers of welfare, including food stamps and Medicaid, to mother-only families is over $69 billion a year.[131] (Not only does single parenting result in negative consequences, but even when there are two parents, if both work and leave a child unsupervised, it can prove deleterious to the child's welfare: "eighth grade students who took care of themselves for eleven or more hours a week were twice as likely to be abusers of controlled substances such as tobacco, marijuana, and alcohol.")[132]

When teenage mothers are involved, the situation is even worse.* In 1992, 92 percent of all black and 55 percent of all white teenage girls age fifiteen to nineteen who had children were unmarried.[133] Although the unwed black teenage pregnancy rate is still four times that of white teenagers, it has remained constant since about 1970, while the pregnancy rate for unwed white teenagers has increased by 150 percent.[134] It seems as if white women are determined to follow the same disastrous trend as blacks when it comes to illegitimacy. If the trend continues, we also can expect the same social problems to plague the white community that have devastated the black community. In fact, the situation might get worse with the renewed pressures to restrict abortions through such measures as parental notification.

---

*There is often confusion regarding the data on birth rates of teenagers. Births to teenagers peaked in 1957 when nearly one in ten teenage girls gave birth. But most of those teenagers got married. In 1950 only 23 percent of mothers fifteen to seventeen years of age were unmarried; in 1996 it had risen to 84 percent. The decline in teenage marriages was undoubtedly a positive trend, but unfortunately the rate in teenage births, although declining as well, did not keep pace. The result was the dramatic increase in the rate of births to unmarried teenage girls. The good news is that since 1992 not only has the total rate of teenage births declined, but births to unwed teenagers have also declined.

In absolute numbers, the problem of unwed mothers is greater for women beyond their teenage years. In 1970, about 50 percent of the unwed births were to teenage mothers. The proportion dropped to 31 percent by 1995.[135] The major reason for the drop in the proportion of unwed mothers who were teenagers wasn't due to teens having fewer illegitimate births (such births increased from 5.4 percent of all births in 1970 to 9.9 percent in 1994 before declining slightly), but rather because women of all ages dramatically increased their number of illegitimate births (from 10.7 percent of all births in 1970 to 32.6 percent of all births in 1994).[136]

The evidence indicates that there is a high correlation between low IQ of the mother, poverty, illegitimate births, low levels of educational attainment for the children, higher rates of delinquency and crime, and a host of other socioeconomic problems.[137] However, there is a question as to the direction of the causality. In other words, does poverty lead to low intelligence, illegitimacy, neglected children, higher rates of crime, etc., or does low intelligence lead to poverty and all the associated problems? In all likelihood, there is not a clear causal direction; rather, the various factors are mutually reinforcing.

In the study by Herrnstein and Murray, 95 percent of poor teenage mothers had below average IQs. Moreover, women in the bottom 5 percent of the cognitive ability distribution were six times as likely to have an illegitimate first child as those in the top 5 percent.[139] But there is much more at work here than merely IQ, because the distribution of women's IQ has changed very little during the past thirty years even though illegitimacy has soared. Conversely, the percent of people living in poverty was far higher in the period from 1930 to 1960, yet the percentage of illegitimate babies was quite low and changed little from 3 percent in the 1920s to 5 percent by 1960. Based upon this trend we would have expected the proportion of illegitimate births to rise to about 6 percent by 1990.[140] Instead it jumped to 30 percent. Herrnstein and Murray clearly believe it was the advent of welfare in the 1960s: "The welfare check enables her to do something many young women want to do anyway—bear children."[141]

My own view is that it was more than the money, it was the removal of the social stigma associated with having an illegitimate child. This was part of the whole 1960s moral revolution. Instead of being ostracized as in the past, unmarried mothers were accepted and their pregnancies even celebrated. Young girls were no longer forced out of high school or sent away to bear their child in shame. Even the term "illegitimate child" was dropped in favor of "child of an unwed mother." (Note that in dropping the stigma for the child, which was appropriate, society in effect dropped the stigma on the mother as well.)

Fathers were also left off the hook. Shotgun weddings became a thing of the past. Bearing children not only became a woman's right, but men were absolved from responsibility in the decision and its consequences. Most perversely, it became a sign of virility for some teenage boys to say they had a child instead of hiding the shame that they got a girl pregnant. Clearly, then, what we have is a serious breakdown in conventional morality. Jenks points out that there has been a dramatic shift in the moral norms regarding children in the last thirty years. Thirty years ago couples were not supposed to have children unless they were prepared to get married and the father was prepared to support them. Moreover, if a man got a woman pregnant he was expected to marry her. Jenks believes that this moral norm lost much of its force between 1980 and 1990 because women were expected to control their fertility and had the availability of welfare.[142] Hence, in a bitter twist of irony, two social innovations that should have improved the lives of women—contraception and welfare—may have actually worked to their detriment.

The problem now becomes how to break a vicious cycle of people who are ill-equipped mentally, emotionally, and financially from having babies that are, in turn, condemned to lives of poverty, welfare, and (often) crime. Past policies clearly have not worked. And despite the reduction in inflation-adjusted AFDC per capita, the total social costs of supporting the growing number of unwed mothers has risen substantially. Janet L. Yellen, chair of the White House council of economic advisors estimates that perhaps as much as half the rise in family earnings inequality is due to changes in the composition of households due to divorces, out-of-wedlock births, and later marriages.[143] The last factor yields a net benefit since later marriages usually mean greater savings and earnings. But divorce and out-of-wedlock births are the great economic plagues of post World War II America.

(b) The Rise in the Use of Drugs

The Vietnam War had an incredibly destabilizing impact on America. A large proportion of the youth lost all faith in their government. Although youth is naturally rebellious, they now could cloak their rebellion in righteousness. The steady stream of lies and half truths coming out of Washington provided America's youth with a rationale to discount all governmental policies, especially those concerned with drugs. Adding to the problem were a significant number (but by no means a majority) of disillusioned Vietnam veterans hooked on a variety of drugs. Finally, Hollywood and rock music promoted the emerging drug culture. Movies such as *Easy Rider* made heroes out of drug dealers and users.

Whatever the merits or, as I will show in chapter 11, the demerits of the U.S. drug policy, it succeeded in making the illegal sale of drugs a highly lucrative, if not somewhat risky, career alternative. Why flip hamburgers at $5.15 an hour when you might be making one or two thousand dollars a week tax-free? The result was the development of an underground economy that continues to flourish to the detriment of our society. We have not learned much from either our past efforts to prohibit alcohol or the past thirty years of the failed war on drugs.[144] Although annual drug arrests more than doubled between 1980 and 1995,[145] it has done little to stop the flow of drugs across the borders. The increase in drug arrests did result in saddling hundreds of thousands of men with criminal records who then found it extremely difficult to get a legitimate job upon release from prison. It has also increased the percentage of blacks serving prison time.[146]

(c) The Establishment of the So-called Culture of Poverty

Years ago, anthropologist Oscar Lewis studied the lifestyles of selective Puerto Rican and Mexican families.[147] Although his investigation was anecdotal and so could not be generalized to either culture, further research supports Lewis's conclusion: "By the time slum children are six or seven they have usually absorbed the basic values and attitudes of their subculture and are not psychologically geared to take full advantage of changing conditions or increased opportunities which may occur in their lifetime."[148] In fact, recent research has concluded that growing up in a culturally deprived and threatening environment can negatively affect the physical development of the brain.

Poverty is more than just the absence of wealth. Sociologist Susan Meyer specifically asked the question: How important is money in enabling families to help their children to escape poverty? Her hypothesis was that money played a crucial role. However, she discovered that children of parents with attributes such as skills, diligence, honesty, good health, and reliability do well even if their parents do not have much income.[149]

Minorities and liberals decry the implied notion that poverty may be so endemic that it cannot be altered by social programs. Of course, simply because a person is acculturated to a certain lifestyle does not mean that his behavior cannot be changed. But it does suggest that the process becomes much more difficult than just providing welfare or short-term intervention programs. Moreover, to suggest that a culture may be dysfunctional is a value judgment that also implies that the culture should be radically altered. Many minorities resent the notion that they have a dysfunctional (implying the term "inferior") cultural. William Julius Wilson tried to finesse the issue by substituting the more neutral sounding phrase "social isolation" rather than "culture of poverty." However, the crucial fact is, as Herrnstein and Murray point out, that some people are "induced by family and neighborhood experiences, into a world in which they acquire wasteful consumption patterns, self-defeating attitudes, and an inability to obtain a legitimate job."[150]

Gary Becker contends that intergenerational differences of the distribution of income are due to the unwillingness of poor families to invest sufficiently in the education and training of their descendants.[151] But we know that this is not true for certain groups, such as Asian immigrants who make great sacrifices to invest in education of their children, thus raising them out of poverty. The deeper question is why some families don't invest sufficiently, not only monetarily, but in the time and effort to raise their children.

In the case of black families, it is sometimes said that the problem can be traced to the evils of slavery. However, the evidence indicates that the black family was not destroyed by slavery, but was about as intact as the average white family at the beginning of the twentieth century.[152] Moreover, despite high rates of poverty throughout the first half of the twentieth century, there were far lower rates of inner city joblessness, teenage pregnancy, out-of-wedlock births, female-headed families, welfare dependency, and serious crime.[153] Most families were nuclear families; 70 to 90 percent had a male present, and most female-headed families were the result of their husband's death, not abandonment.[154] As evil as the institution of slavery was, we must look elsewhere for the causes that led to the dissolution of the black family. I suggest that a primary cause was the lack of job availability for the reasons already discussed.

5. Fiscal Policies

(a) The Growth and Decline of Welfare

It is generally accepted today that the welfare system that began with Lyndon Johnson's War on Poverty programs and expanded during the succeeding decade, did in fact reduce the impact of being poor, but it is more questionable whether it mitigated or exacerbated the culture of poverty.

The key question is, does the availability of welfare—even if inadequate to escape poverty—actually exacerbate the problem by subsidizing parental irresponsibility, especially among the young? Conservatives have long answered this question in the affirmative and many liberals are reluctantly agreeing that such appears to be the case. The primary reason is that the welfare system removes a major incentive for the father to remain with his family. In fact, the fear has long been that it encourages men to leave their families. Finally, ***although the amount of welfare may not be the pri-***

mary incentive for having a baby, it may inadvertently send a message that having an illegitimate child is socially acceptable behavior.

The welfare system also probably increased unemployment among the poor for two related reasons. First, many welfare recipients have come to construe welfare as an entitlement. They view their situation as due to causes outside of their control, which may be partially true, but then conclude that they are not responsible for effecting those changes necessary for them to get off of welfare. Second, with welfare providing food, housing, and even medical insurance, it does not make economic sense for people to take jobs that pay only marginally more than a welfare check, while adding the extra expense of child care and enduring the loss of free health care (Medicaid). Here again, immigration also played a major negative role: by depressing wage rates, immigration reduced the net benefit of working versus welfare. In 1996, there were over five million workers earning the minimum wage or below.[155] Many of these were young, part-time workers, but almost half (48 percent) were over twenty-five years of age.[156]

The availability of welfare might also affect the fertility rate of poor women (white or black), and hence the growth in the number of poor. It is not that poor women have babies to get welfare, as is often claimed. Women have babies for a number of sociobiological reasons. However, knowing that they will be supported by welfare does blunt the negative consequences of having a baby. Therefore, the absence of welfare would act as a disincentive to having children.

Even if, however, the various forms of welfare have helped support a culture of poverty, in the short run, eliminating welfare altogether may worsen the impact of being poor (at least when the poor are forced to compete with immigrants). As mentioned earlier, forcing women off of welfare to take a minimum wage job that does not provide health insurance or child care will result in a lower living standard for the poor. In the next chapter we will see if there are any better solutions to poverty and the growth of income inequality. However, one way of mitigating the negative impact of low wage jobs is through tax policy as explained below.

(b) Changes in the Tax Structure

The Earned Income Tax Credit (EITC) is a refundable tax credit of up to 40 percent of earnings (it declines as earnings increase) that was increased in 1990 and 1993. The impact of the EITC in 1996 was to lift four million families out of poverty.[157]

The progressive nature of the national income tax rate reduces overall income in equality by 6 percent, while the cash and noncash transfers (such as the EITC, welfare, Medicaid, housing allowances, and the like) reduce inequality by an additional 18 percent.[158] Although the 24 percent reduction in inequality is substantial, inequality is far less than in European countries. Virtually every European country has some form of family allowance or child tax credit built into its tax system that is far in excess of the U.S.'s dependent deduction.[159] But this begs the question: is the more generous tax and welfare system of Europe better for society in the long run than what the United States offers? Or in the long run will it create more disadvantages than advantages for Europeans ?

This is not an easy question to answer. U.S. citizens in the bottom 10 percent of earnings distribution had a lower living standard than did similarly situated people in fifteen European countries (England being the exception).[160] But the generous welfare system has had a serious negative impact on European employment. Freeman observes that although the employment to population ratio was about the same in the United States and Europe in 1974 (65 percent), by 1995 the European ratio had declined to 60.1 percent while America had significant increased to 73.5 percent.[161] We know that the average duration of unemployment in Europe is substantially longer than in the United States. Therefore it would appear that more generous unemployment benefits in Europe acts as a disincentive to going back to work. The evidence suggests that the generous welfare provided by most European nations has resulted in high unemployment. It also appears that most European nations are beginning to recognize that they cannot stay competitive in world markets if they continue their present welfare polices. With 20 million Europeans unemployed and 50 million below the poverty line, Europe is reexamining its welfare systems.

On the other hand, while high rates of employment are generally considered desirable, we need to question whether many of the two-earner families in America are necessary for survival. Americans work many more hours than Europeans, averaging an additional 200 to 400 hours per year (that's five to ten weeks)![162] Are the only alternatives working longer hours at stagnant real wages (as in the United States) or higher unemployment (as in Europe)? Gary Burtless contends that even if all the growth in wage inequality were due to the growth in international trade and changing technology, it would still explain much less than one-half the rise in family income inequality.[163] I believe his estimate is low since he excludes the impact of increasing returns to investment that have occurred in the bull market of the past twenty years. ***Yet one major reason for the higher returns have been the ability of businesses to increase returns by moving jobs abroad to take advantage of low-wage labor while using that threat to hold down wage increases at home. The result has been that the proportion of wages and salaries to total income declined from 64 percent in 1970 to 54 percent in 1997.***[164] Hence, as explained in chapter 7, in the completely open global marketplace and with mass migration, we can expect the spread of wage rates to narrow throughout the world, much to the disadvantage of the American (and European) workers. Sir John Goldsmith's recommendation to permit free trade only between roughly comparable economies while negotiating bilateral trade agreements between noncomparable economic regions seems to be a prerequisite to protecting the standard of living in the advanced economies. However, as we will see in chapter 9, there are additional policies that America can and must implement if we are to negotiate the narrow channel between the scylla of stagnant or falling real wages and the Charybdis of high unemployment.

6. Racial Impacts: Past and Present

In his book *Faces at the Bottom of the Well*, Derrick Bell argues that the income disparity between blacks and whites is prima facie evidence of past and present discrimination.[165] Bell believes that blacks will never gain full equality in this country because racist policies are necessary for the success of whites.[166] The past success of whites was due to unjust enrichment due to slavery and exploitation of blacks. If whites were serious about helping blacks attain equality they would pay reparations for past exploitation and injustice. But, according to Bell, the limited improvement in civil rights for blacks in the last couple of decades was a mere cyclical trend that soon will be reversed; there is no long-term trend to greater equality. He even goes so far as to state that blacks provide all other racial groups with something in common, "someone to look down upon."[167] Since there is no hope that black people will ever gain full equality in this country, Bell suggests that we ought to sell licenses to discriminate and provide the blacks with the proceeds.[168] (It is doubtful that Bell offers this last suggestion seriously; it appears to be more an expression of frustration.) Ultimately, Bell believes that blacks can only look to each other for help; the white community can never be relied upon to provide the needed support to end black poverty.

A totally different perspective is offered by black economist Thomas Sowell. In *Race and Culture: A World View*, Sowell notes that immigrants from China, Italy, and Japan moved up from poverty in every country they migrated to despite initial discrimination.[169] Of course none of those groups incurred the debilitating effects of slavery. Even prior to slavery, however, blacks might not have had the same work ethic as whites because their environment did not demand the drudgery of intensive work. "Geological settings which seemed very favorable in presenting spontaneous abundance of food, or lands and streams easily farmed and fished, may be less favorable in the long run than natural settings in which people must develop in themselves discipline, work habits, and frugality merely in order to survive."[170] Moreover, the lack of navigable streams and difficulty of overland travel in Africa prevented trade and the commensurate exchange of ideas and cultural influences as well as the evolution of a mercantile class. Whatever negative work incentives existed prior to slavery would be greatly augmented by slavery: "Among the many aftermaths of slavery has been a set of counterproductive attitudes toward work, among both slaves and their descendants." The consequence of slavery was "not even laziness, but a positive sense of being above various kinds of work performed by slaves, or an aversion to any kind of toil or working under the direction of others, because these, too, were reminiscent of slavery."[171]

Yet despite possible negative consequences of the environmental setting for blacks both in Africa and in this country, it doesn't explain the retrogression in black culture that occurred after the end of slavery. Sowell points out that most black children were raised in two-parent families even during slavery, and blacks had higher rates of marriage during the early part of the twentieth century.[172] ***Moreover, every U.S. census from 1890 to 1950 shows that blacks had higher labor force participation rates than whites.***[173] What caused the regression since then? I suggest that it was several of the factors already discussed, including the negative incentives of increased welfare availability, the loss of good-paying manufacturing jobs to the suburbs and to low-wage countries, the need for higher-educated employees, competition with immigrants willing to work for less, the growth of drug use, the decline in acceptance of personal responsibility, the increase in mother-only families, and other related factors. The far more difficult question is how to reverse the trend.

In summary, there are demographic, economic, and sociological reasons for the cultures of poverty that have developed, especially among the less educated and less skilled, a disproportionate number of whom are minorities. Many of the causes of growth in poverty are subtle and reflect the failure of the government to take appropriate action many years ago. If we did not have the wave of immigration at the beginning of the twentieth century and chose to follow the advice of Booker T. Washington instead, we would have provided job opportunities to blacks and may have started them up an entirely different trend line. However, by creating a society that forced blacks to live hand-to-mouth, blacks have developed a much lower propensity to save and invest. Moreover, throughout their history in Africa and in America, blacks never had an opportunity to develop a mercantile class such as that which gradually evolved in Europe over several centuries.

The stereotypical poor European immigrant lives in a basement apartment and saves his money until he buys the apartment building. The stereotype of the poor American black is one who lives in a slum apartment, buys a flashy car on credit, loses the car by defaulting on his payments, and is evicted from his apartment. Such stereotypes are resented because they are by no means typical of all members of a race, but unfortunately they are too often true. Saving does not come naturally. It is a cultural tradition that differs significantly from culture to culture. Americans as a whole are poor savers, and blacks are exceptionally poor in this regard.

Dysfunctional behavior can become self-perpetuating: very low income can be both the effect and the cause of poor work performance. Lawrence Mead argues that it is not the lack of jobs but the high turnover rate that keeps the poor from advancing.[174] Even Jenks admits that with regard to blacks, "if young black men approach their work in the same way that they approach contraception and parenthood, employers would have good reason to avoid hiring them for responsible jobs."[175]

There are many factors which affect the work ethic, not the least of which is how it is perceived that wealth is achieved in the first place. If it is thought that wealth is attained by fortuitous birth (rich parents), chance (as in the case of lotteries), wheeling and dealing (as in the case of charlatans), or innate talent (such as rock stars or athletes), rather than the belief that hard work is the key to success, then increasing opportunity by ending discrimination and offering greater opportunities to those who apply themselves academically and through hard work will be an insufficient incentive to improve the work ethic and productivity. ***Hence, society must change the reward systems that determine behavior if we want the poor to act differently.*** Can our society take any action to break up these cultures and migrate the poor into the mainstream American culture?

Is There a "Cure" for Poverty and Income Inequality or Is it such a Complex Issue That it Defies Social Intervention?

According to Goldsmith, the money expended on poverty programs in the United States since the 1960s could have bought the entire assets of the Fortune 500 companies and virtually all of our nation's farmland.[176] Yet here we are nearing the next millennium with 36 million Americans still in poverty and income inequality near the postwar high. Is there anything that can be done? Or, even more basically, should we care?

First, I think it is important that we separate the issue of poverty from that of income inequality. It might be argued that, although we do not want to see people mired in grinding poverty through no fault of their own, it is obvious that equality of income has proven not only to be an impossible social objective to achieve, but every effort to do so has resulted in greater misery for the societies that sought it, as communism proved all too well.

Certainly, I would agree that total income equality is an impossible, even counterproductive, social goal. Moreover, I would admit that no one knows what the optimal inequality should be. However, as we concluded earlier, happiness is a function not only of a person's absolute standard of living, but after the basic necessities of life are met, happiness is very much affected by a person's relative standard of living. Hence if the goal of our society is, as stated in the Declaration of Independence, the pursuit of happiness, we should seek to provide people with the *opportunity* to improve their standard of living in both absolute and relative terms. (There are no guarantees of success in this regard.) Moreover, the experience with other societies indicates that concentration of wealth in the hands of a small minority is destabilizing to a society and, since wealth equates to power, such wealth can even threaten the very basis of a democracy.

Therefore, social policy should at a minimum seek to ensure that to the extent possible people have the opportunity for success in both absolute and relative terms. This was a major reason for the Civil Rights Act of 1964 and the affirmative action policies that were implemented afterward. Let's close this chapter by examining whether affirmative action policies have made progress toward the goal of providing more equal opportunities for Americans and whether those policies should be continued.

Have Affirmative Action Policies Reduced Poverty and Should They Be Continued?

In the late 1960s when jobs were plentiful and job discrimination was one of the biggest roadblocks for women and minorities, I was a staunch supporter of affirmative action policies to force companies to end their discriminatory practices. After the passage of the 1964 Civil Rights Act there was initially little effort on the part of most businesses to end discriminatory practices. There were a hundred bogus reasons for black job applicants to be turned away and women to be passed up for promotion. When I first went to work for Illinois Bell in 1964, and for several years thereafter, there were virtually no women who made it past the position of second-level manager (lower-middle management). Out of seven thousand management employees only a handful were black. In fact, there were few black employees even at the craft level aside from telephone operators or maintenance personnel.

It was clear to me at the time that the passage of the Civil Rights Act of 1964 was not going to have much impact on the firm's discriminatory hiring and promoting practices. In fact, even as late as 1972, when I was charged with determining the location of new operator services offices that would maximize the supply of available labor, there were managers who tried to convince me to relocate our offices away from black communities so that we could avoid having to hire blacks, even though my studies indicated that black communities provided the most sustainable supply of labor for operator jobs. As the manager of demographic and economical studies, I had the additional responsibility of providing the statistical basis for setting reasonable and attainable affirmative action objectives. I recommended objectives that could only be met by remaining near sources of black labor, thus forcing the firm to accept my office location recommendations. My action did not win me any friends.

It wasn't until affirmative action goals were set, and managers were held responsible for progress toward those objectives, that the company began to hire blacks as phone installers and service representatives and began a serious effort to train and promote blacks and women. Based upon my own experience and that of business acquaintances in many other firms, there is little doubt in my mind that most companies would never have actively sought to recruit and hire qualified minority workers had there not been aggressive enforcement of the affirmative action policies, including the use of numeric goals. However, I watched in dismay as ***the numerical quotas soon became a license to discriminate not only against white males, but minority males.*** Since there are many times more white women than black males, the quota for white women was far higher than black males, thus making it legal to discriminate against a black male in favor of a white woman. To show how perverse the situation became, after Illinois Bell met its objective for black male telephone installers, additional blacks were denied jobs while the company searched for women to fill the openings. To attract women the company redesigned several aspects of the installers job, such as replacing heavy wood ladders with fiber glass and assigning women to the safer neighborhoods. In management ranks, well-educated women raised in affluent suburban communities, educated at the best schools, and coming from a rich cultural and home environment as well, had little trouble beating out blacks from the inner city for job opportunities.

It soon became apparent that the basis for the affirmative action implementation was terribly wrong. The original justification for setting affirmative action goals was two-fold. First, was the belief that positive action would be required to make up for the grievous harm done to blacks by two hundred years of slavery and another hundred years of economic and cultural discrimination that locked them into grinding poverty while unjustly enriching whites. Second, it was believed that it was too difficult to enforce the Civil Rights Act of 1964 by placing the proof of discrimination on the plaintiff. A far easier method of enforcement was to assume that companies that failed to meet certain predetermined quotas were prima facie guilty of discrimination.

The situation with women was obviously quite different. In days when the norm was to have large families, the vast majority of women saw their position as full-time mothers and housewives as a natural and acceptable division of labor. If someone had suggested to my mother that she take a job outside the home she would have thought it absurd and grossly unfair. Men whose wives had to work were viewed as inadequate supporters of their families. Furthermore, women shared in the wealth of their husbands, even though they may not have had an equal say in how that wealth was used.

So in the case of women, discrimination was not nearly as deleterious to their health and welfare. Thus, while it was right and fair to end job discrimination against woman, there was no justification for society to have sought reparations through preferential hiring and promotional polices. But fair or not, white women were the primary beneficiaries of affirmative action and the reverse discrimination policy that it demanded. Today, to carry on discrimination in favor of women is to tacitly assume that women cannot compete with men, and to foster the discriminatory hiring of white women over black men. Moreover, as British authors Anne Moir and David Jessel conclude in their book *Brain Sex: The Real Difference Between Men and Women*: "To maintain that [men and women] are the same in aptitude, skill, or behavior is to build society on a biological and scientific lie."

Frequently the difference in average wages is used as prima facie evidence of discrimination. But men are more likely to get degrees in engineering and business while women are more likely to earn degrees in education, liberal arts, communications, and sociology. Engineers earn more than school teachers. In 1996, the federal Glass Ceiling Commission complained that 97 percent of senior executives at the largest one thousand industrial corporations were men. But Stephen Chapman points out that in 1970 when today's senior management was just getting started, men accounted for 96 percent of the MBAs in the country. Even today women earn only 36 percent of the MBAs. Moreover, to their credit women are generally less inclined than men to put professional success above every other concern. Only 14 percent of women managers indicate that they want to be CEOs compared to 45 percent of males.[177] As demonstrated in *The Science of Morality*, since women have evolved to be more nurturing and less aggressive and competitive than men, it is not surprising that women and men have different career outcomes on average. In some professions this will work to the advantage of women. For example, based upon present trends there will probably be more female doctors than male doctors within fifty years. In short, although no doubt sexism still exists, on the part of women as well as men, there is no persuasive evidence to justify discrimination against men just because they are more successful in certain areas than women.

As explained in chapter 4, another blow to the ability of blacks to take advantage of affirmative action policies has been the steady growth of immigration since 1970. Since the vast majority of the immigrants in the last twenty years have been Asian and Hispanic, blacks are once again being pushed to the back of the bus. Thus affirmative action legalizes discriminating against blacks in favor of women, Asians, and Hispanics, who many employers prefer hiring for a variety of reasons, not the least of which, in the case of immigrants, is that they are willing to work for lower wages. In an informal poll I conducted of small businessmen, they admitted that their preferential hiring order was Asians first, then whites, Hispanics, and, lastly, blacks. To make matters even worse, employers who are immigrants themselves are most likely to be guilty of flagrant discrimination against blacks.

There is no doubt that affirmative action has enabled many blacks as well as other minorities to get into college, especially the best colleges, than would have otherwise been the case. Even though the gap in SAT scores between whites and blacks closed by one-third by the mid-1980s,[178] the major reason for blacks gaining admission to the nation's top colleges has been the universities' willingness to accept blacks with far lower SAT scores than whites. For the top twenty-six universities this meant lowering their SAT requirements for blacks by an average of 180 points (1.3 standard deviations).[179] However, the results have not always been beneficial to blacks. Because they are admitted to colleges where the competition is tougher than lower-rated colleges for which they might be qualified, blacks have higher failure rates. About 70 percent of the students admitted to Berkeley under the preferential treatment program dropped out of college before graduation.[180] Even when they succeeded, there is a question as to whether they really earned their success or were given some slack to keep from flunking out. The result has been a hardening of racial attitudes on college campuses and a perceived devaluation of a college degree. Since California adopted Proposition 209 effectively outlawing any form of discrimination, including affirmative action, there has been a substantial decline in the number of blacks admitted to Berkeley and UCLA, while the number of Asian-American admissions increased.[181] But, many blacks who did not gain access to Berkeley or UCLA did get into second-tier colleges, and my guess is that there will be a higher proportion of blacks entering college who will graduate. Those who do graduate will know that their degree represents meaningful accomplishment, not just the filling of a quota.

A similar situation exists in the workplace. There is no question that affirmative action has resulted in more opportunities for minorities. Economists such as Becker and Sowell argue that employers always make the economically rational decision in the choice of labor.[182] Sports provides an excellent example. As long as all teams kept blacks from playing baseball, no team was relatively disadvantaged. But once Branch Rickey broke the color barrier by hiring Jackie Robinson, giving his team a distinct advantage due to Robinson's extraordinary ability, no team could afford to pass up hiring a talented black athlete. Today there are a disproportionate number of black athletes because they possess a greater proportion of those skills necessary for success in sports. Although it would be simplistic to believe that racial discrimination has ended, in a competitive world with tight labor supplies, few companies would be so foolish as to pass up a highly qualified engineer because of his color. However, if a company has a choice of several equally highly qualified candidates, as in periods of labor surplus, then they may discriminate based upon color.

There is little doubt that affirmative action programs were initially responsible for partially closing the gap in job opportunities and wage rates between minorities and whites. But according to Harvard economist Glenn Loury, the benefits of affirmative action have primarily accrued to blacks in the higher-paying occupations.[183] In some occupations the results have been dramatic. For example, there are six times as many black doctors and high school teachers as there would be if selection were made by cognitive ability scores rather than race.[184] In general, there may be over twice the number of blacks and 50 percent more Hispanics in high-IQ occupations then would be expected based on average IQ scores.[185] Although blacks on average still earn only 77 percent of what whites earn, after controlling for differences in the average IQ, blacks earn 98 percent.[186]

In the lower-skilled jobs, the difference in employment is given as evidence that racism is still prevalent in the work place. But Wilson believes that it is more the result of past than present racism. He argues that past racism forced blacks into low-paying, low-skilled jobs for decades. These are the jobs most likely to be mechanized or transferred to lower-wage, underdeveloped countries and, hence, blacks stand a greater chance of being displaced.[187]

Egalitarians won't be satisfied unless the average wages across races are the same irrespective of differentials in cognitive ability. But do we want equality even if it means hiring unqualified people in sensitive jobs? For example, in Miami and Washington, D.C., 90 percent of police officers dismissed or suspended within one year of instituting aggressive affirmative action programs had been hired despite their marginal qualifications.[188]

Lowering standards to hire people puts an organization in a bind later. If the less-qualified employees fail to perform equal to their coworkers they will have more dismissals and fewer promotions. This will be taken as prima facie evidence that the organization is discriminating. In 1994, of the 114 Chicago police officers promoted to sergeant based upon the results of an exam, only six were African American or Hispanic. Not surprisingly, there were charges that the test was racially biased.[189] It may be that relying solely on a written exam is not the optimal method of choosing who is best-qualified for promotion. But any other method is more subjective and, unless there are more minorities selected for promotion, you can be certain that there will be charges of prejudice in the selection. To avoid such charges there will be a tendency to promote less-qualified minorities. The result of such misguided policies will be a lowering of the general effectiveness of an organization and a general public mistrust of those minorities who have legitimately merited their promotions or professional status.

Despite the initial benefits of affirmative action programs for blacks, the programs have resulted in a form of discrimination which may still benefit women to some degree, definitely helps Hispanics and Asians who get preference over poor whites and oftentimes blacks, but probably now hurts blacks more than it helps them. Since Hispanics are fast overtaking blacks in total population, and blacks can, in effect, be legally discriminated against in favor of Hispanics, if present trends continue blacks will find their job prospects declining, as demonstrated in chapter 4. Ironically, despite the opinion of 80 percent of Americans that immigrants should receive no special favors,[190] at the time of this writing affirmative action policies still virtually guarantee minority immigrants job preference over nonminority American citizens.

Not only do the present affirmative action laws effectively justify discrimination against blacks, but they cause white resentment as well. When people are out of a job, it is just as painful whether they are white, black, yellow, or red. Pain turns to resentment when people believe that they were discriminated against in the hiring or promotion process. How do we logically explain to a white youth that society has decreed that, because his great grandfather might have benefited directly or indirectly from discrimination against blacks (even if his great grandfather was an abolitionist), we are going to try to even the score by discriminating against whites? Ironically, in any specific case it may not even be true that a deserving white male has been passed over to provide a job or a promotion to a less qualified woman or minority. But affirmative action policies support the perception.

Although in theory quotas have been outlawed by the Civil Rights Act of 1991, there are still de facto quotas since guidelines imposed in 1978 assert that it is prima facie evidence of discrimination if members of protected groups are not hired or promoted at 80 percent or more of the rate achieved by the group with the highest rate of success.[191] Taking a contrary view, economist Sowell flatly states, "Segregation as an employee policy cannot be inferred from group representation statistics, which are readily influenced by varying skills and choices of the groups themselves."[192] In college, too often women and minorities avoid the hard sciences in favor of easier social science courses. It is not an employer's fault if they cannot find minority engineers to hire. As any minority engineering or computer science graduate with reasonably good grades knows, obtaining a well-paying job is a piece of cake.

But even equal opportunity is not enough for some liberals. Political philosopher James Fishkin demands that all people be guaranteed an equal chance for success at birth. If we can predict with a high degree of accuracy where individuals will end up in the competition for preferred positions in society "merely by knowing their race, sex, or family background, then the condition under which their talents and nationality have developed must be grossly unequal."[193] While this may be true, it does not follow that this reflects racial discrimination or that the best way to rectify this inequality is to hire less-competent minorities over better-qualified whites.

It is my contention that present affirmative action laws have become a major source of continued racial antagonism in America. It may even be costing blacks job opportunities since some employers may be less likely to hire a black for fear of being sued if they need to dismiss him or her. ***Revoking the present affirmative action laws is not to abandon the principle of civil rights and equal opportunity.*** Far from it, it is to make the practice agree with the words by rigorously prosecuting all forms of discrimination. But isn't this ignoring the disadvantaged position inherited by blacks? I submit that the road to true equal opportunity is through socioeconomic policies, such as those discussed in this and subsequent chapters, designed to provide greater opportunities for all people regardless of race or gender.

The accomplishments of blacks in sports and entertainment should be the new paradigm for black success. Jackie Robinson faced enormous obstacles in major league baseball. But from that point on it was athletic abilities that determined success or failure of blacks in sports. Similarly, it has proven difficult to get blacks accepted in other vocations. But now it is time to let blacks and other minorities demonstrate that they have the capabilities to succeed. They may or may not replicate their phenomenal success in other disciplines as they did in sports and entertainment. I have no idea how the distributions would look a century from now assuming the end of racial discrimination in hiring, but I would be very surprised to find that the normal distributions of achievement would coincide for men, women, and minorities in every discipline. Nevertheless, the present practices are demeaning to blacks and other minorities and discriminatory against whites and, hence, it is time to abandon any form of preferential hiring or promotion based solely upon race or sex. (It is interesting to note that most blacks also agree with the notion of being judged on their capability rather than given preferential treatment.[194])

Similarly, contract set-asides for minorities should also be scrapped. Often the contractor just has a minority figurehead. I agree with Christopher Jenks who favors requiring employers to justify any selection criteria that eliminates a disproportionate numbers of blacks. But he also argues against reverse discrimination (i.e., discrimination against whites) once valid selection criteria are established.[195]

In his presidential campaign, Robert Dole argued for basing affirmative action on economic disparity rather that race. I have no idea how such a theory could be put into practice. Do we give special preference to the poor, just because they are poor? That's nonsensical. On the other hand, if he would suggest, as I did in the last chapter, that they not be denied the opportunity to an adequate education just because they are poor, or that we provide loans for exceptional children to attend schools they may not otherwise afford, I would support the concept. However, providing additional support for improving a person's skills, is far different than preferential hiring based upon characteristics other than merit.

California has taken the right step in moving to end all forms of discrimination and ***judge people solely on the basis of their individual capabilities and performance rather than as a member of a group.*** Some observers point out that only one black student was admitted to Berkeley's law school in 1997 as evidence of the harm that true nondiscrimination causes. They fail to add that fourteen others were admitted but chose to go elsewhere, such as Harvard, Stanford, and the like. They also fail to mention that black, Hispanic, and Native American admissions to the University of California at San Diego actually went up. And because the minorities admitted will be better able to compete with the other students at UC San Diego, we might expect them to succeed there instead of failing at Berkeley. Hence, dropping affirmative action will work to the benefit of minorities.

Unlike author Dinesh D'Souza, I am not calling for the repeal of the Civil Rights Act of 1964.[196] Rather, all discrimination based upon race, sex, ethnicity, religion, or sexual proclivities must be prohibited. We will never end prejudice by continuing the practice of legalized discrimination against any group.

Summary

Even after adding increased fringe benefits, the total increase in real compensation during the last two decades has been minuscule, and income inequality in the United States is increasing. The number of people living in poverty has increased significantly since the late 1960s and although it dropped slightly in the late 1990s, it remains unacceptably high, especially among children. Although middle-class blacks have improved their income relative to whites, an increasingly larger number of blacks are falling further behind.

The causes for the failure of the underclass, and especially low-income blacks, to improve their economic situation in the last twenty years are many and include: major demographic trends, especially immigration; the growth in international competition; the shift to the postindustrial information age; and major cultural changes, including the rise of the drug culture and the growth in mother-only families. Although federal policies have reduced the impact of poverty, they may have inadvertently weakened the concept of personal responsibility and supported the culture of poverty.

There is no doubt that past discrimination has been detrimental to blacks, but there is less reason to believe that it continues to be the major factor hampering black advancement. In the postindustrial age cognitive capabilities will become increasingly relevant to economic success. Although cognitive abilities are in part inherited, they can be significantly increased or retarded depending upon the child's early environment. However, although childhood intervention can improve a child's capabilities, society lacks the resources to provide the necessary degree of intervention for the tens of millions of children who could benefit from it.

Affirmative action laws have greatly aided women and minorities in the past twenty-five years. However, they now appear to be counterproductive. Because they lead to discrimination against whites, present affirmative action laws are exacerbating racism in the United States. Prejudice means prejudging people on the basis of their race, ethnicity, sex, or the like—a characteristic not relevant to the person's ability—in other words, as members of a group rather than by their individual capabilities. It is time to end all prejudice in the work place. The goal of society must be to judge people based upon their individual capabilities and performance rather than as members of a group. Although I have many criticisms of professional sports, they appear close to the ideal of hiring and paying people based upon individual performance. Any reparations to minorities for past discrimination should be in the form of increasing investment in youth such as increased expenditures on education (especially early childhood programs such as Operation Headstart) and vocational training.

Now that we have clarified the major causes of poverty, and shown that neither massive childhood intervention nor affirmative action is the answer, we will explore some solutions that hold more promise.

NOTES

1. President, *Economic Report of the President Transmitted to Congress, February, 1998* (Washington, D.C.: U.S. Government Printing Office, 1998), table B–31, p. 317.

2. U.S. Bureau of the Census, *Statistical Abstract of the United States, 1997* (Washington, D.C.: U.S. Government Printing Office, 1997), table 1355, p. 836. Luxembourg had the highest per capita income due to the growth of its banking industry. Estimates are on a purchasing power parity basis.

3. Christina Duff, "Mothers' Jobs Spurred 25% Increase in Couples Income from 1969 to 1996," *Wall Street Journal*, September 1, 1998, p. A4.

4. President, *Economic Report of the President Transmitted to Congress, 1991*, table B–44, p. 336 and *Economic Report of the President to Congress, 1998*, table B–43, p. 336.

5. Bruce Bartlett, "Decline in Wages Offset by Hirer Fringe Benefits," *Human Events* (October 27, 1995): 976.

6. President, *Economic Report of the President Transmitted to Congress, 1998*, table B–48, p. 337.

7. Richard B. Freeman, "The Facts About Rising Income Disparity," in *The Inequality Paradox: Growth of Income Disparity*, eds. James A. Auerbach and Richard S. Belous (Washington, D.C.: National Policy Association, 1998), p. 22.

8. Ibid., p. 30.

9. U.S. Bureau of the Census, Historical Income Tables, 1966–1967. www.census.gov/hhes/income/historic/503.html.

10. Ibid., www.census.gov/hhes/income/historic/502.html.

11. Janet L. Yellow, "Trends in Income Inequality," in *The Inequality Paradox*, eds. Auerbach and Belous, p. 13.

12. Freeman, "Growth of income Disparity," in *The Inequality Paradox*, eds. Auerbach and Belous, p. 20.

13. Dan L. Boroughs et al., "Winter of Discontent," *U.S. News and World Report*, January 22, 1996, p. 49.

14. Arthur Okum, *Equality and Efficiency: The Big Tradeoff* (Washington, D.C.: Brookings Institution, 1975), p. 1.

15. Korten, *When Corporations Rule the World* (West Hartford Conn. and San Francisco: Kumarian and Press Berrett-Koehler Publishers, Inc., 1995), p. 22.

16. I add the adjective "perceived" because it is possible that people perceive themselves as relatively worse off even if they are not. For example, if they view televisions as an accurate representation of reality, and the characters on TV all appear to have much more than the average person has, then they might feel disadvantaged, even if in realty they are not.

17. Paul Krugman, *The Age of Diminished Expectation* (Washington, D.C.: The Washington Post Company, 1990), p. 19.

18. Joseph L. Daleiden, *The Science of Morality* (Amherst, N.Y.: Prometheus Books, 1998), chapter 15.

19. U.S. Bureau of the Census, Current Population Survey, "Poverty Status

of People" (March, 1999), table 2. www.census.gov/hhes/poverty/histpov/hstov2.html.

20. Earnest Morgan "Humanizing the American Economy," *The Humanist* (November/December 1988): 27.

21. John McCarron, "Days of Unrest," *Chicago Tribune*, September, 4, 1995, sec. 1, p. 11.

22. Don L. Boroughs et al., "Winter of Discontent," p. 47.

23. Morton Bahr, "Collective Bargaining Bridges the Income Gap," in *The Inequality Paradox*, eds. Auerbach and Belous, p. 4.

24. "Running to a Standstill," *The Economist* (November 10, 1991): 22.

25. Frank James, "White House Touts Study on New Jobs," *Chicago Tribune*, April 24, 1996, sec. 1, p. 8.

26. R. C. Longworth, "As Middle Class Splits, U.S. Loses Balance," *Chicago Tribune*, August 20, 1995, sec. 1, p.14.

27. Ibid.

28. Robert Samuelson, "How Safe Is Your Job?" *Chicago Tribune*, February 9, 1996, sec. 1, p. 29. Citing a study by Louis Jacobson of the consulting firm Westat.

29. David Dembo and Ward Morehouse, *The Underbelly of the U.S. Economy: Joblessness and the Pauperization of Work in America* (New York: The Apex Press, 1992). Cited in *Future Survey*, p. 9.

30. Carl Quintanilla, "Work Week," *Wall Street Journal*, July 14, 1998, p. A1.

31. Robert J. Samuelson, "Immigration and Poverty," *Newsweek* (July 15, 1996): 43.

32. Charles Murray, *Losing Ground* (New York, Basic Books, 1984), p. 88.

33. President, *Economic Report of President Transmitted to Congress, 1998*, table B–33, p, 320.

34. President, *Statistical Abstract of the United States, 1991*, table 730, p. 454

35. U.S. Bureau of the Census, *Money Income in the United States: 1996*, Current Population Reports, Series P-60, Consumers Income, no. 197 (Washington, D.C.: U.S. Government Prining Office, 1996), table B–4, pp. B–9, B–10..

36. U.S. Bureau of the Census, *Statistical Abstract of the United States, 1996*, table 81, p. 66.

37. Data for 1983–1994 calculated from *Statistical Abstract of United States, 1997*, table 645, pp. 410–412, which shows that whites in these occupations increased by 38 percent while blacks increased by 62 percent. Earlier data showing a similar results is provided in Christopher Jenks (New York: HarperPerennial, 1992), p. 148.

38. President, *Economic Report of the President Transmitted to Congress, 1998*, table B–43, p. 331. I am indebted to William Julius Wilson for first demonstrating using this ratio in his book, *The Truly Disadvantaged: The Inner City, The Underclass, and Poverty* (Chicago: University of Chicago Press, 1987), p. 30.

39. Bureau of Labor Statistics, *Employment and Earnings* (January 1997), table A-3.

40. George J. Church, "We're #1 and It Hurts!" *Time Magazine* (October 24, 1994): 52.

41. President, *Economic Report of the President Transmitted to Congress, February, 1998*, table B–48, p. 337, total private compensation adjusted for changes in the Consumer Price Index. If I had used the changes in the prices of all nonfarm products as the deflator instead of just changes in the prices of consumer goods, productivity and real compensation track much more closely. The problem is that using all compensation averages in the huge increases in executive compensation with the minimal increase in compensation of production workers. Only men in the top 7 or 8 percent of wage earners enjoyed increases in real hourly pay between 1979 and 1996 while the bottom 10 percent of male workers saw their real wages decline 18 percent. Although women in the top pay levels increased their earnings faster than men, poor women suffered the same fate as their male counterparts. See Burtless et al., *Globaphobia* (Washington, D.C.: Brookings Institution, 1998), pp. 60–64, 77–78.

42. Ibid., table B–43, p. 330.

43. Leatha Lamison-White, *Poverty in the United States: 1996*, Current Population Reports, Series P-60, Consumer Income, no. 198 (Washington, D.C.: U.S. Government Printing Office, 1997), table A, p. vii.

44. U.S. Bureau of the Census, *Statistical Abstract of the United States, 1996*, table 733, p. 473. Data for 1996 from *Economic Report of President to Congress*, 1998, table B–33, p. 320.

45. Lamison-White, *Poverty in the United States: 1996*, table E, p. xii.

46. Ibid., table A–2, p. A–4.

47. Harrel R. Rogers and Gregory Weither, *Rural Poverty: Special Causes and Policy Reforms* (Westport, Conn.: Greenwood Press, 1989). Cited by *Future Survey* (November 1990).

48. "Shift to Service Jobs Spur Homelessness," *Chicago Tribune*, December 29, 1991, sec. 1, p. 4.

49. Jason De Parle, "Sharp Increase Along the Border of Poverty," *New York Times*, March 31, 1994, p. A–1, Cited by Korten, *When Corporations Rule the World*, p. 246.

50. Lamison-White, *Poverty in the United States: 1996*, table 2, pp. 3–5.

51. William Neikirk, "Midwest-fueled Drop in Poverty Raises Smiles on Clinton's Team," *Chicago Tribune*, September 27, 1996, sec. 1, p. 4.

52. U.S. Bureau of the Census, *Statistical Abstract of the United States, 1991*, table 746, p. 462, and Lamison-White, *Poverty in the United States: 1996*, table 2, pp. 3–5.

53. U.S. Bureau of the Census, *Statistical Abstract of the United States, 1996*, table 731, p. 472, and Lamison-White, *Poverty in the United States: 1996*, table 2, pp. 3–5.

54. U.S. Bureau of the Census, *Statistical Abstract of the United States, 1995*, table 753, p. 484.

55. When there are a dozen different factors it becomes extremely difficult to quantify the relative importance of each factor since the factors may influence one another. The situation, known by the dreadful name of multicollinearity, is especially likely when examining trends over time.

56. U.S. Bureau of the Censes, *Statistical Abstract of the United States, 1991*, table 13, p. 13.

57. President, *Economic Report of the President Transmitted to Congress, 1998*, table B–39, p. 327.

58. *American Demographics* (May 1991): 46.

59. U.S. Bureau of the Census, *Statistical Abstract of the United States, 1991*, table 635, p. 386. President, *Economic Report of the President to Congress, 1996*, table B–31, p. 316.

60. President, *Economic Report of the President Transmitted to Congress, 1998*, table B–35, p. 322.

61. Christopher Jenks, *Rethinking Public Policy: Race, Poverty, and the Underclass* (New York: Harper Perennial, 1992), p. 50.

62. William Julius Wilson, *The Truly Disadvantaged: The Inner City, the Underclass, and Poverty* (Chicago: University of Chicago Press, 1987), p. 172.

63. Ibid., p. 58.

64. Ibid., p. 122.

65. John D. Kasarda "Implications of Contemporary Redistribution Trends for National Urban Policy," *Social Science Quarterly*, no. 61 (1980): 303–322. See also Bernard L. Weinstein and Robert E. Firestein, *Regional Growth and Decline in the United States* (New York: Praeger, 1978).

66. Ibid., p. 37.

67. Maritza Marrero, "Need Link Between Welfare and Work," *Chicago Tribune*, December 12, 1997, sec. 1, p. 26.

68. "Business Bulletin," *Wall Street Journal*, April 16, 1998, p. A1.

69. Ibid.

70. David T. Ellwood, "The Spatial Mismatch: Hypothesis: Are There Jobs Missing In the Ghetto?" in *Black Youth Employment Crisis*, eds. R. B. Freeman and H. J. Halzer (Chicago: University of Chicago Press, 1986).

71. Michael M. Phillips, "Welfare's Urban Poor Need a Lift—To Suburban Jobs," *Wall Street Journal*, June 12, 1997, p. B1.

72. John Kain, "Housing Segregation, Negro Employment, Metropolitan Decentralization," *Quarterly Journal of Economics* 82 (1968): 175–197.

73. Vernon M. Briggs Jr., "Income Disparity and Unionism: The Workplace Influences of Post-1965 Immigration Policy," in *The Inequality Paradox: Growth of Income Disparity*, eds. James Auerbach and Richard S. Belous (Washington, D.C.: National Policy Council, 1998), p. 117.

74. U.S. Department of Labor, Bureau of Labor Statistics, *Geographic Profile of Employment and Unemployment, 1983–1994*, table 6.

75. James K. Tribble and Carl Gallman, "NAFTA Costly to Illinois Workers," *Chicago Tribune*, June 16, 1997, sec. 1, p. 13.

76. For example, in Minnesota 104,000 seekers will compete for 40,000 low-paying jobs. In Indiana the ratio is 133,000 job seekers for 44,800 jobs, and in Ohio 324,800 people will compete for an estimated 80,500 jobs. Based upon analysis by Paul Kleppner, Northern Illinois University Office of Social Policy

Research, as reported by Merrill Goozneer, "Leaving the Dole, Many Call, Few Chosen," *Chicago Tribune*, July 20, 1997, sec. 1, p. 4.

77. Morton Bahr, "Collective Bargaining Bridges the Income Gap," *The Inequality Paradox*, eds. Auerbach and Belous, p. 34–43.

78. U.S. Bureau of the Census, *Statistical Abstract of the United States, 1997*, table 688, p. 440.

79. Briggs, "Income Disparity and Unionism" in *The Inequality Paradox*, eds. Auerbach and Belous, p. 117.

80. David A. Jaeger, "Skill Differences and the Effect of Immigrants on the Wages of Natives," BLS Working Paper No. 273 (Washington, D.C.: DOL Department of Labor Statistics, December, 1995, p. 21. Cited by Briggs, "Disparity and Unionism," p. 123.

81. Gary Burtless, "Technological Change and International Trade: How Well Do They Explain the Rise in U.S. Income Inequality?" in *The Inequality Paradox*, eds. Auerbach and Belous, p. 62.

82. William M. Dugger, *Corporate Hegemony* (New York: Greenwood Press, 1989, p. x. Cited by Korten, *When Corporations Rule the World*, p. 207.

83. Merrill Lynch, *Weekly Economic and Financial Commentary*, February 11, 1993.

84. Donald L. Bartlett and James B. Steele, *America: What Went Wrong?* (Kansas City: Andrews and McMeel, 1992), p. 202.

85. Burtless et al., *Globaphobia*, p. 85.

86. Gary Burtless, "Earnings Inequality over the Business and Demographic Cycles," in *A Future of Lousy Jobs? The Changing Structure of U.S. Wages*, ed. Gary Burtless (Washington: Brookings Institution, 1990), pp. 106–109.

87. According to Marcus Alexis, former business college dean of University of Illinois at Chicago, as quoted by Patrick T. Reardon, "In the '80s the Rich Did Get Richer," *Chicago Tribune*, January 13, 1991, sec. 1, p. 3.

88. President, *Economic Report of the President Transmitted to Congress, 1994*, table B–33, p. 306.

89. Ibid., table B–44, p. 318

90. Sherman Stein, "Decline of Middle Class 'Frightening' to Blacks," *Chicago Tribune*, August 23, 1995, sec. 1, p. 4, quoting University of Maryland sociologist, Bart Landry.

91. David C. Korten, *When Corporations Rule the World*, p. 240.

92. President, *Economic Report of the President Transmitted to Congress, 1994*, p. 101.

93. Jacob M. Schlesinger, "A Slide in Factory Jobs: The Pain of Progress," *Wall Street Journal*, April 28, 1997.

94. John D. Kasarda points out that in the mid-1980s the modal category among black men was less than high school for all regions of the country except the West. "Regional and Urban Redistribution of People and Jobs in the U.S." paper prepared for the National Research Council Committee on National Urban Policy, National Academy of Sciences, 1986, pp. 18–19. Cited by William Julius Wilson, *The Truly Disadvantaged*, p. 102.

95. Herrnstein and Murray, *The Bell Curve: Intelligence and Class Structure in American Life* (New York: Free Press, 1994), p. 158.

96. Ibid, pp. 276, 278.

97. Ibid, p. 107.

98. Ibid, p. 311.

99. Joan Beck, "The Case Against Linking Intelligence to Race and Class," *Chicago Tribune*, November 13, 1994, sec. 1, p. 31.

100. Ellen Goodman, "Latest IQ Book Adds Fuel to Minds of Racists Bigots," *Chicago Tribune*, October 25, 1994, sec. 1, p. 23.

101. Bernie Devlin, Michael Davis, and Kathryn Roeder, "The Heritability of IQ," *Nature* 388 (July 31, 1997): 468–71.

102. Thomas Sowell, *Race and Culture* (New York: Basic Books, 1984), p. 171.

103. Howard Gardner believes that there are seven distinct intelligences: linguistic, musical, logical, mathematical, spatial, bodily, kinesthetic, and two forms of personal intelligence: the intrapersonal and interpersonal. Howard Gardner, *Frames of Mind: The Theory of Multiple Intelligences* (New York: Basic Books, 1993), p. 278. But others such as Herrnstein and Murray think the term "talents" better describes such attributes, p. 18.

104. Herrnstein and Murray, *The Bell Curve*, pp. 64–65.

105. T. W. Teasdale, T. I. A. Sorensen, and D. R. Owen, "Social Class in Adopted and Nonadopted Siblings," *Behavioral Genetics* 14 (1984): 587–93. Cited by Herrnstein and Murray, *The Bell Curve*, p. 54.

106. Herrnstein and Murray, *The Bell Curve*, p. 389.

107. Sandra Scarr and Richard Weinberg, "IQ Test Performance of Black Children Adopted by White Families," *American Psychologist* (October 1976): 731–33. Cited by Sowell, *Culture and Poverty: A World View*, p. 168.

108. R. Plomin and C. S. Bergeman, "The Nature of Nurture: Genetic Influences on 'Environmental' Measures," *Behavioral and Brain Sciences* 14 (1992): 373–427. Herrnstein and Murray, *The Bell Curve*, p. 412.

109. C. Locutto, "The Malleability of IQ as Judged from Adoption Studies," *Intelligence* 14 (1990): 275–92. R. Plomin and J. C. DeFries, "Genetics and intelligence: Recent Data," *Intelligence* 4:15–24. Cited by Herrnstein and Murray, *The Bell Curve*, p. 411.

110. S. J. Schoenthaler et al., "Controlled Trial of Vitamin-Mineral Supplementation: Effects on Intelligence and Performance," *Personality and Individual Differences* 12 (1991): 351–62. Cited by Herrnstein and Murray, *The Bell Curve*, p. 392

111. Ibid., p. 215.

112. Ibid., p. 367.

113. Ibid., pp. 404–409.

114. Rochell Sharpe, "To Boost IQs, Aid Is Needed in First Three Years," *Wall Street Journal*, April 12, 1994, p. B–1.

115. Ibid.

116. Jeanne Brooks-Gunn, Pamela Klebanov, and Greg J. Duncan, *Child Development* (April 1996). Cited by Joan Beck, "The IQ Gap Begins at Birth," *Chicago Tribune*, April 28, 1996, sec. 1, p. 19.

117. Sharpe, "To Boost IQs, Aid Is Needed in First Three Years," pp. B1, B4.

118. Herrnstein and Murray, *The Bell Curve*, p. 522.

119. Ibid., p. 327.

120. Ibid., p. 16.

121. Daleiden, *The Science of Morality*, chapter 2.

122. Linda Seebach, "Who Would Choose Single Motherhood?" *Los Angeles Daily News*, April 8, 1993. 1994 data from the *Statistical Abstract of the United States, 1997*, table 97, p. 97.

123. Chritiana Duff, "Census Finds Striking Shift in Families," *Chicago Tribune*, May 28, 1998, sec. B, pp. 1, 13.

124. Lamison-White, *Poverty in the United States: 1996*, table 2, pp. 2–5.

125. Deborah A. Dawson, "Family Structure and Children's Health: United States, 1988," Vital Health Statistics, series 10, no. 178 (Washington, D.C.: National Center for Health Statistics, 1991), p. 62. Cited by Amitai Etzioni, *The Spirit of Community* (New York: Crown Publishers, 1993).

126. Douglas J. Beshman, "The Other Clinton Promise—Ending Welfare as We Know It," *Wall Street Journal*, January 18, 1993.

127. *American Demographics* (February 1992): 14.

128. Amitai Etzioni, *The Spirit of Community* (New York: Crown Publishers, 1993), p. 62, citing a 1991 study for National Center for Health Statistics.

129. Linda Seebach, "It's Time We Faced up to the Consequences of Single Motherhood," *Chicago Tribune*, April 9, 1993.

130. National Center for Health Statistics, *Health, United States, 1996–97 and Injury Chartbook* (Hyattsville, Md.: U.S. Department of Health, 1997), table 717, p. 722. See also *Statistical Record of Health and Medicine*, ed. Charity Anne Dorgan (New York: Gale Research, 1995), table 21, p. 17.

131. U.S. Office of Management and Budget, *Budget of the United States Government 1995* (Washington, D.C.: U.S. Government Printing Office, 1995), p. 109.

132. Etzioni, *The Spirit of Community*, p. 69.

133. Irving Kristol, "Family Values—Not a Political Issue," *Wall Street Journal*, December 7, 1992. Reprinted in *AEI*, no. 55 (1992).

134. The correlations have been well-documented by Richard J. Herrnstein and Charles Murray, *The Bell Curve*; see particularly pp. 183–980, 200–201, 210, 229–30.

135. National Center for Health Statistics, *Health, United States, 1996–97 and Injury Chartbook*, table 8, p. 86.

136. U.S. Bureau of the Census, *Statistical Abstract of the United States, 1991 and 1997*, table 92, p. 67, and table 97, p. 79.

137. The correlations have been well documented by Herrnstein and Murray, *The Bell Curve*, see particularly pp. 183–90, 200–201, 210, 229–30.

138. Ibid., p. 387.

139. Ibid., p. 167

140. Ibid., p. 178.

141. Ibid., p. 180.

142. Jenks, *Rethinking Social Policy*, pp. 190, 196.

143. Janet L. Yellen, "Trends in Income Inequality," in *The Inequality Paradox: Growth of Income Disparity*, eds. James A. Auerbach and Richard S. Belous (Washington: National Policy Association, 1998), p. 12.

144. See Joseph L. Daleiden, *The Science of Morality*, chapter 10 for a more complete discussion of the consequences of prohibiting drugs.

145. U.S. Bureau of the Census, *Statistical Abstract of the United States, 1997*, table 332, p. 211.

146. Ibid., table 354, p. 220.

147. Oscar Lewis, *La Vita: A Puerto Rican Family in the Culture of San Juan and New York* (New York: Random House, 1965). *The Children of Sanchez: Autobiography of a Mexican Family* (New York: The Modern Library, 1961).

148. Oscar Lewis, "The Culture of Poverty," in *Understanding Poverty: Basic Perspectives from Social Science*, ed. Daniel Patrick Moynihan (New York: Basic Books, 1968), pp. 187–200.

149. Susan Mayer, *What Money Can't Buy* (Chicago: University of Chicago Press, 1997).

150. Herrnstein and Murray, *The Bell Curve*, p. 315.

151. Gary Becker, *A Treatise on Families* (Cambridge, Mass.: Harvard University Press, 1991), p. 231.

152. Herbert G. Gutman, *The Black Family in Slavery and Freedom, 1750–1925* (New York: Pantheon Books, 1976), p. xvii.

153. Wilson, *The Truly Disadvantaged*, p.3.

154. Ibid., p. 64.

155. U.S. Bureau of the Census, *Statistical Abstract of the United States, 1997*, table 675, p. 433.

156. Ibid.

157. Yellen, "Trends in Income Inequality," in *The Inequality Paradox*, eds. Auerbach and Belous, p. 14.

158. Ibid.

159. Timothy M. Smeeding, "U.S. Income Inequality in a Cross National Perspective: Why Are We so Different?" in *The Inequality Paradox*, eds. Auerbach and Belous, p. 211.

160. Ibid., pp. 203–204.

161. Freeman, "Growth of Income Disparity," in *The Inequality Paradox*, eds. Auerbach and Belous, p. 19.

162. Ibid., p. 228.

163. Burtless, "Technological Change and International Trade," in *The Inequality Paradox*, eds. Auerbach and Belous, p. 61.

164. Gail Fosler and Lynn Franco, "Perspectives on Income Disparity," in *The Inequality Paradox*, eds. Auerbach and Belous, p. 45.

165. Derrick Bell, *Faces at the Bottom of the Well: The Permanence of Racism* (New York: Basic Books, 1992).

166. Ibid., p. 154.

167. Ibid.

168. Ibid., p. 60.

169. Thomas Sowell, *Culture and Poverty: A World View* (New York: Basic Books, 1994), pp. 82–83.

170. Ibid., p. 239.

171. Ibid., p. 216.

172. Ibid., p. 220.

173. Ibid., p. 95.

174. Lawrence M. Mead, *Beyond Entitlement: The Social Obligation of Citizenship* (New York: Free Press, 1986), pp. 4, 61.

175. Jenks, *Rethinking Social Policy*, p. 40.

176. Goldsmith, *The Trap*, p. 99.

177. Stephen Chapman, "Women and the Decline of Affirmative Action," *Chicago Tribune*, July 11, 1997, sec. 1, p. 23.

178. Herrnstein and Murray, *The Bell Curve*, p. 294.

179. Ibid., p. 245.

180. Dinesh D'Souza, *Illiberal Education: The Politics of Race and Sex on Campus* (New York: The Free Press, 1991).

181. At Berkeley, the number of so-called underrepresented minorities accepted for the fall of 1998 had declined 57 percent, at UCLA the decline was 36 percent, *Wall Street Journal*, April 1, 1998, p. A1.

182. Sowell, *Race and Culture*, pp. 87–89. See also Gary Becker, *The Economic Approach to Human Behavior* (Chicago: University of Chicago Press, 1976), p. 19.

183. Glenn Loury, "On the Need for Moral Leadership in the Black Community," paper presented at the University of Chicago, April 18, 1984, pp. 13–14. Center for the Study of Industrial Societies and the John M. Olin Center. Cited by W. J. Wilson, *The Truly Disadvantaged: The Inner City, the Underclass, and Poverty*, p. 110. This is particularly true of set-aside programs for minority business. Wilson adds that he is aware of no evidence that such set-aside programs have led to a significant increase in employment for lower-class blacks. p. 116.

184. Herrnstein and Murray, *The Bell Curve*, p. 321.

185. Ibid., pp. 321–22.

186. Ibid., pp. 323, 324.

187. Wilson, *The Truly Disadvantaged*, p. 12.

188. E. J. Delattre, *Character and Cops: Ethics and Policing* (Washington, D. C.: American Enterprise Institute, 1989). D. K. Sechrest and P. Burns, "Police corruption: the Miami Case," *Criminal Justice Behavior* 19 (1992): 294–313. Cited by Herrnstein and Murray, *The Bell Curve*, p. 496.

189. *Chicago Tribune*, August 16, 1994, sec. 5, p. 2.

190. 1994 poll of National Opinion Research Center at University of Chicago, *Chicago Tribune*, September 4, 1995.

191. Herrnstein and Murray, *The Bell Curve*, p. 482.

192. Sowell, *Race and Culture*, p. 84.

193. J. Fishkin, *Justice, Equal Opportunity, and the Family* (New Haven, Conn.: Yale University Press, 1983, p. 4.

194. Herrnstein and Murray, *The Bell Curve*, p. 505.

195. Jenks, *Rethinking Social Policy*, p. 63.

196. Dinesh D'Souza, "Separation of Race and State," *Wall Street Journal*, September 12, 1995, p. A22.

9

Poverty and Welfare: Solutions

Sociologist Charles Murray believes that things are never so bad that government programs can't make them worse. He claims that the growth in poverty and most of the other problems facing us today can be traced to the War on Poverty programs initiated under Lyndon Johnson and expanded under succeeding presidents. The initial government aid programs created under Franklin Roosevelt's New Deal gave us Social Security, Workman's Compensation, Unemployment Compensation, and Aid to Families with Dependent Children (AFDC). Their aim was to provide temporary support for those beset by unforeseeable misfortunes such as a severe recession or depression. However, according to Murray, the War on Poverty went far beyond that modest goal by adding food stamps, public housing, Medicare and Medicaid, manpower training, and the expansion of a variety of entitlement programs that were available on a permanent rather than temporary basis. Of course, that was never the intention of Lyndon Johnson, who made it clear that the goal of the War on Poverty was to enable people ultimately to achieve self-sufficiency.

Regardless of the good intentions of Johnson and his successors, Murray argues that the consequence was just the opposite. He points out that, although social welfare costs increased twenty times between 1950 and 1980 in constant dollars, 13 percent of Americans lived in poverty in 1968 and 13 percent lived in poverty in 1980.[1] This is typical of the sometimes questionable statistical analysis Murray employs. By going back to 1950, he selects a year before the establishment of welfare programs to a year after the institution of the War on Poverty. Naturally going from virtually nothing to any significant number will involve a large multiple.

Next, he compares 1968, a year which culminated a decade of rapid economic growth with a recession year—1980. Not surprisingly, the percentage of people whose income was below the poverty level was quite similar. He should have compared 1968 to 1978 or 1988 to make a valid comparison of years of comparable economic activity. Interestingly, comparing 1968 to 1978 would have shown a significant decline in the percentage of people in poverty (11 percent), while 1988 had the same poverty rate as 1968 (13 percent).[2] As we saw in the last chapter, the increase in poverty in the 1980s was more due to demographic and technological changes than the availability of welfare.

To get a truer perspective on the long-term trend consider that, in 1960, before the War on Poverty was launched, 22 percent of Americans lived in poverty.[3] Going back still further—to 1950—30 percent of the population lived in poverty. Compare that rate to the 1997 rate of about 13.7 percent (only about 10 percent if we had held immigration to the level of 1970) and the poverty programs would appear to be at least partly successful. (Murray would no doubt argue that any improvements were made despite the poverty programs rather than because of them.)

Murray is correct in stating that the rapid economic growth of the 1950s and early 1960s did more to reduce poverty than the welfare programs. However, those years of rapid growth occurred when America was the only economy in the world not ravaged by the Second World War and faced with tight labor markets. Once the other nations of the world had rebuilt their economies and could successfully compete with us, our growth rate began to slip, and it is extremely doubtful that we will ever return to these extraordinary years of world economic dominance and prolonged rapid growth in the median income for the American people.

Nobel Prize winning economist Milton Friedman uses similar selective statistics by comparing Health, Education, and Welfare expenses in 1953 when it was only $2 billion a year to 1978 when it reached $160 billion a year.[4] The growth is astounding, but it starts from a time when there was little social welfare except social security, and then ignores both the impact of inflation and population growth. As we saw in chapter 6, there was indeed substantial growth in federal spending in the late 1960s and throughout the 1970s. However, when we control for defense spending, social security (which is a function of the aging population and inflation), and retirement income for federal employees and the military (which are no more a form a welfare than corporate pensions are), we find that the lion's share of welfare growth is due to Medicare and Medicaid. Expenditures for traditional welfare programs such as food stamps, AFDC, housing subsidies, and the like, have grown about 4.1 percent a year during the past decade after adjusting for inflation.[5] The fastest growing component was

Supplemental Security Income (SSI) for the elderly and disabled who do not qualify for social security. The bulk of this growth was due to the increase in elderly immigrants. In California 50 percent of the Chinese and 66 percent of elderly Russian immigrants are receiving SSI. If we control for SSI, growth in welfare per capita was less than 2 percent per year between 1984 and 1995.

Aside from overstating the growth in what is considered by most Americans to constitute welfare, Murray argues that welfare has had no positive effects in reducing poverty. However, his assertion is not supported by the data.[6] In 1960, 58 percent of the working-age blacks lived in poverty. By 1970, this number had dropped to 30 percent, but no further improvements were made between 1970 and 1980.[7] Murray argues that the reduction in poverty between 1960 and 1970 was not due to the welfare programs, because the funding for the programs credited for the reduction in poverty was much higher in later years even though no comparable decline in poverty occurred. Again, he ignores the offsetting impact of the growth in the labor force due to the entrance of the baby boomers, women, and minorities, as well as all of the factors discussed in the last chapter. Yet it is the extraordinary growth in the labor force coupled with increased world competition that depressed wage growth and were the major factors for the increased poverty beginning in the 1970s.

Similarly, recipients of Aid to Families with Dependent Children (AFDC) rose from 2 percent of the population in 1965 to 6 percent in 1974. However, by 1995 the percentage of recipients had actually declined slightly to about 5.4 percent (two-thirds of which are children). Several other facts place AFDC in the proper perspective. First, after adjusting for inflation, AFDC payments have actually declined in recent years. While the $23 billion spent on AFDC is no trivial amount, it now accounts for less than 1 percent of the total federal budget.[8] Moreover, it should be noted that over half of the women receiving AFDC do so for less than one year, and only 9 percent of women who receive AFDC do so for more than eight years.[9]* This is less than half a million women. Finally, it should be noted that three-fourths of the women living in poverty receive no child support.

The 1996 Welfare Reform Bill may be successful in getting women off welfare. However, it may require additional expenditures on training and child support allowances. Moreover, since most of these women will be earning little more than the minimum wage, they will receive additional federal support in terms of the Earned Income Tax Credit. Hence, even if the Welfare Reform Bill is successful in getting women off welfare, it will not

---

*However it may be that many women continually enter and exit the labor force, thus receiving welfare benefits frequently, although not continuously. We do know that women on welfare usually have high job turnover rates. It is an area that requires further study.

have a major impact on the federal budget. It may be that only by ending most forms of assistance that we can force people to end their dependency on welfare. But it would be foolish to think that *by itself* such a policy will reduce poverty.

Murray's Three Laws

Charles Murray strongly supports the conservative view that social programs will inevitably make matters worse, rather than better for society. His conclusion is predicated on three so-called laws (in reality they are hypotheses):

1. *Law of Imperfect Solution*: "Any objective rule that defines eligibility for a social program will irrationally exclude some persons."[10] This is no doubt true, but so what? It can just as truthfully be stated that any governmental regulation or law is bound to be unfair in some circumstance. Based upon this criterion we would dump the entire system of criminal justice. Conversely, no law or convention can insure justice for every person under every circumstance. Carried to its logical conclusion, Murray's first law would justify a state of anarchy—a classic case of *reductio ad absurdum.*

2. *Law of Unintended Rewards*: "Any social transfer increases the net value of being in the condition that prompted the transfer."[11] The problem with this assertion is that it infers that people will deliberately seek to change their behavior so that they are in the position to receive social benefits. This need not follow, however; it depends upon what options are available. The real question is whether the transfer of income or wealth is so great that people find it better to be in the condition that prompted the transfer than in a situation that would make the transfer unwarranted. No doubt there are some who will work only if the alternative is starvation. However, most people who do not have jobs either cannot find work for which they are qualified or cannot find work that would pay enough to offset the cost of employment (such as transportation and child care), or they have an alternative source of illegal income that pays better than a legal job (such as drugs, prostitution, etc).

It is not surprising that jobs paying only $5.00 to $6.00 an hour fail to attract applicants, especially if they are located in suburbs, far away from the poor who have no public transportation to those jobs. When the Ameritech Corporation moved offices from locations in downtown Chicago to a far northwest suburb, some clerical employees living on the south side of Chicago had to travel two hours each way (even more in bad weather) to get to work. (Most management personnel could afford the more expensive housing in the northwest suburbs.) After trying to keep their jobs by getting up at 5:00 A.M. and getting home at 8:00 P.M., secretaries and clerks with young children had the option of giving up their job or, for all practical purposes, giving up their family. Not surprisingly, many quit.

There are times, no doubt, when welfare will act as a disincentive to accepting low-paying and otherwise undesirable jobs. Liberals often assume that all people want to work and will perform reasonably well if given a chance. But let's face it, some people are lousy workers. Some of the chronically unemployed simply don't like to work. They have terrible attendance records, are frequently tardy, resent taking orders, are surly and ill-tempered, or dumb as a post. In short, they have no job because no one wants to put up with them. Its going to take some very grave consequences to get them to perform even minimally well. But the major reduction in unemployment in the 1990s provides evidence that the unemployment problem from the early 1970s to the mid-1990s was primarily the result of surplus labor due to the post World War II baby boom.

3. *Law of Net Harm*: "The less likely it is that the unwanted behavior will change voluntarily, the more likely it is that the program to induce change will cause net harm."[12] Murray accepts the fact that behavior can be changed by positive and negative reinforcement. However, he fears that if the positive reinforcement is large enough to affect behavior, it will encourage others to place themselves in the socially undesirable position to benefit from the positive reinforcement reward. For example, he alleges that any program that would succeed in helping the hardcore unemployed will make hardcore unemployment a desirable state to be in. This is entirely possible, but not necessarily so. Studies by Leonard Goodwin show that, in general, the poor want to work.[13] The problem is (at least in the case of black males), they often have such a poor self-image that they strongly believe they are incapable of succeeding at a job, and their belief becomes a self-fulfilling prophecy.

Murray's third law also suffers from the same weakness as his Law of Unintended Rewards: i.e., while it may be true, *all other things being equal*, in the real world it depends on what other options are available to people. For instance, a critical factor in determining how people will behave is the level of pay relative to welfare. A two-year study by Manpower Demonstration Research Corporation of what was considered to be a generally successful federally subsidized jobs program in Riverside, California, revealed that although 63 percent of those in the program got jobs, only 35 percent still held them at the end of two years. The reason was not hard to find: those who did keep working were found to be no better off financially than those who went back on welfare.[14] Hence, it is not surprising that self-interest would result in a person choosing not to work when working does not provide a net financial benefit.

Murray's unspoken assumption is that the welfare payments are sufficient incentive for people to prefer welfare to work. This seems to be the case in Europe. In countries such as England, Italy, Sweden, the Netherlands, Germany, and France, unemployment and welfare assistance offer far more generous benefits and, hence, the average time between jobs is much longer than in America. Consequently, the average unemployment rate is also much higher.* In other words, welfare can diminish the incentive for some people to find work.

In the United States the situation is somewhat different. AFDC per capita has been falling short of inflation for the past two decades.[15] If Murray's theory is correct, we would expect all the evils caused by welfare to be reversed as the benefits fall. This has not been the case. The reason may be that until 1995 real wages (adjusted for inflation) have also been falling. This is especially true of minimum wage jobs. Therefore, the relative benefit of working versus welfare has not improved.

The solution which Murray proposes to end all the evils he attributes to welfare and income support is to scrap all such programs for the working age population, including AFDC, Medicare, food stamps, unemployment insurance, worker's compensation, subsidized housing, disability insurance, and the rest. "It would leave the working age person with no recourse whatsoever except the job market, family members, friends, and public or private locally funded services."[16]

He seems to be proposing a return to nineteenth-century America, where there was no such security net and people somehow survived. There are just a couple problems with Murray's vision. In the nineteenth century, even up to the First World War, America was primarily an agrarian and manufacturing economy with a large need for unskilled labor. We also had extremely high tariffs to protect our emerging industries. This enabled the industrial sector to grow at an astounding rate, much as it did in Japan following World War II. Nonetheless, life was far from easy for most Americans. ***It wasn't until World War II and the subsequent shortage of labor during the next twenty years that the unions were able to substantially increase the share of***

*In general, European nations have decided to accept high unemployment, high wages, and high taxes to finance the high unemployment benefits. The United States, conversely, has implemented policies that result in lower unemployment and welfare benefits, lower unemployment, lower wages, and lower taxes needed to fund the unemployment benefits. See Robert Reich, *The Next America* (New York: Random House, 1983, chapter 10). However, the European model is beginning to falter. The higher wage rates have to be met with continued high productivity, or else rising prices of exports will result in reduced demand and slower economic growth. Europe is now plagued with chronic unemployment, over 10 percent in 1996. Only Japan has been able to sustain low unemployment rates in the face of slow growth, but it is doubtful that Japan can continue such a policy in the face of international competition.

national income and wealth for the working man. That trend slowed in the 1970s, however, when the factors mentioned earlier—especially the rapid increase in the supply of labor relative to demand—resulted in labor again losing its bargaining advantage.

The model that Murray seems to be advocating is somewhere between industrialized England of the 1850s and the situation facing migrant farm workers in America today (who are ineligible for most welfare benefits). In short, Murray is advocating a social Darwinism that would completely ignore the plight of the mentally or environmentally disadvantaged. Adam Smith's "invisible hand" is wielding an invisible club to smash anyone who cannot compete.

The Murray view is based upon the correct premise that people must be held responsible for their actions, but ignores the determining factors over which a person has no control. It attempts to turn back the clock to those socioeconomic conditions that gave rise to communism. Yet Murray has become the intellectual godfather of the conservatives. Just how far they were prepared to go was demonstrated when the Reagan administration tried to cut school lunch milk rations from six to four ounces and compel families in need of public aid to first dispose of all household goods of value in excess of $1,000.[17]

Reducing Unemployment and Poverty

Liberals and conservatives alike agree that any system of assistance should be temporary rather than permanent, with the ultimate goal of getting people back on their feet and gainfully employed. We cannot afford to allow the welfare rolls to continue to grow. The value of work is more than just a means of obtaining sustenance. Work fosters those social values necessary for preserving society, such as self-discipline and cooperation. Moreover, work is essential to self-esteem and happiness. Most people think of themselves in terms of what they do. For many, if a person does nothing, that person is nothing. Therefore, reducing unemployment and welfare dependency should be a primary goal of any society.

We can end welfare by simply cutting off all benefits and forcing a person to take a job at any rate of pay or starve. Although such a simplistic approach will necessarily reduce welfare, it will do little if anything to reduce poverty. To reduce joblessness, welfare, and poverty, six essential steps need to be implemented simultaneously:

1. ***Increase the economic differential between work and welfare, even for low-skilled jobs.***

2. ***Improve physical access to jobs.***
3. ***Reduce the supply of low-skilled labor relative to the demand.***
4. ***Increase public infrastructure investment to reduce long-term unemployment during chronic periods of excess labor.***
5. ***Reduce the number of unwed mothers and mother-only families.***
6. ***Revamp America's educational system.***

This last point is so important and complex that I have devoted the entire next chapter to it. Now let's examine the other five steps needed to reduced poverty.

1. Increase the Economic Differential Between Work and Welfare

A minimum wage of $5.15 an hour equates to $10,700 a year. (An increase to $6.15 an hour in September 1999, as proposed by President Clinton would raise annual income to $12,800. This would still leave the minimum wage 5.5 percent below the 1974 level after adjusting for inflation and 16.7 percent below the $7.38 high reached in 1968, expressed in constant 1997 dollars.[18]) But a woman who receives all the possible financial support from all sources of welfare for herself and her newborn, including AFDC, food stamps, Medicaid, and a housing subsidy, would have to earn almost $15,000—about $7.20 an hour—in 1997 to have the same standard of living as when she isn't working. No wonder, then, that so many women on welfare have little incentive to get or keep a job.

If we force women to work at the minimum wage by denying them welfare, we are effectively condemning them to even greater poverty. Employment alone is not sufficient to end poverty. Moreover, changing welfare will not necessarily force women into employment. The percent of single mothers collecting AFDC was 29 percent in 1964, 63 percent in 1972, and 45 percent in 1988. But, as Jenks points out, these wide fluctuations had almost no effect on the proportion of single mothers who worked during those years.[19] Training and education are also of no benefit if there is a lack of decent paying jobs.

We can provide incentives for women to work while not condemning them to even greater poverty. The Earned Income Tax Credit (EITC) was a major step in the right direction. Having a job did not mean the loss of all welfare benefits. Welfare benefits were reduced with increased earnings, but on a sliding scale up to $27,000 for a family of four. This addressed

Murray's concern that under the old system it was to the economic advantage of a family to break up rather than stay together. (Although, as we will see, increased income does not always work to prevent a family breakup.) Unfortunately, in their effort to balance the budget in 1996, Congress sought to cut EITC.[20] By reducing the benefit of working, we are simply encouraging people to either not work or not report income. Instead of reducing the benefit of working we should increase the incentive to work by also providing that all workers can obtain low-cost health insurance at least equal in quality to what they can get under Medicaid.

In 1980, the National Longitudinal Study of Youth asked unemployed sixteen to twenty-one-year-olds what would be the lowest wage they would accept. About half indicated they would not work unless they received a wage more than 50 percent higher than the minimum wage at the time.[21] In today's terms that would be about $8.00 an hour. This also assumes that the job is accessible by public transportation. Therefore, it is not surprising that at pay rates less than $7.00 to $8.00 an hour, a large number of inner-city youth would opt for illegitimate jobs, especially in the potentially lucrative drug rackets. It should also be noted that, according to the Labor Department, two-thirds of those now earning the minimum wage are not teenagers but adults who are often the sole breadwinners of their families. These include child care providers, retail sale clerks, farmworkers, and janitors.[22]

The liberals' answer to the problem of poverty is to raise the minimum wage. Many businesspeople argue that arbitrarily raising the minimum wage will decrease the number of jobs. They are partly right. Certainly, some small businesses might no longer be profitable by raising the minimum wage, and some businesses might find it cheaper to mechanize the higher-paying jobs. But there is no evidence that an increase in the minimum wage to $6.15 (or $6.65 by the year 2000) would significantly decrease the number of jobs. Conservatives raised the specter of massive layoffs when it was raised the minimum wage from $4.25 to $4.75 in October 1996 and again when it rose to $5.15 in September 1997. On the other hand, one hundred economists, including some Nobel laureates, endorsed the 1996 initiative to increase the minimum wage by ninety cents, concluding that the overall impact on workers and the economy would be positive.[23] As of 1999 no noticeable decline occurred in the employment growth in occupation groups with a disproportionately large number of minimum wage workers.[24] Bear in mind that at $6.15 an hour the minimum wage will still be less than in 1968, when it peaked at $7.38 (recalculated in constant 1997 dollars).[25] Furthermore, throughout the period when the minimum wage was declining in real dollar terms, the number of low-skilled workers dropped in relative and absolute terms compared to high-skilled workers.[26] Finally, ***a study by the OECD***

reached the conclusion that there is no connection between low wages and low unemployment, especially among low-skilled workers. Some high-wage countries have high unemployment; others don't.[27] No doubt there is some level where increases in the minimum wage will reduce employment, but we certainly are not there yet. (You can be certain, however, that during the next recession when unemployment rises, some businessmen will argue that the minimum wage is too high.)

America has lower wage rates for unskilled jobs than European countries and appears to have lower unemployment as well. But we also have a large number of people who, because they have exhausted their unemployment benefits, are no longer counted as part of the labor force, hence, they are no longer counted as unemployed. In 1995 economist Lester Thurow estimated the U.S. unemployment rate would be closer to 14 percent if we included all those who are excluded from the work force plus the millions of part-timers who want full-time employment.[28] Even in the tighter labor market of 1998, Thurow's definition of unemployment would yield a rate around 11 to 12 percent compared to the government estimate of 4.8 percent.

The empirical evidence in the United States fails to demonstrate a convincing relationship between wages and unemployment. There has been significant job growth since 1973 along with the decline in real weekly earnings, but it cannot be ascertained how much of that job growth can be attributed to the decline in weekly earnings as opposed to the tremendous economic stimulus caused by the deficit spending, the aging of the baby boomers and their associated increased consumption and investment, and other factors.

Liberals also seek to increase the differential between work and welfare by providing federally funded day care for women with children below school age. However this remedy is problematic. In the first place it may not be feasible since even now there is a serious shortage of qualified day care centers. According to one study, "most child care is mediocre in quality [and] sufficiently poor to interfere with children's emotional and intellectual development."[29] Only 14 percent of child care centers in the study were determined to be developmentally appropriate. Part of the problem is that child care providers are among the poorest paid in the workforce. In 1995 over half of all child care providers earn less than $5.00 an hour. More companies are providing day care or dependent care assistance plans, but these are mainly large corporations, whereas most jobs are being created by small businesses that cannot afford the expense of subsidizing day care centers. Again, a labor shortage resulting in higher wage rates would allow women to pay more for day care, thus attracting better qualified people to day care work.

In 1998 President Clinton proposed a $21 billion child care package.

But providing federally funded day care poses another Catch-22. Although we want to encourage poor women to work, we do not want to provide financial incentives to have children. Therefore, it is essential that parents bear the lion's share of the cost of day care. For the same reason, if society is going to subsidize day care cost at all, it is in the best interests of all not to subsidize the care for more than two children. (Such a restriction would have to be phased in so as not to penalize women who already have more than two children at the time of the law's inception.) Most of the sociologists such as Jenks and Wilson who are strong proponents of increasing federal expenditures for day care completely ignore the potential long-term impact on population growth, especially among the poor.

2. Increase Access to Jobs

The second prerequisite to getting the poor off welfare is the capability to get from the central city to jobs in the suburbs. Increased investment in public transportation to the suburbs would help. A more difficult, but far more effective remedy would be to relocate people to areas where jobs are available. This is not as far-fetched as it may seem. During past periods of tight labor supply, businesspeople have gone to extraordinary lengths to attract and retain labor. During World War II, tire plants in Akron, Ohio, coped with a shortage of labor by recruiting and relocating labor from Appalachia. When AT&T lost many of its telephone operators to better paying defense jobs, it hired women who could barely speak English, and taught intensive English classes. Employers can be remarkably resourceful if they have to be.

A factory owner in Wisconsin complained to me about a lack of available labor. I suggested he had two options: he could relocate his factory in or near an inner city area, or he could pay to relocate inner city minorities to live near his firm. He rejected both options, contending that his managers would quit if he moved to Chicago, and that minorities would not move to take a job in Wisconsin if they could remain on welfare in Illinois.

Maybe the first of these concerns explains why the federal government has not had much success with tax incentives to encourage businesses to relocate to the inner cities. In part, it might be that businesses do not want a minority work force. Moreover, with the availability of immigrant labor they can, for the most part, fill their labor needs without the necessity of moving to the inner cites. Again, reducing immigration would pressure factory owners to recruit and train minority workers.

Offering an opportunity for unemployed inner city residents to relocate to suburban and rural areas would also be advantageous to the poor since it breaks up a dysfunctional culture of poverty. Of course, we might expect the residents of suburbs and rural towns to fight tooth and nail to prevent the construction of low-income housing, through restrictive zoning laws and land use policies. The key is to disperse the poor widely enough so that they don't threaten any given community. Rewarding the towns that permit the necessary housing with federal and state aid for local projects might provide an additional incentive.

Ironically, it is not only the suburban and rural communities who oppose relocating the inner city poor. When the Chicago Housing Authority recommended scattered-site housing, it was the black politicians who opposed tearing down the high-rises. All sorts of spurious arguments were put forth, such as the loss of black identity and culture. The identity of being destitute, powerless, and totally lacking in self-respect? The culture of crime, poverty, and ignorance? It appears that some black politicians were more interested in protecting their electoral base than the welfare of their constituents. If any white person said they thought it was in the best interest of blacks that they stay in their segregated, crime infested ghettos, that person would rightly be called a racist. The very term "ghetto" implied that it was discrimination, not free choice, that trapped blacks in their high-rise slums. Now black politicians argue that it is in the best interest of poor blacks to stay trapped in their ghettos. Who would ever have thought that some black politicians would advocate the same racial policies as the KKK?

One valid concern is that there may not be enough low-cost housing available to replace the high-rise housing being torn down. The answer is for the federal government to provide the poor with housing vouchers equivalent to what is being spent on public housing. If, at the same time, we could strike down discriminatory zoning regulations, the market would make less expensive housing more available in middle-class suburban and rural communities.

William Tucker suggests that we: "Double the number of housing vouchers to the poor. They help twice as many people per dollar as building public housing. Require municipalities that exclude apartments and multifamily homes to compensate property owners, and support the construction of multifamily housing in other communities. Abolish rent control except for national wartime emergencies."[30] Unlike many libertarian proponents, Tucker is not merely advocating an abandonment of the poor to force them to fend for themselves. His recommendations are designed to increase the supply of housing. Adequate supervision must be established in any voucher process to avoid fraud in obtaining vouchers. Fraud is always a potential problem in any government activity from defense spending to issuance of treasury securities.

A more difficult problem is the feasibility of implementing Tuckers's second recommendation. As a practical matter I don't see any way of compensating property owners for the money they lost if they could have sold their property for low-income, multifamily housing. Nor is it necessary to do so. If we can create the conditions where labor is in short supply, businesses will locate in areas that have access to labor. In cases where business is located in rural areas and they wish to attract labor, businesses would fight any building codes that prevent labor from relocating close to the businesses.

In addition to suburban resistance and the concerns of black politicians, there was yet a third obstacle to moving blacks to suburban and rural areas: the misgivings of blacks themselves. As one black newspaper editor told me: "Most blacks are more afraid of moving to a white rural community where they would feel totally estranged, than remaining in their dangerous high-rise ghettos. The only way you could get them to move is in the face of starvation. As long as they can receive some governmental support to stay where they are, they won't budge." In short, in addition to the carrot of available jobs and housing, there must be the stick of ending rent support for those who refuse to take advantage of an opportunity to relocate.

Despite the difficulties and legitimate concerns, it still seems to me that the most feasible way of getting the poor closer to where the jobs are and breaking the culture of poverty, is to tear down the inner city high-rise ghettos and spread the availability of low-income housing throughout the suburban and rural areas. Such a policy would have the additional advantage of infusing the poor with the values of the suburban neighborhoods. My daughter, who was a social worker in both the city and suburban areas, has been struck by the different outlook of inner city and suburban poor blacks. While many inner city blacks feel a sense of hopelessness and are resigned to a life of poverty and crime, low-income blacks located in the suburbs are much more likely to aspire to escape their socioeconomic situation and demonstrate a willingness to work their way out.

In addition to providing transportation or improving proximity to work, it is also necessary to provide information concerning the availability of jobs. I already mentioned the problem of employers deliberately not advertising in certain areas to avoid attracting minorities. I also mentioned the networking of other ethnic groups that provides them with instantaneous knowledge of job openings. If all employers were required to notify state employment agencies of all job openings and hold jobs open a minimum of two weeks, there might be a greater possibility of finding jobs for inner city minority candidates.

Florida has achieved some success in emphasizing job placement over training. Too often training fails to lead to jobs because the wrong skills are taught. Many programs are short term and pay less than the prevailing wage rate for low-wage jobs. Nor do they train people for better-paying jobs. Frequently, they train people for jobs that are not even available.[31] In general, job training has failed to move people off of welfare. Moreover, emphasis on placement is less costly than training. However, here again there must be jobs available. This might require relocation to jobs elsewhere in the country or, only as a last resort, temporary public service jobs.

3. Reduce the Supply of Low-skilled Labor Relative to the Demand

We mentioned that one way to increase wage rates is simply to increase the minimum wage. ***However a far more effective way of increasing wage rates across the board is to reduce population growth and immigration, thus creating tighter labor markets. By allowing market forces to raise the equilibrium between supply and demand for labor (i.e., a reduction in the quantity of labor relative to the demand), wage rates will be bid up.*** However, for such a plan to work we have to avoid increasing the number of poor. ***Under present immigration polices, we will double the number of poor from today's forty million to eighty million or more within the next thirty years.*** At that number the game is over. We begin to resemble an LDC with the most rapidly growing segment of society being the urban poor.

An increase in wage rates for the lowest-paid workers would occur faster if at the same time we temporarily slowed or even reversed the decline in tariffs on imports. As pointed out chapter 7, the notion of trade restrictions is anathema to economists who try an apply Ricardo's theory of comparative advantage to the modern-day international economy. Although the models of comparative advantage also indicate that free trade works to the benefit of both countries, it does not work to the advantage of all workers. We must be careful when using economic models not to be only concerned with the total or even the average impact. If we adopt the perspective of Rawlsian justice as discussed in *The Science of Morality*, we would not support an economic policy that increased the average welfare by exploiting the most disadvantaged group in society.

Economist Alan Blinder's response to this concern is that it would be cheaper to gain the benefit of comparative advantage and then redistribute some of the benefit to the poor. But even if we redistributed the monetary advantages through some form of welfare, this ignores the devastating societal impact of unemployment and underemployment. My position is that it is better to minimize unemployment than to maximize GDP, and it is better to improve the lives of the least favored through jobs rather than welfare. Still, I am not arguing for stiff new tariffs, but a reduction in immigration and no further reduction in tariffs until we absorb the unemployed and increase the minimum wage jobs to a livable level through market forces rather than legislation.

Many economists worry about the inflationary impact of such a policy. However, in the 1950s economists thought that inflation would not become a problem unless unemployment dropped below 4 percent. This was known as the full employment rate. Then, because in the 1970s unemployment rose along with inflation, many economists thought it necessary that the nation accept an unemployment rate of 6 percent to avoid inflationary pressures. This may not sound like much of a difference, but it equates to almost three million workers. Hence, setting the appropriate noninflationary target for unemployment is extremely important.

One reason for raising the goal from 4 to 6 percent is that it took the heat off of Washington to develop policies to ease unemployment. Employers also like higher unemployment rates (as long as they do not get so high as to reduce purchasing power for their products), because it makes hiring easier and reduces pressures on wage rates and, hence, profits. Actually, as explained in Appendix D, the relationship between inflation and unemployment is complex and changes over time. By the end of 1998 the unemployment rate dropped to 4.4 percent with no sign of inflation. My contention is that, with a reasonably constant growth in the money supply equal to the growth in productivity, and with no artificial stimulus caused by a huge increase in federal spending, unemployment can drop to below 4 percent without significant inflation, as it did between 1951 to 1958.

When labor markets get tight, employers will go to extra lengths to hire and train those people who they previously considered incapable of performing satisfactorily. A shortage of labor caused Marriott International, Inc., to create a welfare-to-work program called Pathways to Independence. The program, which runs for 120 days, involves a great deal of nurturing such as driving employees to work, arranging day care, assisting in buying clothes, negotiating with a landlord, and coaching the employee in everything from banking skills to self-respect. The training program does not come cheap. It costs about $5,000 to put a person through the program, of which $2,700 is paid by the federal government. Since it costs $900 to train the average new employee, Marriott comes out ahead if their program keeps a worker 2.5 times longer than average. It has put over 600 people through the program and in New Orleans, where Pathways began. The annual turnover rate has dropped to only 15 percent compared to the overall Marriott turnover of 37 percent.[32]

Lower unemployment, if coupled with reduced availability of welfare, prompts those who have given up looking for work to again seek employment. As word spreads about the availability of jobs, and wage rates increase to the level that makes work more attractive, more and more of the unemployed seek work. The additional income they receive and subsequent increased consumption acts as a further spur to economic growth, which creates still more jobs.

Lower unemployment would be particularly beneficial to blacks who, despite affirmative action, are the last to be hired. When total unemployment in Boston dropped to 3.0 percent during a 1985 military spending boom, black unemployment dropped to 5.6 percent.[33] This is similar to what all of America experienced during World War II and for a decade thereafter. The high demand for labor in relatively high-paying defense industry jobs raised wage rates, while the extremely progressive income tax reduced inequality.

4. Increase Public Infrastructure Expenditures to Reduce Long-term Unemployment

As I said, reducing welfare is easy—just cut benefits. The real trick is to reduce welfare *and* poverty. All of our efforts to achieve this twin goal will be of little avail if there are not enough decent-paying jobs to absorb the low-skilled unemployed. A study in Milwaukee found that there was roughly ***ten times more unemployed people than the number of jobs available.***[34] So how can society create more jobs? Milwaukee is suggesting that combining the various forms of welfare and turning that money over to the cities could provide the funds necessary to provide community service jobs to employ all welfare recipients unable to find jobs in the private sector. In Oregon, a six-month pilot program called Jobs Plus will package the money from AFDC, food stamps, and unemployment compensation and give the funds to private employers to hire welfare recipients and the unemployed. Importantly, workers would retain health and child care coverage and earn at least as much as they did from public assistance.[35] While such a plan sounds more equitable and feasible, it is not without its problems: there is still a significant cost to the taxpayer for health care and child care; it does not discourage women from having additional children; and it doesn't solve the problem of high job turnover among the poor.

Even Milton Friedman admits the potential value of a jobs program such as the Civilian Conservation Corps, but only as a temporary expedient during a depression, not as a permanent solution.[36] The public works programs of the New Deal were specifically designed to be a temporary expediency to avoid the formation of a permanent welfare class. However, ***public works should be used only to attack long-term unemployment in periods of chronic labor surplus, not the short-term unemployment expe-***

rienced during a recession. The use of public works as a means of reducing unemployment during a recession is totally ineffective because it takes too long to plan and fund the projects for the effect to be countercyclical. The average length of a recession is about two years, and it takes at least that long to implement a nationwide jobs program, so it ends up kicking in when the economy is recovering, thus overheating the recovery and possibly creating inflationary pressures.

In effect, we do have one huge permanent jobs program that tends to expand and contract depending on the state of the economy. It is the Interstate Highway System. Economist Hazel Henderson notes that it is the most costly public works project since the pyramids and the Great Wall of China.[37] Earlier, I showed that there was insufficient public infrastructure expenditure to even maintain the existing infrastructure, let alone expand it. Much of the nation's public transportation system, as well as public buildings and other public works, were constructed by the Works Projects Administration (WPA) during the Depression. Public works programs are essential to the economy because they provide needed infrastructure. WPA projects of the 1930s included:

651,000 miles of roads
16,000 miles of water and sewer lines
78,000 bridges
2,300 stadiums
35,000 public buildings
353 airports[38]

Today, a significant portion of this infrastructure needs to be replaced. It is an ideal opportunity to put the unemployed to work. Public service jobs in the 1960s succeeded in helping unskilled and uneducated workers gain valuable work experience and benefit from it. One study showed that the average compensation of those who were hired into public service jobs was 86 percent higher two years after the jobs program than a year before entry into the program.[39]

Despite the value of public service jobs, too often they are simply pork-barrel programs to gain votes with little thought of their eventual, or even temporary, value to the nation. As a means of employing the unemployable on a permanent basis, they will be counterproductive in the long run if they result in permanent civil service jobs. The primary reason is that, without the incentive of a competitive work environment determined by the marketplace, government projects have no inducement to improve efficiency. Anyone who has watched city workers repairing streets knows what I am talking about. ***If the government is going to help reduce unemploy-***

ment through investment in infrastructure, the infrastructure projects must be constructed by private contractors who win the projects through the bidding process. The result would be increased employment, while at the same time bringing the job discipline that can only be generated by a market system.

In addition to providing jobs for adults, it is essential that appropriate job habits be developed in young people. This especially requires the provision of job opportunities for inner city youth. To this end we need to sponsor radically upgraded school-based vocational training linked to craft apprenticeship programs. A Community Service Corps or Youth Conservation Corps should be modeled after the Army's training program. The key is establishing self-discipline and pride.

With the decline in military employment, even more kids need a viable alternative to college. Some of the defense money could be reallocated to vocational training and the Corps programs mentioned above. The Corporation for National and Community Service provides opportunities for 750,000 jobs whereby participants will receive an education award of up to $4,725 per year for up to two years. The money can be used for post-secondary education, approved training, or to pay off education loans.[40] This is a step in the right direction, but it needs to be expanded to provide on-the-job training that is directly applicable to private sector jobs.

One of the key problems in reducing welfare dependence is keeping prior welfare recipients on the job. In the case of Project Match, a job placement program designed to employ AFDC mothers in Chicago, 60 percent of the project's participants lost their first job within six months.[41] As pointed out in *The Science of Morality*, whether people are six or sixty years of age, if we are to create desirable social behavior it is essential that they are forced to live with the consequences of their behavior. An able-bodied person who refuses to work for a living must be allowed to starve. Let me illustrate how necessary this is from my own experience.

Although utilizing many volunteers and a few paid craftsmen on their housing projects, Habitat for Humanity in Chicago also employs some minimum wage, unskilled workers. While working as a volunteer, I was struck by the wide divergence in job performance of the minimum wage workers. Although some of the employees were hardworking and capable, others were lazy, surly, and undependable. Some came to work stoned, drunk, or hung over. The foreman tried a variety of tactics to shape these guys up, but even though it was the middle of winter and losing their jobs meant that they would be literally thrown out onto the street, a few of the incorrigibles seemed not to care. Finally, when all else failed, the foreman had to fire them or else lose the respect and dedication of the other workers, who rightly felt that they had to make up for the idleness of their no-account fellow workers. The lesson I learned is that no matter what approach is utilized, some people cannot be saved. We cannot hope to protect them from their own folly without providing a disincentive to others.

Therefore, any program of welfare reform must include negative consequences for nonperformance. If people fail to perform, they must be dismissed. If loss of job means that a person can no longer care for their children, they must give up custody. The alternative is to teach our children that people need not suffer the consequences of their actions—a prescription for ultimate social dissolution.

The concern that we do not want to punish children for the actions of their parents is valid. But, regrettably, as we have shown, the children of women on welfare are often already suffering. Moreover, by perpetuating a bad system, the numbers just continue to grow. I've listened to some of these permanent welfare mothers describe their plight. Although sympathetic to their suffering, one cannot help but be struck by how incredibly dull-witted many of these people are. It is not just a lack of education; they suffer a serious lack of basic intelligence. They cannot even take care of themselves let alone the needs of their children. Their children would be better off in foster care or an orphanage. Many women are so deficient in basic child care capabilities that to leave children in their care is comparable to exposing the children to a contagious disease. If it were a disease, we would not hesitate to remove the children to protect their heath. We should view conditions of abuse and neglect in the same light. It is one way, albeit a harsh one, of breaking the cycle of poverty.

5. Reduce the Number of Unwed Mothers and Mother-only Families

This is the most difficult, but probably the most important, of all the steps necessary to end poverty. Implementation of all of the previously mentioned recommendations are necessary but not sufficient if we are to significantly reduce the culture of poverty. But the problem of illegitimate children and mother-only families has become so much a part of our culture that it will be extremely difficult to reverse, and will necessitate an attack on several fronts.

Teenage pregnancy in particular is an almost certain prescription not only for the poverty of the mother and her children, but of succeeding generations as well. Not surprisingly, more than half of all AFDC assistance is paid to teenage mothers.[42] Moreover, according to a Government Accounting Office study, "teenage mothers tend to have more children and less education than other women on welfare—and are much poorer."[43] As demonstrated in the last chapter, teenagers as a rule make terrible parents. They are most likely to end up on public aid, and more likely to be guilty of child abuse. "The children of teenage mothers are at greater risk of lower intellectual and academic achievement, social behavior problems, and problems of self-control than are the children of older mothers."[44] Of the 62 children under age fifteen murdered in Chicago in 1993, fifty were born to teenage mothers.[45]

Despite the increase in sexual activity of teenagers beginning in the 1960s, in 1994 births per 1,000 teenage girls were 15 percent lower than in 1960, thanks to the greater availability of contraception and abortion.[46] The birth rates dropped for both white and black teenagers. But in 1994 two-thirds of teenage mothers were unwed, compared to only 20 percent in 1957.[47] Ironically, teenage mothers who marry may end up in even worse shape than those who do not marry. Leaning on a husband, the girls are more likely to drop out of school and get pregnant again.[48] Moreover, years ago teenagers could get fairly well-paying factory jobs. Now they can only get poorly paying service jobs or retailing. So what can be done to substantially reduce teenage pregnancies?

Gary Becker, the Nobel prize winning University of Chicago economist, believes that AFDC recipients would have fewer children if economic incentives were diminished.[49] Becker attempts to show that the demand for children is in large measure a function of the price of children and real income. His econometric model explains why rural families tend to be larger than urban families (farm children contribute to the running of the farm and hence enhance family income), why an increase in the wage rate of working women reduces their fertility (assuming no paid maternity leave, the lost wages due to dropping out of the labor market increase the effective cost of each additional child), and why government programs such as AFDC result in increasing the demand for children and lowering the demand for a husband (AFDC reduces the cost of additional children; and the presence of husbands and males over age sixteen reduce potential welfare benefits).

Yet there is significant evidence that suggests that the relationship between welfare and child bearing is more complex than Becker would leave us to believe. Wilson cites numerous other studies that support the conclusion that women do not have children to get on welfare, or have more children simply because they are on welfare.[50] In the first place, the illegitimacy rates in the South are only slightly lower than in the North, despite AFDC rates at less than half the rest of the country.[51] Secondly, although AFDC benefits adjusted for inflation have fallen steadily since 1975, illegitimacy rates continue to rise.[52] Moreover, women are not primarily on welfare to avoid work. In a survey of fifty welfare mothers in

Chicago, it was discovered that all fifty had other sources of income usually from part-time work (both licit and illicit).[53]

Even though the availability of welfare is not the prime consideration in a woman's decision to have a baby, Jenks and others have shown that welfare does affect women's living arrangements. Without welfare, women are more likely to live with a relative.[54] Surprisingly, income maintenance experiments providing benefits to two-parent families *increased* the likelihood of divorce.[55]

A survey by Melvin Zelnik and Jonathan Kantner indicated that 82 percent of premarital pregnancies were unwanted.[56] The problem is that they were not *sufficiently* unwanted. According to sociologist Kenneth Clark, "In the ghetto, the meaning of the illegitimate child is not ultimate disgrace."[57] ***The increased social acceptability of unwed motherhood is probably the single most important factor leading to the increase in unwed mothers.*** It may have started in the ghetto, but it is growing among all socioeconomic segments of society. For the past two decades, Hollywood appears dedicated to destroying the notion that two-parent families is the desirable social norm. Under the false guise of tolerance, many liberals have been persuaded to embrace the mother-only notion despite the wealth of empirical data showing that mother-only families are far more likely to have problems in child raising.

We can conclude that teenage girls do not get pregnant to get welfare, for the simple reason that most mothers under eighteen are not eligible for public aid. They live with their parents who are working or already on public aid. Nevertheless, sooner or later most of these young women will end up on public aid. Married or not, two-thirds of teenage mothers will have a second child. Moreover, their children must be educated, and the mothers will eventually be eligible for AFDC, food stamps, subsidized housing, and the like. The total bill for taxpayers to subsidize teenage births in 1992 was $34 billion.[58]

In having babies, teenage girls are following their biological instincts. Throughout history, many women became mothers during their teens; they are hormonally conditioned to begin procreation at this age. Hence, to discourage teenage sex and parenthood, society must introduce strong incentives that work against the biological urge to procreate.

It is of interest to note that studies indicate sexual activity among both European and American teens skyrocketed in the last twenty years. However, ***although European teenagers are about as sexually active as American teens, they get pregnant at a only a fraction of the rate.***[59] ***The reason for the difference is that a far greater percentage of European teens use contraception.*** This in turn is due in large measure to sex education and the availability of contraception in Europe. Sweden is a case in point. It offers sex education in schools covering all grade levels and links the schools to clinics that provide birth control to adolescents. Since starting their program, birth rates and abortions have fallen dramatically. By 1991 the teen birth rate in Sweden had fallen to only 20 percent of that of the United States.[60]

The information and availability of contraception in America is still hampered by religious organizations, especially fundamentalists and the Catholic Church. These institutions still operate on the myth that they can turn back the clock on sexual promiscuity and rely solely on moral persuasion to keep teens from having sex. It is an utterly futile notion. But, despite all the evidence to the contrary, the churches persist in their failed polices.

In large measure due to the opposition by religious groups, most schools in this country do not offer contraception or even information about it. For example, in Illinois no suburban schools distribute state-funded birth control, and in 1994 only four schools in Chicago dispensed contraceptives[61] even though ***three quarters of all unintended teenage pregnancies occur to adolescents who do not use contraception.***[62] ***Furthermore, contrary to popular belief, research shows that the availability of contraception does not result in lowering the age of first intercourse.***[63]

There is still an incredible amount of ignorance on the part of American girls with regard to the need for contraception. The churches are focusing on the wrong problem. Sex may not be appropriate for teenagers (especially for kids in their early teens), but the real evil is having babies that the parents are totally unprepared to care for. ***The focus of moral education should be to viscerally instill the conviction that it is morally reprehensible to have sex without contraception, and totally unacceptable to bear a child out of wedlock.***

The use of shame as a negative motivator has been virtually lost in the last two decades. We are so compassionate for unwed mothers that we forget the incredible damage they are doing by bringing a baby into a world of misery. As countries like Japan well know, shame can be a powerful motivator. Teenage pregnancy—or any unwed pregnancy—should therefore be met with strong censure rather than compassion. This no doubt seems harsh to some readers: a return to a time when we blamed the girl for getting pregnant. Of course, both boys and girls should bear the blame. But simply accepting unwed motherhood as a valid "alternative family" has proven to be a disaster.

Although the primary emphasis should be on avoiding pregnancy, teenage sex should be discouraged as well. Young teens should be encouraged to refrain from having sex as long as possible because of the powerful passions it involves and the potential emotional harm that can come when one is not mature enough to deal with it. The average teenage boy is little more than a six-foot putz driven by the huge surge of testosterone. Most teenage girls have all of the instincts but none of the capabilities required for successful mothering in our post-industrial society. However, since it is impossible to ensure that they will refrain from having sex, every child should be given condoms by their thirteenth birthday. It is a cliché to say better safe than sorry, but true nonetheless.

The twin thrusts of encouraging abstinence and providing contraception have proven quite successful in a number of pilot projects in schools across the nation and may be responsible for the decline in teenage births since the early 1990s. These programs also emphasize the difficulties in having and raising a baby. A Planned Parenthood project in Chicago Vocational High School is credited with having cut pregnancies by 64 percent.[64] A Baltimore program combining education and medical programs reduced pregnancy by 38 percent in the schools where it was implemented, while pregnancies citywide went up 30 percent.[65] A California program called "Reducing the Risk" introduced to about a dozen high schools was credited with delaying intercourse and deterring unprotected sex for those students who had not yet been sexually active. However, it had little impact on those who were already sexually active.[66]

Such programs may be having an impact. The illegitimate birth rate fell in 1995 for the first time in two decades. That year marked the second year of decline in teenage birth rates.[67] The reasons for the decline have not yet been established, and it is too early to call it a new trend, but it is cause for optimism.

The key is to start early, in elementary school. The cost/benefit of such programs fully justifies their implementation. For every federal dollar invested in providing contraception, $4.40 is saved in the cost of unplanned pregnancies. A study in California showed that publicly funded family planning saved $7.70 for every dollar invested.[68] Another study by the Center for Population Options showed that more than $13 billion could have been saved in national welfare expenditures if all births to teens had been delayed until women were in their twenties.[69] Yet despite all the evidence, the religious right persuaded the Reagan and Bush administrations to cut funding for contraceptive services by one-third in the 1980s. In 1996, Newt Gingrich tried to gut the entire Title X program, which provides family planning to the poor.

But even programs that encourage abstinence and provide contraception will not be enough to reach many teenage children who are just too dumb, rebellious, or emotionally disturbed to heed the advice. In the Less Developed Countries (LDCs), many women have babies even when they have access to contraception and know that their children will be born into desperate poverty. In many respects, the inner cities of our country are more like the third world than mainstream America. As harsh as it sounds, these are the last people we want having babies. They will make the worst parents and start the vicious cycle of succeeding generations of dysfunctional parents and children.

In trying to persuade unqualified people not to have children, we are bucking an incredibly strong biological and psychological motivation. Therefore, stronger disincentives might need to be employed. Certainly, the Clinton administration's plan to provide two years of cash benefits, education, and training prior to forced enrollment in a work program, would not appear anywhere near strong enough to provide a motivation not to have children. In fact, it might backfire. As columnist Joan Beck points out: "If government pays for training, guarantees a job, and subsidizes it with health care, child care, and transportation to get people off of welfare, wouldn't others be encouraged to take two years off to go on welfare and then get a better deal than those who don't? Wouldn't these benefits give welfare recipients an unfair advantage over the working poor, many of whom are making great efforts and sacrifices to avoid taking government handouts?"[70] This is the concern Murray expresses in his Law of Unintended Rewards: those who are just above some threshold where they receive the benefits will have an incentive to reduce their earnings to the point where they receive those benefits.

To avoid such a possibility, a better policy is one that attacks poverty at its source, by strongly discouraging unwed motherhood and teenage pregnancy. Specifically: ***(1) no girl under the age of eighteen should be allowed to raise a baby. She should be given two choices only: adoption or abortion. (2) Unwed women over the age of eighteen who get pregnant can keep their babies as long as they demonstrate that they can adequately care for them. Otherwise they should lose custody.*** I can hear the hue and cry from the civil libertarians and the religious right at such a suggestion. But there is no Constitutional guarantee that a woman has the right to procreate irrespective of the harm she might do to a child. It is a shame that many organizations care more for the rights (but not the responsibilities) of teenage and other unwed mothers than the rights of a child to receive adequate parental care. Yet even the teenage mother herself would benefit from giving her baby up for adoption. "Unmarried adolescent mothers who place their children up for adoption, when compared to mothers who were single parents, are less likely to live in poverty, more likely to complete high school or be employed twelve months after birth, and more likely to eventually marry."[71]

Today only 3 to 6 percent of unmarried teens give their babies up for adoption. According to the National Council of Adoptions, the number of adoptions has remained steady at about 50,000 per year since 1974, while an estimated one to two million couples or individuals nationwide are seeking to adopt. Unfortunately, there is more difficulty in finding enough families to adopt minority or older children. But even if minority children could be placed, with over one million births to teenagers each year, adoption demand would soon be saturated. On the other hand, the use of orphanages is extraordinarily expensive. Estimates are that it can cost as much as $36,000 annually to adequately house and care for a child. Hence, it would cost $72,000 to care for two children in an orphanage, compared to $8,000 in welfare and food stamps under the present system.[72] Nevertheless, orphanages or foster care are better than leaving a child with an abusive or neglectful parent. Naturally, it would be better still if such people never had a child in the first place. Of course, it may be that most unwed mothers are not guilty of abuse or neglect. Nonetheless, given the high probability of a negative outcome when a child is raised by a teenage mother, society should do all it can to discourage teenage girls from having children. Just as importantly, all unwed women should be strongly discouraged from having children.

Some tentative steps in this direction, such as demanding that women reveal the name of her baby's father and then demanding the father pay child support, do not go far enough. ***Not every woman should have the right to have a baby, but every woman should have the right not to have a baby, i.e., the right to abortion.* Teenagers and unwed mothers should be encouraged to have abortions.*** At present, there are about 400,000 abortions for teenagers each year. With appropriate support and the lack of

---

*The entire abortion debate has been confounded by confusing human life with personhood. The primary characteristic of personhood is self-awareness. Where the courts are getting confused is in considering every fetus as a potential person. Such a statement holds true only in the trivial sense of meaning "a possibility." Every sperm has a possibility of impregnating an ovum. (For that matter, since the discovery of cloning, every cell has the potential to become a person. Does that make every cell sacred?) But such a possibility or potential is relevant only if there is the intention to actually create a future person. Therefore, it would make sense to hold a woman responsible for the care of a fetus if she plans to bring it to term. But if she plans to abort she has no such responsibility. It may be right to punish a woman whose excessive drinking while pregnant results in a child with fetal alcohol syndrome. But if she agrees to an abortion, she has no responsibility to the fetus.

Taking it a step further, a woman who has a seriously damaged a fetus may have a *moral* obligation to undergo an abortion to avoid bringing a child into the world if the child would be condemned to much pain and suffering. Whether or not the woman has a *legal* obligation to have an abortion is a far more difficult question. To avoid the slippery slope regarding governmental control of abortion, my tentative conclusion is that as long as a woman can support her child, society should not have a say in the decision. However, if she is going to ask society to support her child, then society might determine under what conditions it will do so.

Such a cursory treatment of the topic of abortion does not do it justice. For an in-depth analysis, I refer the reader to *The Science of Morality*, chapter 15.

opposition from religious groups this number could double, with a commensurate reduction in misery for future people, their mothers, and society in general. Since the 1973 *Roe* v. *Wade* decision, there have been over forty million abortions, the majority to single women. This represents a tremendous reduction in unwanted children, the vast majority of whom would have been faced with the prospect of miserable lives. Had they survived they would have engendered an even larger number of unhappy people as a result of the ever-growing number of dysfunctional offspring. Abortion is not nearly as desirable a solution to the growth in the number of unwed mothers as contraception, but it is far better for the happiness of present and future people than raising children in poverty.

To encourage teenagers not to get pregnant in the first place, Noel Perrin of the *Washington Post* suggests paying a teenager $500 at age thirteen for not getting pregnant and then raising the payment $100 a year so that by age twenty the incentive would be $1,200.[73] This sounds expensive, but if we were paying all the thirteen to twenty-year-old girls in the nation this amount, the total cost would be about $10 billion a year. When compared to the $34 billion a year presently paid to subsidize teenage births, it appears to be a good investment.

Taking a very different approach, the county prosecutor in the small town of Emmett, Idaho, has used a 1921 law forbidding fornication to prosecute teenagers who get pregnant. It carries with it a maximum penalty of six months in jail and a fine of $300. In practice it has been used to sentence a twenty-five-year old pregnant girl to thirty days in jail and parenting classes. Similarly, the prosecutor has been using the statutory rape law against over-eighteen-year-old boys who get under-eighteen-year-old girls pregnant.[74] Tying such laws to pregnancy is a step in the right direction because it sends a strong message that pregnancy is not an unconditional right, may be morally reprehensible, and under certain conditions, should be illegal. However, rather than go at the situation obliquely through laws regarding fornication or statutory rape, society should simply pass laws making pregnancy illegal when the parents have no means of support, are underage, or are addicted to crack or alcohol; in short, under conditions that will cause permanent harm to a future child.

The studies of Becker and others indicate the size of the family is inversely related to the success of the children because investment per child declines (not only in direct dollars, but in terms of time and energy on the part of the parents). This goes contrary to the conventional wisdom, which hails the virtues of large families. Robert B. Zajonc of the University of Michigan and James V. Higgins have independently found that there is a significant inverse correlation between IQ, SAT scores, and family size. Moreover, even adjusting for IQ, children from large families tend to receive less schooling than children from small families.[75] Becker suggests that the relatively low Jewish birth rate of the last 200 years may have much to do with the greater investment in education for Jewish children and their subsequent success both intellectually and economically.[76]

The nagging question of intelligence and responsible behavior won't go away no matter how hard politically correct liberals try to wish it away. Based upon analysis of the extensive data provided in the National Longitudinal Survey of Youth,* white women were classified in five cognitive categories from very bright to very dull. Only 6 percent of those rated very bright or bright had a illegitimate birth, whereas 49 percent of those rated dull or very dull gave birth to an illegitimate baby.[77]

Education, which is highly correlated with IQ but also has an independent impact as well, is also a significant factor. The illegitimacy rate for black women was 21 percent for college graduates compared to 83 percent for high school dropouts.[78] However, it is important to note that from 1920 to 1960 the percentage of all women having illegitimate children rose only 3 percent (from 3 percent to 6 percent). Contrast this small increase to the epidemic increase in illegitimacy since then: from 6 percent in 1960 to 30 percent by 1995. We cannot blame the increase on lack of education, since average education rose substantially during this period, nor to a decline in intelligence, since average IQ didn't change much. What else could account for the soaring increase in mother-only families?

The Shortage of Marriageable Black Men

According to Charles Murray, it was the availability of welfare. But there were two other key factors. The first, already discussed, was the social acceptability of unwed motherhood. The other factor, as postulated by William Julius Wilson, was a decline in the pool of marriageable black men. As unemployment and underemployment rose among black men, black women had less and less to gain from marriage, irrespective of welfare. Wilson points to the decline in the ratio of employed black men to total black women between 1954 and 1982.[79] I have updated the data for 1996.[80]

*The National Longitudinal Survey of Youth (NLSY) is a large, nationally representative sample of American youths (originally 12,686 people), who were age fourteen to twenty-two when the study began in 1979 and have been followed ever since.

Employed Men per 100 Women

	1954		1982		1996	
Age	*Black*	*White*	*Black*	*White*	*Black*	*White*
20–24	47	50	45	70	52	80
25–34	70	85	60	85	66	91
35–44	73	90	65	85	66	90

Note that the gap widened in every age group between 1954 and 1982. As might be expected with the absorption of the baby boom into the labor force, the ratio has improved for both blacks and whites between 1982 and 1996. Nevertheless, the ratio for blacks in 1996 was still far below the white ratio and, except for those aged twenty to twenty-four, was still worse than 1954.

Even when they have jobs, many black men are not earning enough to adequately support a family. Jenks points out that in 1987, 2.5 million black women between ages twenty-five and sixty-four headed families, but there were fewer than 600,000 unmarried black men in this age range with incomes as high as the average married black man.[81] Although the growing shortage of marriageable men contributed to the declining rate of marriage, Jenks concludes that the increase was not large enough to account for the huge increase in single parenthood.[82] But when we combine all the factors, including high unemployment, low wages, the growth of the drug culture, the social acceptance of illegitimacy, and the availability of welfare, we have a cumulative impact that may be greater than the sum of its parts. At some point, the cycle feeds on itself, producing the culture of poverty we mentioned earlier.

Only a Tough, Comprehensive Solution Will Reduce Welfare and Poverty

With so many negative factors, it would be absurd to think that any single policy could effectively reverse the tailspin. Like waging a war, we need to attack simultaneously on several fronts. To be effective, we need to implement all of the policy recommendations we have discussed in this chapter. Drastic problems call for drastic measures. Hence, in addition to the other policy recommendations we discussed, it is time to eliminate aid to mothers under eighteen, and to make welfare benefits contingent on reducing the rate of illegitimate births. These latter two revisions to welfare reform were passed by the House in 1995, but rejected by the Senate as being too harsh on children. But such policies can work. New Jersey froze AFDC for women with three children (it should have been two children to reduce growth in population) instead of providing them with an extra $64 for each additional child. While such an amount seems trivial, preliminary results show a 19 percent lower birth rate when compared to a control group of women who were not being denied the extra income.[83] Again, it may be that the message of disapprobation that the cutoff sends is more important than the actual dollar amount.

Many other states are following New Jersey's example. Illinois is demanding that to receive welfare benefits, (a) teenage mothers have to live at home and stay in school; (b) able-bodied parents of babies must seek and find work; and (c) no additional cash will be paid to mothers on welfare who have more children.[84] Massachusetts and Virginia have adopted welfare reforms that will provide welfare for up to two years, in which time the welfare recipient must get a job in the private sector. They will provide health care for one year after a person gets a private sector job. (Unfortunately, there are two serious flaws with this proposal: first, the minimum wage is not enough for a family to live on; and second, it penalizes a woman for taking a job by denying her subsidized health care.)

Under the 1996 Welfare Reform Bill, within five years the states were to have 50 percent of their present welfare recipients working at least thirty hours a week. This is going to be extremely difficult, if not impossible, if we continue to follow the present immigration polices. Welfare rolls have been dropping since 1994 due to both economic growth and the time limit placed on receiving welfare—a maximum of five years nationwide and two years in some states, such as Florida. By June 1998, welfare recipients had declined to 8.4 million from the 1994 peak of 14.3 million.[85] Fewer than 4 percent of the U.S. population were on welfare, the lowest percentage since 1970.[86] Still, many of those who obtained jobs were making so little money that they continued to receive some welfare support.

Indiana achieved one of the biggest drops in welfare rolls—a 30 percent decline between 1993 and 1996.[87] In large part it was due to a robust state economy, but it also appears to be a result of welfare reform, which included time limits, job requirements, sanctions for noncompliance, and a cap on benefits to discourage out-of-wedlock births. Of particular importance is the requirement that those women who are able bodied and have children older than three have a two-year limit on cash assistance. Since most jobs pay only $5.00 to $6.00 an hour, and an estimated $9.00 an hour is required to live on, the state is still paying the difference through AFDC. In the long run, increasing wages through tight labor markets is the major precondition for ending this form of supplemental assistance.

Despite the decline in women on welfare, the first study of the effect of the new welfare rules was not encouraging. In Florida, as the two-year deadline was reached, 52 percent of the people subject to the time limits were working compared to 44 percent who would have dropped off the welfare rolls under the old program.[88] There were no horror stories about those who were denied welfare, but the number that obtained and kept full-time jobs was discouraging. Still, it is too early to assess welfare reform. After thirty years of a welfare state, it may take many years to develop the discipline necessary to keep a job. In many cases, employers are dismayed to find that just getting an ex-welfare recipient to regularly show up for a job on time is a struggle.

Thus far I have mainly addressed the problem of women on welfare. But before I am lynched by feminists who will accuse me of placing all the burden on women, let me turn to the problem of irresponsible, deadbeat fathers. Even those women who are married when they have their first child run a high risk that they will be raising that child alone—especially if they are poor and black. In the all-black Wentworth Avenue neighborhood in Chicago, 93 percent of the families with children were headed by a single parent.[89] Even if we are successful in forcing women off of welfare and into the workforce, the low levels of pay for many jobs will not be sufficient to lift many women and their children out of poverty. Hence, the other part of welfare reform has been to go after the fathers for child support. Identifying the father at birth and going after him for child support is useful. It's a little like bringing back the old shotgun marriage. This may work if the father has a job. But what if he is an out-of-work drug user, or serving time in prison as an increasing larger number of men are?* Throwing deadbeat fathers in jail may cause other men to take more care to avoid getting a woman pregnant. However, a father in jail can do little to support his child. This is all the more reason to severely limit the number of unskilled people by reducing the birth rate of poor women and severely limiting the number of immigrants, especially unskilled immigrants.

Do the Poor Have an Inalienable Right to Procreate?

It is sometimes argued that it is only lack of education and job opportunities that result in poor women deciding to have babies. Liberals often

---

*We could enforce vagrancy laws and also bring jobs into prison. We condemn the Chinese for using prison labor to produce manufactured goods at extremely low cost. In the past, American manufacturers had the same complaint against U.S. prison labor. Because of this complaint and the fact that sometimes wardens used prison labor for their own enrichment, the practice was halted in this country. The uncompetitive practices could be addressed by paying prevailing wage rates, deducting an amount for a portion of the cost of the convicts' imprisonment, and reimbursing their victims when appropriate. The use of independent auditors and inspectors could insure the integrity of the system.

choose to deny the fact that many unwed mothers, especially teenagers, are not very intelligent. But irrespective of socioeconomic background, the lower the IQ of a woman, the greater the probability of an illegitimate birth. If a woman has a low IQ and is also poor (a high correlation in itself), the chances of having an illegitimate child soars.[90] Social philosopher Garret Hardin points out that students of poverty often note that many of the poor seem to be deficient in their ability to defer gratification of their desires to a distant (and somewhat uncertain) future.[91] They mindlessly follow their biological motivation. Biologist Galton Darwin warned that if such impulsive women have more children than socially responsible women, natural selection will ensure that their offspring with a similar incapacity for responsible breeding will eventually dominate society. It's a prescription for social disaster. Consequently, it is essential to discourage reproduction among the socially irresponsible. In the area of animal eugenics, scientists have recognized the importance of eliminating bad parent strings: "once you eliminate bad parent strings, you automatically eliminate their offspring, the offspring of their offspring, and so on. . . ,"[92] as well as the harm they do others.

Again I can hear the hue and cry of liberals who will accuse me of promoting Nazi-like eugenics. But I suggest nothing of the kind. I am proposing that people who cannot afford to care for their children adequately have a moral obligation not to have children. It is difficult to know how to legislate what constitutes an adequate capability for child care; it's difficult, but not impossible. We do it even today when we take children out of the homes where they are being seriously abused or neglected.

An Illinois court found a woman guilty of trying to smother her infant son. The judge ordered the woman not to get pregnant for four years in order to stay out of jail. The ACLU and anti-abortion groups rushed to defend the woman. The decision was overthrown by the appellate court because of an Illinois law that forbids judges from ordering women to take contraception.[93] The judge could send the woman to jail to prevent her from having babies, but he could not simply demand that she refrain from bearing children. Where does this unrestricted right to bear children come from? A women has the right of privacy over her own body—the right not to have children. But this right does not imply a concurrent right to bring another person into the world.

We need not go so far as forbidding any woman from having a child. All that I am suggesting is that we end all economic incentives to have babies, and perhaps even provide incentives to people who are not able to financially or psychologically afford a child to refrain from doing so. Moreover, if a woman does have a baby and wants society to support it, then society has some right to determine the conditions under which it will do so. For example, it would be eminently reasonable for society to demand that as long as a woman is receiving social welfare that she accept subdermal implants or some other passive contraceptive means to insure that she has no more children.

In December of 1990, the *Philadelphia Inquirer* made a similar suggestion that welfare mothers be offered incentives to use contraceptive implants. The paper did not propose that any women would be forced to have an implant. However, the suggestion was quickly labeled racist and, unable to take the heat, the paper retracted its editorial.[94] Aside from the mistaken notion that there were more blacks on welfare than whites, those who oppose encouraging contraception among welfare recipients apparently choose to ignore the eventual outcome of most children of welfare mothers. Hiding behind a facade of ill-conceived principles, they ignore the pragmatic considerations to the detriment of those most affected. A woman addicted to crack or who is an alcoholic should be willing to accept a subdermal implant as a condition for receiving any form of welfare, to ensure that she does not have babies born addicted or suffering from fetal-alcohol syndrome.

The Elizabethan Poor Laws of 1601 forbade a man to marry who could not maintain a wife. The purpose was to avoid the suffering of children who would be born into grinding poverty. Today we don't have any laws forbidding people from having children regardless of how deficient or even dangerous they may be as parents. We are so obsessed with individual rights and the dangers of the slippery slope that we are willing to sacrifice the welfare of children to the selfishness and stupidity of some parents. But the slippery slope works both ways. Fear of allowing the government to dictate who may have babies has resulted in permission for anyone to have a baby regardless of their qualifications. The same person who would be denied a driver's license due to mental incompetence or a history of reckless driving will be allowed to have a baby—even subsidized with a tax credit—even though the odds are overwhelming that it will result in a disaster for the child.

Liberals keep pushing for childhood intervention as the answer to the problems of poverty. Unfortunately, no amount of intervention will work when the parents are of very low intelligence or too culturally deprived to be able to reform. Oprah Winfrey decided to personally tackle the problem of poverty by financing a program to move one hundred families out of public housing, off of public aid, and into better lives. But after two years and an expenditure of $1.3 million, only five families completed the program, and even Oprah judged her experiment to be a failure. The reason given was that "the lives of the poor are so chaotic and infused with a 'mind frame of entitlement' that they defy even programs especially designed to overcome these obstacles."[95] As even some liberals are beginning to admit, welfare and intervention will not significantly reduce poverty, and may even make it worse. ***It is time that we attempt to reduce poverty directly by providing the incentives—both positive and negative—to persuade the poor not to have children.*** Rawlsian justice offers the moral justification of such a policy. Children from families earning less than $15,000 are twenty-two times more likely to suffer maltreatment than kids from families making over $30,000.[96] It is in the interest of future generations that they have parents at least minimally qualified to provide for their children's needs.

Many liberals also argue for increased child care services for poor women. They cite a Government Accounting Office study that indicates that three-fourths of the women on welfare would be willing to work if free child care were available.[97] However, they can't afford to leave welfare for work even with a $9.50 an hour job if they have to support three children. There are several major problems with the idea of providing free child care for large numbers of working poor. The first, mentioned earlier, is the shortage of qualified child care providers. In general, child care providers are the poorest paid, and oftentimes the poorest qualified workers in our society. They get paid less than zoo keepers, so it is no wonder that their qualifications are often less than zoo keepers. Yet to try to generate sufficient numbers of highly qualified well-paid child care professionals would result in significantly increased social costs.

The second problem is that free child care would provide an incentive (or at least remove a disincentive) for having children to the people least able to care for them. It is one thing to try to improve the quality of child care, or even to partially subsidize child care for up to two children, in order to get women off of welfare. But recall the free-rider problem discussed in chapter 5. ***Public policies should never permit an individual to reap a benefit while the public absorbs the cost.*** This principle applies to children as well. Parents must expect to bear the costs of having children. Conversely, it cannot be overemphasized that every effort must be made to discourage childbearing by those unable to adequately care for the financial and developmental needs of their children.

We have to balance the personal right to bear children with the moral and legal responsibility for their care. The message must be forcibly brought home: all people must live with the consequences of their actions. It is my hypothesis that two decades of such a policy, coupled with the immigration curbs mentioned above to reduce the labor surplus, would result in a dramatic reduction in unwed mothers, neglected children, and the culture of poverty now so ingrained in the American underclass.

The Role of Marriage in Reducing Poverty

As mentioned in *The Science of Morality*, ***in any relationship between men and women there are three distinct decisions: when to have sex, when to make a long-term and exclusive commitment to each other, and finally when, if ever, to have children.*** These are three distinct and sequential commitments. The primary purpose of marriage is not to sanctify sex as moral theologians contend, but to ensure the optimal child-raising strategy. As Herrnstein and Murray point out, marriage is the legal institution through which rights and responsibilities regarding children are expressed.[98] The belief that marriage is of no particular value in child raising is reflected in the destruction of the family since the 1960s. During the 1950s only 15 percent of the marriages ended in divorce. By the 1960s the number of first marriages ending in divorce soared to 60 percent.[99] Many of these people ended up in a new marriage, but many did not. In addition to unwed mothers, many women who were married were left holding the bag, or more precisely the children, after a divorce. In total, one out of four children today—19 million—are living with mom only.[100] Why the huge increase in the divorce rate?

According to Gary Becker, the increase in wage rates during the Sixties, coupled with the jump in the labor force participation rate for women, allowed them to be more self-sufficient.[101] Initially, higher income women were more likely to obtain a divorce.[102] At the same time, when wives entered the labor force, husbands lost one of the alleged incentives to stay married: the benefit of division of labor, since men were now expected to assume some of the household duties.[103] Additionally, the availability of welfare encouraged women to go it alone while permitting men an excuse to avoid their financial obligations after divorce.[104] Finally, no-fault divorce lowered the cost of divorce in both emotional and financial terms. "No-fault" came to be equated with "no-blame," removing an important disincentive to divorce.[105]

However, viewing the benefits of marriage and the reasons for divorce in strictly economic terms, as Becker does, ignores the many other factors that drive human behavior. Even Becker admits that compatibility is a major factor: marriages are more likely to last when the two people are better matched in terms of education, IQ, religion, income, family background, and the like.[106] Many marriages fail during the first few years because of lack of adequate information before marriage to make informed choices.

Probably one of the most significant reasons for the increase in divorce is that it became socially acceptable, much as being an unwed mother became acceptable. Divorce is no longer considered a mark of failure for either party.

But whatever the reasons for the increase in divorce, there is no doubt that it has had a negative consequence for child raising. Although many women are very successful at raising their children without benefit of a husband, and while an abusive or irresponsible husband can be worse than no husband at all, it is still a far easier and more efficient means of raising a family when the marriage is successful. It is doubtful, however, that any change in federal policy or social attitudes will result in divorce rates returning to the lower levels of the 1950s. So what can be done?

First, the importance of marriage in child raising must be reaffirmed. Just as unwed motherhood must be strongly discouraged, divorce should be made more, not less difficult. Marriage can offer valuable protection both economically and emotionally to women. As mentioned earlier, the number one cause of poverty in this country is single parenting. According to David Popenoe, a Rutgers University sociologist, households with children suffer a 30 percent drop in income after divorce. ***Children of divorces run a two to three times greater chance of dropping out of school, becoming delinquents, having illegitimate children, and getting divorced themselves.***[107] Given the advantage of marriage, waiting periods and counseling should be required before a divorce is granted, unless there is evidence of spousal or child abuse.

Second, waiting periods should be encouraged *prior* to having children. In effect, many couples are selecting this option today by living together prior to getting married. Rather than discouraging such a trend, as many religions do, we *may* want to encourage it. Whether or not living together prior to marriage leads to more durable marriages is an empirical question that requires in-depth study. However, irrespective of whether people live together before they get married, the more important consideration is that they don't rush into child bearing. The motivation for sex is so great that it overwhelms all other considerations. It is only after the initial obsession with sex wears off that two people can decide whether they have enough in common to want to make the permanent commitment necessary for child raising. It is at this point that the decision to have a child should be made.

Therefore, I am recommending a two-tier commitment: the first is the commitment for an exclusive sexual relationship during which time two people can get to know each other, to decide if they are suitably matched so that they can have a reasonable expectation of a long, relatively happy life together. Dissolution of such a commitment should be relatively easy —no-fault divorce with no alimony or palimony involved. The second commitment is a prerequisite to having children should include a legal contract and the traditional marriage ritual. Once children are involved, divorce should be more difficult, involving waiting periods and counseling. The key consideration is to tie the right to bear children with the obligation to maintain a two-parent home if at all feasible.

Summary of Policies to Reduce the Number of Inadequate Parents

In summary, there are several messages that must be viscerally instilled in all people from the earliest age by a variety of means, including education, economic (dis)incentives, and moral sanctions:

1. It is socially and morally reprehensible to have children when they cannot be raised in an environment that includes two parents, financial security, and emotional stability.

2. Men that father children have an obligation for their support. To father a child one cannot adequately support is not a sign of virility, but indicative of stupidity, meanness, and cowardliness.

3. Having babies will generally not improve a young unmarried woman's self-image or happiness. More likely it will rob her of her youth and condemn her to a lifetime of poverty and regret.

4. Every dumb animal can procreate. To be a morally responsible person requires the self-discipline not to have children, unless the prospective parent has attained the education, financial security, and maturity necessary to successfully raise a child.

5. To optimize the chances for successful childraising, marriage should be considered a moral and legal prerequisite for childbearing. Eighteen should be the minimum age for marriage. The state should discourage childbearing outside of marriage by denying welfare to unwed mothers.

6. Children (anyone under age eighteen) should not be permitted to raise children. Girls who get pregnant prior to age eighteen should have only two options—adoption or abortion.

7. Divorce should be made more difficult when children are involved, to discourage capricious divorces and emphasize the seriousness of the commitment to raise children.

We need a public campaign against irresponsible pregnancy as strong or stronger than the campaign against drugs. We need sports heroes like Michael Jordan stressing the values of the two-parent family, and the dissemination of the stories of women who go through the pain and frustration of attempting to raise children in poverty. Unless we can reduce the number of mother-only families, our society will self-destruct.

Homelessness

No discussion of poverty would be complete without addressing the homeless. The number of homeless in America is not known with any degree of certainty. One government report estimates that there are seven million homeless Americans, although the Census Bureau estimates only 600,000.[108] In general, there are three groups of homeless people: the traditional vagrants who cannot or will not hold a job due to alcohol or drug addiction, the working poor who cannot make enough money to provide housing for themselves or their families, and the mentally ill who comprise perhaps 30 to 40 percent of the homeless.[109] The first group we have always had and will always have. The second group, the homeless working poor, is a more recent phenomenon, and will only be changed when a decline in population growth (especially that from immigration) results in a labor shortage that drives up wage rates.

The third group, comprised of the mentally ill, is the result of a poorly conceived public policy. In 1955, there were approximately 559,000 people in public psychiatric hospitals. By 1981 the number had dropped to 122,000, while the number of mentally ill homeless jumped to somewhere between 250,000 to 350,000.[110] The increase was due to government policies predicated on the premise that it was an infringement of the rights of the mentally ill to keep them confined against their will. This was partially the result of the popular myth fostered by books and movies, such as *One Flew Over the Cookoo's Nest*, that the mentally ill were the helpless victims of unscrupulous psychiatrists and psychologists who subjected their patients to oftentimes harmful and inhumane treatment.

There is no doubt that certain treatment has subsequently been found to do more harm then good. This is true of many medical remedies. But the popular notion that psychologists and psychiatrists were gleefully lobotomizing or administering shock therapy indiscriminately is as much a Hollywood myth as the caricature of the mad scientist. (As a matter of fact, shock therapy need not be particularly painful and has proven to be quite helpful in treating certain forms of depression, as people I know personally can testify.) Given the chemical complexity of the human body, it is not surprising that every person reacts somewhat different to a given drug, hence there will always be instances when a certain drug can cause an unfavorable, and in rare occasions, an even fatal reaction. Even aspirin can have that effect.

But the post-1960 radical individualism movement, with its excessive focus on individual rights, resulted in permitting patients to refuse medication even when they are certifiably mentally ill. This presents an interesting paradox. How can we expect severely mentally ill people to know what treatment will be best for them? If at one time society erred in trying to medically treat every eccentricity, today we err on the other side by failing to treat those who cannot possibly care for themselves.

Since the 1970s, unless people posed a danger to society, they were sent to a halfway house. For some mentally ill people the halfway house is indeed a better solution from both a cost and treatment standpoint. There are also many people suffering from mental illness such as schizophrenia and manic depression who can, with the right medical treatment, function successfully outside of an institution. For example, people suffering from schizophrenia have a distorted view of reality that makes them extremely fearful of their environment, especially anything new and different. Contrary to the popular myth, they are far from dangerous and, although the disease is incurable, they can be helped with certain drugs. What these people require is housing, sheltered workshops, and limited supervision to allow them to function with a measure of independence. I served on the board of directors of one such organization whose clients were able to do repetitive tasks quite effectively, and who with help functioned reasonably well outside of a mental institution.

But for many others the halfway house is simply a low cost means of dealing with mental illness. From the halfway house to the street is a short walk that many take. Many of these people should be institutionalized, not because they are a threat to society—few of the mentally ill are—but to protect them from starving, freezing, or being attacked by those who prey on the weak.

A large proportion of homeless who are not suffering from mental illness are drug addicts and ex-cons. In the case of the former, emphasis on rehabilitation should take precedence over criminalization. In the case of the latter, community programs, such as Chicago's Safer Organization that helps ex-cons find jobs, have proven extremely effective. Nevertheless, the sad reality is that there will always be certain people who cannot be salvaged. Even in Japan with its deeply ingrained work ethic there are those who are destitute. We must admit the reality that there are those people who cannot be rescued from their own self-destructive tendencies.

Of greater concern are those who are unemployed or so severely underemployed that they cannot afford even the minimal amenities of life. During recession and times of labor surpluses there is an increase in the number of homeless families who have lost everything with the loss of the primary provider's job. History has shown time and again that economist Arthur Okum's concern for the consequences of an unconstrained marketplace was right.

In attacking the problem of this latter group of homeless, as in other forms of poverty, the first necessity is to reduce the supply of labor relative to the number of jobs, thus reducing unemployment and driving up wage rates. This again speaks to the necessity to reduce immigration, particularly of low-skilled people. The second step is to reduce the birth rate of the poor and, especially, the mentally ill. In the case of the severely mentally ill or retarded, this may mean forced temporary or permanent sterilization, depending upon the severity of the illness and the prognosis of recovery. This goes against the grain of civil libertarians, but they should think more of the life facing a child of a severely retarded mother, especially if the retardation is inheritable. Safeguards of due process can be built in to prevent indiscriminate use of coercive measures.

In addition to increasing employment, the nation's stock of adequate low-income housing must be increased. But, as pointed out earlier, we do not want to expand the failed high-rise projects. Rather, we need to increase scattered site housing. There are two ways of increasing the supply of low-income housing. The first is to build more public housing and employ rent control. This has been tried and must be judged to be a failure. The second is to try to stimulate the marketplace to build more housing through the use of housing vouchers. Expanded use of housing vouchers not only provides greater freedom on the part of the voucher recipient, but reduces the likelihood that a person will squander rent money on alcohol, drugs, or frivolous pursuits.

Summary

A cursory view of the unemployment and income trends since 1960 might easily give a person the impression that Charles Murray is correct in supposing that the Great Society programs, launched by President Johnson and expanded in subsequent administrations, has increased poverty rather than reducing it. However the causes of the growth in unemployment and the culture of poverty is due to a complex interaction of trends in demographics, worldwide economic competition, and a variety of ill-conceived social policies that tacitly weakened the responsibility of both men and women toward their children.

People will act socially and morally responsible only when they are held accountable for their actions. ***Hence it is imperative that all socioeconomic policies are based upon this premise. Hence any form of welfare must emphasize that (a) welfare is never a right, but is a gift from society, and (b) welfare is always a temporary expedient to help people get back on their feet.***

Ending most forms of welfare will not come cheap. It is estimated that the overhead to manage a workfare program will be about $3,400 a person, about the same as AFDC.[111] Putting all welfare recipients to work will also not help the problem of latchkey kids, nor necessarily improve parenting skills. In the final analysis, reducing the birth rate of the poor, especially teenagers, is a much more cost-effective and socially beneficial means of reducing poverty. Equally important, we must seek ways to ensure that those seeking employment have access to the available jobs. This requires economic incentives that encourage either relocation of people to where the jobs are, or the jobs to where the people are.

Instead of implementing the prerequisites mentioned above, some congresspeople propose a radically different approach that can only be characterized as mean spirited. They intend to force the poor to work under conditions that will make them poorer still. In addition to cutting the Earned Income Tax Credit, some conservatives in Congress have proposed to cut Medicaid, child care assistance for low-income families, food stamps, child nutrition programs, energy assistance, and job programs for youth. They also oppose efforts to raise the minimum wage while continuing historically high levels of immigration. Many of the proposed cutbacks are rationalized by the need to reduce the national debt. Yet Congress has no trouble supporting funding of the space station or B-2 bombers that the Defense Department says it neither needs nor wants.

Welfare must be replaced with jobs even if there is no initial governmental savings. To break the cycle of poverty requires that the incentive to work must be far higher than the disincentive. No such incentive exists under the present welfare system. However, if we are to force people to work there must be a sufficient number of jobs available that pay a living wage. This requires a reduction in immigration to eliminate the labor surplus, and the creation of federal and state infrastructure jobs to absorb surplus labor until a labor shortage develops.

Long-term welfare recipients often tend to have many other problems, such as low IQs, that make their success as parents problematic. A number of intervention studies show that parenting skills might be improved somewhat with training and counseling. Such programs might be feasible if we were dealing with a relatively small number of parents. But as the numbers grow, the ability of society to effectively cope with the problem diminishes. We are now in a vicious spiral where the sheer number of inept parents are overwhelming our social services, and the resulting numbers of dysfunctional children are dragging down the children who might otherwise have made it out of poverty.

Michigan provided exactly the wrong incentive when it joined several other states in denying welfare to employable, but childless adults, thus effectively encouraging births.[112] Becker's models clearly indicate that we do not solve the problem of poverty by creating economic incentives for people to have children. Rather, it will require policies and a societal attitude that strongly discourages unwed women from having children. Social policy must also foster greater responsibility among men both for avoiding unwanted pregnancies, and for providing for any children that result from their actions.

It also means an expanded role for sex education starting at a very early age, with particular emphasis on the psychological and ethical dimensions of sexual involvement, and the availability of contraception and abortion to teenagers. In effect, our polices must state: ***"People should not have children they cannot afford to adequately raise. They cannot expect help from the government, except in emergency circumstances and only then on a very short-term basis. If they cannot adequately care for their children, children will be removed from their custody."*** This policy is in keeping with the principle that public polices generally should seek to avoid an outcome where certain individuals receive a benefit for actions that generate a cost to be covered for society as a whole. It also emphasizes that a person must forego a right if they cannot fulfill the corresponding responsibility.

Notes

1. Charles Murray, *Losing Ground* (New York: Basic Books, 1984), pp. 8, 14.

2. Eleanor Baugher and Leatha Lamison-White, *Poverty in the United States: 1995*, Current Population Reports, Series P-60, Consumer Income, no. 194 (Washington, D.C.: U.S. Government Printing Office, 1996), table C–1, p. C–2.

3. U.S. Bureau of the Census, *Statistical Abstract of the United States, 1993* (Washington, D.C.: U.S. Government Printing Office, 1993), table 735, p. 469.

4. Milton Friedman, *Free to Choose* (New York: Avon Publishing, 1981), p. 87.

5. U.S. Office of Management and Budget, *Budget of the United States Government, Historical tables, Fiscal Year 1995* (Washington, D.C.: U.S. Government Printing Office, 1995), table 11.3, pp. 172, 176.

6. Murray, *Losing Ground*, pp. 57–66

7. Ibid., p. 62

8. *Budget of the United States Government, Fiscal Year 1996*, p. 26.

9. Ibid., p. 26.

10. Murray, *Losing Ground*, p. 211.

11. Ibid., p. 212.

12. Ibid., p. 217.

13. Leonard Goodwin, *Do the Poor Want to Work?* (Washington, D.C.: Brookings Institution, 1972)

14. Rogers Worthingham, "Milwaukee Program Could Provide Antidotes for a National Malady," *Chicago Tribune*, March 20, 1994, sec. 4, p. 1.

15. For example, AFDC and food stamps for a family of four adjusted for inflation fell from $577 in 1972 to $495 in 1980. House Committee on Ways and Means, "Background Material and Data on Programs within the Jurisdiction of the Committee on Ways and Means" (Washington, D.C.: U.S. Government Printing Office, 1985). Cited by Jenks, *Rethinking Public Policy: Race Poverty and*

the Underclass, p. 79. By 1984 the combined payments were only 4 percent higher than 1960 levels and 24 percent lower than 1972. Sheldon Dawzinger and Peter Gottschalk, "The Poverty of Losing Ground," *Challenge* (May/June 1985): 36.

16. Murray, *Losing Ground*, p. 228.

17. Robert Lekachman, *Greed Is Not Enough: Reagonomics* (New York: Pantheon Books, 1982), p. 4.

18. Stephen Franklin, "Prospects a Bit Brighter for a Minimum-wage Rise," *Chicago Tribune*, January 21, 1999, sec. 3, p. 1.

19. Jenks, *Rethinking Social Policy*, p. 167.

20. *Chicago Tribune*, September 20, 1995, sec. 1, p. 8.

21. Richard Freeman and Harry Holzer, "Young Blacks and Jobs: What We Know," *Public Interest* (Winter 1985): 18–31. Cited by Jenks, *Rethinking Social Policy*, p.127.

22. Ronald E. Yates, "Small Firms Struggling With Minimum Wage Hike," *Chicago Tribune*, January 13, 1997, sec. 1, p. 8.

23. Ibid. p. A2.

24. Janet L. Yellen, "Trends in Income Inequality," in *The Inequality Paradox: Growth of Income Disparity*, eds. James A. Auerbach and Richard S. Belous (Washington, D.C.: National Policy Association, 1998), p. 14. Also Mark Weisbrot reports a study by the Economic Policy Institute used four different statistical methods to look for job loss following the 1996–97 increase, but found none. "Penny Pincher: The Stinginess of America," *Chicago Tribune*, July 7, 1998, sec. 1, p. 13.

25. John McCrone, "Why We Shouldn't Be Afraid of Raising the Minimum Wage," *Chicago Tribune*, February 23, 1998, sec. 1, p. 15.

26. Freeman, "Is the New Income Inequality the Achilles Heel of the American Economy?" in *The Inequality Paradox*, eds. Auerbach and Belous, p. 222.

27. R. C. Longworth, "Higher Wages Don't Necessarily Cost Jobs," *Chicago Tribune*, August 21, 1996, sec. 1, p. 16.

28. Ibid.

29. "Cost, Quality, and Child Care Outcomes in Child Care Centers," January 1995, Oakton Community College presentation, March 7, 1995.

30. William Tucker, *The Excluded Americans: Homelessness and Housing Policies* (Washington, D.C.: Regnery Gateway, 1990). Cited by *Future Survey* (November 1990): 8.

31. Elliott Currie, *Confronting Crime* (New York, Pantheon Books, 1985), p. 139.

32. Dana Milbank, "Hiring Welfare People, Hotel Chain Finds, Is Tough But Rewarding," *Wall Street Journal*, October 31, 1996, pp. A1 and A14.

33. Jenks, *Rethinking Social Policy*, p. 125.

34. Rogers Worthington, "The Welfare Challenge," *Chicago Tribune*, March 20, 1994, sec. 4, pp. 1–2.

35. Ibid.

36. William Julius Wilson, *The Truly Disadvantaged: The Inner City, the Underclass, and Poverty* (Chicago: University of Chicago Press, 1987), p. 119.

37. Hazel Henderson, *Creating Alternative Futures: The End of Economics* (New York: Perigee Books, 1978), p. 279.

38. Sar A. Louitan, "Does Public Job Creation Offer Any Hope?" *The Conference Board Report* (August 1975): 58ff.

39. Ibid.

40. U.S. Office of Management and Budget, *Budget of the United States Government, 1995*, p. 108.

41. Rogers Worthington, "The Welfare Challenge," *Chicago Tribune*, March 20, 1994, sec. 4, pp. 1–2.

42. Kristin Moore and Steven B. Caldwell, "Out of Wedlock Pregnancy and Childbearing," Working Paper No. 999–02 (Washington, D.C.: Urban Institute, 1976). Cited by Wilson, *The Truly Disadvantaged*, p. 29.

43. *Chicago Tribune*, June 2, 1994, sec. 1, p. 5.

44. V. Dion Haynes, "Providing a Safety Net Can Prevent a Lifelong Fall," *Chicago Tribune*, May 25, 1994, sec. 1, p. 14.

45. Colin McMahon, "Babies Born into Peril," *Chicago Tribune*, May 22, 1994, sec. 1, p. 1.

46. U.S. Bureau of the Census, *Statistical Abstract of the United States, 1991*, table 84, p. 63, and *Statistical Abstract, 1997*, table 90, p. 75.

47. McMahon, "Babies Born into Peril," p. 1.

48. Ibid., p. 17.

49. Gary Becker, *A Treatise on Families* (Cambridge, Mass.: Harvard University Press, 1991), pp. 135–54.

50. Wilson, *The Truly Disadvantaged*, pp. 78–79.

51. D. E. Vining Jr., "Illegitimacy and Public Policy," *Population and Development Review* (September 1983): 105–110.

52. P. Cutright, "Illegitimacy and Income Supplements," David T. Ellwood and Mary Jo Bane, "The Impact of AFDC on Family Structure and Living Arrangements," prepared for the U.S. Department of Health and Human Services under grant no. 92A-82, 1984. Cited by Wilson, *The Truly Disadvantaged*, p. 78.

53. Jenks, *Rethinking Social Policy*, p. 206.

54. Ibid., p. 83.

55. Wilson, *The Truly Disadvantaged*, p. 80.

56. M. Zelnik and Jonathan N. Kantner, "Sexual Activity, Contraception Use, and Pregnancy Among Metropolitan Area Teenagers 1971–1979," *Family Planning Perspectives* (December 1980): 230–37.

57. Kenneth B. Clark, *Dark Ghetto: Dilemmas of Social Power* (New York: Harper Row, 1965), p. 32. Cited by Wilson, *The Truly Disadvantaged*, p. 73.

58. McMahon, "Babies Born Into Peril," p. 17.

59. Colin McMahon and Carol Jouzaitis "Taboos Leave Many Teens Unprotected," *Chicago Tribune*, May 24, 1994, sec. 1. p. 14.

60. Ibid.

61. Ibid.

62. Ibid.

63. McMahon, "Babies Born into Peril," p. 17.

64. Ellen Warren, "To Solve Problem, We Must Face It," *Chicago Tribune*, May 26, 1994, sec. 1, p. 28.

65. Ibid.

66. Ibid.

67. Data from Centers for Disease Control and Prevention, "Out of Wedlock Birth Rate in U.S. Declines for 1st Time in 2 Decades," *Chicago Tribune*, October 10, 1996, sec. 1, p. 3.

68. Warren, "To Solve Problem, We Must Face It," *Chicago Tribune*, sec. 1, p. 28.

69. Ibid.

70. Joan Beck, "Still Too Many Questions on Welfare Reform," *Chicago Tribune*, June 9, 1994, sec. 1, p. 31.

71. V. Dion Haynes, "Providing a Safety Net Can Prevent a Lifelong Fall," p. 14.

72. Amitai Etzioni, "Cruelty to Kids," *Chicago Tribune*, December 1, 1994, sec. 1, p. 31.

73. Noel Perrin, *The Washington Post*, July 8, 1990. Cited by *Future Survey* (January 1991): 8.

74. Quentin Hardy, "Idaho County Tests New Way to Curb Teen Sex: Prosecute," *Wall Street Journal*, July 8, 1996, pp. A1, A6.

75. J. Greenberg, "Family Size Tied to SAT, IQ Scores," *Science News* 127 (June 1, 1985): 340.

76. Becker, *A Treatise on Families*, p. 147.

77. Richard J. Herrnstein and Charles Murray, *The Bell Curve: Intelligence and Class Structure in American Life* (New York: Free Press, 1994), p. 181.

78. Jenks, *Rethinking Social Policy*, p. 194.

79. Wilson, *The Truly Disadvantaged*, pp. 84–89.

80. U.S. Bureau of the Census, *Statistical Abstract of the United States, 1997*, table 21, p. 21, and table 633, p. 405.

81. Jenks, *Rethinking Social Policy*, p. 32.

82. Ibid., p. 133.

83. Mike Doring, "Welfare Cap on Families Shows Signs of Success," *Chicago Tribune*, March 12, 1995, sec. 1, pp. 1, 14.

84. *Chicago Tribune*, February 17, 1995, p. 1.

85. Associated Press, "L.A.'s Welfare to Work Project Hailed," *Chicago Tribune*, August 20, 1998, sec. 1, p. 21.

86. "Welfare Roles Are Smallest in 28 years," *Chicago Tribune*, January 21, 1998, sec. 1, p. 8.

87. Carol Jouzaitis, "In Indiana's Welfare Plan 'Work Works'," *Chicago Tribune*, June 17, 1996, sec. 1, p. 1.

88. Associated Press, "Cities Welfare Time Limits Did Little to Reduce Rolls," *Chicago Tribune*, March 24, 1998, sec. 1, p. 4.

89. *Chicago Housing Authority Statistical Report, 1983* (Chicago: Chicago Housing Authority Executive Office, 1984). Cited by Wilson, *The Truly Disadvantaged*, p. 25.

90. Herrnstein and Murray, *The Bell Curve*, pp. 185–88.

91. Garrett Hardin, *Living Within Limits: Ecology, Economics, and Population Taboos* (New York: Oxford University Press, 1993), p. 115, ref.

92. SRI International, *Scan* (July 1992): 2–4.

93. Janan Hanna, "Judge's No Pregnancy Order Made News But Ignored Rights," *Chicago Tribune*, sec. 2, p. 5.

94. Jonathan Rauch, *Kindly Inquisitors* (Chicago: University of Chicago Press, 1993), p. 22.

95. Louise Kiernan, "Oprah's Poverty Program Stalls," *Chicago Tribune*, August 27, 1996, sec. 1, pp. 1, 16.

96. Reported in a 1996 study by the Department of Health and Human Services, Associated Press, *Chicago Tribune*, September 10, 1996, sec. 1, p. 25.

97. Laurie Abraham, *Chicago Tribune*, September 23, 1994. sec. 1, pp. 1, 14.

98. Herrnstein and Murray, *The Bell Curve*, p. 545.

99. Becker, *A Treatise on Families*, p. 1.

100. Carol Jouzaitis, "Study Finds 25% of U.S. Kids Live with Mom Only," *Chicago Tribune*, April 24, 1995, sec. 1, p.1.

101. Becker, *A Treatise on Families*, p. 354

102. Ibid., p. 336.

103. Ibid., p. 55.

104. Ibid., p. 335.

105. Diana Milbank, "No-Fault Divorce Law Assailed in Michigan and Debate Heats Up," *Wall Street Journal*, January 7, 1996, p. A–1.

106. Becker, *A Treatise on Families*, pp. 327–28.

107. Milbank, "No Fault Divorce Law Assailed in Michigan and Debate Heats Up," p. A–1.

108. *Wall Street Journal*, May 18, 1994, p. 1, col. 3.

109. *Future Survey* (November 1990): 8

110. Charles E. King, "Homeless in America," *The Humanist* (May 1989): 8.

111. Douglas J. Besharov, "That Other Clinton Promise—Ending Welfare as We Know It," *Wall Street Journal*, January 18, 1993. Reprinted in *AEI*, no. 4 (1993).

112. Vern and Bonnie Bullough, "Is the Family in Crisis?" *Free Inquiry* (Fall 1992): 7.

10

Meaningful Education Reform

The Problem

At first glance the educational system in the United States does not appear as bad as its critics contend. The proportion of the population twenty-five to twenty-nine years of age who have graduated from high school has increased steadily for over fifty years. This is especially true for blacks, as figure 10.1 shows.

Figure 10.1[1]
Percentage of People Graduated from High School

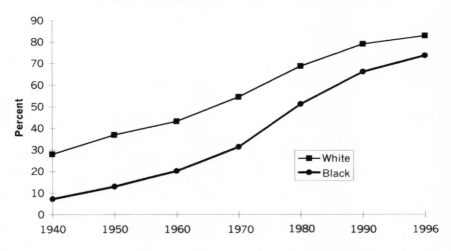

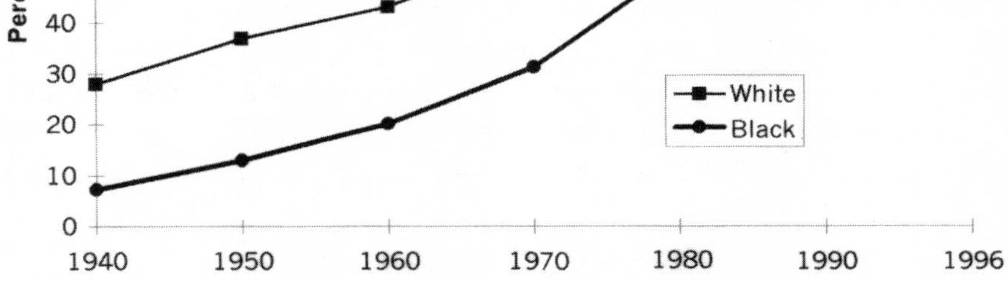

In the course of the past fifty years the proportion of blacks graduating from high school has soared from 7 percent in 1940 to 74 percent by 1996, only 8 percent less than the proportion of whites. The percentages completing high school would be even higher for both whites and blacks if we looked only at younger people, because years ago the dropout rate was higher. The high school dropout rate was at an all time low in 1990 before it increased slightly. In 1995, the dropout rates were 13.6 percent for whites, 14.4 percent for blacks, while Hispanics showed a distressing rate of 34.7 percent.[2] In at least one respect the education of those remaining in school has improved as well. In 1971, 18 percent of black and 2 percent of white seventeen-year-olds still in school could not read at what the National Assessment of Educational Progress determined was a basic level. A teenager who cannot read at this level comes close to being an illiterate in the traditional sense of the word. By 1988 all but 2.9 percent of blacks and 0.5 percent of whites could read at the basic level.[3]

During the past four decades there was an equally impressive growth in the number of students entering college. Between 1955 and 1995, enrollments in public colleges rose from 1.4 million to 11.1 million students, more than a sevenfold increase. By 1996, 24 percent of all people over the age of twenty-five had completed four years of college, compared to only 6.0 percent in 1940. The proportion of blacks with four years of college rose even faster, from only 1.6 percent in 1940 to 13.6 percent in 1996.[4] Still, in 1996 the college graduation rate for blacks was only about half the rate of whites.

Percentage Over Age 25 Who Completed Four Years of College or More[5]

	White	*Black*	*Hispanic*
1960	8.1	3.1	NA
1980	17.1	8.4	7.6
1996	24.3	13.6	9.3

Despite these impressive statistics, there is the underlying worry that in our effort to push more minorities through high school and college, schools have lowered their standards. In the 1970s, many inner-city public schools switched to an automatic pass system.* The results were predictable: many students advanced without learning basic skills. Moreover,

*The automatic pass system advanced students from grade to grade regardless of their performance, hence graduating from elementary school or high school was no indication of what knowledge or skills a student had learned. By 1996, Chicago and some other cities reversed this ill-conceived policy.

the policy that was designed to prevent dropouts did not have the desired effect. One study that tracked 25,000 black and Hispanic students from ninth grade found that only 9,500 graduated and of these only 2,000 could read at or above the national average.[6]

The decline in scores on college entrance exams has also promoted concern. From 1967 until 1980 verbal SAT scores dropped from an average of 543 to 502, then remained almost constant; the 1996 average was 505. Math scores did not drop as much, declining from 516 in 1967 to 492 in 1980, and then rebounding slightly to 508 in 1996.[7]* ACT composite scores reflect a more encouraging trend: after declining from 19.9 in 1967 to 18.5 in 1980, the scores rose significantly to 20.9 by 1996.[8]

International comparisons also indicate that the United States has cause to worry. Of the twenty-one countries participating in the Third International Math and Science Study, U.S. twelfth graders only scored ahead of Cyprus and South Africa. Among the top 10 percent to 20 percent of each country's participants, Americans scored second from the bottom in math and dead last in science.[9]† Part of the reason wasn't hard to discover. Our high school students tend to spurn advanced math and science. Even worse, many of the high school teachers are not qualified to teach these subjects. According to Education Secretary Richard Riley, 28 percent of high school math teachers, 18 percent of science teachers, and nearly half of all physics teachers have neither a college major nor minor in those subjects.[10] The reason for the shortage of teachers in these areas can be laid right at the feet of the teachers union, as we shall see.

The persistently low results with regard to verbal scores are particularly depressing in light of our efforts to combat the decline. Between 1960 and 1995 the average student-to-teacher ratio was forced down from 26.3 to only 17.[11] Education expenditures were increased by over 50 percent in constant dollars between 1980 and 1995[12] but failed to improve test scores. In 1992 the United States devoted a greater proportion of its GDP

---

*In 1995, SAT scores rose significantly, but since the test was changed it is debatable whether the change represents a real improvement in learning or just an easier test. Comparison of present test scores with past trends is further complicated by "recentering," the process by which 75 points were added to the verbal score and 25 points to the math score. The historical scores mentioned above have all been recentered to provide some continuity of the series.

†As further evidence of the sorry state of science in America, a poll conducted by the National Opinion Research Center in 1994 indicated that 23 percent of Americans reject the idea of human evolution and another one-third are undecided. See Edward O. Wilson, *Consilience* (New York: Alfred A. Knopf, 1998), p. 129. There are few theories in science backed by more conclusive evidence than evolution, yet Americans appear to be reverting to a level of scientific ignorance prevalent at the time of the infamous Scopes trial.

to education than any other industrialized country except Switzerland.[13] On a per student basis (using purchasing power parities), the United States leads the world for both K through 12 and for higher education, as figure 10.2 shows.

Figure 10.2[14]
Educational Expenditures per Student (1992)

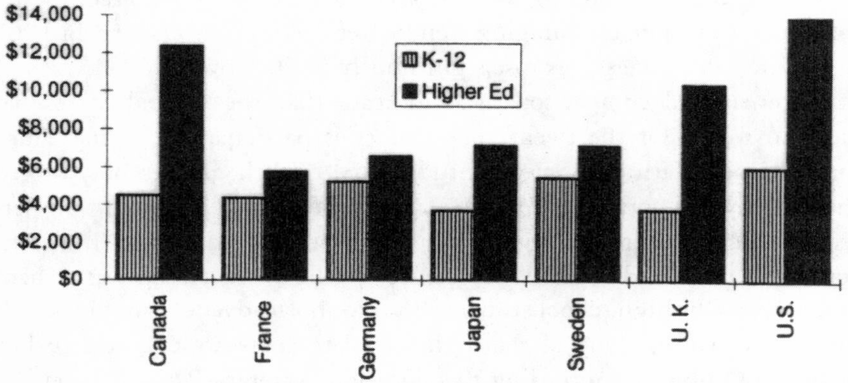

One reason for the drop in the SAT scores was the larger proportion of high school seniors taking the tests. Obviously, if more of the less qualified students take the SATs, the average score should be expected to decline. Another major cause of the decline of average test scores, and the one people are most loath to discuss for fear of being labeled a racist, is the changing racial mix of those taking the tests. In 1960 the high school population was 12 percent nonwhite,* but by 1991 the percentage of nonwhite students rose to 22 percent. During the 1960 to 1991 period the number of white students rose about 14 percent (from 9.0 million to 10.3 million) but during this same period the number of nonwhite students rose 130 percent (from 1.2 million to 2.8 million).[15] Most of this increase occurred in the 1960 to 1980 period when test scores were dropping. The increase in nonwhites slowed significantly between 1980 and 1990 and the decline in average test scores stopped.

However, the averages obscure the impact of the growing number of immigrants. Almost 85 percent of today's immigrants are Hispanics or Asians. Vernon Briggs observes that immigrants have a bimodal distribution in terms of education. Although a higher proportion of immigrants

*Nonwhites include Blacks, Asians, Native Americans, and others; however, the vast majority of this category is comprised of blacks.

have graduate degrees than native-born Americans (3.8 percent and 2.4 percent respectively), and immigrants have about the same proportion of college degrees, about 40 percent of immigrants had less than a ninth grade education.[16] Since children's education performance reflects in large measure that of their parents, it is not surprising that the children of Asian immigrants tend to be high performers while Hispanic children have a school dropout rate exceeding that of blacks.

In the previous chapter we noted that blacks and Hispanics are on average more environmentally deprived than whites, are far more likely than white children to live in households with a female head, and often attend schools with poorer facilities and less qualified teachers. Therefore, it is not racist to conclude that if the population of disadvantaged youth is growing faster than the total population, we would expect achievement results to decline.

To make matters worse, there is ample evidence to show that colleges lowered their admissions standards beginning in the late 1960s to accommodate minorities. A review of SAT data for twenty-six of the top universities reveal that by 1991 the median difference between white and black SAT scores was 180 points or 1.3 standard deviations.[17] The 1960s was also the era when student activism, which initially opposed genuinely racist policies on the part of many colleges, attempted to dictate course curricula and standards. Too often college administrators capitulated. Core curricula got decimated and grading was often replaced with a system of pass/fail, where failure was considered more the fault of the professor than the student. Where grades were still given, grade inflation often occurred both to keep students from failing and getting shipped to Vietnam, and to reduce the dropout rate of blacks. Students soon felt that they had a right to high grades. Professors were afraid of being criticized or even sued for racial discrimination for giving low grades to minority students.[18] Stanford University issued no failing grades for twenty-five years and abandoned the bell-shaped curve for grading. An amazing 91 percent of all grades were As and Bs (99 percent in the Education Department, of which 81 percent were As). Stanford finally reinstated the concept of failing in June of 1994. At Brown University there are no Ds or Fs as a matter of school policy.[19] Although these universities might be exceptional, there has been such general grade inflation that many employers now view a college degree as substantially devalued and grade point averages as almost meaningless. Grade inflation might also explain why a 1996 report by a national panel found more than 25 percent of U.S. teachers were underqualified.[20]

Falling academic standards were accompanied by a general disenchantment on the part of many blacks with the value of education. In addition to growing competition for jobs due to the baby boom and corporate downsizing, blacks also had to compete with an increasing number of women entering the labor market to take advantage of the opportunities offered by affirmative action. Moreover, most of the women were from typical white backgrounds, and hence more affluent and environmentally advantaged than black males. Even the traditional blue-collar jobs were being taken by women, and therefore black males faced more competition for jobs than white men did prior to the advent of civil rights. As discussed earlier, affirmative action, whose original intent was to overcome past racial discrimination, degenerated into a new form of discrimination which as presently construed is working against the interests of the very group of people it was supposed to help. Designed initially to help blacks overcome the effects of 400 years of slavery and discrimination, affirmative action eventually threw its net so wide that 80 percent of all new immigrants—who have no claim to past discrimination—qualified under the affirmative action umbrella.

Coupled with this trend was the flight of jobs from cities to the suburbs, and also from northern cites to the centers of defense spending in the Southwest and West. Disillusioned with the lack of opportunity, many blacks found that selling drugs rather than succeeding in school was a more certain path to wealth. More common than selling drugs was using drugs as a means of escaping the reality of their plight.

Another disincentive for those at the bottom of the socioeconomic ladder, both black and white, was a welfare system that at one time paid more for a man to leave his family then it did if he stayed. As long as the man's income could disqualify a woman from receiving welfare, it was more economically reasonable for a man to leave—or at least for the woman to allege that he was gone. (However, as we will see in the next chapter, this was only one of a dozen factors resulting in the breakdown of the black family.) The result was a further weakening of the family structure for both poor whites and blacks. With absent fathers and working mothers, there was a general breakdown in discipline, whether it pertained to doing homework or just keeping out of trouble. The lack of discipline at home was compounded by law suits which threatened any teacher who dared to physically discipline children in school. The inability to either effectively discipline or expel any student no matter how unruly, or to enforce academic standards, resulted in many inner-city classrooms degenerating into near anarchy.

Psychologist Richard Herrnstein and political scientist Charles Murray dispute the impact of changing demographics on average student performance, citing the fact that whites show the same decline in test scores as blacks, and have also not improved on the verbal test scores.[21] They admit, however, that there was a generally "dumbing down" of verbal material in the public educational system, partially in response to the desire to avoid flunking more black students.[22] To make it easier for minority students to pass, many schools lowered standards for all students. Moreover, students spend a fraction of the time on homework compared to thirty years ago. So what we see happening may not be directly due to changing demographics (although the results of the IQ analysis that Herrnstein and Murray report would strongly support that demographics played a major role), but may be more subtly due to the desire to graduate more minority students at any cost. Furthermore, Murray and Herrnstein's data includes Hispanics with whites, although the academic results of Hispanics more closely approximate those of blacks.

An article in the *Chicago Tribune* illustrated the sad state of education in Chicago. Two girls who always made above-average grades throughout high school and were considered good students, flunked the admissions test to a local community college. It was learned that they read at sixth-grade level.[23] This is all too common an experience with inner-city schools, where the primary goal is to keep kids in school at all costs. ***If the standards required to get a high school diploma (or college degree) were the same today as in 1960 there might well be 20 percent fewer high school graduates (about the 1960 level), but they would be better prepared and the average SAT test results would be far higher.***[24]

Perhaps even more distressing is the attitude on the part of many educators that excelling in school should not be the major objective of education. This reflects the anti-intellectual line of the radical left in the 1960s, many of whom subsequently invaded and have eventually taken over many schools and universities. Several of the new gurus of education are proposing the primary purpose of education should be to build self-esteem, not excellence in academics. Charles Willie, a professor of education at Harvard, believes that schools should be concerned with students attaining mere academic adequacy rather than excellence, and should weigh nontraditional types of "intelligence" such as singing and dancing as heavily as communications.[25] Alfie Kohn, author of *Punished by Rewards: The Trouble with Gold Stars, Incentive Plans, A's, Praise, and Other Bribes* wants to do away with all grades.[26] Peggy McIntosh of Wellesley College believes that excellence is a dangerous concept and reflects an outmoded white male culture of "vertical thinking" (whatever that is).[27] This is all reminiscent of the 1960s view that children must never be allowed to fail. In 1969, William Glasser wrote *Schools without Failure*, in which he argued that during the first six years of schooling no child should ever be failed regardless of their efforts or their skills.[28] This spawned the so-called free schools and organic learning experiments that almost inevitably were failures. Caught up in the spirit of the time and seductive logic of the new thinking, my wife and I sent one of our own children to such a school for a couple of years. By any standard, it was an unmitigated disaster. Most of the children, although brighter than average in terms of IQ, fell behind their peers who attended the Evanston public schools. The lack of structure not only failed in teaching the basic three Rs, but also resulted in a notable loss of self-discipline, as well as an unhealthy increase in egoism due, I believe, to an environment that emphasized individual rights while almost ignoring responsibilities.

Despite a lack of any sound empirical foundation for their theories, many schools are experimenting with a variety of techniques that seem bound to level academics to the lowest common denominator. In Fairfax County, Virginia, seven high schools have decided to dump class rankings. Los Angeles schools abolished the grade of "Outstanding." "Satisfactory" became the highest grade, followed by "Growth" and "Needs Improvement." Other schools are dropping the practice of grouping students according to ability for fear that those in the lower groupings will feel bad despite evidence that students had higher self-esteem in classes designed to work at their pace and compete with students of similar capabilities.[29] But empirical findings are of no concern to liberal educators preaching the new religion of academic egalitarianism. Loyd Hastings, a principal from Texas, contends that "The ability grouping of students for educational opportunity in a democratic society is ethically unacceptable."[30] Why? I always thought that democracy had to do with the right to vote, a system of government. When did egalitarianism become a synonym for democracy? When did the American Dream get transformed from the right to pursue happiness to a guarantee of equal results?

As was demonstrated in *The Science of Morality*, separating consequences from actions is always a prescription for disaster. Any effort to force equality of outcome is implicitly based upon the premise that if we can't raise the worst students to the highest levels, we can damn well drag the best students down to the lowest level.

Grades are a measure of relative performance. They provide information to parents and students as to how well they have performed relative to their peers in regard to academic achievement. If parents mistakenly use this information as somehow an indicator of a student's personal worth or potential, it is the parents who need to be educated as to the function of grades. If used correctly, grades, along with measures of intelligence, can tell the parents if the child requires additional tutoring, is working up to his or her potential, or may have other psychological problems that could be interfering with performance. A child who simply does not have the cognitive ability to achieve top grades may be offered many other areas to demonstrate high achievement: arts, sports, crafts, or other forms of physical work requiring less cognitive skills. If letter grades prove unproductive, we may want to do away with the concept and report more quantitative results (numerical scores). But the information on performance must be conveyed to parent and student if we are to maintain the essential tie of consequences to performance.

Considering the trends of increased welfare dependency, mother-only families, the dumbing down of schools, and the weakening of personal responsibility, it is hard to imagine a group of factors better designed to ensure failure in all aspects of life, not only education. Now we have the second generation of the results of these trends. Without a family structure there is no discipline or role model so essential to success in school. A Michigan University study sought to understand why children of Vietnamese boat people did so much better when they attended the same poor inner-city schools as blacks.[31] The answer was simple: the Vietnamese had a strong family affiliation and discipline. Parents (there were almost always two) made their children do three hours of homework every school night. Television was out. It is exactly the same prescription that most of children of past generations had to follow—with excellent results.

This is not rocket science. It doesn't take a $50 million study to figure out. It is just common sense. Unfortunately, there is nothing so uncommon as common sense. I am constantly amazed that in the millions of words written on why today's children do so poorly in school, discipline is rarely mentioned. Yet Amitai Etzioni reports that virtually every study on the subject concludes that ***"the single factor that separated effective schools from ineffective schools was the existence of discipline—and that the discipline had to be perceived by the students as legitimate rather than capriciously imposed."***[32] As a society we still are obsessed with rights and virtually ignore responsibilities. The ACLU and the courts continue to place the rights of the individual over the rights of the community, which is to say that they effectively place the rights of one person over those of all other people.

We should be far more concerned with the right of the majority of students to receive an adequate education rather than the right of an individual student to avoid punishment, especially corporal punishment, regardless of how egregious his behavior might be. It might be argued that corporal punishment is rarely an answer, but rarely does not mean never. In the past, there have been excessive punishments, but these were comparatively rare and in no way justify the notion that it is somehow wrong to ever physically discipline a student. Having been raised in a Catholic school system where corporal punishment was rare, but the threat was always there, I can testify firsthand that order in the classroom was never a problem. However, in recent years the threat of civil suits have resulted in private school teachers also refraining from any form of corporal punishment. As a consequence, they, too, feel there has been a substantial loss in classroom discipline. Children have to learn that there are negative consequences for socially disruptive acts. But if they don't learn it at home and they are prevented from learning it in school, where will they learn to accept the consequences of their actions?

Our national predilection to focus on individual rights at the expense of the community is affecting all aspects of education. As parents insist on mainstreaming children with serious physical or mental handicaps, the excessive demands on the teacher's time makes it increasingly difficult to meet the needs of the rest of the students. We cannot sacrifice the learning of a whole class to care for the special needs of one or two individuals. That is why special schools were created for the seriously handicapped. Admittedly, such schools might present certain disadvantages, particularly in the socialization of the disabled into the larger society. But we would do well to heed Immanuel Kant's Categorical Imperative: *each person must be counted as one and no more than one*. From the slightly different perspective of the Three Harmonies articulated in the introduction, we must weigh the incremental advantage that accrues to the disabled individuals against the incremental disadvantage that meeting their needs creates for all other children as well as for the taxpayer who foots the bill.

At a recent city council meeting I listened to all the needs and wants of different special-interest groups. I was amazed that none of them (most of whom I knew to consider themselves liberals) considered that, in fulfilling their aggregate desires, tax rates would be driven so high as to force some low-income people (especially the minorities in our city) to have to give up their homes. In another example, our local high school board was under pressure to do away with the current practice of placing students with comparable abilities together (the so-called tracking system) on the basis that it discriminates against those who have learning problems. The result, if implemented, would have integrated students who cannot do basic arithmetic with those who are capable of learning calculus. The interests of neither group would have been served.

There are solutions to America's educational problems. The question is whether we as a nation are willing to make the difficult trade-offs to implement them.

To Improve Education We Must Look to the Past

The solutions to the educational decline of the past three decades are relatively obvious but are not being implemented. The reason is twofold: they go against the popular bias originating in the 1960s of defining new rights without corresponding responsibilities, and they do not serve the narrow self-interest of some teachers, students, parents, religious groups, or the taxpayers. Specifically, teachers often want the guarantee of job security regardless of job performance; students often want unlimited freedom; parents often want to abdicate their responsibility for educating their children—especially regarding values that oftentimes the parents themselves lack—by placing the entire burden on the schools; religious groups are more interested in obtaining financial aid for their own schools than saving the public schools; and the taxpayers often do not want higher tax rates to finance education, particularly if those taxes are to support inner-city schools rather than their own. Ironically, because each group seeks to maximize it own narrow, short-term interest, the long-term interest of all groups suffers.

In the world of international competition, the success of any nation ultimately rests on the education of its people. Therefore, the decline in U.S. education is cause for grave concern. The increased reliance on well-educated immigrants from Asia and India is no more than a short-term expedient to avoid dealing with our failure in education. Furthermore, like each of the problems discussed in this book, education cannot be considered in isolation. The problem caused by the failure of the educational system, as well as its solution, is integrally intertwined with the solution to each of the other issues we are discussing, i.e., unemployment, welfare, income distribution, crime, and so on.

The two prescriptions for improving the education system most commonly advocated today are local control of the schools and educational vouchers. I will argue that neither solution will solve the educational crisis. Their popularity lies in that they provide the appearance of doing something and cost most interest groups little.

The Placebo of Local Control

"Local control" has a noble ring to it, not unlike "grassroots democracy." In Chicago, school reform was initially based upon parental involvement in local school councils. But the empirical evidence and my personal experience leads me to question the ultimate value of such experiments. In the early 1970s "free schools"—where parents and students took an active role in running the school—were thought to be able to provide a less structured and richer environment than public schools. Several of the parents who founded the alternative school that my wife and I joined were in the educational field themselves, some even teaching education at the university level. Virtually all of the parents involved were college educated and many had advanced degrees. We handpicked the teachers and were involved in every decision of the school. We felt quite confident that our kids were going to have the very best education possible. But after two years most of us were prepared to admit that our school was a dismal failure. When everyone is involved in the decision process, decisions either don't get made or, in trying to please everyone, the worst kinds of compromises were the result. The teachers found that it was intolerable having parents looking over their shoulder every minute. And although a few exceptional students worked well in an unstructured environment, most did worse than they would have in the local public schools. Our experience was by no means unique, and by the 1980s free schools gradually went the way of communes.

When considering the benefits of local involvement, we must consider what the parents can bring to the schools to benefit the students. Certainly parent volunteers can provide a valuable assistance to teachers on field trips and certain projects. But are parents always capable of deciding the qualifications of a good teacher, what subject matter should be taught, the most efficacious manner of presenting it, or how students' progress should be assessed? I doubt it. In many schools, particularly those of the inner city, the parents are often little better educated than the students. How can we expect someone who knows nothing about the theory or practice of teaching to decide how to run a school? It is absurd on the face of it, and I contend that it is no more than a sop to the communities with substandard education; an effort to placate parents and taxpayers without having to tackle the real problems. To ask such parents to select principals and teachers or set school policies is sheer foolishness.

I once asked my daughter, who was a teacher in an inner-city school, if she noticed the difference after Chicago began their program of local community control of the public schools. Her response was, "I don't really notice any difference. I still can't get most parents to even help on a field trip. They can't even help their kids with their homework, how can we expect the parents to help manage the school? Our problems are as basic as burned-out lights, insufficient heating, and lack of toilet paper. Community control has done nothing to rectify even these basics." It should be apparent to anyone that the problems of education are not to be solved by the simple placebo of local control. After several years of local control proved a failure in Chicago, the state legislators forced Mayor Richard Daley to assume responsibility for managing meaningful school reform. Since then there has been the first inklings of real progress in improving the Chicago school system, as will be shown shortly. Every successful business manager knows the lessons that American schools are learning the hard way: to get results you have to hire people you can hold responsible;

those people must have the authority to implement their decisions; and there must be agreed upon measures to evaluate their results.

The Real Intent of School Vouchers

The other frequently proposed remedy, school vouchers, while initially appealing because it also involves no additional cost or effort on the part of the parents, is equally useless. Like many advocates of vouchers, Charles Murray has an almost child-like faith in their efficacy. He believes that by giving parents vouchers, "we will observe substantial convergence of black and white test scores in a single generation."[33] It is true that, generally speaking, private and parochial schools outperform public schools. The question is, why? As a product of sixteen years of Catholic schooling, I think the reasons are obvious:

1. Parochial schools have far more rigorous discipline. At least up until recently, they could use disciplinary measures that are forbidden in public schools, including corporal punishment. According to the research of Michael Rutter, a British professor of child psychology, ***a primary characteristic of good schools is a classroom ethos that involves a teaching style that emphasizes the value of schoolwork, rewards good performance, and uses fair but firm disciplinary procedures.***[34] Moreover, according to Wilson and Herrnstein, this "warm but restrictive" environment is far more likely to be found in private and parochial schools than in the public schools.[35] Given the litigious nature of today's society, this is less true today than in the past, much to the chagrin of many teachers who report that even in Catholic schools classroom discipline has weakened. Still, parochial schools have the threat of expulsion both as a means of keeping students in line and as a way of eliminating incorrigible students who threaten the learning experience of others. Additionally, as Wilson and Herrnstein point out, expulsion may not increase the propensity of the kids expelled to commit crime, as is commonly thought. In fact, as much as we worry about dropouts, the evidence suggests that after adjusting for socioeconomic background and IQ, dropouts are no more responsible for crime than those who stay.[36] In short, keeping troublemakers in school simply drags other kids down with them.

Chicago is finally stepping up to the issue of troublemakers. Kids possessing weapons or drugs will get thrown out and sent to a special school for delinquents. If they are really dangerous, they will be sent to a "reform school." Hardly an original idea—that is the way it was done in the 1950s and it worked. It has been argued that reform schools never really reformed anyone. Maybe, but they at least kept the bad apples from spoiling the whole barrel. The mistake that many of us made in the 1960s is thinking that all children can be saved. We believed the adage, "There is no such thing as a bad boy." Nonsense, there *are* bad kids, whether due to genetics or environment, or more probably the interaction of the two. We can't save every child, but we can prevent the worst of them from taking others down with them.

2. The students of parochial schools generally came from families supportive of the school policies and education experience. In the school, the teacher acted as the parent (*in loco parentis*). The proliferation of student rights has now threatened this tradition even in parochial schools. If a student was not performing in a satisfactory manner, teachers most often could count on the parents to get involved in taking remedial action. Furthermore, most often the student in parochial schools had a richer home environment, both monetarily and culturally, than the average kid from a public school. Parochial school parents usually had high expectations for their children, and this translated into a demand that children perform to meet those expectations.

3. Although the nuns and priests are largely gone from Catholic schools, parochial school teachers still reflect the spirit of dedication as evidenced by their willingness to teach at wages substantially below public schools. Of course, many of the elementary teachers are married women and can afford the poor wage because their husbands provide another source of income. However, such idealism will always be in short supply, as well it should be. There is no reason why a teacher should accept economic exploitation just because he or she is devoted to education. On the other hand, schools should not have to retain teachers who are ineffective, incompetent, or burned out.

4. Standards in parochial schools were maintained independent of the socioeconomic background of the students. In the last three decades, the erosion of standards by those who have sought to give a break to those of deprived socioeconomic backgrounds has actually worked to the disadvantage of the very people they sought to help. We already discussed the elimination of grades and the attack on excellence. In 1995, it was decided to inflate SAT scores by 100 points (awarding 75 more points on the verbal and 25 more points on the math portion of the exam) in such a way that we can no longer differentiate the very brightest students from those slightly less bright (since they did not raise the maximum scores achievable), nor easily assess long-term trends in educational achievement.[37]

Moreover, as economist Thomas Sowell points out, both in underdeveloped countries and among lagging groups in industrialized nations, there has been a proliferation of easy, self-flattering courses, such as Maori Studies in New Zealand, Malay Studies in Singapore, and a variety of ethnic studies in the United States. "The claim is often made that the morale boosting effects of such courses will enhance a student's academic performance in other fields, but this claim remains wholly unsubstantiated."[38] Often these courses do little more than confirm the past victimization of minorities, romanticize their past cultures, and virtually ignore the new freedoms and opportunities that presently exist. Additionally, such cultural identification may inhibit assimilation and seal off the minority group from the advantages of the larger culture. While indigenous minority students flock to these easy courses that do little to prepare them for careers, white and foreign students are taking the difficult math and science courses that will prepare them for the most lucrative jobs.

Contrary to the supposed benefits of school vouchers, freedom of school selection had nothing to do with the success of the parochial system. In grades K through 8 there was little freedom of choice in school selection for Catholic kids: you attended your local parish school, and that was that. Moreover, the achievements of schools varied widely; not surprisingly, those schools that were located in affluent areas achieved much better results that those in poor neighborhoods. The Catholic high school that I attended was taught by the order known as the Christian Brothers, many of whom did not have a college degree, and consequently offered an inferior education to that of the neighboring Jesuit school which not only had more qualified teachers, but a much more affluent student body.

The Carnegie Foundation's School Choice study concluded that there is little evidence to support the view that educational choice programs would improve American education. The Carnegie report was especially critical of the Milwaukee voucher experiment that includes private nonsectarian schools, since such schools are not responsible to the public.[39] However, the final verdict is not in. Although one study indicated that students in the school choice program did no better than other students in the city's low-income schools, another study suggested that the choice students started out with lower reading and math scores than other low-income students and were brought up to the average of all low-income students' results.[40] But such an unimpressive accomplishment is hardly reason for dismantling the public education system when other remedies are at hand. Hartford, Connecticut, tried a more ambitious experiment, turning thirty-two schools over to be managed by a private corporation known as Educational Alternatives, Inc. Not only did the firm fail to improve performance or run the schools in a more cost-effective manner, but after 1.5 years the company threw in the towel because it could not make a profit and left Hartford's educational system in chaos.[41]

It should be kept in mind that under a voucher plan, all religious affiliated schools will be subsidized, as would other forms of elitist education. Not surprising, religious fundamentalists and segregationists are vocal supporters of vouchers. Of course, religious schools argue that they will not force their religious beliefs on their students. But this is nonsense. The raison d'être for a church-run school is to impress its particular beliefs on the students. Bishop James W. Malone of Youngstown, Ohio, is very clear on this point: "[I]n the end there is no other reason for us to maintain a system of Catholic schools than to participate in the process of change known as evangelization."[42] New York's Cardinal Bernard Law echoes this belief that the primary purpose of parochial schools is indoctrination. His opinion is based on the Vatican's often repeated urgings that Catholic educators strive to maintain a strong Catholic identity in their schools. This, of course, is their right. But they have no right to demand that the larger society subsidize their proselytizing efforts. Based upon my personal experience, it would seem to me that it is virtually impossible that a Catholic curriculum can avoid providing biased views on history, literature, ethics, and even science (as in the discussion of the psychology of human behavior).

Finally, providing vouchers will drain both resources and the better students from public schools (since private schools will not have to accept the worst performers). As a result, the problem of schools, especially those in the inner city, will become even more intractable. Therefore vouchers not only are unnecessary for solving the underlying problems of education but, in the long run, will undermine the educational effort.

Having said all this, there is one extremely cogent argument for school vouchers: to break the hold of the teacher's union. Like most unions, the teachers union initially had a just and reasonable goal: to improve the pay and working conditions of teachers. When that goal was generally accomplished, however, like many unions, the goal of the teachers union evolved into sustaining its own bureaucracy. The leadership has learned that the best way to ensure its own reelection is to promise job protection and to oppose any form of pay for performance. This allegation is well documented by Myron Lieberman. Lieberman was a long-time member of the National Education Association and American Federation of Teachers, labor negotiator in about 200 school district contracts in seven states, and a professor of graduate courses devoted to teacher bargaining at several universities. In his 1997 book, *The Teachers' Unions*, Lieberman charges that the NEA and AFT have sabotaged every effort for meaningful school reform in an effort to maintain the status quo.[43] While many of his allegations are debatable, one is not: the effect of a pay schedule based on seniority rather than marketable skills and performance. We will see how pernicious the effect of such a system is when we review the recommendation for improving teacher quality.

The Keys to a Better Education

There are eight essential ingredients to a successful K through 12 education system:

1. High expectations on the part of parents and teachers
2. The total amount of time spent on schoolwork
3. Discipline in school and home
4. High quality teachers, especially in math and science
5. Early childhood development
6. Adequate spending on vocational training
7. Use of computer-enhanced learning
8. Reduced inequality in spending per pupil

The ordering of these eight elements is crucial. As we shall see, the parent plays the most important role, and expenditures per capita, while not inconsequential, is the least significant.

1. Parental and Teacher Expectations

All parents have high hopes for their children's success, but all too frequently parents fail to translate these hopes into high expectations for current performance. Despite the decline in SAT scores—especially among the brightest students—91 percent of American parents say that their schools are doing an "excellent or good job."[44] They appear to want their kids to get decent grades, even if the test results show they aren't learning much. They all want their children to graduate, even though today graduation is more a function of time served than of educational achievement. National tests demonstrate this over and over again. Having their children graduate from college is important to parents as a matter of their own prestige, although just about anyone can get into college and, if they take easy courses, graduate. The value of college education has declined to the point where many degrees are of little more value than a high school degree was thirty years ago.*

*Some might argue that our society has become so sophisticated that a college degree is now a necessity, not a luxury. The problem with this argument is that the requirements for obtaining a college degree have been so discounted that it is questionable whether the degree really represents increased learning or simply more time spent in school. As for a high school diploma, most businessmen have come to view it as little more than an indication that the possessor hung around for four years. It certainly is not an indication of literacy.

It is ironic that, because students in Chicago had such a poor showing on the Iowa Skills Test, school officials were considering dropping the test.[45] A classic case of shooting the messenger! Recently, a more pragmatic approach was proposed to deal with children who fail to learn the skills appropriate to their grade level: *don't pass them*. What a radical idea: *tie advancement to achievement!*

Unless parents significantly raise their expectations with regard to their children's true performance (as measured by achievement on national tests in terms of skills development, information retained, and critical thinking), any form of school reform will be meaningless.

2. Time Spent on Schoolwork

It is significant to note that even the top 1 percent of American students would rank in the fifteenth percentile in Japan on academic achievement tests. The reason is simple: Japanese students, and students of most other countries, spend far more time in school:

Number of Days in School Year[46]

Japan	240
South Korea	222
Germany	226–240
England	192
U.S.	180

American public schools have been shrinking the school year for the past three decades. The difference between the United States and Japan in the number of school days per year is as much 60 days. ***By the time the students have left twelfth grade in Japan, they have been in school 720 more days—the equivalent of four more years in American schools.*** No wonder they know as much graduating from high school as U.S. students do graduating from college. And the difference does not end there. The school day in Japan is 8 hours compared to 6.5 for U.S. schools. American schools have even depreciated the hour: their class periods run an average of fifty-one minutes each. It gets worse: ***American schools spend less than half the time compared to their Japanese, German, and French counterparts on core subjects such as language, math, and science.***

Homework has almost become a thing of the past in many schools. In one middle school examined, teachers report that 80 to 90 percent turned in homework nearly two decades ago, but only 50 percent do so today. Many children average only twenty minutes to an hour on homework nightly, although in the best college preparatory schools, such as New Trier, an affluent suburban high school north of Chicago, 4 to 5 hours a night are assigned.[47] At the other end of the scale, so many students fail to do homework in inner-city schools that many teachers no longer even bother to assign it. Given the overall decline in time spent on basic education, it is no wonder why U.S. students compare more closely to those of the third world than to the advanced nations.

Again, however, the pendulum may be swinging back. The Chicago School Reform Board of Trustees has established a tougher homework policy that asks teachers to impose homework increasing in time from 15 minutes in kindergarten to ninety minutes by seventh and eighth grades, and 150 minutes for high school seniors.[48]

3. Discipline at Home and in School

The reduction in hours spent on homework over the past two decades also reflects a general breakdown in discipline in the home. In trying to understand how to improve the quality of education, we should take a lesson from the children of Vietnamese boat people who, although they most often attended the same impoverished inner-city schools, performed far better than their peers. As mentioned earlier, they perform better in large part because their parents greatly valued their children's education and insisted that they put in an average of three hours of homework a night.[49] This explanation has been reinforced by other studies. Asian Americans from families with low incomes score much higher on the quantitative portion of the SATs than did African American, Mexican American, and Native American students from families earning several times as much.[50] Chinese and Japanese Americans also outperform white Americans both academically (including SAT scores) and economically. The usual explanation is that Asian Americans are just smarter. However, the bulk of the evidence would suggest that any small advantage in IQ is insufficient to explain the higher achievement of Asian Americans in academic results.[51] The reason for their success again appears to be due to the high expectations of the parents coupled with greater discipline and many more hours spent on home study. What a surprise—studying is conducive to academic success!

Competition from TV is particularly devastating to academic learning. The average U.S. student spends under 1,000 hours in school annually but averages 1,300 hours watching TV. It gets worse as they get older. By graduation from high school, the typical youth has spent 22,000 hours watching TV—double the number of hours devoted to schooling.[52] I suggest that it is not a spurious correlation that SAT scores decreased with the increase in TV watching over the years.

Several hours of homework was the rule in most families prior to the 1960s. It was also the practice my wife and I used to raise our three children. Two of our children had slight learning problems, but through their exceptional diligence made possible by limiting TV viewing to only a few hours a week, and by demanding that school nights be devoted to homework, they overcame their deficiencies and went on to succeed in college.

The role of the parent is first and foremost in determining the success of the children. Evanston, Illinois, is a bastion of liberalism, where spending for education is the highest priority. The Evanston School District spends over $13,000 per high school student, more than all but two other school districts in Illinois. Yet their minority students have fared poorly on national tests. For example, the median score for white students on the verbal section of the PSAT was in the sixty-fourth percentile, while African Americans scored only in the tenth percentile and Hispanics the twenty-eighth percentile.[53] The results shocked many people in the town and an investigation into the cause of such unexpected results was undertaken. The investigation was forced to conclude that "Financial support in the schools is a poor substitute for parental support at home."[54] Should this come as a surprise? Or is it just common sense that failure of the students is guaranteed when parents are more interested in indulging their children rather than challenging them to live up to their potential? Any teacher in the Evanston school system can cite examples where a student is thrust upon them by parents who expect the school system to miraculously transform their spoiled, undisciplined brat into a responsible student. It can't be done. In the inner-city public schools, most of the children do not have a father to enforce discipline. Some mothers can cope, many cannot. How can the students be expected to do homework when the parents let them watch TV or go out on school nights?

Social philosopher Amitai Etzioni points out that character formation is essential to success in life. This involves "acquiring the capacity to control one's impulses and to mobilize oneself for acts other than the satisfaction of biological needs and immediate desires."[55] A primary purpose of education, then, is to develop those personality traits that characterize effective individuals, and acquire values that promote social cohesion.[56] This is a tall order and one that must be the primary responsibility of parents. It is obvious, however, that many parents lack the capability of self-discipline themselves and are, therefore, totally incapable of transmitting it to their children. The schools can never completely make up this deficit. Indeed, it is at least debatable whether they can have much of an impact at all. But the first step is to *make students accountable for their behavior.* ***The***

rules must be straightforward. Students who don't complete assignments will not get passing grades. Students who don't maintain a C average will not be allowed to participate in sports. Students who don't achieve certain basic skills as determined on nationwide standard tests will not pass. Students who misbehave will be punished. Students who are seriously disruptive will be removed from class, suspended from school, or dismissed. This may sound harsh, but what is far more cruel in the long run is passing students without forcing them to develop the skills necessary to succeed in a competitive world.

Some may object that I have overly stressed negative incentives. What about the positive incentives? Getting high grades and recognition, such as making the honor role, is no doubt valuable, especially when reinforced by parental approval. But if high grades are easily obtained without any effort, they are little value as an incentive; in fact they can work to support underachievement.

It has been suggested that we provide monetary incentives such as the program designed by West Georgia College that offers students two dollars for each book they finish. Educator Alfie Kohn strongly disagrees, arguing that it sends a subliminal message that anything that you must pay a child to do must not be intrinsically of value: "If these people have to bribe me to do it, it must be something I won't like."[57] Kohn believes the way to get children to read is to offer them real literature appropriate to their age level. This may work for reading, but how do you give kids "interesting" arithmetic?

There is no doubt that any subject matter may be made more interesting by a gifted teacher, improved texts, and, sometimes, by fast-paced interactive computer programs. Yet, it may also be true that using positive incentives such as financial rewards have a role. Contrary to Kohn's belief, a child might reason, "If they are willing to pay me, it must really be worth while." Some teachers I talked to have used play money to reward improved performance. The play money could be used at a school "store" to purchase donated items. The question as to the efficacy of financial rewards is an empirical one and it would be useful to try the various approaches to see which works best. However, neither approach is a substitute for the values that come from the practice of self-discipline and learning to do what is right for its own sake.

Kohn says that the research indicates that children who are frequently rewarded for good behavior tend to be somewhat less generous than their peers. They learn that the only reason to help is to get something in return. Yet, as we learned in *The Science of Morality*, self-interest taken in the broadest sense is the motivation for all human behavior. Whether working for a cash reward, or to gain praise associated with good grades, or for the intrinsic pleasure of reading well-written prose, it is always the person's perceived self-interest that motivates action. The problem is that many people do not have the capacity of appreciating excellent prose when they read it. ***Kohn makes the basic error common to many intellectuals: he assumes that all people are intellectually like he is.*** The actual fact is that most people are not intellectuals. No matter how hard we try to teach people to appreciate art, wisdom, or critical thinking, only a rather small proportion of them have the intellectual capacity to reach that stage. Most others are encouraged to learn through the use of short-term motivators, such as the desire to please teachers or parents, or conversely, fear of disapproval. As the military has demonstrated most persuasively, people can be taught discipline through the use of conditioning techniques. Employing extrinsic and intrinsic motivations can be mutually reinforcing. We should make the content of education interesting and, to the extent possible, even entertaining. However, in the final analysis, children are best motivated by the expectations and demands of parents they love and have learned to respect. It takes discipline to achieve any worthwhile goal, and discipline must begin at home.

The breakdown in discipline in school has many causes, the most significant being the breakdown of the family. However, lack of discipline is at least partly the result of the civil libertarian movement (which is focused on creating rights while ignoring responsibilities), bolstered by the glut of lawyers seeking new reasons for a lawsuit. Quite often teachers have to compromise their effectiveness as teachers to protect themselves from a potential lawsuit. In some more extreme, cases teachers have become so intimidated that they have surrendered control over their classrooms.

In the environment of the parochial high school of the 1950s, students were at times treated harshly. I've seen students thrown against lockers, slapped across the face, made to do pushups or run laps until they vomited. I was once struck across the backside with a two-by-two piece of lumber wielded with such force that I was knocked to the floor and was in pain for several days—all for throwing an eraser between classes. Such disciplines were no doubt excessive—but for all that, I was never in danger in high school of being shot, stabbed, beaten, or robbed by a classmate. Schools were safe, and learning did take place.

There is no reason to return to the extreme punishments of the past. At the same time, there are times when corporal punishment, such as a rap across the knuckles with ruler or a paddle on the backside, would establish an element of fear which, for some children, may be the most effective way of ensuring obedience. To those who worry about the potential harm of corporal punishment, I ask, where is the empirical data to support your concern? Conversely, there is ample evidence to show that the lack of discipline in schools has made them a dangerous place. When all else fails, fear is a powerful motivator. But in most schools today, any form of corporal punishment is strictly forbidden. In Illinois, when a bill was introduced permitting mild corporal punishment to be administered by a principle in the presence of a witness, the liberals had an apoplexy. You would think that we were reinstituting the Inquisition. The bill was quickly defeated. Would such corporal punishment have helped or hindered the maintenance of discipline in the schools? We don't know since the experiment was never tried.

In *The Science of Morality*, I posited that domination was a driving force in human nature, particularly among males. Nowhere can this be better observed than in the adolescent who is challenging the dominant position of the teacher. It is essential that the teacher is not so handcuffed that the students can dominate the classroom. The desire to dominate—a natural urge of the male of the species—must be diverted to the athletic field, or even better, to domination of peers through academic and extracurricular achievements. Furthermore, a primary function of socioeconomic policies must be to provide the incentives and disincentives necessary to bring the wants of individuals in congruence with the needs of society. Nowhere is this more important than in school where habits are formed that will accompany individuals throughout their entire life.

Again, the problem with liberal theorists is that they are often intelligent, well-disciplined individuals who mistakenly assume that all people are like them. Because they can assess the long-term consequences of their actions and are motivated accordingly, they assume that all people can similarly be motivated. Further, because they have the imaginative capacity to know how another person might feel under certain circumstances, they can develop the empathetic understanding that inhibits them from being cruel to a fellow human. However, people of extremely low intelligence do not assess the long-term consequences of their actions, nor in general can they imagine how other people feel. The myth of Forest Gump—the low intelligent, heart of gold personality may be entertaining, but bears little resemblance to the truth. It is far more common for people of low intelligence to be impulsive, exhibit extremely narrow self-interest, and unable to empathize with their fellow humans. Hence, the only effective motivators to create socially appropriate patterns of behavior for such people must be immediate rewards or punishments. Sometimes the most effective punishments are physical. Singapore does not have a juvenile delinquency problem, in part because of its severe punishments, including caning. American liberals abhor the notion of caning, but then they usually don't live in the urban ghettos. Who do we imagine are happier, the citizens of Singapore or the citizens of America's inner cities?

Both liberals and conservatives are also concerned about any policy that might possibly lead to a loss of freedom. But there is no freedom in a state of near anarchy that exists in some inner-city schools. We hear much about child abuse, but often fail to recognize that ***the most prevalent form of child abuse is the abuse of one child by another.*** It's not usually sexual abuse, but having someone beat the hell out of you or threaten your life does not make it any more palatable. It is time to stop this obsessive concern with teachers abusing children and begin worrying about the far more significant danger of children abusing children (or even children abusing teachers). This requires limiting children's rights and returning the authority in the classroom to the teacher.

This might all seem elementary to some people and unduly harsh to others. But consider the present situation. American students are getting cheated. A high school education means little anymore. The economic differential between a high school diploma and a college degree has increased in recent years, not because of the knowledge associated with a college degree means so much, but because a high school degree means so little. In absolute terms, the value of a college degree has declined as well. One need only note the kinds of jobs average college graduates are ending up with these days. It reflects the real value the degree represents to the employer. When reviewing job applications for our company, I was not alone in expecting a graduate degree to represent the level of achievement once indicated by a college degree. The whole educational system has been devaluated.

It is far better to educate 75 percent of our children well rather than provide a mediocre education to 100 percent of children. There is no inherent reason why we can't educate almost all of the children well, but that will require more than additional schooling and greater discipline at home and at school; these two requirements are essential but not sufficient.

4. Improving the Quality of our Teachers

A 1996 report by a national panel indicated that 25 percent of U.S. teachers were underqualified.[58] The panel called for a $4.8 billion program to improve teacher quality and the firing of incompetents. We all know that better teachers are a prerequisite for a better education, but there is little economic incentive for the best college students to want to be teachers in the first place, and even less incentive to teach in the inner city. Linda Darling-Hammond, co-director of the Center for School Reform at Columbia University, observes that, "the number of college students earning education degrees declined 55 percent between 1972 and 1987 and only three-fourths [of those] graduating from teacher training actually entered teaching; of those who did enter the profession nearly half left during the first five years."[59] In the past, one of the primary reasons for leaving teaching was the poor pay. That has changed in many school districts. Starting pay in the Chicago elementary schools for a teacher with a bachelor's degree was $31,000 in 1996 (for nine months work). A teacher with 12 years of experience will receive $49,778. A master's degree will increase the annual salary by $2,000. In addition, many teachers supplement their basic wage by coaching sports or other extracurricular activities. In some of the more affluent suburbs, teachers earning over $60,000 annually are not uncommon.

Still, most schools systems do not pay nearly this well, and when comparing the pay for teaching to other jobs, teachers, in general, are economically disadvantaged. A 1996 study by the Organization for Economic Opportunity and Development concluded that U.S. teachers' pay ranks high worldwide, but loses economic status when compared with other jobs. When starting salaries of teachers were compared to other occupations, America fell below all but three of the eighteen countries studied. If we want to get the best people into teaching, we must pay them salaries comparable to what they could make in business.

A major shortcoming of the foregoing study—and of most studies assessing the adequacy of teachers' salaries—is that they use averages. This is not just carelessness, it is a function of the policy of the teachers' unions. They insist on one pay scale where the only two variables are seniority and the number of extra courses or degrees obtained (even if the courses or degrees have no relevance to the area in which the teacher is instructing).

Earlier we saw that a major reason for the poor showing of American twelfth graders compared to other countries in the areas of math and science was due in large part to a shortage of qualified teachers in these areas. In a free market economy this would not happen. The shortage of qualified math and science teachers would drive up the wage rates for these positions high enough to attract the needed teachers. This is exactly what happens in the universities, where the demand for science professors relative to the supply results in science professors making far more money than liberal arts professors, of which there is more than ample supply.

But if a high school has trouble recruiting a few extra science teachers, they must raise the pay of all teachers to the level necessary to attract the science teachers. Myron Lieberman offers the example of a school district of one thousand teachers that needs ten new math teachers. If the average pay for teachers is $40,000, but math teachers can make $50,000 in other occupations, to recruit the ten math teachers the district needs to raise salaries of all teachers by $10,000. So, instead of costing the district

$100,000 in higher salaries to get the ten math teachers, the district would have to pay an additional $10,000,000.[61] In actual practice, the district would probably raise salaries enough to overpay the one thousand teachers, but not enough to recruit top quality math teachers. The result would be higher property taxes for the school district, a continuing shortage of qualified math teachers, and high school students who are poorly educated in mathematics, exactly the situation in most school districts throughout the United States today. ***In short, if we are to attract higher-caliber teachers in areas where there are shortages without overpaying all teachers, we must scrap single salary schedules.***

Money is not the only, and maybe not even the major, problem when recruiting and keeping high-quality teachers. A major reason for people leaving teaching today is sheer frustration. Many ex-teachers and those who stay but hate their jobs say the reason is the lack of control they have over their classrooms. The effort to continually expand students' rights, often at the expense of the teachers, and the pressure to pass students irrespective of their performance, has made a difficult job almost impossible. In addition, many white teachers are concerned that any effort to discipline or fail minority students can raise the charge of racism. Indeed, several white teachers I interviewed have admitted that after years of teaching inner-city youth, they have developed extremely negative attitudes toward minorities. Hence, we must rebalance students' rights with the need for teachers to be able to enforce discipline and maintain appropriate classroom standards. This includes the power to discipline or dismiss a disruptive student.

Similarly, principals must be given control over their schools, including the power to reward extraordinary achievement and fire incompetent teachers. In the Chicago school system, principals do not even have control over the maintenance staffs, and it can take over two years to get rid of an incompetent teacher—just one more example that as a society we have placed too much emphasis on individual rights while ignoring the counterbalancing responsibilities.

To justify higher salaries for elementary and high school teachers, school systems need to raise standards on teacher competency exams, with no allowance for racial preference. We cannot afford to have an incompetent teacher just to satisfy the desire of racial balance. If it takes prospective teachers an extra year to acquire the knowledge to pass the exam, so be it, but nothing justifies having teachers who don't know their subject matter transmitting their ignorance to their students.

Higher salaries also warrant a lot more than 180 school days each year. The school year should be lengthened to at least 210 days. This would mean shorter Christmas, spring, and summer vacations, and fewer holidays. Cutting vacations shorter would have an additional benefit. A 1998 University of Chicago study found that not only do shorter vacation breaks reduce the amount of learning that children forget, but actually improves the skills that determine intelligence. Imagine that: more schooling can make a kid brighter![62]

Another quid pro quo for higher wages is that only those teachers who perform well should continue to be employed—tenure should be eliminated for K through 12 teachers. However, in eliminating tenure, the teacher must be guaranteed a significant degree of academic freedom. The only reason for dismissing a teacher (other than the elimination of the job) would be failure to perform. Admittedly, this is a difficult area to measure. It is sometimes suggested that we measure teachers' performance in terms of their students' results relative to nationwide standards. However, students from deprived socioeconomic backgrounds or low IQs are less likely to meet national standards regardless of the teacher's capabilities. Hence, there should be *norming* at each school—determining a basic level of achievement reflecting the difference between the average student at a given school and the national standard. Teachers whose classes exceed the norm should get bonuses. Teachers whose classes consistently fall below the norm would get dismissed. This may sound severe, but it is unfair to the students to subject them to an incompetent teacher.

Another idea that has been suggested that merits further study is making teachers take competency tests every five years or so. This would be especially important in the area of science, where new discoveries are being made almost daily.

National testing is essential to correctly evaluate student performance, but tying classroom or school results to school funding—unless tied to student improvement rather than absolute levels of achievement—will only result in the most culturally and economically deprived areas being further impoverished. Any national tests should be objective and limited to basic courses, i.e., math, science, reading, vocabulary, and English. Unfortunately, this is not the case with the national tests being proposed. They allow answers that are "close enough" (fuzzy math) and also try to insinuate values assessment into the tests. Values testing would not be so bad if it was limited to "core values" such as the importance of honesty, truthfulness, self-discipline, tolerance, promise keeping, hard work, and the like. Such virtues have been recognized for more than two millennium. But when the so-called virtues really mask a political agenda, such as multiculturism or egalitarianism, it is stepping over the line. Admittedly, it is controversial where to draw the line.

5. Early Childhood Development

In attempting to explain why children don't learn, James M. Healy of Cleveland State University observes that "electronic media, fast-paced lifestyle, unstable family patterns, environmental hazards, junk food diets, and current educational practice *may affect the actual physical structure of the brain*."[63] We are just beginning to learn of the impact of early childhood environment and the development of the brain, but the evidence suggests that environment prior to the age of three can have a major impact on cognitive functions. The Education Commission of the States sums up the findings of neurologists that during the first few years of life the brain develops trillions of synaptic connections largely due to the learning stimulation of the environment. Unused synapses gradually die off until about half are gone by age ten, leaving the rest to last a lifetime.[64] The value of Head Start programs has been clearly demonstrated,* but we now realize that we need to start caring about a child's development even earlier. There have been more than fifty research projects using a variety of curricula and methodology that show that early childhood intervention works.[65] There have also been special programs for older children, including high school kids, that show encouraging results.[66]

However, there are three problems with such programs. First, they are extremely expensive and involve a very small number of kids. Many of the programs are simply not able to incorporate the millions of children who might benefit from them. Some of the programs, such as the Milwaukee Project and the Abecedarian Project, have student/teacher ratios as low as three to one.[67] There is simply no way the nation could hire a sufficient number of qualified teachers to extend coverage to all the students who would benefit from these programs.

Second, oftentimes the effects of the programs are not permanent. Because the children are still in an environment detrimental to their development, once they leave a temporary program they begin to regress, and oftentimes by the time they are in fifth grade or so they have lost the ben-

---

*President Clinton's 1995 Budget mentions that tracking the students of one high-quality preschool program through age twenty-seven found a $7.16 return for every dollar spent. Participants had half the crime rate, increased labor force participation rates, and increased earnings relative to the control group who lacked the benefit of Head Start. However, it cautions that, "Unfortunately, not all Head Start programs deliver the high-quality services needed to produce such results." Indeed, it would be more truthful had it said that no other Head Start program has been this successful. Head Start has proved its value; we need not exaggerate the benefits. U.S. Office of Management and Budget, *Budget of the United States Government*, 1995 (Washington, D.C.: U.S. Government Printing Office, 1995), p. 92.

efits of the program. A study of eleven high-quality experimental programs, including the celebrated Perry Preschool Program, concluded that after several years of follow-up, "the effect of early education on intelligence test scores was not permanent."[68] The proponents of such programs argue that there are other benefits that are not reflected in IQ, but such impacts are at least questionable. No doubt the students would benefit if the programs were extended beyond the early years, but here we not only run into cost considerations but the third problem: an issue of equity. People whose children are not so deprived as to qualify for the programs may well ask why they should be paying taxes so that another person's child benefits more than their own.

I am not suggesting that we abandon efforts to help disadvantaged children. The Head Start program is indeed a worthwhile investment even if it does not permanently raise a child's IQ or have the outstanding results of the best-run programs. It might produce long-term educational benefits if it were followed by an education that incorporated the other reforms discussed in this chapter. Nevertheless, we cannot rely upon childhood intervention programs to take the place of effective parenting.

Before the age of three, a child's mind is physically affected by the environment. For this reason, it is particularly troublesome to note the drastic decline in parenting since 1965, from an average of thirty hours a week to only seventeen hours by 1993.[69] The difference has been made up for the most part by childcare facilities. There is evidence that children who are institutionalized have less of a chance of growing up into well-adjusted adults.[70] Even the Israeli Kibbutzim, once hailed as a successful alternative to the nuclear family method of child raising, has now been recognized as no replacement for the home care of a nuclear family, and for the most part has been abandoned. In America, the childcare facilities are of far less quality than the Kibbutzim. Childcare workers earn in the lowest ten percent of all workers. Their average salary is far less than janitors or zoo keepers.[71] No wonder why we are having so much trouble with children when they start school.

The conclusion of a study by educator Patricia Graham is that schools have generally done well with healthy, well-motivated children of stable families, but they do not do well with unhealthy, unmotivated children from unstable families.[72] Simply getting women off of welfare and into the workforce will do little to solve this problem. In general, group child care is less than an optimal solution. It might work sufficiently in the affluent suburbs that employ relatively educated women caring for only a few children, and the day care in the inner city might be better in some instances than having a child cared for by a dysfunctional mother. In the final analysis, however, no program will remedy the harm caused by unqualified parents—women and men too ignorant or mentally damaged to properly care for their children. As already mentioned, the answer is to discourage such women from having children, to take children from parents guilty of abuse or neglect, and to prevent such parents from having more children by either threatening them with jail or forcing them to take some form of contraception.

On the other hand, the working mother has been the norm for the last twenty years. Some women may wish to take time off from work during the first few years of their child's life, but this will continue to be the exception, not the rule. Most women simply can't afford it, even with a two-earner family. Moreover, given the findings of neuroscience regarding the crucial importance of early childhood learning, we cannot afford to simply dump children in day care centers that are little more than holding tanks for the nation's toddlers. Rather, we need to start childhood education by at least three years of age, perhaps along the lines of the Montessori school.* Such an educational program is not a substitute for effective parenting. Rather, it may supplement it. The idea of a universal early education program removes the issue of one segment of society subsidizing another. Adding a couple of years of education would not come cheap, however. Therefore, before embarking on any national program we need to develop more pilot programs and assess the results.

Some money may need to be diverted from college funding. Additional funds would eventually come from lower costs of remedial learning and the social benefits generated over the lifetime of more productive people. The potential return is far greater from investing in education during early childhood than investing in remedial courses later in life.

To avoid providing an inadvertent incentive for women to have children, it is important that any program of childhood education be limited to two children and/or tuition is charged on an progressive scale, i.e., proportionally greater tuition for each additional child. This is in sharp contrast to many tuition plans that provide discounts for additional children.

Finally, since many parents could provide an educational experience superior to any that may be received in a childcare program, childhood education programs must be strictly voluntary.

---

*Maria Montessori was the first woman in Italy to receive a medical degree. She also studied psychology and became a professor of anthropology at the University of Rome. In 1907 she opened her first school in the slums of Rome. Her method stressed development of a child's initiative and sense and muscle training by means of specially prepared teaching materials and games. The child's interest is maintained by a sense of accomplishment. Her method also developed responsibility by such seemingly elementary techniques as making a child put away any toys that he or she was playing with before taking out another toy.

6. Expanding the Vocational Training and Apprenticeships

In his 1998 State of the Union message, President Clinton proposed a major increase in spending on education. He said that he wanted to expand the opportunity for students to attend college. This is "feel good" sounding nonsense. We should be spending less on college and far more on vocational training. (I would argue that learning computer languages is a form of vocational training.)

Economist Lester Thurow notes that the United States is the only industrial country that does not offer a postsecondary education for those not going to college. There is a bias toward sending kids to college: "for every dollar of taxpayers' money invested in the noncollege bound, fifty-five dollars is spent subsidizing those going to college."[73] Although as Dean of MIT's Business School, you might expect Thurow to argue for an increase in the number of students attending college. But Thurow states that "the problem with the U.S. is that there are too many people in college and not enough qualified workers."[74] This would seem to be certainly true when comparing the 60 percent of U.S. high school students who go on to college to only 32 percent in Germany and 30 percent in Japan.[75]

The percentage of high school graduates enrolled in college increased from 45 percent in 1960 to 62 percent in 1994.[76] This primarily reflects the greater percentage of females and blacks going on to college. The increase in blacks is due in large measure to implementation of affirmative action polices. In an effort to get minorities into college, enrollment requirements have fallen significantly in the last twenty years. Availability of financial aid has also expanded significantly. The result is that hundreds of thousands of kids who would never have made it into college, let alone graduate, are now doing so. In 1976, 42 percent of black high school graduates were entering universities; by 1994, 51 percent were college bound. Today, there is greater opportunity for blacks than for whites with equivalent SAT test scores,[77] but the consequences are at best a mixed blessing. First, admitting many minorities to college who are not qualified results in a much higher dropout rate. Controlling for IQ, black and white dropout rates are about the same.[78] Second, the devaluation of college degrees due to grade inflation has resulted in many college graduates being qualified only for menial jobs that years ago would have been given to high school graduates. I have employed several college graduates as secretaries. In general, their capabilities were no better than, and frequently not as good as, those of the last generation with high school diplomas.

The inevitable consequence is a high level of frustration for many college graduates. Blacks thought that their college degree was a ticket to good careers in highpaying jobs. They were wrong. This is particularly true of those majoring in liberal arts and nontechnical disciplines. As economist Thomas Sowell warns, "The result of blindly processing more people through the schools may not promote economic development, and may well increase political instability. A society can be made ungovernable by the impossibility of satisfying those with a passionate sense of entitlement—and without the skills or diligence to create national wealth from which to redeem their expectations."[79]

Other nations, such as Germany, avoid the futility of trying to prepare the majority of high school students for college, and make much more extensive use of apprenticeship programs. In Germany, 70 percent of the youth enter the job market through the apprenticeship system. During the seventh to ninth grade, boys and girls are exposed to various occupations. In tenth grade they can choose an apprenticeship or opt for a purely academic education.[80] In the eleventh and twelfth grades, apprentices would mix training at work sites with high school courses. The many advantages of such a system include providing students with adult mentors (their job trainers), offering a very tangible incentive for succeeding in the academic aspects of school, integrating disadvantaged youth into the economic mainstream, and creating a better trained workforce.

Americans think of apprenticeships as applicable only to various forms of manual labor. But apprenticeships should include every form of technical training from computer maintenance to nursing. Although the United States spends twice as much of its GDP on higher education as Germany and Japan, and we send proportionally twice as many of our children to college, it is apparent from cross-culture tests that our general population is not better educated.

The economic benefits of vocational training are significant. According to a study by Ohio University economist I. A. Ghazulah, vocational school graduates earn 20 percent to 55 percent more than high school students in male-dominated jobs, and 50 percent to 80 percent in female-dominated jobs.[81] The Cincinnati Technical College, a two-year state school, finds skilled jobs for 98 percent of its technical students.[82] I doubt if many four-year colleges can make that claim. The key is to coordinate training with employer needs. The Clinton administration has recognized the value of vocational training with the School to Work Opportunities Act that would provide on-the-job experience leading to a diploma and industry-recognized credentials for a job.[83] However, financing more vocational programs at the federal level is difficult given the need to reduce the national debt. The best way to come up with the needed funds is for the states to divert funding from state colleges, but this will be fought tooth and nail by the colleges and college teacher unions. In a discussion with the president of a college teachers' union concerning the problems of unemployment for unskilled workers, his suggested solution was to send more kids to college. He seemed completely oblivious to the high unemployment and under-employment rate among recent college graduates.

Around the corner from where I live, a help wanted sign has been up for several weeks seeking a trained plumber. On my street are kids whose parents have sunk $80,000 into their children's liberal arts education at out-of-state universities. After graduation, most of these kids ended up as bartenders, waitresses, and eventually, in some mediocre white-collar job that required only a good high school education years ago. I belong to an association of philosophers in which there are several experienced college teachers who can only find part-time positions paying $2,000 to $3,000 a course. At eight courses a year, an adjunct professor with two children is earning at about the poverty level. Again we see the inescapable law of supply and demand at work.

Finally, it is often argued that focusing on career training as a primary goal of college misses the whole point of a college education. The purpose of college, we are told, is to broaden a person's capacity for critical thinking. Maybe so, but if this is true, our colleges are indeed failing miserably. Today, as years ago, only a small fraction of college students appear capable of critical thinking. The vast majority learn by rote and get good grades by feeding back to their professors what they are taught. Even worse, many colleges have become an ideological straight jacket where students are conditioned to unquestionably accept unverified propositions as dogma. Political correctness has displaced intellectual discourse. This is true as much in some of America's most-noted universities as it is in fundamentalist Christian colleges. The message may be different, but the effort to stifle debate and accept unverified principles as sacred truths is the same.

Worst of all, the students graduate from college believing that because they spent four years being spoon-fed some intellectual pap, they are educated. They fail to recognize that there is no such thing as "being educated," as if it were a task that one can complete. True education would instill the realization that knowledge is a lifetime quest that can never be completed. Ask the average college graduate how many nonwork related, nonfiction books they have read since graduating, and you may begin to realize why I feel that college education has become little more than four years of indoctrination and escape from reality.

7. Computer-Enhanced Teaching

Much more could be done using the computer in an interactive learning process. To this end, Northwestern University created the Institute for

Learning Sciences. The first director of the institute, Roger Schank, is convinced that recording the best teachers lecturing and responding to questions can be incorporated into systems whereby each student is, in effect, interacting with the finest teachers. Moreover, since children are attuned to interacting with fast-paced electronic media, such as video games, the schools should fight fire with fire. One study showed that computer-based instruction resulted in 30 percent more learning in 40 percent less time and 30 percent less cost compared to traditional classroom teaching. Lewis J. Pearlman believes employing computer-based instruction could save U.S. schools $100 billion a year. This may be somewhat optimistic, but many suburban schools are already experiencing the advantages of computer-based leaning. The problem is that this requires a costly initial investment that inner-city schools can ill afford.

It greatly helps if the computer-enhanced skills can be reinforced at home, but few inner-city residents can afford a computer for the home. In Indianapolis, the state has provided free computers for an extended trial. The computers are also linked to local libraries and some university libraries. The results thus far indicate that when supplied with computers, even inner-city students will spend more time doing homework and significantly enhance their learning. The results are so encouraging that the Indiana legislature has set a goal of eventually providing a subsidized home computer to every student in the state. Whether they will follow through with the necessary funding remains to be seen.

8. Changing Educational Spending Priorities

One of the reasons that the number of school days have declined is an effort to reduce costs. In this regard, proponents of vouchers point out that it often costs considerably less to operate parochial schools. What they fail to say is that parochial schools cost less because: (a) parochial schools do not have to offer services to the disadvantaged and the handicapped; (b) teachers can effectively have larger class sizes since they do not have to put up with discipline problems, extremely slow or disabled students; and (c) most significantly, parochial schools generally underpay their teachers. In the past, of course, nuns were cheap to support; today lay teachers are beginning to rebel against slave wages, and that is one of the reasons why the Catholic schools are so desperate for public subsidies.

Federal spending on human capital as a percent of total GDP declined in the 1980s as did state and local spending.[85] The often cited cliché that money by itself will not solve the problems of the American education is only partly true. When coupled with reforms in discipline, more time spent in school and on homework, and improving early childhood development, money could help. Earlier I pointed out that although few countries devote a higher portion of their GDP on total educational expenditure, the United States spends a smaller portion of its GDP on K through 12 education than most of the other Western nations.[86] On the other hand, it might be noted that because our GDP per capita and taxes are so high, in absolute dollars only the Swiss spend more per student.[87] Furthermore, because K through 12 education is so inferior in the United States compared to other countries, ***many students spend up to one-half of their college education mastering the basic skills and knowledge that students of other nations learn by the end of their secondary education.*** If we could improve primary and secondary education we could reduce the cost and increase the effectiveness of a college education.

The famous 1966 Coleman Report concluded that student performance depended on the student's background and the background of classmates more than resources spent on education.[88] Ever since then, we often hear that additional spending on schools is not the answer to the decline in academic performance. A *Wall Street Journal* report concluded that increasing investment per pupil by $1,800 in five years during the mid-1980s "hasn't paid off."[89] And as the Evanston experience demonstrates, *by itself*, increased spending will have little effect on improving education. Like almost every factor of production, there is a point of diminishing returns where an added dollar of expense will make little if any difference in output. But at the other extreme, there is a point of increasing returns, where an added dollar can yield very high benefits.

It may be that school districts such as Evanston that have a high per capita expenditure have reached the point of diminishing returns. But it is simplistic to suggest that increased spending makes no difference. If expenditure per pupil has nothing to do with education, it would appear absurd that the richest school districts would choose to spend six times more per pupil than the lowest-spending districts.[90] Although it is by no means the only variable affecting student achievement, or even perhaps the most important, money does matter. A comprehensive study conducted by the University of Chicago concluded that "Educational policy should be based on the presumption that per pupil expenditure, smaller class sizes, smaller schools, and more experienced and well-educated teachers are all positively related to student achievement."[91] All of these factors are also related to money.

In 1995, the difference in expenditure per student between the richest district and the poorest district in Illinois was startling:

Illinois Spending Per Student[92]

	Elementary	*Secondary*
Poorest District	$2,500	$4,302
Richest District	15,014	13,848

In San Antonio, the situation was even more inequitable, ranging from $2,000 per student in the poorest districts to $19,000 per student in the most wealthy areas.[93] Can anyone seriously believe that a difference in spending of this magnitude does not make a difference in the quality of education a child receives? If so, let's review some of the differences that money can make.

Teachers—as a way of saving money, one of the nation's poorest districts, East St. Louis, fills 70 percent of its positions with substitute teachers who are paid only $10,000 a year.[94] Even in Chicago, about one-quarter of the teachers are substitutes. The number of teachers over sixty years of age is twice that of teachers under thirty.[95] Very old and very young are often not the best teachers; older teachers may be burned-out and young teachers often lack experience. In the Chicago area, as in most cities, teacher turnover is extremely high; many of the best teachers seek jobs in the suburbs. Some cities such as Chicago compound the problem by mandating that all Chicago teachers live in Chicago, thus excluding a pool of qualified teachers. Rather than paying less for inner-city teachers than their affluent suburban counterparts, we should be paying more. To attract and retain the best teachers in the inner city might require a 50 percent to 100 percent premium in pay over the suburban rate. Combat soldiers get additional pay, why not more pay for teachers in inner-city "combat zones"?

Class Size—Chicago has been able to drop average class size in elementary schools from thirty students to twenty-four in recent years, and in the wealthy suburb of Winnetka the class size is down to seventeen students.[96] In Goudy School—one of Chicago's poorest—a remedial class holds thirty-nine students; slow learners in the affluent New Trier District have the benefit of only fifteen in their class.[97]

Textbooks and Supplies—In some Detroit schools it is not until the sixth grade that every student has a textbook.[98] In contrast, the libraries and resource materials in the wealthiest schools resemble those of a small college. In one Chicago inner-city school, teachers receive a $125-a-year allowance to spend on "extras" for their classrooms, such as graphic arts and special teaching aids. In the affluent suburb of Highland Park, teachers receive $2,000 annually for their classroom.

In many schools the basic textbooks are also allowed to become woefully outdated. This is not only due to the financial situation of some school districts but the controversy that inevitably arises regarding the content of books from groups seeking to advance their specific social agenda. Educators are rarely allowed to select books based solely on the findings of science and the scholarship involved in developing the text.

Physical Plant—Every suburban parent should visit a typical inner-city Chicago school. The buildings are often in depressing disrepair: windows cracked or broken, lights out, heat so inadequate in winter that the students sometimes have to keep their coats on, playgrounds that look like prison yards, flaking paint, and oftentimes no toilet paper in the washrooms. Going into some of these schools, you feel that you are in a third world country.

Having better teachers, smaller class sizes, adequate books, and physical facilities can promote the learning experience. Moreover, it violates the Rawlsian notion of fairness that the present tax system, in effect, provides a greater subsidy for the wealthy to finance their schools than it does for the poor. The primary source of revenue for K through 12 education comes from property taxes that are deductible from income taxes. The mortgage interest deduction also provides a nice federal subsidy for the wealthy that indirectly enables them to pay for better schools.

It isn't that the poorer school districts do not try to provide a better education for their children. Their property tax rates and, hence, the proportion of their income directed to financing their children's education, is far higher than the rates of the wealthy school districts.[99] But since the value of the property in poor districts is far less, so are the tax dollars collected. Oftentimes, the lack of industry or businesses to facilitate the tax base places the poor districts at a further disadvantage. In San Antonio, the richest school district has an assessed tax base of $14,000,000 per student, while the poorest tax base averages only $20,000.[100] Relying on property taxes to fund schools guarantees gross inequality in education and all the evils commensurate with perpetuating a culture of poverty.

In the last chapter we argued that affirmative action was not the answer to solving the disparity that has resulted from centuries of discrimination. A far better solution is to increase investment in the children of the poor, whether white, black, Asian, or Hispanic. If we are to provide greater equality of opportunity, we must start with greater equality of education at the primary level (and even earlier, as Head Start has demonstrated). One method of rectifying the inequality in education for the nation's children is to create metropolitan taxing districts where the taxes of all the communities are pooled and each child allocated an equal expenditure. Minneapolis-St. Paul, Indianapolis, and Toronto have experimented with this concept with favorable results. Toronto consolidated thirteen independent municipalities into six governmental bodies to manage local affairs. In addition to regionalizing educational taxing and spending, a metropolitan council administers regional services such as transportation, waste collection, and planning. The result is far less bureaucracy and more equality of services, benefiting all the people living in the area. Portland, Oregon, is probably the prime example of the value of metropolitan planning, and might become the paradigm for the twenty-first-century megalopolis. At the other extreme, the eight-county Chicago area has 1,299 governmental bodies, including municipality, village, school, and county taxing districts.

The federal government should encourage the elimination of excessive taxing entities and the formation of single taxing districts by tying federal aid to creation of such districts. For example, it could be stipulated that federal educational funds will only be provided to schools that are part of such a metro district. However, even metropolitan area consolidation is not enough. It will just encourage businesses and individuals to relocate just outside the metropolitan areas to reduce their property tax liabilities. In general, funding education through state and federal income taxes, rather than the regressive property taxes or state lotteries, would provide far greater equality of opportunity than do the counterproductive busing and affirmative action programs in place today.

California tried a different approach by establishing a statewide foundation program—a minimum of expenditure for each school district. However, there was a fatal flaw in the California plan. The minimum funding was set so low that the poorer districts could not offer a decent education at that level. After Proposition 13 was enacted, the share of state income tax going to schools declined to 3.8 percent, placing California 46th among the fifty states. This did not pose a problem for the wealthier districts because their citizens provided tax-deductible contributions to make up for the shortfall. The result was that the wealthiest districts still spent more than twice as much per student as the poorer districts.[101]*

More equal spending does not mean that we can expect equal results. As we learned in Evanston, when the students come from educated and disciplined home environments, they will succeed far better than when they come from lower socioeconomic backgrounds. Hence, we cannot expect the educational outcome of the poorest communities to approximate that of the wealthiest communities. However, increasing expenditures on the poorest communities, if accompanied by the other recommendations in this chapter, should improve results significantly.

A major reason for increased costs in schooling in recent years has been

---

*In 1988, the State of Michigan passed a law to equalize expenditures per public across all school districts in the state. At the time of this writing it was too early to evaluate the results.

a number of unfunded mandates from the federal government, especially the demand that learning disabled or physically disabled students be educated with mainstream students. Without getting into the pros and cons of this decision, I will only point out that it is extremely costly and places an additional burden on teachers. Reducing class sizes does not accomplish much if a teacher also has a few students who take up a disproportionate amount of time.

Before leaving the subject of equality of spending, we should note that the inadequate funding of inner-city schools is in part the fault of big-city mayors. The Chicago school budget is being stretched thinner and thinner as the schools are forced to offer bilingual education to tens of thousands of new immigrants. Every major city is, or will soon be, facing the same crisis. The big-city mayors seek political support by catering to the wants of immigrant voters, ordering their police departments not to cooperate in the apprehension of illegals, and offering bilingual education in dozens of different languages instead of the cheaper and more effective English as a Second Language program.* At the same time, they whine that federal and state governments must increase funding for the city schools. The state should say to their big-city mayors, "no more state funding until you help the INS apprehend illegal aliens."

Rethinking College

Up to now my remarks have been directed primarily to the problems of elementary and high school education. Now let's examine some issues concerning college education in America. As noted earlier, during the 1960s our colleges underwent a radical transformation, and unfortunately, not for the better. First, there was grade inflation. This was in part an effort to keep students out of the draft. How could a professor flunk a student knowing that if he did so the student might wind up being killed in Vietnam? Higher grades were also an effort to accommodate minority students who were often environmentally and educationally deprived. Many colleges dropped grades altogether replacing them with a simple pass/fail

*To be fair, Chicago's bilingual education program was the result of a 1973 Illinois General Assembly mandate demanding that bilingual education be offered in any school with twenty or more students of the same language. It is a classic example of an unfunded mandate. By 1995, Chicago was offering bilingual education in nineteen different languages including Gujarti, Hindi, Hmong, Khmer, Mandarin, and Urdu. With 1,600 bilingual teachers now in Chicago schools, the teachers' union will oppose any effort to change the failed bilingual education program in favor of the more successful, and less resource intensive, English as a Second Language program.

system. Colleges thought that they were offering an opportunity to make up for past discrimination. Actually, they were depreciating the value of a college education to the point of irrelevancy.

Second, in order to ensure peace on campus, many colleges allowed the students a role in the administrative process,* even so far as determining course curricula. Core curricula was out, letting the students design their own curricula was in, although how people who are uneducated can decide what should constitute an education remains a mystery to me. Western rationalism and scientific thinking were often placed on a par with Eastern mysticism. To some extent this trend continues, frequently under the guise of multiculturalism. The reason is that many of the students of the debased academic system of the late 1960s and 1970s are now themselves in control of our colleges and universities. In some schools the new multicultural studies have resulted in myth masquerading as history. The latest fad in some African American studies is to allege that the ancient Egyptians were really African blacks, the Greeks stole their ideas from these black Egyptians, and what Western civilization regards as history is only a biased European perspective that deliberately discredits all black accomplishments.[102] Although there is little, if any, evidence to support such claims, they frequently are unopposed for fear that the challenger be accused of racism. This is just one more example of spineless college administrators and professors failing in their primary duty of teaching their students to think critically.

The New Age movement is the logical outcome of this rejection of critical thinking. Bennett W. Goodspeed proclaimed in his best selling book *The Tao Jones Averages*: "The cognitive era appears to be in its twilight." Rather than lamenting the fact, Goodspeed hails the decline in college scores as socially beneficial.[103] According to Goodspeed, formal education is itself a waste of time because, in the words of the illustrious Lao Tsu, "Those who know do not speak, those who speak do not know." What a prescription for institutionalizing ignorance!

Goodspeed's anti-intellectual approach could be dismissed as so much sophomoric thinking were we not finding colleges graduating students

---

*Evaluation of teachers by students can be of value, but if not used with circumspection, it can also pose a danger to the quality of education. While it can prove useful for students to express their views on what a teacher could do to improve his or her method of elucidation, the value of students actually grading teachers is questionable. A professor of a top-ranked Chicago area university told me that even though the performance of his students was generally declining year by year, he was afraid of giving too many low or failing grades lest he get a bad evaluation from his students. One way to mitigate this problem is to make certain that the student evaluation is made before students receive their grades. Also, students must be asked to support any general evaluation of a teacher with specific observations.

with so little capability for critical thinking. In the 1980s, the declining job market forced students to take their education more seriously, but by education they mostly meant job training. Not just any jobs—they wanted jobs to make them rich. Masters degrees in business administration and law degrees became the passkey to wealth. The best salaries were paid to professors in these disciplines, and students enrolled in these areas in greater proportions than ever before. The MBAs soon produced such a glut on the market that rather than becoming a key to advancement, employers could make it a necessary prerequisite for many entry-level white-collar jobs. Although lawyers also proliferated like rabbits—from 260,000 in 1960 to about 900,000 by the turn of the century—they have the advantage of being one of the few occupations that create their own work. Their prodigious efforts to turn every problem into a lawsuit is cited by London's *Economist* magazine as one of the factors that has seriously impeded economic progress during the past two decades.[104] This is particularly true for the United States, which has four times the number of tort suits per capita than European countries and gross per capita awards that are ten times higher.[105]

While America continued to produce lawyers and MBAs in mind boggling numbers, European and Japanese universities were turning out scientists, engineers, and computer programmers. In Germany and Japan, 40 percent of the graduates have engineering degrees, compared to only 15 to 17 percent in the United States.[106] Because of an inability to stimulate sufficient numbers of American students to enter the rigorous disciplines of science and engineering, we had to import talent. By the late 1980s, 60 percent of our engineers were foreign born. More than half of all mathematics and engineering Ph.D.s were awarded to people who were not U.S. citizens.[107] Given the lowering of academic standards and the propensity of American universities to turn out bureaucrats rather than innovators of science and technology, is it any wonder that we had to rely on imported labor to maintain our technological edge? As pointed out earlier, seeking to import talent is not the answer. Much of the talent comes from third world countries who need to retain their best and brightest if they are to succeed.

If we want better educated students coming out of colleges and universities, we might have to provide them with higher caliber students in the first place. Rather than lowering standards, we should be raising them. Albert Shanker, former president of the American Federation of Teachers, points out that the efforts to raise the national level of education will come to nothing unless students recognize that they have a stake in improving their performance.[108] Shanker points out that grade inflation has resulted in evaluations having little to do with performance. College-bound students in England, Wales, France, Germany, and Japan take very tough examinations to get into college, and only 25 to 36 percent of those taking the test pass them. In the United States the equivalent exam would be the Advanced Placement Test that only 7 percent of American eighteen-year-olds take and only 4 percent pass.[109] Luckily (or perhaps unluckily) for American kids, it is not required for college entrance. The result, according to Shanker, is that the few kids who pass the Advanced Placement Test get to go to the best colleges, get a top-rate education, and become part of the American elite. A great proportion of other kids go to second-rate colleges that have dropped their entry standards to take in just about anyone with a high school degree, give out grades that have little to do with what the student has actually learned, and provide a degree that isn't worth the paper it is printed upon. These graduates more often than not find to their dismay that they have no marketable skills.

Despite the drastic easing of requirements, the dropout rate of American colleges is 29 percent compared to 6 percent in Japan and 9 percent in Germany.[110] Clearly, we are admitting too many people who do not have the ability to succeed in college. The result is a waste of money and a frustrated group of kids.

Shanker proposes that entrance to college should be dependent on how well a student performs in high school, not just SAT scores. Some colleges do take high school performance into consideration. The problem is that at present there is no way of interpreting high school results given the tremendous variation in standards. Meaningful nationwide high school standards must be indicative of accomplishment, not just of time spent in a classroom. The net result would be fewer students going to college, but those that do enter college will have a far greater chance of succeeding. Lester Thurow argues that a better admission criteria would be *standardized achievement tests* rather than the present IQ oriented SAT tests or high school grades, since neither intelligence (as measured by IQ scores) nor academic grades reflect accomplishment.[111]

It is not only the college-bound that must demonstrate a mastery of basic subject matter. In many countries students who are not headed for college can study for special certificates that entitle them to additional technical training or qualify them for certain jobs. Shanker suggests that if every employer specified the standard that must be achieved to qualify for a job, students would have some very specific goals to aim for, rather than the present notion of obtaining a high school degree that employers generally find almost meaningless.[112] The high school dropouts that take the trouble to go back to school to get a GED learn that their odds of finding a job are little improved because most employers feel it does not represent a sufficient level of learning to qualify for any but the most menial of tasks.

In order to make a marked difference in the quality of those graduating from college, we must improve the quality of those going to college. In the first place, we must scrap any affirmative action programs that employ racial quotas. Sending unqualified students to college and then passing them with inflated grades is actually quite unfair since it provides them with a worthless college diploma. Moreover, as explained in the previous chapter, affirmative action overlooks the fact that selecting students based upon race rather than achievement is just another form of discrimination. ***A far better policy is one that improves the quality of education in preschool and K through 12, as I have outlined earlier, and also ensures that no one who qualifies is denied college because they cannot afford it. Rather, student loans should be provided to any one who meets the performance tests necessary to enter college. Outstanding students should be provided loans sufficient to enter outstanding universities.*** The qualification tests would not be IQ-related as they now are, but solely a function of mastering prerequisite skills and knowledge. This allows for students to make up with extra effort what they might lack in natural ability. The loans could be repaid in one of three ways: a flat repayment of principle and interest, a percentage of future earnings, or through a two-year work program, depending on the nation's needs. For example, if there is a shortage of doctors or nurses in rural areas, that is where new doctors or nurses may have to devote two years of their initial practice to repay their loans.

One last point: although there is present emphasis on each of the fifty states setting their own standards, in a mobile country such as ours the result will be chaos. Employers will not be able to evaluate the standards of fifty states to determine which are meaningful and which are just so much fluff. Although it is a good idea to see what different states would recommend, ultimately there should be one national standard if we are to be able to make distinctions in hiring that reflect achievement.

The Goals of Higher Education

In order to improve the educational system in this country it is first necessary that we be clear on the goals we expect of a college education. Thurow contends that it is not the function of education "to confer skills and therefore increased productivity and higher wages on the worker; it is rather to certify his (or her) 'trainability' and to confer upon him (or her) a certain status by virtue of this certification. Jobs and higher income are then distributed on the basis of this status."[113] I believe this goal is too narrow. The purpose of education is not just to turn out good employees, but good parents, good citizens, and to some extent, people who can appreciate and benefit from art and culture. I suggest that the following six goals be established for higher education in America:

1. Mastering job preparation skills
2. Establishing habits of critical thinking
3. Understanding human nature
4. Establishing the desire for lifetime learning
5. Creating a system of values to enhance social and ecological harmony
6. Developing the basis for an avocation

1. Mastering Job Preparation Skills: The first goal of education should be to prepare a person to earn a living, for without the requisite skills a person is doomed to a dismal state of existence, and so is society. This does not always mean that people are trained so narrowly that they are technically ready to step into a specific job, but that they have demonstrated the prerequisite skills that ensure employers that such a person has an excellent probability of learning to perform a job in their chosen field. Particular emphasis should be given in producing more scientists and engineers and fewer MBAs and lawyers.*

Education should equip a person to enter into a lifetime of learning. Education at the undergraduate level should also provide a testing ground in different disciplines to segregate people by aptitude. For example, by taking courses in computer science, the student can learn whether he or she has the aptitude to master this discipline. On the other hand, postgraduate education, such as in medical school, or for that matter any Ph.D., indeed must certify a minimum level of qualification to perform certain functions.

Much more emphasis needs to be expended on developing technical skills that do not require a full four-year education. Oakton Community College in Des Plaines, Illinois, has an excellent program of surveying local employers to determine what skill sets they require. When the college learned that there was a shortage of labor with the capability of using Computer Aided Design (CAD) and Computer Aided Manufacturing (CAM) equipment, it developed a course curriculum to train students in these areas.

Many community colleges and some four-year colleges are in effect guaranteeing job preparation of their students by offering twelve to fifteen hours of remedial instruction to students earning a degree but failing to perform the skills they were taught. St. John Fisher College, a private four-

---

*The software industry has successfully lobbied the federal government to double the number of temporary visas for foreign computer scientists and software engineers, citing a serious shortage of American students with such skills. However, when it was suggested that they pay a fee to bring in foreign engineers—the fee to go for training more American software specialists—they adamantly refused. The market solution to any shortage is to let wages increase to whatever level is necessary to attract more American students to major in computer science, or to hire other majors and train them to be software engineers.

year liberal arts school in Rochester, New York, offers up to $5,000 in refund payments to students who are unable to find a job within six months of graduation. The necessity for such guarantees is all too apparent. The college degree is often not even an indicator of proficiency in basic skills. According to a study by the Educational Testing Service, 21 percent of two-year college graduates and 11 percent of four-year graduates have such poor literacy skills that they have difficulty writing a simple letter protesting a billing error.[114]

It isn't just a lack of basic skills that is a problem; it is a lack of relevant skills. Colleges argue that it isn't their function to train people to earn a living; they see their purpose as to create educated people. Actually, it is absurd to think that the two goals are antithetical. To gain one but not the other is a waste of social resources and does a serious disservice to the students. The core curricula for any major should include introductory courses in statistics, finance, and economics.* Lacking such basic knowledge, liberal arts and social science majors should be provided a warning: "Mastering the requirements of this degree will not ensure that you will be able to earn a living." This is not to say that social sciences or liberal arts courses have no value. They can make a major contribution to the other goals of education that I've listed. By themselves, however, they are not sufficient in preparing people to earn a livelihood. Most colleges are not particularly concerned if their students will succeed economically. They generally fail to assess the job market or advise students where future career opportunities lie, despite a wealth of information provided by the federal government projecting job needs in the decades ahead.

All schooling from day one through college should also focus on developing the proper work habits, self-discipline, and interpersonal skills.[115] But, most importantly, by making grades a meaningful assessment of accomplishment, a college degree will again have value to both the recipient and potential employers.

2. Establishing Habits of Critical Thinking: Perhaps the most important function of education is to promote critical thinking. In recent years much has been made of the two kinds of thinking, creative thinking and critical

---

*The number of Americans without even a rudimentary understanding of economics is of particular concern. Virtually every public policy issue has an economic dimension. Yet I have discussed issues with Ph.D.s who have never had a course in economics and, as a consequence, haven't the foggiest notion of how wealth is created, the implications of supply and demand for labor relative to wage rates, or the purpose of the Federal Reserve System. I even had one supposedly well-educated woman tell me in the course of a debate that I was citing statistics, and statistics don't matter. The innumeracy of many who consider themselves intellectuals is frightening.

thinking—the right brain, left brain dichotomy (which is itself a terribly oversimplified model of how the brain works). The emphasis has been placed on the need for developing more creative thinking, but for all the hundreds of books written on how to think creatively, I have seen no compelling evidence to suggest that creativity is teachable. My own experience with hundreds of employees and co-workers over the past thirty years forces me to confess that I still do not know how to detect creativity in employment testing or interviews, but after observing a new employee for two weeks on the job I can usually identify whether he or she has creative capabilities. Moreover, it appears that those who don't have it seem incapable of developing it. Personnel organizations at major corporations are suckers for consultants hawking seminars that purport to improve management's creativity.* If education can develop creativity it would be wonderful indeed, but to my knowledge there is no convincing evidence that such is the case.

On the other hand, by focusing on merely imparting information, colleges almost completely ignore the teaching of critical thinking. This is evident by the increase in recent years in students' willingness to accept the most ludicrous New Age beliefs, such as the existence of ghosts, angels, and demons; the belief in all forms of pseudoscience from psychic predictions to astrology; and affirmation of the most ridiculous forms of mysticism, including past life regressions, out-of-body experiences, and psychic healing. (Some of the ultrafeminists have even attacked the notion of critical thinking as part of a male conspiracy to prevent women from advancing.) The ability to use the scientific method to test hypotheses is teachable, and with practice can be mastered by anyone of average intelligence. Unfortunately, it is all but ignored in most schools, yet, if we are to be a successful democracy, we must have a populace who is capable of electing leaders who will enact policies based upon empirical evidence rather than fanciful theories that ignore reality. Absolutely no one should be able to graduate from college without demonstrating a firm understanding of the scientific method. Knowing the method of science will not guarantee that a person is capable of critical thinking, but critical thinking is extremely difficult without the foundation in the method of science.

3. Understanding Human Nature: An educated person should have a basic understanding of the nature of the human species—biological, psychological, and sociological. It is only by understanding the motivations of human

---

*Unfortunately, personnel departments are typically composed of people with little analytical expertise and so they fail to demand verification of these claims. Consequently, I have witnessed the expenditures of millions of dollars on such seminars at Ameritech, with never once seeing some post-seminar evaluation to test their efficacy. Once again faith wins out over empiricism.

behavior that the correct social and economic policies can be formulated for a specific time and place. Such instruction should not be narrowly focused cultural indoctrination such as European, African, Hispanic, or Asian studies programs. Rather, students need to understand the motivating factors common to all people and how they gave rise to past socioeconomic systems, with emphasis on why past cultures arose and fell. Strengths and weaknesses of our own and other cultures need to be critically examined.

Special attention needs to be paid to the prerequisites for social harmony. This is much more than the study of civics. It is understanding the impact of present trends at the local, national and international level, and the impact they are having on our society. It is understanding how business, religion, the media, politicians, and even academia work to shape society to meet their own ends. It is understanding the need to balance rights with responsibilities, and individual wants with societal needs. It is understanding the individual's role in shaping our culture to meet the needs of the next century.

4. *Establishing the Desire for Lifetime Learning*: Education should instill in the individual a sense of intellectual humility—a realization that college or even graduate school alone does not produce an educated person. Too many kids come out of college or graduate school believing that they have acquired knowledge that is sufficient for a lifetime, supplemented with the evening news, *Time* or *U.S. News & World Report*, the *Wall Street Journal*, and perhaps some professional publications. Many fail to read books other than fiction or works required to keep current in their chosen careers. Colleges should convince students that, at best, a degree means that they have acquired some limited information, the capability of evaluating the truthfulness of propositions, and an appreciation of learning that should enable them to continue to deepen and broaden their education throughout their lives.

5. *Creating a System of Values to Enhance Social and Ecological Harmony*: Many of the science courses in high school and college are so narrowly construed that they are of little value in a person's later life unless he or she is pursuing a specialized science discipline. Conversely, in today's environment every citizen should have an appreciation of the ecological implications of their individual actions, as well as the consequences of socioeconomic policies. For example, if a person is studying an economic issue, such as the impact of a change in the tax structure, it is essential to understand not just the impact of taxes on the distribution of wealth, investment or consumption, but also the second-order impacts on resource consumption, pollution, population growth and dispersion, and related matters.

It is also apparent from the growing lack of parental involvement in child raising, that from kindergarten through college, schools have a more difficult and comprehensive role to play than in the past. It was a major failure for schools to abdicate the teaching of moral values to religious institutions. As demonstrated in *The Science of Morality*, morality is as proper a subject of research and training as any other academic discipline. The correct moral behavior for a given time and circumstance can be derived empirically. General norms can be formulated that are most conducive to the happiness of present and future generations. It is not enough, however, that this information be disseminated so that it can be intellectually appreciated. It must be ingrained in the students viscerally as well. To do so requires that the instruction on values and norms must permeate many areas of learning from childhood. For example, history courses can demonstrate the value of self-sacrifice and long-term commitment to the welfare of society by individuals who fought for democracy and equal rights. Biology should emphasize the ecological interdependence of all species. Literature courses can include selections of works that demonstrate especially admirable virtues or show the tragic individual and social consequences of pursuit of narrow self-interests.

Parochial schools to some degree inculcate a code of morality into their students, but there are two problems with sectarian education. First, the moral norms promoted are not necessarily arrived at through an empirical process but rely primarily on dogma and traditions. Therefore, the moral dictums may be totally inappropriate for the needs of a given society at a certain time in history. Second, because religious schools do not teach critical thinking (although they would surely deny the allegation), social mores that are irrelevant, inappropriate, or downright harmful to either society or the individual will nevertheless be unquestioningly accepted.

Again, education cannot and should not be value neutral. In the 1960s, there was an aborted attempt to imbue in students a sense of obligation to the broader society. This gradually got distorted into preoccupation with narrow self-actualization, and in the 1980s, mere unenlightened self-interest. Educators must return to providing an understanding of the interrelationships people have with their society and environment, and thereby demonstrate that, in the long term, self-interest must be congruent with the interests of society and environmental sustainability.

The city of Chicago has introduced value education in 154 elementary schools. Critics fear that the curriculum will be used to promote a particular religion or impinge on the private rights of individuals.[116] Such fears are groundless. It is more likely that we will find that attempting to instill values in school which are not reinforced at home, or which are contradicted by the overwhelming negative values of the media, will have little impact.

Today, at the college level there is a danger that courses which discuss values will degenerate into cultural relativism or political indoctrination, whether liberal or conservative. Ideally, in grades K through 12 the schools will do the proper job of inculcating the basic values such as truth, honesty, keeping of promises, temperance, kindness, prudence, and so forth. In college the discussion should involve the goals of society and the optimal means of achieving those goals. Rather than providing pat answers, the education process should demand that students back up their opinions with the weight of logic and empirical evidence. For example, take the statement "all men are created equal." What does it mean? Is it a truism? An objective? A delusion? Is there any empirical basis for the assertion? How has it been interpreted historically and today? What does it imply for social policy? What policies have been followed by various societies with regard to that statement and what have been the consequences? How should such a statement be regarded in the future? Obviously, these are extremely difficult questions, and forcing students to explore the range of possible answers will hopefully teach them to question any doctrinaire responses to this and the thousand other issues which each society must continually review in the context of new information regarding humankind and the world in which we live.

6. Developing the Basis for an Avocation: Finally, an appreciation of the various arts provides not just an outlet for human expression, but a visceral understanding of the human condition. The philosopher Arthur Schopenhauer believed that art and art alone can make life worth living. This may be a little strong, but an appreciation of art certainly can help make life more enjoyable, and at times even be therapeutic. Moreover, for the most part art is environmentally benign. It is neither resource constrained nor a source of pollution. Hence, developing an appreciation of painting, music, dance, theater, and the many other forms of artistic expression can divert people from more environmentally damaging forms of consumption.

Is all this too much to expect from the system of education? Many would probably say so, but in my opinion, such a list can and must form the essence of the educational experience.

Summary

It is sometimes argued that we cannot expect the schools to improve the education of students if the parents do not do their part to support and reinforce what is taught in the schools. This is in part true, but then the question becomes how do we break the cycle of poor parenting and poor educational results? In the previous chapter we discussed the need to reduce poor parenting by discouraging teenagers and unqualified parents from having children. But there will always be parents who are ineffective, at best, in the art of child raising. Schools cannot totally make up for inadequate parents, but they can make a marginal difference, and if the American culture is going to improve rather than disintegrate, it will be due to marginal improvements in each generation. Therefore, to break the culture of poverty we must not only provide the necessary incentives discussed in the chapter 9, but we must improve education in the country as well. While it is true that simply increasing educational expenditures is not the answer, the adequate funding of schools—especially the nation's poorest schools—is a necessary, although far from sufficient, prerequisite to educational reform.

If American education is going to pull itself out of its current despair, the following recommendations need to be implemented:

1. The number of school days must be extended to at least 210 per year. Lester Thurow is calling for the high school year to be extended to 220 days. (For those who say this is impossible, we note that Holy Angels Elementary school in Chicago has extended its school year by 40 days. The initial results are encouraging.)[117] In addition to longer school years, several hours of homework should be demanded every night.

2. Parents must be held responsible for their children attending school and doing their homework. Teachers must have the right to call in parents of truant or failing students. Parents who refuse to meet with teachers should face penalties, such as charges of neglect, fines, or the denial of welfare payments. In extreme cases, parents who do not cooperate with school authorities might be forced to give up their children. Society has a vested interest in protecting children and may determine the minimally acceptable standards with regard to their health and education, as well as physical and emotional well-being.

3. Control of the classroom must be returned to the teachers. Students who seriously disrupt the educational experience of others and cannot be corrected by appropriate disciplinary measures must either be sent to special schools (if under the age of sixteen) or have their education terminated.

4. Similarly, control of the schools must be returned to the principals, including the right to dismiss teachers or maintenance personnel who fail to perform adequately. Tenure should be reserved only for college professors who may publish unique or unpopular treatises or theories, but tenure must never be used to protect inept teachers. The single-schedule wage rate must be scrapped and teacher salaries determined in the marketplace.

5. If the results of pilot programs of early childhood education prove as beneficial as some studies suggest, we should consider universal implementation. Educational funding must be reprioritized to provide more money for

early childhood education as well as K through 12 education. Funding for colleges should be cut and admissions requirements raised so that fewer, but better-qualified, students are permitted to enter college. Entrance should be based upon achievement tests rather than IQ tests and racial quotas.

6. Per capita educational funding must be equalized among school districts to insure equality of opportunity. This will require that more funding come from state and federal sources, i.e., more funding from income taxes and less reliance on local property taxes. (However, funding should be denied to any city where education expenditures are rising because the city refuses to allow their police to cooperate in the apprehension of illegal aliens.)

7. Teachers' salaries in primary and secondary education need to be competitive with jobs in industry. Contrary to the common belief, and distasteful as it seems, the success of America's defense department has showed us that throwing money at a problem can work when it attracts the most qualified personnel.

8. There should be national achievement exams for students and their teachers. If students don't pass, they'll have to repeat the grade. If teachers don't pass, they will not be allowed to teach until they meet competency requirements.

9. Beginning in tenth grade, a system of vocational apprenticeships should be set up for the more technically, less academically oriented students. This would include not just the traditional crafts such as building trades and mechanics, but might include computer maintenance, dental hygienists, nurse aides, and the like. The vocation programs must be integrated with the needs of business. Trade unions must not be allowed to control the supply of craftsmen by preventing qualified vocational students from getting their journeymen card in a reasonable time.*

10. Values and moral education must be incorporated in all relevant courses from preschool through college. Basic values such as honesty, truthfulness, prudence, kindness, and the like, can be taught without relying on religious instruction. Appropriate prosocial (i.e., moral) behavior must reflect the increasing knowledge of human nature as well as the needs of present and future generations. As in the case of any human behavior,

*Under union contracts, only journeymen are allowed to perform the more difficult tasks. There is logic in this since using an apprentice to perform more complex or skilled tasks could result in shoddy workmanship or present a danger to either the apprentice or the customer. At times, however, unions have sought to keep the wage rates of journeymen high by controlling or preventing apprentices from obtaining journeymen status. For instance, it may take four years of job experience for an apprentice to make journeyman. The key words here are "job experience." If there is an excess supply of labor, it may take much longer than four calendar years for apprentices to gain four years credit of actual job experience. Hence, not only do apprentices earn less money because they are working less often, but they will receive a lower hourly wage rate as well.

moral norms are the proper subject matter for scientific investigation, and the findings of science with regard to morals should be transmitted through education. Correct moral behavior is too important to be left solely to religious institutions, which often base their moral codes on ancient beliefs, the whims of those who think they speak for God, and dangerously outmoded worldviews.

11. Affirmative action for college admission should be scrapped. Special classes and additional tutoring should be provided for any person at any age who seeks to improve his or her educational skills, but only after the minimum standards are met should the person be allowed into an institution. This means that for a while the very best schools would probably be predominantly white. So what? The very best basketball teams are predominately from minorities, but there are some great white basketball players and no doubt there will be great minority students. If a pure meritocracy does not result in proportional numbers of people in various academic, athletic, artistic, or technical careers, then so be it.

12. Educational attainment should not be a function of wealth insofar as ability to pay is a factor. At the college level, every student who qualifies should be able to finance his or her education by government loans. To qualify, a student must demonstrate mastery of the prerequisite knowledge (not just the intellectual capacity to learn as ascertained by SAT scores). The loans should be repaid as cash repayments of principle and interest, by providing a percentage of future earnings, or through a two-year civilian work program.

13. Incentives should be added to encourage more students to elect technical degrees, especially science and engineering. We need far fewer MBAs and lawyers. Unfortunately, market forces by themselves are particularly ineffective in reducing the number of lawyers who are able, to a large degree, to create their own demand. The answer may be a reform of the tort system, such as implementing the European practice which does not allow lawyers to work on a contingency basis and, hence, significantly reduces lawsuits.

14. At the college level a balanced core curriculum should be created that advances the six goals of education: 1) developing basic job skills, 2) developing habits of critical thinking, 3) understanding human nature, 4) establishing the desire for lifetime learning, 5) creating a system of values to enhance social and ecological harmony, and 6) developing the basis for an avocation and appreciation of the arts.

Admittedly, this is an extraordinarily ambitious group of educational reforms. But unless such a total revamping of the educational system is undertaken, what now passes for education reform will accomplish little to reverse America's educational decline or meet the nation's needs for the next century.

NOTES

1. U.S. Bureau of the Census, *Statistical Abstract of the United States, 1991* (Washington, D.C.: U.S. Government Printing Office, 1991), table 223, p. 138, and *Statistical Abstract of the United States, 1996*, table 241, p. 159.

2. U.S. Bureau of the Census, *Statistical Abstract of the United States, 1997*, table 272, p. 175.

3. Jenks, *Rethinking Social Policy: Race poverty and the Underclass* (New York: HarperPerennial, 1992), p. 177.

4. U.S. Bureau of the Census, *Statistical Abstract of the United States, 1997*, table 243, p. 159.

5. Ibid.

6. "The Bottom Line: Chicago's Failing Schools and How to Save Them," *Designs for Change* (1985): 2, 5. Cited by Wilson, *The Truly Disadvantaged: The Inner City, the Underclass, and Poverty*, rev. ed. (Chicago: University of Chicago Press, 1987), pp. 57, 58.

7. U.S. Bureau of the Census, *Statistical Abstract of the United States, 1997*, table 276, p. 177.

8. Ibid., table 277, p. 177.

9. John Kronholtz, "U.S. 12th Graders Rank Near Bottom in Math, Science," *The Wall Street Journal*, February 25, 1998, p. B2.

10. Adam C. Holland, "Report Says Test Scores Lag After 4th Grade," *Chicago Tribune*, February 25, 1998, sec. 1, p. 7.

11. U.S. Bureau of the Census, *Statistical Abstract of the United States, 1996*, table 249, p. 164.

12. Ibid., table 235, p. 156.

13. U.S. Bureau of the Census, *Statistical Abstract of the United States, 1995*, table 1370, p. 853.

14. Ibid. The latest data available was for 1992. It was not reported in the 1996 Abstract.

15. U.S. Bureau of the Census, *Statistical Abstract of the United States, 1993*, tables 228 and 229, p. 152.

16. Vernon Briggs, "Income Disparity and Unionism: The Workplace Influences of Post 1965 Immigration Policy," in *The Inequality Paradox: Growth of Income Disparity*, eds. James A. Auerbach and Richard S. Belous (Washington, D.C.: National Policy Association Report, #288, 1998), p. 116.

17. Richard J. Herrnstein and Charles Murray, *The Bell Curve: Intelligence and Class Structure in American Life* (New York: Free Press, 1994), p. 451.

18. Carol Jouzaitis, "College A's Become Rampant," *Chicago Tribune*, May 4, 1994, sec. 1, p. 19.

19. Ibid.

20. *Wall Street Journal*, September 13, 1996, p. A1.

21. Herrnstein and Murray, *The Bell Curve*, pp. 426–27.

22. Ibid., pp. 429–31.

23. Jacquelyn Heard, "Reformers' Biggest Hurdle," *Chicago Tribune*, September 6, 1995, sec. 2, p. 1.

24. Interestingly, as Herrnstein and Murray point out, it would be the brightest students—those who suffered most from the consequences of dumbing down—who would benefit from higher standards. Herrnstein and Murray, *The Bell Curve*, pp. 428–29.

25. Charles J. Sykes, "The Attack on Excellence," *Chicago Tribune*, August 27, 1995, p. 18.

26. Alfie Kohn, *Punished by Rewards: The Trouble with Gold Stars, Incentive Plans, A's, Praise, and Other Bribes* (New York: Houghlin Mifflin Co., 1993). Kohn confuses the use of grades as rewards—which would indeed be inappropriate—and the use as means of providing a student with an indicator of relative performance. It is this latter function which is crucial if we are to maintain the link between actions and their consequences. The fact that some students will perform academically worse than others regardless of their effort is a fact of life that must be recognized and dealt with in other ways—such as finding other areas where hard work can produce excellent results.

27. Sykes, "The Attack on Excellence," p. 18.

28. William Glasser, *Schools Without Failure* (New York: Harper and Row, 1969).

29. Sykes, "The Attack on Excellence," p. 23.

30. Ibid.

31. Nathan Caplan et al., "Indochinese Refugee Families and Academic Achievement," Institute for Social Research, University of Michigan, *Scientific American*, 266 (February 1992): 36–42. Cited in *Future Survey* (November 1992): 11.

32. Etzioni, *The Spirit of Community* (New York: Crown Publishers, 1993), p. 95.

33. Charles Murray, *Losing Ground* (New York: Basic Books, 1984), p. 224.

34. M. Rutter, B. Maughan, P. Mortimore, and J. Ouston, *Fifteen Thousand Hours: Secondary Schools and Their Effects on Children* (Cambridge, Mass.: Harvard University Press, 1979).

35. James Q. Wilson and Richard J. Herrnstein, *Crime and Human Nature* (New York: Simon and Schuster, 1985), p. 283.

36. Ibid., p. 278.

37. Ron Grossman, "SATs Get Dumber," *Chicago Tribune*, sec. 4, p. 1.

38. Thomas Sowell, *Race and Culture* (New York: Basic Books, 1984), p. 24.

39. *Church and State* (December 1992): 17.

40. *Chicago Tribune*, February 16, 1995, sec. 1, p. 1.

41. Joseph A. Kirbey, "Hartford Failure Raises Doubts about School Privatization," *Chicago Tribune*, January 28, 1996, sec. 1, p. 8.

42. Rob Boston, "Vouchers for Evangelism," *Church and State* (June 1991): 9.

43. Myron Lieberman, *The Teachers' Unions* (New York: Free Press, 1997).

44. H. Stevenson et al., "Mathematics, Achievement of Children in China and the United States," *Child Development* 61 (1990): 1053–66. Cited by Richard J. Herrnstein and Charles Murray, *The Bell Curve,* p. 437.

45. *Chicago Tribune*, February 15, 1995, sec. 1, p. 1.

46. Marvin Creton and Margaret Gayle, *Educational Renaissance: Our Schools at the Turn of the Century* (New York: St. Martin's Press, 1991). Cited in *Future Survey* (March 1991): 111.

47. Gabrielle Stern, "Kid's Homework May Be Going the Way of the Dinosaur," *Wall Street Journal*, October 11, 1993, p. B–1.

48. Michael Martinez, "City Schools Alter Homework Policy," *Chicago Tribune*, June 27, 1996, sec. 2, p. 3.

49. Caplan et al., "Indochinese Refugee Families and Academic Achievement," p. 36.

50. "Race, Class, and Scores," *New York Times*, October 24, 1982, sec. 4, p. 9. College Entrance Examination Board, *Profile, College-Bound Seniors, 1981* (New York: College Entrance Examination Board, 1982) pp. 27, 36, 45, 55. Cited by Sowell, *Race and Culture*, p. 16.

51. Sowell, *Race and Culture*, p. 181. Herrnstein and Murray, *The Bell Curve*, p. 269.

52. Mark Heyman, "A Mystery in Our Schools," *Illinois Issues* (January 1977): 33.

53. Jon Hilkevitch, "Evanston High Admits Minority Gap," *Chicago Tribune*, June 6, 1995, sec. 2, p. 5.

54. Ibid., p. 1.

55. Etzioni, *Spirit of Community*, p. 91.

56. Ibid., p. 90.

57. Alfie Kohn, "Dubious Rewards for Reading," *Chicago Tribune*, July 11, 1995, sec. 1, p. 17.

58. *Wall Street Journal*, September 13, 1996, p. A1.

59. Linda Darling Hammond, "Achieving Our Goals: Superficial or Structural Reform?" *Phi Delta Kappan*, 72, no. 4 (December 1990): 286–95, cited in *Future Survey* (June 1991): 4.

60. *Chicago Tribune*, December 10, 1996, sec. 1, p. 8.

61. Lieberman, *The Teachers' Unions*, p. 213.

62. Ronald Kotulak, "Shorter Breaks, Smarter Kids," *Chicago Tribune*, August 12, sec. 1, p. 3. Study by Janellen Huttenlocher, Susan Levine, and Jack Vevea, to be published in *Child Development* (August 1998).

63. James M. Healy, *Endangered Minds: Why Our Children Don't Learn* (New York: Simon and Schuster, 1990). Cited by *Future Survey* (March 1991): 13.

64. Education Commission of the States, *Bridging the Gap Between Neuroscience and Education*, October 1996, cited by Joan Beck, *Chicago Tribune*, October 17, 1996, sec. 1, p. 23.

65. For example, the Perry Preschool Program spent $7,252 in 1992 per child, but for every dollar spent society expended $7.16 on nonprogram children by age twenty-seven. Charles Leroux and Cindy Schreuder, "Preschool—Worth the Cost," *Chicago Tribune*, November 1, 1994, sec. 1, p. 12.

66. For example, the Boston-based "Better Chance" program takes students from inner city schools and provides private scholarships to top college preparatory schools in the country. And the University of California developed

a precollege enrichment academy in a South Central Los Angeles neighborhood. But of the fifty-nine people who started the program only twenty-six remain. *Wall Street Journal*, "Two Approaches One Goal: Saving Kids," August 15, 1994, pp. B1, B4.

67. Herrnstein and Murray, *The Bell Curve*, p. 415.

68. I. Lazer and R. Darlington, "Lasting Effects of Early Education: A Report from the Consortium for Longitudinal Studies." Monographs of the Society for Research on Child Development 47, 1982, Issues 2–3, p. 47. Herrnstein and Murray, *The Bell Curve*, p. 405.

69. Etzioni, *Spirit of Community*, p. 64.

70. Ibid., p. 59.

71. Ibid., p. 57.

72. Patricia Albjerg Graham, *S.O.S. Sustain Our Schools* (New York: Hill and Wang, 1992). Cited by *Future Survey* (November 1992): 11.

73. U.S. Department of Commerce, *Survey of Current Business*, July 1989. Cited by Thurow, *Head to Head*, p. 275.

74. Thurow, *Head to Head* (New York: William Morrow and Company, 1992), p. 275.

75. George Bush, "Agenda for America," Renewal, speach delivered to Economic Club of Michigan, September 10, 1992, p. 6.

76. U.S. Bureau of the Census, *Statistical Abstract of the United States, 1998*, table 279, p. 180.

77. Herrnstein and Murray, *The Bell Curve*, p. 469.

78. Ibid., p. 473.

79. Sowell, *Race and Culture*, p. 24.

80. Robert I. Lerman and Hillard Pouncy, "The Compelling Case for Youth Apprenticeships," *The Public Interest* 101 (Fall 1990): 62–77. Cited in *Future Survey* (March 1991): 14.

81. *Wall Street Journal*, March 4, 1992, p. 1.

82. Ralph T. King Jr., "Job Retraining Linked Closely to Employers Works in Cincinnati," *Wall Street Journal*, March 19, 1993, p. 1.

83. U.S. Office of Management and Budget, *Budget of the United States Government, 1995* (Washington, D.C.: U.S. Government Printing Office, 1995), p. 105.

84. Lewis J. Pearlman, "Luddite Schools Wage Wasteful War," *Wall Street Journal*, September 10, 1990. Cited in *Future Survey* (March 1991): 14.

85. David W. Haverback and Lester M. Salamon, *Human Capital and America's Future: An Economic Strategy for the Nineties* (Baltimore: John Hopkins University Press, September 1991). Cited by *Future Survey* (November 1991): 12.

86. U.S. Bureau of the Census, *Statistical Abstract of the United States, 1991*, table 1444, p. 840.

87. U.S. Bureau of the Census, *Statistical Abstract of the United States, 1995*, table 1370, p. 853.

88. James S. Coleman, Earnest Campbell et al., *Equality of Educational Opportunity* (Washington, D.C.: Office of Education, 1966).

89. Editorial, *Wall Street Journal*, June 27, 1989.

90. Illinois State Board of Education, "Illinois Elementary and Secondary School Statistics," 1995.

91. Eric Zorn, "Money Does Make a Difference in the Quality of Schools," *Chicago Tribune*, April 16, 1996, sec. 2, p. 1.

92. Illinois State Board of Education, "Illinois Elementary and Secondary School Statistics," 1995.

93. Jonathan Kozol, *Savage Inequalities* (New York: Crown Publishers, 1981), p. 223.

94. Ibid., p. 24.

95. Ibid., p. 51.

96. Ibid., p. 17.

97. Ibid., p. 66.

98. *Detroit Free Press*, March 6, 1988. Kozol, *Savage Inequalities*, p. 198.

99. Kozol, *Savage Inequalities* p. 134.

100. Ibid., p. 225.

101. Ibid., p. 221.

102. For an excellent and frightening exposé of this trend, see: Mary Lefkowitz, *Not Out of Africa: How Afrocentrism Became an Excuse to Teach Myth as History* (New York: Basic Books, 1996).

103. Bennett W. Goodspeed, *The Tao Jones Averages* (New York: E. P. Dutton, Inc., 1983).

104. "Running to Stand Still," *The Economist* (November 10, 1989): 20.

105. Peter W. Huber and Robert E. Litan, ed. *The Liability Maze: The Impact of Liability Law on Safety and Innovation* (Washington, D.C.: Brookings Institution, June, 1991).

106. Thurow, *Head to Head*, pp. 276–77.

107. Sowell, *Race and Culture*, p. 41.

108. Albert Shanker, "Making Standards Count," *American Educator* (Fall 1994): 16.

109. Ibid.

110. Thurow, *Head to Head*, p. 276.

111. Ibid., p. 278.

112. Shanker, "Making Standards Count," p. 18.

113. Lester C. Thurow, "Education and Economic Equality," in *The Inequality Controversy: Schooling and Distributive Justice*, eds. Donald M. Levine and Mary Jo Bane (New York: Basic Books, 1975), p. 172. Cited by Herman E. Daly and John B. Cobb Jr., *For the Common Good* (Boston: Beacon Press, 1989), p. 403.

114. Mike Dorning, "Colleges Issue Diplomas with Guarantees for Employers," *Chicago Tribune*, August 20, 1995, sec. p. 6.

115. Sowell defines such dispositions as the basis for cultural differences and believes that changes in such behaviors are essential for ending a culture of poverty. Sowell, *Race and Culture*, p. 9.

116. Kristina Marlow, "V for Values Now Joining 3 R's," *Chicago Tribune*, September 16, 1994, sec. 6, p. 6.

117. *Chicago Tribune*, July 27, 1994, sec. 2, pp. 1, 8.

11

Reducing Crime

The Problem

Getting accurate estimates of the change in crime rates over time is difficult since collection of national crime data was woefully deficient years ago. For example, in 1973 twice as many crimes were reported to police than the police reported to the FBI. By 1987 this difference had shrunk to 8 percent. Hence, FBI crime data reflects an improvement in compilation of crime statistics as well as any change in the rate of crime.[1] However, the report rates for the most serious crimes, especially murder, appear to be more consistent over time. Accordingly, we can accept the homicide rate as fairly reliable and it is probably an acceptable surrogate for violent crime in general.

Figure 11.1 shows the trend in homicide rates in the twentieth century. It is interesting to note that there were two distinct waves, the first beginning at the turn of the century and peaking in the early 1930s, and the second beginning in the mid-1960s and cresting about 1991. There is no doubt that homicides and violent crime have declined significantly in the 1990s. The more difficult question is why the drop occurred and whether it will continue.

One explanation frequently offered for the increased rate of crime in the post World War II era was that the nation got soft on crime. The almost complete elimination of executions after 1965 is commonly cited as evidence of this permissive attitude. However, if we compare the rate of homicides with the rate of executions throughout the twentieth century, as in figure 11.2, there appears to be little correlation between the two. While the homicide rate soared between 1900 and the early 1930s, the execution

Figure 11.1[2]*

(Rate per 100,000 population at five-year intervals)

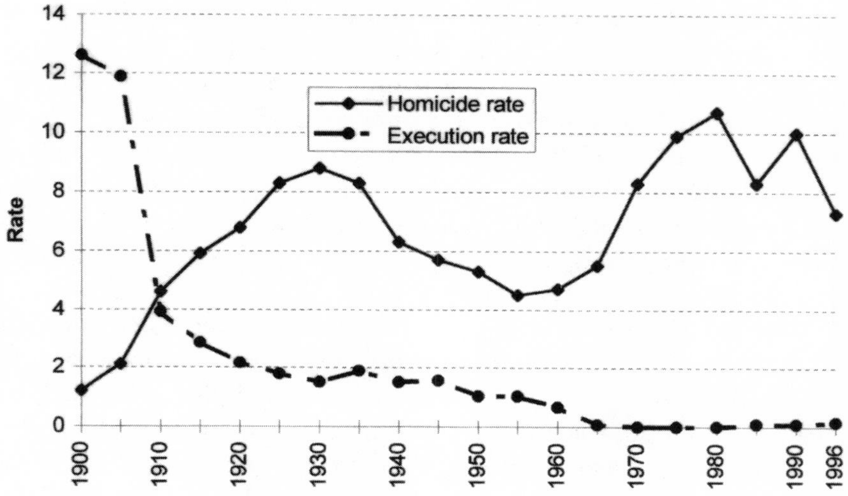

*Homicide rate per 100,000 population. Execution rate per 100 homicides.

rate declined from 12 people per 100 homicides to less than 4 per 100 by 1915. It might therefore be thought that the decline in the execution rate contributed to the rise in the homicide rate.

Note, however, that with the end of Prohibition, the homicide rate dropped from a high of over 8 per 100,000 population to less than 5 per 100,000 by the mid-1950s. Yet by this time the chance of a murderer being executed was only about 1 in 100. There then occurred a sharp rise in the murder rate in the late 1960s—concurrent with the increase in the sale and use of illegal drugs—before levelling off around the mid-1980s, and dropping steadily after 1991. During this latter period, although many of the states reestablished the death penalty, the chances of being executed were still well less than 1 in 100 (actually, about 1 execution per 500 homicides). There may be valid reasons for inflicting the death penalty, such as retribution, but deterrence does not appear to be one of them.

What makes understanding the causes of crime so difficult is that the trend in crime rates correlates with so many other trends. For example, during the two periods of rapid increase in crime, we had major demographic shifts, including large numbers of immigrants in the first twenty years of the century and the period beginning around 1970, but we also had a large increase in the number of teenagers resulting from the post World War II baby boom about this same time. Between 1917 and 1933 the nation experimented with Prohibition; the late 1960s gave rise to the drug culture and the War on Drugs. During both cycles, disparity in income between the richest and the poorest increased. And so on.

But there were major differences between the two cycles as well. During the first cycle average incomes generally rose. The second cycle was marked by relative stagnation in the growth of real per capita income. During the first cycle there was virtually no public welfare. The second cycle was marked by a huge increase in welfare recipients. The second cycle also saw emphasis on civil rights, the movement of women into the labor force in greater numbers, a surge in mother-only families, and an increasing depiction of graphic violence in the media. The impact, if any, that each of these factors contributed to the growth in crime is difficult, if not impossible, to reliably quantify.

Moreover, since many factors are to some extent interrelated, it may be that individually any specific factor would not be very significant, but collectively they become overwhelming (i.e., the whole is greater than the sum of its parts). All this indicates that understanding the causes of crime is difficult, and we should be suspicious of any facile or simplistic explanation. Although statisticians use sophisticated collection analyses in an effort to quantify the relative impact of each factor, there are a host of conceptual and data problems that make any statistical inference far from certain. In this chapter, we will see if it is possible to disentangle the many factors affecting crime rates and suggest socioeconomic polices that can reasonably be expected to further reduce crime rates in the future.

Post World War II Crime Trends

Let's begin by getting a little sharper focus on the crime trends since the Second World War. As the foregoing figure indicate, crime rates generally continued the decline that began after the repeal of Prohibition until about the mid-1950s. It stayed at relatively low levels and did not begin its precipitous climb until the mid-1960s, as Murray and others who try to demonstrate a correlation between crime and welfare are quick to point out. It should be noted, however, that the crime rate began to pick up even before the increase in welfare, and was in full swing by the time the welfare programs were being more generously funded.

After 1980, the murder rate fell slightly until turning upward again after 1985. In 1991 it was close to its 1980 high, but then began a steady decline. By 1997 the homicide rate had dropped to 6.8 per 100,000, falling well below the rate of 8 to 10 per 100,000 that the nation had maintained between 1970 and 1995.[3] The violent crime rate also has declined steadily since 1991, falling by about 15 percent by 1996.[4] While this improvement in crime rates is welcome, the homicide rate is still 25 percent higher than in 1965, while the violent crime rate is still more than three times as high as 1965.[5] (Some of the increase in the violent crime rate since 1965 may be due to better data collection.) Given the aging of the population, we might have expected the decline in crime since 1990. Although demographics played a major role, a decline in crime is due to more than just the aging of the population. The improved performance of the economy may have played a significant role, as did the 40 percent increase in law enforcement officers between 1982 and 1996.[6] As we will see, the prospect of increased income through honest means combined with the increased chance of being apprehended and incarcerated changed the risk/reward ratio for crime versus noncrime, and, hence, the propensity to commit crime.

Looking at who the victims of homicides are, we see from the table below that black males are almost seven times more likely to be murdered than white males.

Homicide Victimization Rates per 100,000 People[7]*

	White Males	*White Females*	*Black Males*	*Black Females*
1970	6.8	2.1	67.6	13.3
1980	10.9	3.2	66.6	13.5
1990	9.0	2.8	69.2	13.5
1995	7.8	2.7	56.3	11.1

In 1995 handguns were used in 58 percent of the nation's 20,220 murders.[8] Another estimated 20,000 people were wounded.[9] There were an additional 917,000 nonfatal crimes committed with handguns. It is fortunate that criminals appear to be bad shots, missing their intended victims four out of five times, but with the increase in the number of semi-automatic weapons, they may be able to improve their accuracy. Of particular concern is the continued drop in the age of those committing crimes with handguns. Between 1985 and 1990, the likelihood of a black male between fifteen and twenty-four getting killed by a gun tripled, accounting for one out of four deaths in this age group.[10] Moreover, until recently the increase in homicides for this group correlated closely with the increase in availability of firearms.[11]

Although the number of homicides increased 14 percent over the period 1985 to 1995, the number of juveniles between ten and seventeen who committed murder doubled from 1,384 to 2,753 over this period.[12]

---

*Separate data for Hispanics is not available. The vast majority of Hispanics are included in "white" estimate.

Even worse, the Justice Department warned that the number of juvenile murders could double again in the next fifteen years due in part to the growth of the juvenile population as the echo birthrate of the baby boomers become teenagers.

It is well known that U.S. crime rates are the highest of the industrialized nations. For example, the murder rate here is at least seven times higher than most European countries.[13] What is less well known is that the U.S. incarceration rate is also among the highest in the world. We are expected to jump ahead of Russia in a year or so.[14]

As shown below, the prison population tripled between 1980 and 1994. This does not include the 490,000 local jail inmates. By mid-1997, over 1.7 million Americans were behind bars.[15] We were spending over $100 billion annually on corrections—more than twenty times the cost in 1975.[16] Between 1980 and 1995 the total number of people under correctional supervision (prisons, jails, probation, or parole) also tripled to 5.2 million.[17] By 1995 almost three of every one hundred Americans were in prison or on probation.[18] The majority of these had been involved in some crime related to drugs. California now spends more money on prisons than higher education. Projections are that by the year 2000, 3 percent of the male workforce will be incarcerated and 9 percent under supervision of the criminal justice system.[19]

Federal and State Prisoners[20]

1960	213,000
1970	196,000
1980	316,000
1990	740,000
1995	1,085,000
1997	1,245,000

The primary perpetrators and victims of violent crime are blacks, and the primary reason for homicides is gang-related turf wars over the sale of crack cocaine.[21] It is reminiscent of the battles over bootlegging liquor during the Prohibition era. Drug arrests increased from 256,000 in 1980 to 536,600 by 1990.[22] This also explains the large increase in arrests of blacks. For example, in Michigan drug arrests doubled between 1985 and 1990, while drug-related arrests of blacks tripled.[23] In Washington, D.C., where in 1988 there were 372 murders, 98 percent of the victims were black and the overwhelming proportion of the crimes were drug related.[24] By 1993, there was approximately one black man under supervision of the criminal justice system for every three to four black men in the workforce.[25]

Clearly, although the War on Drugs has done little to reduce the flow of drugs or reduce the number of frequent users, it has yielded significant results in terms of imprisonments, and this trend is expected to continue. The problem is, what do we do with this burgeoning prison population? Even during the height of our present economic prosperity, black unemployment remains unacceptably high. As James Johnson and Melvin Oliver note, having a prison record is the "Scarlet Letter of unemployability."[26] We have learned from past experience that prison rarely reforms anyone. This is particularly true when the convict has no job skills and little hope of getting a job upon release. In 1991, 81 percent of state prison inmates were recidivists (repeat offenders).[27] At a cost of $18,000 per inmate per year,[28] this is a very expensive method of dealing with the nation's drug problem. Is there a more cost-effective way of reducing drug-related crimes in America? Many criminologists contend that there is, but first we have to dig deeper into the causes of crime.

THE FACTORS AFFECTING CRIME RATES

Crime theories can be classified into three general categories: (A) genetic, (B) environmental, and (C) economic. All three factors are interrelated, and it may be argued that economic factors should be included under environmental; however, to aid our understanding we will consider them separately.

A. Genetic Factors Contributing to Crime

The primary genetic factors summarized in the work *Crime and Human Nature* by John Q. Wilson and Richard J. Herrnstein are body types, intelligence, and personality.[29]

Body Types

At first blush the notion of body types affecting behavior seems a throwback to the discredited anthrometry of Cesare Lombroso, the Italian physician of the late nineteen century. The notion that a person's body type can affect their predisposition to crime seems absurd, and it is extremely doubtful that body type is a major cause of crime. But Wilson and Herrnstein summarize a number of statistical studies that demonstrate that there is a relationship between body type and crime.

William Sheldon classified body types (somatypes) in terms of *endomorphic*, *mesomorphic*, and *ectomorphic*.[30] An endomorphic build tended toward roundness; mesomorphic toward heavy-boned muscularity; and ectomorphic toward linearity—tall and lean. Most people may have elements of all three characteristics to some degree, but one or another characteristic may dominate. Sheldon studied the somatypes of two hundred delinquent youths and found that a disproportionate number were mesomorphic, i.e., muscular and neither fat nor lean. Many subsequent studies have confirmed his findings. There are two plausible explanations. First, a heavily muscled young boy would have a greater possibility of forcibly getting his own way, and therefore develop the traits of a bully or, conversely, fail to develop the discipline to achieve his goals through more patient, although less certain, means. Second, extreme masculinity could indicate a higher level of male hormones such as testosterone, and a subsequent increased level of aggressiveness.

However, even if either of the above is true, the overwhelming majority of people who could be classified as mesomorphic are law-abiding people. Many of the studies of somatypes are of delinquents or criminals. Usually these people also have a host of other disadvantages such as low IQs, an impoverished socioeconomic background, child abuse, and more. So, about all we can conclude from body typing is that those who are unusually muscular and masculine may require extra effort on the part of parents and society to teach them to control their desire for dominance. As explained in *The Science of Morality*, males have a natural desire to dominate, but the strength of that desire falls along a bell-shaped curve: most men have a fairly strong desire to dominate, with a relatively few number of men demonstrating either a much stronger or much weaker desire to dominate than the average. It is a function of family and society to train all males (and to a lesser degree females) to control their desire to dominate and to channel this tendency into socially accepted outlets rather than destructive endeavors. In the case of highly aggressive males, special efforts might be required in this regard, such as drug therapy to reduce excessive testosterone. There is relatively little research into this area, however, and it would be premature to make any recommendation in this regard. It may be that the right type of prosocial conditioning could also yield the desired results. Unfortunately, in our culture there are all too many positive reinforcers of aggressiveness, from contact sports to the violent content of television and the movies.

Intelligence

Herrnstein and Wilson emphasize the correlation between crime and low intelligence.[31] They show that on average there is a ten-point gap between offenders and nonoffenders.[32] Their findings are confirmed by other studies of repeat offenders.[33] Jenks explains that "[T]he prevailing view among sociologists is that children with low intelligence learn less in school, earn low grades, and react negatively to this experience. In order to protect their self-respect, many reject the standards of the adult world that defines them as incompetent."[34]

Correlations of crime with IQ fail to explain several extremely important facts, however. First, crime rates rose dramatically between 1970 and 1990, although average IQ changed very little over this time (in fact, it rose slightly).[35] Second, it should be remembered that the vast majority of low-IQ people are law abiding. Third, crime rates differ among societies far more than average IQ does, suggesting that culture itself has a far greater impact on crime rates. Finally, we are now beginning to understand that IQ itself is a function not only of heredity but also socioeconomic factors.

Taking this last relationship first, studies by Terrie E. Moffitt, a psychologist at the University of Wisconsin-Madison, indicate a close link between delinquent behavior and deficiencies in two neuropsychological realms—verbal skills and verbal memory.[36] This deficiency may be due to poor prenatal or postnatal care, especially basic nutrition. Untreated prenatal infections of a mother and exposure of a child to lead have been found to be especially harmful to a child's mental development and later behavior.[37] Behavior can also be affected by alcohol, drugs, or tobacco taken by a child's mother during pregnancy. Moffitt says she would increase expenditure on public health programs to improve prenatal care and infant health as the best ways to prevent delinquency.[38]

The role of intelligence is no doubt important. A very low IQ person may have trouble thinking ahead to the possible consequences of his actions. On the other hand, a very bright person might evaluate the risk and rewards correctly and decide that, under situations where the probability of apprehension is low, a decision to commit a crime is economically rational.

Personality

Personality exerts an impact on criminality independent of intelligence. A study by Edna Erez of Philadelphia jail inmates found that only 21 percent of all offenses had been planned.[39] Conversely, 79 percent of the offenses were the result of an undisciplined person acting on impulse. The Porteus Maze Test,* developed by S. D. Porteus to supplement conventional intel-

*The Porteus Maze Tests were developed by S. D. Porteus for cross-culture comparisons of intelligence. The tests use a series of paper-and-pencil mazes graded in difficulty. The mental ability score depends on how far a person can successfully advance and how many attempts are necessary to solve each maze. Since Porteus believed his tests would measure, among other things, planning ability, judgment, and impulsiveness, he anticipated that it also might be capable of predicting delinquency, job stability, and other signs of social adjustment.

ligence tests, indicates that a single cut off score identified over 70 percent of delinquents.[40] The delinquents were more impulsive and less socialized, i.e., cared little for the feelings of others.

Even here there is an interaction between environment and a person's personality development. For example, we know that the level of certain chemicals such as serotonin or testosterone is associated with aggression, but the specific form that the aggressive tendency takes—whether through sports or gang-related violence—is heavily influenced by environmental conditioning. Neuroscientist Bruce McEwen of Rockefeller University explains that "the environment—external influences from conception onwards—has a major role in shaping our individuality by shaping the expression of our genes."[41] ***Recent evidence shows that the environment can actually affect the development of the brain, resulting in dispositions ranging from depression to epilepsy, and certainly a predisposition to violence.*** We must be concerned, therefore, when a study of students from poor Chicago neighborhoods indicates that 74 percent had witnessed a murder, shooting, stabbing, or robbery. Nearly half were victims.[42] It should not be surprising, therefore, when an inner-city first-grade student comes to school with a knife for self-protection; he has seen firsthand what happens if a person can't protect himself.

Two facts clearly stand out: the great portion of crimes are committed by a relatively few people and such people frequently demonstrate deviant behavior at very early ages. A study by sociologist Marvin Wolfgang and colleagues of 10,000 children born in 1945 indicates that ***6 percent of the boys in the study accounted for one-half of all crimes, three-fourths of all rapes, and three-fifths of all aggravated assaults.***[43] ***A second study by Wolfgang of children born in 1958 indicated that 7.5 percent of kids accounted for 69 percent of all serious crimes and were arrested on average five times or more.***[44] Finally, numerous studies have indicated that people who were viewed as highly aggressive as children were far more likely to be convicted of a crime.[45] We must not assume that all delinquent children grow up to be criminals. No more than half of the children displaying childhood conduct disorders, however extreme, engaged in criminal behavior as adults.[46] However, the large number of offenders from this deviant juvenile population suggests that much more effort needs to be expended on how to alter antisocial behavior that is clearly discernible in childhood.

A review of the myriad of studies searching for a genetic basis for crime indicate that genetics is an important but not determining factor. It has been pointed out that children of repeat offenders commit twice as many crimes as the children of nonoffenders.[47] In cases of adopted children, there is a higher incidence of delinquency where the biological father was convicted of a crime.[48] However, most children whose fathers are convicted of a crime do not themselves commit crimes, and again it is difficult to adjust for all the other socioeconomic variables. The strongest evidence for inheritability are studies of identical twins (who have 100 percent identical genes) that show a higher likelihood of identical twins being involved in criminal behavior than fraternal twins (who share only 50 percent of their genes). *The most notable observation regarding heredity is that while body type, low IQ, or a high level of impulsiveness may increase a person's disposition toward crime, it does not explain the difference in crime rates between Houston and Milwaukee, or the changes in crime rates in the United States over the last thirty years.*

B. Environmental Factors Contributing to Crime

Is there something about the culture in the United States that causes violence? Contrary to common belief, we are not the most violent country in the world, but we do compare very poorly to other industrialized countries.

Male Homicide Rates per 100,000 People for Selected Countries[49]

Japan	0.7	China	2.7	Lithuania	11.2
Ireland	0.8	Singapore	2.8	Trinidad & Tobago	12.1
United Kingdom	1.2	Canada	2.9	Latvia	14.6
Denmark	1.4	Italy	4.5	United States	15.9
Germany	1.4	Poland	4.5	Russia	24.9
France	1.5	Costa Rica	6.6	Mexico	31.5
Netherlands	1.6	Bulgaria	7.5		
Australia	1.9	Argentina	8.5		

In general, we find that Europe and Asian countries have very low rates of homicide and violent crime. Violent crime in the Balkan nations and Russia jumped dramatically after the fall of communism. Perhaps most surprising is the homicide rate of Mexico, which is far higher than other South American countries and double that of the United States. We also find a high incidence of crime in the most underdeveloped countries in Africa, Latin America, and South America, particularly as peasants migrate from rural areas to urban slums. In part they may simply be following the same trend as Europe where pre- and early-industrial crime rates were far higher than today.[50] We also find that some poor countries, such as India, Saudi Arabia and some other Arab counties, and especially Asian nations, have very low (but in many cases rising) crime rates. In these instances there is usually a very close supportive family, a strong authoritarian government, or both.

How can an understanding of these different trends explain the relatively high level of crime in a country as developed as ours? The key to understanding the U.S. crime rate is to recognize that it reflects in part the averaging of various socioeconomic subcultures. For example, blacks in America are more likely to live in socioeconomic conditions similar to underdeveloped counties. Hence, it is not surprising that blacks are far more likely to be both perpetrators and victims of crime. Nationwide in 1994, 8.5 white males were murdered per 100,000, while black murder victims were 8 times higher—65.1 per 100,000.[51] Among inner-city blacks the rates were far higher. In 1995, blacks were only 13 percent of the population but 46 percent of jail inmates.[52]

Although we are experiencing a temporary decline in crime rates, it is doubtful that they will return to the levels of the 1950s; more likely they will begin increasing again as the children of the baby boomers hit their peak crime years. As more immigrants come from nations with high crime rates such as Mexico, we can expect crime rates here at home to increase. Such has certainly been the case in California, where the overall state homicide rate has increased faster than any other state in the Union, from 5.1 in 1965 to 9.0 by 1994.[53] Such data also demonstrate that crime rates are in large part a function of culture.

Family Structure

It comes as no surprise that the home environment has a major impact in developing patterns of behavior. A Rand Corporation study of prison inmates revealed that 56 percent came from broken homes,[54] but the relationship may not be as straightforward as it seems. Elliott Currie, a criminologist and sociologist from the Center for Law and Society at the University of California at Berkeley who has done extensive research on the causes of crime, points out that it may be the discord in the home, of which divorce is only the final step, that leads to delinquent children. Families who suffer the death of one of the parents do not appear to have higher rates of delinquent children.[55] However, the age of the child at the time of the death of a parent is relevant. The younger the child, the more likely that problems will develop.[56] One of the consequences of a family breakup is often substantial loss of income for the single parent. In general, women who are better educated, older, and better employed might be better able to fill the gap caused by a divorce.[57]

Having an intact, but dysfunctional, family can be worse than a single-parent family. One study indicated that in cases of violent children, the father was unusually likely to have been violent to the children's mother as well as to the children themselves—***62 percent of the fathers of violent***

children were violent.[58] Ethnographer Mark Fleischer's studies of 194 West Coast street criminals led him to conclude that they displayed "fragile and undependable social ties that weakly bound children to parents and other socializers." Nearly all of their parents abused alcohol or drugs or both.[59]

Cathy Spatz Wisdom, professor of criminality and psychology at the State University of New York in Albany, found that childhood abuse or neglect increased the likelihood of arrest as a juvenile by 53 percent, as an adult by 38 percent, and for a violent crime by 38 percent.[60] One particularly distressing study found that 76 percent of serial rapists were sexually abused as children, 73 percent were psychologically abused, and 38 percent were physically abused.[61]

As we saw in chapter 8, the evidence is overwhelming that the ideal family is a functional, two-parent family. There was a much higher percentage of poor people in the Depression than today but much lower crime rates. One difference is that despite poverty, the family stayed intact. In the 1960s, the California neighborhood with the lowest income, the least educational attainment, the highest tuberculosis rate, and the highest rate of substandard housing was Chinese. Yet at the time, only five people of Chinese ancestry were committed to prison in the entire state of California.[62] Compare that situation to that of inner-city black neighborhoods today and we immediately sense that there are other factors at work than just poverty. Perhaps the most significant is that the mother-only family is extremely rare among the Chinese, but endemic among black families. A longitudinal study of 1,000 black children from Chicago's Woodlawn neighborhood shows that children from mother-only households were more likely to be judged by teachers as "maladapting" than those from mother/father families.[63] Race is not the key factor here; the absence of the natural father is.

A 1998 study by Cynthia Harper of the University of Pennsylvania and Sara McLanahan of Princeton University tracked a sample of 6,000 males age fourteen to twenty-two from 1979 to 1993. They found that boys whose fathers were absent from home had double the odds of being jailed even when other factors such as race, income, parental education, and urban residence were held constant. Even though white children have a lower rate of father absenteeism, when families do split, white youth are at an even higher risk of incarceration than blacks. Surprisingly, remarriage does not seem to help, as boys who grow up with a stepfather in a home were at roughly three times the risk of incarceration than children who remain with their natural parents.[64]

Worldwide studies all conclude that a father plays an essential role in child raising, especially for boys. A study of forty-eight preliterate societies found that theft and personal crime were fostered by customs that limited a young boy's contact with this father.[65] Even in other animals the lack of adults to influence behavior results in "delinquency." Zoologists in South Africa were puzzled when young elephants displayed very unusual behavior by killing white rhinos. They soon learned that the bizarre activity occurred because there were no adult elephants in the area for the young elephants to test their skill against. Eventually all the young rogue elephants had to be destroyed.[66] So, too, it appears that in humans when there are no male adults to check the aggressive urges in adolescence or socially acceptable outlets for aggression, it can result in a variety of antisocial activities.

In our attempt to find causes that explain the increase in crime since the mid-1960s, the breakup of the family becomes a major factor. As mentioned earlier, in the case of black families, from the end of slavery until the 1920s there was not a disproportionate number headed by females.[67] The number of families headed by women began to increase slowly but steadily from the 1920s, but did not reach epidemic proportions until the 1960s. The rates of crime among blacks coincided with the demise of the two-parent household. According to James Q. Wilson, "Children raised by mothers, black or white, who have never married are more likely to be poor, to acquire less schooling, to be expelled or suspended from school, to experience emotional or behavioral problems, to display antisocial behavior, to have trouble getting along with peers, and to start their own single-parent families."[68] The consequences for children of teenage mothers are even worse, including cognitive defects, hyperactivity, hostility, and poorly controlled aggression.[69]

It might be argued that to some extent these problems are at root genetic—people deficient in intelligence or who have impulsive natures are more likely to have children suffering from the same problems. However, whatever the reason, the solution is the same: there must be strong incentives for single women, especially teenagers, not to have children, and for families to try to stay intact as long as the parents are not causing more harm than good.

The general decline in the number of parenting hours even in two-parent families has resulted in a decline in parental control. The average white parents spend ten hours less per week with children than they did in 1960.[70] The poor quality of day care in general has exacerbated the problem. According to a study by Jay Belsky at Pennsylvania State University, "entry into day care in the first year of life for twenty or more hours per week creates a 'risk factor' for the development of insecure attachment in infancy and heightened aggressiveness, noncompliance, and withdrawal in the preschool and early school years."[71] It must be admitted, however, that it is not at all clear how better day care would alleviate the problems cited by Belsky. ***It may be that it is not day care, per se, that increases the risk factor, but the fact that so many daycare centers are staffed by incompetent people.*** As indicated previously, day care is among the lowest paid occupations, and many of the providers are inadequately trained.

As in the case of poverty and educational attainment, the size of the family is also relevant, even when the father is present. In families where the father is a manual worker, the size of family has a considerable correlation with crime for boys.[72] If we can simply reduce the average number of children per woman, we might reduce delinquency.

Before leaving the subject of family, I would like to note two caveats proposed by Currie. The first is what Currie calls the *fallacy of autonomy*—that what goes on inside a home is independent of what goes on outside of it. Even in an ideal two-parent family the children must deal with the community in which they are raised. Additionally, as the Coleman report discovered long ago, the success of children in a classroom is heavily influenced by their classmates. Raising a child in the inner city is fraught with formidable obstacles even given the best family environments.[73]

Currie terms his second concern the *fallacy of intractability*—the belief that because delinquency problems begin early in life they are irreversible. There are numerous instances when intervention of various sorts have turned around a kid who looks certain to be headed for a life of crime.[74] Nevertheless, a successful public policy needs to play the odds. It must recognize that a strong family increases the odds of a child avoiding crime in any environment, and the best predictor of a child's behavior in later life is behavior in early childhood. Hence, again, the proper public policy will seek to forge strong, competent two-parent families.

A review of parenting studies by Wilson and Herrnstein concluded that the most effective parents are those who can be described as "*warm and restrictive*." A *warm* parent "is approving and supportive of the child, frequently employs praise as a reinforcement for good behavior, and explains the reasons for rules."[75] A *restrictive* parent is one who "states clear rules, monitors behavior to ensure that it conforms to those rules, and reinforces compliance by consistent and contingent use of reinforcers."[76] The children of warm-restrictive parents are most likely to value adult approval, readily internalize rules, and be rule abiding.[77] Such parenting skills require maturity, intelligence, and self-discipline from the parents. Hence, it is unlikely that children of self-indulgent, ignorant, immature, socially maladjusted parents will be well-adjusted, law-abiding citizens.

Finally, the evidence suggests that in the case of delinquent children, early childhood intervention is essential. Yet in a society where parents have the right to reject assistance, and with limited resources available to help relative to the number of cases that would benefit from help, it is easy to see how difficult it is to alter a trend when an entire subculture begins to plunge downward in an ever-worsening spiral of dysfunctional families raising dysfunctional children.

Drugs

When Murray tries to link all social evils to the increase in U.S. welfare during the 1960s, his theory fails to account for the increase of crime during the 1900–1933 period, a time when there was no social welfare. Nor does Murray's theory account for the fact that most European nations have a far more extensive welfare system than we do, but have experienced little increase in crime. (England is the major exception.)

As an alternative explanation of the increase in crime since the 1960s, we noted that a significant factor was the changing demographics. However, James Q. Wilson argues that the increased murder rate was more than ten times greater than what we would have expected from the changing age structure of the population alone.[78] I don't know how he derived his estimate; it may be high for reasons to be discussed later, but there is no doubt that America's increased crime rate is due to more than demographic factors alone.

When viewing figure 11.1, the similarity between increased crime during Prohibition and the period of the War on Drugs suggests that America's drug policies may be a major factor in the increased crime since the mid-1960s. Many European nations also have high drug usage, but have not experienced a significant increase in crime, especially violent crime. Of particular interest is the experience in Holland, a nation that is extremely permissive with regard to drug use and yet has crime rates that are 92 percent *less* than ours. Although per capita drug use is about the same in Amsterdam and New York, New York has ten times the murder rate.[79] The prohibition on drugs in the United States, like the prohibition on alcohol in the 1930s, has spawned a whole new industry of lucrative crime.

Drug-related crimes can be classified into four categories: (1) crimes related to sale and possession of drugs per se; (2) crimes related to efforts of rival gangs to control the drug trade—a leading cause of the increase in murders during the 1970s and 1980s; (3) crimes committed by those under the influence of drugs—particularly by users of crack cocaine; and (4) crimes caused by drug addicts attempting to get money to buy drugs. This last factor is particularly significant. The number of crimes committed by addicts attempting to get money for drugs is astounding. A study by John C. Bell and colleagues estimates that *243* addicts had accumulated *473,000* crimes over their lifetimes—that's almost 2,000 crimes per addict![80] ***The controlled availability of drugs would eliminate three of the four reasons for crime listed above. Moreover, the availability of drugs other than crack cocaine would reduce the use, and hence the crime, associated with crack.*** Legalizing and controlling the sale of drugs through state-owned or controlled outlets would not eliminate all drug-related crime, any more than legalization of alcohol eliminated all alcohol-related crime. But based upon the experience of other countries, it might reduce drug-related crimes by as much as 70 percent and the overall crime rate by over 40 percent.

On the other hand, legalizing drugs without an extensive and focused program aimed at discouraging both drug and alcohol use may result in an increase in crime related to those under the influence of drugs. A Rand Corporation study indicated that almost one-third of state prisoners reported being under the influence of an illegal drug before committing the crime that put them in prison. Another one-third had had four ounces or more of alcohol.[81] Disincentives for drug use have not worked very well. It is time we attempt to increase the incentives for not using drugs. As will be explained, the primary means of achieving this end is to increase the opportunity to obtain good paying jobs.

Television and Movies

In the United States, we do a marvelously effective job in conditioning our citizens to accept violence as an appropriate response to adversity. Those who have not experienced violence directly can view it with a mind-numbing regularity on TV. During their three to four hours of TV watching every day, children can view every imaginable type of violence. Even the seemingly innocuous types of violence such as the that of the Morphin Power Rangers can lead to habits of acting out aggression. In one poll, 96 percent of teachers said they witnessed Morphin-inspired acts of aggression.[82]

Psychologist L. Rowell Huesmann, a leading researcher into the impact of television on children's behavior, and his associate Jessica Moore, reviewed over one hundred laboratory studies, all of which conclude that at least some children exposed to films of dramatic violence act more aggressively afterwards. Additionally, more than fifty field studies found that "children who habitually watch more media violence behave more aggressively and accept aggression more readily as a way to solve problems." The connection shows up regardless of age, sex, social class, and previous level of aggression.[83]

TV may have a secondary impact. As mentioned, studies show that a major cause of criminality, independent of low IQ, is impulsiveness—a personality disposition to act without forethought, to seek instant gratification, to shift attention quickly, and to overreact to minor frustrations.[84] Wilson and Herrnstein express the concern that TV "might so dispose viewers to individual gratification that they become unable to work for distant goals or engage in disciplined activity."[85] This would be especially true in the case of those viewers with a propensity to impulsiveness.

There is also a substantial body of research indicating that not just young people are affected by sex and violence in the movies. Laboratory tests with college students viewing movies depicting aggressive behavior of men toward women, especially when the woman appears to welcome it (as in pornographic movies where the woman is actually "turned on" by her assailant), have the effect of increasing aggressiveness and hostility, especially toward women.[86] It might be noted that movies where rape is depicted as a cruel and disgusting act has the opposite effect, making men more sensitive toward the vulnerability of women and less likely to act aggressively.

In addition to a propensity toward violence, the media has many other adverse impacts. By depicting lifestyles that are basically hedonistic and wholly materialistic, it significantly impacts people's wants and values. Its characters often undermine prosocial norms. The TV character Murphy Brown was the first of a succession of sit-com unwed mothers who in effect sanctioned the notion of unwed motherhood. Another common theme is the right of superheroes to place themselves above the law in judging people and meting out punishment. As a promoter of self-discipline and prosocial values, TV is almost totally wanting.

TV acts as a constant source of diversion for people to avoid their civic and family responsibility. Studies tracking behavior in remote areas where TV was unavailable until the advent of satellite transmission indicate that the citizens become less involved in social and civic activities, and developed entirely new sets of wants.[87]

Finally, there is no greater disincentive for students to do homework than the example of their parents plunked down in front of the TV every evening. While some TV can be a positive experience, as shows such as *Barney* and *Sesame Street* demonstrate, there are extremely few programs that foster the essential and woefully inadequate capability of most people to engage in critical thinking. Quite the contrary, given the average viewer's willingness to accept the veracity of the media, the recent trend of pseudoscience programs purporting to investigate claims of the paranormal increase viewer credulity.

All in all, TV has become a mental virus infecting our nation with self-centered, antisocial values. In the long run, it is probably far more dangerous to America's future than AIDS. Yet to-date there is no serious effort to cope with the pernicious effects of TV other than labeling programs for content.

C. Economic factors contributing to crime

James Q. Wilson believes a major paradigm shift in morality occurred in the 1920s. The emphasis shifted from discipline and suppression of basic instincts to the Freudian notion that suppression of basic instincts was psychologically dangerous. This notion was amplified by the more permissive child-raising practices suggested by the works of John Dewey. Aside from the mischaracterization of the work of these two men, it is easier to see the changes that occurred in the 1920s as stemming from a combination of economic prosperity and the negative consequences of Prohibition than from Freud and Dewey. Elliot Currie also proposes a moral paradigm shift, contending that it occurred in the 1960s, and was due to a rise in economic inequality. As we will see, both Wilson and Currie's theories are oversimplifications of the numerous factors that merged to impact crime rates.

We did have a paradigm shift in the 1960s and TV was a significant factor, but it is not clear whether it was the cause or the effect of the factors we have identified. Moreover, if a morality shift is the major cause of the increase in crime, we have a difficult time explaining why crime rose so much for the poor and so little for the wealthy.

Inequality and Poverty

Some economists and sociologists offer this explanation for the inverse relationship between crime and income: the opportunity costs of crime are much less for the poor than the wealthy. The greater the perceived potential economic benefits of crime relative to the benefits of an alternative (such as jobs), the greater the incentive for crime will be. The economic foundations of crime are backed by substantial empirical support.

Many liberal sociologists believe that crime is a product of economic inequality. Currie notes that countries with greater equality of income have less crime, especially homicides, and that the economically disadvantaged account for a disproportionate share of all crime.[88] A study by Stephen Messner of Columbia University concludes that income inequality in thirty-nine countries explains 35 percent of the variance in homicide rates among the countries even after adjusting for the level of economic development, population density, and the degree of urbanization.[89] Sociologists Judith and Peter Blau found high murder rates in cites where whites worked in much more skilled and better-paid jobs than blacks, and in cities where the difference between rich and poor was unusually high.[90] Surprisingly, ***it was inequality of income rather than the absolute level of poverty that made a difference.**** Currie notes that the homicide rate in Texas was six times that of Wisconsin. He proposes that one reason for the difference in homicide rates is that Texas had five times the number of poor people but only slightly more AFDC recipients than Wisconsin. In addition, AFDC for a Texas family in 1980 averaged only $109 a month compared to Wisconsin's $366.[91] Therefore, the poor of Texas were worse off relative to the average Texan than the poor in Wisconsin were relative to the average Wisconsin resident.

Despite the high correlation between crime and income inequality, it does not necessarily prove cause and effect. Is there high crime because of high inequality? Or are both crime and inequality the result of other factors such as a difference in IQs or personality as suggested by Herrnstein, Murray, and Wilson?[92] Or is crime primarily a cultural phenomenon? In India there is a much wider gap between rich and poor, but much less crime.[93] Although the poor in many other countries have higher rates of crime, their crime rates are still generally less than the poor in the United States. It is true that U.S. crime rates increased in the 1920s, the 1970s, and the 1980s along with increasing inequality of income. But then why has the homicide rate declined in the mid-1990s even though inequality continues to increase? The conclusion I reach is that income inequality may play a role in crime, but the weight attached to this factor is probably not very great.

Unemployment

The relationship between unemployment and crime is by no means clear. During the late 1960s and early 1970s, there was a large increase in crime rates among blacks even though poverty rates were falling and unemployment had not yet risen.[94] In one review of studies relating crime and unemployment, three studies found a relationship between crime and unemployment, seven did not, and four gave equivocal results.[95] One reason for the ambiguity is that just looking at jobs tells us nothing about the nature of the jobs: are they part-time or temporary? Do they pay a living wage? Do they offer opportunities for advancement?

Currie suggests that the key is to look at structural, i.e., long-term,

---

*This would support the hypothesis in *The Science of Morality* that beyond the subsistence level of living, it is relative rather than absolute level of wealth that determines people's happiness and behavior.

unemployment. The increase in long-term unemployment for teenagers in the 1960s when the overall rate of unemployment was dropping explains the increase in the crime rate, according to Llad Phillips and Harold Votey of the University of California at Santa Barbara.[96] In 1952, the unemployment rate for nonwhite males eighteen to nineteen years of age was 10 percent; by 1967 it had risen to 20 percent. In 1966, when unemployment in the New York City area was under 5 percent, subemployment (defined as unemployment, labor force dropouts, and those working at poverty-level wages) was 33 percent in East Harlem.[97] Ann Drydan Witte argues that the availability of jobs providing economic viability is required to reduce crime.[98] European countries provide "economic viability" to even the unemployed by supplying much higher unemployment benefits for a longer period of time. As already pointed out, the downside of this policy is higher and more prolonged unemployment.

Risk and Rewards

Criminal behavior theories advanced by Becker as well as Wilson and Herrnstein hold that behavior is largely determined by its consequences—the greater the ratio of net benefits from crime relative to the net rewards of noncrime activities, the more likely a person will commit a crime.[99] Hence, we could expect higher unemployment and underemployment rates to lead to higher rates of crime. The incentives also include the positive psychological reward a person may get from feeling he is "beating the system," or negative feelings due to pangs of conscience. *The Science of Morality* presented a model of human behavior based upon the hypothesis that the desire for power, achievement, and affiliation are key motivations in determining human behavior.[100] These genetically induced desires can explain why teenagers join football teams, debating societies, and gangs. While many of us may look down on a person who traffics in drugs, his peers might look up to him. In his 1980 study, sociologist Charles Tittle concluded that the ability of communities to exercise social control is "rooted almost entirely in how people perceive the potential for negative reaction from interpersonal acquaintances." According to Tittle, formal sanctions are "largely irrelevant."[101] ***Therefore, when the net economic and/or psychological desires are more readily fulfilled by crime then by legitimate activities, we would expect crime rates to rise.***

Demographics and the Risk of Apprehension

Crime will increase if a society weakens the beneficial consequences for socially acceptable behavior. An increase in crime in the 1970s was in part predictable from the demographics in a way that Wilson fails to appreciate when he looks at a linear relationship between the increase in young people and the increase in crime rates. Recognizing that the postwar baby boom would result in a huge increase in teenagers and those in the twenty to twenty-four-year-old bracket—which traditionally has the largest incident of lawlessness—the nation should have been better prepared.

However, the nation failed to increase law enforcement efforts commensurate with the changing demographics of the late 1960s and 1970s. The nation's criminal justice system was soon overwhelmed. Insufficient police, courts, and jails resulted in a declining prosecution rate, and a declining probability of a defendant having to serve a sentence. To clear the court backlogs, plea-bargaining became the common practice. At the same time we had to cope with a whole new class of crime due to the rise of the drug culture. Becoming a drug seller may seem an economically rational alternative to unemployment or a dead-end minimum-wage job, even after factoring in the odds of getting caught or getting killed by a rival drug gang.

Furthermore, when the baby boomers were not provided jobs, an increase in crime was inevitable, but we went out of our way to exacerbate the problem. We built a welfare system that weakened the correlation between work and reward, and even provided a financial incentive—in terms of increased welfare payments to women—for a man to desert his family by denying aid to families with able-bodied males of sixteen years of age. (The man did not get the financial reward, but he could more easily rationalize leaving his family.) The increase in the mother-only family correlates all too well with the increase in crime.

Furthermore, I have long held that the number of teenagers relative to the number of their adult controllers is a significant factor in explaining the growth in juvenile crime. Especially when teenagers are concentrated in a small area—such as the high-rise public housing located in Chicago's notorious Cabrini Green—where there may be several hundred teenagers in a square block, we may achieve critical mass.[102] As density increases the criminal opportunities increase as well, and when potential offenders become more numerous, the chances of getting caught decline.

In addition to the increased population associated with the baby boom, there was continued migration to the cites from rural areas, particularly black migration from the rural South to inner cites in the North. From 1960 to 1970, the number of whites between the ages of fourteen and twenty-four increased by 23 percent, but black youth in this age group jumped 78 percent.[103] One study argued that, contrary to Wilson's opinion, all of the increase in crime in Pittsburgh between 1967 and 1972 could be explained by demographic changes.[104]

The huge increase in crime and the subsequent overwhelming of the criminal justice system became a major impetus for even greater increase in criminality. The street soon became aware that a criminal justice system was unable to keep up with the crime rate, which meant that the odds of apprehension, conviction, and sentencing would be increasingly in the criminals' favor. Between 1962 and 1979, the chances of a serious crime resulting in an arrest fell from 32 percent to 18 percent. The shift in the odds of actually serving time was considerably greater than this, dropping from 10 percent to only 2 percent.[105] By the mid-1970s, the average Cook County, Illinois, youth would be arrested more than thirteen times before going to reform school. ***With the chances of serving time dropping to 1 out of 50, is it any wonder why rational people might view crime as a more certain course for economic advancement than an honest job?*** And even if they are sent to prison, there is always time off for good behavior, making the time served as little as one-third of the sentence. There is evidence that youthful offenders are quite sophisticated about the probabilities regarding their apprehension and conviction.[106] All other things being equal, states in which the probability of going to prison is high have lower crime rates than states in which the probability is low.[107]

Wilson and Herrnstein cite numerous studies which conclude that, all other things being equal, punishment is an effective deterrent to crime. For example, criminal behavior changed when abusive spouses were arrested instead of merely being counseled, when Chicago delinquents were placed in more restrictive rather than less restrictive institutions, and when the penalties for carrying guns or driving while drunk were made either more certain or more severe.[108] The studies show that, in general, the key is not the *severity* of punishment so much as the *certainty* of punishment, especially if it is well publicized.[109] Although statutory penalties in Japan are less than in the United States, the clearance rate (i.e., the percent of crimes solved) for serious crimes in Japan is 60 percent compared to 20 to 22 percent in America.[110] Once apprehended and prosecuted, a criminal in Japan has a 90 percent chance of serving time. Japan has only 6 percent of the lawyers per capita that we have. The offender does not have access to the huge array of defenses to prevent him from receiving punishment since the Japanese, like most Asian societies, are more concerned with responsibilities than rights. The overemphasis of rights in America, and the commensurate reduced likelihood that a guilty person will serve time, is just one more reason why we have four times more serious crime per capita than Japan has crime of any sort, excluding traffic violations.[111]

Yet even if we increase arrest and conviction rates, imprisonment by itself will not succeed in significantly reducing crime. When American criminologist Lee Bowker studied crime and imprisonment rates between 1941 and 1978, he found that the correlation was not always in the direction expected. In fact, in some periods crime went up even though imprisonment rates increased.[112] Australian criminologist David Biles studied crime and imprisonment in England and Australia from 1960 to 1979. Although trends in crime were very similar in the two countries over the period, the trends in imprisonment were exactly opposite.[113] Such results need not surprise us, since we have seen that crime rates are a function of a whole host of variables.

Genetics, Environment and Economics are not Independent Variables

The point of the foregoing discussion was to show that crime rates are not a function of any single cause, but an interaction of many mutually reinforcing factors.* Therefore, no single change in social policies will significantly reduce crime. As the astute reader has gathered by now, it is impossible to separate the impact of genetics, environment, and economics in determining their relative impact on crime rates since they interrelate. Together they form a self-perpetuating reinforcing spiral of crime and poverty—a culture that worsens in each succeeding generation. It is futile to try and quantify the impact of each factor, but let's summarize the several trends that together have resulted in the increased crime rate.

1. *Migration from rural South to Northern urban areas.* Blacks migrated from rural to urban areas, especially to Northern cites, in record numbers in the 1940s to obtain well-paying factory jobs made available due to the labor shortage during World War II. By the 1960s, however, a growing number of manufacturing jobs were moving to the suburbs, the South, and eventually to other countries. The interstate highway system facilitated the migration of jobs to the suburbs, while discriminatory housing policies prevented minorities from following.

2. *Declining wage rates.* Lower-average real hourly earnings since 1973 have reduced the economic payout of legitimate work relative to criminal activities.

---

*Even weather seems to play a role. The highest crime rates are in Southern cities, where they don't have the crime dampening effects of winter. There may be other factors operating as well, but the highest homicide rates are in the Southeastern, South Central and Southwestern states. The Pacific Coast states follow close behind, while North, North Central, Mountain, and New England areas all have far lower homicide rates, and they have had for the last thirty years. The largest increase in crime in the last three decades has been in California, which not coincidentally has also had the largest increase in immigrants. Dobin, *Statistical Handbook on Violence in America*, p. 35.

3. *The post World War II baby boom.* The huge increase in the number of youths due to the baby boom, and the concentration of the poor in high-rise ghettos, destroyed the sense of community and increased the opportunities for crime. The increase in youth was not initially accompanied by a commensurate increase in police, courts, and jails—the result being a dramatic decline in the ratio of arrests and convictions to crimes, making it less risky to commit crimes.

4. *The anti-establishment movement.* A loss in respect for the nation's government and its laws resulted from a greater awareness of the nation's history of racial discrimination brought about through the Civil Rights movement, the disastrous Vietnam War, the resignation of Vice President Spiro Agnew and then President Richard Nixon, and numerous government scandals that have followed.

5. *The profitability of illicit drugs.* The growth of the drug culture together with the prohibition on drugs ensured enormous profits to drug sellers. Occurring at the same time as higher unemployment, these events resulted in a major shift in the risk and reward ratios for legal versus illegal activities. As we saw, affirmative action resulted in a depreciation of education and a college degree thus further reducing the reward side of the ratio.

6. *Overemphasis on rights rather than responsibilities.* A shift to a more liberal perspective that de-emphasized personal responsibility resulted in the disconnecting of actions and the consequences of those actions. This can best be seen in efforts to legitimize unwed motherhood. The growth in the number of unwed mothers and single parents as a result of fathers shifting their responsibility to society at large resulted in the further breakdown of the family. Even in the case of two-parent families, the number of latchkey kids and a reduction in parenting hours has been detrimental.

7. *Cultural norms and mores determined by the media.* Television and the movies reinforced sexual promiscuity and irresponsibility. The promiscuous male was held up as the new role model. Depictions of violence and sex reached new heights (or depths). Perhaps more importantly, television both raised materialist expectations and augmented impulsive tendencies. At the very least, it became a major impediment to homework and the educational process.

8. *Twenty years of excessive immigration.* All of the above problems have been exacerbated in the last two decades by the influx of tens of millions of immigrants and their children, who have displaced American workers, decreased wage rates, increased inequality of income and wealth, placed a

huge new burden on an already failing school system, and increased crime and interethnic conflict.

The difficult question now is, how do we reverse the course of social disintegration? Liberals and conservatives seek entirely different solutions based upon very conflicting suppositions of human behavior and the ability of society to alter that behavior. (I realize that the following are gross generalizations and liberals and conservatives fall along each of these continuums.) In general, liberals emphasize the environment as the primary factor affecting behavior; conservatives emphasize genetic characteristics. Liberals believe that people are infinitely malleable; conservatives emphasize the difficulty in changing basic character dispositions. Liberals emphasize the carrot of reward; conservatives emphasize the stick of punishment. Liberals like to believe that with the proper social polices every child can be saved; conservatives believe that social engineering will only make matters worse.

There is some truth in each of these opposing positions, but both involve gross generalizations that offer little guidance on how society can foster prosocial behavior. If we are to significantly reduce crime without turning our nation into a police state, we must first understand the determinants of human behavior, as discussed in *The Science of Morality*. Only then can we develop an optimal set of polices that recognize the limitations of social engineering to shape human nature, as well as the potential benefits of carefully constructed policies that effect the risk/reward ratio and the psychological conditioning that fosters prosocial behavior.

Since this topic was discussed at length in *The Science of Morality*, I will just offer the conclusion of that discussion here. There are two essential prerequisites to promoting prosocial behavior. First, people must have a relatively high degree of certitude with regard to the consequences of their behavior in terms of reward and punishments. Second, because we cannot always guarantee that behavior will receive the merited reward or punishment, it is equally as important that we instill in our children a moral sense—the feeling of internal satisfaction from prosocial behavior and guilt when considering antisocial acts. This has long been the goal of religion, but it needs to be one of the foremost goals of government and education as well.

Policies to Reduce Crime

Crime rates can be reduced to the rates of the 1950s, but it will take a different set of policies than at present either liberals or conservatives are prepared to endorse because of their limited view regarding the determinants of crime. There are several steps that must be taken *concurrently* to have any substantial impact on crime:

1. Increase the certainty of apprehension, conviction, and imprisonment.
2. Decriminalize consensual acts by adults that fall within the purview of personal morality. This would include prostitution and drug use.
3. Increase the rewards for noncriminal behavior relative to the benefits of criminality.
4. Use behaviorism to alter the psychological benefits of crime versus noncrime.
5. Implement effective means for reducing aggressive behavior—especially rape and spousal abuse.
6. Recognize the limited potential of rehabilitation.
7. Slow America's internal "arms race."
8. Redefine civil rights to preserve society.
9. Eliminate the culture of poverty.

This last point was discussed at length in previous chapters, and so I will only reiterate that as a society we must do all we can to discourage single parenting, and to treat parental neglect and abuse as the most serious of crimes. We know that single parenting greatly increases the chances that the children will live in poverty and become more likely to engage in delinquent behavior. We know that neglected and abused children are more likely to engage in criminal behavior. In addition to the soaring rate of single parenting discussed earlier, there has been an even greater increase in child abuse and neglect: an increase of 45 percent just between 1990 and 1995.[114] Although, thankfully, most abused children do not become criminals, this epidemic of child abuse will certainly increase the number of future criminals. To stem the tide, society must accelerate its efforts to remove children from dysfunctional parents who pose a serious threat to their children. If there is a shortage of foster parents, bringing back the orphanage must be considered as a more reasonable alternative to leaving children with parents who are doing them great harm. Of course we must also protect children from overzealous social workers who might wish to take children away from parents who, although far from perfect, may still be better than the alternative of a foster home or orphanage. For example, not all forms of physical punishment are cause for separating children from their parents. At times, parental education may work, especially in the case of immigrants where the action of parents, while not acceptable in our society, might reflect the norms in the country of origin.

Certainly it is a far better solution to reduce the likelihood of abusive or neglectful parents from having children in the first place. We are back to the argument for increasing the availability of contraception and abortion services as well as the use of forced contraception—such as subdermal implants—to prevent women convicted of repeated instances of abuse from having additional children. In the 1970s, five million unwanted pregnancies were averted through family planning programs without the use of abortion.[115] The result was no doubt the avoidance of a lot of unhappy children and many future criminals. It disgraceful that the pressures of the religious right and a mistaken sense of budget priorities has seen a steady reduction in federal assistance to family planning efforts. Every year the reactionary Senator Jesse Helms of North Carolina leads the crusade to strip Title X funding—the primary source of family planning services for poor women. ***We should double Title X funding and reestablish federal aid for abortion services for all women.***

Now let's turn to the other eight recommendations which would result in fewer crimes.

1. Increase certitude of apprehension, conviction, and imprisonment.

When the United States failed to increase policy, courts, and prisons in proportion to the increase in criminality in the 1970s, the odds of incurring the negative consequences of crime dropped significantly. Moreover, the relationship between crime and punishment may be nonlinear, i.e., a small change in the ratio of the reward of crime to noncrime might result in a much greater that proportional increase in a people's willingness to commit crime. Hence the change in demographics triggers a far more than proportional increase in crime rates.

Conversely, in recent years not only did the eighteen to twenty-four-year-old cohort drop relative to the total population, but we increased the number of police, courts, and prison cells. Therefore, we achieved a much greater drop in crime than we would expect from either the changing demographics or the increased certainty of apprehension taken separately.*

*In statistical terms, the explanatory variables are multiplicative rather than additive.

2. Decriminalize consensual acts by adults that fall within the purview of personal morality.

An inordinate amount of law enforcement is devoted to apprehending and prosecuting people involved in victimless crimes. The result is a diversion of resources that could be devoted to reducing all other crimes. Consenting adults should be able to engage in any activity they wish regardless of how immoral it may seem to others. One outstanding example of this is prostitution. If two adults freely consent to engage in sex for pay, there is no victim and hence should not be judged a criminal act. A woman would be victimized if she is forced or coerced into the occupation, or her customer could be victimized if a women knowingly infected him with a disease. Some European countries, such as France and Germany, have effectively coped with both of these conditions by requiring prostitutes to get frequent medical examinations and by prosecuting those who threaten or coerce women in any way.

Wining and dining a woman in the hope of getting her into bed is legal, but paying her outright is not. Why? Although many people would consider both seduction and paying for sex immoral, immorality *per se* is not justification for declaring an action illegal. If it were we would have hundreds of additional laws on the books.

It is particularly noteworthy that Japan and France have very low incidents of rape. Given the wide disparity in their cultures, one reason for the low incidence of rape may be that prostitution is far more socially acceptable in these countries than it is in America.[116] Of course, not all sex crimes arise out of frustrated sexual desire, but it is equally incorrect to assume that rape only rarely reflects sexual desire. (Especially in recent times, it is often posited that rape is motivated by the desire to dominate, humiliate, or otherwise harm a woman, and sexual desire plays only a minor role. However, although this is sometimes true, it is not usually the case, as will be explained later in this chapter.) The net effect of an enlightened policy toward prostitution would be reduced policing costs and might result in less violence toward women. Whether or not a society would benefit by legalizing prostitution is, like any moral issue, an empirical question demanding the appropriate study and analysis. At present, virtually all religions will refuse to reconsider the taboo on prostitution. The basis for the prohibition made sense when sex frequently led to unwanted pregnancies. Now that we can effectively prevent unwanted procreation, the religious taboo should be reviewed. Regretfully, given the dogmatic tendencies of most religions, they will refuse to reconsider the issue of prostitution irrespective of the evidence.

Some feminists argue that sex for money is inherently demeaning to women, and that it discriminates against poor women who would be disproportionately enticed into prostitution. I would counter that whether or not sex for money is demeaning is a matter of attitude. In many cultures courtesans were greatly respected. As to whether more poor women would be drawn into prostitution, I cannot say, but suppose that is the case. It would be nice to think that there are better jobs available for all women and none would have to resort to prostitution to earn a livelihood. This might be the ideal situation and we should work to provide better education and job opportunities for all women. However, in the final analysis, many jobs are far from enjoyable or rewarding. Working on an assembly line or as a farm worker in 100 degree heat is far from pleasant. Moreover, I would submit that even if every woman was offered a job paying a minimum of $20 an hour doing relatively easy work, there would still be many women who would opt for a much higher-paying job as a prostitute. The real crime with regard to prostitution is that those who engage in this oldest of all professions are not offered any protection under the law.

3. *Increase the rewards of noncriminal behavior relative to the benefits of criminality (e.g., the case for decriminalizing drugs).*

The increase in drug-related crime was totally predictable from the theory of self-interest discussed in *The Science of Morality*,[117] as well the criminal behavior theories advanced by Gary Becker,[118] and James Q. Wilson and Richard J. Herrnstein.[119] When the risk-adjusted rewards for crime exceed those for noncrime, we can expect an increase in crime rates. The time value of the behavior also plays a role: a payoff today is valued more highly than a payoff in the distant future (or a possible penalty in the distant future). Personalities that desire instant gratification are especially likely to heavily discount future rewards or penalties. If the alternative facing the impoverished inner-city teenager is a minimum-wage job flipping hamburgers or the possibility of earning several hundred dollars a week pushing drugs, the more entrepreneurial youth may opt to sell drugs even after considering the risk of apprehension. He simply makes a judgment based on the relative economic incentives.*

*Elliot Currie argues for "generous support of nonemployment" to ensure that the rewards of noncrime exceed those of crime (*Confronting Crime*, p. 271). Although generous benefits to the unemployed, as is the case in Europe, may reduce crime, it also results in longer-term unemployment. If there is little incremental benefit to work, many people will choose not to work, and the result is a prescription for economic and social disaster. Europe is finding its high number of unemployed people increasingly more difficult to support. I suspect that idleness is conducive to alcohol and drug use, sets a bad example for children, and ultimately will result in higher rates of crime than a fully employed society would incur. This is, of course, an empirical question, and Europe has not experienced the crime rates of

Despite increasing the federal spending to fight drugs from $1 billion in 1980 to $17 billion in 1996, the price of drugs dropped faster than the amount of money spent on policing could rise to meet it, indicating that supply is increasing faster than demand.[120]* In 1980 one kilogram of cocaine cost $60,000; by 1988 it had dropped to $12,000.[121] The cocaine supply multiplied 10 times between 1980 and 1988.[122] According to one estimate, cocaine profits amount to $95 billion annually—tax free. That kind of economic incentive will guarantee that there will always be willing dealers. Even those who had a regular job found the sale of drugs a lucrative way of supplementing their income. In 1992, two-thirds of drug dealers had a regular job. However, the median wage for a straight job was $7 an hour, while the median hourly earnings for drug dealing was $30 an hour—tax free, with an up-side potential of many times that amount.[123] Moreover, during the last twenty-five years the decline in real wages has increased the relative value of crime. Wilson and Herrnstein suggest that the reason why there has been no change in heroin traffic despite the greater number of arrests and more severe penalties is that a person who sells significant quantities of heroin is still likely to make far more money than he would in any straight job.[124]

The odds of a drug dealer getting caught rose dramatically in the 1980s as drug arrests doubled, but by then the sale and use of drugs had become a way of life for inner-city, and even many suburban, residents. A Rand Corporation study projects one in four black men will be arrested for drug dealing before his thirtieth birthday.[125] By the year 2000, it is estimated that as many as 80 percent of imprisonments will be drug-related.[126] Selling drugs is like other forms of gambling: despite the fact that the odds are against you, the chances of winning big will attract many people to make the bet.

Controlling the supply of drugs is a hopeless illusion. ***The effect of our drug policy has been to keep the value of growing poppies, cocoa, and marijuana above that of any other crop.*** Hence, it is economically rational for people to produce these substances. It is not only people who get addicted to drugs, it is entire economies. *Washington Post* Rensselaer W.

---

the United States. But until a compelling case can be made that high levels of unemployment compensation will not lead to net negative consequences in the long run, we should take the conservative approach of doing all we can to discourage unemployment.

*The $17 billion is a very conservative estimate because it does not include the huge cost of incarcerating all of those convicted of crimes related to the selling and possession of drugs. As many as 50 percent of all U.S. jail inmates may be serving time for drug-related crime (William Buckley, *National Review*, February 12, 1996, p. 35). The cost of drug-related crime has been estimated as high as $150 billion annually—considerably more than the entire U.S. budget for welfare and social services (*Chicago Tribune*, January 29, 1996, sec. 1, p. 14).

Lee explains: "the cocaine industry directly employs hundreds of thousands of people in the Andean region. . . . If the industry shut down tomorrow, economic and political chaos would reign in Bolivia and Peru and possibly Colombia as well."[127] There is little chance of shutting down the drug industry, however. To try to police Colombia, Peru, and Ecuador requires covering an area equal to 43 percent of the United States.

By almost any measure, the War on Drugs has been a monumental failure. While the U.S. drug policy had little or no effect on the supply—other than to make the drug trade lucrative—it is a major stimulus to crime, especially violent crime. During the 1980s, Washington, D.C. alone averaged ten murders a week, almost always related to drug trafficking. For every dealer taken off the street, two are ready to take his place. It is a simple matter of economics. High rewards will always warrant high risks. Ironically, one of the reasons offered for the decline in violent crime in the mid-1990s is that the gang-controlled drug territories had become more stable, resulting in less gang warfare.

There has been a slight drop in the number of users of all forms of drugs, but this has not been because of a decline in the supply but rather an increase in awareness of the dangers of drugs. The educational aspect of the drug war has met with limited success. Despite all efforts to discourage the use of drugs, however, there still will be a proportion of the population that will attempt to escape from reality through intoxication, whether it be drugs, alcohol, or some other harmful addiction. Ironically, aside from the criminal aspects associated with drug laws, the use of drugs is not nearly as dangerous as the use of tobacco or alcohol. Drug policy scholar Mark Kleinman, of the University of California at Los Angeles, notes that alcohol is the drug on which kids "are most likely to get pregnant, commit crimes, get in fights, or drive recklessly."[128] Tobacco causes 400,000 deaths annually, and alcohol is responsible for about 100,000 deaths, while drug deaths from all causes amount to between 10,000 and 15,000.[129]

The peasants in Pakistan cannot understand the Western prohibition on opium. They have been growing it and using it for centuries with little negative impact. Yet the Americans and Western European countries pressure the Pakistani government to outlaw the growing of poppies. On the other hand, alcohol is forbidden by their Moslem religion. How would the Western nations react if Moslem nations demanded that the Western nations cease growing and fermenting hops and barley? A similar situation exists in South America, where Indians and peasants have been using coca for hundreds, if not thousands, of years.

The citizens of less developed countries have a right to feel that the entire drug effort is hypocritical and misfocused. They wonder why Western nations, particularly the United States, do not seek to tackle the much more serious drug problem of alcohol abuse. The statistics of drinking dwarf those of illicit drugs:

- Three times as many teenagers drink alcohol regularly than use any other drug.
- Alcohol results in 25,000 highway deaths.
- Alcohol costs $136 billion due to lost productivity, excess mortality, additional health care, property loss, and crime.
- Alcohol is a major factor in 50 percent of emergency room visits and 20 to 40 percent of all in-patient hospital admissions.[130]

Despite these huge social costs, America learned in the 1930s that prohibition is not the answer. Although the era of prohibition did reduce drinking and its commensurate ills, it also threatened to undermine our entire society. The huge profits to be made through the black market sale of alcohol spawned a crime syndicate that is still a major problem in America. Similarly with gambling: most states did prohibit most forms of gambling in the past, but in so doing they greatly augmented the economic benefits of illegal gambling. The prohibition on drugs has had the same effect. It has undermined the work ethic of countless numbers of people, particularly those of the inner city.

Holland has taken a more enlightened approach to drugs, choosing to control their sale and quality, even collecting tax revenue from the sales. By also providing free syringes, there are far fewer cases of AIDS or hepatitis deaths due to drugs or infected needles. Most importantly, there is no role for organized crime in the sale of drugs and very little if any drug-related crime. Has this laissez faire approach resulted in all Dutch children becoming drug addicts? Not in the least. Despite the problem of Holland's unique approach to drugs attracting drug addicts from other parts of Europe, there is still a smaller percentage of drug users in Amsterdam than in New York City.

By far the most dangerous aspect of illegal drugs is not the direct effects on the users. As bad as they are, they do not affect nearly as many people as alcohol or tobacco. The major evil of illegal drugs is the crime that they spawn, and no amount of policing and increased imprisonment will solve this problem. There is only one reasonable solution, and that is to decriminalize and control the sale of *all* dangerous drugs.

Won't decriminalization lead to more users and abusers of drugs, more crack babies? For all its negative consequences, Prohibition did reduce the number of alcoholics. Alcohol consumption increased by about 25 percent after prohibition,[131] and the decriminalization of drugs may very well lead to an increase in the number of drug users. However, it is doubtful that anyone who wants to abuse drugs today has any problem getting them. If people want to get high or escape form reality, they will always find a way. The plain fact is that there is no way a society can prevent people from getting high on some drug or another.

The best that a society can do is try and curb the demand for drugs by:

1. mitigating the circumstances that exacerbate drug use, such as joblessness (assuming that is a causative factor rather then the reverse);
2. engaging in a sustained effort to discourage drug use through negative advertising and education;
3. if drugs are decriminalized, prohibit advertising their use (this prohibition should extend to alcohol and tobacco as well);
4. implementing policies that prevent drug users from becoming a danger to others (such as providing heroine addicts methadone);
5. reallocating money from apprehension to rehabilitation of drug users;
6. taxing decriminalized drugs to finance efforts to discourage their use and to subsidize rehabilitation efforts; and
7. implementing programs that would reduce the likelihood of addicted women from having children, such as encouraging women using cocaine to accept a subdermal implant to avoid conception.

The answer to drug abuse, first and foremost, is education. The slight decline in American drug use over the last decade was not due to increased efforts to reduce supply, which, as I have shown, was a failure despite the highly touted drug busts, but rather was due to education. In the 1960s, we were told that marijuana use would result in addiction and an urge to commit all sort of crimes. It was untrue. Consequently, and unfortunately, all government information concerning drugs was dismissed by youth as a fabrication. Since that time, we have learned that habitual marijuana use is not without psychological and physiological dangers, and the many dangers of other drugs are quite real. So are the dangers of alcohol use. Unfortunately, while as a nation we are doing a better job of educating our children on the true dangers of marijuana, cocaine, and other illegal drugs, and even the dangers of smoking, we are terribly remiss in educating them of the dangers of alcohol. In addition, the alcohol and tobacco industries are permitted to spend billion of dollars to push their drugs.

Education can have little impact if it is swamped by the billions of dollars spent to create enticing ads that equate alcohol consumption with being cool, sophisticated, and, especially, attractive to members of the opposite sex. The beer company executives know exactly what they are doing with their fast-paced, extremely imaginative ads, which say, in effect, beer=party=sex=happiness. Note especially that the beer ads are viewed by children thousands of times before they become teenagers. By that time they are quite effectively conditioned to drink.

If this nation is at all serious about reducing drug availability and use, we must step up to the issue of alcohol consumption. Otherwise, the best we can hope to do is to switch people from illegal drugs to legal drugs at great social cost. ***Therefore, it is imperative to ban all forms of advertising (including TV, radio, or the printed media) for alcohol, tobacco and any drugs that are legalized.*** Admittedly, the evidence is somewhat mixed with regard to the effectiveness of reducing advertising. In the United States when we banned the advertising of tobacco on TV and radio, the percentage of Americans who smoked declined from 42 percent in 1964 to 26 percent in 1994.[132] Conversely, Norway, Canada, and New Zealand have had a more comprehensive ban on tobacco ads that have achieved little or no decline in smoking.[133] It is apparent that by itself, banning advertising of tobacco and alcohol is insufficient; it must be part of a larger strategy including negative advertising.* The alcohol and tobacco industries will howl that it is an infringement of their right of free speech. Too bad. As pointed out time and again, there is no such thing as an unequivocal right of free speech. The First Amendment was not written to permit patent medicine salesmen to hawk dangerous bogus remedies. Nor was it the intention to allow businesses to profit from peddling dangerous drugs.

The more difficult task is to discourage TV shows and movies from depicting the use of drugs as a cool form of rebellion. Unlike simply banning advertising, we cannot ban all depiction of drug use without seriously threatening the First Amendment. What we can do is launch an all-out counterattack through advertising. There have been some pathetically inadequate efforts in this direction. (Remember the frying egg—"Here is your brain on drugs"?) To succeed, we need a massive advertising campaign, analogous to the U.S. savings bond drives of World War II. The War on Drugs could be waged more successfully if more of the $17 billion allocated to fight drugs in 1996 were diverted from attempting to interdict illicit drugs to reducing demand through education and negative advertising. Powerful ads could be developed showing the effects on babies of crack-using mothers. By legalizing drugs, we could save $25 to $50 billion a year in police, courts, and incarceration costs. This savings would be more than enough to mount an effective education and negative adver-

*It should go without saying that any government subsidies, such as those for tobacco farmers, should be ended.

tising program. It should involve the enlistment of major sports and entertainment celebrities. Michael Jordan and Oprah Winfrey carry far more weight among teenagers than the president of the United States.

The use of drugs, especially nicotine, can be further reduced through increased taxation such as that being considered in Congress at the time of this writing. According to one estimate, a 10 percent increase in the price of cigarettes will result in a 12 percent reduction in consumption.[134] However, as we know from the Canadian experience, we must be careful not to tax drugs so high as to create a black market. When taxes resulted in the price of cigarettes approaching $5 a pack, smuggling picked up so fast that Canada had to quickly reduce cigarette taxes. In addition to funding negative advertising, the proceeds from the taxes should be used for drug rehabilitation programs.

The sale of drugs should be controlled through licensed facilities, where control over sale to minors can be enforced. Again, the goal cannot be to completely eliminate minors obtaining dangerous substances, but merely to discourage use. Efforts should also be directed at reducing pregnancies among known alcoholics and drug users. Women who give birth to crack babies or babies suffering from fetal alcohol syndrome should be denied welfare benefits unless they are willing to have a subdermal implant or sterilization to ensure that they do not get pregnant again. Alcoholics and drug users who do get pregnant should be encouraged to get an abortion. ***Most importantly, the education program should feature frequent TV ads indicating the dangers of alcohol, cigarettes, and illegal drugs on fetal development.*** The evidence suggests that these drugs are the reason that such a large number of U.S. women have low-birth-weight babies, and it is the number of these at-risk babies—not inadequate medical treatment—that results in the higher infant mortality rate in the United States compared to other Western nations.[135]

Perhaps the most controversial policy is one which actively seeks to prevent addicted women from having children. In Anaheim, California, an organization provocatively called C.R.A.C.K. (Children Requiring a Caring Community) offers addicts who continually get pregnant a $200 incentive to get sterilized. Liberals are aghast at the program, but consider the alternative. The *Chicago Tribune* reported the story of a drug addict who got pregnant fifteen times. The result: four children dead, ten in foster care, and one son left in her custody. The founder of C.R.A.C.K., Barbara Harris, had adopted four babies born to a heroin addict. She knew that babies of addicts are frequently born with AIDS, brain damage, attention deficit disorder, and a variety of other problems. She decided to try and stop drug addicts from getting pregnant in the first place by offering them a cash incentive to get a tubal ligation or a five-year birth control implant.[136] Incentives for sterilization are also available for male addicts. Critics argue that the program takes advantage of the addicts' "vulnerability." They would do well to concern themselves with the vulnerability of the addict's children.

The more difficult consideration is whether to ever make sterilization mandatory. There have been a couple of sentences for repeat drug offenders who were also guilty of child neglect to accept a subdermal implant as an alternative to a jail sentence. So far all such sentences were overturned by higher courts. The concern is that in the past there have been forced sterilization programs that targeted low-income women and women of color. This is certainly a valid concern. However, if protections could be built in against bias in sentencing, the idea of sterilization of drug addicts who have children that are subsequently abused or neglected should not be dismissed out of hand as "cruel or unusual punishment." Often society must decide on policies that are the lesser of two evils, while at the same time remaining cognizant of the dangers of the slippery slope.

4. Use behaviorism to alter the psychological benefits of crime versus noncrime

We have for the most part abandoned the notion that a primary objective in child raising is to develop in children the prosocial habits necessary to make them responsible citizens. As Wilson and Herrnstein point out: "The notion that social institutions dealing with the youth were chiefly intended to convert young people into conforming adults has been replaced by the view that such institutions primarily exist to protect the young from adults."[137]

Even if nature is deterministic and people are not ultimately responsible for their actions in the philosophical or psychological sense, we must treat them as if they were truly responsible, because in so doing we provide the necessary motivation to behave in a prosocial manner. Currie points out that American society makes relatively little effort to discourage physical aggression among young males, whereas France and Japan punish physical aggression.[138] The results are predictable.

When a person evaluates the cost/benefit ratio of crime versus noncrime activity, one of the costs must be the psychological feelings of guilt for breaking the law, and one of the benefits should be a feeling of satisfaction when behaving in a prosocial manner. This requires intensive inculcation of prosocial values throughout a child's education. It should come from the home, but because we know that such education is not happening to the extent that it should be, we need to use the school system to undertake this activity. Values training should permeate every course of study from history to literature.

The conservative model suggests that increasing certitude of apprehension is sufficient to deter crime. We have already shown how the decline in the odds of getting arrested and serving time dropped in the 1960s and 1970s, thus encouraging increased criminal activity. The converse also seems to be true. Between 1980 and 1990, the total number of crimes rose 11 percent while the number of prisoners in federal, state, and local jails rose 125 percent; between 1990 and 1995, crime declined by 4 percent while the number of prisoners continued to rise by 39 percent.[139] Given the extremely high rates of recidivism, there is a concern as to what will happen to crime rates when many of the recently convicted are released.

By the mid-1980s, almost 50 percent of all black men were arrested once by age fifty-five for a serious crime. Of these, 85 percent to 90 percent were arrested for a second offense.[140] Currie points out that the conservative model of crime deterrence is based on the assumption that there is a high incidence of crime among a relatively small portion of the population. Hence, all we need to do is keep these criminals off the street and society will be safer. However, with so many minorities being arrested, the problem is not so much the incidence of crime committed by a small number who are responsible for most crimes, but the prevalence of crime among a specific segment of society, namely inner-city minorities. We are back again to the problem of a culture of poverty.

Therefore, increasing apprehension and punishment is necessary but not sufficient to significantly reduce crime rates. In addition, we must provide the monetary and psychological incentives to discourage crime. British psychiatrist Michael Rutter found that schools with fewer delinquents were fortunate to have teachers and staff who displayed responsiveness and encouragement and ample use of rewards, praise, and appreciation, along with a focus on good behavior.[141] This directly contradicts American educators such as Alfie Kohn who want to get rid of all rewards and praise for a child's accomplishments.

The use of rewards to alter behavior is not as straightforward as it might seem. Behavior psychologists have long ago learned that once a reward is associated with a certain form of behavior, the behavioral response is *actually strengthened* by not giving it every time an action is performed. As any one who owns a pet knows, it only takes an occasional reward or punishment to reinforce a habit once it has been established. In fact, once the stimulus/response is firmly established, it is difficult to alter the response even if the reward is dropped altogether. Of course, human behavior is far more complex than that of dogs. We are smart enough to recognize when there is no longer a possibility of a reward/punishment for certain forms of behavior. Under such circumstances, the psychological benefits or guilt associated with certain behavior will probably not be strong enough to overcome a huge reward for a criminal act, but we are often surprised. Almost every year we read about someone who finds a large sum of money and voluntarily turns it in just because it is the right thing to do. We should never underestimate the power of prosocial conditioning.

Another area where behavioral conditioning could be used effectively is in developing job habits. Many job placement programs have demonstrated that as difficult as it is to find jobs for low-skilled people, often an even greater difficulty is keeping them on the job. Many people have never developed the habit of coming to work every day, being on time, and putting in a full day's work. They expect to fail and they inevitably do. One way to foster better work habits and also prosocial attitudes in all of our citizens is through *universal compulsory civic service.*

In the past, one of the benefits of military service was inculcating habits of discipline and self-sacrifice, as well as developing a sense of nationalism as contrasted to the divisive nature of being ethnocentric. These same benefits could come from civic service. In addition, the "draftee" could see the positive value of his/her work on society. The notion of compulsory civic service for all people would serve two ends: it would develop disciplined work habits necessary to succeed on any job, and it could provide assistance in a number of areas where social needs are the greatest. ***We should demand one year of civic service from all people, and an additional year for those who receive government assistance to go to college.*** The possible jobs could include conservation projects, training of new parents, medical assistance, tutoring (especially English for immigrants), and even policing.[142]

5. Implement effective means for reducing aggressive behavior—especially rape and spousal abuse.

It is difficult to assess how much rape may have increased in America during the past three decades because some of the increase may have to do with a greater willingness of women to report the crime. However, the incidence of rape in America is 5 to 7 times more than any European country.[143] There are a number of actions the United States could take to greatly reduce the number of rapes if we only had the will.

As mentioned previously, it is a common misconception that most acts of rape are not sexually motivated but are the result of a man's desire merely to commit an act of violence against a woman. Actually, rapists fall into five categories.[144] First are the losers, men who have little chance of attracting women into any voluntary sexual liaison. Second are those who have been sexually abused as children and view force as an acceptable way of fulfilling sexual desires. Third are the opportunists, who find themselves in a situation where they think that they can rape a woman with impunity. They may have chanced upon a woman in an isolated situation or taken advantage of a woman's inebriated state. A fourth group is comprised of people who have had a sexually suppressed youth. They often come from extremely religious backgrounds where any encounter with nudity or material even remotely suggestive of sex has been suppressed. Their reaction can be sexual obsession and perversion. Finally, the fifth group are those men whose primary desire is to violate and abuse women, and rape is only a means to this end. The psychological reason for such behavior is complex and may be due in part to hormonal imbalances.

The five reasons are not mutually exclusive; a man may fall into more than one category. However, it is important to note that it is very likely that greater availability and social acceptability of prostitution may reduce the propensity to rape for a large number of potential offenders. The female availability argument is bolstered by the fact that the highest rape rate in the United States is found in Alaska, which is double the U.S. average, where the ratio of females to males is the lowest of any state.[145] Hence, there are fewer opportunities for legitimate sex. Moreover, as mentioned, in cultures where prostitution is socially more acceptable, such as France or Japan, the incidence of rape is far less.

Legalizing prostitution would probably not eliminate rape but it might reduce the incidents. There would still be rapes motivated by aggression against women rather than sexual desire. Further, the evidence suggests that incarceration per se will have little effect in reducing the incidence of rape other than the obvious consequence of preventing the rapist from committing the crime (at least against women) while serving time.[146] Nevertheless, the threat of imprisonment might be a deterring factor for many men, so I am not suggesting that we reduce sentences.

Recent research indicates that aggression can be reduced by lowering the testosterone levels of the offender. This leads to methods that promise to be far more effective in reducing rape and especially sexual molestation of children. Recidivism rates for pedophiles can be as high as 64 percent.[147] Prison by itself is not an effective deterrent to repeat offenders. Of particular interest is the so-called medical castration—the use of drugs that reduce the production of testosterone and other hormones that can cause aggressive behavior. Many European countries have been more willing to treat rapists with testosterone-reducing drugs such as the antiandrogen drug, cyproterone acetate. Such drugs have proved highly effective in suppressing abnormal sexual desires, although there may be side affects including gallstones and diabetes.[148] Another difficulty is ensuring that the offender continues the medication. It has to be administered by some agency that can threaten re-imprisonment if the person fails to show up to receive medication. Nevertheless, the results in some studies have been encouraging, equaling those of physical castration.[149]

When medical castration fails, physical castration may be the answer. The results of past experiments in Denmark, Czechoslovakia, Holland, Switzerland, Norway, Iceland, Sweden, and Finland have been extremely successful. One Danish study indicated a very low recidivism rate, only 4.3 percent over a period of eighteen years among 117 surgically castrated sex offenders, whereas 58 noncastrated offenders were ten times more likely to reoffend. Another Danish study, involving 900 castrated sex offenders followed for periods as long as thirty years, reported a recidivism rate of only 2.2 percent. A Swiss study reported a 7.4 percent recidivism rate for castrated offenders compared to a 52 percent rate for men who were not castrated.[150]

Castration is not a physical stigma since the testicles can be replaced with prostheses. Moreover, the surgery need not mean the end of a man's sex life, since hormones can be injected to provide sexual adequacy, but at a lower level than prior to castration. A 1991 Czech study demonstrated that after castration, 21 percent of the men lived in a stable heterosexual relationships.[151] Despite its success, the use of physical castration has been dropped in all countries at the insistence of civil rights activists. One study arguing against the use of castration points to the Danish study in which 2 to 3 percent continued to offend, and another 2 to 3 percent committed suicide.[152] (However the study did not track the suicide rate of any control group of convicted rapists.) I find this argument specious, since it gives more weight to the welfare of the criminals than to their victims. Which is better, a 2 to 3 percent suicide rate or a 58 percent recidivism rate? Unfortunately, social policy must often select the lesser of two evils.

Religion has also played a significant role in defeating any reasonable castration program. For a short time, Canada gave multiple sex offenders the option of physical castration or a long jail sentence. In the three cases where men opted for castration, they lost their aggressiveness to women and caused no more trouble. Nevertheless, the Catholic Church and civil libertarians objected to this "unnatural" and "excessive" punishment and put a stop to what appeared to be an effective and humane deterrent to rape. Once again religion and an unwarranted obsession for individual rights frustrates efforts to benefit society.

One of the most absurd cases in recent years was that of the Texas child molester Larry Don McQuay, who confessed to attacking almost 200 children. Before his release from jail he begged to be castrated, stating that he would undoubtedly attack another child, and to avoid being identified and apprehended he would probably kill the child.[153] Regrettably, because the U.S. Supreme Court ruled mandatory castration unconstitutional as "cruel and unusual punishment" (whereas the death penalty is not), he was released without the castration. Now while he is under virtual house arrest, he is having trouble finding a doctor willing to perform the operation.

Castration, whether physical or chemical, should be considered a viable alternative to extended jail sentences.* That it would reduce male aggressiveness cannot be disputed; however, such a severe remedy should be reserved only for multiple offenders. Moreover, castration must not be used as an alternative to imprisonment because victims and others in society might feel that the perpetrator has avoided sufficient punishment. (For many men, however, castration would be considered a far more serious punishment than a long prison sentence, since they would feel that it effectively robs them of their manhood.)

Imprisonment and castration is after the fact; what about identifying those individuals with abnormally high levels of testosterone and providing medication to reduce their testosterone level? The problem with such a suggestion is that high levels of testosterone also correlate with success in many fields where aggression is of value. This can run the gamut from contact sports to entrepreneurship. Many highly successful businessmen, professionals, law enforcement officers, military personnel, athletes, and the like will often, I suspect, be found to have high testosterone levels. Moreover, we don't want to have the government decide the level of testosterone that males must have.

A better method to harness aggressive tendencies is by educational conditioning. It has been shown that men can be conditioned to oppose the idea of rape by films that depict the pain and humiliation that a women experiences. Conversely, films that perpetuate the myth that some women are "just asking for it," or secretly will enjoy being violated, are the most pernicious form of pornography.

In *The Science of Morality*, I discussed the issue of pornography and what has been learned from research in this area, so I will not repeat the discussion here.[154] I will interject, however, that the issue of concern is violence, not sex per se. The Canadian Supreme Court has defined obscenity as that which is harmful to women. Certain feminist groups have interpreted "harmful" as anything that some women may find offensive. Such a ridiculously broad interpretation can result in a serious and unwarranted curtailment of free speech.

A different approach was offered by U.S. Senator Mitch McConnell

---

*In 1996, California became the first state requiring either chemical or surgical castration of repeat child molesters. The measure would require that anyone convicted twice of sexually assaulting a child be injected during the week before parole with a drug containing female hormones (most commonly Depro-Provera) that reduce sexual drive, or the parolee could choose physical castration at the state's expense. The law is certain to be challenged by the ACLU and other groups that oppose forcibly medicating people.

(R-Ky). He proposes a Victim's Compensation Bill that would allow victims of sex crimes to claim damages from pornographers if they can establish a link between the crime and the obscene material.[155] Most studies indicate that it is probably not the linkage with depictions of sex per se that results in violent behavior, but the linkage with depictions of violence.[156] As such, any violent crime that can be shown to be precipitated by gratuitous depictions of violence might be cause for a victim's claim for damages from the producers of such material.

The notion of censorship is abhorrent to most Americans. Civil libertarians, especially, fear that once we begin down that slippery slope it will inevitably lead to the loss of free speech. But the censorship laws of England or Canada have not led to any curtailment of free speech on political matters in those countries. There will always need to be trade-offs between freedom and security. It is absurd to think that free speech can be absolute. Again we are faced with balancing rights and responsibilities.

As a society we must especially be concerned with the movie and television programming that our children consume. There is evidence to support the contention that the thousands of violent acts to which we expose children have at least three negative effects:

1. At the very least it provides a false notion of reality. Studies have shown that frequent watchers of TV of any age group believe the world to be an even more violent place than it is. Suburban whites estimate their chances of being the victims of violence as far higher than the actual odds and thus live in unrealistic fear.

2. Ironically, despite the heightened sense of fear, people who have watched thousands of TV and motion picture murders by the time they enter high school have developed a passive acceptance of violence as an inevitable state. As a nation we have come to accept the 25,000 murders a year as a natural state of affairs, like the children of Northern Ireland or Lebanon who were so used to perpetual war that it became their favorite make-believe game.

3. For a small number of people at one end of the bell-shaped curve of normalcy, graphic portrayals of violence may indeed become a motivating factor to commit violent acts.

With regard to this latter group, the trend in movies is particularly disturbing. In the three decades from 1930s to the 1950s, although bad guys were romanticized in the roles of James Cagney and Humphrey Bogart, they always were caught and punished in the end. In the 1960s, opposing the "establishment" even by illegal means was romanticized and justified in the interest of "reforming" a corrupt society. Then, beginning in the 1970s, even this rationale for portrayal of violence was discarded and appeal of many movies became the amount of gratuitous violence that could be crammed into ninety minutes. The formula for movie success was combining the most imaginably grisly depictions of murder with a wisecracking hero who is justified in acting outside the law to apprehend the murderous thugs (often racially depicted as Arab terrorists). Movie violence has become the ultimate entertainment for a jaded society—a society without an ennobling purpose. Movies like *The Wild Bunch*, *Bonnie and Clyde*, or *Thelma and Louise* try either to justify violence or at least make its perpetrators palatable. Sylvester Stallone, Chuck Norris, and Arnold Schwarzenegger have introduced spectacular effects to make violence a major spectator experience. It is the modern form of watching gladiator combat. The Roman arena marked the decay of the Roman society. The alarming increase in movie violence is signaling the degeneration of American society.

As the work of L. Rowell Huesman and colleagues demonstrate, there is already enough evidence to link media violence with aggressive behavior.[157] Our society must decide which is more important: unlimited freedom of expression even when it causes great harm, or greater public safety. The First Amendment does not guarantee a person's right to yell fire in the theater. It does not guarantee the right of a person to provoke a riot. It does not guarantee the right of a person to instigate violence directed against another. It could well be that there are movies that instigate violence and must therefore be censured. For instance *The Science of Morality* reviewed several studies demonstrating that male college students showed an increasingly aggressive attitude toward women after watching films depicting women as if they secretly enjoyed being raped.[158]

The most common form of violent crime in America is spousal abuse. The criminal justice system often appears to turn a blind eye to it. There is a reluctance to get involved in family matters. Yet wife abuse might be significantly reduced if we were to take it as seriously as any other crime. However, spousal abuse is treated with such leniency in this country that it is not discouraged: one in four victims suffer from repeated incidents involving the same offender.[159] In a Minneapolis study of family violence, Lawrence Sherman and Richard Berk found that ***victims of assault by family members were about twice as likely to be assaulted again if police made no arrests, even though very few arrests result in convictions.***[160] Hence, to reduce spousal abuse we must treat it as any other form of violence and seek arrests and convictions. Even if the jail sentences are relatively short (we have to consider the impact on family income), we will be sending a clear message that marriage does not convey the right to abuse a spouse.

In the final analysis, the most effective way of reducing violent crime is to inculcate the right set of values in our youth. I return to the theme that I mentioned in discussing education. Our schools must impart basic values. This is much more than the present "value clarification" discussions which oftentimes give students the impression that the values of any person or culture are equally valid and must be respected (moral and cultural relativity). We need an ongoing program from preschool through the university to instill in our youth prosocial values, including a respect and toleration for the rights of others; an aversion to violence; a willingness to stand up for the dignity of all people; a firm belief that the virtues of honesty, truthfulness, and the keeping of promises are essential to the maintenance of any society; and that kindness and generosity rather than dominance are the hallmarks of excellence in humans. Because of their ubiquity, the TV and movie media have a responsibility for value creation as well. If they fail to exercise that function in a socially responsible manner, society may curtail their freedom of expression by virtue of its preeminent right of self-preservation.

6. Recognize the limited potential of rehabilitation.

There was a time when we thought that a primary purpose of prison was rehabilitation. The success of rehabilitation efforts is open to debate. No doubt many individual cases may be cited, but the overall evidence casts doubt on the efficacy of rehabilitation efforts. A review by Lipton, Martinson, and Wilks of thirty-one accounts of criminal rehabilitation programs through individual or group psychotherapy efforts to reduce recidivism rates of delinquents or criminals found little consistent evidence that such programs had a beneficial effect.[161] In another review of twenty-four programs for youths by Ross and McKay, all the programs appeared successful while kids were in the institution. However, only four studies followed the subjects after they returned to the community, and three of the four reported no lasting effect on crime reduction.[162] This is a common problem with studies on rehabilitation: many fail to track the participants long enough after they return to the community. It is easy for participants to feel that they have changed their lives while incarcerated, because the potential rewards of crime are absent and the costs all too apparent. Unfortunately, back in the community, if the perceived benefits of crime exceed those of noncrime activities, recidivism will be the consequence.

Rehabilitation does work some of the time, especially for youthful offenders. Some programs ranging from only six weeks to two months have proven superior to imprisonment, judging from later delinquency. Examples include camps where youth were put to work on construction, attended alternative schooling, and even outdoor training, involving hiking and camping, with some counseling thrown in.[163] According to several studies, successful rehabilitation is not so much a function of the particular program per se, but the conditions under which it is offered, especially whether the program is closely linked with other community services—schools, employers, social service agencies, networks of relatives, and community organizations.[164]

It seems clear that successful rehabilitation depends on three key factors. First is the nature of the offense. For example, as we saw, perpetrators of crimes of rape or molestation have a very different motivation than sellers of drugs. Selling drugs is motivated by economics, just as crimes of theft are, whereas sex crimes may be due to any one of several motivations, each requiring a different rehabilitative response to effectively deter further offenses. The second factor is the environment and incentives that await the convict upon release. Studies show that, regardless of treatment, if offenders return to the same negative influence of family and community, they have little chance of rehabilitation.[165]

The third factor—which is particularly important in deterring future economic crimes such as theft and drug trafficking—is whether there is any change in the ***perceived*** rewards of crime versus noncrime. For example, if a delinquent or ex-con has little opportunity for any meaningful employment, whereas the sale of drugs or car theft still offers a chance to get rich, we can expect a high recidivism rate. Note that I italicized "perceived." Even if the true odds of getting rich through crime are very slight, impulsive people or those with low intelligence might still opt for crime.

Concern for the contingencies associated with crime is also a reason why Charles Murray and Louis Cox worry that even if alternatives to prison sentences successfully reduced recidivism, if they are not punitive in nature they will not act as a deterrent to potential new criminals. Why should someone refrain from a crime if the worse that could happen is that they go to a work camp in the country that offers fresh air, exercise, alternative education, and counseling?[166] On the other hand, there is little evidence to suggest that jail sentences are successful for either rehabilitation or deterrence. Lyle Shannon's review of studies of youth crime in Wisconsin found an increase in frequency and seriousness of misbehavior in periods following imprisonment.[167] Donald West also found that imprisonment of youthful offenders increases their likelihood to commit crime again.[168] The problem with these studies is that they can't really say that those imprisoned would not have continued to commit crimes anyway. At the very least, they were unable to commit crimes while they were in prison, and the older they are when released, the less likely they are to commit violent crimes again.

However, imprisonment is at best a very expensive social expedient. The average cost of imprisonment is now about $20,000 a year. Moreover, increasing the number of arrests and imprisonments may not be the most economic or effective means of reducing crime. Currie estimated in 1984 that tripling the number of imprisonments would reduce crime rates 20 to

25 percent while requiring $70 billion for the construction of new prisons and increasing operating costs $14 billion a year. For that same $14 billion, Currie argued that we could create jobs for 750,000 people.[169] Interestingly, ***the United States has more than doubled the number of imprisonments between 1984 and 1997 and yet by 1997 the total crime rate had dropped only about 15 percent from its 1991 peak and was just slightly lower than the 1984 rate.***[170]

Obviously I am not arguing against imprisonment for criminals. An increased number of imprisonments will reduce crime if for no other reason than that a person in prison is at least temporarily unable to commit crimes (at least crimes outside of prison). I do contend, however, that imprisonment is the final and least effective stage in the process of fighting crime. If we are to maintain the recent decline in crime rates, we need to adopt the other recommendations in this chapter. For instance, the proven way to reduce recidivism is to relocate offenders in another community and provide them with decent paying jobs. However, it should be obvious that if we can do that for offenders, why not try the same approach before an offense is committed? In other words, ***why not develop a national jobs bank and offer relocation to unemployed people before they begin a life of crime?***

7. *Slow America's internal "arms race."*

With the changing demographics resulting in an aging population, we would expect crime to decrease, as indeed it has in almost every category, including murder. But murder is still the number one cause of death among young blacks. The availability of handguns greatly facilitates killing due to murders and accidents. In 1995, there were 13,790 gun-related murders, amounting to 68 percent of all murders; 11,300 murders were committed with handguns.[171] To these deplorable statistics should be added the more than 1,400 gun-related fatal accidents each year, of which 200 are children.[172]

Every effort to bring a minimum of sanity to the nation's gun laws has been fought by the efforts of one of the nation's most powerful lobbies, the National Rifle Association. The NRA and other pro-gun political action committees spent $26 for every $1 spent by the proponents of handgun control.[173] Hiding behind the Second Amendment,* they have opposed

---

*The NRA likes to quote the Second Amendment which states, "the right of the people to keep and bear arms shall not be infringed." But the NRA and gun proponents ignore the preceding words: "A well-regulated militia, being necessary to the security of the free state. . . ." Obviously, allowing every yahoo to own a gun hardly qualifies as a "well-regulated militia." Eighteenth-century militias were organized military forces subject to the legal requirements of the states. They were eventually phased out and replaced by the National Guard.

bills to impose waiting periods to determine if the purchaser of a gun is a felon, bills to outlaw semi-automatic weapons and "Saturday Night Specials" (the little snub-nosed guns that were the weapon of choice for holdups before the greater fire power of the semi-automatic handguns appeared on the scene), bills to prohibit steel jacket "cop killer" bullets that can pierce police safety vests, and any other regulation to which no true sportspeople or hunter could reasonably object. In the 1994–95 period, of the ninety police officers killed in the line of duty where the murder weapon was identified, thirty-three were by weapons included under the assault weapons ban.[174]*

By the time the Brady Bill finally got passed instituting a waiting period to check the background of a gun buyer, the nation was so swamped with guns that teenagers could get an illegal handgun almost as easily as a stereo. We are now the only country in the civilized world where teachers are afraid to go to class in many schools until metal detectors screen for guns. In 1987, it was reported that 135,000 students carried a gun to school.[175] To curb this extraordinarily dangerous trend, many high schools had to install metal detectors. Firearm possession arrests for kids under age eighteen jumped from under 20,000 in 1976 to more than 31,500 by 1989. Their access to high-technology guns like Tec–9s is increasing. The predictable result was a comparable increase in teenage murders. ***Nationally, the number of murders of those under the age of eighteen rose 73 percent in the nine years from 1985 to 1994. During this same period the percentage of teenage murders due to guns rose from 40 percent to 60 percent.***[176] Beginning in 1995, the teenage homicide rate has declined, but remains at a relatively high and totally unacceptable rate. There is no doubt that the increase in teenage murders during the preceding two decades was due in part to the greater fatality rate of those who are shot as opposed to stabbings or other forms of attack. Despite the deplorable state of affairs in our schools, our obsession with rights over responsibilities resulted in a Cook County, Illinois, judge dismissing weapons possession cases involving high school students whose arrest involved the use of metal detectors. He ruled that the students' constitutional protection against unreasonable search and seizure had been violated.[177]

The mixture of guns and drugs is deadly: 20 to 25 percent of kids who shot people were high on crack or PCP (angel dust). Perhaps even more disquieting is the fact that 75 to 80 percent of the teenage murderers were not high at the time of their crime. It was cold-blooded murder. More often

---

*The assault weapons ban prohibited only a handful of the roughly 500 kinds of semi-automatic weapons. Despite its limited nature, the House voted to repeal the law in 1995, but the Senate would not go along.

than not, the murder was gang-related, either for control of the drug trade or an effort to get money to buy drugs.

The psychological effect of carrying a gun is worth commenting on. In college I was president of my college's rifle club. I was amazed to see the transformation that often came over even the most mild mannered kid when he got his hands on a gun, especially a handgun. He was suddenly ten-feet tall and willing to take on the world. While walking through the woods behind the college, I've seen guys lob shots into a nearby town just "to wake them up," and take pot shots at any bird or other animal they came across. One fellow even threatened to "draw down" on me because I made fun of him while he was practicing his quick draw. (I wasn't too worried since he couldn't hit the side of a barn.) My experience with young people and guns demonstrated to me that many teenagers, especially those from an urban environment, were not mature enough to have a gun, especially a handgun. The NRA absurdly says, "Guns don't kill, people do." The empirically correct observation is that people with guns are more likely to kill than people without guns.

Part of the reason for the proliferation of guns in this country is for protection. Florida points proudly to the fact that since it allowed almost anyone to carry a gun there was a 21 percent decline in murders.[178] But New York City had a similar decline although it prohibits concealed guns. It appears that other factors are at work, such as the changing demographics, a decline in joblessness, and tougher law enforcement.

Does a gun offer protection? The protection of a gun is hotly debated. Opponents point out that the chances are far greater that a person with a gun will be killed; to be precise, eight out of ten who get held up and respond with a gun get killed.[179] But proponents tell us that the probability of a serious attack is 2.5 times greater for a woman resisting without a gun than resisting with a gun.[180] Note that neither of these statistics really answer the question. The first case may indicate that if an attacker has a gun and you respond with a gun you have a good change of getting killed. The second statistic may indicate that if a woman with a gun is attacked by a person without a gun, she has a good chance of defending herself. Of course neither of these statistics address the issue of whether or not increasing the number of concealed handguns will reduce or increase crime on the streets.

Do guns make a home safer? Here again there are conflicting statistics cited. A study published in the *New England Journal of Medicine* reports that homicides were three times more likely in households where guns were present than in households where they were not.[181] The increased danger of having a gun in the house has prompted the *Chicago Tribune* to suggest that a warning label be placed on all guns: "Caution: Having a gun in your house can greatly increase your risk of being shot or having your teenager commit suicide."[182] On the other hand, the higher rate of gun ownership in America appears to result in a much lower rate of burglaries when the occupants are at home (called "hot burglaries"). Almost half of all burglaries in Canada and Britain occur when the occupant is home compared to only 13 percent in the United States.[183] Neither of these statements differentiate between handguns, rifles, or shotguns. It might be that reducing "hot" burglaries is a legitimate argument for owning a rifle or shotgun, but would not require ownership of a handgun.[184] It might be that handguns rather than rifles and shotguns significantly increase the chances of getting killed in one's home.

In recent years there have two widely cited studies that emphasized the defensive value of guns. Florida State University criminologist Gary Kleck in his controversial book, *Point Blank* states that based upon his surveys, 2.4 million Americans annually use guns successfully to deter criminals compared to the 500,000 crimes committed with guns each year.[185] This is a far higher estimate than the 80,000 to 82,000 defensive uses reported by the U.S. Justice Department's National Crime Victimization Survey.[186] Other surveys by the *Los Angeles Times*, Gallop and Peter Hart Research Associates imply that there may be anywhere from 760,000 to 3.6 million defense uses of guns per year.[187] However, all of these surveys fail to differentiate the use of handguns from rifles and shotguns. If a person wants to protect his home, a rifle or shotgun will do as well and yet are far less likely to be used in commission of a crime since they cannot as easily be concealed.

Kleck also uses time series analysis* to determine if the growth in gun ownership is correlated with homicide rates. His results do not show a correlation. But again, his methodology is questionable. Since the United States has always had a huge number of guns outstanding and has made it so easy for any adult to get a gun, it is difficult to make any determination from time series analysis of national data. On the other hand, international comparisons indicate that those countries where handgun control is very rigid have very few deaths from handguns. Switzerland and New Zealand are often cited as countries where a high proportion of the population has guns and yet there are very few murders. However, most of the guns owned in these countries are not handguns, but hunting rifles in the case of sparsely populated New Zealand, and military weapons in the case of Switzerland, which has a citizen-army. Neither country is at all comparable to America.

---

*Time series analysis examines changes in the trends of various data series (variables) over time and, using sophisticated mathematical techniques such as regression analysis, attempts to determine whether a change in one variable is related to changes in the other variables.

John Lott Jr. and David Mustard of the University of Chicago examined the records of all 3,054 U.S. counties over eleven years between 1977 and 1992 to ascertain whether gun laws saved or cost lives. Based upon their cross sectional and time series analysis of the counties, they concluded that if all fifty states permitted the carrying of concealed guns in 1992 murders would have declined by 1,839 (7.7 percent), rapes by 3,727, aggravated assaults by 10,990, robberies by 61,064, and burglaries by 112,665.[188]

These are a startling conclusions, but before we all rush to buy a handgun, there are several concerns with their studies that need to be answered. First, it must be noted that they had data before and after a change in the law for only Arizona, Oregon, and Pennsylvania. Second, there were several trends occurring at the same time that states began to permit the carrying of concealed weapons: an aging population, a greater number of arrests and convictions, and increased law enforcement budgets. Lott and Mustard tried to disentangle these various factors (except for the increased law enforcement) but until their results are replicated in further analysis, their conclusions must be viewed with some skepticism. For example, many of the states that authorized concealed gun laws are in the South where population growth is spurred by immigration of retirees who obviously have very low crime rates, thus reducing the states' average crime rates.

Another cause of skepticism is the result that the percent of victims killed by family members declined when states passed laws allowing concealed handguns.[189] Are we to believe that arming members of a family make them safer from each other? On the other hand, there was only a 2.2 percent decline in robberies, the crime statistic we would think would be most deterred by concealed handguns.

Even a 7.7 percent decline in murder is trivial compared to the extremely low murder rates in countries that have very restrictive handgun laws. Moreover, at the present time relatively few people in any state carry concealed handguns. Pennsylvania has about the highest rate of concealed handgun permits at 5 percent while the Florida rate is only 2 percent. An intriguing argument might be made that there is an optimum number of concealed weapons. For example, it may be that if 5 percent of the population is licensed to carry a concealed handgun, the potential criminal feels that the risks are too high. On the other hand, if 30 or 40 percent carry concealed weapons it would pose an unacceptable risk to all citizens, especially law enforcement officials. The problem is that once we got to that level it would be extremely difficult to reduce the rate. It will be like the old West: no one will want to give up his or her gun when they think most other people are armed.

In short, before we begin arming the public we better study the issue in far more depth. Some of the data we need to get a better handle on are (a) the differential effect of concealed guns versus guns in the home, (b) the differential effect of owning handguns versus rifles or shotguns, and (c) the comparative positive effect to be achieved with less deadly protection (for example, carrying pepper spray or stun guns). Even if we permit some people to carry concealed handguns, is there an optimum number?

Although John Lott and Gary Kleck have not established the case for handguns, they have raised issues that need to be answered. Just as it is wrong to dismiss studies examining the relationship between IQ and poverty out of hand, it would be wrong to dismiss studies suggesting an inverse relationship between gun ownership and crime. Lott demonstrates that there is indeed much we can learn by examining the data rather than our preconceived notions:

- There is only one recorded incident in the thirty-one states that permit concealed handgun laws of a permitted concealed handgun being used in a shooting following a traffic accident, and that involved self-defense.[190]
- Only 17 percent of all murders in Chicago between 1990 and 1995 involved family members, friends, neighbors, or roommates. Most data on acquaintance murder includes rival gang members who the victim might have known or someone the victim just met.[191]
- In 1988, in the largest seventy-five counties in the United States, over 89 percent of adult murderers had criminal records, and 77 percent of juvenile murderers had prior criminal arraignments.[192]

Such observations lend some support for the NRA opinion that the vast majority of people are not going to murder regardless of the availability of guns. Murderers are different than most of us.

At the same time, we cannot forget that based on their rate of violent crime, Americans are the most violent people of the industrialized nations. Each year there are more homicides in Chicago than in all of Canada. Proponents of handgun control argue that the ease of getting a gun facilitates violence. Canada has tight restrictions on guns and outlaws over 200 types of weapons.[193] The United States, on the other hand, prior to the enactment of the 1994 Brady Law, had more gun dealers than automobile dealers. There were over 248,000 gun dealers in 1993. Anyone who could fork over $10 got a license to peddle guns. The 1994 Brady Handgun Violence Prevention Act raised the fee to $60 and the number of dealers dropped to 124,286 by 1997.[194] The Clinton administration unsuccessfully tried to raise the fee to $600, which they believe would eliminate most of the remaining small-time dealers.[195] Still, it is questionable whether it is now possible to significantly reduce criminal possession of handguns. There are over 300,000 guns stolen every year, and there are so many guns out on the streets today—an estimated 200 million[196]—that even if we were to stop manufacturing guns now, there is a supply to last over 100 years.

So what can be done? In 1997, England passed a law to outlaw private ownership of any handguns of larger caliber than a .22. Even .22 caliber handguns are allowed only in gun clubs, not in an individual's residence. There are tens of thousands of handguns in England. It will be interesting to note England's success in enforcing the law, and even more interesting to see what effect it has on crime rates. However, England does not have America's devotion to gun ownership.

In this country it is probably not practical to ban ownership of handguns. There are just too many handguns out there to make enforcement of a ban possible; and many of the owners are fanatics who would fight to the death before surrendering their beloved handguns. However, we could outlaw the manufacture, import, and sale of handguns and semi-automatic weapons carrying more than six rounds. Congress has banned nineteen types of so-called assault weapons, including weapons carrying more than ten rounds of ammunition (such as the AK–47 assault rifle, which carried 150 rounds). But Congress continued to allow the sale of 500 other semi-automatic models, functionally similar to the banned weapons.

Will regulations such as this keep handguns and assault weapons out of the hands of criminals? Not completely, but it makes a start. Between the passage of the Brady Act and the end of 1997 of the 10 million applications reviewed, 242,000 handgun purchases were denied—about 2.3 percent. Felony convictions or indictments accounted for 61.7 percent of the rejections, 9.1 percent were denied to people who had misdemeanor domestic-violence convictions, and 5.9 percent turned out to be fugitives from justice.[197]

The NRA says that if we ban guns only criminals will have guns. Of course, not even most supporters of gun control suggest that all guns should be banned, and it is true that criminals can always obtain a gun. Most murders are not committed by career criminals, however, but result from disputes between relatives or acquaintances where immediate access to a handgun facilitated the killing. Lack of immediate availability of a gun would reduce such spontaneous murders. Stricter control of the manufacture and sale of handguns would also reduce the number of weapons in the hands of teenagers. On the other hand, I have nothing against a store owner being licensed to conceal a gun while in his store.

With the number of handguns now owned by the public, a ban on handguns is no longer feasible, but we still might reduce the number of semi-automatic rifles and handguns that hold more than eight bullets in their clip before they, too, proliferate out of control. Incredibly, despite the pleas of the nation's law enforcement officers, rather than extend the ban to cover more semi-automatic weapons, some congressmen sought to reverse the 1994 ban on assault weapons. The argument is that not enough people have been murdered by assault weapons to warrant a ban. The reasoning is analogous to arguing that that there is no reason to vaccinate people against a disease until it has spread throughout the population. When the number of murders reaches the point to justify a ban, then Congress will argue that, like handguns, there are too many available to realistically control them—the perfect Catch-22.

If we were serious about reducing the number of murders in this country, we would control the ammunition used by assault weapons and handguns. Guns last almost forever, but it is estimated that there is only a four- or five-year supply of ammunition. Since it is almost impossible to effectively regulate the sale of ammunition, the key is to halt the manufacture and import of certain kinds of ammunition, or at least control it so that it is only available to the military and police. Such a ban would not be 100 percent effective. Again, since other countries will continue to manufacture weapons and ammunition, there will always be a black market. However, the supply would be reduced and the cost driven up to the point where teenagers will find it much more difficult to get hold of the required ammunition.

Finally (and in this case the NRA is correct), we must decrease the threat of crime if we are to reduce the feeling of many Americans that they need a gun for self-defense. We must continue to increase spending for law enforcement and institute legal reforms to greatly increase the odds that criminal acts will result in incarceration. Charles Krauthammer reports that in 1996 only 4 percent of all robberies in the United States resulted in time served. "Tell your stick-up man, 'You can go to jail for this' and he can correctly respond, '25 to 1 says I don't.' "[198] In addition to increasing the likelihood of apprehension and conviction, we must eliminate the most common reasons for the criminal use of guns: illegal drugs, gangs, the growth of single-mother households, and joblessness (especially among youth). This requires implementation of the policies recommended previously.

8. Redefine civil rights to preserve society.

It is imperative that we rebalance the rights and responsibilities equation. Philosopher Amitai Etzioni has taken the lead in trying to redress the imbalance between rights and responsibilities by founding the Communitarian Movement, the purpose of which is to refocus attention on responsibility.

Civil libertarians are quick to oppose any law that curbs the rights of Americans for fear that it will begin the slide to restrict all of our rights. While appreciating their concerns, I demonstrated in *The Science of Morality* that rights are a creation of society. Therefore, rights are not absolute but must be modified from time to time to preserve society. We must always weigh the benefits and liabilities of each right and make a decision as to where to draw the line. The decision must shift to fit the circumstances.

The murder rate in New York City has dropped 40 percent during the last couple of years; the robbery rate declined 30 percent and the burglary rate 25 percent. There has been a 64 percent reduction in felonies in the city's subways. Among the reasons suggested for the significant decline have been a rigid enforcement of the gang loitering law and aggressive attack on "public order" offenses such as aggressive panhandling, public drunkenness, vandalism, and prostitution.* In other cities, gang loitering laws have been struck down as an unconstitutional infringement of the right to peaceful assembly. In Illinois, a citizen has to file a complaint alleging that a group is breaking some other law before the police can break up a gathering of teenagers. Hence, the police have their hands tied until after the trouble starts. A more reasonable approach is to offer facilities where young people can gather to socialize in a supervised indoor area, such as a gym, while also allowing the police to break up gangs hanging around just asking for trouble. It is not a threat to peaceful assembly for political purposes, since there is no evidence that municipalities deny permits to hold rallies or demonstrations.

In New Orleans, crime rates in public housing dropped 70 percent after the city decided it had had enough. In 1994, the city imposed a dusk-to-dawn curfew on all those under age seventeen, forbidding them to leave the immediate vicinity of their home unless accompanied by an adult after 9:00 P.M. on Sunday through Thursday, and 11:00 P.M. on Friday and Saturday. New Orleans also made major reforms in the police department, cracking down hard on corruption, increasing the standards for hiring, and implementing community policing in public housing complexes.[199] The result was a 27 percent decrease in juvenile crime the first year of the crackdown. Perhaps the pendulum is swinging back from the excessive emphasis on individual rights to a more optimal balance between rights and responsibilities.

---

*As pointed out earlier, based upon the experience of other countries where prostitution is more or less accepted, it is at least questionable whether this last factor is related to other types of felonies.

Summary

Although at the time of this writing crime rates are declining in America, our violent crime rates are still much higher than other industrialized nations and still high by our own historical standards, especially for youthful offenders.

The reasons for the increase in crime rates over the past thirty years are complex and include: the changing demographics, especially the growth in the number of young people relative to adults and the relative density of young people in high rises; the reduction in the chances of apprehension and conviction of offenders; the growth in mother-only families; a lessening in accountability during child raising; the increase in the rewards of crime, especially the sale of drugs; and a reduction in wage rates and an increase in unemployment and underemployment. All of these factors resulted in a change in the net benefit of crime relative to noncrime activities. In addition, America has failed to integrate blacks into the mainstream socioeconomic culture. As a result, blacks (and increasingly, Hispanics as well), have developed separate cultures of poverty that are dysfunctional and hamper these groups from moving up the socioeconomic spectrum.

Several policy actions need to be taken immediately, all of which will increase the reward of noncrime activities and decrease the reward for crime. They include:

1. Changing the benefit ratio for crime versus noncrime activities. This requires increasing the chances of getting apprehended and serving time. But it also requires reducing the growth of the labor force, especially the number of the low-skilled, by reducing immigration. Tighter labor markets will increase wage rates, thus increasing the benefits of noncrime.
2. Decriminalizing consensual acts by adults will allow police to focus on true criminal activity. By concentrating on crimes involving victims, the certitude of apprehension and conviction will increase.
3. Decriminalizing the use of drugs and regulating their sale to reduce the net benefit of drug-related crime.
4. Understanding the causes of aggression, and learning how to either reduce aggressiveness or channel it into socially acceptable outlets.
5. Dismantling the dysfunctional culture of poverty by tearing down the inner-city high rises and scattering new low-income units among suburbs and rural areas. A major societal objective should be the socioeconomic integration of all minority groups into the main-

stream. The present emphasis on multiculturalism frustrates that goal.

6. Overcoming the hysteria of the NRA and enacting legislation to outlaw the manufacture or importation of handguns and semi-automatic weapons that can carry more than eight rounds (except for military or police use). Ammunition for such banned weapons should also be banned.
7. Renewing our emphasis on values as part of the educational experience of every American youth. We must inculcate the notion of shame for dishonorable actions to provide the psychological motivation for prosocial behavior.
8. Balancing the rights of the individual more carefully against the needs of society.

In addition, we must reduce birth rates among those not qualified to raise children (e.g., teenagers, drug and alcohol abusers, and mothers with a history of child abuse or neglect). This is yet another reason to provide federally subsidized contraception and abortion on demand, and to deny welfare to teenage mothers. Since we can never prevent all unqualified women from having babies, society must also increase the effectiveness of child raising by training parents.[200] In cases of abuse and neglect, including the inability to adequately support children, we may have to increase the number of orphanages to house children removed by court order.

Finally, there is still much we must learn about the causes of crime if we are to formulate effective policies to combat it. Special emphasis should be given to possible biological causes of aggressive and impulsive behavior, and their treatment. It might be that hormonal or other chemical imbalances that precipitate criminality in some people are medically treatable. Wilson and Herrnstein call for longitudinal studies from birth to adulthood. (Actually, we need to know about the child's prenatal care as well.) The National Institute of Justice has sponsored one such study: the Project on Human Development in Chicago Neighborhoods. It will collect data on individual traits, community characteristics, school and family settings, and peer groups for nine age groups from birth to age thirty-two. It will involve a sample of 11,000 people and track them for eight years (which is probably not long enough). The initial, tentative findings of the study indicate the important role of a father in adolescent development.[201] Although this comes as no surprise, it may help quell the recent assumption of yet another right without a commensurate responsibility, the "right" to have a baby even without benefit of a husband.

The project also indicates predictable results: areas that have high concentrations of poor, unemployed, and female-headed families, coupled with residential instability, will lack social control. This result bolsters the argument for scattered site housing for the poor.[202]

Notes

1. Jenks compared the U.S. Bureau of Justice Statistics, *Sourcebook of Criminal Justice Statistics, 1988* (Government Printing Office, 1989), pp. 283, 427, and the "Bulletin: Criminal Victimization, 1988," p. 5, in Jenks, *Rethinking Social Policy: Race, Poverty, and the Underclass* (New York: Harper Perennial, 1998, 1991), p. 186.

2. Sources: U.S. Bureau of the Census, *Historical Statistics of the United States, Colonial Times to 1970,* Series H 971–86, p. 414. U.S. National Center for Health Statistics, "Vital Statistics of the United States, as published in *Statistical Abstract of the United States, 1991, 1993, 1998*, "Homicide Victims by Race and Sex," table 341, p. 204. Data for 1996 from *Statistical Abstract, 1998*, table 335, p. 210.

3. *Chicago Tribune*, "FBI Reports Crime Rates Again Drop Dramatically," June 2, 1997, sec. 1, p. 3.

4. U.S. Bureau of the Census, *Statistical Abstract of the United States, 1997*, table 313 (Washington, D.C.: U.S. Government Printing Office, 1997), p. 201. Estimates for 1996 from *Chicago Tribune*, "Murder Rate Declines to 30-year Low," November 23, 1998, sec. 1, p. 13. Executions from *Statistical Abstract, 1998*, table 382, p. 231.

5. U.S. Bureau of the Census, *Statistical Abstract of the United States, 1975*, table 248, p. 150, 1985; table 275, p. 166, 1997; table 313, p. 201.

6. Data for 1982–1992 from the *Statistical Abstract of the United States, 1997*, table 338, p. 213. 1992 to 1996 estimate from "What's News," *Wall Street Journal*, June 8, 1998, p. A1.

7. U.S. Bureau of the Census, *Statistical Abstract of the United States, 1997*, table 341, p. 213.

8. U.S. Bureau of the Census, *Statistical Abstract of the United States, 1997*, table 317, p. 204.

9. *Chicago Tribune*, May 16, 1994, sec. 1, p. 4, reported 21,000 in 1993; my estimates reflect the decline in all crime.

10. Center for Disease Control Report, *Wall Street Journal*, March 24, 1993, p. 1.

11. "Personal Security: Crime, Illegal Immigration, and Drug Control," *Budget of the United States Government, 1995* (Washington, D.C.: U.S. Government Printing Office, 1995), p. 198.

12. U.S. Bureau of the Census, *Statistical Abstract of the United States, 1997*, table 313, p. 201, and table 329, p. 209.

13. "Report: U.S. Has Top Jailing Rate," *Chicago Tribune*, January 6, 1991, sec. 1, p. 5.

14. "U.S. Leads World in Imprisonment," *The New York Times*, January 7, 1991, cited in *Future Survey* (March 1991): 8. The United States rate in 1990 was 645 of every 100,000 compared to 590 per 100,000 for Russia. European rates range from 35 to 120 per 100,000.

15. New York Times News Service, *Chicago Tribune*, January 19, 1998, sec. 1, p. 7.

16. U.S. Bureau of the Census, The 1992 estimate of costs at all levels of government was $92 billion. *Statistical Abstract of the United States, 1997*, table 338, p. 213. The estimate of an increase of 20 times over the 1975 cost came from "U.S. Leads World in Imprisonment," *The New York Times*, January 7, 1991, cited in *Future Survey* (March 1991): 8.

17. U.S. Bureau of the Census, *Statistical Abstract of the United States, 1997*, table 358, p. 222.

18. *Chicago Tribune*, July 1, 1996, sec. 1, p. 4.

19. Richard B. Freeman, "Is the New Income Inequality the Achilles Heel of the American Economy?" in *The Inequality Paradox: Growth in Income Disparity*, eds. James A. Auerbach and Richard S. Belous (Washington, D.C.: National Policy Association, 1998), p. 225.

20. U.S. Bureau of Justice Statistics, "Prisoners in State and Federal Institutions on December 31." The data for 1970–1993 from *Statistical Abstract of the United States, 1997*, table 355, p. 220. The 1997 data from "What's News," *Wall Street Journal*, August 3, 1998, p. A1.

21. Patrick Reardon and William Rechtenwald, "Chicago Among Top in U.S. Violent Crime Rankings," *Chicago Tribune*, October 3, 1993, sec. 2, p. 7.

22. *Statistical Abstract of the United States, 1997*, table 332, p. 211.

23. "Report: U.S. Has Top Jailing Rate," *Chicago Tribune*, January 6, 1991, sec. 1, p. 5.

24. *Sunday Times of London*, reprinted in *World Press Review*, May, 1989, p. 34.

25. Richard B. Freeman, "Why So Many Young Americans Commit Crimes and What We Might Do About It," *Journal of Economic Perspectives* 10 (1996): 25–42. Cited by James H. Johnson Jr. and Walter C. Farrell Jr., "Growing Income Inequality in American Society: A Political Economy Perspective," in *The Inequality Paradox*, eds. Auerbach and Belous, p. 144.

26. James H. Johnson Jr. and Melvin L. Oliver, "Structural Changes in the Economy and Black Male Joblessness: a Reassessment," in *Urban Labor and Job Opportunity*, eds. G. E. Peterson and W. Vroman (Washington, D.C.: Urban Institute Press, 1992), pp. 113–47.

27. U.S. Bureau of the Census, *Statistical Abstract of the United States, 1993*, table 345, p. 211.

28. "Report: U.S. Has Top Jailing Rate," *Chicago Tribune*, January 6, 1991, sec. 1, p. 5. (The cost per inmate is the U.S. average. It is far higher for those in maximum security facilities.)

29. James Q. Wilson and Richard J. Herrnstein, *Crime and Human Nature* (New York: Simon and Schuster, 1995).

30. William H. Sheldon, S. S. Stevens, and W. B. Tucker, *Varieties of Human Physique* (New York: Harper, 1940).

31. Wilson and Herrnstein, *Crime and Human Nature*, pp. 148–72. Richard J. Herrnstein and Charles Murray, *The Bell Curve: Intelligence and Class Structure in American Life* (New York: Free Press, 1994), pp. 235–52.

32. Wilson and Herrnstein, *Crime and Human Nature*, p. 154.

33. See, for example, Bruce Bower, "Criminal Intellects," *Science News* (April 15, 1995): 232–33.

34. Jenks, *Rethinking Social Policy: Race, Poverty, and the Underclass*, p. 108.

35. Herrnstein and Murray, *The Bell Curve*, p. 238.

36. Bower, "Criminal Intellects," p. 222.

37. See for example the studies of Herbert Needleman, *Journal of American Medical Association* (February 7, 1996). His study of 212 boys in Pittsburgh public schools found that what distinguished the most aggressive children from peers with similar backgrounds was a high level of lead in their bones. *Chicago Tribune*, February 7, 1996, sec. 1, p. 11.

38. Ibid., p. 232.

39. Edna Erez, "Planning of Crime and the Criminal Career: Official and Hidden Offenses," *Journal of Law and Criminology* (Spring 1980): 71.

40. Wilson and Herrnstein, *Crime and Human Nature*, p. 174.

41. *Chicago Tribune*, April 14, 1993, sec. 1, p. 18.

42. Ibid.

43. Marvin Wolfgang, Testimony in U.S. Congress, Senate Committee on Juvenile Justice, "Violent Juvenile Crime Hearing," 97th Congress, 1st Session, July 1981, p. 132. Cited by Elliot Currie, *Confronting Crime* (New York: Pantheon Books, 1985), p. 84.

44. Wolfgang, "Violent Juvenile Crime Hearing," p.133. Cited by Currie, *Confronting Crime*, p. 84.

45. See for example Leonard Eron, "The Consistency of Aggressive Behavior Across Time and Situations," paper presented at meeting of American Psychological Association, August 27, 1983. Cited by Currie, *Confronting Crime*, p. 212.

46. Lee N. Robins, "Childhood Conduct Disorders and Later Arrest," in *The Social Consequences of Psychiatric Illness*, eds. Lee Robins, Paula Clayton, and John Wing (New York: Brunner-Mazel, 1980), p. 249.

47. Jenks, *Rethinking Public Policy*, p. 102.

48. Wilson and Herrnstein, *Crime and Human Nature*, pp. 95–100.

49. Adam Dobrin, Brian Wierseman et al., eds., *Statistical Handbook on Violence in America* (World Health Organization 1994), p. 3. *World Health Statistics Annual* (Geneva, Switzerland, 1993). It is interesting that a March 1991 Senate Judiciary Committee report concluded that the United States is the most violent and self-destructive nation on earth. Morton Yant, "War Against Crime Is a Crime—and a Waste," *Free Inquiry* (Winter 1991–92): 13. This comparison shows that as violent as the United States is, we do not hold the title of "most violent."

50. Currie, *Confronting Crime*, p. 173.

51. U.S. Bureau of the Census, *Statistical Abstract of the United States, 1997*, table 319, p. 204.

52. U.S. Bureau of the Census, *Statistical Abstract of the United States, 1997*, tables 354, p. 220.

53. U.S. Department of Justice, *Uniform Crime Reports for the U.S., 1965–1995*.

54. Joan Petersila, Peter Greenwood, and Marvin Lavin, *Criminal Careers of Habitual Felons* (Washington, D.C.: National Institute of Law Enforcement and Criminal Justice, 1978), p. 74. Cited by Currie, *Confronting Crime*, p. 194.

55. Currie, *Confronting Crime*, p. 195.

56. Ibid.

57. Ibid.

58. Dorothy Otnow Lewis et al., "Violent Juvenile Delinquents: Psychiatric, Neurological, Psychological and Abuse Factors," *American Journal of Psychiatry* 137 (1980): 1211–16. Cited by Currie, *Confronting Crime*, pp. 205–206.

59. Cited by John J. Dilulio Jr., "Moral Poverty," *Chicago Tribune*, December 15, 1995, sec. 1, p. 31.

60. Michael A Lev, "Robert—100% Victim," *Chicago Tribune*, September 4, 1994, sect. 2, p. 1.

61. Linset Myers, "U.S. Ahead in Incidence of Rape Too," *Chicago Tribune*, November 22, 1995, sec. 1, p. 14.

62. P. Tagaki and T. Platt, "Behind the Gilded Ghetto: An Analysis of Race, Class and Crime in Chinatown," *Crime and Social Justice* (September 1978): 2–25. Cited by Wilson and Herrnstein, *Crime and Human Nature*, p. 473.

63. However, there is a heredity factor as well: boys who were aggressive at an early age were likely to be delinquent regardless of the kind of family they lived in. S. G. Kellam, M. E. Ensminger, and J. Turner, "Family Structure and the General Health of Children," *Archives of General Psychiatry* 34 (1977): 1012–22. Wilson and Herrnstein, *Crime and Human Nature*, p. 478.

64. Reuters, "Jail More Likely for Males who Grow Up without Fathers, Study Says," *Chicago Tribune*, August 21, 1998, sec. 1, p. 8.

65. Margaret Bacon, Irving Child, and Herbert Barry, "A Cross-culture Study of Correlates of Crime," *Journal of Abnormal and Social Psychology* 66 (1963): 291–300. Cited by Wilson and Herrnstein, *Crime and Human Nature*, p. 452.

66. Liz Sly, "Who's Killing the White Rhinos of South Africa?" *Chicago Tribune*, October 2, 1994, sec. 1, p. 19

67. Herbert G. Gutman, *The Black Family in Slavery and Freedom, 1750–1925* (New York: Pantheon, 1976). Cited by Wilson and Herrnstein, *Crime and Human Nature*, p. 480.

68. James Q. Wilson, *The Moral Sense* (New York: Free Press, 1993), p. 176.

69. Isabel Sawhill, "Young Children and Families," in *Setting Domestic Priorities: What Can Government Do?* eds. Henry J. Arron and Charles L. Schultz (Washington, D.C.: Brookings Institution, 1992), pp. 147–84. Cited by Wilson, *The Moral Sense*, p. 176.

70. Wilson, *The Moral Sense*, p. 159.

71. Jay Belsky, "The Effects of Infant Day Care Reconsidered," *Early Childhood Research Quarterly*, no. 3 (1988): 257. Cited by Wilson, *The Moral Sense*, p. 160.

72. Donald West, *Delinquency: Its Roots, Careers, and Prospects* (Cambridge, Mass: Harvard University Press, 1982), p. 37. Cited by Currie, *Confronting Crime*, p. 188.

73. Currie, *Confronting Crime*, p. 185.

74. Ibid.

75. Wilson and Herrnstein, *Crime and Human Nature*, p. 237.

76. Ibid.

77. Ibid., p. 238.

78. James Q. Wilson, *Thinking About Crime* (New York: Basic Books, 1975), p. 17.

79. Dane Archer, "Cities and Homicide: A New Look at an Old Paradox," *Comparative Studies in Sociology*, no. 1 (1978): 84. Cited by Currie, *Confronting Crime*, p. 167.

80. John C. Bell et al., "Lifetime Criminality of Heroin Addicts," *U.S. Journal of Drugs* (Fall 1982). Cited by Currie, *Confronting Crime*, p. 70.

81. Mark A. Peterson, Harriet B. Braiker, and Suzanne Polick, *Doing Crime: a Study of California Prison Inmates* (Washington, D.C.: National Institute of Justice, 1980), p. xii.

82. *Wall Street Journal*, December 7, 1994, p. A5.

83. Rowell Huesmann and Jessica Moore, "Media Violence Is a Demonstrated Health Threat to Childhood," *Harvard Mental Health Record* 12, no. 12 (1996): 5.

84. Bower, "Criminal Intellects," p. 232.

85. Wilson and Herrnstein, *Crime and Human Nature*, p. 354.

86. Joseph L. Daleiden, *The Science of Morality* (Amherst, N.Y.: Prometheus Books, 1998), chapter 18.

87. Tannis MacBeth Williams, ed., *The Impact of Television: A Natural Experiment in Three Communities* (Orlando, Fla.: Academic Press, 1987).

88. Currie, *Confronting Crime*, pp. 144–72.

89. Stephen Messner, "Income Inequality and Murder Rate: Some Cross National Findings," *Comparative Social Research*, no. 3 (1980). Cited by Currie, *Confronting Crime*, p. 169.

90. Judith and Peter Blau, "The Cost of Inequality: Metropolitan Structures and Violent Crime," *American Sociological Review*, no. 47 (February 1982): 114–29.

91. Currie, *Confronting Crime*, p. 170.

92. Herrnstein and Murray, *The Bell Curve*, pp. 375–76, 93–94, 98–100.

93. Dave Archer and Rosemary Gartner, *Violence and Crime in Cross-National Perspective* (New Haven, Conn: Yale University Press, 1994), table 5.2. Cited by Jenks, *Rethinking Social Policy*, p, 115.

94. Jenks, *Rethinking Social Policy*, p. 19.

95. Robert W. Gillespie, *Economic Factors in Crime and Delinquency: A Critical Review of the Empirical Evidence* (Washington, D.C.: National Institute of Law

Enforcement and Criminal Justice, 1975). Cited by Wilson and Herrnstein, *Crime and Human Nature*, p. 312.

96. Llad Phillips and Harold Votey, "Crime Generation and Economic Opportunity for Youth," in *The Economics of Crime Control* (Beverly Hills: Sage Publications, 1981).

97. Michael Harrington, *Toward a Democratic Left* (Baltimore: Penguin Books, 1969), pp. 55–57. Cited by Currie, *Confronting Crime*, p. 118.

98. Ann Drydan Witte, "Unemployment and Crime: Insights from Research on Individuals," U.S. Congress Joint Economic Committee, Hearing on Social Costs of Unemployment, 96th Congress, 1st Session, 1979, p. 30. Cited by Currie, *Confronting Crime*, p. 112

99. See, for example, Wilson and Herrnstein, *Crime and Human Nature*, pp. 44–45. See also Gary Becker, *The Economic Approach to Human Behavior* (Chicago: University of Chicago Press, 1976).

100. Daleiden, *The Science of Morality*, chapter 10.

101. Charles Tittle, *Sanctions and Social Deviance* (New York: Praeger, 1980), p. 4. Cited by Currie *Confronting Crime*, p, 68.

102. I note that Wilson and Herrnstein have also used this expression (p. 427) that I have been using in lectures on demography since 1978.

103. U.S. Bureau of Census, *Social and Economic Characteristics of the Population in Metropolitan and Nonmetropolitan Areas, 1970 and 1960*, Current Population Reports, Series P-23, no. 37 (Washington, D.C.: Government Printing Office, 1971). Cited by Wilson, *The Truly Disadvantaged: The Inner City, the Underclass, and Poverty*, p. 36.

104. A. Blumstein and D. Nagin, "Analysis of arrest rates for trends in criminality," *Socio-economic Planning Science* 9 (1975): 221–227. But although Wilson and Herrnstein agree that the changing age structure accounted for a significant increase in crime, they doubt that it explains most of it.

105. Wilson and Herrnstein, *Crime and Human Nature*, p. 425.

106. Sally E. Merry, *Urban Danger: Life in a Neighborhood of Strangers* (Philadelphia: Temple University Press, 1981). Cited by Wilson and Herrnstein, *Crime and Human Nature*, p. 392.

107. James Q. Wilson, *Thinking About Crime*, rev. ed. (New York: Basic Books, 1983), chapter 7. John Lott's analysis of Pennsylvania data indicates that changes in arrest rates explained 15 percent of the variance in violent crime rates. Lott Jr., *More Guns, Less Crime*, p. 103.

108. Wilson and Herrnstein, *Crime and Human Nature*, p. 402.

109. See, for example, K. I. Wolpin, "An Economic Analysis of Crime and Punishment in England and Wales, 1984 and 1967," *Journal of Political Economy* 86 (1978): 815–840. Also H. I. Rose, *Deterring the Drinking Driver: The Legal Policy and Social Control* (Lexington, Mass: Lexington Books, 1981). Wilson and Herrnstein, *Crime and Human Nature*, pp. 392–399.

110. W. Clifford, *Crime Control in Japan* (Lexington, Mass.: Lexington Books, 1976). Cited by Wilson and Herrnstein, *Crime and Human Nature*, p. 454.

111. D. H. Bayley, "Learning About Crime: The Japanese Experience," *Public Interest* 44 (1976): 55–68. Wilson and Herrnstein, *Crime and Human Nature*, p. 453.

112. Lee H, Bowker, "Crime and the Use of Prisons in the United States: A Time Series Analysis," *Crime and Delinquency*, April 1981, p. 211. Cited by Currie, *Confronting Crime*, p. 58.

113. David Blis, "Crime and Imprisonment: A Two Decade Comparison Between England and Wales and Australia," *British Journal of Criminology* 23, no. 2 (April 1983): 171. Cited by Currie, *Confronting Crime*, p. 59.

114. U.S. Bureau of the Census, *Statistical Abstract of the United States, 1997*, table 352, p. 218.

115. Jacqueline Darrock Forrest, "The Impact of U.S. Family Planning Programs on Births, Abortion, and Miscarriages," *Social Science and Medicine* 18, no. 6 (1984).

116. For a fuller discussion of this issue, see *The Science of Morality*, chapters 17 and 18.

117. Ibid., chapters 3 and 10.

118. Gary Becker, *The Economic Approach to Human Behavior* (Chicago: University of Chicago Press, 1976).

119. Wilson and Herrnstein, *Crime and Human Nature*, pp. 43–45.

120. *Chicago Tribune*, January 29, 1996, sec. 1, p. 14.

121. *The Economist* (September 2, 1989): 21–23.

122. Jeane J. Kirkpatrick, "Drugs: Failure Here at Home," *Washington Post*, March 19, 1990. *AEI*, no. 11 (1990).

123. Robert MacCoun et al., "Money for Crime: A Study of the Economics of Drug Dealing in Washington, D.C.," *American Demographics* (January 1992): 16–17.

124. Wilson and Herrnstein, *Crime and Human Nature*, p. 401.

125. Ibid., p.17.

126. John J. DiIulio Jr., *No Escape: The Future of American Corrections* (New York: Basic Books, 1991). Cited in *Future Survey* (March 1991): 8.

127. Renesselaer W. Lee III, "The White Labyrinth: Cocaine and Political Power," *Washington Post*, March 19, 1990. *AEI*, no. 11 (1990).

128. Stephen Chapman, "The GOP's Bogus Drug Attack," *Chicago Tribune*, August 25, 1996, sec. 1, p. 15.

129. Eric E. Sterling, "What Should We Do about Drugs? Manage the Problem Through Legalization," *Vital Speeches of the Day* 57, no. 20 (August 1, 1991): 626–32. Cited In *Future Survey* (December 1991): 15.

130. Diana Chapman Welsh, "The Shifting Boundaries of Alcohol Policy," *Health Affairs* 9, no. 2 (Summer 1990): 47–62. Cited in *Future Survey* (March 1991).

131. John McCarron, *Chicago Tribune*, January 29, 1996, sec. 1, p. 15.

132. Charles Krauthammer, "Why Stop at Tobacco? Let's Go After All the Sins of Society," *Chicago Tribune*, June 10, 1994, sec. 1, p. 31.

133. Ernest Beck, "Ad Bans Haven't Snuffed Out Smoking," *Wall Street Journal*, June 12, 1997, p. B1.

134. Amitai Etzioni, *Spirit of Community* (New York: Crown Publishers, 1993), p. 181.

135. Nicholas N. Eberstadt, "America's Infant Mortality Problem," *Wall Street Journal*, January 20, 1992. Cited by *AEI*, no. 9 (1992).

136. V. Dion Haynes, "To Curb Pregnancies, Project Pays Addicts $200 to be Sterilized," *Chicago Tribune*, May 3, 1998, sec. 1, p. 3.

137. Wilson and Herrnstein, *Crime and Human Nature*, p. 435.

138. Currie, *Confronting Crime*, p. 103.

139. U.S. Bureau of the Census, *Statistical Abstract of the United States, 1991*, table 292, p. 176, tables 333, 334, p. 193. U.S. Bureau of the Census, *Statistical Abstract of the United States, 1997*, table 313, p. 201, and tables 354, 355, p. 220.

140. Currie, *Confronting Crime*, p. 86.

141. Michael Rutter, *Changing Youth in a Changing Society* (Cambridge, Mass.: Harvard University Press, 1980), pp. 168–69. Cited by Currie, *Confronting Crime*, p. 45.

142. Adam Walinsky and Jonathan Rubinstein have suggested providing college scholarships in exchange for three years as police officers. *New York Times*, January 27, 1985, p. 20E. Cited by Currie, *Confronting Crime*, p. 233.

143. Linset Myers, "U.S. Ahead in Incidence of Rape Too," *Chicago Tribune*, November 22, 1995, sec. 1, p. 14.

144. For a summary of the research regarding the various determinants of rape, see Daleiden, *The Science of Morality*, chapter 18. Also *Pornography and Sexual Aggression*, eds. Neil M. Malamuth and Edward Donnerstein (New York: Academic Press, 1984) and *Pornography and Censorship*, eds. David Copp and Susan Wendell (Amherst, N.Y.: Prometheus Books, 1983).

145. Rape data from *Statistical Abstract of the United States, 1995*, table 310, p. 200.

146. It might also have the indirect benefit of preventing those more disposed to crime from procreating. Wilson and Herrnstein report that chronically criminal biological parents (those with three or more convictions) are three times more likely to produce a criminal son than are biological parents with no convictions. Wilson and Herrnstein, *Crime and Human Nature*, p. 97.

147. Dr. Fred S. Berlin, "The Case for Castration, Part 2," *The Washington Monthly* (May 1994): 28.

148. D. A. G. Cook, "There Is a Place for Surgical Castration in the Management of Recidivist Sex Offenders," *British Medical Journal* (September 25, 1993): 791. See also "Help for Sex Offenders," *The New Yorker*, May 7, 1994, pp. 6–7.

149. *World Press Review* (July 1992): 44.

150. Dr. Fred S. Berlin "The Case for Castration, Part 2," p. 29.

151. "Help for Sex Offenders," *The New Yorker*, May 7, 1994, p. 7.

152. John Gunn, "Castration Is Not the Answer," *British Medical Journal* (September 23, 1993): 790.

153. Larry Don McQuay, "The Case for Castration, Part 1," *The Washington Monthly* (May 1994): 26.

154. Daleiden, *The Science of Morality*, chapter 18.

155. Anna-Liza Kozma, "Porn Ruling," *Chicago Tribune*, June 14, 1992, sec. 6, pp. 1, 11.

156. For a review of studies examining the link between pornography and sexual aggression, see *Pornography and Sexual Aggression*, eds. Neil M. Malamuth and Edward Donnerson, and *Pornography and Censorship*, eds. David Copp and Susan Wendell.

157. See L. Rowell Huesmann, "Television Violence and Aggressive Behavior," in *Television and Behavior: Ten Years of Scientific Progress and Implications for the Eighties*, vol. 2, eds. D. Pearl, L. Bouthilet and J. Lazar (Rockville, Md: *NIMH*, 1982).

L. R. Huesmann and L. D. Eron, "Structural Models of the Development of Aggression," Development of Aggressive Behavior, D. Magnusson, Chair, symposium at the International Society for the Study of Behavioral Development, *Tours* (July 1985).

L. R. Huesmann, L. D. Eron, M. M. Leftowitz, and L. O. Walder, "Television Violence and Aggression: The Causal Effect Remains," *American Psychologist* 28 (1978): 617–20.

L. R. Huesmann and L. D. Eron, "Intervening Variables in the Television Violence-Aggression Relation: Evidence from Two Countries," *Development Psychology* 20 (1984): 746–75.

158. Daleiden, *The Science of Morality*, pp. 453–56.

159. "Nonstranger Violence Study, cited in U.S. National Institute of Justice Study," *Justice Assistance* (April 1983): 6. Currie, *Confronting Crime*, p. 230.

160. Lawrence Sherman and Richard Berk, cited in *San Francisco Chronicle*, May 19, 1984. Currie, *Confronting Crime*, p. 231.

161. Douglas Lipton, Robert Martinson, and Judith Wilks, *The Effectiveness of Correctional Treatment: A Survey of Treatment Evaluation Studies* (New York: Praeger, 1975). Cited by Wilson and Herrnstein, *Crime and Human Nature*, pp. 377–87.

162. R. R. Ross and H. B. McKay, "Behavioral Approaches to Treatment in Corrections: Requiem for A Panacea," *Canadian Journal of Criminology* 20 (1978): 279–98. Wilson and Herrnstein, *Crime and Human Nature*, pp. 381–82

163. Currie, *Confronting Crime*, p. 240.

164. Ibid.

165. Ibid., p. 241.

166. Charles A. Murray and Louis A. Cox, *Beyond Probation: Juvenile Correction and Chronic Offenders* (Beverly Hills, Calif.: Sage Publications, 1979).

167. Lyle W. Shannon, *Assessing the Relationship of Adult Criminal Careers to Juvenile Careers: A Summary* (Washington, D.C.: U.S. Office of Juvenile Justice and Delinquency Prevention, 1982), p. 8.

168. Donald West, *Delinquency: Its Roots, Careers, and Prospects* (Cambridge, Mass.: Harvard University Press, 1982), pp. 104–108.

169. Currie, *Confronting Crime*, p. 89.

170. Between 1984 and 1995, the prison population increased from 454,000 to 1.1 million, yet crime rates in 1995 were 5,278 per 100,000 population compared to 5,031 in 1984, a 5 percent increase. Particularly distressing was the

increase in violent crimes from a rate of 539 per 100,000 in 1984 to 685 in 1995, a 27 percent increase. Based upon preliminary data for 1997, the drop in crime rates has continued and is now probably less than the 1984 rates; but it took a doubling in the number of incarcerations just to get back to the prior crime rates of the early 1980s, and they are nothing to crow about. U.S. Bureau of the Census, *Statistical Abstract of the United States, 1997*, table 313, p. 201. Since 1991 there has been a decline in violent crime; however, the increase in youth crime—especially violent crime among ever younger children is a major cause for concern.

171. U.S. Bureau of the Census, *Statistical Abstract of the United States, 1997*, table 317, p. 204.

172. John R. Lott Jr., *More Guns, Less Crime* (Chicago: University of Chicago Press, 1998), p. 9.

173. Etzioni, *Spirit of Community*, p. 220.

174. *Chicago Tribune*, December 17, 1995, sec. 1, p. 20.

175. Gordon Witkin et al., "Kids Who Will Kill," *U.S. News and World Report*, April 8, 1991, pp. 26ff.

176. U.S. Department of Justice, *Uniform Crime Reports for the U.S. 1985–1995*. Unfortunately, the data prior to 1985 uses different age groupings. But I have little doubt that if we tracked the trend back earlier, it would add even greater support to the conclusion that the availability of guns is highly correlated with the number of teenage murders.

177. *Chicago Tribune*, June 24, 1994, sec. 2, p. 2.

178. Stephen Chapman, "Make My Day," *Chicago Tribune*, January 26, 1995, sec. 1, p. 23.

179. Sydney J. Harris, *Chicago Daily News*, July 19, 1979.

180. Lott Jr., *More Guns, Less Crime*, p. 4.

181. Arthur Kellerman and Fred Rivera, *New England Journal of Medicine* (October 7, 1993). Cited in *Center for Handgun Violence* (January 1994): 3.

182. *Chicago Tribune*, October 31, 1993, sec. 4, p. 5.

183. Lott Jr., *More Guns, Less Crime*, p 5.

184. John R. Lott Jr. and David B. Mustard, "Crime Deterrence, and the Right-to-Carry Concealed Handguns" (University of Chicago, August 15, 1996). Published in the *Journal of Legal Studies* (January 1997).

185. Paul Galloway, "Under the Gun," *Chicago Tribune*, sec. 5, p. 4.

186. P. J. Cook, "The Technology of Personal Violence," *Crime and Justice: Annual Review of Research* 14 (1991): 57, 56, n. 4. Cited by Lott Jr., *More Guns, Less Crime*, p. 11.

187. Lott Jr., *More Guns, Less Crime*, p. 11.

188. Ibid., p. 54.

189. Albert W. Alschuler, "Two Guns, Four Guns, Six Guns, More: Does Arming the Public Reduce Crime?" *Valparasio University Law Review* 31 (1997): 369. Cited by Lott Jr., *More Guns, Less Crime*, p. 148.

190. Lott Jr., *More Guns, Less Crime*, p. 12.

191. Ibid., p. 8.

192. Ibid.

193. Bob Green, *Chicago Tribune*, sec. 5, p. 1, April 7, 1993.

194. *Wall Street Journal*, January 30, 1997, p. A1.

195. U.S. Office of Management and Budget, *Budget of the United States Government, 1995*, p. 201.

196. Paul Galloway, "Under the Gun," p. 4.

197. Associated Press, "Brady Law's Presale Rules Stopped 69,000 Handgun Sales Last Year," *Chicago Tribune*, June 22, 1998, sec. 1, p. 5.

198. Charles Krauthammer, "Disingenuous Debate on Repeal of Assault Weapons Ban," *Chicago Tribune*, April 8, 1996,

199. Joseph A Kirby, "Big Easy Gets Tough on Crime and Crooked Cops," *Chicago Tribune*, June 7, 1996, pp. 1 & 24.

200. G. R. Patterson, P. Chamberlain, and J. B. Reid, report that children in parent training programs displayed a sharp drop in the frequency of aversive behavior, while those in conventional programs showed no change on average. "A Comparative Evaluation of a Parent Training Program," *Behavior Therapy* 13: 638–50. Wilson and Herrnstein, *Crime and Human Nature*, p. 387.

201. Christy A. Vishen, "Understanding the Roots of Crime: The Project on Human Development in Chicago Neighborhoods," *National Institute of Justice Journal* (November 1994): 9–15.

202. "Research in Brief: Project on Human Development in Chicago Neighborhoods: A Research Update," *National Institute of Justice Journal* (February, 1997).

12

Health Care and Social Security

The fiscal 1999 budget agreement achieved between the Clinton administration and Congress was hailed by both political parties as a great success because it promised a budget surplus by 1999. However, the budget agreement was actually a shameful fraud because, not only is the inclusion of the temporary Social Security surplus misleading as discussed in chapter 6, but, in typical Washington fashion, it deferred taking on the two most troubling financial problems facing the nation in the years ahead: the looming shortfalls in Medicare and Social Security. Instead of taking the painful action of dealing with these issues by either raising taxes or cutting benefits, a jointly duplicitous White House and Congress once again deceived a gullible American public by ignoring the inevitable. As we shall see, neither problem is unsolvable, but they both require financial sacrifice.

Health Care

Like so many indicators, measures of health care can be viewed from more than one perspective. Liberals will lament that the United States is only twenty-second in the world in terms of infant mortality rates, seventeenth in male life expectancy, and sixteenth in female life expectancy.[1] Babies in the United States are more likely to die in their first month compared to other industrialized nations, and also far more likely to suffer mental retardation and learning problems.

Conservatives will boast that progress in providing adequate health care is demonstrated by the significantly increased life expectancy of all Americans in the post World War II era. It is lifestyle, especially improper diet, that results in many Americans dying earlier than they should. Conservatives will also point out that infant mortality rates have dropped significantly since 1970.[2] The relatively high infant mortality rates are due in large part to low birth weight, which in turn is due to mothers who smoke or who use alcohol and drugs.[3] In fact, although our infant mortality rate is twice as high as Japan's, any group of high-risk babies has a greater chance of surviving in the United States than in Japan.[4] Therefore, they conclude that it is lifestyle, not lack of medical care, that results in the high U.S. infant mortality rate.

It has recently been discovered, however, that a significant fraction of premature births can be linked to the bacterial vaginosis infection.[5] The risk of premature birth is about the same for women with the infection as for those who smoke. About 25 percent of all women have the infection, which can be cured by standard antibiotics. With adequate prenatal care the infection could be diagnosed and cured. Hence, like most issues there is some truth on both sides of the issue. Providing more universal prenatal care would help reduce America's infant mortality, but so would changes in the lifestyle of poor mothers.

In general, most people will agree that Americans have the best health care in the world—for those who can afford it. The problem is that an increasing number of Americans cannot afford it. At the end of 1997, one in six had no health care insurance.[6] Many other working Americans have grossly inadequate policies. These are not people on welfare; welfare recipients are covered by Medicaid. Rather, the uninsured are comprised of millions of hard-working lower- and middle-class citizens, not covered by employer-provided health care, who simply cannot afford the huge healthcare premiums. It is patently unfair and a major disincentive to leaving welfare if in so doing a person loses health care by taking a job. Yet, three-fourths of uninsured children live in families where both parents work.[7] For the parents any family illness can be a financial disaster.

The healthcare issue smoldered throughout the 1980s and then erupted in the 1992 presidential election. Both parties recognized that something had to be done; the Democrats responded to the need of the uninsured, the Republicans recognized that healthcare costs were spiraling out of control. In 1993, Clinton proposed a new healthcare plan that involved two key components: (1) a universal, private healthcare plan paid for by making all companies directly or indirectly contribute to their employees' health insurance, and (2) government regulated "managed ...petition" in which both Health Maintenance Organizations (HMOs) ...r healthcare providers would compete for business, including the ...of those subsidized by Medicare and Medicaid.[8]

...hough the bill was rejected by Congress, several pieces of it have been instituted in subsequent legislation. The Health Care Reform Bill passed in 1996 guaranteed insurance to workers who change jobs or have preexisting medical conditions. It also allowed individuals to establish Medical Savings Accounts, and allowed them to keep their unspent balances, thus providing an incentive to minimize health costs.

The 1998 budget included a new $24 billion initiative to extend health coverage to some of the nation's 10 million children who lack medical insurance, but at the time of this writing it was uncertain just how many would be covered. The estimates ranged from the Clinton administration's claim of five million to the Congressional Budget Office estimate of only five hundred thousand. In the Fiscal 1999 budget, Clinton sought to let people between ages fifty-five and sixty-five buy into Medicare, i.e., get healthcare insurance at significantly reduced rates. Clinton also established a patient's "bill of rights" that would end some of the worst abuses of managed health care. Among other provisions, it guarantees that patients whose health care is federally financed will receive full information regarding the risks, benefits, and costs of alternative treatments, provides coverage for emergency treatment when lack of such coverage would cause serious jeopardy; and provides access to specialists for patients with serious medical problems.[9] Despite all of these changes, 43 million Americans (16 percent) still have no health care.

Each year an increasingly larger share of GDP is being devoted to health care. In 1950, 4 percent of GDP was being expended on health care; by 1995, the proportion rose to 14.2 percent. Medicare and Medicaid became the fastest-growing parts of the federal budget: together they reached $314 billion by 1997.[10] The total U.S. expenditure on health care passed the $1 trillion mark in 1996 and, according to a 1998 study by the Health Care Financing Administration, it is expected to double to more than $2.1 trillion by the year 2007.[11] The 14 percent of GDP spent on health care in this country is higher by far than any other country in the world.[12]

Health Care as Percentage of GDP (1995)[13]

United States	14.2%
Canada	9.6
Finland	7.7
France	9.8
Switzerland	9.8
Germany	10.4
Italy	7.7
United Kingdom	6.9
Japan	7.2

Many causes have been identified as contributing to the rising healthcare costs, including:

- unnecessary procedures
- administrative inefficiency
- malpractice insurance
- fraud and abuse
- an aging population
- overspecialization of doctors
- conflicts of interest.

(This last cause refers to the many doctors who own facilities such as x-ray or diagnostic labs and thus may overprescribe tests.)

Of the above list of causes, a *Consumer Reports* investigation concluded that improvements in the first two—unnecessary procedures and administrative inefficiency—offered potential savings amounting to 20 percent of total healthcare costs ($130 and $70 billion, respectively).[14] The General Accounting Office estimates that as much as 10 percent of healthcare costs might go for fraudulent practices, including not only the unnecessary treatment covered in the *Consumer Report* estimates, but inflated billing, billing for services not rendered, falsifying reimbursement codes to collect higher fees, and other activities.[15] *Consumer Reports* argued that a carefully constructed national healthcare system can realize enormous savings in these areas.

Canada has demonstrated that a national healthcare system can reduce waste and inefficiency, and thus reduce healthcare costs with only a small reduction in the quality of health care received. However, a system such as Canada's limits the options on health care, which effectively prevents a person from receiving specialized care even if the patient is willing to pay extra for it. Moreover, as we will see, even if such savings can be realized, and the long-term growth rate of medical costs slowed, health care will continue to consume a larger and larger proportion of our national output unless we take a fundamentally different attitude to the purpose of health care.

In addition to the problem of not covering a large portion of our population, the nation's public healthcare program for the aged (Medicare) is running out of funds.

Medicare's Part A trust fund (hospital insurance for those over sixty-five)—the part funded by the 2.9 percent payroll tax—will slip into the red within the next year or so. ***During the next decade when the first baby boomers reach age sixty-five, the program's deficit will explode, soaring to $12 trillion by the year 2030, more than twice the national***

debt. So far a timid congress has proposed pushing eligibility back to age sixty-seven, which will do little to solve the problem.

Congressional proposals to cover Medicare Part B (doctors' fees) include allowing premiums to rise over time to cover 25 percent of doctors' fees and outpatient services. Premiums will rise for the elderly with income above $50,000 ($75,000 for couples); individuals with income above $100,000 ($125,000 for couples) will see their premiums rise from $43.80 a month to $200. Such a proposal will certainly be opposed by the wealthy.

Although such proposals are a start in the right direction, so far Congress has just nibbled at the edges of the issue. The basic problem is that, as medical technology continues to advance, we can spend an unlimited amount of money to extend life, even though death remains inevitable. We hate to put a price on life, but the inescapable fact is that as a society we must decide how much of our limited resources we will spend on improving health or extending life. Individuals are willing to make this decision when it is their own money they are spending, but they fail to consider this trade-off when public funds are being expended. It is time to take the same hard look at health care as any other economic choice.

The Three Approaches to Providing Health Care

There are basically three approaches to providing universal health care: (a) permit the creation of tax-free medical savings accounts (MSAs) similar to the current IRA, (b) institute nationalized health care such as that adopted by Canada or England; or (c) provide some form of subsidy that allows people to purchase health care insurance through the private market. As we will see, these need not be mutually exclusive alternatives.

Medical Savings Accounts (MSAs)

Under an MSA, individuals would be allowed to deduct $4,800 each year from their income taxes. This is average that the government now spends per capita on health care. With the deduction, the person could buy catastrophic insurance from a private insurer for about $3,000 a year and put the $1,500 in a special savings account to pay expenses below the deductible. Those earning so little that they don't pay taxes would receive a tax credit, an addition to the earned income credit. The advantage of MSAs is that they give people the maximum freedom to select the doctors and health care they want and encourages people to seek only necessary health care, since they can keep the money they don't spend.

There are counterarguments suggesting that the MSA is not the panacea that its proponents claim. In the first place, many healthy people would opt for lower premiums by dropping out of the standard insurance risk pool. If they leave, the premiums of those who remain would have to increase to reflect the higher average medical expense. An additional problem is the concern that people will not actually save the money, but spend it frivolously, and then still not have the necessary medical coverage when they need it. We are back to a basic issue that separates liberals and conservatives: how much personal responsibility should we expect from individuals? It would be nice if we could compel people to accept responsibility for their actions, but we know that there are a lot of stupid and impulsive people who will always eat their seed corn. Should one role of government be to protect people from their own stupidity? Conservatives say no, it just fosters irresponsibility. Liberals say yes, some people can't help being irresponsible.

We need a compromise, since there are people who do not have sufficient intelligence to insure themselves against future illness, and even more people who will never earn enough to afford catastrophic health care insurance. Therefore, the ideal system needs to provide better health care for those who save for future medical care and take care of their health, but also provides a basic system of health care for those who are unable, through no fault of their own, to care for themselves, such as the mentally retarded or physically disabled.

National Healthcare System

A national healthcare system similar to Canada's is supported by many liberals. They argue that the cost of health care could be significantly reduced and coverage increased by focusing on preventive medicine. To cite but one example: it is alleged that every dollar spent on prenatal care can save $3.38 during the first year after birth.[16]

On the other hand, some doctors will argue that, should a national healthcare system such as that found in the United Kingdom or Canada be instituted in this country, it would result in many doctors leaving the country, as was the case in Britain. Is this threat real? Where will they go? Chile? Korea? South Africa? Relatively few doctors left Canada for the United States when Canada put in its system, and there is no developed country left for U.S. doctors to run to in an effort to escape any form of nationalized health care.

If the pay for doctors decreases, won't fewer people seek to enter the profession? This an empirical question and I don't know of any study that answers it. So far the effect on the supply of U.S. doctors regulating doctor's fees through HMOs is unclear. The medical association points to a reduction in the number of students choosing a career in medicine and infers that it is due to a decline in the average annual income of physicians. While doctors' incomes have declined, the drop is due in part to the large number of foreign doctors who have migrated to America to increase their earnings.

Canada does not appear to have a shortage of qualified doctors. In part the answer depends upon the monetary return that can be expected relative to the cost of becoming a doctor. If we lower the return, we must lower the cost of medical school as well. This could be achieved by more government loans that could be paid back in the form of public service. Before this remedy is sought, however, we should first explore how much of a doctor's time is used performing routine activities that a nurse or nurse practitioner could perform just as well. It could be that we could reduce the demand for doctors, thus being able to pay the fewer number of doctors higher salaries.

Subsidized Private Health Care

So far the United States has adopted a market solution through private HMOs that determine what healthcare service is provided, the fees that doctors can charge, and how much of a hospital bill will be reimbursed. The guidelines for payments is based upon what the government is willing to pay under Medicare and Medicaid. Although no one is happy with this solution, it has reduced the growth in healthcare costs.

There is no doubt that America could provide some form of *universal* health care, but not *unlimited* health care. There is also a concern that any form of nationalized health care will build in the inefficiencies that seem inherent in any form of government-run bureaucracy where there is no market competition to spur innovation and greater efficiency. The answer that most economists would support is a market-based system where the government provides some basic subsidy, but leaves individuals the option to choose their specific health service provider.

A healthcare policy that prevents individuals from purchasing private healthcare plans, such as that in England, is based upon the premise that if people could opt out of a public plan in favor private plans, the healthy low-risk people would opt out—taking their premiums with them—and leave only the high-cost people to be supported by the public plan. We could get around this problem by creating a mandatory plan of basic insurance to cover the usual medical procedures for everybody financed out of general tax revenue. Those who wish to buy additional health services, or pay a premium to see a specific doctor, would be permitted to do so.

Society has no need to limit how much heath care an individual may wish to purchase with their own money. The resulting two-tier system is still more preferable than the present two-tier system that provides extraordinary medical treatment to those who can afford it and no medical treatment to those who cannot.

A doctor should be allowed to work for an HMO or on a fee-for-service basis. This may mean that those who can afford the very best doctors will do so and those who cannot will get second-best service. Paying for a better-quality product is the hallmark of a market economy. There is no more reason to argue that everyone should have the same quality medical care than that everyone should have the same quality house, eat the same food, or receive the same quality education. (Which is not to say that everyone who works should not be able to afford *adequate* housing, food, education, or medical care.) To treat all doctors equally would remove a major incentive for those with the best potential to put in the extra effort to maximize that potential.

America is gradually moving toward a variety of two-tiered systems, including Health Maintenance Organizations (members must use physicians employed under the plan), Preferred Provider Organizations (members choose care from physicians who are affiliated with the organization or pay a premium for services or doctors not included in the basic plan), and Point of Service Plans (HMO-type plans that allow patients to choose physicians outside the plan on a fee-for-service basis).

There is no question that managed care reduces the cost of health care. U.S. healthcare costs decreased 1.1 percent in 1994 and rose only 2.1 percent in 1995, well below the inflation rate.[17] Part of the reason for the small increase was that large- and medium-size employers had cut the percentage of full-time, permanent employees who received benefits, from 92 percent as recently as 1989 to 82 percent in 1996, producing a savings of $10 billion annually.[18] In addition, a greater proportion of those who do have health care were pushed into managed care programs. The problem that people experience with managed care is that patient treatment is driven by the profitability of the system rather than the best possible treatment for the patient.

The larger problem is that none of these options provides health care for the working poor. One reason is that most low-paying jobs are with very small businesses that are not able to obtain the favorable insurance rates that larger businesses can negotiate with healthcare providers. The same, of course, holds true for the self-employed. Representative Harris Fawell (R-Ill) tried to set up a system to allow small business associations like the Farm Bureau or the National Restaurant Association set up self-insurance plans like those that have helped large corporations cut costs.

Such plans would have to be exempted from state-by-state insurance rules and placed under federal (ERISA) jurisdiction. Unfortunately, Fawell's excellent proposal was killed by a Congress dead set against expanding federal regulation at the expense of state regulation, and the lobbying of regional insurers who sought to protect their captive markets.

No matter what form of medical care we adopt, we still must face difficult trade-offs. In a world of economic constraints, there is no perfect healthcare plan. For example, under HMOs doctors are limited by an annual cap on expenditure per patient (called capitation). Their profits are a function of how much they can keep medical treatment expense under that cap. Hence, they will be encouraged to avoid expensive treatments that reduce their profits. To avoid doctors seriously short-changing their patients with regard to medical treatment, basic procedures might need to be outlined in a manual. Moreover, the managed care providers might be required to conduct annual surveys of patients' satisfaction with the plan.[19] In a competitive market, those HMOs that do not provide adequate service will lose membership to those that do.

Providing Universal Health Care

The cost of universal health care is the subject of much debate. The Clinton administration contended that its 1993 plan would be deficit neutral in the first four years and deficit reducing after that.[20] The reasoning was that, in addition to large savings in administrative overhead and reduced growth in fees for medical services and prescription drugs, a large amount of healthcare costs are already being incurred by the uninsured. In 1994, the average uninsured person incurred $1,200 of medical costs, 60 percent of which was paid by the federal government and private payers. This compares to the $2,300 average medical costs incurred for insured payers.[21] However, part of the lower amount is due to the lower average age of uninsured recipients. Since, in general, the uninsured are younger and healthier, providing them coverage would initially increase the federal government's cost by only 10 percent.[22]

Moreover, a universal health care system would encourage people to leave welfare to take a job. At present, when a welfare recipient takes a job, she incurs a tax of two-thirds or more on earnings resulting from the loss of AFDC, food stamps, and medical benefits.[23] Thus, insuring the ex-welfare recipient incurs no net increase in health care costs, while removing the incentive of staying on welfare would result in reduced welfare costs.

However, in order for total healthcare costs not to increase under universal health care, the system must be designed not to encourage greater usage of health care. For example, there is a danger that providing for the cost of a baby will remove a disincentive of the poor from having more babies. ***To avoid this unwanted incentive to procreate, it is essential that maternity benefits not be provided to anyone under the age of 18, nor extended to cover more than two children.*** (Or, conversely, the share of the premium paid by the individual for health care would rise steeply for additional children.) This was not the case in the Clinton proposal. On the other hand, it is economically beneficial if healthcare benefits include contraception and abortion services to all people of any age. But getting abortion services funded will be fought tooth and nail by the anti-abortion groups.

It is also essential that universal health care not act as a magnet encouraging more legal and illegal immigration. To discourage illegal immigration, it is essential that neither the illegal immigrant nor any children subsequently born in the United States be automatically eligible for health care. Health care should be for U.S. citizens only.* This also implies that children of illegals will not automatically become citizens.

Finally, there should be some minimal out-of-pocket cost for all treatments and prescription drugs to discourage wasteful use. Even Russia had to adopt this method during the heyday of communism to avoid people taking all sorts of unneeded drugs.

Reducing Healthcare Costs

There are several other changes that could significantly reduce the rising health costs. The savings could be used to reduce insurance premiums and provide universal coverage.

Reducing Overhead Costs: In 1987, the proportion of health care absorbed by overhead was 117 percent higher in the United States than Canada. U.S. hospitals spent about 20 percent on billing administration compared to 9 percent in Canada.[24] Reducing America's overhead to the level of Canada's would have saved $63 to $83 billion in 1987, enough to provide healthcare insurance to all uninsured Americans.[25] Although this estimate is somewhat dated, there has been no effort to standardize all insurance-related forms across the industry, which would be a major step in reducing overhead.

Reducing Unnecessary Procedures: According to a Rand Corporation study, a substantial portion of surgeries are unnecessary: 27 percent of hysterec-

*This assumes passage of the legislation recommended in chapter 4 ending automatic citizenship to children born in the United States whose parents are here illegally.

tomies, 32 percent of operations to remove artherosclerotic plaque from arteries, 14 percent of heart by-passes, and so on.[26] Demanding second opinions as a prerequisite for reimbursing surgical costs is now being employed by many insurance companies to reduce unnecessary surgery.

Increasing the Number of General Practitioners: Per capita expenditures for physical exams are $347 in America compared to $202 (USD) in Canada. The number of patients per physician is roughly comparable in the two countries: 463 patients per physician in Canada compared to 488 in the United States. But Canadian physicians are much less likely to specialize: 50 percent of the physicians in Canada are general practitioners compared to only 10 percent here. Not surprisingly, the higher proportion of specialists lead to 237 percent higher fees. If U.S. physicians charged at Canadian levels, we would save $100 billion a year.[27]

The AMA will argue that the benefit of the high number of specialists is a major factor in providing Americans with the most advanced medical treatment in the world. However, the present healthcare system doesn't provide even adequate care for the working poor, and increasingly more so, the middle class. We may give an eighty-year-old patient a new heart while pricing routine physicals out of the reach of many people.[28] However, since HMOs are less likely to refer a patient to highly paid specialists, the fees of specialists should fall and, hence, fewer doctors will wish to spend the extra time and money required for the additional training.

Reducing Fraud and Abuse: It has been estimated that healthcare fraud may run as high as $50 to $80 billion a year. One of the major sources of abuse arises from the conflict of interest when doctors own other medical facilities such as diagnostic/imaging centers, clinical labs, physical therapy or rehabilitation centers, and the like. Studies have shown that where such facilities are owned by doctors, there is a far higher likelihood that they will refer their patients to them.[29] While not banning doctors from making investments in other medical facilities, a regulation could be implemented forbidding doctors from referring patients to facilities in which the doctors have a financial interest.

Particularly vexing is that in many cases the medical treatment involves only cosmetic surgery. In California, it has become popular to give cosmetic surgery as presents. If a kid doesn't like the shape of his nose or jaw or breasts or butt, mom and dad will fix it. Now people have the right to spend their own money any way they like, but oftentimes what is purely cosmetic surgery is justified by superfluous medical reasons. For example, it is not unusual to justify operations that are performed to correct an overbite for cosmetic reasons by claiming temporal mandibular joint disease.

The result is that insurance companies—which means all of the rest of us—are forced to pay for it.

Use of Nurse Practitioners and Expert Systems: To some extent, the problem of rising healthcare costs is due to the growth in the number of doctors per se. Between 1970 and 1995, the number of U.S. doctors doubled.[30] In 1970, there was one doctor for every 613 Americans; by 1995, there was one doctor for every 369 people. This increase in supply should have reduced doctors' fees if the additional doctors were evenly dispersed throughout the population. Quite often, however, the new doctors are not interested in working in rural areas or serving the poor. There is far more money to made today being a specialist in an urban area. In addition, the growth in medical knowledge and technology means that many more conditions are treatable today that in the past just had to be endured.

To bring adequate health care to the greatest number of people, we need to break the doctors' monopoly on treatment of many common minor ailments. Nurse practitioners—who receive additional medical training but not as much as a doctor—could be utilized in performing many of the routine physical examination functions, most of which are simply a matter of reading the results of blood tests, electrocardiograms, or X-rays, and comparing the results with a table of normalcy, or detecting changes from previous results. Expert systems—computer programs that simulate the judgment of an expert based on the rules that experts utilize in making their judgments—could be employed to aid the nurse practitioner. For any diagnostic result there are just a finite set of possibilities. The probability that a particular test result is indicative of a certain illness could be estimated statistically. Based upon that probability, a recommended course of treatment or a further set of tests could be ascertained. Such computer-aided diagnostics are used in many industries with excellent results. Computers don't forget or overlook a possibility. With the aid of computers, the use of doctors could be reserved for the truly ambiguous or novel symptoms, cases requiring direct observation, and of course those involving surgery. The supply of nurse practitioners has increased in the 1990s and should continue to do so, much to the chagrin of the AMA.

Limiting Malpractice Suits: Yet another cause of the rising medical expense is the soaring cost of malpractice insurance, whose premiums soared in the 1980s, doubling in just the four years between 1984 and 1988. Insurance premiums amounted to 6 percent of a doctor's gross pay in 1988 and were climbing rapidly. Premiums differ dramatically by type of practice and location—an obstetrician in Long Island would be paying $200,000 in 1990.[31]

Malpractice suits no doubt raise the cost of health care, but the amount is subject to dispute. The U.S. Department of Health and Human Services puts the cost of malpractice at less than 1 percent of total health outlays, which would be about $10 billion in 1996.[32] However, many doctors would argue that much of the unnecessary medical treatment discussed above is the result of their overly conservative approach to medicine to avoid any potential charges of malpractice, e.g., they test for very unlikely but possible conditions. So the threat of malpractice suits might have very large second-order impacts.

The growth in litigation is primarily the result of the oversupply of lawyers and the legal system that permits lawyers to charge a fee contingent on winning the case and proportioned to the award. They don't have to win often; as long as when they do win, they win big. Moreover, if a lawyer is working on a contingency basis, patients have nothing to lose when they sue. Hence the rule is "when in doubt, sue." The ratio of civil claims filed per 100 doctors rose from about 1 per 100 in 1960 to 17 per 100 at end of 1980. It then dropped slightly, to 13 per 100 by 1990.[33] ***Nevertheless, the U.S. should follow the practice of many European countries and outlaw contingency suits.*** The result would be far fewer frivolous medical law suits. Lawyers would only accept law suits for which they are certain to get paid. People will tend to sue only when there is a reasonable likelihood that they will win.

Certainly there are doctors whose negligence has resulted in much pain and suffering, and in some cases even death. However, it is more important to remove an incompetent practitioner from the profession than to present an award so high that we substantially increase the cost of medical care for all of society. Most often, a medical mistake is not a matter of willful negligence or gross incompetence as much as human error. Doctors are fallible; sooner or later they all will make a mistake. The question is how much society should pay to compensate the victim of a mistake. The value of a human life may be inestimable, but society's resources are not. The real issue is not what a life is worth, or what is fair compensation for physical and mental suffering, but how much can society afford to compensate without weakening health care for the rest of us.

We need guidelines on awards to provide juries with some idea of what is fair in given situations. Some of the criteria would include the age of the patient, future earnings potential lost, and the degree of negligence involved. Punitive damages should only be awarded when there is willful negligence demonstrated. Under such conditions we would expect that the doctor in question would also lose his/her license. An alternative is to ***have juries only decide if the defendant is guilty of inadvertent or willful negligence, but let the judge make the monetary award, analogous to criminal proceedings in which the judge determines the sentence.*** Again, however, there should be some guidelines both for the sake of equity and to keep malpractice insurance premiums from rising so high as to discourage people from entering the medical profession. A final option would be to admit that the average lay jury is in no position to assess whether a doctor was negligent in his/her diagnosis or treatment and turn such cases over to either a blue ribbon jury of experts or special courts with the necessary experience to make such determinations. In any case, frivolous suits should be discouraged through the imposition of stiff fines against both lawyer and client in such instances. The point to be made is that the tort law is in need of reform. Admittedly, this is easier said than done. Illinois passed a bill to reform tort law, but it was thrown out by the state supreme court.

Limitation on Treatment: All of the aforementioned problems contribute significantly to the rising cost of heath care, but ***the most significant cause is not due primarily to greedy doctors, unscrupulous insurance companies, or shyster lawyers. Rather, it is due to people's desire to have access to the most effective health treatment regardless of the cost to society.*** At the same time as our population is aging, major technological breakthroughs are occurring with breathtaking speed and at breathtaking cost. Today we can provide organ and bone morrow transplants, open heart surgery, unconstrained access to CAT scans and Magnetic Response Imaging (MRI) machines, chemotherapy and radiation therapy, and on and on. Millions of people who would have died two decades ago can now be cured or kept alive for an extended period of time. These technological marvels are extremely costly, however, and the chronically ill generate the greater part of healthcare costs. For example, end-stage treatment of renal disease (including dialysis and/or kidney transplant) is projected to reach $14 billion by the year 2000.[34]

Average life expectancy has increased by five years between 1960 and 1990, but such a statistic tells us nothing about the quality of those extra years. Look into most nursing homes and you will see a distressing sight. As often as not, the huge expenditures to care for many people are not to extend an active, fulfilling life but to lengthen the dying process. According to a study published in *The New England Journal of Medicine*, ***about 27 percent of total Medicare expenditures are for patients sixty-five or older in the year they die.***[35] This partly accounts for the fact that 8.1 percent of the population generate 51.3 percent of the total costs.[36] However, oftentimes it is not known whether expensive treatment will turn out to be futile unless it is tried. If we just eliminated obviously futile intervention of the terminally ill, the savings would only be about 3.3 percent of healthcare costs.[37] To make major savings then, society would have to provide treatment only when the *probability* is that it would be effective. (Of course this does not prevent an individual from investing his or her own money on any potential remedy as long as the risks are accurately presented.) That would mean denying certain treatments that *might* save or extend life but have little chance of doing so. For example, one study shows that 79 percent of infants born prior to 25 weeks of pregnancy will die or have severe brain damage and major disabilities if they survive.[38] To make matters worse, physicians often have a difficult time predicting the outcome for such early neonates. Therefore, it makes sense to refuse heroic measures for all babies born this prematurely, as practiced in some European countries.

Again we face the question of trade-offs. We could design a car that was virtually indestructible at 20 mph. We could then make 20 mph the maximum speed limit throughout the nation. Even though tens of thousands of lives would be saved every year, as a society we have decided that the trade-off isn't worth it. Nor are we willing to spend $100,000 to purchase a safer auto, although we may spend an extra couple thousand or so for air bags, seat belts, and antilock brakes. Just as we make trade-offs between lives and what we are willing to spend for transportation, we must make trade-offs between lives and what we are willing to spend on health care. We could have a complete medical checkup every month so that we detect certain forms of heart disease or cancer as early as possible and thus reduce the mortality rate even further, but the small increment in reduced mortality would not justify the huge increase in medical expense. We must reevaluate the purpose of medicine: is it to extend life under all circumstances, or is it to eliminate pain and extend life when the cost of doing so is within some reasonable limit?

About 80 percent of conventional healthcare policies have a lifetime limit on reimbursable expenses of between $250,000 and $1 million.[39] However, the universal health care proposed by the Clinton administration would have no lifetime limit. This could result in unlimited growth in healthcare costs. It ignores the basic economic problem: how do we allocate scarce resources to meet the unlimited wants of humankind? Ultimately, like any other product or service, there must be some way to allocate health care. This is just another way of saying there must be a rationing mechanism.

The Oregon Health Care Plan addresses this issue by deciding which medical procedures it will pay for and which it will not. The plan identified 709 medical conditions ranked according to seriousness and likelihood that treatment will restore the patient to long-term good health. Based upon how much money the state decided to devote to health care, 587 conditions were selected for reimbursement. All others would not be covered. For example, Oregon's plan will not pay for life support for babies born before twenty-three weeks of gestation or weighing less than 1.1 pounds.[40]

This is a rational way to both control healthcare costs and insure the greatest social benefit for the dollars spent.

Permitting Voluntary Euthanasia: Paul T. Menzol, professor of philosophy at Pacific Lutheran University, believes that people have a moral responsibility to die cheaply—i.e., to conserve resources in the course of treatment they chose when dying.[41] (This argument is a corollary to the concept of conservation of resources as a requirement of intergenerational equity.) At the very least, this means that individuals must make a decision as to how much to spend on treatment which at best will extend their lives a few months. Frequently, however, a dying individual is not mentally alert enough to make such a decision. The answer is to have delegated that responsibility to someone else through a living will and power of attorney.

We need to make a clear distinction here between the rights of the individual and those of society with respect to medical treatment. While I might feel that people should not waste their money on expensive medical treatment that will extend their lives only a short period of time, and even argue that it is morally wrong for them to do so, from a legal and a moral perspective it should still be their decision. I also might think it is immoral to spend $200,000 on a vintage Rolls Royce, but I am not about to grant the right to the government to determine how an individual spends his/her money. On the other hand, when an individual decides to obtain insurance against catastrophic illness, the insurer, whether private or government, can determine the conditions under which an illness is covered. The insurer could say, for example, that it will not cover a lung transplant for smokers, or will not cover treatment when consulting physicians agree that it will probably not extend the patient's life more than a few months. In the case of taxpayer-funded programs, taxpayers should have a say in determining the types of treatment provided. ***In the interest of intergenerational equity, we must establish one crucial constraint: we should not institute a plan that forces future generations to subsidize the present generation, i.e., health insurance should be fully funded.*** As a practical matter this is easier said than done, and is not the case today under Medicare and Medicaid.

Many Americans believe they should have the right to actively terminate their life under certain conditions if they so wish. About one-third of those surveyed believe that people have the moral right to end their lives if they become "extremely heavy burdens" on their family.[42] In my last book I discussed the necessity for society to grant the right of an individual to go beyond merely refusing treatment that prolongs dying and request assistance from a doctor to shorten the dying process.[43] The issue of euthanasia was discussed at length in that work and so will not be repeated here. The conclusion reached was that it is in the best interests of society and the individual that each of us have the right to determine how and when we will die. Dr. Jack Kevorkian was practicing the highest degree of humanitarianism, and following the moral philosophy advocated by Socrates, Plato, and Aristotle, by assisting terminally ill people to end their lives painlessly and with dignity.

In the instances where people have lost their mental capacity, a member of the family or a friend with power of attorney should be able to make that decision, provided there is no obvious conflict of interests. For those who worry that such a law would lead to all sorts of evils, we have the experience of the Netherlands. In that more enlightened nation, voluntary euthanasia (terminating life at the request of the person concerned) and assisted suicide have been permitted since 1984. Critics have alleged that there have been hundreds of non-voluntary cases of euthanasia, but it turns out that these were instances in which the dying person was in a coma or no longer mentally competent (such as advanced Alzheimer's disease) to make a decision. Here the patients' families were consulted, as was a second physician. It is further alleged that the Netherlands is sliding down a slippery slope since it now allows physician-assisted suicide for those in unbearable suffering, including psychological suffering. However, the slippery slope argument is a red herring that has been hauled out by the Catholic Church and the religious right to oppose every attempt to question the Church's authority on moral issues. The real question is whether the new law is *likely* to lead to the imagined evils. As discussed at length in *The Science of Morality*, restrictions on involuntary euthanasia can be written to prevent such abuse. And indeed, an editorial in the *New England Journal of Medicine* concluded that there is no basis to assert that the Netherlands' policy has led to abuses.[44]

Laws to legalize voluntary euthanasia have been introduced in Washington, Oregon, and California, but so far only Oregon has a law permitting voluntary euthanasia in terminal cases. This is not surprising since the idea is staunchly opposed by most religious groups. These are the same organizations who opposed contraception for so many years, and still oppose abortion. They continually seek to force their theological beliefs on the rest of society.

In the first year under Oregon's assisted suicide law, fifteen people used it to end their lives, and there was no evidence that any of the fears raised by those who argued against the law were realized. Thirteen of the fifteen who took lethal drugs were cancer patients. The others were suffering from heart or lung disease. The average age of those who took their lives was sixty-nine.[45]

Nevertheless, it is only a matter of time before terminally ill people will be permitted to determine how they should die. With scientific advances, we are reaching the point where life can be maintained almost indefinitely—if by life all we mean is that the respiratory, circulatory, and digestive systems are kept functioning. For most people, however, there is a qualitative aspect of life which must be maintained as well, and if it cannot, the mere extension of days, months, or even years can be a form of inhuman torture. David C. Thomasma of the Loyola School of Medicine correctly observes that the aim of medicine in the technological age should be to preserve life as a *conditional value*—as a good that permits us to pursue other values.[46] ***When the quality of life is so constrained that we have no chance to pursue happiness, then we have the right to not only refuse medical assistance to sustain life, but also to request medical assistance to end life.*** If that option cannot be exercised by a person, then a designated relative or friend should be able to make that choice for the patient. The purpose of the law should be to provide proper safeguards so that such a decision will not be made merely for the advantage of the person making the decision.*

In summary, then, although there are many steps that can be taken to slow the increase in healthcare costs, ultimately there must be a mechanism for rationing health care just like any other economic good or service. If we believe that the free market would be too cruel to those with lower incomes, we must find another mechanism. The Oregon Plan rations health care based upon a predetermined allocation of money to be expended for health care and a cost/benefit analysis of those types of treatments found to be most efficacious. It does not preclude a person from spending their own money on additional health care. However, it is also in the interest of both the individual and society that people who face debilitating incurable illness have the right to terminate their lives.

Social Security Reform

The older generation has done exceedingly well in expanding Social Security benefits. They are getting back out of the program many times what they put in or could have made with an alternative investment of equal risk, such as treasury bonds.† ***The number of aged living under the poverty level dropped from 55 percent in 1955 to 10.5 percent by 1995.*** On the other hand, the number of children living in poverty bottomed out in 1973

*For a complete discussion of this complex issue see *The Science of Morality*, chapter 16.

†Oftentimes comparisons are made between the return on Social Security and the stock market. However, the stock market has a significantly higher risk, which is why it must offer a higher return to attract investors.

at 14.2 percent of all children, and then soared 44 percent between 1973 and 1993 to 22 percent, before declining slightly to 20 percent in 1995.[47] ***One reason for the different results in the fortunes of the young and the aged is that Social Security benefits were linked to inflation and welfare benefits were not.*** Score one for the old folks. These were oftentimes the same people who had their representative in Congress vote against the Family Security Act and Children's Survival Bill (which would have set minimum benefit levels and link them to inflation). Neither bill passed.[48]

Even more discouraging was the opposition of the majority of senior citizens to a bill providing benefits to aged people who were not covered by Social Security. When it was proposed that seniors pay taxes on Social Security if their total income exceeded some level so that coverage could be extended to the less fortunate, they quickly killed the bill. Self-interest worked with a vengeance here. Eventually Social Security benefits were subject to taxation over the objections of the elderly, but the extra tax dollars did not benefit the aged not covered by Social Security. The additional revenue was used to balance the budget. At the time of this writing, higher income people may have up to 85 percent of their Social Security benefits subject to income taxes.

Despite its critics, Social Security did accomplish what it was set up for—to help people in their old age. In the short term, the increased Social Security receipts, coupled with a relatively small number of elderly, will result in a huge surplus in the Social Security Trust Fund. This is necessary to provide benefits to the baby boomers when they are ready to retire. The Brookings Institute has estimated that the surplus could reach $12 trillion by 2030,* and then decline rapidly as the baby boomers retire and are sup-

---

*Some people dispute the notion of a surplus as an accounting fiction since the money paid into the Social Security Trust Fund is not actually maintained in a separate account, but is used to offset the rest of the budget deficit. They would prefer to see the money reinvested in corporate bonds and stocks. But when we buy the stock or bonds of corporation, what is it we own? The firm can take that money to pay off its other debts just as the government does. All we really have with a stock or bond is a claim on future earnings or the liquidation value of a firm, which in the case of many companies is virtually nil.

So, too, when we buy a government bond we are simply making a claim on the future revenue (i.e., taxes) of the government. In the case of a federal trust fund, the Treasury Department takes the money and issues a note of indebtedness to the fund. That note in turn has to be financed by either future taxes or additional federal borrowing, e.g., the issuance of treasury bills. A treasury note is backed by the government's future revenue generating capabilities just as a company's bond is ultimately a claim against future revenue. The only difference is that a business might not be able to raise the revenue if no one buys its products, whereas the government would not be able to pay off its bonds if society decided not to pay the taxes necessary to cover the debt. As we saw in chapter 7, as long as the total debt of the government is declining as a proportion of total output (GDP), this should not be a problem.

ported by a relatively smaller population cohort. Between 2035 and 2060, Social Security would run a deficit equal to 3 percent of GDP, about the size of the total deficit today. To cover the benefits of the baby boomers, payroll taxes will have to reach 21 percent compared to the 13 percent today (adding employee and employer contributions), but that is only if we wait until the deficit hits before trying to solve it.

This prospect doesn't bother some economists who agree with Robert Eisner's position that Social Security is not really an insurance system where the benefits received are a function of the premiums paid. Rather, Social Security is the means by which each generation takes care of the preceding generation in its old age. In a sense this is the socialization of an honored tradition. There are two problems with Eisner's logic. First, in the past, the older generation generally did not live very long. The vast majority died before they ever quit working, so their liability on their children was often not very much. Second, with a growing population and increased production, each generation had more total product with which to care for the preceding generation. However, if we constrain population growth, future economic growth must eventually come solely from increased productivity. Can we assume that productivity growth will always be sufficient to provide the need of both the current generation and the aged of the preceding generation? The answer is yes *if* the current generation exercises some constraint in seeking to fulfill their unlimited wants.

Conservatives initially opposed Social Security on the grounds that it discourages personal savings and rewards people for being irresponsible with regard to planning for their own retirement. However, there is no empirical support for this opinion. To the contrary, econometric studies and national data suggest that personal savings have not been affected by Social Security.[49] Generally speaking, people do not save because they believe they will receive Social Security when they get old. Moreover, it is unfortunate but true that many people are not very good at long-term planning. My own father was an entrepreneur who worked six days a week all his life. He assumed that he would amass sufficient wealth to retire on, but he made some errors in judgment and ultimately went bankrupt, losing his life savings as well. If it were not for Social Security, he and my

---

In any case, it is future revenue (i.e., taxes paid by future generations) that will have to pay for future Social Security benefits. Even if we increase taxes today to cover the future deficit, the taxes will reduce not only today's consumption but also today's investment. The increased taxes reduce government borrowing, allowing more capital funds available to the private sector, but the reduced after tax income reduces savings and, hence, investment. The only way to increase the economy's capability to fund future Social Security payouts is to increase the nation's productivity and the total production of future products and services.

mother would have been totally dependent on their children.* For many millions of other people who only make enough money to live hand to mouth, Social Security is the only support that keeps them from ending years of hard work in abject poverty.

It is often overlooked that Social Security performs two other crucial functions: providing benefits to more than 5 million disabled workers and their families and supporting more than 7 million family members of deceased workers. In 1996, Social Security disability benefits had the same value as a $203,000 disability insurance policy to an average worker with a spouse and two children. Survivor coverage for the same family is equivalent to a $295,000 life-insurance policy.[50] Most low-income earners could never afford such coverage. Those who would like to turn Social Security into some sort of mandatory IRA fail to note that it would eliminate this coverage for very low-income people.

The problem with Social Security is two-fold. First, the changing demographics mean that the ratio between those who will be recipients and those who support the system will continue to decline dramatically. In 1934, when Social Security was established, there were 10 employed people for every retiree. By 1990, this ratio had dropped to 5 workers per retiree, and by the year 2030 there will be only 2.5 workers for every retired person.[51] Consequently, unless benefits are reduced or real per capita income rises dramatically, Social Security taxes will have to be raised. If we rely solely on FICA taxes, they will take a bigger and bigger chunk out of the paychecks of those who are working. In 1997, the payroll tax rate was 12.4 percent divided equally between employee and employer, but unless we take action quickly, by the year 2025 increased taxes necessary to close the deficit could reach as much as 21 percent of total wages.[52] Although only half of this amount shows up on the employees' paycheck (the other half being paid by the employer), arguably the entire incidence of the tax falls on the employee, because it is all associated with the cost of labor. Hence, increases in FICA taxes to the firm will be offset by reduction in the growth of wage rates and an increase in the price of products/services sold.

The second problem is that by tying Social Security increases to the growth in the Consumer Price Index (CPI), we have allowed Social Security payments to grow too fast. The problem is that the CPI is heavily weighted by the price of new homes, whereas a retiree does not buy a new home every year. Many never need to buy another home. (On the other

---

*My parents were fortunate to have children who collectively earned enough to support them even if they did not have Social Security, but who supports parents who have no children or whose children earn only enough to support themselves?

hand, local property taxes have been growing even faster than the cost of housing in many areas. This problem will be addressed in the next chapter.) In short, the benefits per retiree grew much faster than the true effect of inflation and retirees made out quite well.

In the past, Congress has addressed the future deficits in Social Security by raising FICA taxes. What it should have done was to slow the increase in payments by tying them to the portion of the CPI that relates to annual consumption of necessities such as rent, food, and clothing. Such a rational solution was politically unpopular among the aged, to say the least.

That is water over the dam now. Regarding the future, there are four questions to answer with regard to Social Security:

1. Should Social Security be an insurance system for disability and old age providing only life's basic necessities (the original intent of the program), or should it be some sort of national pension plan eligible to all people who pay into it and offer a middle-class lifestyle (as it has evolved)?
2. Who should pay for the benefits of Social Security, the present generation or the next generation?
3. Will present tax rates generate enough revenue benefits for future retirees?
4. Will the surplus funds created today actually be available for the retirees of the future?

With regard to this last question, there is a worry that the money will be spent on other government budget needs and not be available to the retirees of the future. Moreover, the answer to the last two questions depends on the answer to the first two questions.

Should Social Security Be an Insurance System or National Retirement Plan?

This is one of those issues that has no right or wrong answer, since society can opt to make it either. The reason we have a problem today is that Social Security was originally set up and funded as a kind of insurance, but evolved into a pension plan without making the necessary changes in funding.

Society appears to want a pension plan available for everyone. Yet many people already have good pension plans through their unions or employers. Should these people be forced to subsidize those who do not? How do we cover those who had good pension plans but who voluntarily or involuntarily are forced to change employers? In the case of health insurance, Congress decided to guarantee insurance for workers who change jobs. Similarly, pension plans could also be made portable.

Moreover, the amount of a pension should be proportional to the number of years worked. This eliminates the unfair feature of many plans which provide a tiny pension until a person reaches twenty-five or thirty years of service, after which he/she hits the jackpot. The problem is not so much that it is an incentive for employers to get rid of their older employees before they reach pension age (age discrimination laws and seniority systems largely take care of this), but that when there are work force reductions for whatever reason, employees can loose sizable pensions for being laid off a month or even a day before they become eligible for a full pension. Again, simple vesting* is often insufficient to remedy this problem even if the pension payout is also proportional to years of service.

If we make pensions proportional and portable, how does this solve the problem of an employee who has no more than five years of service with several different companies? One answer is to allow the person to take the accumulated accrued pension with them, i.e., make the funds transferable from job to job. The alternative is to ensure that an IRA is available which allows sufficient annual contributions by the employee to build his/her own pension plan. In fact, there is no reason that we can't do both: ***company pension allotments should be paid directly into the employee's IRA where they can be supplemented as necessary—up to certain annual amount—by an employee's contribution.***

The 401(k) plan is a step in this direction. Section 401(k) of the Internal Revenue Code allows employees who participate in an employer-sponsored 401(k) plan to defer part of their salary. The employees themselves determine how much money to defer and how it should be invested. The benefit to the employee is that taxes on the deferred salary and any subsequent investment earnings are also deferred, and if employees change employers, the 401(k) investments go with them.

It is not required, however, that every company offer a 401(k) plan, nor that the company contributes any pension money to the plan. Without any employer contribution, lower-paid workers are not likely to save a sufficient amount to provide a worthwhile pension.

---

*Vesting is the practice of guaranteeing a pension after a certain length of employment even though a person leaves the company prior to retirement age. The problem is that the vested amount is not paid until the person reaches retirement age and by that time even if inflation is only 3 to 4 percent a year, the pension can be heavily discounted in constant dollar terms. For example, if inflation averages 3 percent annually, a $100,000 vested pension granted at age forty, but not paid out until age sixty, would only be worth $55,368; at a 5 percent average rate of inflation, the pension would be worth only $37,689.

Unless we are willing to allow many elderly people to live in poverty, we need a form of Social Security that provides a pension floor. I would argue that everyone must pay into such a system (this keeps the premium low), and everyone is entitled to the payouts when they reach retirement age or are disabled. This helps ensure that such a system receives broad support.

However, the more problematic issues are: how generous should such a system be and how do we finance it? ***In order to encourage people to save for their old age and be primarily responsible for their futures, Social Security payouts should be no more than the poverty level.**** This ensures that no one starves or is homeless, but yet maintains the incentive to save for one's old age.

Which Generation Should Pay for the Benefits of Social Security?

Determining how to fund Social Security is an even more complex issue. In discussing health insurance we argued that, in the interests of intergenerational equity, we should not make one generation subsidize another. But it might be argued that investments made for education of the young are, in effect, the present generation subsidizing future generations. Therefore, I see nothing conceptually wrong with having future generations pay back something to the present generation. Since future generations have no say in estimating the reciprocal trade-offs, there is the concern that the present generation would always seek to increase its present benefits more than the investment in its children's future. This also recognizes that since many people don't have children, they are not motivated by the genetically induced altruism to sacrifice for one's children.

Therefore, any pension plan should be largely financed by balancing present taxes against accrued future benefits. Indeed, that is the reason for running a large surplus in the Social Security Trust Fund today. The problem is that today's surplus is not enough to balance the accrued shortfall when the baby boomers retire. Hence, to balance today's taxes against future benefits, we need either to reduce benefits or increase taxes, or some combination of both.

---

*It has been suggested by a colleague, Walter Buchmann, that the poverty level for a single person should not be based upon the cost of a person living alone. Rather, it should be based upon the more economical form of group living. While it might be difficult for one person to make ends meet on $700 a month, if three people pooled their resources, they could rent a nice apartment and live well on $2,100 a month. Moreover, they could help one another and be an answer to the problem of loneliness which afflicts many older people. This idea has merit and needs to be explored further.

What Will Be the Shortfall When the Baby Boomers Retire?

Unfortunately, this is not an easy question to answer. In the first place, there are two ways of assessing a potential gap between Social Security tax receipts and benefits: the "closed gap" and the "open gap" method. The *closed gap* method uses estimates of taxes paid and benefits received by all people now age fifteen or older who will become workers or beneficiaries over the next seventy-five years. This methodology yields a funding shortfall of $7.6 trillion over the next seventy-five years.[53] However, some economists argue that this mind-boggling amount is unrealistic because many new children will be born during that time and as they enter the labor force, they will contribute additional tax revenues. The *open gap* method includes the future taxes of people under the age of fifteen and estimates of taxes of those not yet even born. This method results in a much smaller shortfall of $1.9 trillion. Although even this estimate sounds quite large, remember that it is the *cumulative* shortfall over seventy-five years. To put it into perspective, Robert Eisner estimated that it would have taken a payroll tax increase of only 1.46 percent to close the gap in 1993.[54] The longer we wait, however, the larger will have to be the tax increase to close the gap. By 1997 payroll taxes would have needed to be increased by 2.2 percent (1.1 percent from the employee portion).[55] Such an increase would be unwelcomed, but by no means a real hardship on workers or their employers.

Before we become too sanguine with this rather modest increase in taxes, there are several caveats to keep in mind. The estimate of the shortfall is based upon predictions of population growth, including immigration, job and earnings growth, life expectancy, and so on. Of particular concern is the immigration estimate. We have seen earlier that the Bureau of Census' "middle series" projection (which is most often cited) underestimates immigration because the bureau largely ignores the influx of illegals. Of course all the descendants of illegal immigrants born in this country are citizens and therefore will be entitled to Social Security or supplemental security (SSI) benefits. Now if all immigrants (legal and illegal) pay into the system more money in taxes than they eventually take out, all well and good. This is one reason why some economists favor high rates of immigration. Conversely, if the immigrants withdraw more money from the system than they pay in, the deficit will be just that much larger. Such a case would occur if benefits keep pace with inflation while taxes do not. In recent years, income tax rates have been reduced to reflect inflation in order to avoid "bracket creep" whereby a person whose wages increase due to inflation would be paying a higher portion of income in taxes even though their real earnings have not changed. Since FICA tax rates are not indexed to inflation while Social Security pensions are, the greater the amount of inflation, the greater would be the shortfall.

An increasing shortfall would also occur if the growth in the number of low-skilled workers increase the average unemployment rate or decrease the average wage rates of indigenous workers, as is likely under a high immigration scenario. Additionally, immigrants over the age of sixty-five (usually the parents of recently naturalized citizens who sponsored them), can qualify for $8,000 a year in Supplemental Security Income after becoming citizens and five years of residency.* The states will then determine eligibility for benefits such as Medicaid and food stamps. From 1983 to 1993, the number of immigrants receiving elderly benefits quadrupled while the total number of citizens receiving elderly benefits declined 25 percent.[56] In short, under present immigration policy, immigrants will probably extract much more from Social Security than they put in. Those economists who see immigration as the answer to the Social Security shortfall not only overestimate the benefits from immigrants relative to their costs, but ignore the infrastructure and environmental costs of population growth.

Using different assumptions results in a wide range of possible outcomes. The most optimistic case projects a $5.25 trillion surplus in the year 2025, which continues to grow to $22.2 trillion by 2075. At the other extreme, the most pessimistic outlook projects that the fund will be exhausted by 2017. I can guarantee that the optimistic case will not occur—if the surplus was growing that fast, the government would use the money to reduce the deficit or fund new federal initiatives. The best guess is that if present trends continue, there will be a deficit sometime before the year 2030. Therefore, ***it is essential that we at least cover "closed gap" estimates by a combination of increasing Social Security tax rates and reducing the growth of future benefits. Over the next fifty years, we should go to a fully funded plan by gradually closing the deficit based upon the "open gap" methodology.*** However, to try and resolve the problem in too short a time would require either draconian tax increases or major cuts in other government programs. In chapter 6, it was explained that we already must increase taxes and implement further budget cuts to continue reducing the national debt.

There are a few seemingly less painful ways of closing the Social Security deficit that have been suggested, but they are problematic.

---

*Originally, Supplemental Security Income (SSI) was created by Congress to cover hardship cases, such as disabled people who made so little money during their lifetime that, through no fault of their own, did not pay sufficient Social Security taxes to qualify for Social Security pension. (They also had to have virtually no wealth of their own from other sources). Immigrants have discovered that they could bring over their aged parents, who deed any assets to their children, then once the parents become citizens they can apply for SSI. Congress tried to end this practice in the 1996 Welfare Reform Act, but instances of real hardship among some elderly immigrant parents has caused Congress to backtrack on the restriction.

1. Use the current Social Security surpluses to pay off the national debt, thus stimulating the economy to generate additional tax revenue in the future to cover Social Security needs.

At present, the government is collecting about $70 billion a year more in Social Security taxes than are being disbursed in benefits. One proposal is for the government to use the excess funds to finance today's federal budget deficit, thus reducing borrowings from the private sector. In so doing, it is hoped that more private sector funds will be available for investment to stimulate the economy, thus generating additional income and taxes to cover future Social Security payouts.[57] Of course, if the Federal Reserve Board thinks that the economy is growing too fast and running the risk of increasing inflation, it will take action to reduce growth in the money supply or raise interest rates, thus reducing economic growth. Another possibility is that a large portion of the added money in the private sector may go for increased consumption of imports which will fail to increase U.S. growth and investment. In fact, if for any reason the economy slows, the diversion of the Social Security surplus to balance the federal budget might backfire and the retirees of tomorrow suffer the consequences. Therefore, using the Social Security surplus to reduce the national debt is an unwarranted gamble and should be rejected.

To avoid the temptation of using the Social Security surplus to reduce the nation's debt, Social Security taxes and expenditures should be excluded from the federal budget altogether. Excluding the Social Security surplus from the unified budget has the benefit of revealing the true depth of the current fiscal deficit and encourages further spending cuts or increased taxes to reduce the deficit. If the Social Security surpluses were "off-budget" in fiscal 1997, the annual budget deficit would be $81 billion higher than the estimated $21 billion.[58] In any case, it would force us to deal with the problems caused by the current generation, rather than pushing it onto future generations.

2. Instead of buying bonds from the Treasury Department, invest the Social Security tax receipts in corporate bonds and the stock market.

Some critics of the Social Security system don't like the idea of investing all of the program's present surpluses in government securities. They argue that since the government doesn't produce any salable goods and services, government securities are only based on the faith of the American public on future tax generation capabilities of the government. (See footnote, p. 609).

Those who don't like this reliance on future growth to finance current debt suggest that the Social Security surplus should be invested in corporate bonds and equities rather than Treasury bonds.[59] The concern has been raised, however, that permitting the federal government to have such a large amount invested in the private economy would effectively increase federal control of the private economy.[60] The government might try to influence the stock market. For example the president could threaten not to reappoint the Federal Reserve Chairman if he raises interest rates (which can cause stock prices to fall). Some people fear it may be a backdoor to socialism. Such concerns might be alleviated by creating a semi-autonomous body to manage the investment, just as the Federal Reserve Board was created to manage the money supply. Nor need we invest all the surplus in the private sector. It has been estimated that we might close the future Social Security gap by investing 37 percent of the Social Security Trust Fund in private sector securities that average a 3.8 percent real rate of return.[61] (That's 6.8 percent if the rate of inflation is 3.0 percent.)

One of the suggestions by the presidential advisory panel on Social Security would require each worker to take about half the present payroll tax and put it into a personal investment account and personally administer it. A 1998 Congressional bipartisan panel was less radical, recommending that initially 2.0 percent of the present 12.4 percent of the present payroll tax be diverted to individual investment accounts. Retirees could not begin tapping their accounts until they reach age seventy.[62]

But what happens if the stock market drops precipitously as it did during the Great Depression? We often hear that it couldn't happen again. That's what they thought in Japan before their stock market dropped 55 percent from its 1989 peak and has still not recovered. In the United States, with billions of new Social Security dollars chasing already high-priced stocks, there is a strong possibility that it could result in pushing stock prices to unsustainable heights. The stock market need not tank to cause problems. Even if it goes through a period of stagnation, such as the seventeen years between 1965 to 1982 when the Dow Jones industrials declined 3 percent (a whopping 53 percent after adjusting for inflation), retirees will find that the purchasing power of their investments has dropped dramatically.[63]

Peter Klenow of the University of Chicago Graduate School of Business notes that investing Social Security money in something besides treasury bills will put pressure on the government to artificially buoy up the stock market. Also, during the transition to a fully or partially privatized system, the government would have to issue huge amounts of debt to pay the Social Security benefits. The increased debt (government's private sector borrowing) would likely raise interest rates, thus dropping the comparative advantage of stocks over bonds, pushing stock prices lower.[64]

England's experience is also worth noting. It had the same debate in the early 1980s whether to allow people to invest their retirement funds in equities and decided it was worth a try. Beginning in 1988, higher income workers could opt out of public and company sponsored pension plans to manage their own contributions. Two million workers decided to do so and were immediately deluged by banks, insurance companies, and financial advisors, all of whom offered sure-fire methods of increasing the retirees' pensions. The result was a disaster: by 1998 it was expected to cost British taxpayers $18 billion in compensation payments to nurses, miners, school teachers, and other workers hurt by bad advice. It wasn't that the people made uninformed decisions. The problem was primarily one of "misselling" (that's a British euphemism for being conned). A study that the investment services KPMG Peat Marwick prepared found that 91 percent of the 735 personal pension plans reviewed were "unsatisfactory" or "suspect" in terms of giving clients appropriate advice.[65] To rectify the deplorable situation, England is going to resort to more regulation of the financial services industry.

Finally, and most importantly, investing in the private sector still relies on future economic growth to pay back existing investment plus a return on capital. As we discussed earlier, underinvesting in social infrastructure can also reduce productivity and hence slow future economic growth. The real issue is not whether to invest the present Social Security surpluses in government bonds or corporate bonds, but whether there will be sufficient growth in the economy to make an adequate return on any investment in inflation-adjusted dollars.* There is danger in overreliance on future growth to cover future obligations in either case. ***A better policy is to set today's premiums (tax rates) of levels sufficient to cover tomorrow's benefits, assuming a very conservative return on investment.***

3. Eliminate the limit on earnings subject to FICA taxes.

We ought to admit that Social Security is not a true insurance policy, but a tax to provide a minimal standard of living for every American in old age.

---

*It is sometimes argued that since most government expenditures do not increase productivity, we should therefore invest as little as possible in government and as much as possible in the private sector. However, aside from the fact that we are talking here about how to reduce existing debt, i.e., the money that has already been spent, it is a moot point whether we issue bonds today to get the income to cover the deficit or raise taxes in the future—either way it will reduce private sector investment and spending. Moreover, it is not at all clear to me that society is better off because we invested more money in professional sport teams, casinos, or pollution-producing products, as opposed to government functions that insure the safety of the food we eat and the drugs we consume, protect our lives and homes, educate our youth, and save our environment to benefit future generations. Although there is no doubt waste in government, having worked in both the public and private sector, I am not convinced that there is any *more* waste in government than in the private sector.

Just like Medicare, we should therefore remove the ceiling on earnings subject to taxes. We might also establish a floor below which earnings are not taxed.[66] This latter option would have the added advantage of effectively raising the minimum wage, thus encouraging more people to opt for work over welfare, while not raising the cost to the employer and thus discouraging added employment.

4. Raise the retirement age.

Congress has raised the retirement age as far as reasonable by phasing in the requirement age for receipt of full benefits to age sixty-eight. Although it is true that people are living longer, many are not necessarily healthy by their late sixties. We are able to keep unhealthy people living much longer than years ago. While it is wonderful if a person is healthy and wants to continue working past sixty-five, I view it as a step backward to extend the number of years a person *has* to work. Hence I would argue for moving full benefits back to age sixty-five.

5. Cut payroll taxes and future benefits and encourage workers to begin building their own pension funds.[67]

Supporters of such a plan have cited Chile as an example of how it has appeared to work well—at least until recently. During the 1998 world stock market decline, the head of Chile's retirement system urged workers about to retire to "hold off a little bit."[68]

One plan proposed in the United States would take about half of the present 12.4 percent of payroll tax and credit this to an individual's Personal Security Account (PSA). These would be held by the Social Security Trust Fund but could be invested any way an employee chooses, similar to an IRA or 401(k) plan. At retirement, the employee receives the amount held in the PSA plus its return. The plan would be constructed in such a way that even if some people made such bad investments that they lost it all, they would still receive a pension from the government amounting to about 60 percent of the poverty line.

Naturally, investment houses and corporations love this idea. However, there will be winners and losers under such a plan. Investment theory suggests that on average, investors will about equal the overall stock market average. The basic assumption is that over a long time the market will have a better return than the Social Security system could make by buying only government bonds. The problem is that people retire at different points in time. Depending upon when they retire, they could be hurt if there was a deep and sustained decline on the stock market, such as the 1965 to 1982 period. Also, many people will be dumb investors and loose their shirts on the market. Even if everyone had adequate information and was well-educated in investing, there would be a normal distribution of winners and losers along the bell-shaped curve. Even though most people would equal the market average, what will we do for the losers? Tell them tough luck, you lost, now you starve? I doubt it. What society could do is support the losers by heavily taxing the winners. Such a system of taxation and transfers would be complex and I don't think it would receive wide voter support ahead of time since everyone believes they are going to be a winner.

To make matters worse, what would no doubt happen is that the investment industry would advertise their stocks and funds as vigorously as any other business advertises their products. The boiler rooms (a group of salesmen pushing stock by phone) would be working overtime, cleaning the clocks of unsophisticated investors. The government would need to expand its oversight function to avoid fraud, and the courts would be swamped with both legitimate claims of fraud and thousands of class action cases on the part of those investors who lost money even though no fraud was involved. We could seek to avoid such a nightmare by limiting investment to index funds, treasury bills, and investment-quality bond funds, but even this involves a significant amount of government intrusion into private investment decisions.

The way around all the nightmare scenarios is to compute how much Social Security tax would be required to provide a poverty level income. Then take the difference between that tax rate and the present rate and permit workers to earmark it for an IRA-type account. There have been a number of suggestions similar to this. The thirteen-member presidential Social Security panel recommended that workers be permitted to place 1.6 percent of their paychecks into a personal retirement account that could be invested in a small range of relatively safe stock and bond funds overseen by government officials. Senator Daniel Moynihan has recommended that employees be allowed to divert up to 15 percent of their payroll taxes (that's the equivalent of 1.9 percent of their paychecks) into personal savings accounts.

6. Increase the tax on Social Security benefits.

To close the projected gap, Congress began taxing Social Security income. This was fair in theory since tax rates should be based upon total income. Hence, those who had little income other than Social Security were taxed far less—if at all—than the very rich who had their Social Security taxed at a far higher rate. In 1996, up to 85 percent of Social Security benefits were subject to taxes for those retirees in the top income bracket. This was mistakenly construed by many people as an 85 percent tax on Social Security benefits, whereas it really meant that 85 percent of Social Security benefits were subject to the top tax rate of 39.6 percent.*

A variant of increasing taxes on Social Security is to reduce the amount of earned income people can make before having their benefits reduced. One problem with this solution is that it does not differentiate between those who are living primarily on their Social Security benefits and those who have amassed significant wealth. It also results in different tax rates depending upon the source of income (i.e., from wages versus investments).

The most inequitable part of the present tax law involves the taxes on earnings of those who continue to work after collecting Social Security. The law is hellishly complicated in this regard, but at the very least people who work while collecting Social Security lose $1 of benefits for every $2 earned ($1 for every $3 earned if over sixty-five) plus the amount of income tax on their earned income.[69] If a person under age sixty-six collecting Social Security was in the top income bracket, his effective tax rate would be 89.6 percent (50 percent for the Social Security reduction and 39.6 percent in income taxes). ***The remedy is not to withhold Social Security payout regardless of how much a person makes, but to treat all sources of income equally, when calculating tax liability, including wages, interest, dividends, Social Security income and capital gains (this last adjusted for inflation is discussed in the next chapter). In effect, the tax rate applied to Social Security income would be whatever marginal rate is applicable to a person's total income.***

7. Tie the growth in Social Security benefits to growth in the economy.

Lester Thurow suggests that benefits be limited to per capita growth in GDP.[70] That would result in much slower growth in benefits and future Social Security taxes. The problem with this proposal is that during periods of high inflation and low growth, Social Security recipients would get hammered. It is a financially responsible solution, but makes retirement income somewhat of a crapshoot.

8. Limit Social Security benefits to people in need.

Social Security was originally passed not as a universal pension plan but as an economic insurance policy. Some people suggest that we go back to that

---

*Still, it might be considered unfair because a portion of the Social Security pension is, in effect, a return of the FICA taxes that the wage earners paid during their lifetimes. Hence, it has been suggested that if Social Security pensions are taxed at all, they should only be taxed on the amount the recipient receives over and above the FICA taxes paid.

intent, arguing that it is absurd to give people making a $100,000 of annual income on other investments Social Security payments as well. Milton Friedman proposed that we phase out Social Security taxes and benefits, and replace them with a negative income tax for those whose annual income is below a certain level, just as we are doing for all other low-income people with the Earned Income Tax Credit.[71] Others would link the amount of Social Security payments to wealth since, as mentioned, older people frequently have little income but significant wealth, which they could tap. While I have no theoretical problem with the equity of such a recommendation, I doubt if it is politically feasible. People tend not to support a bill that does not have something in it for them.

Recommendations

In the final analysis, the most prudent and practical solution is to increase Social Security taxes to the point where, using reasonable assumptions regarding the growth in population and the changing demographics of an aging population, we provide payments equal to the amount sufficient to bring future retirees to 125 percent of the poverty level. As inflation increases Social Security taxes, the poverty level would rise and so would Social Security payments, but this increase should be less than the consumer price index, since the CPI does not reflect the market basket of goods older people buy. If there is a shortfall in the Social Security Trust Fund based on this new payment schedule, taxes might need to be raised. Gradually, we need to switch to the "pay-as-you-go" plan that matches receipts to benefits as reflected in the "close gap" methodology.

The Social Security Trust Fund should not in any way be commingled with the rest of the federal budget so the present Social Security surpluses can be used to balance the budget.* The bulk of the trust fund, perhaps 60 percent, should continue to be invested in Treasury bonds. Another 30 percent could be used to purchase investment-grade corporate bonds (AAA to BBB).† The remaining 10 percent could be used to buy an index fund such

*At the time of this writing, the Republican leadership in Congress has recommended "walling off" the Social Security trust fund, in effect forbidding the government from using these funds for any other purpose for a period of ten years. (William Neikirk, "GOP Leaders Agree on Budget Plan," *Chicago Tribune*, sec. 1, p. 5.) Although a step in the right direction, the wall between the Social Security Trust funds and the rest of the budget should be permanent.

†Bonds are evaluated by bond-rating services, such as Moody's or Standard and Poor's, based on the risk of default. They are graded from AAA, AA, A, BBB, BB, etc. Investors who want a high degree of security against default are advised to buy only bonds rated from AAA and BBB, which are considered "investment grade."

as the S & P 500 or Russell 2000. As we test this approach over the next ten to twenty years we may decide to change the mix, but we should always err on the side of caution.

Social Security basic benefits will enable people to live at the poverty level, but since we are taxing at a level to yield 1.25 percent of the poverty level, people should be permitted to earmark 20 percent of their taxes for a personal savings account that could be invested in relatively safe stock and bond index funds. They could receive payouts as an annuity beginning at age fifty-nine.

This solution (or any that threatens to reduce benefits) will not be welcomed by the American Association of Retired Persons. They will fight tooth and nail against any changes that threaten the benefits to which they feel they are entitled. They ignore the fact that they have already benefited by the insurance effect of Social Security, i.e., if they had lost their earning power, they would have had Social Security unemployment or disability income. That is the true purpose of insurance. Do we try to claim accident or illness benefits from an insurance policy even though we never had an accident and have had the good fortune to remain healthy?

However, to be fair, we must gradually enact any reforms that result in a lower base level of benefits, along with the potential for higher returns based upon supplemental personal savings plans.

Summary

There is a major effort underway to reduce welfare by forcing the unemployed to find jobs. It is only fair that people who leave welfare to take jobs do not lose their health care. Even more importantly, we should offer some form of health care to the millions of working poor who at present cannot afford healthcare insurance. Therefore, a universal basic healthcare insurance policy that covers every working person is indispensable. This would not deny any person from buying additional health insurance or paying for additional medical services. But any universal health care must not act as an incentive to have more than two children or attract more illegal immigration. It must also incorporate features to:

- reduce overhead through standardized fees and billing processes
- reduce unnecessary procedures through second opinions or an audit review process
- increase the number of general practitioners relative to specialists
- reduce fraud and conflicts of interest

- encourage the use of nurse practitioners and expert systems
- limit malpractice suits by forbidding lawyers to work on a contingency basis, and having judges determine the amount of the settlement.

Even if all of the above recommendations were implemented, healthcare expense would continue to absorb an increasingly larger portion of our GDP, unless we act to ration health care to those procedures that are most likely to improve the long-term quality of life, as the Oregon Plan proposes.

Finally, we must also allow adults to voluntarily terminate their own lives if they wish, as long as they are mentally competent to make the decision. If they are no longer mentally able to do so, as in the case of a someone who is permanently comatose or in latter stages of Alzheimer's, the decision should pass to whomever they have granted power of attorney, or lacking that, to a Medical Ethics Review Board.* The laws regarding euthanasia should be designed to protect the individual from coercion in making such a decision, not to deny a person the right to control his/her life.

The Social Security system is not as moribund as many critics claim. However, based upon present trends there is a gap that will cause the system to go broke sometime around the year 2030. The gap can be closed by redesigning the program in terms of benefits and funding. Benefits should be tied to the poverty level, and revenues must ultimately be sufficient to close the gap on a pay-as-you-go basis, just as with any other insurance policy. The alternative is to continue to have each generation support the prior generation on the assumption that the total wealth of society will always be increasing, thus making it easier for the next generation to subsidize the present generation. The danger of not implementing a pay-as-you-go system is that the present generation loses any incentive to control benefits.

Although, in one sense, it does not matter whether the Social Security surpluses are invested in government or private sector securities, taking a portion of the fund and investing it in the stock market, just as private pension funds do, should increase the total return and hence, lower the costs of Social Security in the long run. Any investment on the part of the government in the stock market should be in a broad index fund to avoid a conflict of interest on the part of government employees managing the Social Security Trust Fund. Individuals should not have control over any Social Security investment in the stock market, or it no longer becomes an insurance plan but merely another savings plan like an IRA. Hence, there will be a bell-shaped curve of returns, with some people being big winners and some big losers. Those who lose will be in the position of having no

---

*The details of this process are discussed in *The Science of Morality*, chapter 16.

retirement income, exactly the situation that Social Security was created to correct.

To provide a more accurate perspective on the budget and to prevent using Social Security surpluses to finance other federal programs, the trust fund should be maintained separately from the rest of the federal budget.

Finally, whatever solution is decided to close the gap, ***it is essential that we begin to solve the problem today. The longer we wait, the greater the problem becomes.***

NOTES

1. "Wasted Health Care Dollars," *Consumer Reports* (July 1992): 445.

2. Ben J. Wattenberg, "Reading beyond Media Hype Lies," *Washington Times*, May 22, 1991. Reprinted in *AEI* 28 (1991).

3. Nicholas N. Eberstadt, "America's Infant Mortality Problem: Parents," *Wall Street Journal* (January 20, 1992).

4. Ibid.

5. Sharon L. Hillier and Robert P. Nugent et al., "Association Between Vaginosis and Preterm Delivery of a Low Birthweight Infant," *New England Journal of Medicine* (January 1996).

6. U.S Bureau of the Census, as reported by John McCarron, "Too Bad We Ignored Hillary's Health Care Proposals in 1993," *Chicago Tribune*, January 13, 1998, sec. 1, p. 17.

7. *Chicago Tribune*, August 18, 1994, sec. 1, pp. 2–3.

8. McCarron, "Too Bad We Ignored Hillary's Health Care Proposals in 1993."

9. Laurie McGinley, "U.S. Health Costs Are Expected to Double by 2007," *Wall Street Journal*, September 15, 1998, p. A2.

10. U.S. Office of Management and Budget, *Budget of the United States Government, Fiscal Year 1996, Historical Tables* (Washington, D.C.: U.S. Government Printing Office, 1996), table 3.2, p. 59.

11. Associated Press, "Health-care Costs Reach $1 Trillion," *Chicago Tribune*, January 13, 1998, sec. 1, p. 5.

12. U.S. Bureau of the Census, *Statistical Abstract of the United States, 1997* (Washington, D.C.: U.S. Government Printing Office, 1997), table, 1341, p. 835.

13. Ibid.

14. "Wasted Health Care Dollars," *Consumer Reports* (July 1992): 435–48.

15. Ibid., p. 437.

16. David E. Rogers and Eli Ginzberg, eds., Cornell University Medical College Sixth Conference on Health Policy (Boulder, Co.: Westview Press, 1990). Cited in *Future Survey* (July 1991): 12.

17. Ronald Kotulak and Peter Gorner, "Medicine Aches with HMO Fever," *Chicago Tribune*, April 14, 1976, sec. 1, p. 16.

18. David Wessel, "Firms Cut Health Care Costs, Cover Fewer Workers," *Wall Street Journal*, November 11, 1996, p. A1.

19. Carol Jouzaitis and David S. Cloud, "HMO Reforms Delayed; Critics Blame Politics," *Chicago Tribune*, July 9, 1996, sec. 1, p. 8.

20. President, *Economic Report of the President Transmitted to Congress, 1994* (Washington, D.C.: U.S. Government Printing Office, 1994), p. 161.

21. Ibid., p. 135.

22. Ibid., p. 136.

23. Ibid., p. 165.

24. "Wasted Health Care Dollars," *Consumer Reports*, p. 448.

25. Steffie Woolhandler and David U. Hammelstein, "The Deteriorating Administrative Efficiency of the U.S. Health Care System," *New England Journal of Medicine* 324, no. 18 (May 2, 1991): 1253–58. Cited in *Future Survey* (July 1991): 9.

26. "Wasted Health Care Dollars," *Consumer Reports*, pp. 439–41.

27. Judy Heviere, "Medicare," *Mother Jones* (March/April 1981): 50ff.

28. Janice Castro, "Condition: Critical," *Time* (November 25, 1991): 34–42.

29. Ibid., pp. 34–42.

30. U.S. Bureau of the Census, *Statistical Abstract of the United States, 1997*, table 176, p. 122.

31. Paul C. Weiler, *Medical Malpractice on Trial* (Cambridge, Mass: Harvard University Press, 1991), cited in *Future Survey* (July 1991): 11.

32. "Wasted Health Care Dollars," *Consumer Reports*, p. 443

33. Weiler, *Medical Malpractice on Trial*. Cited in *Future Survey* (July 1991): 11.

34. Joan Beck, "Who Should Live, Who Should Die," *Chicago Tribune*, May 26, 1996, sec. 1, p. 21.

35. Joan Beck, "What's a Life Worth," *Chicago Tribune*, March 20, 1994, sec. 4, p. 3.

36. President, *Economic Report of the President Transmitted to Congress, 1994*, p. 143.

37. Based upon a *New England Journal of Medicine* report cited by Beck in "What's a Life Worth."

38. Ibid.

39. President, *Economic Report of the President Transmitted to Congress, 1994*, p. 138.

40. Edwin M. Reingold, "Oregon's Value Judgment," *Time* (November 25, 1997): 37.

41. Paul T. Manzol, *Strong Medicine: The Ethical Rationing of Health Care* (N.Y.: Oxford University Press, 1990). Cited in *Future Survey* (March 1991): 5.

42. Brad Edmondson, "Demanding Death with Dignity," *American Demographics* (November 1991): 14.

43. Joseph L. Daleiden, *The Science of Morality* (Amherst, N.Y.: Prometheus Books, 1998), chapter 16.

44. Marcia Angell, "Euthanasia in the Netherlands: Good News or Bad," editorial, *New England Journal of Medicine* (November 28, 1996): 3.

45. Associated Press, "Suicide Law Painless, Oregon Says," *Chicago Tribune*, February 1, 1999. sec. 1, p. 6.

46. David Thomasma, *Euthanasia: Toward an Ethical Social Policy* (N.Y.: Continuum Publishing Company, 1990). Cited in *Future Survey* (March 1991): 7.

47. U.S. Bureau of the Census, *Statistical Abstract of the United States, 1997*, table 737, p. 475. For children under six the situation was much worse, with 25 percent—one in four—living in poverty in 1996. *Chicago Tribune*, March 15, 1998, sec. 1, p. 11.

48. Joe Davidson, "Differing Social Programs for Young, Old Result in Contrasting Poverty Levels for the Two Groups," *Wall Street Journal*, June, 27, 1985

49. Joseph A. Pechman, *Federal Tax Policy* (Washington, D.C.: The Brookings Institution, 1987), p. 225.

50. Dianne Gambino, Social Security Administration, "Social Security 'Crisis' Exaggerated," *Chicago Tribune*, Voice of the People, April 1996, sec. 1, p. 14.

51. Merrill Lynch, *Economic and Financial Chartbook* (May 1992): 15.

52. Carolyn L. Weaver, "Controlling the Risks Posed by Advance Funding—Options for Reform," *Social Security's Looming Surpluses, Prospects and Implications*, ed. Carolyn L. Weaver (Lanham, Md: University Press of America, 1992). Cited by *American Enterprise Institute*, Book Summary, 1992, p. 4.

53. Robert Eisner, *The Misunderstood Economy: What Counts and How to Count It* (Boston: Harvard Business School Press, 1994), p. 128. Based upon estimates of the Social Security Administration.

54. Ibid.

55. R. C. Longworth, "Debate to Be Over Tinkering, Major Changes," *Chicago Tribune*, January 29, 1998, sec. 1, p. 13.

56. Federation for American Immigration Reform, *FAIR Immigration Report* (April 1995): 1.

57. Carolyn Weaver Testimony Before U.S. House Budget Committee Task Force on Economic Policy. *AEI* Congressional Testimony, 1989.

58. U.S. Office of Management and Budget, *Budget of the United States Government, Fiscal Year 1999, Historical Tables*, table 1.1., p. 20.

59. "The Folly of Raiding the Piggy Bank," *The Economist* (April 8, 1989): 27–28.

60. Eisner, *The Misunderstood Economy*, p. 143.

61. R. C. Longworth, "Social Security Slowly Moving to Center Stage," *Chicago Tribune*, February 18, 1996, sec. 1 p. 6.

62. Christopher Georges, "Overhaul of Social Security Is Endorsed by Panel," *Wall Street Journal*, May 18, 1998, p. A3.

63. President, *Economic Report of the President Transmitted to Congress, February 1997*, table, B–93, p. 406.

64. Bill Barnhart, "Investing Social Security Dollars in Stocks No Panacea," *Chicago Tribune*, January 13, 1997, sec. 4, pp. 1, 4.

65. Steve Stecklow and Sara Calian, "Social Security Switch in UK is Disastrous: A Caution to the U.S.?" *Wall Street Journal*, August 10, 1998, pp. A1, 8.

66. Joseph Pechman, *Federal Tax Policy* (Washington, D.C.: Brookings Institute, 1987), p. 229.

67. This was recommended in legislation proposed by U.S. Representatives John Danforth and Bob Kerry. *Wall Street Journal*, December 12, 1994, p. A1.

68. Robert Lewis, "Privatization Splits Lawmakers, Experts," *AARP Bulletin* (September 1998): 11. Reported quote by Vice President Al Gore.

69. For a complete explanation of the convoluted tax law regarding Social Security and its impact on wages of those collecting Social Security, see Eisner, *The Misunderstood Economy*, pp. 137–41. Eisner points out that under certain scenarios where a person retires before age sixty-five, and thus has delayed benefits but never receive them because he doesn't live long enough, he could actually have an effective tax on additional earnings of over 100 percent. He could effectively lose 103 percent of each additional dollar earned. Pp. 140–41.

70. Daniel Bell and Lester Thurow, *The Deficits: How Big? How Long? How Dangerous?* (New York: New York University Press, 1985), p. 129.

71. Milton Friedman, *Free to Choose* (New York: Avon Publishing, 1981), pp. 112–14.

13

EQUITABLE TAX REFORM

In many respects, this may be the toughest chapter in the book. The impact of taxes are subtle and complex. There are some politicians who argue that a flat rate tax is the answer, but as we shall see, a simple flat rate tax is far from equitable. So I urge readers who may be enamored by the simplicity of a flat rate tax to suspend this judgment until they have worked through the many issues regarding taxes raised here.

When the economic history of the twentieth century is written, the 1981 Reagan tax cuts will be shown to be one of the two greatest economic deceptions perpetrated on the American people in the post World War II era. (The other was Lyndon Johnson's expansion of the money supply to cover his "guns and butter" spending increases.) The 1981 Economic Recovery Tax Act cut income taxes 25 percent over three years. The bulk of the tax reduction benefited the wealthiest Americans who saw the top tax rate, which had already fallen from 35.5 percent in 1977 to 31.7 percent in 1980, slashed to 26.7 percent.[1] (It might be recalled that during the 1950s the top *marginal* tax rate [i.e., the tax rate on the last dollar earned] was 91 percent, but the variety of tax deductions and loopholes meant that few if any Americans actually had any incremental income taxed at the 91 percent rate.)

The justification for the lopsided benefit for the wealthy was that, since they saved the greatest portion of their income, the tax cut was supposed to result in increased aggregate savings, which would be used to stimulate investment and, hence, economic growth. Treasury Secretary Donald Regan argued that 40 percent of the tax cut would be saved. Economist Allan Blinder reports that after the tax cut was enacted, only about

6 percent of the tax savings was actually saved, about in line with the historical average for all saved income.[2]

The economy was stimulated during the 1980s, not by the tax cut per se, but by the unprecedented increase in deficit spending to finance the military buildup and growth Medicare/Medicaid, as discussed in earlier chapters. Concurrent with the increase in spending, Reagan, and later George Bush, slowed the growth in transfer payments to the states and cities which were used to support a variety of local public services. Education and welfare were hardest hit, since these two areas account for about 50 percent of state and local government expenditures, as shown on the table below.

Distribution of General Expenditures of State and Local Governments[3]

Education	34%
Public Welfare	13
Transportation	7
Health & Hospitals	9
Public Safety	9
Administration	6
Interest	9
Other	13

Consequently, states and cities had to raise taxes to fill the gap. Moreover, the impact was by no means proportional throughout the country. Huge increases in federal funds continued to flow to those states such as Texas and California that had large defense industries, whereas the dollars to subsidize those states came from states where federal funding for services were being cut. Illinois, for example, had a net federal tax outflow of $6 billion a year.

As a consequence of this loss of revenue, central cities that were the primary recipients of federal aid had to fill the gap by raising the two most regressive taxes, sales and property taxes. Raising taxes encouraged more white flight to the suburbs, thus reducing the tax base, and hence revenues. Therefore, the outcome of the Reagan tax cut was merely to shift the incidence of taxes from the rich to the poor and middle class and, by generating about four trillion dollars of debt in only ten years, shifted the tax burden from those that created the debt (the present generation) to those who will have to repay the present debt (future generations). Quite a neat little scam. Bush perpetuated the fiction by vowing not to raise taxes. When he was running for president, 75 percent of Americans believed that taxes would have to be raised to cover the Reagan deficits, but they hated the idea. So they were willing to read Bush's lips and make a leap of faith. As the states and cities were forced to raise taxes to replace the lost federal revenue, local officials had to take the heat that should have been directed at the White House. It also should be noted that by shifting the burden to the states and cities, the wealthy suburbs could to some degree forego increasing taxes, since they didn't have the cost of educating and housing the poor which the central cites did.

In chapter 6 we saw that, with the duplicitous practice of including the Social Security Trust Fund, the federal government appears to be headed for budget surplus. Yet we cannot forget that we still have a $6 trillion debt and require hundreds of billions more for infrastructure and toxic waste clean-up. Before we suggest recommendations on how to achieve these goals, we must dispel some commonly held myths about U.S. taxes.

MYTH 1: AMERICANS ARE OVERTAXED

The belief that Americans are staggering under their tax burden simply is not true. Nevertheless, as Alexis de Tocqueville pointed out over a century ago, "When Americans have taken up an idea, whether it be well or ill-founded, nothing is more difficult than to eradicate it from their minds."[4] Given the general feelings of Americans, it may come as a surprise that if we compare the average marginal tax rate on income of U.S. citizens to that imposed by other countries, Americans are quite fortunate:

Marginal Tax Rate on Average Earnings[5]

Belgium	over 60%
Germany	over 60%
Denmark	60%
Sweden	60%
Holland	60%
Italy	58%
Spain	52%
France	50%
Australia	48%
England	45%
United States	40%
Canada	32%
Japan	30%
New Zealand	28%

These estimates include income tax at all levels of government (federal, state, and local) and the Social Security FICA tax. Although the estimates are for 1987, to the best of my knowledge, there have been few major changes in the tax rates in any of these countries.* The tax rates exclude property and sales taxes in the U.S. states and value-added taxes abroad.

Actually, the relative situation for Americans is even better than the above comparison would indicate. The marginal tax rate indicates how much tax is paid on the last dollar earned. A more relevant number would be the average tax rate calculated by dividing total taxes paid by total income. Of course, this would vary considerably from state to state due to the variance in property, sales, and state income tax. Using data on the various state tax rates, I have calculated that in 1994, the average tax on income of $50,000 for a family of four (including federal and state income tax, average property tax, and sales tax) would vary from a low of about 27 percent in Alaska to a high of 34 percent in New York. If the family made $100,000, the average tax rate for those in Alaska and New York would be 34 percent and 37 percent, respectively.[6] To place the income numbers in perspective, the median family income in 1994 was about $37,000. Hence, they would have paid an even lower average rate of taxes—about 30 to 33 percent for the median family nationally. Conversely, some of those in the highest bracket in New York would be paying an average tax of over 50 percent.

If we compare taxes as a percentage of GDP for all countries, we get a similar relative picture:

Government Receipts as Percent of GDP[7]

France	46
Germany	43
Italy	42
Canada	42
England	40
Japan	35
United States	32

It would appear that U.S. citizens are not overburdened with taxes compared to other nations. However, some economists would argue that it is the greater tax burden of European nations that has caused their slower growth in the last decade. But a far greater negative impact on Europe has been their relatively high wage rates coupled with a lowering of their tariff

*The U.S. average marginal tax rate may be about 2 percent higher if we netted out the tax increases of Bush and Clinton and the 1997 tax reduction.

restrictions. Average wage rates are now higher in many European countries than in the United States.

Despite their lower tax burden, Americans still feel overtaxed. Since the average American family pays about one-third of its income in all forms of taxes, we often hear people grumbling that they must work four months of each year just to support federal, state, and local governments. This is a absurdly misleading statement, akin to typical Rush Limbaugh sophistry. The correct statement should be that we work one third of the year for the services that we have demanded of the government, including national defense, education, police and fire protection, sanitation, highways, health research and disease control, security against job loss and disability, old age pensions, environmental protection, and much more. While an individual may not want all these services—and not all of us receive services proportional to what we pay in taxes—we have decided as a nation, through our elected officials, to provide them. Actually, ***based upon who people vote for, it is apparent that most of us want these services and more; we just don't want to pay for them.***

Myth 2: Taxes Continue to Increase Incessantly

Isn't the government grabbing an ever increasing chunk of our collective income? People tend to confuse the fact that the tax dollars they pay increase with the percentage of their income going for taxes, which may or may not have increased. The answer depends more on how tax rates have changed at the local level. As shown in the table below, taxes increased their share of GDP between 1960 and 1970 and then leveled out. The lion's share of the increase was due to state and local governments' educational expenditures, reflecting both the changing demographics and the growth in the number of students attending college. From 1970 until 1993, federal taxes as a percentage of GDP did not increase. They have increased by about 1.8 percent since Clinton became president, primarily due to efforts to reduce the annual budget deficits. Had the Republican administrations and Democratic Congresses in the 1980s not run up the huge national debt, we would not be devoting 20 percent of our annual budgets to interest expense ($285 billion in 1997).

Some proponents of tax reform argue that the ratio of taxes to GDP should be declining since the Cold War has been over for almost a decade and defense spending has declined. What they often forget is that the money for the defense buildup was borrowed and we are paying $285 billion annually for on-budget interest on that debt. Only if we run budget surpluses, the GDP continues to increase, and we add no major new federal programs, will taxes decline as a percentage of GDP.

Taxes as a Percent of GDP[8]

	Federal	*State & Local*	*Total*
1960	18.3%	7.9%	26.2%
1970	19.6	10.2	29.7
1980	19.6	10.1	29.6
1990	18.8	10.7	29.5
1997	19.8	10.7	30.5

The increase in state and local taxes came mostly in the form of sales and property taxes, two of the most regressive taxes. Although the marginal tax rate on the rich was the highest in the 1950s, that decade witnessed the largest increase in the middle class in our nation's history, while the number of people earning more than $500,000 annually grew only modestly. The situation was reversed in the 1980s. This is in large part why the middle class is complaining of their increased tax burden. They have felt a disproportionate share of the tax impact.

The seeming unfairness of the present tax structure might explain in part why tax evasion is now close to $100 billion a year. Much of this evasion comes from those salaried workers who cannot get their share of the $65 billion in tax loopholes.[9] Much also comes from small businesspeople who have dozens of ways of legally avoiding and illegally evading taxes. Ironically, when tax evasion grows this large, it increases the requirement for additional revenues, resulting in still higher taxes. The present resistance to income taxes is becoming so significant that it threatens the entire tax structure. That is why economists and politicians are seeking alternative sources of tax revenue. Before reviewing those alternatives, let me dismiss one last myth.

Myth 3: Increased Taxes Always Slow Economic Growth

It is commonly believed that higher tax rates will slow economic growth. The truth is that the impact on growth depends on what the government does with the tax dollars. I have already made the argument that spending on defense does indeed eventually reduce economic growth, whereas spending on urban and rural infrastructure could increase growth. Now if the government increases its purchases of goods and services by the same amount as it increases taxes, the intuitive reaction would be that the impacts would be a wash, but this is not so for the same reason that reducing taxes will not stimulate enough revenues to offset the loss of tax dollars.

In economic terms, the reason is that the consumption multiplier is stronger than the tax multiplier. By the *multiplier effect*, economists mean the cumulative impact that occurs when a dollar of consumption results in increased production, leading to increased employment and wages, still more consumption, and so on. It is a continuous circle. Therefore, the impact of a sudden stimulus to consumption has a multiple impact that is gradually dampened in each succeeding round as savings are siphoned off.

When the government simultaneously increases its purchases and taxes, 100 percent of the first round of government expenditures goes directly to increase GDP with no loss due to savings. Tax payments, on the other hand, are in part taken out of savings.[10] ***Thus, the net effect in the short term of simultaneously increasing federal spending with an equal increase in taxes is to stimulate economic growth. Conversely, a decrease in federal spending with an equal decrease in taxes will initially result in a decrease in economic growth.***

In the long run, the impact depends on whether the increased taxes result in reduced consumption or savings. (A decrease in savings means reduced investment, all other things being equal.) Therefore, when we discuss alternative ways of increasing tax revenue, I can do so with the clear conscience that a tax increase will not necessarily impair economic growth unless tax revenues are wasted on nonproductive activities such as defense or space exploration. (That is not a value judgment but a simple statement of fact, since such expenditures do not result in higher productivity for U.S. products and services except in terms of some spin-off technologies.) As explained in our discussion of the deficit, if the government diverts personal income from consumption to investment in education and training, infrastructure improvements, or research and development, the effect could be increased economic growth in the long term.

However, although taxes do not necessarily impair economic growth, there may be alternative ways of obtaining the needed tax revenues that would be more equitable and less painful than the present methods. The following discussion also assumes that we have minimized waste in the government, which should, of course, always be a primary goal.*

---

*As a sidebar, I would note that except for defense expenditures, the bulk of federal tax dollars go to transferring income between groups, such as the rich and the poor (welfare), the young and the elderly (Social Security), workers and nonworkers (unemployment compensation), and so on. Most of the goods and services provided directly to the end user are delivered by state and local governments (education, streets and highways, water and waste disposal, fire and police protection, and the like.) If we wish to reduce transfer payments, we should start at the federal level. If we wish to reduce waste, we should focus at the local level.

Alternative Sources of Tax Revenue

To begin with, we need to establish some criteria to judge each tax proposal. Alan Blinder suggests five "commandments" of an ideal tax system.[11]

1. It must raise sufficient taxes to cover government expenditures. This should be obvious, especially to conservatives, but it was certainly not the policy of either Democrats or Republicans during the last thirty years.

2. Taxes should distort economic incentives as little as possible. It is of course true that activities that are heavily taxed will be more discouraged than those that are more lightly taxed. However, I do not agree that it is always good policy to make taxes economically neutral. Taxes that discharge products on activities that pollute (such as consumption of gasoline), or cause death and disease (such as tobacco and alcohol), or bias consumption toward private rather than public goods (such as advertising), can foster the three harmonies discussed in *The Science of Morality* and result in greater happiness for humankind.

3. Tax rates should automatically be adjusted downward to offset increases in the rate of inflation. To do otherwise, in effect makes taxes a function of the inflation rate rather than governmental design. As we will see, inflation can particularly be a problem in distorting the economic impact of capital gains.

4. The tax code should be fair and equitable. While everyone agrees with such a goal, each person will have a different judgment as to what constitutes fairness. For Blinder, it means that the tax system should not introduce "capricious redistributions of income,"[12] but we need a more definite idea of what redistribution, if any, is permitted. Economist John Kenneth Galbraith would add another condition: *all enrichment should be treated alike*, i.e., "to apply a common rate of taxation to every enrichment whether it accrues in the form of salary, capital gains, property income, inheritance, gift, [etc.]. . . ."[13]

5. The tax system should be as simple as possible. No one would disagree, but it is not at all clear that this goal would not often conflict with the previous goals. Many of the deductions built into the tax code are to increase equity. For example, deductions for small business out of one's house were established to offset the expense deductions that large businesses receive for the cost of their rent or depreciation of their office building. However, all too often tax deductions are the result of special interest groups successfully lobbying to give themselves a tax break that has little to do with equity.

Joseph Pechman is a former director of the Brookings Economic Studies program and one of the nation's leading tax experts. In his classic book, *Federal Tax Policy*, Pechman suggests that tax policies should also promote growth, stability, and efficiency in the economy.[14] I can agree with Pechman if by growth he doesn't simply mean the accumulation of economic products and services, but an improvement in human welfare, such as that discussed in chapter 2.

Let's explore a few of these principles a little deeper, beginning with the idea of economic incentives.

As we saw in our discussion of pollution and the environment, a major incentive to past pollution has been the failure of farming, mining, forestry, fishing, and manufacturing to be charged all of the costs associated with these activities. It is essential, therefore, to ensure that the total long-term economic costs be included in each product. This can be accomplished by instituting a *Pigovian tax*—named after the economist A. C. Pigou—which will add a charge equal to the cost of offsetting the environmental damage caused by a product. Such a tax provides an economic incentive to reduce pollution or any negative environmental impact that we wish to discourage.

There are other existing tax incentives that we would do well to eliminate or at least significantly reduce. For example, at present there is a deduction for dependents regardless of how many children a person chooses to have. Since, as argued in chapter 4, we wish to discourage population growth, the tax deduction should apply only to the first and second child (except in the case of adoption).*

At present, the most significant tax deductions for individuals are the home mortgages and property taxes. Capital gains on home sales significantly add to this benefit. Together, the three deductions reduce tax revenues by $35 billion annually (even more after the 1997 tax reform). Such a deduction encourages home ownership, but discriminates against those who cannot afford to own their home. Those who rent effectively have to pay a higher rate of taxes to subsidize those who own. This is blatantly regressive and unfair. Ownership-related tax deductions also encourage urban sprawl and the associated environmental problems. ***At the very least, there should be a cap on the amount of housing related tax deductions (e.g., limiting tax deductions to interest on mortgages below $250,000).*** To allow someone to deduct mortgage and property taxes on a

---

*Bill Clinton's proposal that we should further subsidize children by allowing a tax deduction for child care is going in the wrong direction. It effectively penalizes parents who decide that one of them will stay home to care for their children, since they now have to pay a larger portion of their income for taxes than when both parents work.

multi-million dollar estate serves no useful social purpose. To prevent the shock of eliminating the deductibility of such taxes on those who may be counting on the tax deductions to finance their housing, the elimination could be phased in or the rights of existing owners could be grandfathered (i.e., they are allowed to retain the deduction on their present house only).

Economists talk about horizontal and vertical equity, the former referring to the distribution of the tax burden fairly among people in the same economic circumstances, and the latter referring to taxing wealthier people at higher rates.[15] The justification for taxing wealthier people at higher rates is based on the concept of diminishing marginal utility. Basically, as figure 13.1 shows, the incremental happiness derived from each additional dollar of income declines as income increase.

Figure 13.1
Hypothetical Utility Curve

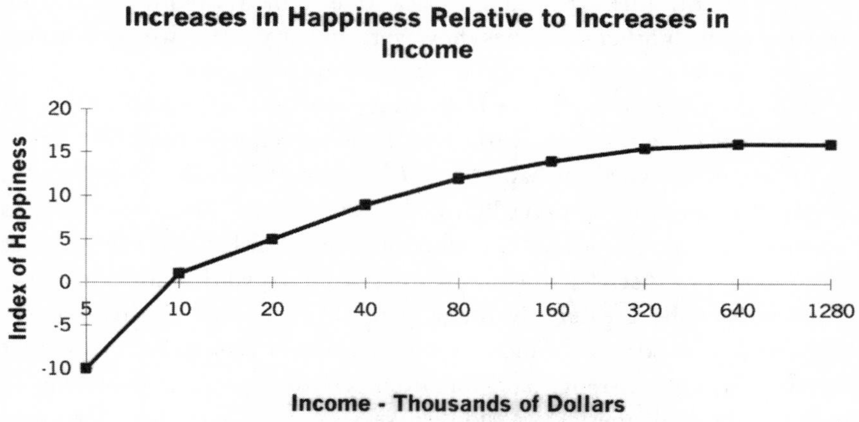

The difference between making $5,000 a year and $10,000 can be the difference between living on the street or in an apartment. However, the difference which an additional $5,000 makes to a person already earning $300,000 would be indiscernible. Consequently, the pain of paying an additional dollar of taxes is theoretically less for a rich person than a poor person. (Although the way some rich people howl about taxes it may not seem so.) Hence, to distribute the pain of taxes fairly, we might select proportionally higher rates of taxation as we move up the income scale.

At some level of taxation, it is generally believed that increased tax rates would discourage additional work. Why bother to strive to increase our income if the government takes 90 percent of each additional dollar? While such an argument probably holds true in the extreme case, there is little evidence to indicate that taxes in this country ever acted as a disincentive to work even when the top marginal rate was 91 percent. (Of course at the time there were so many loopholes that many people in that tax bracket paid little, if any taxes!) A review of the empirical evidence leads Pechman to conclude that "income taxation does not reduce the amount of labor supplied by workers and managers who are primary family earners."[16] To the contrary, there are a few studies indicating that as marginal tax rates decline, at least some members of the labor force prefer to take the benefit in additional leisure time instead of more income.[17] At the upper-income brackets, there are many additional incentives to work besides income: power, prestige, enjoyment of the work itself, and many others. Did basketball players play less hard in the 1960s when they were making only a fraction of the obscene amounts players garner today? Similarly, it is extremely doubtful that their performance would be affected by higher tax rates in the future. The amount of progressivity (higher rates of taxes as income increases) that can be built into the tax structure before work incentives are diminished is an empirical question. It would appear from comparisons with other countries, however, that at present we are not near the threshold where tax rates become a disincentive to work.

Since taxes are, in part, an ethical issue, another way of examining the question of relative tax rates is to employ the principle of modified Rawlsian Justice as discussed in chapter 5 of *The Science of Morality*. From behind our veil of ignorance, we don't know if we are rich as Midas or as poor as the proverbial church mouse. Therefore, we have decided that the goods of society should be distributed equally unless an unequal distribution works to a proportionally greater advantage of the least favored. Since we know that there is a good deal of luck in whether one is very rich or very poor (since brains, good parents, and fortuitous circumstances are not handed out on the basis of merit), we would like to see the extremely fortunate share their good fortune with those who are less fortunate. We do not want to undermine the concept of merit, however, so that people forego work to increase their wealth, because in a society where no one finds value in additional effort, all suffer. The Communist nations have shown that removing the benefits of merit is disastrous for all. Therefore, Rawlsian justice would lead us to conclude that tax rates cannot be so progressive as to threaten merit. Conversely, we must let people live with the consequences of failing to educate themselves, work diligently, and save or invest for the future. The exact amount of progressivity before the consequences offset the benefits is a very difficult empirical question and much more research needs to be conducted in this area.

Of course in real life, none of us hides behind a veil of ignorance. We each know exactly how our income and wealth will be affected by changes in the tax rates and we will be biased accordingly. Because we are motivated by self-interest, we will tend to be very generous at redistributing the income of those who make more than us (or more than we hope to make in the future), but not so generous in redistributing our own income. However, we may be able to see the value of devoting a portion of our income to alleviate conditions of poverty that threaten our own long-term self-interest. We may recognize that it is cheaper in the long run to invest in opportunities to educate the children of the poor, and to help provide them with an environment conducive to their success, than to pay the huge cost of incarceration and increased police protection. On the other hand, we never want to be so generous as to reward parents for having children they cannot afford to raise.

Based on these principles, I believe that, in general, we need to ***avoid any further increases in the regressive property and sales taxes except for "use" taxes that encourage conservation, such as taxes on water, electricity, motor fuel, and garbage collection, or taxes to discourage consumption of dangerous substances such as alcohol, tobacco, or other legalized drugs.*** Then what are our options? As figure 13.2 shows, about 30 percent of taxes come from property and general sales taxes, and 50 percent is derived from personal income taxes:

Since no one likes to increase the tax on their personal income, liberals are especially inclined to recommend raising corporate income taxes, which now account for only about 10 percent of total taxes collected. Does this make sense?

Figure 13.2
Distribution of Tax Revenue by Source, 1994[18]

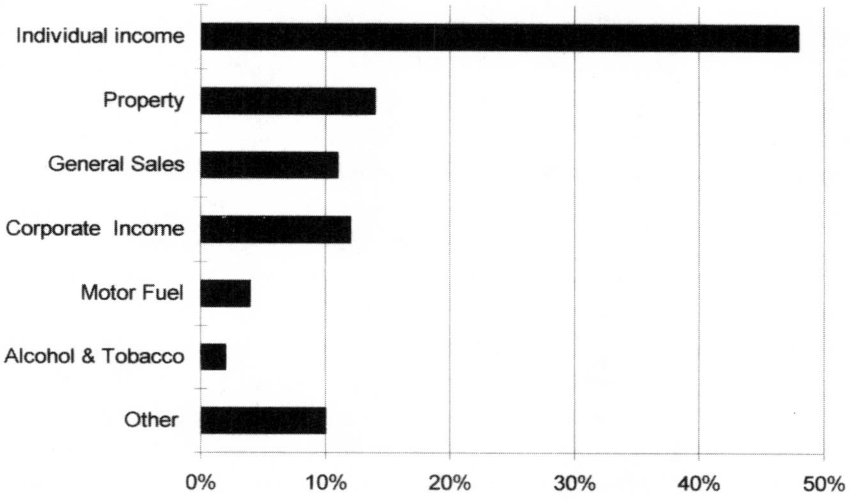

Corporate Income Tax

It must be understood that, in the final analysis, corporations do not actually incur the taxes levied upon them. They merely pass on taxes to employees, customers, and shareowners. Who actually bears the burden of the tax depends on the competitiveness of the corporation, the bargaining power of its workers, and the demands of its shareowners. Since it is impossible to say beforehand who the incidence of the corporate tax falls upon, a corporate tax is an ambiguous method of raising revenue.

Pechman advances the argument that in the long run, lower returns would result if corporations try to pass the tax on to the investors, thus causing capital to move to other countries. Since labor is not mobile like capital, most of the burden of a corporate tax would fall on wage earners in the form of lower wages. But later Pechman points out that under conditions of floating exchange rates, capital would not leave for long. Although an increase in taxes in country X would result in lower returns resulting in an initial outflow of capital, the value of country X's dollar would drop until the demand for its exports increase, thus increasing the return on X's investment. Capital would then flow back into the home country. Pechman concludes, "floating exchange rates . . . permit countries to decide what type of tax structure they wish to have for domestic reasons, without being constrained by fear of foreign repercussions."[19]

Another concern is that, in theory, equity investors get taxed twice, once in the form of taxes on the corporate income and a second time when they receive dividends as personal income. The result is to lower investment returns, thus discouraging growth in savings and investment. However, Pechman concludes that despite the large increase in corporate income tax since World War II, there is no evidence that the rate of investment has been reduced. The reason is that the corporate tax rates have effectively been declining during almost the whole of the postwar era due to increases in capital consumption allowances (deductions for depreciation). ***The result is that, as a percent of before-tax profit, federal corporate income taxes have declined from a high in 1952 of 42.6 percent to around 15 percent by the end of the 1980s.***[20] It is argued that a cut in the capital gains tax would stimulate investment, and hence business growth, ever more.

Despite past improvement in depreciation allowances, there still is a significant potential for underdepreciation during periods of rapid inflation, such as those experienced in the 1970s. During inflationary periods, firms that own assets with long lives find that when they go to replace those assets, they have only recovered a portion of the replacement cost, perhaps as little as 25 percent. Pechman recommends that companies be allowed either to adjust for inflation by using replacement cost (assuming that the rate of inflation is fairly predictable), or allow for an immediate depreciation adjustment before the inflation impact is known.[21] While an improvement over present depreciation rules, neither technique eliminates the difficulty of knowing how to anticipate the potential economic impact of inflation on taxes during periods of changing rates of inflation.

Another potential problem with the corporate income tax is that, to the extent that the individual income tax rate differs from the corporate rate, corporations are encouraged to either retain earnings or pay additional dividends.[22] Either decision, taken solely on the basis of tax policy, can result in a misallocation of resources. For example, if corporate tax rates were deliberately set below the individual tax rate, it might cause the shareowners to demand that a corporation reduce dividends to investors so investors can avoid paying higher personal income tax rate on dividends received. Instead of paying dividends, the company would invest all earnings back into the business. The hope would be that the growth in the business would be reflected in stock appreciation, which would not be taxable unless the stock is sold, and then only at the lower capital gains rate. However, it is doubtful if this theoretical concern is a practical problem. Despite many changes in corporate and individual tax rates over the years, there has been little change in the rate of either personal or corporate savings. As a percentage of GDP, gross corporate saving was 11.8 percent in 1929 and 11.6 percent in 1996.[23] Clearly, there are many factors other than tax rates that determine a corporation's decision whether to invest, retain earnings for future investment opportunities, or pay out earnings in the form of dividends.

Yet another objection to the corporate income tax is that even if it were borne equally by customers, employees, and investors, it is unfair because it effectively taxes all customers or all employees at equal rates despite potentially large differences in their respective incomes or wealth. Therefore it is, in effect, a regressive tax.

Finally, it should be noted that if states try to tax corporate income, there is always the threat that the corporation will move to a state with lower tax rates. As investment becomes more internationally mobile, this same threat holds true to some extent on the international scene. This is particularly a problem because foreign companies that do business in the United States do not have to pay our income taxes. The game multinational corporations play is to shift their costs to countries with high tax rates to maximize deductions, while shifting profits to low-tax rate countries.[24]

It is primarily because of the difficulty in assessing the short-term impact of corporate taxes on labor and investors, as well as the potentially negative impact on investment, that many economists argue that the corporate income tax should be abolished. However, were we to do so, there is a concern that people would seek to avoid income tax by sheltering their investment in corporations. Daly and Cobb suggest that this tax avoidance can be prevented by requiring *all* corporate profits to be distributed to stockholders as income.[25] Future investment not funded out of depreciation would then require continual new issues of debt or equity. New stock issues, not profit, become the source of capital for new plant and equipment. However, this might present problems for corporations during periods of market downturns or inflation. As we will see, a better alternative is to replace the corporate income tax with a value-added tax.

If we retain the corporate income tax, at the very least we should eliminate all deductions for entertainment expenses and advertising expense. This latter would be fought particularly by corporations as an impediment to their First Amendment rights to free speech. However, the First Amendment was intended for individuals, not corporate entities (although unfortunately, the courts have granted rights to corporations as if these legal creations were individuals). More significantly, ***we are not impinging on corporate rights by simply saying that advertising is not tax deductible. After all, the individual cannot deduct his/her expenses associated with exercise of free speech.*** In reality, permitting deductions for advertising expense is subsidizing efforts to increase consumption. Since one of the goals of our society should be to reduce consumption and increase savings, it is only logical that we would refrain from encouraging advertising. If loss of this tax deduction would give foreign competitors an advantage, we could offset such an advantage through tariffs. (Again I can hear the free market advocates scream, but as we pointed out in chapter 7 on trade, free markets are not an end in themselves, but only a means to the end of enhancing human welfare. When free markets impede other socioeconomic goals, such as protection of the environment for future generations, the objective of free trade might need to be modified.)

Another particularly thorny issue is the serious problem of tax evasion practiced by many small businesses. According to the IRS, ***only 68 percent of business owners' income is properly recorded.***[26] This should not come as a surprise to anyone who is familiar with the practices of many small entrepreneurs. I know several, and almost all of them evade taxes by drawing a very small salary to reduce their personal income tax liability, and then charge a variety of personal expenses (such as vacation trips, cars, and a variety of other personal expenses) to their businesses to understate their business income as well. With an understaffed IRS, the chances of getting caught are extremely slim. This flagrant abuse of our tax laws results in higher taxes for the rest of us.

Taxing Interest and Dividends

It is often argued by economists that one of reasons for Japan's high growth rate during most of the post World War II era was its higher savings rate and lower cost of financing. The lower cost was due in part to Japan's lower taxation of capital. Japan exempts from taxation most interest income and capital gains on stocks. As mentioned, in the United States, profits are first taxed as income to the corporation, then taxed a second time when dividends are paid to shareowners. Personal income taxes can be deferred, but not avoided by shareowners, if the corporation lowers dividends and increases retained earnings. The retained earnings will increase the value of the stock and therefore also increase the amount of capital gains tax that must be paid when the stock is sold (albeit today at the lower capital gains rate). Conservatives are right when they say that such double taxation increases the cost of equity financing.

To further bias the financing decision, interest payments are tax deductible to a corporation, making financing with debt far less costly to the firm than equity financing. The differential tax treatment acts as an incentive for firms to "leverage up" (the practice of increasing debt relative to equity), hence increasing financial risk. The additional risk occurs because, unlike dividends that can be suspended if the company has a drop in revenue, interest payments must be met or the company faces bankruptcy.

The unequal tax treatment for debt and equity caused corporations during the 1980s to dramatically increase leverage. Moreover, because corporate acquisitions are financed primarily through debt, and interest payments are tax deductible, the public has been, in effect, subsidizing corporate acquisitions. One study concluded that $92 billion has been shifted from taxes to interest payments.[27] Hence, the unequal tax treatment of debt and equity encourages companies to increase their financial risk while simultaneously shifting taxes to the individual taxpayer.

Tax law does not let individuals deduct interest payments (except interest on home mortgages) and there is no reason why we should allow corporations to deduct interest. Dividends and interest payments should be treated the same for tax purposes. However, this is not as easy as it might seem, because not all profits are paid out as dividends. To the extent that profits are kept as retained earnings, personal income taxes are deferred. Pechman reviews five methods for integrating corporate and individual income taxes, variations of which have been tried here or in other countries.[28] He includes the notion of eliminating the tax deduction for interest expenses so that, in effect, corporate interest payments are taxed at the same rate as profits, at least with regard to corporate income taxes. He also discusses economist John H. Makin's suggestion that only one-half of interest expense should be deductible and only one-half of interest income should be taxed.[29] Makin claims that such a policy would act as an incentive to save while decreasing the incentive for firms to acquire debt. Moreover, the lower interest rates that would result due to lower demand for debt would save the U.S. treasury $75 billion in interest costs over five years. However, Pechman concludes that all of the methods he reviews introduce other problems in terms of allocation of capital among industries and firms, and may encourage firms to act uneconomically by either paying out or retaining too much of their earnings. He also argues that there is no compelling evidence that corporate taxes have impaired U. S. growth.[30]

On the other hand, a study by the Institute for Political Economy estimates that if the United States adopted Japan's tax system, it would lower the cost of capital by 16 percent, which would in turn raise profit margins by five percentage points—an amount greater than the entire corporate tax liability.[31] The study points out that, comparing the cost of capital paid at the corporate level only, the cost of capital in Japan would be 26 percent higher than under the U.S. system, in part because of more favorable U.S. depreciation allowances.[32] However, due to generous tax credits on dividends received, the effective marginal tax rate on dividends to individuals in Japan is only one half of one percent. Moreover, the study points out that most personal interest income in Japan is excluded from taxable income and that capital gains from the sale of stock are exempt from tax. The conclusion is that "capital source income in Japan is virtually untaxed at the personal level."[33]

Therefore, to provide investors with an equivalent return on investment, Japanese firms can pay out less in dividends and worry less about increasing the value of their stock in the short-term. With the pressure off high short-term returns, firms are encouraged to undertake greater investment for the longer term. This adds weight to the argument that the corporate income tax should be dropped altogether in favor of a value-added tax.

Conversely, if a corporate income tax is retained, we should eliminate all tax exemptions for advertising or public "education," lobbying, or political contributions. Corporations have enough power at influencing public policy without the benefit of tax exemptions.

Capital Gains Tax

There are three arguments commonly made against the tax on capital gains. The first is that capital gains should be excluded from taxation since a company's earnings—which are the reason for the increase in the value of a stock—have already been taxed. This may or may not be true. There have been so many changes in the tax law over the years, allowing for accelerated depreciation, write-offs, investment tax credits, and the like, making it extremely difficult to say just how much of a corporation's earnings have been taxed. Moreover, the value of a stock is based upon future earnings, making it even more difficult to assess how much of the earnings will be taxed.

Second, it has been estimated that in 1991 a reduction in the capital gains tax from 28 percent to 15 percent would have reduced the cost of capital from 6.7 percent to 5.3 percent, thus encouraging companies to undertake additional investment, and shifting 20 percent of U.S. companies into the growth category.[34] Therefore, the 1997 tax cut, which actually reduced capital gains from 28 percent to 20 percent (for stocks held longer than eighteenth months) should have had a similar impact. Given such a benefit, why not do away with capital gains taxes completely as conservatives urge?

There is no doubt that capital gains taxes raise the cost of capital, thus reducing profits and, hence, investment. Nevertheless, if we were to do away with capital gains taxes entirely, many wealthy people who have no annual salary income could avoid taxes by getting companies to refrain from paying dividends and buy back stock with excess cash. The result would be to avoid all taxes.

The third concern has been that the value of a stock appreciates in part due to inflation, and to that extent does not reflect a real increase in value. This is a legitimate concern but applies to earnings from whatever source. The federal government is already addressing this issue by protecting taxpayers against the "inflation creep" that pushes taxpayers into higher brackets even though their real earnings might not have changed. The government's tax rate tables are adjusted each year to take account of inflation.

If the tax tables are adjusted annually to correctly reflect inflation, for the purposes of simplicity, we should treat capital gains as any other form of income for purposes of taxes. Of course, this recommendation runs directly counter to the 1997 tax reform that lowered the capital gains tax from 28 percent to 20 percent on stocks held for 18 months, and will further drop to 18 percent for assets purchased after the year 2000 and held for five years. The problem of double taxation can be avoided and the cost of capital reduced by the earlier suggestion of dropping all corporate income taxes. By treating all income equally, regardless of source, we can avoid the problem of having people in widely different income brackets paying the same tax rate on capital gains which seems to me to violate the goal of fairness. (The 1997 creation of a new 10 percent capital gains tax rate for taxpayers in the 15 percent tax bracket was a step in the right direction.)

International Financial Transaction Tax

David Korten argues for a 0.5 percent tax on all international financial transactions to reduce currency speculation. While on the surface this idea has some appeal, I confess that I have not studied the ramifications sufficiently to make an informed judgment on the suggestion. I'll leave it to others to study Korten's suggestion.

Payroll Taxes

The payroll tax is generally thought to be regressive since only $68,400 of earnings are subject to FICA taxes; the more a person earns the lower FICA taxes are as a percentage of income. On the other hand, lower-income people are more apt to suffer periods of unemployment and, therefore, benefit more from unemployment compensation. The same cannot be said of Social Security pensions, since there is no means test for receiving benefits. Nevertheless, since up to 85 percent of a high-income earner's Social Security is subject to income taxes, those with higher incomes, in effect, receive a smaller Social Security payout than a lower-income person. Still, since we need to close the Social Security gap, and one of our principles of taxation is to spread the pain equally, the cap on income subject to FICA taxes should be eliminated to change the tax from regressive to neutral (i.e., the tax remains proportional to income for all people).

Medicare eliminated the cap on taxable payroll income, justified in part by the fact that higher-income people are equally liable to receive benefits some time in their lives. Eliminating the earnings ceiling for Social Security could raise as much as $50 billion of additional federal revenue annually or permit a reduction in the tax rates on those with lower incomes.[35] Generally speaking, however, ***payroll taxes are a poor way to increase tax revenue since they effectively raise the cost of labor, making U.S. firms less competitive in world markets.***

Senators Sam Nunn (D-Georgia) and Pete Domenici (R-New Mexico) have proposed a tax reform plan that would allow taxpayers to deduct FICA taxes from income.[36] Lester Thurow goes a step further and argues that to stimulate investment in both human capital and physical investment, both payroll taxes, and corporate income taxes be eliminated. However, if we drop payroll taxes, we have to make the shortfall up somewhere else, most likely through increased income taxes. There would be a battle regarding how to distribute the incidence of the taxes among the various income levels. Although the poor and middle class would argue that it should be passed on to the rich based on their greater ability to pay, the rich would argue that since the poor are more apt to receive unemployment benefits and will be able to retain a larger proportion of Social Security benefits (since their Social Security will be taxed at a lower rate), the poor should pay their fair share.

Property Taxes

In recent years, increases in property taxes have become extremely burdensome to people with fixed or low incomes. As a result, increases in property taxes have become one of the prime targets of so-called taxpayer rebellions. Unfortunately, property taxes are the prime source of revenue for schools; therefore, some schools districts are feeling the brunt of the backlash.

As explained in chapter 10, to increase equity in financing schools, it is essential that we reduce funding of education through property taxes and shift more of school funding to state income taxes. The amount of state funding should be the basis to ensure a minimally adequate education for every student in the state. Beyond that basic level, communities can decide to spend additional dollars on their children if they can raise the necessary local taxes.

Although property taxes are regressive, Daly and Cobb point out that *higher taxes on land encourage the most efficient use of real estate.* They do not advocate property taxes on buildings since to do so discourages improvements. This is contrary to most tax assessment schemes, which penalize real estate owners for improving structures. Pittsburgh is one city that revised its tax code to increase taxes on land values to 12.55 percent, while decreasing taxes on buildings to only 2.475 percent. This stimulated a building boom that resulted in Pittsburgh being rated the nation's most livable large city, with housing prices the lowest of any major city in the country.[37] Daly and Cobb suggest that even a 2 to 1 ratio between land and buildings taxes will get results. However, while such a differential might be good for efficiently utilizing previously developed land, it might also provoke urban sprawl by encouraging the development of new communities at the edge of urban areas. ***Therefore, to reduce this incentive for urban sprawl and to protect our nation's farmland, we need to maintain a very large property tax differential between previously developed land and undeveloped land.*** The alternative is simply to have a region-wide planning board that would have broad zoning powers. However, this requires a metropolitan government, which has generally not been acceptable to suburban communities.

A credit against state income taxes for property tax payments by the poor and those on fixed incomes is employed in thirty-two states. Such "circuit breakers" as they are called, prevent people from being taxed out of their homes. However, it may be argued that such credits are effectively subsidies to the owners of houses by those who must pay rent, since renters must ultimately pay the incidence of property taxes (in the form of higher rents) while not being able to deduct them from their income taxes. A more equitable program to help the poor would be a housing allowance deduction for which all are eligible rather than just those who are fortunate enough to own homes.

Another reason for the increased property taxes on home owners has been the success of corporations to escape property taxes. By threatening to leave areas where their property is taxed, and by obtaining special exemptions from municipalities seeking to attract new industry, corporations have reduced their proportion of total property taxes from 45 percent in 1957 to only 16 percent by 1987.[38] This demonstrates once again why we must avoid states and localities being coerced by corporations to continue reducing taxes and services in what Korten terms "a race to the bottom." The only way to avoid this problem is to collect the bulk of taxes at the federal level, so moving from state to state offers no advantage.

Finally, at present, property taxes exempt nonprofit organizations, but taking these organizations off of the tax rolls results in higher taxes for all other property owners. These organizations should be required to pay property taxes, or at least a use tax for the local services they do use, such as police, fire, water, garbage pickup, and so on. The only exceptions might be those institutions that provide a direct service to the city, i.e., schools, hospitals, shelters, and the like.

Sales Taxes

The other primary source of state and local revenue is the regressive sales tax. Pechman demonstrates its regressivity by showing that in 1985, a 5 percent tax on all consumption would amount to a 17.6 percent on the income for the 5 percent of the families with the lowest income, but only 2.2 percent of the income for families in the top 5 percent.[39] Most cities have pushed their sales tax to the point where further increases will cause real hardship for those at the bottom of the income ladder. (However, some cities have reduced the regressivity of sales taxes by exempting food, pharmaceuticals, and other basic necessities.) Furthermore, many central cities have reached the point where increasing sales tax rates will drive purchasing into the nearby suburban shopping malls.

One way to lessen the pressure on the central cities from increasing tax revenues through property and sales taxes would be to place more taxation responsibility at the federal level. By having the bulk of taxes collected by the federal government and then turned back to the states and municipalities for administration, we can take away the corporations' leverage while increasing local control of spending decisions. This is exactly the reverse of the trend of the last decade.

The argument against moving the responsibility of tax collection to the federal level is that it removes a major incentive for the cities to be fiscally responsible. Nowhere is this more evident than in the issue of immigration where many so-called sanctuary cities have encouraged illegal immigration and then sought aid from the federal government to help finance the education and medical services of the aliens. However, it cuts both ways; oftentimes the federal government is guilty of creating "unfunded mandates"—federal regulations that place an additional financial burden on the cities. The answer is that ***each political unit must be responsible for the tax revenue associated with the liabilities it creates.*** Of course, this is easier said than done.

Senator Billy Tauzin (R-Louisiana) has been pushing to replace the income tax with a national retail sales tax. At first blush such a notion is appealing, since it would seem to replace the horrendously complex income tax system with the conceptually simple tax on sales. According to Tauzin, a 15 percent sales tax would generate the same total dollars as the present income tax. To avoid the regressivity of a sales tax, Tauzin would rebate 15 percent of wages up to $2,405 for a family of four. (Other versions eliminate taxing on medicine and food, but that results in a higher sales tax rate to make up the shortfall.) By taxing consumption instead of income, the supporters of the national sales tax believe it would increase savings. Finally, they argue that a sales tax would eliminate the much despised Internal Revenue Service.

It all sounds too good to be true—and it is. Experts say that the federal sales tax would have to be at least 17.2 percent to replace the existing income tax, and even higher if family rebates are allowed.[40] The true rate of the sales tax would have to add in the existing state sales tax. Since state income taxes are based upon the federal income tax process, they would also have to be dropped and made up through additions to the sales tax. Therefore, the total sales tax rate would have to be about 25 percent. Such a high sales tax would be a huge incentive for tax evasion and black marketeering. Although the IRS would be eliminated, the sales tax would need to be enforced through the new sales tax bureau at the Treasury Department and greatly expanded state tax departments. Even then, experts believe that the highest sales tax that can be imposed without massive evasion would be about 15 percent. As a result, nearly every country that has imposed a hefty sales tax has abandoned it as unenforceable and switched to a value-added tax. The value-added tax, which is a sales tax collected at each stage of production, will be discussed later.

Inheritance Taxes

The argument against high inheritance taxes usually is based upon the assumption that people should have the right to take care of their children or other beneficiaries in any way they see fit. Furthermore, it is pointed out that very high estate taxes are confiscatory and penalize those people who are frugal and invest rather than spend their income.

On the other side, we have the philosophy of millionaire industrialist Andrew Carnegie, who saw wealth as a social trust, and said that "the parent who leaves his son enormous wealth generally deadens the talents and energies of the son, and tempts him to lead a less useful and less worthy a life than he otherwise would."[41] Of course, many counter-examples may be given of heirs of fortunes who have used the freedom from want to pursue very ambitious objectives.

Nevertheless, from behind the Rawlsian veil of ignorance I believe that most people would find it objectionable that huge fortunes pass to those who have done nothing to earn them. Although parents want to leave something to their progeny—at least enough to protect them against the caprice of ill-fortune—there are limits to what is reasonable. ***The limits are of necessity subjective, but the amount a person may inherit should not negate the requirement that each person work for their livelihood.*** Again, recall that Rawlsian justice demands that all social goods be distributed equally unless an unequal distribution works to the advantage of the least fortunate. We have determined that inequality in earnings due to hard work can provide incentives that ultimately will benefit the least fortunate. It seems more difficult, however, to demonstrate that leaving large sums of money to heirs provides the incentives that will benefit all of society more so than if the wealth were subsequently reinvested in social institutions and infrastructure which benefit all.

One of the major problems with inheritance is that it biases the chances of success in favor of those who are descendents of a person who previously won. A free market economy might be compared to the game of Monopoly®. There comes a point in the game where one player has so many assets that no other player has a chance of winning. In that case, we declare that person the winner and start the game over. No one would want to have to take over the position of the losers. One of the functions of taxation can be to "start the game over" by leveling the playing field—at least to some degree—for each succeeding generation.

Barlett and Steele recommend taxing capital gains at death.[42] This would have the advantage of not discouraging investment while also preventing the next generation from gaining unearned wealth. I would go much further. The 1997 tax revisions gradually increase the amount excluded from state and gift tax from $600,000 to $1 million over ten years. I would go in the opposite direction and recommend a progressive tax beginning at 10 percent for the first $100,000, and rising to 50 percent for amounts over one million dollars and 90 percent for amounts over 100 million. At the same time, we must revise the present gift tax so that people cannot avoid the higher estate taxes by giving away their assets before they die.

Finally, we must remember that money equals power. The concentration of wealth from generation to generation facilitates the concentration of political power as well. Ironically, sometimes the results of this concentration of power have been totally at odds with the intentions of the original progenitors of the wealth. Nowhere is this more evident than in the area of foundations. With hundreds of billions of dollars at their disposal, foundations have become a major new political force in this country, of which most Americans are blissfully unaware. Foundations are not allowed to contribute to political campaigns; however, under the guise of "education," they have numerous ways to shape public opinions.

Although most foundations were set up by conservative millionaires, they are now being run by liberals who frequently use the money in ways that would cause their founders to roll over in their graves. The Ford Foundation has given millions of dollars to create the Mexican American Legal Defense Fund (MALDEF) and La Raza, both left-wing organizations, the latter with a distinctly racist agenda.* ***To avoid the increased concentration of power in perpetuity in the hands of foundations, they should be required to dispense their proceeds within twenty-five years, after which any unexpended funds revert to the U.S. Treasury for the benefit of all Americans.***[43]

Pollution Taxes

I have already discussed the use of taxes on pollutants as an effective means of providing economic incentives to companies to reduce pollution (see chapter 5).

*The Ford Foundation decided that it wanted to create for Hispanics the same political power that blacks attained through organizations such as the National Association for the Advancement of Colored People (NAACP) and the Southern Christian Leadership Conference (SCLC). Hence, the foundation provided tens of millions of dollars over the years to create MALDEF and La Raza. MALDEF was as tremendous success not just for Mexicans but for all Hispanics, gaining for them the same minority job preferences and antidiscrimination protection that blacks won after decades of struggle. MALDEF succeeded in getting Hispanics recognized as a "race" (La Raza) even though there is no anthropological basis for lumping people from Cuba, Argentina, Mexico, and all other Central and South American countries together as if they were one racial or ethnic group. Ironically, the Ford Foundation has paved the way for a new form of discrimination which, as discussed in the chapter 4, threatens to erode job opportunities and political power for blacks.

Gas Tax

In real dollar terms, gas taxes per gallon were no higher in 1998 than they were in 1954. In 1998, federal taxes were 18 cents a gallon and state taxes averaged 18 cents a gallon, for a total of 36 cents.[44] Even an additional 50 cent per gallon tax increase would leave the United States with the cheapest gas of any industrialized nation, and also leave real dollar cost per gallon at the level of the 1950s.[45] Not only would higher gas taxes reduce gasoline consumption, thus cutting both pollution and the reliance on foreign oil, but it could have a major impact in reducing the national debt. A tax increase of only 10 cents a gallon would raise $10 billion of revenue. ***A $1.00 tax per gallon (about a $.64 increase) would be quite reasonable and would reduce the debt by $64 billion a year. A $1.00 per gallon tax would still leave U.S. gas less taxed than Germany ($1.46), Japan ($1.62), Britain ($1.76), and France ($2.41).***[46] Yet Congress raised the tax on gas by only four cents and then tried to roll back this measly increase. It is obvious that they are not really serious about either conservation or reducing the national debt.

To soften the regressiveness of a higher gas tax on the working poor who need to drive to work, the gas tax could be deducted from income taxes on a sliding scale inversely related to income.

A variation of the gas tax is to place a special tax on cars that fail to meet a mileage per gallon standard. The last time this was done, Detroit howled that it was an impossible standard to meet and that no one would buy fuel-efficient cars anyway. In the meantime, the Japanese car manufactures met the standard and Americans were snapping up their cars. Reluctantly, American manufacturers stopped whining and by 1986, every American passenger auto met the standard and no longer was subject to the tax. This shows what can be achieved with the proper incentive. One major hole in the law was to exclude vans, sport vehicles, and recreational vehicles. With the rising popularity of these vehicles, they should also be subject to the same MPG standards.

However, the next time Congress suggested raising the standard, the price of oil had dropped and the short-sighted American public lost interest in conservation of energy. The auto manufacturers lobbied hard to get President George Bush to kill the proposal on the alleged basis that the manufacturers would have to make the cars so light that they would be unsafe. But if equipped with front and side impact air bags, cars would be safer despite their reduced weight. (Of course raising speed limits reduces gas mileage and increases risk regardless of the safety built into the cars. But Americans seem to be willing to accept this added risk.)

Cigarette, Liquor, and Other Drug Taxes

In 1997, federal taxes on a pack of cigarettes were only 24 cents. In constant dollars, federal taxes on cigarettes declined by 72 percent between 1954 and 1997. ***A $1.00 a pack increase in taxes would generate $10 billion in increased revenues.***[47] ***If cigarettes were taxed at the 1954 level in real dollar terms, it would raise $20 billion annually.***[48] The increased taxes would have the additional benefit of discouraging smoking by about 10 percent, thus decreasing the associated healthcare costs.[49] However, there is a limit to how high taxes can be raised before a black market in cigarettes is stimulated. In Canada when the government taxed cigarettes to bring the cost to over $5.00 a pack, almost one-third of the cigarettes were being smuggled in from the United States. Consequently, taxes had to be lowered to about $2.00 a pack to reduce the smuggling. In 1998 there was much talk in Congress of raising cigarette taxes by $1.00 or $1.50. While Congress dithered, the states brought a joint lawsuit against the tobacco industry and won a multibillion-dollar settlement. To pay for their settlement, the tobacco companies had to increase the price of cigarettes about $1.00 a pack. Hence, the states got the equivalent of a tax increase (minus, however, a big chunk of the settlement that went to pay the numerous law firms that handled the suit). Whether or not the federal government could still increase the taxes on cigarettes by $1.00 a pack without creating a black-market for cigarettes is now problematic. At any rate, consideration of further tax increases is a dead issue in Congress.

Like gasoline, federal taxes on alcohol increased only once in the past thirty-five years. ***Federal taxes on liquor were 36 cents per fifth in 1954 compared to an inflation adjusted 8 cents in 1997.*** Moreover, beer and wine are not taxed relative to their alcohol content such as so-called hard liquor. ***A 20 percent increase in the liquor tax and increasing the tax on beer and wine to parity based on alcohol content would raise another $5 billion of tax revenue.***[50]

One reason for not increasing federal taxes on tobacco and alcohol is the opposition of states who wish to raise their own taxes on liquor and cigarettes. However, states face an even greater problem of interstate smuggling if their taxes are out of line with neighboring states. Therefore, it is more practical to institute the tax at the federal level and refund the revenue to the states. At the present time the alcohol and tobacco lobbies have succeeded at preventing any significant increase in taxes on their socially detrimental products.

Another potential source of tax revenues could come from the legalization and taxing of presently illicit drugs. The pros and cons of legalizing drugs was discussed in chapter 11 and need not be repeated here. While an estimate of the amount of revenue to be derived is difficult, it might be equal to that of tobacco and alcohol, i.e., $10 to $20 billion. In addition, there would be billions of dollars in savings from reducing the fruitless efforts to eliminate drug use. These taxes and cost savings could be used for an advertising campaign to discourage drug use, as well as for drug rehabilitation programs.

Personal Consumption Tax

Lester Thurow proposes a tax on personal consumption.[51] Unlike the Value-Added Tax (to be discussed below), Thurow's proposal would not tax expenditures directly; rather, it would effectively tax consumption by exempting all savings from taxes. Since all income must be either saved or spent, by excluding savings from taxes we are effectively taxing spending. Such an idea has much to commend it. It is conceptually simple and it encourages savings, and hence investment. This was the same goal of the tax-deferred Individual Retirement Accounts (IRAs); Thurow just takes it a step further.

Since the poor have less savings, a consumption tax would take a larger proportion of their income and hence be regressive. To avoid this, Thurow's proposal would (a) allow deductions for mortgage interest for one house worth up to $500,000, (b) allow personal exemptions up to the poverty line for families of different sizes, (c) set marginal tax rates from 12 percent for the first dollar of taxable income up to 100 percent for consumption of $85,600, (d) increase tax rates by 1 percent for each $1,000 of consumption beyond $85,600. This latter feature is especially appealing to conservationists since it would reduce environmentally destructive consumption.* The modification I would make to Thurow's proposal is to limit the personal exemptions to two children. At the very least, we need to end subsidies that encourage large families. Thurow's idea has become the basis for several efforts to replace the income tax with national sales tax as discussed earlier. However, Thurow's proposals include increases in the tax rate for higher levels of consumption.

The tax reform plan proposed by senators Nunn and Domenici would, in effect, create unlimited retirement accounts. It retains the progressivity by taxing people at higher rates as income rises, but allows deductions for

---

*However, as a practical matter, I am not certain how it could be implemented. A value-added tax (VAT) would have the same result with regard to reduced consumption and can be implemented as European countries have demonstrated. On the other hand, a VAT is regressive. This is not the case in Europe where the tax benefits to the poor and unemployed are extremely generous. But providing such generous benefits seems to be reducing the international competitiveness of European firms to the point where it is impeding the economic performance of Europe. As such, many European countries are trying to scale back benefits.

every dollar used to purchase stocks or bonds or to start up a small business. College and vocational tuition costs could be deducted up to $2,000 per person and $8,000 per family per year. The only other deductions allowed would be for FICA taxes, mortgage interest, contributions to charity, and alimony payments.[52] This is much closer to the spirit of Thurow's proposal. It is hoped that a major overhaul of the tax system along these lines would significantly increase America's anemic savings rate.

Wealth Tax

Many economists feel that it is more equitable to tax inflation-adjusted wealth rather than income, but they see the practical difficulty of doing so.[53] One method would be through the inheritance tax, which effectively taxes the lifetime accumulation of wealth.[54] Many European countries tax the value of assets less liabilities. The value of exemptions is high to exclude all but the most wealthy individuals. The maximum tax rate is only 3 percent,[55] but applied against net wealth, such a rate is not inconsequential. (In the case of Bill Gates, the tax would be over $1 billion.) While a wealth tax could help prevent the concentration of wealth, it might also be a disincentive to save. Nevertheless, a moderate wealth tax rate used in conjunction with an income tax would prevent the concentration of power that necessarily accompanies the concentration of wealth.

In the United States, a handful of states have an "intangible tax" that is just another name for a wealth tax. Florida and Tennessee employ an intangible tax instead of an income tax. Kentucky and Georgia have both an intangible tax and an income tax. Because they are applied to wealth, which is a far larger base than income, the rates are very low. For example, Florida's rate is 0.1 percent.

The Flat-Rate Income Tax

Some politicians and presidential wannabees such as multimillionaire Steve Forbes and Representative Dick Armey (R-Texas) argue that the income tax is so complicated and unfair that it should be replaced with a flat-rate income tax. Armey's plan calls for a 20 percent tax on wages only, not capital gains, interest, dividends, or inheritance. No deductions are allowed. To avoid raising taxes on lower-income people who are currently paying less than a 20 percent rate, there would be an across-the-board deduction; for example, the first $33,800 of earnings would be excluded for a family of four. Taxes would still be paid through wage withholdings, and the need for the IRS, while reduced, would not be eliminated.

The primary criticism of a flat tax is that, like a sales tax, even with exclusions or a rebate, such taxes lighten the burden of taxes for the wealthiest Americans while increasing it for everyone else. There is no doubt that those who are paying an average annual tax rate over the flat income tax level (such as the 20 percent suggested by Armey) would benefit and those paying below that level would suffer. For example, the working poor who are now receiving the earned income tax credit would lose it—this would effectively take $20 billion a year out of the pockets of America's lowest income earners.[56]

Moreover, a flat tax would present a major problem for the states. It would effectively eliminate the state income taxes since state taxes are based upon the federal income tax forms and procedures. Without the assurance that the fed is auditing income tax filings, the states would each have to replicate the federal government's defunct system, making state income tax collection prohibitively costly to implement. A flat tax would reduce some tax fraud, but would not catch one of the biggest sources of fraud: small businessmen who underreport income by paying themselves very low salaries while charging personal expenditures against their business.

One of the most popular arguments advanced for the flat tax has nothing to do with the flat tax itself; namely, proponents claim that it will stimulate economic growth. Actually, any reduction of taxes would stimulate growth in the short term if we run a budget deficit. ***However, in the final analysis, it is not how much tax is collected that determines economic growth, but how the money is spent, particularly the impact on total U.S. productivity.*** This is an extraordinarily important point and one most often overlooked in the tax debates. As was pointed out earlier, all wealth ultimately comes from increasing productivity. If the government spends $10,000 on defense, there is no increase in productivity and hence no increase in wealth. If the consumer spends $10,000 on snowmobiles, there is no increase in productivity either. On the other hand, $10,000 spent by the government or by private industry on basic research or infrastructure could have a tremendous impact on productivity. Implicit in the arguments that lower taxes increase economic growth is an assumption that what they are spent on will increase productivity. If the dollars go for increased consumption, then it is merely a matter of personal values as to whether the government or the individual makes better use of the money. I personally would rather see the government use tax dollars to clean up toxic wastes than to see individuals use those same dollars to buy gas-guzzling recreational vehicles or power boats. But all this has nothing to do with who pays the taxes, and so we must ignore any claims that a flat tax per se is related to economic growth—with one exception. (In economics it seems that there is always an exception.)

Many economists object to flat and sales taxes because they implicitly fail to recognize that the value of each additional dollar declines as wealth increases. In other words, giving up 15 percent of their income for a family making a million dollars a year is not nearly as painful as it would be for a family making less than $50,000 a year. The people in lower-income groups tend to spend a greater proportion of their income on consumption, while those in upper-income groups tend to invest a greater proportion of their income. Assuming the total tax collected remains the same, simply collecting a greater share of tax dollars from the lower-income groups increases investment by the wealthy and, hence, long-term economic growth. The greater increase in long-term wealth would then trickle down to the poor who have had to curtail their consumption. Sound familiar? It's the old Reagan trickle-down economics. But that, in effect, puts the burden of subsidizing economic growth on the poor and middle class who also are last to receive the benefits.

Personal Income Tax

Today the bulk of federal tax revenue is generated by the personal income tax. It accounts for more than 45 percent of federal budget receipts, a greater proportion than in any other country.[57] It was first adopted in the Revenue Act of 1913 and reinforced by the Securities Act of 1933, but by 1939 still only claimed 1 percent of personal income. Financing World War II resulted in the first significant tax increase, and it gradually rose to today's level, which claims about 10 percent of total United States personal income[58] (which is considerably less than most people would guess). In 1980, the maximum tax rate was 70 percent, but the 1981 Income Tax Act cut that rate to 28 percent. In order to replace some of the revenue lost by the act, and to provide equity with lower-income earners, the top rate was subsequently raised to 33 percent in 1985. In order to reduce the deficit, the Clinton administration raised the top marginal rate again in 1993 to an effective rate of 39.6 percent. (Note that this is the marginal rate; the average tax rate for the top 5 percent of American families was 32 percent in 1998.)[59]

Although the wealthy benefited most from the 1980 income tax cut, all groups benefited to some degree. In 1980, 55 percent of total personal income was subject to tax rates less than 20 percent. By 1988, 66 percent of income was subject to taxes of less than 15 percent.[60] However, this government largess, along with the increased defense and healthcare expenditures, resulted in the explosion of the national debt. Already by 1984 it was recognized that the 1980 tax cut would not generate more revenues than it lost. The net lost revenues in 1984 amounted to $162 billion.[61] A half-hearted attempt to sneak in some small tax increases netted $53 billion by 1985, not nearly enough to fill the gap.[62] Left with the huge deficits, both the Bush administration and the Democratic Congress showed little inclination to tackle the problem by raising taxes. Aided by stronger economic growth, a small tax increase, and slowing growth in the federal budget, Congress and the Clinton administration were able to significantly reduce the annual deficits and slow the growth in the national debt. But substantially higher taxes were never seriously considered both because of the political risk and the concern that a sudden increase in personal income tax would stifle the economic recovery in 1992 and 1993.

Rather than a simple but grossly inequitable flat tax, we need revisions to the federal income tax code that makes taxes more fair, generate additional income, and promote the social goal of a sustainable society. Here are suggestions I find that would have the most significant impact and would advance the goals of increasing average social welfare:

- reinstate the two-earner credit so as not to penalize people for getting married;
- drop or phase out the deduction for interest on mortgages over $200,000;
- limit dependent deductions to two children (and all adopted children), or those elderly and disabled who have no Social Security or other source of income;
- eliminate all other deductions except for the following:
  - property taxes
  - child care up to 5 percent of gross income or $5,000, whichever is lower
  - IRA savings up to $5,000 per person per year (including homemakers)
  - the present medical deduction, until universal healthcare coverage is established
  - a gradually declining deduction for gas taxes *if* they are raised by $1.00.

It should be noted that by eliminating many of today's deductions, tax rates could be reduced for everyone and still generate the same amount of revenue. Note also that no charitable deductions are allowed. There are two reasons for this. First, the vast majority of charitable expenses go to support churches. If someone wants to support a church, that is their right, but that is no reason to make it a tax deduction. Since a key purpose of taxes is to cover governmental expenses, if one person pays less taxes for any reason, other people have to pay more. Hence, a deduction to a religion is effectively a subsidy for that religion.

The second reason is the impossibility of drawing a bright line between charitable and political giving. Listen to many sermons in most churches and you can see the blurring of the line. Churches have the right to preach against abortion and even to organize protests. As tax-exempt organizations, however, churches have a legal obligation not to support or oppose specific pieces of legislation or to do extensive lobbying. Yet churches often engage in such actions because they know that the IRS will not seek to revoke the tax-exempt status of a religious organization (except maybe some small fringe group). To even suggest such action results in the cry of religious persecution.

Of course, there are legitimate charitable services that may initially suffer a decline in contributions because of the absence of a tax deduction, but it is still wrong to force one person to pay additional taxes because another person wishes to support a particular charity.

To lessen the shock to those organizations that presently benefit from tax exempt status (i.e., whose supporters can deduct contributions), the charitable deduction might be phased out over five years.

An alternative approach to taxes is offered by Daly and Cobb, who would eliminate all but four deductions for personal income taxes:

- taxes and cost of repairs and improvements on homes whose rental value is added to income;
- expenses necessary for earning a living, such as child care when necessary for the parent to work (Pechman would drop the childcare credit and use the additional revenue to subsidize facilities for low-income families);
- gifts to private institutions and charitable activities;
- small gifts to politicians.[63]

Another approach would be a variation of a suggestion by Representative Richard Gephart (D-Missouri). He would tax most families at a 10 percent rate, abolish virtually all deductions except mortgage interest, and keep double taxation of investment income (i.e., tax corporate profits and dividend income). The tax rate would increase with income and the highest bracket would be 34 percent.[64] ***I would go further, disallowing interest on mortgages above $200,000 and raising the top rate to 75 percent on income over one million dollars a year. This is not unlike the income tax***

schedule in the 1950s, probably the most egalitarian decade in America's history.

The Negative Income Tax

Essentially a negative income tax (NIT) is calculated so that when income, adjusted for the normal tax deductions, falls below the minimum level where a person must pay a tax, the government would pay a proportional subsidy. Years ago economist Milton Friedman espoused a negative income tax as an alternative to welfare. He felt that if it were structured correctly it would be less of a disincentive to work than welfare is. Under an NIT, people could always increase their total income by working more, unlike welfare in which a person loses benefits by taking a job. The concept of an NIT was finally passed into law under President Gerald Ford and revised in subsequent Republican and Democratic administrations as the Earned Income Tax Credit (EITC).

Basically the EITC is the same as a guaranteed minimum income. As such, it suffers from the same potential drawbacks, most importantly the fear that certain people will prefer to live off the dole. Daly and Cobb believe that this number will be small,[65] but Murray disagrees. He cites studies of experiments in Seattle and Denver indicating that an NIT reduces the "desired hours of work" by 9 percent for husbands and 20 percent for wives.[66] Murray admits that simply wanting to reduce the number of hours worked is not necessarily disastrous, but reductions in average hours of work were primarily due to men opting out of the labor force altogether. Of grave concern was the impact on young males: a decline of 43 percent for those who remained unmarried throughout the seven year experiment, and 33 percent for those who married during this time.[67] Another negative result was the increased length in unemployment between jobs—an increase of nine weeks or 27 percent longer for men, fifty weeks or 42 percent longer for women, and 56 weeks or 60 percent longer for single women. ***Worst of all, divorce rates were 36 percent higher for whites receiving NIT compared to a control group who did not get the benefit, and 42 percent higher for blacks.***[68] Interestingly, in another study of Gary, Indiana, among recipients of NITs, no increase in the divorce rate occurred. Why? According to Murray, the reason was that the couples were under the impression that they would lose the NIT if they separated. This result may indicate how to avoid the potential negative consequences of an NIT.

One important factor that Murray does not mention is the differential in income between the income received from the negative income tax and the *net* income received from working. By net income I mean the income received after deducting the costs associated with work, such as child care and transportation. Child care can be factored into the calculation of the negative income tax, since it is an allowable deduction when computing taxable income, but a deduction for transportation costs is not allowable. In areas where the jobs are a great distance from where the poor live, and public transportation is not readily available, this may require the purchase and maintenance of an auto, which seriously reduces the take-home pay. Consequently, when the costs of employment are factored in, the differential income between working and receiving a negative income tax might be trivial.

What are the tentative conclusions from the experiments with a negative income tax? First, it cannot be denied that any form of welfare for able-bodied people will result in a disincentive to work for some individuals. Whether the disincentive is enough to make them significantly reduce their hours or drop out of the work force probably depends in part on their differential rate of pay. A person making $20 an hour is much less likely to give up a job for welfare than someone making $7 an hour. Consequently, ***to avoid being a serious disincentive to work, it is essential that the minimum wage should be sufficient to provide an economic incentive to work. (In the absence of immigration and excessive welfare benefits, the law of supply and demand would probably ensure this outcome.)*** Second, to argue that the NIT discourages work implies that there are jobs available in the first place. From 1970 until about 1995, this has not been true for the unskilled in many areas of the country. Although I have argued that it is essential that people be held responsible for the consequences of their actions, fairness demands that they have reasonable alternatives. If the alternative is between netting $2 or $3 an hour (after costs associated with working are deducted), or not working and still receiving the equivalent from welfare, it should not be surprising that the latter course is chosen. In our efforts to eliminate long-term welfare dependency, it is essential that jobs be available paying a wage that more than covers the costs of working (such as health insurance, transportation, and child care).

Eighteen percent of those working full time in 1992 earned too little to keep a family of four out of poverty. The Clinton administration's 1995 fiscal year budget expanded the Earned Income Tax Credit to bring a working family of four up to the poverty level. This amounted to a maximum credit of $3,500 for a parent with two children, which, when combined with the $4.25-an-hour minimum wage, would yield an effective hourly wage rate of $6.00.[69] Even with a minimum wage of $6.00 an hour, the total with the EITC would be $16,120 a year, or $7.75 an hour.

Value-Added Tax

Although Lester Thurow's personal consumption tax is reasonable, it does not appear to be politically feasible. A politically more appealing tax is the Value-Added Tax (VAT), which would also tax consumption but less obviously. A value-added tax is a tax on the difference between sales and the cost of supplies and purchases from other firms, i.e., a tax on the value added at each stage of production. Hence, by the time a product gets to the consumer, its price tag includes taxes on all the incremental profit at each stage of production. For example, suppose we are talking about a car radio completely made in America with American parts (admittedly a far-fetched example). A manufacturer buys raw materials to make components for $A and sells the finished components to the assembly plant for $B. He pays taxes on the amount $B – A. Next the assembly plant buys the components for $B and sells the assembled radio to a car dealer for $C. The assembly operator pays taxes on $C – $B. Finally, the car manufacturer pays taxes on the difference between his cost for the radio ($C) and the price he charges the automobile buyer ($D), or $D – $C.

With a value-added tax, unlike corporate income taxes, there is no incentive to play games with stock versus debt financing to manipulate net income, because the company is not taxed on net income. Since value-added nets out the cost of capital equipment, but not labor costs, there is an incentive to increase productivity by substituting capital for labor.

Probably the two most significant advantages of a VAT is that it raises lots of money and it has a built-in incentive to reduce consumption. More than forty countries have adopted a form of the VAT with rates varying between 6 percent and 20 percent.[70] Thurow estimates that ***a 15 percent VAT in the United States would have raised $325 billion in 1982, thus eliminating the deficit at the time, while simultaneously permitting the elimination of the corporate income tax and a reduction in the regressive payroll taxes.***[71]

Despite these advantages, the VAT has been strenuously opposed in this country for several reasons.[72] First, a VAT would not have the countercyclical stabilizers that we get from an income tax. With the present progressive tax structure, when income drops during a recession, a greater than proportional drop in tax liability results, thereby partially offsetting the decline in purchasing power, which mitigates the recession. Since a VAT is a constant rate, it would always act to discourage consumption, thus it might exacerbate an economic downturn.

Second, a VAT competes with a sales tax on consumption, resulting in the federal government tapping the same source of revenues as the state and local governments.

Third, like all consumption taxes, the VAT is regressive: it taxes consumption and, therefore, almost *all* of the income of low-income people, but only a portion of the income of wealthy households. Europe modifies this regressiveness through an extremely progressive income tax, along with much more public spending on welfare and other public programs that benefit the poor and middle classes.

Finally, the critics of the VAT oppose it especially because of the effectiveness with which it raises revenues. They argue that by not showing the direct impact of the tax, it is too easy for the government to keep raising taxes, resulting in less control over federal spending.

On the other side of the ledger, there are several arguments in favor of the VAT. I already mentioned the incentive to save rather than consume, and the large amount of money that could be raised with less chance of public outcry. This would make it easier to generate the tax revenue necessary to retire the national debt. Second, it reduces the major problem we have today with businesspeople who avoid income taxes by charging personal expense to their corporation to reduce their reported income. Under a VAT, they effectively must collect the tax from their customers or else they have to pay it out of their own pockets. The only way to avoid the tax is to not record sales. For producers and wholesalers, this is easy to check by examining the books of their customers. For retailers, fraud detection is more difficult, but still easier to detect than under the present system of income taxes. Third, there is no disincentive to work as alleged of the income tax. Every additional dollar earned benefits its recipient equally. Fourth, since the tax is on consumption rather than income, even those who get income from illegal activities get taxed when they spend their ill-gotten gains. Fifth, since the VAT is rebatable under terms of international trade (i.e., an exporter can claim the VAT on the product he exports as a credit against other taxes he pays), it reduces the price of exports. Other nations have been taking advantage of this rule for years to the disadvantage of U.S. manufacturers. Moreover, to the extent that the VAT can be used to reduce payroll taxes and corporate income taxes, the benefit would be even greater in reducing the price of U.S. exports. Finally, the criticism that the VAT is regressive can be met by incorporating a per-capita refundable tax credit to offset the effect of the tax on the poor.[73] For example, a tax credit could be given for the first $15,000 of consumption for a family of four.

Of all the objections, the most cogent argument against the VAT is that it will make it too easy for the federal government to raise revenues. Those who wish to reduce the role of the federal government see the VAT as a major impediment to their goal. I have argued throughout this book that far from being out of control, the federal government is not carrying out its basic responsibilities such as protecting the environment, providing adequate health insurance for all, and building and maintaining the necessary urban and commercial infrastructure. Moreover, providing more revenue to the federal government would allow it to transfer income from the wealthy suburbs to the central cites, thus effectively providing the benefits of a metropolitan area form of government, which is so difficult to establish in most urban areas of this country. It could also end the competition among the states to reduce taxes and social benefits to attract businesses. (Then again, some people might consider this a liability of the VAT.)

Conclusion and Summary

An ideal tax system should have the following characteristics:

- It should generate sufficient taxes to cover expenditures.
- It should distort economic incentives as little as possible, but add the cost of externalities (e.g., the impact of pollution and environmental degradation) to the cost of production.
- It should adjust for inflation.
- It should be as simple as possible, both to make it understandable and to discourage cheating.
- It should be based on Rawlsian justice, which allows for unequal distribution of income and wealth, and in doing so, acts as an incentive to greater effort that results in benefits for the least favored.
- It should foster stability and efficiency in the economy. Growth may also be a goal, if by growth we mean not just the accumulation of products and services, but an improvement in an Index of Human Welfare such as discussed in chapter 2.

Based upon these characteristics, and the goal of raising sufficient revenues to close the budget deficit, the following revisions to the tax structure are in order:

1. Corporate income taxes should be phased out. In the final analysis, corporations don't pay taxes, they merely pass them on to the customers, employees, and shareowners.
2. Businesses should pay use taxes for any public resources they consume, especially those externalities such as clean air and water. They should also be taxed on the amount of pollutants they discharge.

3. Social Security taxes should be levied on total income with no ceiling on taxable earnings.

4. If taxes remain on corporate income, personal income taxes on dividends received should be dropped to avoid double taxation. Moreover, treating interest expense and dividends differently can bias the financing decisions of corporations in favor of debt rather than equity, thus increasing financial risk. Dropping the corporate income tax completely would avoid double taxation or the biasing of corporate financing while also reducing the cost of capital.

5. If corporate income taxes are dropped, capital gains should be indexed for inflation and taxed at the marginal rate of ordinary income.

6. Property taxes are regressive and should be kept to a minimum. Property taxes also prevent poorer areas from raising the required revenues for their schools unless they tax at a higher rate than wealthier suburbs. Taxes on improvements to existing buildings should be discouraged as incentive for optimal use of existing developed land. However, to conserve farmland, wetlands, and open space, property taxes on undeveloped land should be much less than on developed land.

7. Sales taxes are also regressive and should be a minimum source of revenue. However, excise taxes on luxury goods are warranted.

8. Taxes on tobacco, alcohol, and legalized drugs should be at the highest rate possible, just short of creating a black market for these goods. The average tax rates should be approximately the same among the states to avoid smuggling between states. Better still, the federal government should levy the taxes and refund the states a portion of the taxes collected.

9. Inheritance taxes should be sufficiently steep to avoid what is effectively intergenerational welfare and the concentration of political power. In general, people should not benefit when they provided no service.

10. The Earned Income Tax Credit (a negative income tax) is an important means of aiding the working poor. However, it has to be tied to work so that those who are able to, but do not choose to work, are not subsidized.

11. A value-added tax should be implemented to generate enough revenue to replace the discontinued corporate income tax. It would not only reduce consumption but improve U.S. competitiveness.

12. The personal income tax, if retained, can be much more progressive than at present—particularly for those earning over $200,000 annually—without danger of diminishing work incentives. All deductions should be eliminated except property taxes, interest on mortgages of less than $200,000, childcare expense up to $5,000 or 5 percent of gross income (whichever is smaller), the present medical expense deduction (at least until there is some form of universal healthcare coverage), IRA contributions up to $5,000 per person per year, and if the $1 per gallon gas tax is implemented, a declining deduction for gas taxes. To ease the pain to homeowners and charitable institutions, the elimination of the related deductions could be grandfathered or phased out over a five- or ten-year period.

This cursory treatment of an incredibly complex subject is designed to stimulate further research and discussion with the goal of achieving fair and effieicne tax reform. The key point to remember is that an equitable tax system must generate sufficient revenue to provide the needed public investment in line with the principles of modified Rawlsian justice. This would effectively preclude any form of a flat tax.

Notes

1. *Wall Street Journal*, April 8, 1992, p. 1.

2. Alan S. Blinder, *Hard Heads, Soft Hearts* (New York: Addison-Wesley Publishing Company, Inc., 1987), p. 21.

3. Joseph A. Pechman, *Federal Tax Policy*, 5th ed. (Washington, D.C.: Brookings Institution, 1987), table D–23, p. 392. Data from U. S. Department of Commerce, Bureau of Census.

4. Alexis de Tocqueville, *Democracy in America* (New York: Vintage Books, Division of Random House, 1972), vol. 1, p. 188.

5. *The Economist*, November 21, 1987.

6. Based on state tax rates from *Money Magazine* (January 1995): pp. 92–93, compiled by Kely Smith and Roberta Kirwan with Diane Giles. The data assumes a family of four spending $38,000 on food, clothing, and shelter. Federal income tax assumes the standard deduction.

7. OECD Bank for International Development. Reported in Merrill Lynch, *Weekly Economic and Financial Commentary* (February 27, 1993).

8. U.S. Office of Management and Budget, *Budget of United States Government, Fiscal Year 1999, Historical Tables* (Washington, D.C.: U.S. Government Printing Office, 1999), table 15.1, p. 268.

9. Bell and Thurow, *The Deficits: How Big? How Long? How Dangerous?* (New York: New York University Press, 1985), p. 115.

10. Pechman, *Federal Tax Policy*, pp. 11–12.

11. Blinder, *Hard Heads, Soft Hearts*, p. 162.

12. Ibid., p. 163.

13. John Kenneth Galbraith, *Economics and the Public Purpose* (Boston: Houghton Mifflin Company, 1973), p. 306.

14. Pechman, *Federal Tax Policy*, p. 5.

15. Ibid.

16. Ibid., p. 76.

17. Robert Lekachman, *Greed Is Not Enough: Reaganomics* (New York: Pantheon Books, 1982), p. 61.

18. U.S. Bureau of the Census, *Statistical Abstract of the United States, 1997* (Washington, D.C.: U.S. Government Printing Office, 1997), table 478, p. 300.

19. Pechman, *Federal Tax Policy*, p. 156.

20. Ibid., p. 153.

21. Ibid., pp. 174–75.

22. Ibid., p. 151.

23. President, *Economic Report of the President Transmitted to Congress, 1991* (Washington, D.C.: U.S. Government Printing Office, 1991), table B–28, p. 318, and *Economic Report, 1998*, table B–32, p. 318.

24. Donald L. Barlett and James B. Steele, *America: What Went Wrong?* (Kansas City, Mo.: Andrews and MeMeel, 1992), pp. 43, 95.

25. Herman E. Daly and John B. Cobb Jr., *For the Common Good* (Boston: Beacon Press, 1989), p. 32.

26. Eric Zorn, "For Tax Cheats and the Rich, Dole's Your Man," *Chicago Tribune*, August 8, 1996, sec. 2, p. 1.

27. David C. Korten, *When Corporation Rule the World* (West Hartford, Conn., and San Francisco: Kumarian Press and Berrett-Koehler Publishers, Inc., 1995), p. 211.

28. Pechman, *Federal Tax Policy*, pp. 183–87.

29. John H. Makin, "An Unpopular Appeal for Higher Savings, More Affordable Housing and Lower Deficits," *Testimony to House Ways and Means Committee* (April 19, 1989).

30. Pechman, *Federal Tax Policy*, p. 188.

31. David Brazell et al., *The Cost of Corporate Capital in the United States and Japan* (Newington, Conn: Krieble Foundation, 1985), pp. 4–6.

32. Ibid., p. 34.

33. Ibid., p. 23.

34. Callard, Madden, and Associates, Market Update, 1:12 (December 12, 1991).

35. Merrill Lynch, *Weekly Economic and Financial Commentary* (January 18, 1993).

36. William Neikirk, "Bipartisan Sponsors Unveil Tax-Revamp Plan," *Chicago Tribune*, April 29, 1995, sec. 1, pp. 1, 4.

37. Daly and Cobb, *For the Common Good*, p. 329.

38. Robert Reich, *The Work of Nations* (New York: Alfred A. Knopf, 1991), p. 281.

39. Pechman, *Federal Tax Policy*, p. 204.

40. David Wessel and Greg Hitt, "Anti-IRS Frenzy Gives Republicans a Chance to Road-Test Plans," *Wall Street Journal*, October 10, 1997, pp. A1–A10.

41. Ibid., p. 235.

42. Barlett and Steele, *America: What Went Wrong?* p. 218.

43. I wish to thank Walter Buchmann for pointing out the issue of concentration of wealth and power and offering this suggestion to remedy the problem.

44. Merrill Lynch, *Weekly Economic and Financial Commentary* (January 18, 1993), adjusted for the four-cents-a-gallon increase passed by Congress in 1994.

45. According to AAA spokesman Brian Sterling, by the end of 1998 gas prices, including taxes, were the lowest they have ever been. Michael Ko, "Price Plunge a Gas," *Chicago Tribune*, December 12, 1998, sec. 2, p. 1.

46. Merrill Lynch, *Weekly Economic and Financial Commentary* (January 9, 1989): 3.

47. Merrill Lynch, *Weekly Economic and Financial Commentary* (January 18, 1993): 3.

48. Merrill Lynch, *Weekly Economic and Financial Commentary* (January, 9, 1989): 3.

49. "Audit Finds Tobacco Deal May be Windfall," *Chicago Tribune*, August 17, 1997, sec. 1, p. 7.

50. Merrill Lynch, *Weekly Economic and Financial Commentary* (January 18, 1993): 3.

51. Bell and Thurow, *The Deficits*, pp. 117–19.

52. William Neikirk, "Bipartisan Sponsors Unveil Tax-Revamp Plan," *Chicago Tribune*, April 29, 1995, sec. 1, pp. 1 and 4.

53. See for example, Cobb and Daly, *For the Common Good*, p. 319, and Pechman, *Federal Tax Policy*, p. 253.

54. Pechman, *Federal Tax Policy*, p. 253.

55. Ibid., p. 254.

56. Clarence Page, *Chicago Tribune*, November, 25, 1995, sec. 1, p. 17.

57. Pechman, *Federal Tax Policy*, p. 63.

58. Ibid., p. 64.

59. David Wessel, "Again the Rich Get Richer, But This Time They Pay More Taxes," *Wall Street Journal*, February 23, 1998, p. A1.

60. Pechman, *Federal Tax Policy*, p. 68.

61. Ibid., pp. 40–41.

62. Ibid., p. 41.

63. Cobb and Daly, *For the Common Good*, p. 319.

64. *Chicago Tribune*, July 23, 1995, sec. 4, p. 2.

65. Cobb and Daly, *For the Common Good*, p. 320.

66. Charles Murray, *Losing Ground* (New York: Basic Books, 1984), pp. 150–51.

67. Ibid., p. 151.

68. Ibid., p. 152.

69. U.S. Office of Management and Budget, *Budget of the United States, Fiscal Year 1995*, p. 111.

70. Merrill Lynch, *Economic and Financial Chartbook* (April 1993), p. 11. See also Cobb and Daly, *For the Common Good*, p. 328.

71. Bell and Thurow, *The Deficits*, p. 113.

72. Pechman, *Federal Tax Policy*, p. 207.

73. Bell and Thurow, *The Deficits*, p. 113.

14

Putting It All Together

To prevent the current socioeconomic trends from leading to the dire State of the Union Address in 2050 that was expressed at the outset of this volume will require major changes in public policy. Neither traditional liberal nor conservative polices are the answer because they are both founded on false premises. Liberals see the poor primarily as victims of past injustice and an unfair socioeconomic system. They minimize the substantial inherent differences in capabilities among people and believe that society should strive for a more egalitarian outcome irrespective of a person's behavior. They stress the environment as the primary shaping influence on behavior and greatly discount the weight of genetic predispositions. They believe that a high level of social intervention will correct human deficiencies and wish to assign government that role. Ultimately, they lean toward holding society more responsible for an individual's fate than the individuals themselves. Liberals stress rights over responsibilities, and by breaking the linkage between a person's actions and the consequences of those actions, effectively remove a primary incentive for prudent, prosocial behavior.

Conservatives, on the other hand, tend to discount societal influences, placing greater weight on genetic endowment and individual responsibility. The poor are seen as victims of their own innate deficiencies of intelligence or character. People are believed to be free to determine their own behavior and their ultimate success or failure. For conservatives, the role of government is to see that people play the game by the rules, but not to help people over inequalities of circumstances. A pure meritocracy is thought to provide the necessary and sufficient incentives for the best and brightest to succeed, and their achievements will increase total output, ultimately providing a better life for everyone. It is alleged with dogmatic fervor that the free market is the answer to all human problems. For many conservatives, the ultimate goal of economic polices is growth in economic output (GDP). Like liberals, conservatives tend to stress rights over responsibilities, but their list of rights differ in almost every respect, with property rights being paramount.

The most serious shortcoming of many liberals and conservatives alike is their failure to assess the long-term consequences of their policies. ***Neither maximization of output nor arbitrary efforts to equalize the distribution of that output will result in optimizing human happiness over the long term.***

This volume presented socioeconomic policies predicated on a pragmatic alternative to the usual liberal/conservative dichotomy. While recognizing that in a deterministic world we are a function of our genetic endowment and environmental circumstances, it is acknowledged that people must be held responsible for their actions in order to provide the necessary motivation for prosocial behavior. Although meritocracy is necessary to provide incentives for people to maximize their capabilities, society has a responsibility to help those who strive and fall on their face. Public assistance should be limited to enabling a people to get back on their feet, rather than allowing them to retire from the race.

It was also noted that peoples' happiness depends to a large extent on how well they are able to fulfill their basic needs, but, unfortunately, society can create an ever-increasing list of insatiable wants. Moreover, it appears that after people meet their genetic needs, their happiness is a function of their perceived relative rather than absolute (objective) level of affluence. This is modified to the extent to which people feel that they can increase their relative position. If they believe that they are falling further behind in a relative sense and have no opportunity to improve their position, they will feel frustrated and unhappy.

Several areas requiring policy reform must be addressed simultaneously if we are to avoid condemning our children and grandchildren to a bleak future. The basis for the policy recommendations in this volume are:

A. The assumption that all people ultimately seek happiness and are motivated primarily by self-interest. There appears to be a limited form of altruism, however, particularly within a family or small social group.

B. Perceived self-interest can be modified through social conditioning, but the primary method of producing the social behavior that is beneficial to society is through empirically proven positive and negative incentives.

C. Social happiness will be optimized through a system of modified Rawlsian justice holding that all social goods should be distributed equally except when an unequal distribution works to a greater than proportional benefit to those most disadvantaged.

D. Socioeconomic policies must balance three objectives: (1) permitting people the possibility of satisfying their genetically determined needs to at least a limited extent; (2) promoting harmony between the needs of the individual and those of others in society; and (3) balancing the collective needs and wants of society with environmental constraints. This last objective is the same as saying we must balance the needs and wants of today's generation with the needs and wants of future generations. It is a particularly crucial criterion in formulating socioeconomic policies and, in effect, repudiates GDP growth as the primary measure of social success, since GDP is biased toward trading-off the welfare of future generations to maximize present consumption.

POLITICAL PRECONDITIONS

A host of recommendations have been proposed in this book to achieve these objectives. It is extremely doubtful, however, that our present political system will foster the type of leadership necessary to enact these recommendations. In the 1996 presidential election, less than 50 percent of the voting-age Americans cast ballets.[1] ***In the 1998 primaries, only 16.9 percent of eligible voters cast ballots, of which 9.5 percent were Democrats and 7.4 percent Republicans. This means that as little as 5 percent could determine the outcome of the average Democrat primary and 4 percent of the voters could determine the Republican primary.***[2] No doubt one reason for the poor turnout was that the economy was doing well, so voter apathy was greater. But according to Curtis Gan, director of the nonpartisan Committee for the Study of the American Electorate, "This is not, as some have claimed, a picture of a satisfied electorate. The nation is sliding into a condition in which its voting electorate will become almost exclusively the interested and the zealous, as the impulse to civic duty and engagement vanishes."[3] What we are witnessing is a population that has grown so large that most feel their voice cannot be heard and their vote doesn't matter. And they are right. In effect, since the population has tripled in this century, the individual's vote has depreciated by two-thirds. If the present population trend continues, by the middle of next century a vote will be worth about 15 percent of what it was at the beginning of the twentieth century. As the majority of people drop out of the political process and the special-interest groups take over, the United States will bear little resemblance to the democracy envisioned by our nation's founders. In fact, it might be hard to use the term *democracy* at all.

Another major factor for the low turnout was that many voters listened to both of the candidates and said, in effect, "none of these guys seem to have any real vision for America or even represent my interests." As one letter to the editor expressed it:

> The Democrats are hopeless prisoners of multiculturalism, affirmative action, and quotas determined to turn America into a Balkanized state of rival ethnic and racial groups. The Republicans have become the arch-defenders of the gloating rich, corporate welfare, and poverty wages, disguising them with fashionable slogans like restructuring, downsizing, and being competitive. Until a strong third party emerges, the social and economic deterioration of America will continue.[4]

While I might characterize the two parties a little differently, I think the writer expresses a view shared by millions of Americans. They once hoped that Ross Perot and the Reform Party would represent their views, but Perot had neither the knowledge of what socioeconomic policies were needed to revive the American Dream, nor the political savvy necessary to implement them. I believe that if a political candidate came along and advocated the socioeconomic recommendations discussed in this volume, he or she could galvanize the American people to once again feel proud to vote for the best candidate rather than simply the lesser of two evils.

There are three political prerequisites that must be implemented if we are ever to get a Congress with the courage and foresight to take the action necessary to stem the tide of national disintegration that is slowly sweeping across our nation. The purpose of all three political reforms is to curb the power of special interest groups. To achieve this objective will require (a) eliminating Political Action Committees (PACs), (b) enacting campaign financing reform, and (c) imposing term limits. Although such reforms merit far more discussion than I can provide here, let's take a moment to place them in perspective.

Eliminate Political Action Committees (PACs)

Years ago when votes were exchanged for money we called it bribery and prosecuted those involved. Today, we have effectively legalized bribery in the form of the Political Action Committee (PAC). The basis of any democracy should be "one person equals one vote," but PACs attempt to make the rule "one dollar equals one vote." If we are ever to end the inordinate weight of special-interest groups in determining public policy, we must end the role of PACs.

It is argued that simply contributing to a congressional campaign does not guarantee that the representative will vote the way the contributor wishes, and that is true. But if the contribution is significant, it does gain the contributor greater access to the representative and that person's staff to plead the contributor's case and, as such, provides a distinct and unfair advantage.

It is also argued that without PACs, and with limits on the amount of individual campaign contributions, the political minority on an issue is powerless. To the contrary, my contention is that with PACs, minorities without money have even less power. In fact, a good argument could be made that even the majority of Americans have little influence on political policy today.* If we want wealth to be the determinant of public policy, we are opting for a plutocracy instead of a democracy. To reverse the current trend to a de facto plutocracy requires that we eliminate PACs.

Limit Campaign Spending and Publicly Finance Bona Fide Candidates

In the 1996 election, campaign costs for the average House seat was $560,000; Senate expenditures ran an incredible $3.5 million per seat. In the 1996 elections, Republicans and Democrats raised $2.2 billion, doubling the amount raised in the 1992 elections. Of this amount, over $260 million was "soft money" (money given to the parties, not to candidates), which falls outside of the federal election law's donation limits and ban on corporate contributions.[6] The political parties can use this money to finance "issue advertising," a means of attacking the other candidate's position on the issues without directly promoting their own candidate. Moreover, at present, there are no constraints on how much an individual spends of his own money. The reason is a perverse ruling of the courts holding that restricting the amount of money an individual can spend on self-promotion himself is a violation of the right to free speech. Apparently, the courts have taken literally that age old adage, money talks!

The result has been one more step down the road to a plutocracy. In the 1996 Republican senatorial primary in Illinois multimillionaire Peter Fitzgerald defeated his opponent, Loletta Didrickson, by spending $7 million of his own money. Fitzgerald outspent Didrickson by a four-to-one margin.

To further constrain the dominating role of money in an election, limits should be placed on total campaign expenditures from whatever source, and the campaigns should be funded out of public funds. This suggestion is not as radical or expensive as it first sounds. This system works

---

*Strictly speaking, in any democracy, if individual representatives can be elected by a mere plurality, and the elected representatives can vote any way they want on a specific issue, there is no guarantee that the majority of citizens will get their way.

well in England, where in 1990 campaign expenditures were limited to $15,000 per candidate. Supposing that an average of $1.5 million is spent on each Senate race (split among qualifying candidates) and $200,000 per house race, funding the campaigns for the entire Congress out of public funds would cost less than $250 million per election. Complete funding of national elections for the next five years would cost less than one Seawolf submarine and would be far more essential to the future of our narion.[7]

Finally, as a prerequisite for media licensing, radio and television stations should be required to offer a certain amount of free air time to qualifying candidates (those who have collected the minimum number of signatures). The air time should be in significant blocks—at least fifteen minutes—not the misleading thirty-second sound bites that make winning public office more a function of successful negative advertising than of addressing the issues. In England, the law prohibits political advertising. What a relief that would be to all of us!

Enact Term Limitations

With less money to spend on an election, the name recognition of incumbents becomes an even more important asset. Combined with the capability of the incumbent to deliver the pork barrel benefits to his district, the official in office has advantages that are difficult to overcome. The longer incumbents hold their offices, the more difficult it is to defeat them.

Moreover, it is a human tendency not to change one's position once it is made public, despite new facts. A scholarly uncle of mine once asked me to find a professor in the social sciences who changed his basic theory after once having published his position. There probably are some, but I was unable to come up with one. Most people are naturally reluctant to admit they have been wrong, especially if their previous decision has resulted in the loss of human life. Yet, in order to ensure a steady stream of innovation necessary to reflect the incredibly fast pace of change in today's world, we need an opportunity to bring in fresh ideas.

Therefore, we should limit senators to *two terms of six years each*, and representatives to *three terms of four years each*. Note, I also recommend changing House terms from two to four years. Two years is just too short a time to achieve much. The first year a congressperson is learning the ropes and the second year he is running for office again. One of the biggest problems I encountered in my short stint in government was the inability of congresspeople to take the longer-term view. They were obsessed with how their votes on any piece of legislation would play with the people back home. Even four years is not very long to get anything substantive accomplished in the legislature. To protect against especially inept congressional representation, we could create an expedited recall procedure.

The Referendum

In addition to the three prerequisites discussed above, there is a fourth suggestion that bears further study. It would allow us to take back our nation from the special-interest groups and reestablish a true democracy. This could be done by enacting a referendum system similar to that established in California and employed in some other countries such as Switzerland. In that nation a petition signed by only 50,000 voters can insist that proposals submitted to the Parliament be submitted as a public referendum.[8] Of course, we would want to have substantially more than 50,000 signatures to place legislation in a national referendum, and state referendum criteria would differ depending on the population of the state. But as California found out, such a referendum system does get the public involved, much to the discomfort of the professional politicians and special-interest groups. You can be certain that the notion of referendum voting would be opposed with all the strength politicians could muster, which will demonstrate how much the concept of real democracy strikes terror in their hearts. It is time we have an open discussion on the merits of such a proposal. The only question is, where can we find a politician willing to open the issue?

Twelve Major Recommendations for the Twenty-first Century

With this all-too-brief discussion of the three key legislative prerequisites, we can now review the twelve areas for major socioeconomic policy reform. It is important to note that in some instances, making certain changes recommended in this volume while skipping others could actually make things worse. For example, to end welfare but still allow a large number of unskilled immigrants will eventually result in greater rather than less poverty, crime, and drug use. Similarly, to legalize drugs while not affording greater job opportunities and stepping up the national advertising campaign against drugs will result in more drug use. Allowing the use of crack while not demanding that crack mothers avoid or terminate pregnancy will result in more crack babies. And so on. In short, many of the recommended polices are complementary and must be viewed as such.

These, then, are the twelve major areas for policy reform:

1. GDP must be dropped as the principal measure of changes in social welfare. GDP is primarily just a measure of production. After a basic level of subsistence is met, the relationship between GDP and human happiness is doubtful at best. Happiness is a function of a person's ability to meet basic genetic needs and conditioned wants. The goal of society should be to provide the opportunity for all of its members to obtain employment and the basic necessities of life. Beyond this, there are many other indicators of a society's general welfare that bear a much closer relationship to human happiness than GDP. Some specific objectives to be measured in addition to average real per capita disposable income include, but are by no means limited to:

- changes in the distribution of income;
- unemployment (including those who have given up seeking work when no jobs are available) and underemployment rates;
- measures of health;
- average educational achievement (not simply years of education but measures of learning achievement);
- crime rates;
- divorce rates and the percentage of mother-only families;
- suicide rates, especially among the young;
- changes in pollution of air and water;
- impacts on wildlife, forests, wilderness, and wetlands.

2. Population growth must be stopped not only in the United States, but worldwide, because the demographics and economics of the international community are interconnected in a thousand ways. Contraception should be easily available to all women and men throughout the world at little or no cost. The goal of parents in most countries should be to have no more than two children. In overpopulated countries such as China or Bangladesh, the goal should be one child per family until the population is reduced to the long-term carrying capacity of the nation. It is in the interest of the United States that world population stabilize as quickly as possible. Therefore, we should provide at least $2 billion annually to help make family planning services available to every woman on the planet.

The new reproductive ethic must be that bearing children is not every woman's right; rather it is the moral responsibility of every man and woman to ensure that they do not have more children than they or the carrying capacity of their environment can support.

Sex education should involve in-depth discussions of the moral responsibility to avoid having children one cannot support or adequately care for. The use of abortion to terminate unwanted children should be subsidized and actively encouraged.

In the United States, both legal and illegal immigration must be drastically curtailed to achieve zero population growth. With almost four billion poor in the world, no amount of immigration to the United States will have a noticeable impact on world poverty. In fact, to the extent that we harvest the best and brightest from the less developed countries, we will retard LDC development. However, if the present rate of immigration to the United States continues, we can reliably predict a host of problems for our country, including a devastated environment, depressed wage rates, a decline in educational achievement, higher crime and interethnic conflicts, more congestion, and higher taxes to pay for increased infrastructure needs.

The foolish hope of multiculturalism must be seen for what it is: a trend to foster ethnic and racial segregation. We must return to the concept that has served America so well for the last two hundred years. The concept of a melting pot allowed people to gradually transcend their narrowly construed ethnic and cultural origins and view themselves and their fellow Americans in a larger cultural context. The present Balkanization into groups of hyphenated Americans is the first step toward the dissolution of America.

3. The idea of a sustainable economy must replace the belief that our economic goal is constantly increasing production of material goods. This does not preclude continued economic growth; but the composition of that growth must be comprised of more information and services, and less manufactured products that consume resources and generate pollution and waste as by-products. In the long run, exponential rates of physical goods production cannot continue in a finite world. Educational curriculum must include a basic understanding of ecology and the linkage to consumption. Incentives to conserve must be built into tax laws. Market-based solutions are most effective in reducing pollution, except for highly toxic substances where outright prohibition is the only answer.

4. The defense budget should continue to be reduced in real dollar terms. With the infrastructure of the United States unraveling at an unprecedented rate, it is time we turn to rebuilding America. It is ironic that, proportionally, the greatest increase in the building of schools, public buildings, highways, bridges, and numerous other public infrastructure projects occurred when America was the poorest, during the Great Depression. We have the resources to again rebuild America's crumbling infra-

structure, while at the same time reducing the national debt and long-term unemployment. But it requires rethinking our national priorities.

5. The national debt can and must continue to be reduced relative to GDP. To reduce the debt we can further reduce a defense program that still reflects a Cold War view of the world. Additionally, taxes on gasoline, tobacco, and alcohol should be raised significantly, as well as taxing decriminalized drugs. Tax deductions for more than two children, interest on mortgages over $200,000, and most other deductions should be eliminated (with the exception of a graduated disallowance for the gas tax). The remaining gap can be closed with a value added or consumption tax.

In addition to the national debt, the nation must enact policies that stimulate personal savings, remove incentives for corporations to leverage up their debt, and prevent a repeat of the savings and loan fiasco in the banking industry.

6. Although the present trade deficits are not a major economic problem, we need to rethink the whole purpose of trade, especially in terms of how it affects different segments of our society. It is not enough that free trade results in faster growth in GDP. We must have a plan for easing the dislocation of employment and prevent the rapid concentration of wealth that will accompany free trade. It is especially crucial that we coordinate our immigration policy with our trade policy so that we do not add low-skilled immigrants just when low-skilled jobs are migrating to other countries. Although we cannot turn back the clock on General Agreement on Trade and Tariffs (GATT), we should slow any further tariff reductions until we can absorb the impact of the tariff cuts of the last two decades.

7. One of the primary goals of society should be to provide work for all able-bodied people. Work projects such as a job corps are temporary expedients at best. To deal with long-term unemployment problems like those caused by major demographic changes or shifts in basic technology (such as the present transformation from the industrial to the information age), it should be a national objective that the labor supply does not grow faster than job creation. This is a primary reason for curbing immigration, especially of unskilled and poorly educated people.

A national database of available jobs, relocation allowances, and job retraining should be available to those involuntarily terminated for reasons other than performance. Public works jobs should supplement the job market to ensure that every person, even the disabled, have job opportunities, but all jobs should demand minimal performance requirements. The basic premise that must be understood by every member of society is: if you are capable of work and choose not to work, you will not eat. The flip side of this social contract must be: if people are willing to work, they should receive a living wage. Slow growth in the population and labor markets would assure this result.

Welfare must be tied to incentives to avoid having additional children. Long-term welfare should be phased out. Incentives such as fines, revocation of drivers licenses, or even jail terms may be necessary to encourage men to assume responsibility for family support and child-rearing. We must viscerally inculcate the ethical norm that it is immoral to have a child a parent cannot support either emotionally or financially. Pregnant girls under eighteen years of age should be forced to choose between adoption or abortion. Parents who are guilty of child abuse or neglect should be forced to give up their children to orphanages and denied any form of public aid unless they receive some form of contraception to prevent them from having additional children.

8. The secret to education reform is to return control of the classrooms to the teachers, and control of the schools to the principals. This means allowing them to maintain an atmosphere of care and discipline. It must also allow them to remove incorrigible children. It also requires standardized testing and teacher assessment. Teachers who are ineffective must be removed from their jobs.

Education expenditures must be redirected from colleges to preschools, grades K through 12, and vocational training. Preschool programs such as Head Start and early childhood development should be greatly expanded. Apprenticeship programs should be added to both high school and junior college curriculums. Affirmative action programs in higher education should be scrapped in favor of college entrance determined solely on the basis of achievement tests that measure the candidates' mastery of the requisite knowledge rather than the present IQ/aptitude tests.

To improve elementary educational results also requires greater parental involvement, a school year of at least 220 days, and sufficient time spent on homework.

Although the most important source of values is the home, the school should reinforce the basic prosocial values such as honesty, kindness, self-discipline, the keeping of one's word, temperance, and the like.

More education, welfare, and healthcare programs should be financed at the federal level to avoid the incentive for states to vie for business by reducing tax rates and, consequently, social services. Ideally, city and suburban taxing districts should be merged to equalize the revenues and benefits. However, since there is little chance of this occurring, moving the responsibility for collecting the taxes primarily to the federal level while providing local control of spending would provide more equality in social services. There is a precedent in this regard with the revenue sharing programs of the Nixon administration. However, it was not nearly enough, and was killed by suburban interests who objected to the redistribution of spending from the suburbs to central cities.

9. It is totally unacceptable that even those on welfare have access to healthcare while forty million working poor have no healthcare coverage. Universal health care must be a major objective of social policy. It can be achieved by a two-tiered healthcare structure that provides basic healthcare insurance to all while allowing those who wish to take out supplemental coverage or to pay for additional treatment on pay-for-service basis. The present options of HMOs, PPOs and MSAs are a step in that direction but at present fail to cover the working poor. One approach to provide them coverage would be to allow small business associations like the Farm Bureau or the National Restaurant Association to set up self-insurance plans like those that have let large corporations negotiate favorable healthcare insurance rates.

The rapid increase in medical technology to sustain life requires that the national goal should be to improve the quality of life rather than merely increasing longevity. There are a half-dozen major initiatives that could bring down the cost of health care, but the advance of technology can have the perverse result of spending extraordinary amounts of money in just keeping a person alive. Ultimately, therefore, rationing of medical procedures based upon the patient's prognosis and cost cannot be avoided. The purpose of medical treatment for terminal patients should be to reduce the pain and suffering associated with dying rather than to extend the dying process. Voluntary euthanasia should be the right of every adult. If terminally ill or comatose people are unable to make that decision for themselves, a person with power of attorney or a Medical Ethics Board should be permitted to make the decision for them.

10. Social Security can be saved by a small increase in payroll taxes and a slight decrease in the growth in benefits. However, the fundamental policy question that must be answered is whether Social Security is primarily an insurance system against unforeseen unemployment or disability, or a universal retirement plan. In either case, benefits should be tied to the poverty level and revenues must ultimately be sufficient to close the gap on a pay-as-you-go basis, just as with any other insurance policy. To rely on future growth to pay for future benefits is a pyramid scheme that could result in the eventual collapse of the system.

To provide a more accurate perspective on the budget and to prevent using Social Security surpluses to finance other federal programs, the Social Security Trust Fund should be maintained separately from the rest of the federal budget. Whatever solution is decided, it is essential that we begin to solve the problem today; the longer we wait the greater the problem becomes.

11. To permanently reduce crime rates, the first step is to reduce the incentives for criminality. Victimless acts should be decriminalized. Since over 50 percent of all crime is drug related, decriminalizing and controlling the sale of drugs would not only reduce the crime rate *de facto*, but the fall in the price of drugs would remove a prime incentive to traffic in drugs. Decriminalization should be accompanied by a massive education and advertising program to discourage the use of all drugs, including the most dangerous drugs: alcohol and tobacco. All forms of advertising for alcohol, tobacco, or any dangerous and addictive drug should be prohibited.

12. The tax system should be meaningfully reformed. The corporate income tax should be dropped since it is simply passed on to other groups. Different treatment of interest and dividends biases corporate decisions and increases corporate risk. Capital gains should be indexed for inflation and then treated as ordinary income for tax purposes. Taxes on gasoline, tobacco, and alcohol could generate an additional $125 billion a year. Additional government savings could be realized and additional tax revenue could be generated by legalizing and taxing illicit drugs.

A value-added or consumption tax should be instituted that would raise sufficient revenue to reduce the national debt, discourage consumption in favor of saving and investment, and be consistent with our goal of establishing a sustainable society. However, given the political bias against such a tax and its complexity, an alternative to be considered is a graduated income tax starting at 10 percent for families above the poverty line and topping out at 75 percent for the wealthiest people. Stiff inheritance taxes should be levied above the present $1 million deduction to avoid the concentration of power that accompanies concentration of wealth and to help level the playing field for succeeding generations.

Given the nature of the political process to always deal with crises rather than the underlying trends that ultimately will create a crisis, I am not optimistic that even if these policies were generally agreed upon, Congress could be prompted to take the action necessary to implement them. Given the comprehensiveness and radical nature of some of these policies, some might even criticize this entire effort as quixotic. It might also be argued that more research is needed to test the efficacy of many of these policies.

To this latter concern I would readily agree, and encourage undertaking of such research.

With regard to the former criticism, I have little doubt that as the current trends reach the crisis stage, the appropriate policy decisions will be made. However, it would be nice if just once we would anticipate the problem and avoid much unnecessary grief and suffering. It is analogous to World War II. Although thousands of books have been written on the heroic efforts on the part of America and our allies to win that horrendous conflict—at the cost of over 40 to 50 million lives lost on all sides—the epic tragedy might have been avoided at the Treaty of Versailles, as John Maynard Keynes foresaw at the time. Similarly, the proper polices enacted today can avoid much more draconian policies, and the commensurate amount of pain for society, tomorrow.

NOTES

1. Frank James, "Big Labor, Vows More Spending in '98 to Defeat GOP Candidates," *Chicago Tribune*, November 9, 1996, sec. 1, p. 2.

2. Michael Tackett, "Few Eligible Voters Care Any Longer, Study Finds," *Chicago Tribune*, June 19, 1998, sec. 1, p. 6.

3. Ibid.

4. Michael Wertanen, letter to the Green Bay Press-Gazette, October 23, 1996.

5. New York Times News Service, "Campaign Costs Soar to Record $2.2 Billion," *Chicago Tribune*, November 25, 1997, sec. 1, p. 6.

6. Phil Kuntz, "Money Poured into War Chests for '96 Election," *Wall Street Journal*, January 13, 1997, p. C 14.

7. Ibid., p. 212.

8. Sir James Goldsmith, *The Trap* (New York: Carroll and Graf, Inc., 1993), p. 72.

Appendix A

Summary of *The Final Superstition* and *The Science of Morality*

The Final Superstition[1] demonstrated that we cannot rely upon either the pronouncements of those who pretend to speak for God or the dictums of texts such as the Bible or the Koran as guides to ethical behavior or social policy. Quite the contrary, since religious teachings reflect the beliefs and needs of ancient societies, they are oftentimes inappropriate for dealing with the problems of today. Exponential population growth, genetic engineering, environmental degradation, loss of species diversity, and artificial prolongation or termination of life, are just a few of the issues never faced by ancient peoples and their religions. Therefore, at best, they are unreliable guides for resolving the key moral issues of today.

The time-binding nature of religious dogma will always hamper the ability of religions to properly formulate appropriate moral responses in a dynamic environment. Nevertheless, ***religions might, if kept in the proper perspective, provide a useful vehicle for*** transmitting ***moral values and guidance arrived at by empirical analysis.*** Just as with Aesop's fables, religious myths can be useful to illustrate moral propositions. Religious myths such as the story of Jesus can also portray moral ideals like sacrificing our short-term self-interest for the good of our fellow humans. Such inspiring stories can viscerally transmit values to modify human behavior to the benefit of all members of society.

The second volume, *The Science of Morality*, develops a basic framework for ascertaining appropriate moral norms and socioeconomic policies. It posited the following conclusions:

1. All hypotheses require verification; yet absolute truth is unattainable. The relative degree of certainty regarding a statement or proposition depends upon the amount of empirical evidence, and the degree to which a new proposition fits with the existing body of knowledge. The scientific method of assessing propositions has been the most productive procedure for advancing our knowledge of reality and, although unable to produce certainty, can provide the basis for action.

2. All human choice is a function of the relative motivations affecting the individual at the time the choice is made. These motivations are affected by genetic and environmental factors, both conscious and unconscious. In essence, therefore, humans neither possess free will nor in the final analysis can they be said to be truly morally responsible for their actions in the philosophical sense. However, ***it is precisely because all actions are determined by motivations that society must hold people responsible for their actions and provide effective rewards and punishments.*** In so doing, society provides the necessary motivations for individuals to behave in a prosocial manner, i.e., for the good of the whole rather than their own narrow self-interest.

3. The father of neoclassical economics, Alfred Marshall, wrote that "The economist, like everyone else must concern himself with the ultimate aims of man."[2] As much as it may infuriate those who wish to romanticize or spiritualize the human species, we find that ***the ultimate ends of humans are the same as any other animal: survival of the species and happiness (or at least avoidance of pain).*** However, there are times when these two goals conflict, and one or the other may take precedence.[3] At present, the goal of increasing human happiness requires providing incentives to constrain humankind's genetic predisposition to procreate.

To achieve the two ultimate goals of species survival and personal happiness, humans are driven to pursue two genetically determined strategic objectives: ***dominance and security.*** Each goal necessitates the pursuit of both strategies to some degree, but, in general, males primarily pursue dominance over other males to obtain females for mating, and females primarily pursue security to protect themselves and their children. To achieve the objectives of dominance and security, all people pursue one or more of three tactics: ***power, achievement, and group affiliation.*** These tactics are not always consciously chosen, but have evolved as basic genetic needs. Again both men and women share these needs to varying degrees. Individuals adopt a variety of career roles and personal behaviors to fulfill their genetic needs. The careers and behaviors selected are a function of genetic capabilities and cultural influences.

4. Saying that all people seek happiness is, in a sense, the same as saying that they each seek to promote their self-interest. Economists and sociologists from the time of Adam Smith have recognized that self-interest is the basis of all economic activity. Sociologist Max Weber wrote that "All economic activity in a market economy is undertaken and carried through by individuals acting to provide their own ideal or material interests."[4] He goes on to add that an economic system organized on a socialistic basis is no different than a capitalist system in this respect, even though the decision making may be centralized.

It would be a mistake, however, to argue that self-interest equates with narrowly construed selfishness or implies that we never care about the needs or desires of other people. The foolishness of such a position can be easily demonstrated with the illustration of the character Robinson Crusoe. As the only person on the island, he could do whatever he liked. Despite this unlimited freedom, he was overjoyed to run into the man he called Friday. However, as soon as he meets Friday, Crusoe's freedom is limited somewhat. He cannot now simply act in anyway he pleases, but must consider the needs of Friday as well, and Crusoe must do so for his own self-interest. It is not simply that Friday can provide work to make Crusoe's life easier, but rather that Friday offers him companionship, answering a need that is intrinsic to the nature of humankind. Even if Crusoe was one of those aberrant personalities who does not desire companionship, there are still many other benefits that Friday can offer, such as care and protection in the face of sickness or a common enemy. So it is in Crusoe's self-interest to consider the needs of Friday as well. A sick or vengeful companion would not serve Crusoe's interests as well.

As a practical matter, there are conflicts of interest in the everyday lives of each of us. Psychologist Karen Horney lists three basic conflicts:

- the desire for material goods is so stimulated that it can never be satisfied;
- aggressiveness is so pronounced that it cannot be reconciled with brotherhood (and cooperation);
- expectations of unconstrained freedom cannot be squared with the multitude of restrictions and responsibilities that restrain us all.[5]

Reconciling these conflicts should be the primary goal of socioeconomic policies.

Adam Smith's economic theory assumes that the invisible hand of self-interest might work to the benefit of all if each person in a transaction possessed equal power and equal information. But, ***Smith also recognized that***

self-interest must be tempered by moral sentiments: an empathy for the feeling of others. However, the studies of social biologists such as Konrad Lorenz, E. O. Wilson, and Nikolaas Tinbergen indicate that the natural expression of empathy is strongest within a family or tribe and weakens when the relationship among individuals is more distant.

The danger of allowing individuals to follow their perceived self-interest can become especially disastrous when the benefits accrue to one person while the costs are spread among the public at large, as, for instance, in the case of pollution. Each person following his/her own perceived best interests leads to a what ecologist Garrett Hardin termed "the tragedy of the commons," i.e., the destruction of our shared environment.

The importance of creating a congruence of interests among unrelated individuals was recognized as far back as 1768, when John Dickinson, a delegate to the Continental Congress, wrote, "A people is traveling fast to destruction when individuals consider their interests as distinct from the public. Such notions are fatal to the country and themselves."[6] More recently, economist Hazel Henderson observed that "in a large enough time/space framework, individual, group, and species self-interest are identical."[7] The problem is that the time/space framework may lie beyond the lifetime of an individual or, perhaps more importantly, beyond the scope of the individual's vision.

Important limitations to the benefits of the pursuit of narrowly construed self-interest are not recognized by some of the most adamant proponents of the self-interest view, such as Ayn Rand. However, biological evidence is offered by the social biologists that altruistic behavior—at least extending to members of the extended family and/or tribe—offers a selective advantage to the group. Additionally, behavioral psychologists have demonstrated that people can be habituated to certain forms of behavior so that they will experience extreme mental discomfort when not conforming to conditioned moral values such as truthfulness, courage, benevolence, obedience to authority, and the like. In a broad sense, it might be said that such people are acting in their own self-interests by avoiding the mental distress (or incurring the psychological pleasure) of practicing certain forms of behavior. In this way, the interest of the individual might be brought into congruence with the needs of other members of society. I refer to this seemingly altruist behavior as ***conditioned self-interest.***

5. Human happiness requires balancing the needs of the individual, society, and the environment. In short, human happiness, thus, depends on three harmonious relationships:

- Individuals must balance their short-term and long-term biological needs and conditioned wants.
- The individual's biological needs and conditioned wants must be balanced, to the extent possible, with needs of others in society.
- The aggregate needs of society must be fulfilled in a manner that is in harmony with long-term environmental sustainability.

This last harmony is based upon the requirement of intergenerational equity, since the potential for happiness of future generations is in large part a function of the environment they will inherit. These *three harmonies* become the guiding standards for determining the appropriateness of ethical norms and socioeconomic policies.

6. As an aid in assessing whether a specific action will advance the three harmonies, and thus can be judged as morally desirable, it was concluded that the best chance of optimizing happiness for humankind over the long run is to establish a general guideline (as contrasted to an absolute principle) that would be selected by people who did not know what their particular status in life might be (with regard to income, race, age, health, among other characteristics), and who wanted to ensure the greatest chance that they would be happy under a variety of possible circumstances. The guideline selected is a modified form of a principle of justice proposed by Harvard philosopher John Rawls. ***Modified Rawlsian justice*** holds that ***"All social primary goods (liberty and opportunity, income and wealth, and the basis of self-respect) are to be distributed equally unless an unequal distribution of any or all these goods is to the greater {relative} advantage of the least favored."***[8] I added the qualifier *relative* because people's happiness is influenced in large part by their perception of their situation relative to the rest of society. It is especially important to note that a Rawlsian distribution does not preclude a meritorious distribution of rewards, since tying rewards to effort can benefit all members of society. For example, rewarding additional effort through more income is one way to ensure that each person provides the greatest value to society. If we paid doctors the same as clerical workers, many talented people would decide that the extra effort in becoming a doctor was not worth it. Similarly, if the benefits of not working are close to the benefits of working (such as welfare compared to the minimum wage), many people would choose not to work. Hence, Rawlsian justice would not result in equal outcomes in income or any other social good, including human happiness. Nevertheless, as demonstrated in *The Science of Morality*, its application might increase human happiness for most, if not all, people.

In the United States, even though the middle class has made some modest gains in income during the last twenty-five years primarily through employment of a second wage earner (the wife), the middle class percentage of total wealth has been steadily declining relative to the top 1 percent of the population who now control 36 percent of the nation's total private wealth.[9] Conversely, the wealth of the bottom 20 percent of the population continues to drop in both absolute and relative terms. Consequently, if the goal of socioeconomic policy is to increase human happiness—as I argue it should be—present policies have failed to do so for the vast majority of Americans.

An objection to the Rawlsian criteria is that it ignores the different psychological personalities of the people making decisions from behind Rawls's veil of ignorance. For example, high-risk personalities might assume that others are like them and therefore would select a criterion that the winner takes all. They are willing to gamble that they will be one of the winners, even with the full realization that they might be a big loser. However, while admitting that there would be those willing to establish such a criteria, I believe that the vast majority of people would opt for criteria that would mitigate the extremes of success or failure; if this were not so, the insurance business would not be the huge industry it is.

Unlike utilitarianism, modified Rawlsian justice would not sacrifice the happiness of a disadvantaged minority to increase the happiness of the majority. Nevertheless, in a democracy it is necessary that the majority want a Rawlsian distribution if we are to select socioeconomic policies to support it. That has not been the case during the last two decades, and it is not at all clear why Americans seem to vote for greater inequality of income than would seem to be justified by the benefits of a meritocracy, or that has been selected by the other Western industrialized nations.

7. Rights are a creation of society to help foster the three harmonies and enable individuals to attain happiness. The U.S. Declaration of Independence posits that it is a "self-evident" truth that "men are endowed by their creator with certain unalienable Rights, that among these are Life, Liberty, and the Pursuit of Happiness." (It could be argued that this is somewhat redundant since life and at least some liberty are necessary for happiness.) Are any rights truly "unalienable"? *The Science of Morality* argues that since rights are created by society, in the final analysis there are no absolute or inalienable rights. This is an extremely important conclusion since in recent years everyone wants society to guarantee their freedom to perform some action by claiming it as an á priori right. As Cass R. Sunstein, professor of jurisprudence at the University of Chicago, points out, such claims to certain rights are often "conclusions masquerading as reasons."[10]

If, as a society, we decide to establish certain rights as fundamental, it is because we believe that happiness is unattainable without such rights. However, it is not difficult to show that under certain conditions any predetermined right might actually interfere with the happiness of at least some members of society, because rights often conflict. Therefore, in deciding on specific socioeconomic policies, the concept of rights per se is of little value. As a society, we may wish to deem as rights the most basic policies required to increase happiness and to establish the priority of policies when they conflict. But although we may wish to invest a given policy with the status of a right at a certain time, in no case will these rights be considered absolute, since a change in world environment might necessitate a revision in what are considered rights. The most obvious example would be in a defensive war where to preserve a society many rights have to be temporarily suspended. We also see this need to revise rights in our discussion of reducing dangerous population growth that threatens the well-being of future generations.

8. Finally, *The Science of Morality* explains that to get people to behave in ways that promote the three harmonies, moral education is of value but, by itself, is insufficient. Just knowing what is ethically right is no guarantee that a person will act in that manner. If people act to maximize their self-interest, it is essential that they are encouraged to do so through appropriate rewards and punishments. The primary purpose of this present volume is to assess those socioeconomic policies that encourage the kind of behavior that will lead to an increase in human happiness in the long run by fostering the three harmonies mentioned earlier.

The one overriding perspective of all three volumes is that the conclusions derived are based upon the strength of the evidence rather than any preconceived ideological or doctrinaire viewpoints. Hence, the operative words are ***empirical*** and ***pragmatic***.

NOTES

1. Joseph Daleiden, *The Final Superstition* (Amherst, N.Y.: Prometheus Books, 1994), p. 245.

2. Alfred Marshall, quoted by John Kenneth Galbraith, foreword to *The Affluent Society* (New York: New American Library, 1958).

3. Admittedly this is an anthropocentric view of the universe and some might object that such a view places the interests of all other species second to humans. However, this does not mean that we can be calloused or indifferent to other species or nature in all of its forms. Human happiness ultimately depends in

no small measure on our respect for, and treatment of, all species. But there is no reason to place the interest of any species higher than, or even equal to, humankind. It might be argued from a cosmic perspective that there is no justification for this view. An unconscious cosmos is indifferent as to whether humans or cockroaches inherit the earth, or for that matter, whether the earth continues to exist. But every species on earth places its interests above every other species. Humans are no different in this regard. This is not to say that humans might not act differently regarding other species for a variety of reasons. For example, it might be shown that deliberate inflicting of suffering on another species might result in a more calloused attitude to suffering of humans. But it is still concern for human interests that is the rationale for humane treatment of other animals.

4. Max Weber, *Economy and Society*, vol. 1, eds. Guenther Roth and Claus Wittich (Berkeley, Calif: University of California Press, 1978), p. 202.

5. Hazel Henderson, *Creating Alternative Futures: The End of Economics* (New York: Perigee Books, 1978), p. 25.

6. Quoted by Henderson, *Creating Alternative Futures*, p. 12.

7. Henderson, *Creating Alternative Futures*, p. 152.

8. John Rawls, *A Theory of Justice* (Cambridge, Mass: Harvard University Press, Belknap Press, 1971), p. 303.

9. *Chicago Tribune*, May 23, 1995, sec. 1, p. 16.

10. Cass R. Sunstein, *The New Republic* (September 2, 1991): 34. Quoted by Amitai Etzioni, *The Spirit of Community* (New York: Crown Publishers, 1993), p. 7.

Appendix B

An Abbreviated History of Post World War II U.S. Defense Spending

If we were to examine the U.S. budget by federal agency, we would get a misleading notion of how much is spent on defense each year because many defense dollars are included in the budgets of agencies other than the Defense Department. For example, at one time almost half of the Department of Energy's budget went for developing the plutonium for nuclear weapons. For this reason, the U.S. budget must be examined on a functional, rather than departmental basis. The "functional budget" picks up many additional defense-related dollars, but still fails to capture all the spending related to defense. For example, "International Security Assistance" is military aid to allies—primarily Israel—yet it is not included in defense expenditures. Whether we spend the money or give it to an ally to spend, the dollars should be included under defense, as should expenditures for "foreign information and exchange activities," which also involves national security. It is difficult, if not impossible, to ferret out all the budgetary pigeonholes for hiding defense dollars, from weather satellites that also serve as spy satellites and thus are charged to the Department of Agriculture, to a sizable portion of the General Science, Space, and Technology budget dedicated to military research.

The biggest omission is the exclusion of Veterans Benefits, which were about $43 billion in 1998 and will continue rising well into the next century as aged veterans seek hospital and medical care. These costs are far in excess of the Medicare dollars veterans would have received if they had been employed in the private sector, since many private-sector companies provide medical insurance for their retired employees. Excluding such future costs from defense expenditures would be exactly the same as a company excluding the cost of pensions and benefits from its income statement, except that a private corporation could never get its auditors to overlook such a blatant omission.

Moreover, I've estimated that about 40 percent of the present interest on the national debt is due to the increase in defense spending during the 1980s. Again, when calculating the profits on a line of business, it is common accounting convention to charge the business for any debt it incurred. According to a Center for Defense Information study in 1992, ***adding in the appropriate share of interest, veterans benefits and all the hidden defense costs would raise the defense estimates by 42 percent.***[1] My own calculations came very close to this. In the early 1990s, the federal budget erroneously attempted to portray defense as being about 21 percent of the total budget. However, when the proper costs were added up, it was about 30 percent.

Frequently, supporters of increase defense spending will attempt to relate defense to total GDP and point out that defense spending defined in traditional terms has dropped from 14.6 percent of GDP at the end of the Korean War to 3.7 percent in 1995 and, based upon current projections, will decline to about 3 percent by the year 2000.[2] However, ***there is no reason to believe that defense spending should rise or fall relative to the size of the national economy.*** It is not like education or healthcare expenses that are, in part, a function of growing population or shifts in the demographic mix. Rather, defense expenditures should be a function of the spending of potential enemies. Looked at from this perspective, we can afford to continue cutting defense spending since, at present, the United States spends more on defense than the next six countries combined, all but two of which are our allies. In 1996, we spent about twice as much as Russia and China combined.[3]

Let's examine America's defense spending pattern since World War II. When adjusted for inflation and defined correctly, military spending has remained relatively constant since the Korean War. An examination of defense expenditures adjusted for inflation since the end of World War II reveals the following pattern:

Figure B.1[4]
U.S. Defense Expenditures, 1940–2000
(Constant 1992 Dollars)

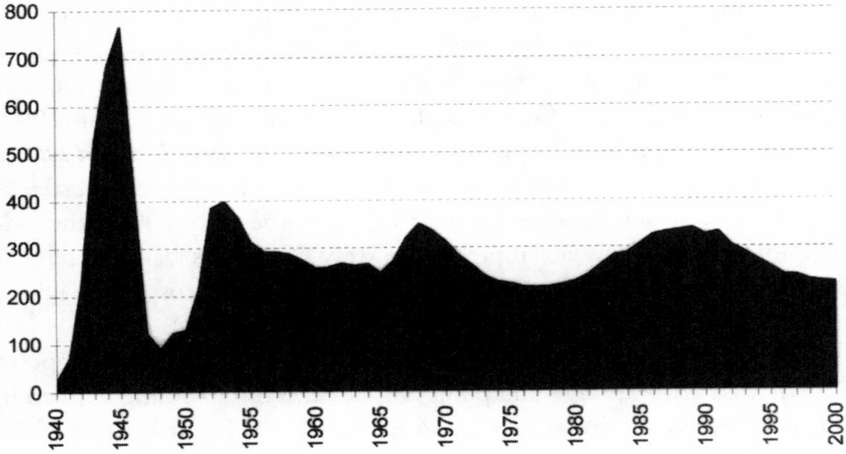

As figure B.1 shows, the Korean War quickly reversed the post World War II cuts in defense spending. After the Korean War, spending was gradually cut by about one-third in constant dollars, but then began slowly to increase even prior to Vietnam. From 1954 until 1966, the level of spending in constant dollars remained at about 80 percent of the Korean War level. The Vietnam era increased spending to 90 percent of the peak Korean War level by 1968. After Vietnam there was a slight peace dividend with expenditures falling to 70 percent of the Korean War level. However, during the Reagan era expenditures soared, until by 1988 defense spending adjusted for inflation was higher than the level of the Vietnam War and, although the Korean War expenditures reached a higher peak, it was only for a couple of years, not a complete decade as in the 1980s.

Even after adjusting for inflation, ***defense expenditures for the period 1982 to 1992 exceeded the total amounts expended on the Korean and Vietnam wars combined and was only 5 percent less than the amount spent between 1940 to 1950, which, of course, included all of World War II.*** This was the consequence of an arms race that ultimately bankrupted the Soviet Union and, as will be shown, seriously undermined the American economy as well. Of particular interest is that ***unlike the 90 percent defense cutbacks that occurred after World War II, the end of the Cold War saw no such dramatic decrease. The military spent $1.8 trillion in the five years before the collapse of the Soviet Union in 1990, and $1.5 trillion in the five years after.***[5]

During this period, while the United States was spending 5 to 7 percent of its GDP on defense, Germany was spending only a little over 3 percent and Japan a very frugal 1 percent of their respective GDPs on defense. For forty years, these two nations were slowly closing the technology gap by focusing on research and development to increase productivity and develop consumer products that qualitatively matched or exceeded American products, and at cheaper prices. For forty years, America was so concerned with the possibility of the Soviets catching up to us militarily, that we all but ignored the fact that the Germans, Japanese, and soon many other European countries, were overtaking us economically in terms of per capita GDP. Even as late as 1994 almost 50 percent of the U.S. defense budget was spent to protect our primary competitors: Germany, Japan, Korea, and Taiwan.[6] For this reason former senator Eugene McCarthy argued that it would be fair if we were reimbursed by means of a tariff on imports from those countries to cover these defense expenditures. (Only Japan pays us an amount comparable to the U.S. cost of defending that country.)

The Impact of Defense Spending on U.S. International Competitiveness

By the late 1980s, America's ballooning national debt could no longer be ignored. The toughest kid on the block was on defense steroids. He was muscle-bound but had none of the economic agility to win in the world marketplace. The United States had won the Cold War but was losing the economic war. In every year between 1951 and 1991 military outlays exceeded the combined profit of U.S. corporations.[7] Countries like Germany and Japan were spending a fraction of what we were on defense. But instead of cutting back, we urged our allies to spend more. They wisely never saw the need, but by 1988 Japan had been pressured to increase its military expenditures slightly, from 10 percent of the U.S. average per capita to 14 percent.

More money spent on defense meant less money for consumer product research. A U.S. Congressional Budget Office study showed that between 1984 and 1988, research and development outlays for private U.S. business were growing at one-half the rate of the a decade earlier.[9] Almost one-half of all research[10] and about 70 percent of federal research was defense related.[11] By the end of the 1980s, the much smaller country of Japan was spending more than the U.S. on nondefense research.[12] It should not have been surprising, then, that in 1987 no U.S. company was among the top three recipients of U.S. patents; all were Japanese: Canon, Inc.; Hitachi Ltd.; and Toshiba Corp. While many of the best and brightest of American

Figure B.2
Expenditures per Taxpayer, 1983 & 1995[8]

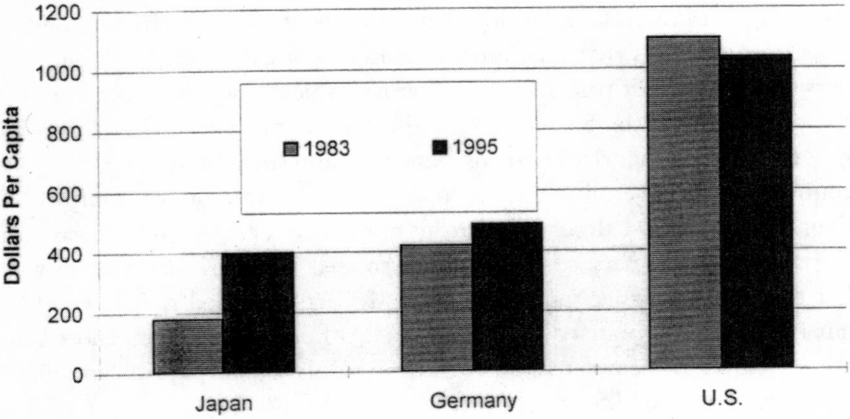

scientists and engineers were being offered lucrative defense jobs, a major shortage of college professors in these disciplines developed. In 1988 there were over 1,800 vacancies in U.S. engineering faculties. In the mid-Eighties defense industries were employing a significant proportion of the nation's brain power:[13]

Mathematicians	30%
Physicists	25%
Aero-astronautical engineers	40%
Computer programmers	11%

With all these resources devoted to defense, it is no wonder that we lost our competitive edge for a while and had to rely on immigration and increased work visas for high-tech employees to make up the difference. In the 1990s, the cutbacks in defense have produced a surplus of engineers and scientists in many fields, and we are quickly moving again to the technological forefront. Still, Simon Ramo, a high-tech entrepreneur and advisor to President Reagan, has estimated that the United States will reach the level of technological sophistication by the year 2000 that could have been attained in 1980 had military research and development been redirected to those areas of science and technology promising the most economic progress.[14]

U.S. Monetary and Fiscal Policy to Support Defense

The brain drain on private R & D and the education of future scientists and engineers is by no means the worst impact of the post World War II military build-up. To understand the full impact of the defense buildup on the U.S. economy, we have to go back to 1965. That was when Lyndon Johnson decided to escalate America's involvement in Vietnam while simultaneously expanding social programs. To do so he had only two legitimate options: raise taxes or run a budget deficit and borrow money. Since neither were going to be popular with the voters, his administration hit on a third option, which was not so legitimate: expand the money supply.* The repercussions were exactly as Robert Heilbroner and other economists had predicted: "Short of a tax program or direct controls of various sorts, it is doubtful that the militarization of the economy could progress very far without serious price rises in every sector."[15] Whenever the money supply increases faster than the economy's ability to produce goods and services for a sustained period, people will bid up prices, i.e., inflation will result.

The practice of devaluing money to finance the military is an age-old trick that was practiced as far back as the emperors of Rome. They did it by debasing coins to get more coins from a given amount of gold and silver. During World War I, such a policy contributed to the collapse of Czarist Russia in 1917.

Inflation in the United States had been running under 2 percent through 1965. From 1965 until 1973, it increased steadily until reaching 6.2 percent. Washington began to get worried about the political repercussions and the Nixon administration officials were looking for someone to blame. Labor unions were singled out for demanding wage increases above the increase in national productivity. But labor, like everyone else, was just trying to keep up with inflation to prevent real wages from declining. It is clear that inflation had been initially sparked by "demand-pull" rather than "cost-push."† However once the spiral had begun, no one had a clear idea how to stop it.

In 1973, the first of the oil shocks hit when the oil cartel cut back pro-

---

*Technically, the White House did not even have this power, since the Federal Reserve System controls the money supply and is independent of the federal government, but this was one time when they cooperated with the president, much to the nation's subsequent regret.

†Demand-pull refers to the situation when the aggregate demand for goods and services increases faster than the economy's capability to produce them. Cost-push refers to the situation where increases in wage rates or other factor costs exceed the increase in productivity. In either case the end result is the same: businesses raise prices and an inflationary spiral is begun.

duction and forced oil prices to jump 33 percent. The nation was ill-prepared to deal with it. Energy conservation had been urged by environmentalists for many years, but their advice fell on deaf ears. We had become so dependent on imported oil, that the oil embargo, short as it was, coming on the back of an inflationary spiral, kicked off by the combination of defense buildup and increased spending on social programs, pushed up consumer prices by 11 percent in 1974.

Defense spending continued to exacerbate the inflationary spiral in more subtle ways. First, the Defense Department was an easy mark for the defense manufacturers to more than pass on their higher costs. Dr. Helen Caldicott notes that more than 90 percent of all contract dollars were not awarded on the basis of price competition. Twenty-five percent of the contracts were awarded on a cost-plus basis where there is no incentive to hold down costs or improve productivity.[16] The free market system so hallowed by conservatives was quietly scuttled when it came to military procurement. Consequently, a 1980 report of the Defense Science Board indicated that inflation in weapons systems was twice the rate of inflation for the economy at large.[17] Additionally, the premium wages that could be paid by defense contractors for both professional and blue-collar workers added yet another inflationary stimulus, since other employers had to match those wage rates to hang on to their best technical employees. The inflated wage rates also impaired America's international competitiveness for over a decade.

Once inflationary expectations are built into the mind-set of a nation, it is extremely hard to shake them. One brutal but effective way is to dramatically cut the money supply, exactly the opposite policy employed by the Johnson administration (or more precisely, the Federal Reserve Bank at the instigation of the administration) that started the inflationary spiral. The problem is that just as an expansive money supply will overheat economic growth, contracting the money supply will ultimately lead to a recession. However, this is exactly what the Federal Reserve did in the late 1970s. Federal Reserve Chairman Paul Volcker decided that a recession was better than runaway inflation and so the Fed deliberately induced the 1980–82 recession. Then, not wanting to rekindle inflation by again rapidly expanding the money supply, but needing to pull the economy back out of the recession, the Reagan administration readily bought into the fanciful notion of supply side economics.

Actually, by expanding defense spending while cutting taxes, Reagan was practicing basic Keynesian economics, but with a vengeance unimagined by Keynes.* Keynes once said that to stimulate the economy, it did

*It should be noted that during this time, while Reagan was expanding defense spending, the Democrat-controlled Congress exacerbated the problem by rapidly expanding expenditures for health care.

not matter what the government chose to spend its money on, even hiring people to dig holes and fill them up again would do the trick. However, in suggesting that deficit spending might serve to stimulate demand to pull a nation out of a recession, Keynes never imagined that a country would be so foolish as to continue to run ever-increasing budget deficits for more than a decade after the economy was growing again. Whereas Johnson had adopted the dishonest policy of printing money, Reagan simply borrowed the money, effectively writing IOUs for the next generation to pay. When the economy slid into the 1990–91 recession, the size of the federal deficits prevented the use of further fiscal stimulus to aid the recovery. With only monetary easing—primarily lowering interest rates—to stimulate the economic recovery, it was not surprising that the initial years of the recovery phase were the slowest of any post World War II recession.

With the economy operating so far below capacity in 1990 and 1991, there was no fear that an expansive monetary policy would be inflationary. However, the lost increases in productivity for a decade that resulted from diversion of so much intellectual and investment capital to defense will haunt us for years to come. In particular, the diversion of investment to defense resulted in a continual balance of trade deficit with Japan because (a) Japan was investing in better and cheaper methods of production while we were investing in better missiles, and (b) Japan was collecting fat interest payments from the treasury bonds it bought to finance the U.S. defense buildup. In addition, the diversion to defense forced cutbacks in the physical infrastructure for America, which for more than a decade has been deteriorating faster than our willingness to replace it. Finally, in order to remain competitive, we had to hold the lid on growth in real wages. Thus, for twenty-five years the standard of living for the average American was declining relative to our major trading partners.

The key point is that the defense buildup of the past 40 years, and the dishonest way of financing that buildup, was one of the major causes of the slow growth in the economy and particularly of wage rates since the end of the Vietnam War until the mid–1990s.

WHATEVER HAPPENED TO THE "PEACE DIVIDEND"?

With the fall of the Soviet Union some of the more naive political pundits began speaking of the peace dividend—the money that could now be cut from the defense budget. ***But there could be no peace dividend for the simple reason that the money for the growth in defense in the 1980s was borrowed in the first place.***

Moreover, further cuts in military spending are at present unlikely. At a 1990 conference on developing computer-based planning processes I half-jokingly asked some Army brass if they were worried about their jobs with the breakup of the USSR. They replied that it was the furthest thing from their minds. "There will always be an enemy," I was reassured. "With Russia out of the way we can now turn our attention to Iran and Iraq, and then there are all those nasty drug dealers and Communists in South America." Within ten months after this prophetic conversation, the United States had invaded Iraq and had offered military assistance to Colombia and Peru to fight the drug cartels (which fortunately was rebuffed). One U.S. senator declared that the break-up of the Soviet Union had left the world in an even more precarious position than before and will necessitate an increase in defense spending. This comment came despite the removal of one million Soviet troops from Eastern Europe and an 80 percent reduction in Soviet military expenditures.[18] But it is not surprising. Both Republican and Democratic congresspeople hate cutting defense expenditures because it can cost jobs and hence, votes, in their home states.

It is possible to spend too little on defense, but the more common historical examples for Western societies has been the opposite. In his classic work, *The Rise and Fall of Great Powers*, Yale university historian Paul Kennedy has documented that each of the great powers of the last 500 years rose and fell in part because of expansionist programs that required huge defense outlays, eventually weakening their economies to the point that the nation fell behind its more economically competitive rivals.

After World War II, our effort to be the dominant military power in the world, and the Soviet challenge to that position, resulted in a Cold War cost to the U.S. Treasury of $5.4 trillion spent on defense (in inflation-adjusted 1993 dollars, expenditures would be over $10 trillion). With the economic collapse of the Soviet Union and the political collapse of Communism, there is no longer any justification for the continuing high levels of military spending. In our obsession with the arms race, the nation has paid insufficient attention to maintaining U.S. competitiveness in world markets; environmental problems; crumbling urban infrastructure; growing inequities in the distribution of income; and a host of growing social ills including joblessness, a declining literacy rate, and rising juvenile crime. All of these issues need to be urgently addressed to prevent us from following the path of so many other nations who, in their efforts to dominate the world militarily, sowed the seeds of their own economic and social collapse.

Notes

1. Center for Defense Information, *Defense Monitor*, XXI, no. 4 (1992), p. 2.

2. U.S. Office of Management and Budget, *Budget of the United States Government, Fiscal Year 1995, Historical tables* (Washington, D.C.: U.S. Government Printing Office), p. 85.

3. J. Whetfield Larrabee, "Black Holes," *The Humanist* (May/June 1996): 14.

4. U.S. Office of Management and Budget, *Budget of the United States Government, Historical tables* (Washington, D.C.: U.S. Government Printing Office), p. 85. Rebased to constant 1995 dollars.

5. Robert Borosage, "Imagine Peacetime," *Mother Jones* (January/February 1992): 20–23.

6. Eugene McCarthy, *A Colony of the World* (New York: Hippocreene Books, 1992), p. 84.

7. *World Press Review* (September 1992): 13.

8. *Economist* (August 6, 1988): 15, for 1983 data. Data for 1995 calculated from *Statistical Abstract of the United States, 1997*, table 1334, p. 829, and table 1389, p. 861.

9. Lindley H. Clark and Alfred Malabre Jr., "Slow Rise in Outlays for Research Imperils U.S. Competitive Edge," *The Wall Street Journal*, November 16, 1988, pp. A1, A10.

10. Jeremy Rifkin, "Turning Arms into a Green Dividend," *The Washington Post*, "Outposts," April 15, 1990, D3. Cited in *Future Survey* (December 1990): 15.

11. Dr. Helen Caldicott, *Missile Envy* (New York: Bantam Books, 1986), p. 47.

12. Paul Kennedy, *The Rise and Fall of the Great Powers* (New York: Random House, 1987), p. 463.

13. Caldicott, *Missile Envy*, p. 33.

14. *Los Angeles Times*, August 11, 1981, pt. IV, p. 3. Cited by Robert Lekachman, *Greed Is Not Enough: Reaganomics* (New York: Pantheon Books, 1982), p. 142.

15. Robert L. Heilbroner, *The Future as History* (New York: Random House, 1960), p. 137.

16. Caldicott, *Missile Envy*, p. 67.

17. Lekachman, *Greed Is Not Enough: Reaganomics*, p. 148.

18. *Chicago Tribune*, March 13, 1994, sec. 1, p. 4.

Appendix C

The Neo-Marxist Theory of Defense Spending

Some Neo-Marxist economists argue that capitalism invariably results in monopoly corporate power capable of producing a surplus of output over production costs, but fails to provide the sufficient consumption required to absorb the rising surplus in output. Therefore, since managers can see that such a surplus will not be absorbed, they decide not to produce it in the first place. The result is that the natural state of monopoly capitalism is stagnation. To alleviate the situation, the state intervenes with expanded military expenditures that can absorb the surplus. To support their argument, the Neo-Marxists show that military expenditures as a percent of GDP usually rise after a recession year. They further demonstrate that U.S. military expenditures do not correlate with Soviet expenditures or changes in political parties. On the other hand, there is a tendency to increase military spending just before an election.

Although they cite anecdotal evidence, the arguments of Neo-Marxists are not supported by the weight of the empirical evidence. First, if their theory was correct, we should observe that militarism correlates with economic growth, but there is no evidence to suggest that most capitalist societies follow this pattern. During the longest period of sustained economic growth in Great Britain, there was no significant military action and defense expenditures were reduced to only 2 or 3 percent of GDP. In our own country, the hundred years between the War of 1812 and World War I was characterized by incredibly small military expenditures, with the exception of the Civil War. Prior to World War I, the United States had an army of only 26,000.[1] Yet in the period from 1812 to 1914, America rose from the status of a small colony to the leading economy in the world.

Many other countries, such as those of Scandinavia, have spent relatively little on defense and appear to have benefited economically by *not* diverting a large portion of their output on the military. Even Japan's period of strongest economic growth coincided with five years of peace after World War II and very little spending for defense.

Second, as I have argued in chapter 6, excessive military spending will actually produce a stagnant economy by diverting intellectual and physical resources from more productive uses, ultimately resulting in a nation losing its competitive edge. While it is true that past military expenditures usually increase in election years, it was not primarily to stimulate the economy, but to fend off the rhetoric of the party seeking power who usually alleged that the incumbents were soft on Communism. This spurious accusation worked extraordinarily well for both John Kennedy and Ronald Reagan. Nothing was easier, it would appear, than to gain political mileage by scaring the American people with the bogeyman of the red menace (or yellow menace) from time to time. After the fall of Communism, the new scare raised was the supposed dangers of such militarily insignificant nations such as Iran and Iraq.

Even though the evidence does not support the claim that military expenditures are essential for growth of capitalistic economies, there is one linkage that cannot be denied. During a recession, increased federal spending for any purpose will temporarily stimulate the economy. However, it has been shown that to develop a new public works program and implement it can take over two years. Furthermore, it is often difficult to garner public support for such programs. Certainly, during the 1980 recession when the budget was already in a deficit and the Republicans had been arguing against increased social programs for four years, the only form of spending where conservatives could gain quick public support was in the area of defense. Recalling our discussion of self-interest, most Americans do not see how it is in their self-interest to support social programs that appear to benefit only the poor and minorities. It was far easier to convince people that it is in their self-interest to be protected from the scourge of Communism. Therefore, as a matter of political expedience, it was easiest to increase defense spending to stimulate the economy.

Nevertheless, based on the continued increases in defense spending that occurred under Reagan even after the economy was out of the recession, I can only conclude that his primary motivation was not to provide economic stimulus. Rather, conditioned by the experience of World War II, the Reagan generation saw the world in terms of good and evil. Dictators such as Hitler and Stalin were clearly evil. America defeated Hitler, therefore we must be on the side of the angels. (This can be taken literally since atheistic Communism must be, by definition, the work of the devil.)

For Reagan, no expense would be too great to defeat the Red Menace, or in his case, the Evil Empire. Through their past conditioning it was absolutely impossible for the Reagan administration to conceive that by 1980 Communism posed little threat to any country beyond those which bordered the Soviet Union.

Although increased defense spending is not tied as neatly to economic growth as the Neo-Marxists suggest, decreases in defense are difficult to achieve because of their short-term negative impact on growth. Although in the long run the economy will greatly benefit from less defense spending, there is a lag between the cut in defense and the benefits to be accrued. We have become a nation of defense expenditure junkies. Roger Bolton suggested that the industrial structure of a nation can become suited primarily for further increases in defense spending. This is particularly true at the local level where certain areas of the nation are almost totally dependent on defense. Bolton refers to this dependency as "dynamic adaptation."[2] The dramatic impacts of defense cuts can be seen in the effect on the Massachusetts economy when the Navy cut back its shipbuilding program in 1990. Similarly, the West and Northwest are heavily impacted by aircraft expenditures. When it comes time to cut programs or close bases every congressperson says "fine, but not in my district." Hence, the difficulties of switching military production capacity to alternative consumer products may result in an inertia toward defense spending that is difficult to reverse.

NOTES

1. Paul Kennedy, *Rise and Fall of the Great Powers* (New York: Random House, 1987), p. 248.
2. Roger Bolton, "Impacts of Defense Spending on Urban Areas," 1979, Conference on Urban Impacts of Federal Policies.

Appendix D

The Mythical Philips Curve

Economists have expended a huge amount of effort trying to establish how low the unemployment rate can be pushed before triggering increased inflation. In the 1960s, the rate was thought to be about 4 percent, but the estimate of this so-called Non-accelerating Inflation Rate of Unemployment (NAIRU) was raised by conservative economists in the 1980s to between 6 and 7 percent. Much of the controversy concerning estimates of the trade-off between unemployment and inflation ignores the difference between ***cyclical*** and ***structural unemployment***. Cyclical unemployment is due to swings in the business cycle from growth to recession to recovery, while structural unemployment refers to long-term factors such as population growth or increases in the labor force participation rates that have nothing to do with the business cycle. Cyclical unemployment is largely a self-correcting problem due to the built-in economic stabilizers such as unemployment compensation and deficit spending that help support consumption and investment even when tax revenues fall, thus preventing a downward spiral of unemployment leading to a depression.

In light of these built-in stabilizers, it is usually unnecessary and unwise to try to use discretionary federal programs to reduce cyclical unemployment. In fact, some studies show that it takes two to three years to legislate and implement major federal programs such as public works. Hence, by the time they are implemented they can overstimulate an economic recovery and can create inflationary pressures. Therefore, deciding upon the appropriate federal policy to reduce unemployment requires an analysis as to what is causing the growth in unemployment. The 1972–73 recession masked the more serious structural trend in unemployment caused by the baby boomers entering the labor force, increased labor force participation rates of women, the decline in U.S. tariff barriers, and the rise in technological competitiveness of European and Japanese economies. Inflation, on the other hand, had been ignited by the expansion of the money supply to finance the Vietnam War and then exacerbated by the major oil shocks in 1973 and 1979.

The notion in a constant relationship between unemployment and inflation, whereby decreases in unemployment beyond some certain level would result in rapid growth in inflation, was first proposed by A. W. Philips in the 1950s. During the 1970s and 1980s, the so-called Philips Curve appeared to have shifted, resulting in higher levels of unemployment required to avoid inflation. Some economists, such as Milton Friedman and Edmund Phelps, argued that there was no long-run Philips curve; the effect, if any, was a temporary one.[1] However, economists such as Alan Blinder and Paul Krugman held that to reduce inflation by 1 percent, the United States must hold the unemployment rate to between 2 and 2.5 percent above the full-employment rate for a year (i.e., unemployment would have to run 6.5 percent).[2] In 1990, Krugman argued that to get price stability would require an average unemployment rate of 7 percent.[3] However, the national unemployment rate fell to 4.7 percent by the end of 1997, at the same time the rate of inflation was close to zero. Krugman also believed that to reduce inflation 1 percent a year required the economy to run 4 percent below capacity,[4] but in the 1990s the Federal Reserve Bank has been able to hold inflation below 3 percent per annum while allowing the economy to grow in real terms by almost 3 percent per year.

Other economists, such as Hazel Henderson, question the assumption that inflation is due to wages and believe that the Philips Curve has been inoperative for some time now.[5] Henderson argues that rising social costs and the worsening population/resource ratio drove inflation in the 1970s, not wage rates. There is little doubt that the cost of pollution control, legal expenses associated with the complexity of modern living, control of crime, and the like, result in increased costs. Over the past years, however, such pressures have been more than offset by a decrease in real wages. A surplus of labor coupled by increased world-wide pressures on the United States to improve its productivity have offset the higher social costs.

I submit that there is a relationship between unemployment and inflation, but it is a shifting one caused by the interaction of several factors at any point in time especially, demographic trends, trade policies, and the situation in other parts of the world economy. In 1995, economist Robert Gordon revised his view that inflation would be triggered by unemployment of 6 to 6.5 percent and suggested that it could drop to between 5 and

5.5 percent before inducing inflation.[6] My opinion is that since the mid-1990s the U.S. economy has been in a situation analogous to the 1950s (but for different reasons), and unemployment could drop to between 3 and 4 percent before inflationary pressures would become significant. In addition to the foregoing reasons, the official unemployment estimates fail to include the numerous discouraged workers who are no longer seeking work and, hence, true unemployment is significantly understated, while recent analysis indicates that the Consumer Price Index, as presently calculated, overstates actual inflation. Moreover, we must not make the mistake of equating increased wage rates with inflation. Inflation occurs when unit prices are increased. ***As long as wage rates do not increase faster than productivity growth, it is not necessary for businesses to raise prices to maintain profit margins.*** The greatest pressure on employment is in the information technology area, but that is also where productivity is the greatest, so substantial increases in wages could be absorbed with little inflationary stimulus. Hence, at the time of this writing there is room for unemployment to decline further before necessarily resulting in price increases.

The primary weakness of the Philips Curve theory is that it is a correlation of two variables that assumes the direction of causation is the same over time. It actually is always changing. Sometimes low unemployment can increase wages and inflation. Oftentimes, however, the cause is the other way around: inflation due to expansionary monetary policies or external shocks such as the oil embargo can lead to lower consumption, reduced investment, and higher unemployment. As explained, during the Vietnam era the initial impetus to inflation was the increase in the money supply, which outstripped the productive capacity of the economy. At that time, increases in wages trailed increases in prices as labor sought to have its earnings catch up with inflation. During the next phase, beginning with the slowdown in the 1973 recession, there was not excess demand pulling up prices; rather, we entered a phase of cost-push inflation. It was the sharp increase in energy cost that was the primary push. At the same time, however, labor was seeking to regain lost purchasing power and continued to push for higher wage rates despite an increase in unemployment, contrary to the predictions of the Philips Curve.

Once an inflationary spiral has begun, everyone keeps it going by trying to get ahead of the game. The inflationary spiral of the 1970s was finally checked by the Federal Receive Board's decision to drive up interest rates to the point where investment was choked off. The economy was subsequently thrown into a recession: producers could not demand higher prices and labor could not demand higher wages.

Since 1973, labor earnings have not kept pace with inflation even though total employment costs have been approximately equal to inflation.

In 1973, weekly earnings in the private sector averaged $315. By 1997, after adjusting for inflation, average weekly earnings adjusted for inflation had fallen to $261, a 21 percent decline that cut weekly earnings to the level of 1959.[7] The reason that employment costs have risen slightly faster than wage rates is due to the increasing cost of benefits, particularly health-care costs. Yet, as shown earlier, even though U.S. wages and fringe benefits are now below those of Japan and Western Europe, they are still well above those of Eastern Europe and the emerging nations in Southern Asia and Latin America. This results in continued pressure to hold down wage rates and inflation.

The enhanced international flow of technological information and capital results in a significant change in the unemployment/inflation relationship. In effect, what is developing is a world labor market. Either relative wage rates decline in the United States or jobs will migrate elsewhere as capital migrates abroad. Such dynamics seriously undermined the ability of labor to increase its wage rates above increases in national productivity. Hence, for the foreseeable future there will be little cost-push inflation for any internationally traded products, since it would lead immediately to higher unemployment. Moreover, as long as wage rates do not exceed growth in average national productivity, there can be no cost-push inflation due to increased labor costs. If wages increase faster than productivity, prices will rise and the demand for exports will slow, thus resulting in U.S. exporters reducing costs or going out of business. The demand for U.S. dollars will also decline, and the falling value of the dollar will result in further reducing inflationary pressures.

Inflation could result if the federal government sought to finance the real dollar value of the debt by increasing the rate of growth in the money supply (the so-called monetarizing of the debt). An increase in the money supply will not lead to inflation if the economy is operating at less than full employment or productive capacity. On the other hand, if the money supply is expanded to finance the debt when the economy is at full capacity it would trigger a renewed inflationary spiral. So far Federal Reserve chairman Alan Greenspan has resisted any effort on the part of the president and Congress to spur money supply growth when it might increase inflation.

How can American labor maintain its standard of living in the face of greater worldwide competition? Those who possess skills that cannot be shifted abroad—such as educators, professional people, and many types of services—will not be as significantly impacted initially. In fact, they benefit from lower-priced goods that are produced abroad. But, eventually, other people will seek to enter those fields where the wages are rising, resulting in downward pressure on wages in those fields as well. Moreover, lower wages on average mean that those who purchase the services of the higher-waged people are less able to pay. So in the long run everyone's wages will decline relative to those in other nations of the world. At the same time, there will be more income inequality in this country, as the providers of capital (investors) receive a greater share of the fruits of production relative to labor.

Low-skilled workers are going to be the group most negatively impacted. On one hand, relatively good paying, low-skilled jobs are migrating to third world countries. Mechanization is further reducing the need for low-skilled workers. At the same time, the higher birth rate of the poor and the highest level of immigration in U.S. history is flooding the labor market.

When unemployment dropped to between 6 and 6.5 percent, some economists were calling upon the Federal Reserve Board to raise interest rates to slow economic growth. If that policy had been followed, it would have resulted in unnecessarily high rates of unemployment. The view that 6 to 6.5 percent was the noninflationary rate of unemployment was based on an outdated conception of the labor force dynamics. An unemployment objective of 3 to 3.5 percent would go far to provide jobs paying a livable wage to the almost 20 million unemployed and underemployed people in the United States

We can do little to stem the long-term trend to world-wide equalization of the labor rate, any more than the regions of our country could prevent incomes from reaching a rough parity during the last thirty years as jobs migrated from the North to the South. At best, we can slow the trend by delaying additional tariff reductions, but the various rounds of GATT have pretty much already dismantled our tariffs. Jobs will continue migrating from the Western hemisphere to the Eastern hemisphere, and also to some extent from the Northern hemisphere to the Southern hemisphere. (Africa will continue to suffer due to the lack of political stability which discourages investment there.)

Some economists argue that the Federal Reserve Board will have increasingly less ability to control the money supply and economic growth in the future because hedge funds* will have a greater impact on foreign exchange and interest rates than any nation's central bank.[8] The world's central banks can only muster about $14 billion a day to protect a currency from speculative attack, whereas daily currency trading now amounts to $800 billion.[9] Moreover, monetary policy generally works through bank loans, but bank loans continue to decline as a source of credit. In short, the international economy is taking on a life of its own, and individual efforts

*Hedge funds are private investment partnerships invested primarily in stocks and various contracts involving stocks, such as short selling, buying and selling options, warrants, and convertible bonds.

of governments to regulate it are falling by the wayside. This does not augur well either for international monetary stability or the future of the American worker.

NOTES

1. Robert Eisner, *The Misunderstood Economy: What Counts and How to Count It* (Boston: Harvard Business School Press, 1994), p. 175.

2. Alan S. Blinder, *Hard Heads, Soft Hearts* (New York: Addison-Wesley Publishing Company, Inc., 1987), p. 39.

3. Paul Krugman, *The Age of Diminished Expectations* (Washington, D.C.: Washington Post Brief Company, 1990), p. 41 (See also p. 25).

4. Ibid., p. 39.

5. Hazel Henderson, *Creating Alternative Futures: The End of Economics* (New York: Perigee Books, 1987), p. 29.

6. *Wall Street Journal*, January 24, 1995, pp. A1, A6.

7. President, *Economic Report of the President Transmitted to Congress, 1998* (Washington, D.C.: U.S. Government Printing Office, 1998), table B–47, p. 336.

8. Felix Rohatyn, "World Capital: The Need and the Risks," *New York Review of Books* (July 14, 1994): 51–52. Cited by David C. Korten, *When Corporations Rule the World* (West Hartford, Conn. and San Francisco: Kumarian Press and Berrett-Koehler Publishers, 1995), p. 199.

9. Joel Kurtzman, *The Death of Money* (New York: Simon and Schuster, 1993), pp. 89–91. Cited by Korten, *When Corporations Rule the World*, p. 201.

Appendix E

Reversing the Plight of the Less Developed Countries (LDCs)

A complete discussion of the steps necessary to solve the manifold problems of the LDCs would merit a book by itself, and indeed many have been written on the subject. However, we can outline several prerequisites that must be implemented if the LDCs are going to have a chance of being lifted out of their grinding poverty without destroying their environment to do so. The essential policy initiatives include:

- dramatic slowing of population growth;
- debt forgiveness and a freeze on future World Bank loans;
- a rollback of military sales to the LDCs; and
- institution of sustainable, people-oriented development.

Slowing population growth

A dramatic decline in population is the sine qua non of the LDCs' survival, let alone development. The Cairo Conference on Population emphasized the *right* of women to control their procreation but failed to mention anything about the *responsibility* of couples to control the number of births. The new ethic for the twenty-first century must be "two is enough" for developed and undeveloped countries alike. If developed countries average more than two children, they will continue to absorb a disproportionate amount of the world's resources and create a disproportionate amount of waste and pollution. Undeveloped countries, on the other hand, will never improve their average standard of living if their population continues to outstrip the carrying capacity of their environment.

Many LDCs should seek to adopt the Chinese goal of averaging one child per family. This need not involve forced abortions, but it would require strong incentives, such as encouraging late marriages, no state aid for the second child, and even a tax on a third child. Naturally, family planning services, including free and safe abortion, should be readily available. Such policies will be fought tooth and nail by the Vatican and the Religious Right. If history is a guide, it will take the hierarchy of the Catholic Church 200 to 300 years to recognize its error. Unfortunately, the LDCs have to accomplish their demographic transition to a zero (or in some cases, negative) population growth scenario in a matter of a few decades if they are going to avoid a catastrophe on a hitherto unimaginable scale.

Removing the Shackles of Debt

As a one-time supporter of the concept of a World Bank* providing loans to the LDCs, it pains me to admit that the bank's loan policies have been a colossal failure. One of the major functions of the bank was to make loans to private investors in the LDCs backed by the guarantee of the Bank's member nations. They would undertake projects too risky for private lenders. This was analogous to the disastrous policy followed in the United States when the Reagan administration began deregulating American savings and loans while still providing insurance against default. It had the same tragic results. The guarantee against default encouraged funding a disproportionate number of incredibly risky projects.

To make matters worse, the World Bank had a bias toward huge projects—such as major dams that forced the relocation of millions of people who mainly fled to the cities—and resulted in unforeseen environmental problems on a massive scale, often destroying entire ecosystems. Aside from their environmental consequences, many projects were financial disasters. ***One study found that 37.5 percent of bank-funded projects completed in 1991 were already deemed failures at the time of their completion.***[1] Another study that followed up on projects four to ten years after

---

*The World Bank, known officially as the International Bank for Reconstruction and Development, is an agency affiliated with the United Nations whose purpose is to finance projects that promote economic development in member nations. The stated purposes of the International Monetary Fund (IMF), also affiliated with the UN, include creating international monetary cooperation, stabilizing currency exchange rates and assisting member nations who have balance of payment difficulties.

completion found that twelve out of twenty-five projects initially claimed as successful subsequently turned out to be failures.[2]

Such failures, coupled with the disastrous export-led development, have resulted in a crushing level of international debt that will preclude many LDCs from climbing out of poverty in the foreseeable future. By the 1990s, LDC debt was $1 trillion.[3] ***Repayments of principle and interest equaled $150 billion a year—far more than the $40 billion of foreign aid of all the developed countries combined.***[4] To meet the interest payments on their debt, the LDCs shifted to cash crops, driving up the cost of basic food staples, some of which may be imported.[5] The result was increased poverty.

The first reform for the World Bank is to refrain from funding projects that a prudent financier would not fund. Second, they must stop funding projects that result in massive relocation of people. David C. Korten contends that the World Bank can't show a single bank-related project where relocated people enjoy a standard of living comparable to what they enjoyed before displacement.[6] In our country, the principle of eminent domain gives the state the right to expropriate property if fair compensation is provided. However, if people cannot obtain an equivalent standard of living elsewhere, we have to question whether fair compensation was provided.

There is simply no way that the LDCs are going to pay off all of their loans so we might just as well write it off and take the debt off their backs. Many of the commercial banks have already written off a substantial portion of the loans. In chapter 6, we discussed Lovejoy's plan of debt-for-nature swaps. This would cost the developed countries relatively little—since we will never see the repayment of the loans anyway—and at the same time protect some of the ecologically endangered areas.

In 1996, the World Bank and the International Monetary Fund finally took a major step in reducing LDC debt. They got the lender nations to pledge to contribute $7.7 billion to a "multilateral debt" trust fund.[7] There are rigid criteria for receiving debt reduction including political reform and sound economic polices. Many of the poorest nations are in such political turmoil that they will not qualify for debt relief. However, holding out this economic carrot might encourage these nations to take the steps necessary to save themselves.

Rollback of Military Exports

One of the most effective policies for improving the LDCs' chances of survival would be an international ban on military exports. The billions of dollars spent by the LDCs on military hardware has cost millions of lives in internecine warfare and wasted the hard currency necessary to build their counties. Instituting such a ban would be extremely difficult—the vested interests of every developed country would oppose it. Yet unless something is done to curb the destructive power of the LDCs, the loss of life in the twenty-first century will run into the hundreds of millions of people.

Institution of Sustainable, People-oriented Development

Korten defines true international development as "a process by which people increase their human, institutional, and technical capacities to produce goods and services needed to achieve sustainable improvement in their quality of life using the resources available to them."[8] Such development does not mean merely increasing GDP, but, as explained in chapter 2, improving the measures associated with human happiness. It involves not just making an elite group wealthier, but spreading the benefits of development as broadly as possible. It questions the wisdom of the export-led model of the World Bank. Instead, it follows the path taken by Japan, South Korea, and Taiwan: beginning with land reform, followed by establishing small rural factories to slow the flight to urban areas and their associated problems, development of self-sufficiency in basic necessities, such as food, protection of infant industries until they can compete worldwide, education of a business class,* and only then, gradually increasing exports and opening markets to world trade.[9]

The failure of the present export-led development promoted by the World Bank and the International Monetary Fund is illustrated by Costa Rica. Of all the Caribbean countries, Costa Rica was by far the most successful. By eliminating its army, it saved tens of millions of dollars. Its general level of education was relatively high and income distribution far less skewed to the wealthy than other Caribbean nations. In short, it was an exceptional country in a troubled region.

Enter the World Bank and the IMF to provide economic incentives to improve agricultural productivity to increase exports. The result was a shift away from the small farms to the large estates producing cash crops for export rather than meeting the food requirements of Costa Rica. This was followed by an increase in crime and violence as rural small farmers were forced to migrate to urban areas, an increase in public expenditures to

---

*This includes a major redirection of the career of choice for the upper classes, who traditionally have chosen to become government bureaucrats rather than seeking careers in business.

meet the needs of the unemployed, and a doubling of foreign debt as the country became dependent on imports to meet basic food requirements.[10]*

Costa Rica is simply an example of the larger problem. From 1980 to 1992 the excess of imports over exports for low-income countries increased from $6.5 billion to $34.7 billion. The World Bank and the IMF responded by lending more money to carry out "structural adjustments" i.e., reducing government expenditures to help the poor. Countries such as Mexico cut government spending on health and education from 20.2 percent of government expenditures in 1980 to less than 8.5 percent by 1988.[11] Despite these draconian cuts in public welfare, over the 1980–1992 period the LDC collective debt rose from $134 billion to $473 billion.[12]

The answer proposed by the World Bank is for the European Community, Japan, and the United States to cut their tariffs by another 50 percent. The result, according to the World Bank, would be to raise exports from the LDCs by 50 percent a year—which is more that the entire flow of foreign aid.[13]

Of course, unless the LDCs immediately and significantly reduce their birth rates, they face a bleak future irrespective of any economic polices they choose to adopt.

Notes

1. Pratap, Chatterjee, "World Bank Failures Soar to 37.5% of Completed Projects in 1991," *Third World Economics* (December 16–31, 1992): 2. Cited by David C. Korten, *When Corporations Rule the World* (West Hartford, Conn., and San Francisco: Kumarian Press and Berrett-Koehler Publishers, Inc., 1995), p. 171.

2. Michael Cernea, "Farmer Organizations and Institutions Building for Sustainable Development," *Regional Development Dialogue* 8, no. 2 (Summer 1987): 1–19. Cited by Korten, *When Corporations Rule the World*, p. 171.

3. Nicholas Eberstadt, *The Tyranny of Numbers* (Washington, D.C.: AEI Press, 1995), p. 212.

4. Ibid., pp. 212, 197. Note that the total of foreign aid equals only about $10 a year per person in the LDCs.

5. Al Gore, *Earth in the Balance* (Boston: Houghton Mifflin Company, 1992), p. 54.

6. Korten, *When Corporations Rule the World*, p. 49.

7. *Chicago Tribune*, October 10, 1996, sec. 1, p.20.

8. Ibid., p. 168.

---

*All these problems were exacerbated by the failure of Costa Rica to bring down its birth rate sufficiently. If it does not rapidly halt its population growth, no economic policy will save Costa Rica from eventual ruin.

9. Japan gave freehold tenure to 4.7 million tenant farmers and raised the proportion of owner-farmed land to over 90 percent. Taiwan underwent a similar massive land reform. Paul Johnson, *Modern Times* (New York: HarperPerennial, 1983, 1991), pp. 731, 735.

10. Korten, *When Corporations Rule the World*, p. 49.

11. Eberstadt, *The Tyranny of Numbers*, p. 232.

12. *World Debt Tables, 1992–93: External Finance for Developing Countries* (Washington: D.C.: World Bank, 1992), p. 212. Cited by Korten, *When Corporations Rule the World*, p. 165.

13. Alen Murray, "Attention Agenda for Rio Summit," *Wall Street Journal*, June 8, 1992, p. A1.

Selected Bibliography

Aaron, Henry J., and Joseph A. Pechman, ed. *How Taxes Affect Economic Behavior.* Washington, D.C.: The Bookings Institution, 1981.

Armstrong, Robert, and Janet Shenk. *El Salvador: The Face of Revolution.* Boston: South End Press, 1982.

Aschauer, David Alan. "Is Public Capital Stock Too Low?" *Chicago Fed Letter* (October 1987).

———. "Prescription for Productivity: Build Infrastructure, " *Chicago Fed Letter* (September 1988).

Auerbach, James A., and Richard S. Belous, eds. *The Inequality Paradox: Growth of Income Disparity.* Washington, D.C.: The National Policy Association, 1998.

Auster, Lawrence. *The Path to National Suicide.* Monterey, Va.: The American Immigration Control Foundation, 1990.

Barfield, Claude E. "US R & D Spending: Getting Behind the Numbers." *New York Times* (March 4, 1990). Reprinted American Economic Institute, #15 1990.

Bartlett, Albert A., "Fusion and the Future." Negative Population Growth, *Human Survival* (Fall 1990).

Barlett, Donald L., and James B. Steel. *America: What Went Wrong.* Kansas City, Mo.: Andrews and McMeel, 1992.

Batra, Dr. Ravi. *The Myth of Free Trade: A Plan for Economic Survival.* New York: Charles Scriber Sons, 1993.

Becker, Gary. *The Economic Approach to Human Behavior.* Chicago: University of Chicago Press, 1976.

———. *A Treatise on Family*, Cambridge, Mass.: Harvard University Press, 1991.

Beck, Roy. *The Case against Immigration.* New York: W. W. Norton and Company, 1996.

———. *Re-Charting America's Future.* Petosky, Mich.: The Social Contract Press, 1994.

———. "Immigration: No. 1 in U.S. Growth." *The Social Contract* (Winter 1991–92).

Bell, Daniel, and Lester Thurow. *The Deficits: How Big? How Long? How Dangerous?* New York: New York University Press, 1985.

Bell, Derrick. *Faces at the Bottom of the Well: The Permanence of Racism*. New York: Basic Books. 1992.

Berke, Meredith. "An Environmental Income Statement for Immigration." *Social Contract* (Summer 1993).

Berman, Karl. *Under the Big Stick: Nicaragua and the United States Since 1948*. Boston: South End Press, 1986.

Blinder, Alan S. *Hard Heads, Soft Hearts*. New York: Addison-Wesley Publishing Company, Inc., 1987.

Bluestone, Berry, and Bennett Harrison. *The Deindustrialization of America*, New York: Basic Books, 1982.

Bolch, Ben W., and Harold Lyons. *Apocalypse Not: Science, Economics, and Environmentalism*. Washington, D.C.: Cato Institute, 1993.

Borjas, George J. *Friends or Strangers: The Impact of Immigrants on the U.S. Economy*. New York: Basic Books, Inc., 1990.

———. "Know the Flow." *National Review* (April 17, 1995).

———. "The New Economics of Immigration." *Atlantic Monthly* (November 1996).

Borjas, Geroge, Richard B. Freeman, and Lawrence F. Katz. "On the Labor Market effects of Immigration and Trade." In *Immigration and the Work Force.* Chicago: University of Chicago Press, 1993.

Boston, Rob. "Vouchers for Evangelism." *Church and State* (June 1991).

Boulding, Kenneth E. *The World as Total System*. Beverly Hills, Calif.: Sage Publications, 1985.

Bouvier, Leon F., and Linsey Grant. *How Many Americans?* San Francisco: Sierra Club Books, 1994.

Bower, Bruce. "Population Overload: Mice Advice." *Science News* (May 31, 1986).

Branscomb, Lemis M. "Does America Need a Technology Policy?" *Harvard Business Review* (March/April, 1992).

Brazell, David, et al. *The Cost of Corporate Capital in the United States and Japan*. Institute for Political Economy, The Krieble Foundation, 1985.

Briggs, Vernon, Jr. *Mass Immigration and the National Interest*. New York: M. E. Sharpe, 1992.

———. "Mexican Migration and U.S. Labor Market." Center for the Study of Human Resources and the Bureau of Business Research, University of Texas, Austin, 1975.

Brimlow, Peter. *Alien Nation*. New York: Random House, 1995.

Brown, Lester. *Building a Sustainable Society*. New York: W. W. Norton and Company, 1981.

Brown, Lester R., et al. *State of the World*. New York: W. W. Norton and Co., 1989, 1990, 1991, 1992, 1993, 1994, 1995, and 1996.

———. *Vital Signs*. New York: W. W. Norton and Company, 1993, 1994, and 1996.

Burtless, Gary, Robert Z. Lawrence, Robert E. Litan, and Robert J. Shapiro. *Globaphobia*. Washington, D.C.: Brookings Institute, 1998.

Budiansky, Stephen. "10 Billion for Dinner Please." *U.S. News & World Report* (September 12, 1994).

Caldicott, Helen. *Missile Envy*. Toronto: Bantam Books, 1986.

Camatora, Steven A. and Mark Krikorian. "The Impact of Immigration on the U.S. Labor Market, Center for Immigration Studies." Washington, D.C., 1997.

Center for Defense Information. "Nuclear Threat at Home, the Cold War Lethal Leftovers." *The Defense Monitor* XXIII, no. 2 (1994).

———. "International Arms Sales: Race to Disaster." *Defense Monitor* XXII, no. 9 (1993).

Center for Immigration Studies. "The Cost of Immigration: Assessing a Conflicted Issue." No. 2–94 (September 1994).

Cohen, Joel E. *How Many People Can the Earth Support?* (New York: W. W. Norton and Company, 1995).

Coleman, James S., Earnest Campbell, et al. *Equality of Educational Opportunity*. Washington, D.C.: Office of Education, 1966.

Commoner, Barry. *The Closing Circle*. New York: Knopf, 1971.

Conference on Population and Development. The Final Document, Cairo, 1994

Consumer Reports. "Wasted Health Care Dollars." (July 1992).

Costanza, Roberta. "Balancing Humans in the Biosphere: Escaping the Overpopulation Trap." *NPG Forum* (July 1990).

Cross, Harry E., and James A. Sandos. *Across the Border: Rural Development in Mexico and Recent Migration to the United States*. LaJolla, Calif.: Institute of Government Studies, University of California, 1982.

Currie, Elliott. *Confronting Crime*. New York: Pantheon Books, 1985.

Curver, Philip C. "Lighting the 21st Century." *The Futurist* (January/February 1989).

———. "Hydrogen, Tomorrow's Limitless Power Source." *The Futurist* (November/December 1989).

Cuttler, Blyne. "World's Choices for Birth Control." *American Demographics* (June 1991).

Daly, Herman E., ed. *Toward a Steady State Economy*. San Francisco: W. H. Freeman and Company, 1973.

Daly Herman E. and John B. Cobb Jr. *For the Common Good*. Boston: Beacon Press, 1989.

DeGrasse, Robert W., Jr. (Council on Economic Priorities). *Military Expansion, Economic Decline*. Armonk, N.Y.: M. E. Sharpe, Inc., 1983.

Doerr, Ed. "Suppression of NSSM 200." *The Humanist* (September/October 1992, p. 25.

Douglass, Frederick. *My Bondage and My Freedom*. New York: Dover, Black Rediscovery Series, 1969.

Douglis, Carole. "Images of Home." *Wilderness* (Fall 1993).

Drew, Lisa, "25 Messages from Wildlife." *National Wildlife* (April/May 1995).

Durning, Alan Thein. "Are We Happy Yet?" *The Futurist* (January/February) 1993.

———. "Limiting Consumption." *The Futurist* (July/August) 1991.

———. "Saving the Forests, What Will it Take?" *Worldwatch Paper*, no. 117 (December 1993).

Eckes, Alfred, Jr. *Opening America's Market: U.S. Foreign Trade Policy Since 1775*. Chapel Hill, N.C.: University of North Carolina Press, 1996.

The Economist. "Running to a Standstill." (November 10, 1991).

Eberstadt, Nicholas. *The Tyranny of Numbers*. Washington, D.C.: AEI Press, 1995.

Edmondson, Brad. "The 'Boomlet' Still Booming." *American Demographics* (June 1991).

———. "Demanding Death with Dignity." *American Demographics* (November 1991).

Eisner, Robert. *The Misunderstood Economy: What Counts and How to Count It.* Boston: Harvard Business School Press, 1994.

Etzioni, Amitai. *Spirit of Community.* New York: Crown Publishers, 1993.

Federation for American Immigration Reform. *A Tale of Ten Cites*. Washington, D.C., 1995.

Filer, Rander K. "The Effects of Immigrants' Arrivals on Migratory Patterns of Native Workers." In *Immigration and the Work Force*. George Borjas and Richard Freeman, eds. (Chicago: University of Chicago Press, 1993).

Findley, Paul. *They Dared to Speak Out*. Chicago: Lawrence Hill Books, 1989.

Fishback, Murray, and Alfred Friendly Jr. *Ecocide in the USSR: Health and Nature Under Siege*. New York: Basic Books, 1992.

Fornos, Werner. *Gaining People, Losing Ground.* Washington, D.C.: The Population Institute, 1987.

Fox, Robert W. "Neighbor's Problem, Our Problems: Population Growth in Central America, " *NPG Forum*, Negative Population Growth (June 1990).

Freeman , R. B., and H. J. Halzer, eds. *Black Youth Employment Crisis*. Chicago: University of Chicago Press, 1986.

Frey, William H. "Immigration and the Changing Geography of Poverty." *Focus*, University of Wisconsin–Madison, Institute for Research on Poverty, 18, no. 2 (Fall/Winter 1996–97).

Frey, William H., and Kao-Kee Liaw. *The Immigration Impact on Population Redistribution within the United States.* Population Studies Center at the University of Michigan, Research Report Series, December 1996, no. 96–376.

Friedman, Milton, and Rose Friedman. *Free to Choose*. New York: Avon Publishing, 1981.

Galbraith, John Kenneth. *The Affluent Society*. Boston: New American Library, 1958.

———. *Economics and the Public Purpose*. Boston: Houghton Mifflin Company, 1973.

Gardner, Howard. *Frames of Mind: The Theory of Multiple Intelligences*. New York: Basic Books, 1993.

Georgescu-Roegen, Nicholas. *The Entropy Law and the Economic Process*. Cambridge, Mass.: Harvard University Press, 1971.

Geyer, Georgie Anne. "America Into Splinters." *Social Contract* (Summer 1993).
———. *Americans No More*. New York: The Atlantic Monthly Press, 1996.
Gever, John, et al. *Beyond Oil*. Cambridge, Mass.: Ballinger Publishing Co., 1986.
Gilder, George. *Wealth and Poverty*. New York: Basic Books, 1981.
Gilliam, Harold. "Bursting at the Seams." *Social Contract* (Summer 1993).
Glasser, William. *Schools Without Failure*. New York: Harper and Row, 1969.
Glynn, Lenny. "Global Debt." *Global Finance* (September 1990).
Goldsmith, Sir James. *The Trap*. New York: Carroll and Graf Publishers, Inc., 1993.
Goodspeed, Bennett W. *The Tao Jones Averages*. New York: E. P. Dutton, Inc., 1983.
Goodwin, Leonard. *Do the Poor Want to Work?* Washington, D.C.: Brookings Institution, 1972.
Gore, Al. *Earth in the Balance*. Boston: Houghton Mifflin Company, 1992.
Gowdy, John, and Sabrine O'Hare. *Economic Theory for Environmentalists*. Delray Beach, Fla.: St. Lucie Press, 1995.
Grant, Lindsey. "Free Trade and Cheap Labor: The President's Dilemma." *NPG Forum* (October 1991).
Gregg, Alan. "A Medical Aspect of the Population Problem." *Science* 121 (1955).
Gutman, Herbert G. *The Black Family in Slavery and Freedom 1750–1925*. New York: Pantheon Books, 1976.
Haberstan, David. *The Next Century*. New York: William Morrow, 1991.
Handy, Jim. *Gift of the Devil: A History of Guatemala*. Boston: South End Press, 1984.
Hardin, Garrett. *Living Within Limits: Economy, Economics, and Population Taboos*. New York: Oxford University Press, 1993.
———. *The Immigration Dilemma: Avoiding the Tragedy of the Commons*. Washington D.C.: Federation For American Immigration Reform, 1995.
———. "There Is No Global Population Problem." *Humanist* (July/August 1989).
Harrison, Paul. "Slower Population Growth Stimulates Economic Growth." World Population News Service, *Popline*. (May/June 1992).
Hatton, Timothy J., and Jeffrey G. Williamson. "International Migration 1850–1930: An Economic Survey." In *Migration and the International Labor Market 1850–1939*. Edited by Hatton and Williamson. New York: Routledge, 1994.
Heilbroner, Robert L. *The Future as History*. New York: Harper and Brothers, 1960.
Henderson, Hazel. *Creating Alternative Futures: The End of Economics*. New York: Perigee Books, 1978.
Herrnstein, Richard J., and Charles Murray. *The Bell Curve: Intelligence and Class Structure in American Life*. New York: Free Press, 1994.
Hervey, Jack L. *Chicago Fed Letter,* Federal Reserve Bank of Chicago (November 1990).
Howe, Neil, and Philip Longman. "The Next New Deal." *Atlantic Monthly* (April 1992).

Hubbert, M. King. "The World's Evolving Energy System." *American Journal of Physics* no. 49 (1981): 1006–29.

———. "Energy from Fossil Fuels." *Science* no. 109 (1949): 103–9.

Huber Peter W., and Robert E. Litan, eds. *The Liability Maze: The Impact of Liability Law on Safety and Innovation*. Washington, D.C.: Brookings Institution, 1991.

Huddle, Donald L. "Immigration, Jobs, and Wages: The Misuses of Econometrics." *NPG Forum* (April 1992).

———. "Immigration and Jobs: The Process of Displacement." *NPG Forum* (May 1992).

———. "The Net National Cost of Immigration in 1993." Updated June 27, 1994, methodology, notes, and exhibits.

Hughes, James A. "Understanding the Squeezed Consumer." *American Demographics* (July 1991).

Jaeger, David. "Skills Differentials and the Effect of Immigrants on Wages of Natives." Working Paper 273, Office of Employment Research and Program Development (December 1995).

Japan Productivity Center. "Survey: U.S. Puts Profit First, Japan Favors Employment." *Productivity in Japan* (Winter 1989).

Jenks, Christopher. *Rethinking Social Policy: Race, Poverty, and the Underclass.* New York: HarperPerennial, 1992.

Johnson, Bonnie. "Overpopulation and Reproductive Rights." *Free Inquiry* (Spring 1994).

Johnson, Paul. *Modern Times*. New York: HarperPerennial, 1983, 1991.

Kasarda, John D. "Implications of Contemporary Redistribution Trends for National Urban Policy." *Social Science Quarterly* no. 61 (1980).

Kaufman, Jonathan. "Immigrant Businesses Often Refuse to Hire Blacks in Inner City." *Wall Street Journal* (June 6, 1995).

Kennedy, Paul. *The Rise and Fall of the Great Powers*. New York: Random House, 1987.

Kendell, Henry W., and Steven J. Nadis. *Energy Strategies Towards a Solar Future.* Cambridge: Mass.: Ballinger Publishing Company, 1980.

Kester, W. Carl, and Timothy A. Luehnman. "The Myth of Japan's Low-Cost Capital." *Harvard Business Review* (May/June 1992).

Keynes, John Maynard. *Essays in Persuasion*. New York: W. W. Norton and Company, 1963.

King, Charles E. "Homeless in America." *The Humanist* (May 1989).

Kohn, Alfie. *Punished by Rewards: The Trouble with Gold Stars, Incentive Plans, A's, Praise, and Other Bribes*. New York: Houghton Mifflin Company, 1993.

Komanoff, Charles. *Power Plant Cost Escalation: Nuclear and Coal Capital Costs, Regulation and Economics*. New York: Komanoff Energy Associates, 1981.

Korten, David, C. *When Corporations Rule the World*. West Hartford, Conn., and San Francisco: Kumarian Press and Berrett-Koehler Publishers, Inc., 1995.

Kozol, Jonathan. *Savage Inequalities*. New York: Crown Publishers, 1981.

Krugman, Paul. *The Age of Diminished Expectations*. Washington, D.C.: Washington Post Briefing Company, 1990.

Lamb, Richard. "Immigration: The Shifting Paradigm." *The Social Contract* (Fall 1994).

Lekachman, Robert. *Greed is Not Enough: Reagonomics*. New York: Pantheon Books, 1982.

Lefkowitz, Mary. *Not Out of Africa: How Afrocentrism Became an Excuse to Teach Myth as History*. New York: Basic Books, 1996.

Leopold, Aldo. "Some Fundamentals of Conservation in the Southwest." *Environmental Ethics* 1, no. 2 (Summer 1979).

Lerman, Robert I., and Hillard Pouncy. "The Compelling Case for Youth Apprenticeships." *The Public Interest* no. 101 (Fall 1990): 62–77.

Lewis, Oscar. *La Vita: A Puerto Rican Family in the Culture of San Juan and New York*. New York: Random House, 1965.

———. *The Children of Sanchez: Autobiography of a Mexican Family*. New York: The Modern Library, 1961.

Lieberman, Myron. *The Teachers' Union*. New York: Free Press, 1997.

Locutto, C. "The Malleability of IQ as Judged from Adoption Studies." *Intelligence* 14 (1990): 275–92.

Lott, John R., Jr. *More Guns, Less Crime*. Chicago: University of Chicago Press, 1998.

Lott, John R., Jr. The Concealed Handgun Debate." *Journal of Legal Studies* 27 (January 1998).

Louitan, Sar A. "Does Public Job Creation Offer Any Hope?" *The Conference Board Report* (August 1975): 58ff.

Lutton, Wayne, and John Tanton. *The Immigration Invasion*. Petoskey, Mich.: The Social Contract Press, 1994.

Magaziner, Ira C., and Robert B. Reich. *Minding America's Business*. New York: Vintage Books, 1983.

Mann, Donald. "Why We Need Smaller U.S. Population and How We Can Achieve It." *NPG Forum* (July 1992).

Marshall, Adrianna. "Immigration in a Surplus Worker Labor Market: The Case of New York." New York University, Research Program in Inter-American Affairs, 1983.

McCarthy, Eugene. *A Colony of the World*. New York: Hippocrene Books, 1992.

McKenzie, James J., et al. *The Going Rate: What It Really Costs to Drive*. Washington, D.C.: The World Resource Institute, June 1992.

McKibben, Bill. "An Explosion of Green." *Atlantic Monthly* (April 1995).

McNamera, Robert S. "The Population Explosion." *The Futurist* (November/December 1992).

Mumford, Stephen D. *The Life and Death of NSSM 200*. Research Triangle Park, N.C.: Center for Research on Population and Security, 1996.

Munson, Dick. "Philosophical Differences." *Northeast-Midwest Economic Review* (September 24, 1990).

Murray, Charles. *Losing Ground*. New York: Basic Books, 1984.

"Newcomers in American Schools: Education Needs of Immigrant Youth." *The Social Contract* (Summer 1993).

Nordhaus William, and James Tobin. "Is Growth Obsolete?" In *Economic Growth*. National Bureau of Economic Research, General Series No. 96E. New York: Columbia University Press, 1972.

North, David. *U.S. Congressional Record*, U.S. Senate (S 19523-S 19525), December 20, 1979.

Okum, Arthur. *Equality and Efficiency: The Big Tradeoff*. Washington, D.C.: Brookings Institution, 1975, p. 1.

Passel, Jeffrey S., and Rebecca L. Clark. "How Much Do Immigrants Really Cost? A Reappraisal of Huddle's 'The Cost of Immigrants.' " The Urban Institute (February 1994).

Pechman, Joseph A. *Federal Tax Policy*. Washington D.C.: The Brookings Institution, 1987.

Pechman, Joseph A., and P. Michael Timpane, eds. *Work Incentives and Income Guarantees*. Washington, D.C.: The Brookings Institute, 1975.

Plomin, R., and J. C. DeFries. "Genetics and Intelligence: Recent Data." *Intelligence* 4 (April 1980): 15–24.

President. *Economic Report of the President Transmitted to Congress*, 1993, 1994, 1995, 1996. Washington, D.C.: U.S. Government Printing Office.

Raspail, Jean. *The Camp of the Saints*. Translated by Norman Shapiro. New York: Charles Sribner's Sons, 1975.

Rauch, Jonathan. *Kindly Inquisitors*. Chicago: University of Chicago Press, 1993.

Ray, Dixie Lee with Lou Guzzo. *Environmental Overkill: Whatever Happened to Common Sense?* Lanham, Md.: Regnery Gateway, 1993.

Reich, Robert. *The Work of Nations*. New York: Alfred A. Knopf, 1991.

Rensberger, Boyce. "A Reader's Guide to the Ozone Controversy." *Skeptical Inquirer* (Fall 1994).

Ricardo, David. *On the Principles of Political Economy and Taxation*. London: John Murray, 1817.

Roosevelt, R. T. "Taking Contraception to the World's Poor." *Free Inquiry* (Spring 1994).

Robins, Lee N., Paula Clayton, and John Wing. *The Social Consequences of Psychiatric Illness*. New York: Brunner-Mazel, 1980.

Rutter, M., B. Maughan, P. Mortimore, and J. Ouston. *Fifteen Thousand Hours: Secondary Schools and Their Effects on Children*. Cambridge, Mass.: Harvard University Press, 1979.

Ryerson, William N. "What's Needed to Solve the Population Problem?" *The Social Contract* (Summer 1993).

Schlesinger, Arthur M., Jr. *The Disuniting of America: Reflections on a Multiculture Society*. (New York: W. W. Norton and Company, 1998).

Schmookler, Andrew Brad. "The Insatiable Society." *The Futurist* (July/August 1991).

Schumacher, E. F. *Small Is Beautiful: Economics As If People Mattered*. New York: Harper and Row, 1973.

Select Commission on Immigration Policy and the National Interest. Washington, D.C.: U.S. Government Printing Office, 1981.

Shanker, Albert. "Making Standards Count." *American Educator* (Fall 1994): 16.
Sherman, Howard. *Radical Political Economy*. New York: Basic Books, 1972.
Simon, Julian. *The Economic Consequences of Immigration*. Cambridge, Mass.: Basil Blackwell, Inc., 1991.
Sivard, Ruth Leger. *World Military and Social Expenditures*. 14th ed. Washington, D.C.: World Priorities, 1991.
Sowell, Thomas. *Race and Culture*. New York: Basic Books, 1984.
Spenser, Gregory. "Demographic Implications of an Aging United States Population Structure During the 1990 to 2030 Period." *Futures Research Quarterly* (Fall 1990).
Stroch M., and J. Raloff. "The Dirt on Erosion." *Science News* (April 4, 1992).
Sullivan, John. "Immigration: Effect on Poor Blacks." *Social Contract* (Fall 1993).
Swartout, John G. "The Free Trade Charade." *The Social Contract* (Fall 1993).
Sweeney, Catherine. "UNICEF Says Family Planning Saves Lives." World Population News Service, *Popline* (January/February 1991).
Sykes, Charles J. "The Attack on Excellence." *Chicago Tribune Magazine* (August 27, 1995).
Tanton, John. "End of Migration Era." *NPG Newsletter* 18, no. 1 (Fall 1992).
Thurow, Lester C. *Head to Head*. New York: William Morrow and Company, 1992.
———. *The Zero-Sum Society*. New York: Penguin Books, 1981.
———. "Why the Ultimate Size of the World's Population Growth Doesn't Matter." *Technology Review* (August 1986).
Tierney, John. "Betting the Planet." *The New York Times Magazine* (December 2, 1990).
Uher, Richard A. "Levitating Trains." *The Futurist* (September/October 1990).
Unger, Sanford, J. *Estrangement: America and the World*. Oxford: Oxford University Press, 1985.
U.S. Bureau of the Census. *Statistical Abstract of the United States, 1993, 1994, 1995, 1996, 1997, 1998*. Washington, D.C.: U.S. Government Printing Office.
U.S. Commission on Immigration Reform. *Legal Immigration: Setting Priorities*. 1995 Legal Immigration Report to Congress (June 1995).
U.S. Commission on Population Growth and the American Future. *Report of the Commission on Population Growth and the American Future*. Washington D.C.: U.S. Government Printing Office, 1972.
U.S. Congress, Office of Technology Assessment, USGPO. "Improving Automobile Fuel Economy: New Standards, New Approaches." (October 1991).
U.S. General Accounting Office. "Illegal Aliens: Limited Research Suggests that Illegal Aliens May Displace Native Workers." Washington, D.C.: (April 1986).
U.S. Office of Management and Budget. *Budget of the United States Government, Fiscal Years, 1994, 1995, 1996, 1997*. Washington, D.C.: U.S. Government Printing Office.
———. *Budget of the United States Government, Fiscal Year 1995, Analytical Perspective*. Washington, D.C.: U.S. Government Printing Office.

Vishen, Christy A. "Understanding the Roots of Crime: The Project on Human Development in Chicago Neighborhoods." *National Institute of Justice Journal* (November 1994).

Washington, Booker T. "Cast Down Your Bucket Where You Are." Speech delivered to the Atlantic Cotton States and International Exposition (September 18, 1895). Reprinted in *The Social Contract* (Summer 1995).

Weaver, Carolyn L., ed. *Social Security's Looming Surpluses: Prospects and Implications*. Lannham, Md.: University Press of America, 1992.

Weber, Max. *Economy and Society*. Edited by Guenther Roth and Claus Wittich. Berkeley Calif.: University of California Press, 1978.

Weeks, John R. "How to Influence Fertility: The Experience So Far." *NPG Forum* (September 1990).

Weiner, Jonathan. *The Next One Hundred Years*. New York: Bantam Books, 1990.

West, Donald. *Delinquency: Its Roots, Careers, and Prospects*. Cambridge, Mass.: Harvard University Press, 1982.

White, Lynn, "The Historical Roots of Our Ecological Crisis." *Science* (March 10, 1967).

Williams, Tannis MacBeth, ed. *The Impact of Televison: A Natural Experiment in Three Communites*. Orlando, Fla.: Academic Press, 1987.

Wilson, Edward O. *Consilience*. New York: Alfred A. Knopf, 1998.

———. *On Human Nature*. Toronto, Canada: Bantam Books, 1978, 1982.

Wilson, Franklin D., and Gerald Jaynes. "Immigration and Labor Market Outcomes for Native Workers." *Focus*, University of Wisconsin-Madison, Institute for Research on Poverty, 18, no. 2 (Fall/Winter 1996–97).

Wilson, James Q. *The Moral Sense*. New York: The Free Press, 1993.

———. *Thinking About Crime*. New York: Basic Books, 1975.

Wilson, James Q., and Richard J. Herrnstein. *Crime and Human Nature.* New York: Simon and Schuster, 1985.

Wilson, Peter, "Net Loss: Fish, Jobs, and Marine Environment." *Worldwatch Paper* no. 120 (July 1994).

Wilson, William Julius. *The Truly Disadvantaged: The Inner City, the Underclass, and Poverty*, rev. ed., Chicago: University of Chicago Press, 1987.

Williams, Linda, and William Pratt. "Wanted and Unwanted Childbearing in the United States: 1973–88." *Advance Data*, NCHS (September 26, 1990).

Wolfe, Alan. *America's Impasse*. Boston: South End Press, 1981.

World Resources Institute. *World Resources 1992–93*. New York: Oxford University Press, 1992.

Young, Kenneth B., and Jerry M. Coomer. "Effects of Natural Gas Price Increases on Texas High Plains Irrigation, 1976–2025." Agricultural Report No. 448, Washington, D.C.: USDA, Economics Statistics, and Cooperative Service, February, 1980.

Zolotas, Xenophon. *Economic Growth and Declining Social Welfare*. Athens: Bank of Greece, 1981.

Index